Constructive Java Programming

S Sagayaraj
Associate Professor, Department of Computer Science
Sacred Heart College (Autonomous), Tirupattur, Tamil Nadu

R Denis
Assistant Professor, PG Department of Computer Science
Sacred Heart College (Autonomous), Tirupattur, Tamil Nadu

P Karthik
Assistant Professor, Department of Computer Science
Sacred Heart College (Autonomous), Tirupattur, Tamil Nadu

D Gajalakshmi
Assistant Professor, PG Department of Computer Science
Sacred Heart College (Autonomous), Tirupattur, Tamil Nadu

Universities Press

CONSTRUCTIVE JAVA PROGRAMMING

UNIVERSITIES PRESS (INDIA) PRIVATE LIMITED

Registered office
3-6-747/1/A & 3-6-754/1, Himayatnagar, Hyderabad 500 029, Telangana, India
info@universitiespress.com; www.universitiespress.com

Distributed by
Orient Blackswan Private Limited

Registered office
3-6-752 Himayatnagar, Hyderabad 500 029, Telangana, India

Other offices
Bengaluru, Chennai, Guwahati, Hyderabad, Kolkata
Lucknow, Mumbai, New Delhi, Noida, Patna, Visakhapatnam

ISBN: 978-93-89211-77-1

Typeset in Times New Roman PS 10/12 *by*
Cameo Corporate Services, Coimbatore, Tamil Nadu, India

501743

Printed at
B B Press, Noida 201 301

Published by
Universities Press (India) Private Limited
3-6-747/1/A & 3-6-754/1, Himayatnagar, Hyderabad 500 029, Telangana, India

Dedicated

to our respective families

and

to the learning community

Preface

Constructive Java Programming is designed for those readers who wish to start learning to program in an object-oriented programming language. It has been designed primarily as a first programming text. However, it also fulfils the needs of learners ranging from novices to experts. It is suitable for those who already have some experience with another programming language, and who now wish to move on to an object-oriented one. Indeed, much of the material is based on courses delivered by the authors to students with a wide range of both non-programming and programming backgrounds.

Our approach is to regard Java as a language that readers will want to use as a primary tool in many different areas of their programming work—not just for creating programs with graphical content within Web pages. This book aims to bring all the basic concepts with some advanced concepts of Java under a common roof so that engineering/science students can easily find relevant information whenever necessary and can become experts in this field.

The fundamentals cover the primary technical issues that every Java expert should understand, such as Data types, Decisions, Loops, Arrays, Class and Objects, Methods, Inheritance, Interface, Packages, String Handling, Exception Handling, File Handling, Applets, AWT Controls and many others. The advanced topics covered include multithreading, GUI (Graphical User Interface) programming, JDBC (Java Database Connectivity), Java Servlet, Java Server Pages, Collections, Design Patterns, Generics, Autoboxing and unboxing, Metadata (Annotations) as well as MVC Patterns. These features make it a unique textbook for the undergraduate students of all universities in India. Each chapter provides detailed worked out examples illustrating the functioning of these technologies and how they can be used to build robust Java-based applications. This book provides real-world examples supported with screenshots so that readers can understand and easily apply them to Java-based applications they would develop in the future. Such coverage ensures that the book also serves as a basic reference for software engineers and practitioners working in IT and other industries.

Every chapter comes with an extensive set of Short questions, Comprehensive questions, Solved Programs and Programming Exercises. We encourage students to try these out by themselves to test and enhance their understanding of the subject. To encourage students to put the concepts learned in this book into practice, we have added two appendices on the App and on the website (Appendix A: Getting started with NetBeans IDE, Appendix B: Database access with MySQL).

BRIEF OVERVIEW OF EACH CHAPTER

The book is organised into twenty chapters, each covering a unique topic in detail.

Chapter 1 provides an introduction to the field of computer science, and covers the fundamentals of hardware, software and programming languages. An overview of entering source code, compiling and executing it, is presented. A brief history of Java is also given. The chapter concludes with a primer on OOP.

Chapter 2 gets the student started in Java by introducing data types, identifiers, variable declarations, operators, constants and comments. The conventions of programming style are also introduced. The student learns to read console input with the Scanner class.

Chapter 3 discusses conditional statements and loops in detail. First, the *if* statement is explained with true or false blocks and then it is elaborated with an *else* part followed by *if-else-if* statements. More conditions are applied to the *if* control statement using logical operators. The use of multiple *if* statements is illustrated and the *switch* statement to replace such statements is described. The emphasis on the two unary operators – the increment and decrement operators – is discussed. The loop statement and its types *while*, *do–while* and *for* are explained in detail. To enter and exit the loop, *break* and *continue* statements are described. These programming notions are explained with their structure, program flow and sample programs.

Chapter 4 introduces the student to classes, objects and access specifiers. The concept of overloading methods and constructors has been dealt with. Static methods and fields, interaction between objects, passing objects as arguments and returning objects from methods are discussed. Further, the concepts of Wrapper Classes, Generics, Autoboxing and Unboxing, Metadata (Annotations) are also covered.

Chapter 5 allows students to learn to create and work with single and multidimensional arrays. Numerous array-processing techniques are demonstrated, such as summing the elements in an array, reading the values of an array and displaying it in a pyramid structure. Other topics, including passing arrays as arguments to methods, String array and array of objects are also discussed.

Chapter 6 covers non-numerical data types—characters and Strings. The String, StringBuffer and StringBuilder classes are briefly explained. More String class methods are covered, including the StringTokenizer class to tokenize strings.

In **Chapter 7** the study of classes continues with the subjects of inheritance and polymorphism. The topics covered include superclass and subclass constructors, method overriding, classes that inherit from different classes, polymorphism and dynamic binding, abstract classes and final class.

Chapter 8 explains the concept of interfaces, packages and various types of Access specifiers or Modifiers. An interface is used to solve the problem of multiple inheritance by declaring the abstract methods in the interface and implementing these methods in the inherited classes. A package is used to group the classes and interfaces. Common functionality of classes is grouped together in one package and accesses the package classes in other packages. Inheriting the class from another class is done by providing restriction on accessibility of the classes. This can be achieved using various types of modifiers.

Chapter 9 teaches the student to develop enhanced error trapping techniques using exceptions. It helps programmers to understand what exceptions are and how they are handled. It also gives a brief description of exception classes and their hierarchy. Techniques like try…catch, multiple catch blocks, nested try, finally, throw, throws clause as well as developing and throwing custom exceptions, are also discussed.

Chapter 10 describes the multi-threaded processes in Java. A multi-threaded process has two or more parts which can run concurrently and each part can do a designated task at the same time. Multi-threading enables us to write programs in a way where multiple activities can proceed concurrently in the same program. The topics covered in this chapter include thread creation, life cycle, joining a thread, thread scheduler, thread priority, thread synchronisation, inter-thread communication, thread control, thread pool, thread group and daemon thread.

Chapter 11 first introduces simple file operations for reading and writing text files. Further, it briefly explains the File class, I/O Stream Classes, File Streams, File I/O Streams, Filter Streams and RandomAccessFile class.

Chapter 12 introduces the programmers to the world of Windows-based programs through applets. This chapter discusses applet fundamentals, life cycle of an applet, steps to develop an applet program, passing values through parameters, graphics in an applet and finally, complete event handling with the applets through packages such as java.util, java.awt.event.

Chapter 13 provides the various user interface components to develop window-based applications which provide a high end Graphical User Interface (GUI) environment to the user for easy interaction with the application. Java provides a predefined set of graphical components to design the GUI application with the help of the AWT (Abstract Window Toolkit) package. AWT is used to develop system-dependent window applications. Independent Windows applications can be developed using the Swing package. This chapter also discusses the components of Swing packages to develop GUI applications.

Chapter 14 continues the study of GUI application development. Fundamental Swing components and the concepts of event handling by demonstrating more components on AWT, special AWT classes such as Color, Font, Image and advanced Swing components such as JTable, JTree, JOptionPane, JColorChooser, JFileChooser, JSlider, JProgressBar and JTabbedPane are briefly discussed.

Chapter 15 discusses an important technique called Java DataBase Connectivity (JDBC), which allows us to access databases through Java programs. It explains types of drivers, JDBC architecture, Java classes and interfaces to fire SQL to process results and perform other operations common to databases.

Chapter 16 explains a powerful unified architecture, known as a collection framework, provided by Java. Java provides high-quality implementation of collection interfaces resulting in unquestionable performance and quality of programs. Java not only provides the different implementations of an interface, but also allows us to interchange these implementations seamlessly.

Chapter 17 talks about the idea behind design patterns, which is to develop a standardised way to represent general solutions to commonly encountered problems in software development. The benefits are that over time, catalogues of patterns are built up. This enables newcomers to software development to more effectively benefit from the experience gained over the years. Standardising patterns makes it easier for all development professionals – beginners and experts alike – to explicitly understand the implications of their decisions. This makes communicating decisions to developers easier.

Chapter 18 explains the powerful Java server-side technology called Servlets. They usually run inside a Java-enabled web server and extend its capabilities. Since servlets are written in Java which is an extremely powerful language, even a simple web server bundled with servlets becomes unquestionably powerful. This chapter covers servlet alternatives, servlet strength, architecture, life cycle, Generic/HTTP servlet, creating the first servlet application in NetBeans IDE, passing and retrieving parameters in servlet, working with JDBC from a servlet, cookies and problems with servlets.

Chapter 19 describes the Java Server pages which is an extension to Servlets. It is one of the many server-side technologies used to build a dynamic web application that has caught the attention of web developers due to several reasons. The working of JSP, the components of JSP, implicit objects and so on, are briefly explained.

Chapter 20 discusses some preliminary concepts of the MVC pattern and the idea of a software framework. It also explains the need of an MVC framework for web application development, structure of the MVC framework, developing web application with MVC design pattern and concludes with MVC DB access.

Acknowledgments

First and foremost, we are grateful to our colleagues for contributing their time, effort and understanding during the preparation of the book. We offer our sincere gratitude to the management of Sacred Heart College (Autonomous), Tirupattur, for support and encouragement. Most of the contents of this book have evolved over a period of time from our own experience of teaching Java.

We thank our family members for their love and understanding during the preparation of the book.

We sincerely thank the external reviewers commissioned by the publisher for their critical comments and suggestions that helped in improving the presentation and organisation of the book, in the process adding value to it.

Finally, we are indebted to the editorial team at Universities Press Pvt Ltd, for their enthusiastic support and guidance during the preparation of the book. Their team inspired us to take up this project and set the publication process in motion. Mr Kallol Das managed the manuscript review process and ensured that it covers the topics prescribed in the syllabi of most educational institutions. Dr Gita S Dattatri guided us in updating the book to enrich the content. Her editing ensured that the book is well presented, error free and typeset in an elegant form. They were wonderful to work with!

S Sagayaraj
R Denis
P Karthik
D Gajalakshmi

Table of Contents

About the Authors

Dr S Sagayaraj, MCA, M Phil., Ph.D, is Associate Professor, Department of Computer Science, Head, PG Department of Computer Science and IQAC coordinator, Sacred Heart College (Autonomous), Tirupattur, TN, India. He has over 32 years of experience in teaching computer science courses. His research interests include Knowledge Engineering, Semantic Web, Big Data, E-Learning and Semantic Web Services.

R Denis, MCA, M Phil., is Assistant Professor, PG Department of Computer Science, Sacred Heart College (Autonomous), Tirupattur, TN, India. He has over 10 years of experience in teaching computer science courses. Currently he is pursuing a Ph.D in the field of Data Security and he has published research papers in reputed journals. His areas of specialisation include Java, Python, Compiler Design and Artificial Intelligence. He also holds an Indian patent in image processing.

P Karthik, MSc, M Phil., BEd., PGDIS, is Assistant Professor, Department of Computer Science, Sacred Heart College (Autonomous), Tirupattur, TN, India. He has nearly 9 years of experience in teaching computer science courses and he has completed the TNSET in 2012. His areas of specialisation include Java, Software Engineering and Data Communication and Networking.

D Gajalakshmi, MCA, M Phil., is Assistant Professor, PG Department of Computer Science, Sacred Heart College (Autonomous), Tirupattur, TN, India. She has nearly 7 years of experience in teaching computer science courses and has qualified in the Tamil Nadu State Eligibility Test in 2017. Her areas of specialisation include Java, Python, J2EE Technologies and research interests include Data Science, Blockchain and Machine Learning.

CHAPTER

1

Foundations of Java

Java is an extensive, well-established language that is still growing with its competencies and associated libraries. Java is still popular for these reasons: it is a simple and powerful language, it provides an amazing range of programming features and the system-independent nature makes it an efficient and easy-to-use language. Java is the choice for novices, experts and for major application development. Java programs are easy to develop and maintain, compared to those in other languages. It also provides the capability to run programs on different types of computers and operating systems, without making changes. Java provides a lot of facilities, more quickly and more easily.

The features of C and C++ have been highlighted to understand and explain the move from these languages to Java. Also, the comparison between the object-oriented languages such as C++ and Java, enables the C++ programmer to see how it is easier to learn Java. The need for Java, the initial purpose of the language and how it was accepted in the internet world, is discussed. In the introduction, three predominant challenges are explained—security, portability and platform independence. The important features of the language are—it is simple, object-oriented, compiled, architecture neutral, multi-threaded, garbage collection, robust and extensible. Since Java is an object-oriented language comprising objects and classes, these concepts are elaborated along with the three principles of encapsulation, inheritance and polymorphism.

1.1 STAGE FOR JAVA

Java provides various programming features. The two main reasons for the popularity of Java are, the platform independence and the vibrant and interactive web environment it provides. C language was developed by Dennis Ritchie in 1969 in Bell Labs. It is a popular programming language, used as a general-purpose language, and is often learnt as the first programming language. C++ was developed by Bjarne Stroustrup in 1979 in Bell Labs. C++ is a general-purpose OOP language. There are numerous similarities in terms of features, between Java and C/C++. Learning Java is easy and simple if the reader has had exposure to C and C++. However, it is simpler to learn Java afresh without the user having to adapt the concepts learned for one language to another language.

Java derives its syntax from C and object-orientation from C++. This section is intended for C/C++ users to understand how the user can migrate to Java and understand the similarities and differences.

- C++ is a platform-dependent language while Java is platform-independent. A program written using C++ will run in one system and may not run in another system, but a Java program written for one system will run on any system.

- C++ was used mainly for system programming, but Java is used for application programs as well as in Windows, web-based, enterprise and mobile applications.
- Getting class information from two classes is permitted in C++ as multiple inheritance, but Java does not support multiple inheritance that can be achieved with the help of an interface.
- Performing arithmetic operators on objects is supported by C++ as operator overloading, while Java does not support operator overloading.
- C++ supports pointers and it can be used within programs, but Java supports pointers implicitly and they cannot be used in programs.
- C++ programs are only compiled but in Java the programs are first compiled and then interpreted.
- To pass arguments to functions in C++ both *call by value* and *call by reference* may be used, but Java supports only *call by value*.
- In C++ there is no provision for threads but Java provides built-in support for thread handling for manipulating many tasks concurrently.
- The memory de-allocation in C++ is done by calling its destructors. In Java that is taken care of by *garbage collection*. It keeps track of the programming parts and automatically de-allocates memory when it is not used.
- A few features of C++ are not supported by Java for security purposes, because the language is for the internet.

1.2 ORIGIN OF JAVA

The growth of the internet greatly impacted society in the 1990s. It changed the way computers were used and started the revolution of the use of computers in communication. The internet is a collection of various computers on different platforms and thus the need was felt for a language to handle communication between computers across platforms. Java emerged as a language for programming the internet as well as a general-purpose programming language. This language was initially not developed for the internet. Java was developed by a team from Sun Microsystems in 1991, led by James Gosling, and was initially designed for programming home appliances such as washing machines, microwave ovens, televisions, and so on. They started designing an application using C++. The multiple inheritance of classes and runtime programing errors of C++ made it unsuitable for the intended design of applications for home appliances. Hence the team started evolving a new language to overcome these issues raised by C++. But C++ was taken as a model for the design of the new language which was called *Oak*. The development team faced two challenges. The first was that the appliances were controlled by various types of processor chips and there was a need for a common language to work on these processors. The second was that the compilers to be used in the home appliances were costly. The programs developed for these machines would first be compiled using a compiler and then executed to control the appliances. To simplify the task of writing compilers for each appliance, the development team adopted a two-step process. The first step was that the programs written for the appliances were translated to intermediate code which was the same for all appliances. The second step involved the execution of the intermediate code in a step-by-step manner for a particular appliance. Hence the cost of translating to multiple machine languages was saved. However, programming the appliances did not appeal to appliance manufacturers. However, this concept was adopted in computers.

There are several types of computers that use various operating systems. Programs written for one computer may not work on another computer. Writing a program for one computer and executing it on another is called *portability*. The problem is similar to that of programming home appliances and Java designers used it to solve program portability. The two-step process was adopted for programming. The first step is that the written program is translated by a Java compiler into standardised machine language called *bytecode* which is the same for all computers. The bytecode is a machine-independent intermediate code. The second step is to translate this bytecode into machine language using an interpreter for a particular computer. The bytecode is interpreted and executed on any platform having a Java Virtual Machine (JVM). To run the bytecode it needs a JVM that serves as a language interpreter. The JVM reads the bytecode instructions and translates instruction by instruction into machine language code that is executed by a particular computer. Bytecode is interpreted one instruction at a time, which is different from compiling the entire program at one go.

The complete compilation and translation process is presented in Fig. 1.1. Java programs are translated by the compiler into bytecode which is common to all types of computers. The JVM for Windows interprets the bytecode for Windows. Similarly, the respective JVM interprets the bytecode into the respective computer's machine code. This diagram implies that the bytecode can be executed on any computer that has a JVM to interpret it. This provides the flexibility to the programmer to write the program once and execute it on several computers.

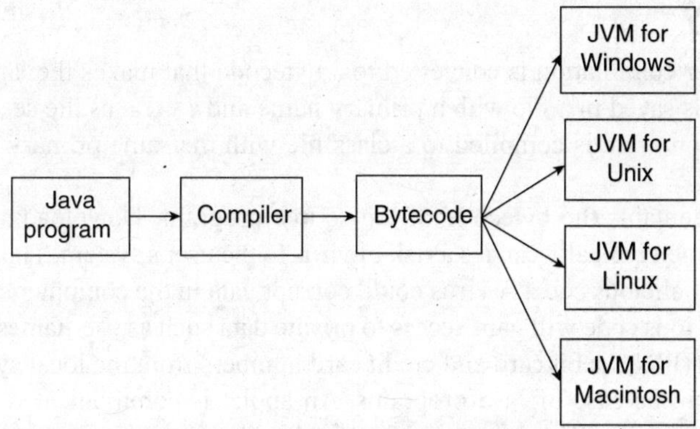

Fig. 1.1 Java compilations and interpretation model

In other languages the compiled machine code is directly executed. In Java the computer cannot execute the bytecode; for that it must execute the JVM to interpret each bytecode instruction into instructions it can run. The JVM reads each bytecode instruction and gives the computer the corresponding set of operations to execute. The computer executes the bytecode at a slower pace compared to the execution of machine code. The bytecode is portable to any computer but at the same time the bytecode execution is slower. Because of this advantage of portability, it has evolved as a widely used programming language.

By the time the language evolved, the name *Oak* had already been claimed and the name was changed to Java. Java is now owned by Oracle Corporation. In 1994, Patrick Naughton and Jonathan Payne developed HotJava, which is a web browser to execute Java programs in the internet. That is why Java is known as the programming language for the internet.

There are two types of programs in Java, namely, *applications* and *applets*. The standalone program written for any common problem is called an application and it does not need a browser to run. The program executed in a browser is called an applet. An applet is a program designed to be executed within a Java-compatible browser or applet viewer. There are a few differences between applications and applets. They are compiled in a similar fashion and created differently. Classes and methods can be used in both applets and applications. The code size of an application program is large while the length of an applet is less. Applications are executed on a standalone computer but an applet is executed on a client browser. Application execution needs the Java Development Kit (JDK) and JVM to be installed on a client system but an applet is executed by any Java supported browser. All the resources of a computer are accessed by an application while an applet is executed in a restricted environment. Applications are created using the `main()` method but applets are created by extending the `java.applet.Applet` package. Using a browser gives an applet access to a range of services, such as linking an applet to another web page or using browser resources like the status bar. An applet is restricted by a browser's security constraints and has no freedom to perform file and network operations as supported by application programs. Details of applet programming are explained in Chapter 12.

1.3 CHALLENGES OF JAVA

Java faced many challenges during its design; the prominent three challenges being security, portability and platform independence. This section explains how these challenges were overcome by Java.

1.3.1 Security

The Java program after compilation is converted to a bytecode that makes the language secure. As the program is written, it is saved in a file with a primary name and `.java` as the secondary name. During compilation, the java program is compiled to a class file with the same primary name and `.class` as the secondary name.

This `.class` file contains the bytecode of the source program. Downloading programs from the internet is an action which typically carries a risk of virus to the user's system. The program may contain any type of virus and malicious code. A virus could corrupt data in the computer system and slow down its performance. Malicious code will gain access to private data such as usernames, passwords, Personal Identification Number (PIN), debit card and credit card numbers from the local system. However, there is a level of security in the case of Java programs. An applet is communicated over the internet and automatically executed by the Web browser. Virus and malicious code attacks are prevented by the applet. The reason is that the bytecode generated is secure and can be executed in any computer which contains the JVM. Different types of JVM are available for each type of platform. In other words the bytecode is the same but the JVMs for various platforms are different. The bytecode is tested by the JVM for viruses and any malicious code, during the program interpretation and execution. The applet executed by the JVM will not allow access to authorised parts of the computer. Hence, an applet will not harm the computer and the fact that security is not broken is an important feature of Java. Thus, Java provides the construction of virus-free programs based on the public-key encryption technique for authentication. The language provides access to computer resources based on authentication.

1.3.2 Portability

Since Java is a programming language for the internet, it needs to communicate with various types of computers. Each computer has its own instruction set. Generally, programs written for one computer will not run on another computer. If a program written for a computer is to be executed on another, lots of changes have to be made to the source program. Most programming languages are not portable and pose a problem for multi-platform users. Portability means being able to write it once and run it anywhere. It facilitates programs being executed on any platform without making changes to the code. Java programs are not directly converted to machine code; instead they are converted to bytecode. To run this bytecode there is a need for a Java interpreter. Such an interpreter is available for all platforms, which make Java portable.

1.3.3 Platform Independence

The most important characteristic of Java is that it was designed to be machine independent. Java programs can run unchanged on any machine and platform that supports Java. An internet environment is a collection of various systems with different processors and different platforms. Over the years, platforms have changed and processors have been upgraded, which makes Java program execution tougher. Unlike other programming languages, Java is not compiled into a platform-specific code; rather, it results in platform independent bytecode. The bytecode is supported by any computer which has JVM installed, which makes Java a platform-independent language. In comparison, programs of other languages like C or C++ after compilation get translated into an object code which is processor- and platform-dependent. That is why C and C++ are called platform-dependent and Java is called a platform-independent language.

1.4 JAVA FEATURES

The basic features learnt in the previous sections have made Java a powerful tool for programming the internet. As mentioned earlier, *Java is a simple, object-oriented, compiled, architectural neutral, multi-threaded, garbage collection, robust and extensible language*. These descriptions have been explained here in order to provide a better understanding of the language.

- Simple—Learning Java will be simple for those who have programming experience in languages such as C and C++. The syntax of C is followed in Java and the knowledge of an object-oriented language will help programmers to migrate easily from C++ to Java. Many unnecessary features of other programming languages such as pointer, math, implicit type casting, structures or unions, operator overloading, templates, header files, or multiple inheritance have been excluded in Java.
- Object-orientation—This language uses classes to organise a program into logical components. The program must define the classes before they are used, which helps the compiler to locate and report type conflicts. These defined classes act as templates for the creation of objects during program execution. Classes can inherit members from other classes, but inheriting from multiple classes is not allowed in Java.
- Compiled—After writing the program it must be compiled by the Java compiler. The compilation translates the source program into a bytecode, which is similar to machine-code. The bytecode can be executed on any platform that has a Java interpreter. This interpreter reads bytecode and translates the commands into machine language commands that are executed on a computer. All other programming languages are only compiled but Java is both compiled and interpreted.
- Multi-threaded—Most programming languages will execute one task at a time in a uniprocessor. If an instruction contains many tasks to be performed, they will execute sequentially. A Java program however handles several tasks concurrently by using multiple threads. For example, a multi-threaded program can display a series of prime numbers on the screen using one thread while continuing to accept keyboard input from the user, using another thread. Any Java application has at least one thread to execute its program.
- Garbage collection—An object created for a class in a program will occupy space in the memory and will remain there till it is deleted. The unused objects that become garbage in the computer memory were handled in C++ by special functions called destructors to free the memory held by those objects. Java's garbage collection automatically handles the de-allocation of memory held by the unused objects, which relieves the programmer from memory management problems.
- Robust—Run-time errors in C/C++ sometimes make the program get into an endless loop and program control is transferred to the operating system. As a result, the program is unable to handle

the situation. The reasons for such situations lie either in the memory management or errors in the program which surface during program execution. The memory management is handled by the Java interpreter that checks all system access performed within a program. Java programs cannot end up in infinite loops during program execution. Instead, Java identifies run-time errors and creates an exception which is captured and managed by the program without risking the system.

- Extensible—The functions written in other languages can be used in Java, that is, can be linked dynamically during the program execution. In this manner, Java supports native methods, which are functions written in C++ that may execute faster than the equivalent methods written in Java.

The attributes of Java show that a great deal of thought has gone into development of the language that is easy to use and so popular. Because of the garbage collection feature, programmers can focus more on developing their program instead of wasting resources on handling memory management errors. Java is object-oriented and multiple threading to execute multiple tasks concurrently. It also has other attributes that collectively ensure that the language is up-to-date and powerful.

1.5 OBJECT-ORIENTED PROGRAMMING

Before using actual object-oriented programming, there is a need for introducing its basic concepts. This section will discuss the basic foundation of object-oriented programming. The discussion is not only for the foundations of Java but for understanding any OOP language. The most important characteristics of OOP are classes and objects. Just as botany students visualise all the vegetables they come across and refer to them by their botanical names, after learning Java completely, users will visualise everything as objects. For example, in a train reservation system, passenger, train and bank details for payment are objects. An *object* is a concept or abstract or thing with boundaries and gives meaning to the problem. Objects have two purposes,

- to promote understanding of the real world, and
- to provide a practical basics for implementation.

An object contains *data* and *methods* which manipulate this data. A passenger data has a name, age, ticket number, gender, source station, destination station, date of travel, train name and number, credit/debit card number, PIN number, date of expiry of the card, and so on. Methods can perform a number of functions such as receiving these data, storing, allotting seats based on the availability, payment, printing a ticket, displaying ticket on the screen, sending a Short Message Service to the passenger's mobile, and so on. In a train there will be many passenger objects travelling and they reserve their seats. These objects have their own unique identity. For example, Passenger-1 details are Mohan Kumar, 46, 789068, male, New Delhi, Chennai, 24/01/2020, 12658, Tamil Nadu Express, and so on, and Passenger-2 details are Soniya, 34,152769, female, Pune, Hyderabad, 18/04/2020, 15534 Hyderabad Express, and so on. All the data in these passenger details are different and exclusive. But the processing method for these objects will be same; the same method can receive values, the same methods can be used for storing, allotting seats, payment, printing, and so on. Hence the data is different for each object and the methods are the same for all objects. Objects are created in a program using a `class`. A `class` is a template for objects with data and methods. A class describes objects with various attributes, common operations, relationships to other objects. An object is an instance of a class. The objects belong to the class. Passenger-1 and Passenger-2 are instances of class Passenger. The program can create any number of objects for a class.

The class provides a template for the objects. Almost all programming languages allow the variables to be declared and then used in a program. There are two types of declarations, one is the predefined data type declaration such as integer, float, characters, and the other is the user defined data type declaration. For example, when a variable is declared as type *int*, the variable is an instance of the int data type. A class is like a data type in that, it is the blueprint upon which an object is based. If a new object is needed in a program, create a class, which is a kind of template for the object. Then, create an instance of the class. This instance is called an object. Classes are really nothing more than user-defined data types. It is easy to declare variables of the pre-defined data types. But for the user-defined data type, it is first defined and then the variables are declared. Also, the pre-defined data type provides mechanisms to perform operations on those data types, such as addition, subtraction, comparisons, and so on. Hence, for the user-defined data types, after the definition, the various operations to be performed on those data must be defined. Class is a user-defined data type where the data is defined and the operations to manipulate those data are provided in the methods. The class definition informs the compiler that a new user-defined data type is created in the program. The variables declared in a program will occupy space in the memory. However, the class definition will not occupy space in the memory but just notifies the compiler about its definition. Objects are the instances of a class. The declaration of an object will occupy space in the memory. For this reason, the class definition is abstract. The class must be defined first, followed by the declaration of the objects. The class is presented in Fig. 1.2 and object is depicted in Fig. 1.3(a) and 1.3(b).

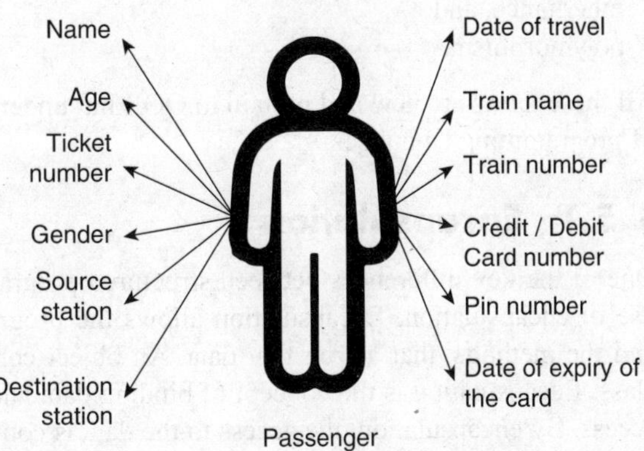

Fig. 1.2 Class representation

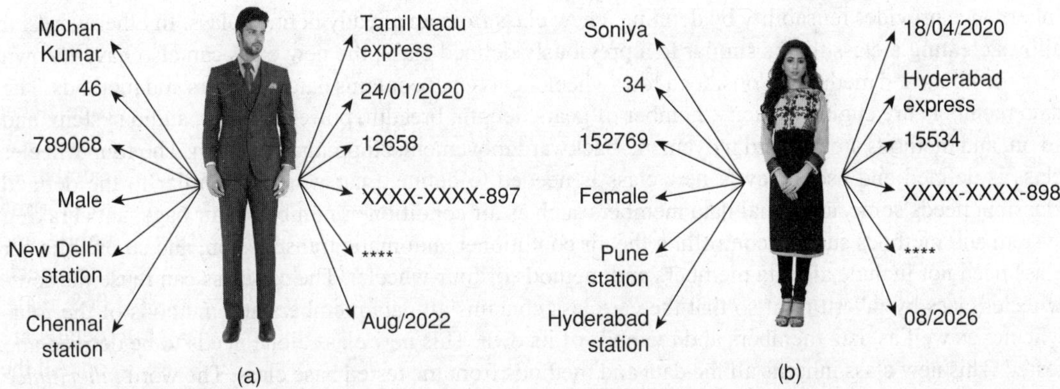

Fig. 1.3 Object representation (a) Passenger 1 (b) Passenger 2

Object-oriented programming allows the programmer to think of program elements as objects. The data in a program in the earlier languages is open and anyone can access it, that is, even an unauthorised user can use the data. But in OOP, the data is protected and can be accessed only by the intended users, that is, an unauthorised user cannot use the data in an object. Apart from hiding data access, the OOP paradigm provides a lot more. Learning about OOP involves three main concepts that are the backbone of OOP. These concepts, which are covered in the following sections, are:

- encapsulation,

- inheritance, and
- polymorphism.

All these terms are new and pertain to OOP, but understanding these topics needs some basic concepts of programming languages.

1.5.1 Encapsulation

One of the key differences between structured programming and object-oriented programming is the use of encapsulation. Encapsulation allows the programmer to hide inside the object, both the data and the methods, that act on that data. An object contains data and methods that are contained in a class. Encapsulation is the concept of binding data and methods together and it prevents unauthorised access. By encapsulation, the access to the data is controlled. On the other hand, to access the data the developers use controlled access (to the data) through the method which acts as an interface.

After providing controlled access, the data can be accessed or modified only through the methods and that too only by authorised users. The data in an object is always private by default in OOP. Other than the objects, the program should never have direct access to the data. In a structured programming language, data is declared in a method as a local variable. If a value of the variable is needed in another method, the variable must be declared as global. This gives any segment in the program access to the variables. In OOP, there is another level of scope that would make the data global to the methods that need it, but still prevent other methods from gaining access. That is the concept of encapsulation. In an object, the encapsulated data members are global to the methods of the object. But still they are local to the object and are not global variables.

1.5.2 Inheritance

Inheritance provides reusability by defining a new class from an already defined class. In other words, it allows creating a class that is similar to a previously defined class; the new class can also have its own data members and methods. Consider a four-wheeler class that contains data members and methods. The data members are engine capacity, number of gears, length, breadth, power steering, audio system, and so on, and methods are forward movement, backward movement, stopping, and so on. The four-wheeler class is defined and used. Now a new class is needed to define a car which is similar to the defined class but needs some additional data members such as air conditioner, number of air bags, anti-braking system and methods such as controlling the air conditioner, automatic transmission, and so on. The car class need not include all data members and methods of four-wheeler. The car class can reuse the four-wheeler class by inheriting it so that the car class contains all data members and methods of the four-wheeler as well as data members and methods of its own. This new class alone needs to be defined and tested. This new class inherits all the data and methods from the tested base class. The word *inheritance* reflects how children inherit many of their characteristics from their parents. But the children also have characteristics that are uniquely their own. In OOP, a base class is seen as a parent and a derived class as a child.

1.5.3 Polymorphism

From birth, a human being takes on different forms such as child, adult, middle aged and senior citizen. All these forms represent the same person. This occurrence of the same person in many forms is called *polymorphism*. In programming languages, polymorphism is the ability of an object to take on many forms. Polymorphism is derived from the Greek words, *poly* and *morphs*, meaning many and forms, respectively. Thus, polymorphism means *many forms*. Polymorphism is one of the characteristics of OOPs. This characteristic is seen in many object-oriented programming languages but its implementations vary from one object-oriented programming language to another object-oriented programming language. In Java programming, the polymorphism principle is implemented with the method overriding concept of Java. The polymorphism principle is divided into two sub-principles. They are:

- static polymorphism, and
- dynamic polymorphism.

Static binding is also called early binding or compiler time binding. Overloading is compile time polymorphism where more than one method share the same name with different parameters or signature and different return type. The overload method should always be part of the same class, with same name but different parameters. The parameters may differ in their type or number, or both. They may have the same or different return types. It is also known as compile time polymorphism. Method overloading is the best example of static binding. In method overloading, your method calls to the methods are decided by the compiler, in the sense that, which function is going to be called is decided by your compiler at compile time.

Dynamic binding is also called late binding or run-time binding. Dynamic polymorphism exists at run-time. Here, the Java compiler does not understand which method is called at compilation time. Only JVM decides which method is called at run-time. Dynamic method dispatch is a mechanism by which a call to an overridden method is resolved at run-time. This is how Java implements runtime polymorphism. When an overridden method is called by a reference, Java determines the version of method to be executed based on the type of object it refers to.

SUMMARY

1. C language was developed by Dennis Ritchie in 1969 and C++ language was developed by Bjarne Stroustrup in 1979 as a general purpose OOP language.
2. Java was developed by a team from Sun Microsystems led by James Gosling in 1991. It is a language for programming the internet. Java is also used as a general purpose programming language on the internet. Java was initially designed for programming home appliances.
3. The program written is translated by a Java compiler into standardised machine language called bytecode which is the same for all computers. The bytecode is a machine-independent intermediate code. The bytecode is translated to machine language using an interpreter for a particular computer. The bytecode is interpreted and executed on any platform having a Java Virtual Machine (JVM).
4. There are two types of programs in Java—*application* and *applet*. The standalone program written for any common problem is called application and it does not need a browser to run. The program executed in a browser is called an applet.
5. Java faced many challenges during its design; the three prominent challenges being security, portability and platform independence.
6. Java is a simple, object-oriented, compiled, architecture neutral, multi-threaded, garbage collection providing, robust and extensible language.
7. Class is a user-defined data type where the data is defined and the operations to manipulate that data are provided in the methods. Objects are the instances of a class.
8. The three main concepts – encapsulation, inheritance and polymorphism – are the backbone of OOP.

SHORT QUESTIONS

1. What is Java bytecode?
2. What is an application program?
3. What is an applet program?
4. Differentiate between application and applet programs.
5. What is the purpose of an object?
6. What is a class?
7. What is inheritance?

COMPREHENSIVE QUESTIONS

1. Compare the features offered by C++ and Java.
2. Why was Java initially not created for the computer? Explain in detail.
3. Discuss the challenges faced by Java during its creation.
4. Describe the various features of the Java language.
5. Discuss the various principles of object-oriented programming.
6. Explain how data is protected in object-oriented programming.

CHAPTER

2

Java Essentials

This chapter discusses the basic elements of Java. Any discussion on a programming language is best started with a simple program followed by elaboration of its various components which are common to all programs. Then the program compilation and execution are explained. In C/C++ the `#include` header files allow certain functions to be used in the program. Similarly, some of the pre-defined classes in Java can be made available to a program using the import statement; various types of variables and literals for storing values are explained. The primitive data types are briefly introduced along with their type and range of values. The input data type for Java is always string type. To handle this data type, a predefined String class is introduced. The language provides a rich set of operators that are explained with the various data types. An essential part of programming which involves the need to convert one data type to another type is also discussed. This chapter discusses the declaration, initialisation and usage of constants along with the scope and lifetime of the variables. The programs are documented with single and multiline comments to help in clarity. The chapter ends with the introduction of how to provide values to the variables through pre-defined classes, which is an important feature of any programming language.

2.1 ELEMENTS OF A JAVA PROGRAM

Now the first simple Java **Program 2.1** involving a lot of concepts is given below.

Program 2.1

```
public class FirstProgram {
public static void main(String[] args)
   {
      // A simple First program in Java
      System.out.println("My First Program in Java");
   } }
```

Output 2.1

```
My First Program in Java
```

The developer is generally at liberty to choose any name for his/her program. But that is not possible in Java. The name given to a program is very important. Program 2.1 is stored in a file with the name 'FirstProgram.java'. Here the file name has two parts—one is the primary filename, that is, `FirstProgram` and then there is a secondary file name which is java. Java insists that the file name for the program uses the `.java` file name extension. Normally a file name extension has three characters but in Java it has four characters. A Java program contains one or more class definitions. The name of the class and the name of the program file to be stored should match. That is why, the primary name of the file is `FirstProgram` and the class name inside the program is also `FirstProgram`. Java is a case-sensitive language because the files `FirstProgram` and `Firstprogram` are two different program files.

To compile the program using the command line argument for the program `FirstProgram.java`, the command is as follows

```
C:\>javac FirstProgram.java
```

The `javac` is the compiler which compiles the program `FirstProgram.java` and converts the source program into bytecode in a file `FirstProgram.class`. The bytecode is the first step in the process of execution of the program. The second step is to execute the `.class` file using an interpreter as follows:

```
C:\>java FirstProgram
```

This command executes the program and the result is shown in Output 2.1. The above program contains only one class name called `FirstProgram`. This is not always the case. The Java program will have many class definitions and during compilation for each class definition a class name with `.class` extension is created. In these classes, one of the class definitions must have `main` method and that class name is given to the name of the Java file name. That is, though there are many classes contained in a file, only one class definition will have the `main` method and that class name is given as the filename. Again looking at Program 2.1, the class name `FirstProgram` has a `main` method that is why the class name `FirstProgram` is used for naming the file. The compilation converts the program into one or more class files and the interpreter executes the class file which contains the `main` method. The second type of compiling program is NetBeans, discussed in Appendix I.

We see that the above program is a simple and small. It contains a number of features which may appear in all programs. The first line starts with the class definition as follows,

```
public class FirstProgram
```

A class is defined with the keyword `class` followed by the name of the class. Here, the name of the class is `FirstProgram`. The members of the class are enclosed inside the open curly brace `{` and closing curly brace `}`. The details of the class definition and its members are discussed in subsequent chapters. Before the class keyword, the access specifier is placed as `public` which informs the compiler that this class can be accessed from anywhere by the user. If the class is declared with `private`, the access to the class is given only to the owner and others cannot access the class. Inside the class, open curly brace `{`, the `main()` method definition starts as follows,

```
public static void main(String args[]) {
```

The `main()` method is a member of the class `FirstProgram` and it is executed by Java. There may be any number of methods defined inside the class definition, but the execution begins only with the `main()` method. As mentioned earlier, this `main()` method also has a public access specifier which allows anyone to access. The reason for making the `main()` method `public` is to allow another code outside of its class to be able to call this method. The purpose of the class definition is to create objects and use the objects to call the methods defined in the class.

The next keyword after `public` is `static` which helps to access the `main()` method without declaring objects for the class. The role of `static` helps Java to execute the `main()` method before any objects are created for the class. The next keyword in the statement is `void`, which informs the compiler that the `main()` method is not returning any value. Since the `main()` method is not returning a value to the calling statements, the return type is `void`; otherwise the `void` will be replaced by the type of data returned.

In the C language, the command line arguments help to pass different types of arguments to the program, which is similar to giving input to the program. But in Java, the command line arguments can pass only string type data using the predefined class `String` and `args` is the name of the parameter which holds a set of strings as an array. The passed strings are stored in the `args` and the program can extract and process the strings. The `String` class stores a set of characters as an object. This program is not passing parameters to the program. After the open curly brace for the `main()` method, the next line is as follows,

```
System.out.println("My First Program in Java");
```

This statement displays the string 'My First Program in Java' as output. `System` is a built-in class that provides access to the computer system and `out` is the output stream connected to the system console. The `println()` is a method defined in the output stream, which outputs the string arguments '`My First Program in Java`' on the console. The console refers to the output which displays the arguments on the computer screen. The `println()` method displays the string argument and display control is brought to the next line, first column. The `System.out.println()` statement ends with a semicolon. The practice in Java is that all statements must end with a semicolon. There are no more statements in the `main()` method, so it is ended by the closing curly brace. Similarly, there are no more methods defined in this class, and it is ended by the closing curly brace. That is the end of the class definition for the class `FirstProgram`. The program structure for a simple Java application is presented in Fig. 2.1.

All Java applications follow the template provided in Fig. 2.1. The first box is for comments which are required for good program writing, but it is optional. Comments have already been introduced in the first simple Java program. The second box marks the import statement and is based on the classes needed for a program, the corresponding packages are imported. For example, the first program has not imported any packages. The next section explains the use of import statements. The third box is for class definition, where the class variables and methods are defined. The first program has no variable but has a `main()` method. A program may contain any number of class definitions but only one class must have a `main()` method.

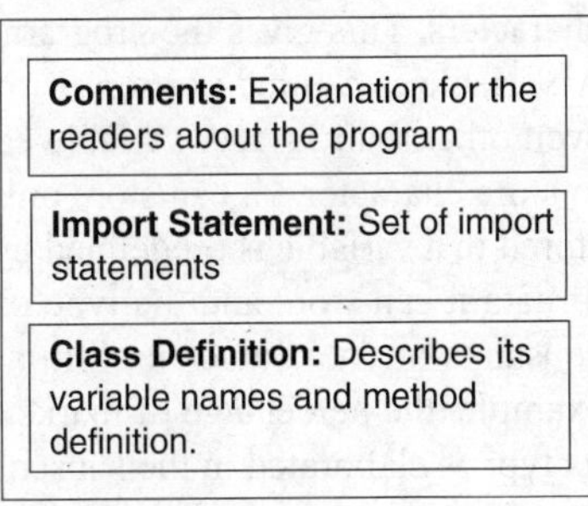

Fig. 2.1 Java application program template

The next section briefs the readers about a few classes used later in this chapter.

2.2 JAVA API

For C programming, using header files is essential for calling certain functions. For example, to use `scanf()` and `printf()` functions, the header file `stdio.h` must be attached to the program. Similarly, Java provides an Application Program Interface (API) which is a collection of classes used to develop programs. The API includes all packages, classes and interfaces. Packages are a library of classes that are used to keep the class name space as a group. Packages are created by grouping classes and then used in a program without moving the classes to the workspace. For doing this, an import statement is needed, which helps the predefined classes to be used in a program from the package. The import statement allows a program to access classes which are declared in other packages. The built-in classes provide access to these members and make use of their methods, fields and constructors in a program. These predefined classes offer vast functionality to a programmer. One must be aware of these classes and should know how to use them. To use a class from Java API, include an import statement at the start of the program. For example,

```
import java.util.Scanner;
```

Here the import statement gets access to the `Scanner` class defined under a subpackage called `util`, which is again grouped in the Java package. Some of the more frequently used packages are `java.lang`, `javax.swing`, `java.awt.event`, `java.util`, `java.io`. For example, `String` class is defined in `java.lang` package and `Scanner` class is defined in `java.util` package. These are the most frequently used classes in most of the programs written in the early stages of Java programming. `String` class permits the creation, use and manipulation of strings and Scanner class allows a program to read input from the keyboard. Each package groups its classes based on a purpose. For example, network programming (`java.net`), input and output (`java.io`), database programming (`java.sql`) and so on. There are plenty of packages defined in Java and explaining each of them will be beyond the scope of this book. A few of the packages are explained in various chapters, based on necessity. The default package in java is the `java.util` package.

2.3 VARIABLES

This section deals with components that are not objects, but are the basic data types such as numbers and characters. This gives the programmer an opportunity to use these elements in numerical calculations. A variable is a titled portion of the memory used to store data that is used in any program, perhaps even other than Java. A variable can store only one type of data. For example, if a variable is declared to store characters, it can store only character data and cannot store numerical values. The type of data stored in a variable is predefined by Java. A variable has a range of values it can accommodate; the type of data it can store and the type of operations performed are verified by the compilation process. The constants or data values used in a program are called literals. Each literal is of a particular type. For example, the percentage of marks for a student is 78.25, which is a literal and is a fractional value and its type is elaborated in the subsequent section. Like other languages, Java also expects the variables to be declared and used. Variables are declared by a name and its type. The name selected for a variable is called an identifier. Though programmers can give names to the variables, they cannot use the keywords defined by the Java as the name of the variable. For example, the previous section used a keyword *class* to define a class, so `class` should not be used as a variable name. The reason for so many restrictions in naming variables is to make the complier distinguish between the user defined variables and the other components in the program. The next section explains the various types of data and its literals.

2.4 PRIMITIVE DATA TYPES

A variable stores values according to its type. There are eight basic data types in Java called primitive data types. These primitive data types store four types of integer values in `int` data type, two types of fractional values in `float` data type, character data type in `char` and true or false values in `Boolean` variables. The `int, float, char` and `Boolean` are keywords that are not to be used as variable names.

2.4.1 Integer Variable

The integer variable to store an integer value is declared as

```
int age;
```

The data type of this variable is `int` and the name of the variable is `age`. The value stored in the variable `age` is only integer. There are four types of integer values stored in an integer variable. These four types are signed variables that can store either a positive or negative value. These four integer data types hold only integer values but differ in terms of range of integer values they store. The four type integers are given in Table 2.1.

Table 2.1 Java integer types

S. no.	Data type	Data range	Bytes
1.	`byte`	–128 to +128	1
2.	`short`	–32768 to + 32767	2
3.	`int`	–2147483648 to 2147483647	4
4.	`long`	–9223372036854775808 to + 9223372036854775808	8

The type of integer chosen by the programmer is according to the needs of their application. But `int` is mostly used to store an integer value and for a bigger range of integer values, `long` integer type is used. Now the four type of integers are declared as follows

```
byte age;
short year;
int placesInWorld;
long mobileUsers;
```

These declarations have declared the integer types according to the range of values they can store. The age of a person is not more than 128, so it is declared as `byte`; years are four digits which can be stored in a `byte` data type; the number of places in the world is in the range of `int` and the number of mobile users at present may be in the range of `long` integer. The number of byte allocated to `byte` data type is 1. Similarly, `short` integer data type holds value in 2 bytes. Java permits the use of declaring and initialising variables of any type. To declare and initialise the `age` variable can be done as follows,

```
byte age = 21;
```

The statement declares age as integer `byte` type and initialises the Right Hand Side (RHS) constant to the variable. It is a good practice to initialise a variable before it is used. If a variable is not initialised, it will have some unknown values and when used in summation or product terms will result in garbage value. If that variable is initialised and used in summation or product terms, it will give the expected result. Java is so flexible in declaring a variable, that it allows the declaration to be placed anywhere in the program, but before the variable is used. So, the program can have a declaration for each block of code. The declaration and initialisation is possible for more than one variable in the same statement. For example,

```
int age = 21, year = 2017;
```

Here, two variables are declared as integer and initialised, but they are separated by a comma. Multiple declarations and initialisations are possible only for a single data type with multiple variables declared and initialised using comma as a separator. But for program readability, it is better to declare and initialise a single variable in a statement. When variables are initialised, the value must be within the range of their types, otherwise the compiler will give an error message. The four types of integers should be used according to the situation which makes the program more efficient in terms of memory utilisation. For each application program, different types of data are used and these values can be stored in the appropriate integer data type which uses less storage space. This situation is applied where there is less memory available for programming. But this is not the case nowadays because programmers have more memory locations available in present day systems for their applications.

2.4.2 Floating-point Variables

Integral values are stored in integer variables and non-integral values (fractional values or values with decimal point) are stored in floating-point variables. The value 56.04512 can be stored in a floating-point variable. The same value is equivalent to 0.5604512×10^2; 56045.12×10^{-3} and 0.005604512×10^4 which reflects that the decimal point is floating and all the representations are equal. That is why the name for the data type is floating-point representation. The number of decimal places after the decimal point is called the precision. There are two primitive data types for floating-point data such as `float` and `double` (Table 2.2).

Table 2.2 Java floating-point data types

S. no.	Data type	Data range	Bytes
1.	`float`	-3.4×10^{38} to $+3.4 \times 10^{38}$ (OR) −3.4 E38 to +3.4 E38	4
2.	`double`	-1.7×10^{308} to $+1.7 \times 10^{308}$ (OR) −1.7 E308 to 1.7 E308	8

The notation of 10^{38} can also be presented as E38 which is used in Table 2.2. The declaration of floating-point variable is,

```
float salary = 156820.50F;
```

This statement declares a variable `salary` by initialising it with a floating point constant 156820.50F. If F is not appended to the constant then the value is by default, `double` type. The declaration for the `double` type is the same as that for the `float` type but will not have the F towards the end of the constant. As seen in the integer declaration `float` and `double` data type can also have multiple declaration and initialisation in a single statement.

2.4.3 Character Variables

Integer and floating-point variables store a range of numeric values. The character variable stores a single character. Character variables are stored as Unicode using 2 bytes of memory. The character variable is declared and initialised as follows

```
char firstName = 'S';
```

The statement initialises the variable `firstName` with the Unicode character representing the character S. The character constant assigned to a character variable must be enclosed within single quotes. The character enclosed within single quotes is treated as a character constant and that without single quotes is treated as a variable by the compiler. Apart from character variables and constants, Java provides *escape sequences* character constants. All the character constants are specified inside a pair of single quotes. Some characters cannot be entered directly using a pair of quotes. A backslash followed by a character informs the compiler that it has a different meaning. Such sequences of characters are called escape sequences or escape characters. The sequence is typed as two characters with no blank in between the characters. The use of backslash suppresses the meaning of an escape sequence character. To display double quotes inside a string, \" is used so that it will display double quotes and not the end of the string. Though the escape sequence is of two characters it is treated as a single character. A list of escape sequences is shown in Table 2.3.

Table 2.3 Escape sequences

S. no.	Escape sequence	Meaning
1.	`\'`	Single quote
2.	`\"`	Double quote
3.	`\\`	Backslash
4.	`\b`	Backspace
5.	`\f`	Form feed
6.	`\n`	New line
7.	`\r`	Carriage return
8.	`\t`	Horizontal tab

2.4.4 Boolean Variables

The Boolean variable has only two values—true or false. These two values are Boolean constants. The Boolean variable is declared as follows

```
Boolean employed = true;
```

The statement declared a Boolean variable `employed` and initialised it with the Boolean value `true`. The Boolean variable can be reassigned by another value as follows

```
employed = false;
```

The statement assigns the value `false` to the variable. The first assignment to the Boolean variable was `true` and the same variable is reinitialised with `false`. The use of Boolean variables seems limited in this section but it is used mainly in the decision-making process of an application. In the above declaration, the Boolean variable `employed` has either the value true or false; based on the state of the variable the execution of the program can be altered. Also, the Boolean operators, AND, OR and NOT produce the result true or false, which helps the program to decide on alternate flow of the program.

2.4.5 Assignment Statement

The variables discussed in this section can be modified by the assignment statement. The equal (=) sign is used as the assignment operator. The assignment statement has the following format,

```
variable = constant (or) variable (or) expression;
```

The assignment operator has a Right Hand Side (RHS) and Left Hand Side (LHS). The LHS must be a variable and the RHS may have constant or variable or expression. If the assignment statement has a constant on the LHS, the value is assigned to the RHS variable. If it has a variable on the RHS constant is assigned to the LHS variable. If it has a variable on the RHS the value of the variable is assigned to the LHS variable. If the RHS has an expression it is evaluated and the result is assigned to the LHS variable. The following statement assigns values to the variables,

```
Course = "Physics";
Balance = previousBalance;
Area = pi * radius * radius;
```

The first statement is to assign a string constant to the variable `Course`, the second assigns the value of `previousBalance` to the variable `Balance` and the last statement calculates the result by multiplying the values of `pi`, and `radius` twice and assigns it to the variable `Area`. Sometimes the same variable may appear on both the RHS and LHS as follows

```
count = count + 1;
```

It is an assignment statement where the RHS is evaluated first by taking the present value of the variable `count`, for example, if it is 4 and it is added with the constant 1 and the result 5 is assigned to the variable `count` on the LHS. Now the value of `count` is 5. The same value can also be assigned to two variable in a single statement, as follows.

```
test1 = test2 = 56;
```

The constant 56 is the marks of a student in two subjects which are assigned to test1 and test2 by which both will have same value.

2.5 THE STRING CLASS

The character variable that stores a single character is not sufficient to accommodate more characters. There is need to store name, address, degree, company name, description, and so on. To store a group of characters, Java provides the predefined class called `String`. The `String` class helps to create and manipulate strings. The `String` class is a default package which is available to all the programs and there is no need to import this package. The characters in `String` are stored as Unicode. Program 2.1 has used a string constant 'My First Program in Java'. A string constant is a sequence of characters between double quotes. The escape sequences character constants can be used inside the string constant to realise its impact. For example, the Output 2.1 can be changed by inserting the escape sequence characters in the string as follows,

```
System.out.println("My \t First \t Program \tin \tJava);
```

displays the output as,

```
My  First  Program  in  Java
```

The `\t` is an escape sequence for tab on the same line. The same Output 2.1 is changed again by using the `\n` escape sequence as follows.

```
System.out.println("My \n First \n Program \n in \n Java);
```

produces the output as,

```
My
First
Program
in
Java
```

The `\n` is an escape sequence for the new line character which places the remaining string into the next line. The first `\n` places `First` in the next line, the `\n` after `First` places `Program` in the next line and similarly the remaining words are displayed in separate lines. The Program 2.1 used `String [] args` which is the `String` class as explained and `args` is an array of String objects. The array of String objects will be discussed in the later part of this section. Till then it is sufficient to learn that String objects are declared and initialised in a similar way as primitive data types as,

```
String country = "India";
```

A more detailed explanation for the creation of objects is provided in Chapter 4 on Classes and Objects. The above statement declares an object `country` similar to a variable and initialises it using a string constant. Like a variable, this String object can be used for processing and display. The following statement displays the string constant and a country.

```
System.out.println("The name of my Country is: " + country);
```

In this statement the string constant 'The name of my Country is:' is displayed and the String object `country` is displayed as India. A new symbol is introduced in the above statement, that is, the + operator which joins or concatenates the string constant and the String object and displays it on the screen as,

```
The name of my Country is: India
```

In a similar fashion the primitive data types are also concatenated in **Program 2.2** with the String constant.

Program 2.2

```
/*
* To concatenate various data types with
* the String constant.
*/
public class SecondProgram {
   public static void main(String[] args) {
      int age = 23;
      double salary = 56075.25;
      String country = "India";
      System.out.println("The Age is: "+ age);
      System.out.println("The Salary is: "+ salary);
      System.out.println("The name of country is: "+ country);
   }
}
```

Output 2.2

```
The Age is: 23
The Salary is: 56075.25
The name of country is: India
```

Now the first four lines are comments for the program and the compiler will not execute those lines. The `public` access specifier indicates that this class can be accessed not only by the owner of the program but also by others. The `class` is a keyword which declares the class `SecondProgram`. Sufficient explanation is given for the next line of the code. The next few lines declare an integer variable `age` which is initialised with the constant 23, declare `double` variable `salary` initialised with the constant 56075.25 and a `String` object is created and initialised with the String constant `India`. The integer value in the variable `age` is converted to string as '23' and concatenated by the + operator with the string 'The Age is:'. Similarly the `double` value is also converted to a string as '56075.25' and concatenated by the + operator and the entire string is displayed. The final output statement has no need to convert the data because the String constant is concatenated with the value of the String object which is again a string. There are a number of methods in the `String` class which will be explained in Chapter 7.

2.6 OPERATORS

An operator is a symbol that informs the compiler to perform some operation on the given data. There are several operators provided by Java. The operators can be classified into four categories such as arithmetic, relational, logical and bitwise. Each category is explained briefly in the subsequent sections.

2.6.1 Arithmetic Operators

Arithmetic operators are used in mathematical calculations. The list of basic arithmetic operators is given in Table 2.4.

Table 2.4 Arithmetic operators

S. no.	Operator	Meaning
1.	+	Addition
2.	–	Subtraction
3.	*	Multiplication
4.	/	Division
5.	%	Modulus

Before using these operators, to realise the operation, some variables are declared and initialised as follows,

```
int a=16, b=5;
```

The variable `a` holds the value 16 and the variable `b` hold the value 5. The following statements make use of the arithmetic operators.

```
int c = a + b;
int d = a - b;
int e = a * b;
int f = a / b;
int g = a % b;
```

The result in these variables is not going to be a surprise to the reader; the value of `c` is 21, `d` is 11, `e` is 80, `f` is 3 and `g` is 1. The value of `f` should be 3.2 but it is 3, the reason is that when dividing 16 by 5 the result is 3.2, but when it is assigned to an integer variable `f`, only the integer part of the result 3 is assigned. The value of `g` is assigned by the modulus operator which actually divides the 16 by 5 and the remainder of the operation is assigned to g as 1, whereas in division the quotient is assigned to the variable `f`. In the same way the other data types such as `float` and `double` can also use arithmetic operators.

2.6.2 Relational Operators

Six relational operators are provided by Java to compare two primitive data values. The comparison may be performed on constants, variables or expressions using the list of operators given in Table 2.5. The result of the comparison can be stored in a Boolean variable and used in decision making as follows

```
Boolean result;
result = marks > 40;
```

The above statements declared a Boolean variable `result` and the value of `marks` is checked to see whether it is greater than 40 or not; if it is, true is assigned to `result` otherwise `result` is false. Based on the value of `result`, a student can be declared as pass or unsuccessful.

Table 2.5 explicitly states the meaning of each relational operator. Each relational operator is used to compare operands and the outcome will be either true or false which helps in making the decisions. Mostly the relational operators will be used in conditional statements or looping statements. When the relational operators are used in conditional constructs, the result of the comparison executes some statements for a true value and executes another set of statements for a false value.

Table 2.5 Relational operators

S. no.	Operator	Meaning
1.	>	The result of the comparison is true if the LHS operand is greater than the RHS operand
2.	>=	The result of the comparison is true if the LHS operand is greater than or equal to the RHS operand
3.	<	The result of the comparison is true if the LHS operand is less than the RHS operand
4.	<=	The result of the comparison is true if the LHS operand is less than or equal to the RHS operand
5.	==	The result of the comparison is true if the RHS operand is equal to the LHS operand
6.	!=	The result of the comparison is true if the RHS operand is not equal to the LHS operand

2.6.3 Bitwise Operators

The value of the variable stored in memory is represented in binary. The bits of an integer value can be operated on bit by bit using bitwise operators. The number of bits used to store an integer value is 32, so to store the decimal number 12, it is converted to 1100 and represented in 32 bits as 000000000000000 0000000000001100. Each bit of this binary number is operated with the corresponding digit of another binary representation of an integer value. The various bitwise operators are listed in the Table 2.6.

Table 2.6 Bitwise operators

S. no.	Operator	Meaning	Operation
1.	&	AND	If the corresponding bits in its two operands are 1, the result is 1, otherwise 0.
2.	|	OR	If either of the corresponding bits in its two operands is 1, the result is 1, otherwise 0.
3.	^	Exclusive OR	If both the corresponding bits in its two operands bits are different, the result is 1, otherwise 0.
4.	~	Complement	Each bit of the operand is inverted.
5.	`n << b`	Shift Left	Number `n` is Shifted to the left by `b` positions, `b` number of zero bits are appended to the lower order bits.
6.	`b >> n`	Shift Right	Number `n` is Shifted to right by `b` positions, the sign bit (MSB) is copied to `b` number of bits in higher order.
7.	`b >>> n`	Shift Right	Number `n` is Shifted to right by `b` positions, `b` number of zero bits are appended to the higher order bits.

To realise the impact of bitwise operations in a simple manner, variables are declared as integer and the binary representations are used for operations as follows

```
int a = 15, b = 10; // a = 1111, b = 1010;
int c = a & b;  // c = 1111 & 1010 = 1010;
```

The integer variables `a` and `b` are initialised with 15 and 10 respectively. The leading 0s in variables `a` and `b` are not shown in this example. The binary value of `a` is 1111 and the binary value of `b` is 1010, and they are operated using the `bitwise AND` operation; the result 1010 is assigned to `c`. Similarly, the same variables are used to perform `bitwise OR`, `Exclusive OR` and `complement` operations in the following statements

```
int a = 15, b = 10;       // a = 1111, b = 1010;
int c = a | b;            // c = 1111 | 1010 = 1111;
int d = a ^ b;            // d = 1111 ^ 1010 = 101;
int e = ~a;
// e = ~1111 = 11111111111111111111111111110000
```

The results are not surprising, because the results of OR and Exclusive OR operations are clear. But the result of NOT operation is something new. The reason is that the integer is represented using 32 bits; when complementing the 1111 the leading zeros are shown as complemented. So, the leading 28 zeros are complemented to 1 and 1111 is complemented as 0000. Combining both results is shown in the above statements. The bitwise shift operations are explained in a similar fashion as follows:

```
int a = 15, b = 2; // a = 1111, b = 10;
int c = a << b;     // c = 1111 << 10 = 111100;
int d = a >>> b;    // d = 10 >>> 1111 = 11;
int e = a >> b;     // e = 10 >> 1111 = 11;
```

The variables `a` and `b` have the same values as in the previous example; the variable `a` is shifted left (<<) by 2 bits. The variable `a` which is 1111 is shifted to the left by 2 bits and the vacant 2 bits are filled with zeros. Hence the result is 111100. The next line is similar but the bits are moved towards the right (>>>) by 2 bits. It is filled by the sign bit of the number that is 0 which represents positive number. The vacant bits are filled with zeros and the result is 0011. But the result is displayed as 11 because the leading zeros are ignored. The last line also shifts the bits to the right (>>) but after shifting 2 bits towards the right, the vacant bits are not filled with zeros. The result is again 0011 and the leading zeros are ignored again and the result becomes 11.

2.7 COMBINED ASSIGNMENT OPERATORS

In an assignment operator the same variable may appear on either side. To simplify the assignment, Java has provided a set of arithmetic assignment operators which are listed in Table 2.7.

To realise the assignment arithmetic operation, one variable is initialised as follows.

```
int a = 20;
```

Table 2.7 Assignment arithmetic operators

S. no.	Operator	Meaning
1.	+=	Addition Assignment
2.	-=	Subtraction Assignment
3.	*=	Multiplication Assignment
4.	/=	Division Assignment
5.	%=	Modulus Assignment

The variable a has the value of 20 and the following statements make use of the assignment arithmetic operators.

```
a = a + 1 (or) a + = 1;
```

The above notations are equal and the usage of these notations is left to the discretion of the programmer. The value of a is 20; it is added with 1 and the result 21 is assigned by the above statements. The next operator is -= which is used as follows.

```
a - = 2;
```

The value of the variable a is 21 is subtracted by 2 and the result 19 is assigned to a. The next operator *= is used in the following statement.

```
a * = 3;
```

The value of the variable a is 19 is multiplied by 3 and the result 57 is assigned to a. The next operator /= is used in the following statement.

```
a /= 4;
```

The value of the variable a is 57 which is divided by 4; the result is 14.25, and the integer part of the result, that is, 14 is assigned to a. The next operator %= is then applied in the following statement,

```
a % = 5;
```

The value of the variable a is 14 and modulus operation with 5 which actually divides the 14 by 5 and gives the remainder 4 which is assigned to a.

2.8 CONVERSION BETWEEN PRIMITIVE DATA TYPES

Type conversion, also called *Type Casting*, takes place when one primitive data type value is assigned to another primitive data type. For example, the value 25 is held in an integer variable x and 4 is in variable y.

By dividing x/y and assigning the outcome to an integer variable z, the resulting value in z is 6 but not 6.25. The result of the division is a floating-point value which is to be assigned to an integer variable z in which case the float value is converted implicitly and assigned to z as 6. The above statement is written as,

```
int x = 25, y = 4, z;
z = x/y;
```

The same statement can be written explicitly as follows and the result of the operation is the same as the previous one.

```
int x = 25, y = 4, z;
z = (int) x/y;
```

This statement divides the integer value by another integer value and the result is float which is explicitly converted to integer, because the LHS variable is an integer. If the type conversion takes place from integer to float, the integer value is appended with a few zeros in the fractional part. In the same way if a float value is converted to an integer, the fractional values are truncated and assigned as explained in the above statements. For example,

```
double p = 12;
```

The above statement assigns 12.00 to the double variable. Simply `p` cannot be assigned with 12, but that is possible with the automatic type conversion called *type coercion*. This type coercion makes the automatic conversion for an integer type to double type, but assigning a double to an integer is not possible, and the compiler will report an error message indicating that as illegal. But it is still possible with the explicit type casting as follows,

```
double p = (int) 12;
```

The above statement is a valid assignment statement. The primitive data types are arranged in a sequence as follows based on the number of bytes each one occupies.

```
byte -> short -> int -> long -> float -> double
```

The type conversion takes place for the above primitive data types in reverse order automatically. But to convert from higher bytes to lower, the explicit type casting is needed.

2.9 SCOPE OF VARIABLES AND BLOCKS

A few lines of code from Program 2.2 are presented in the following lines.

```
int age = 23;
double salary = 56075.25;
String country = "India";
```

These variables are declared in a `main()` method. These variables are specific to this block of code. The block is a code enclosed within the opening curly brace and closing curly brace. The visibility of these variables is only within this block; if these variables are accessed outside the block, the compiler will report an error message 'undefined symbol'. Scope is a block of code where a variable is declared and within which it can be accessed. Whenever a block is created, a new scope is also created for the variables declared inside the block. The lifetime of a variable is only within the block where it is declared. If there are two blocks placed one after another, the first block's variables are not visible to the second block. This situation is presented in the following example.

```
{
    int u=35;
    ...
    ...
    ...
}
{
    int c, d=8;
    c = d // Valid statement
    c = u // Invalid statement
    ...
}
```

The variables declared in the first block are local to itself and not visible to the next block. Hence the variable `u` declared in block one is not visible to block two. If one block is contained in another block as nested blocks, the variables declared in the outer block are accessible from the inner block but the variables declared in the inner block cannot be accessed from the outer block. The scope of nested blocks is explained using the following example.

```
{
    int u=35;
    {
        int c, d=8;
        c = d // Valid statement
        c = u // Valid statement
        ...
    }
    u = d // Invalid statement
    ...
    ...
}
```

The outer block declared the variable `u` and initialised it to 35. It is assigned to `c` in the inner block, which is valid. But the variable `d` declared in the inner block is not accessible to the outer block.

Comments have already been explained in the beginning of the chapter. The following section gives a more detailed explanation.

2.10 COMMENTS

All the statements covered so far instructed the computer to perform certain operations. A comment helps the programmer or non-programmers to understand the purpose and explains the complexity of program segments. There are two ways in which comments can be used in a program. The first is single line comments and the second is block comment. Single line comments start with the symbol `//`. The text between the symbol `//` and the end of the line is a comment. Any text that follows the symbol `//` is identified as comment by the compiler and the text is ignored. For example,

```
// Explains the process of the main() method
```

This comments reflects the purpose of the `main()` method. As the name suggests, this type of comment is for a single line. For commenting a group of lines, a block comment is used. Block comments start with the symbol `/*` on a starting line and can be extended to any number of lines and the block comment ends by the `*/` symbol. The text placed between the pair of symbols /* and */ are treated as comments and the compiler ignores those lines. For example,

```
/*
* To introduce the basic elements of a Java
* in the program FirstProgram.java.
*/
```

The above two lines are enclosed by the symbols /* and */, so the compiler understands that the text is a comment. Program 2.1 presented again, this time with comments added, provides a better understanding of the program.

```
/*
* To introduce the basic elements of a Java
* in the program FirstProgram.java.
*/
public class FirstProgram {
public static void main(String[] args) {
   // process of the main() method System.out.println("My   First   Program in
Java");
   }
}
```

The output of the program is the same as Output 2.1.

2.11 UNDERSTANDING KEYBOARD INPUT

Providing input to the Java program is not as easy as in other programming languages. However, the input to be given to the program is made simple with the use of `Scanner` class API. `Scanner` class is a predefined class used to receive values for the variables in a program as introduced in Section 2.2. The usage of the `Scanner` class API will explain the purpose of API and can be thought of as an example for API learning. The `Scanner` class is defined with a number of variables and methods. This section is not going to use all the members of the class; instead it will be used appropriately to read various data types in the program. Another predefined class `String` API is also used in **Program 2.3** to explain how to use the class to display a message prompt to the user to enter values.

Program 2.3

```
import java.util.Scanner;
public class readingValues
{
   /*
   * The program demonstrates the use of String and Scanner classes
   * to read values and display
   */
   public static void main(String args[])
   {
      String name;
      int age;
      double salary;
      char sex;
      Scanner inp= new Scanner(System.in);
      System.out.println("Enter your Name");
      name = inp.nextLine();
      System.out.println("Enter your Age");
      age = inp.nextInt();
      System.out.println("Enter your Salary");
      salary = inp.nextDouble();
      System.out.println("Enter M for Male
      and F for Female");
      sex = inp.next().charAt(0) ;
      System.out.println("The Employee
      Details are");
      System.out.println("------------------------");
      System.out.println("The Employee Name   :"+name);
      System.out.println("The Employee Age    :"+age);
      System.out.println("The Employee Salary :"+salary);
      System.out.println("The Employee Sex    :"+sex);
   }
}
```

Output 2.3

```
Enter your Name Xavier Maria Doss
Enter your Age
34
Enter your Salary
78458.25
Enter M for Male and F for Female
M
The Employee Details are
------------------------
The Employee Name     : Xavier
                        Maria
                        Doss
The Employee Age      : 34
The Employee Salary   : 78458.25
The Employee Sex      : M
```

Before explaining the program, `Scanner` class usage and methods need to be discussed in detail. The import statement must be placed as the first line of the program (as learned in the Java program template), to make use of the `Scanner` class. The import statement informs the compiler where it can find the definition of the `Scanner` class. The first line of the program also informs the compiler that the `Scanner` class is in the java.util package. A package is a collection classes and interfaces. Here Java is a package and it contains a number of subpackages. The `util` is a subpackage that represents the utility package. This import line makes the `Scanner` class available from these packages to the program. An object of the `Scanner` class is created using the following statement,

```
Scanner inp = new Scanner(System.in);
```

This statement takes `System.in` (keyboard) as a parameter to the constructor of the `Scanner` class and *new* keyword that allocates memory and reference is assigned to the `Scanner` object `inp`. Understanding the previous statement will be difficult at this point, but simply understand that the `Scanner` object `inp` is created and used to read various data types as follows,

```
name = inp.nextLine();
```

The `Scanner` object `inp` invokes the `nextLine()` method to read a string value from the keyboard and assigns it to the variable name. Similarly the following line reads an integer value using the `nextInt()` method from the keyboard using the object and assigns it to the variable `age`.

```
age = inp.nextInt();
```

In a similar way, the double value is also read and assigned to the variable `salary`. The following lines read a character using `charAt( )` method of the `Scanner` class:

```
sex = inp.next().charAt(0) ;
```

The statement reads characters using the above notation. The `next()` method is called from the `Scanner` object and reads a character from the position 0 to the character variable `sex`. Four methods of the `Scanner` class are used to read string, integer, double and character values. The remaining task of the program is to display the values using the predefined `String` class. This class is in the `java.lang` package which is a default package. So there is no need for importing `java.util` package for `String` class. The `System.out.println()` is used to display strings given as arguments. The string to be displayed is enclosed with in double quotes and passed as an argument as follows:

```
System.out.println("The Employee Details are ");
```

The string 'The Employee Details are' is passed as a parameter to `System.out.println()` for display. Sometimes integer, double, objects and so on that are to be displayed can be joined with the passed string using the concatenate operator `+` as follows:

```
System.out.println("The Employee Name :"+name);
```

The integer value is converted to string and joined with the string 'The Employee Name :' by the symbol `+` and passed to `System.out.println()` for display.

SUMMARY

1. A simple Java program has a class definition and a `main()` method as its components.
2. The compilation translates the program into bytecode using `javac` command and the JVM interprets and executes the code.
3. The template of Java application starts with comment, import statement and class definitions.
4. A number of pre-defined packages are provided by Java. The `String` class helps in manipulating a set of characters and the `Scanner` class is used to read various types of data.
5. A variable can hold values, such as `integer`, `float`, `character` and `Boolean`. The type of the variable must be equal to the type of the value stored in the variable. All variables must be declared and used.
6. The integer data type has four types—`byte`, `short`, `integer` and `long integer`. Each type can accommodate values based on its size.
7. The float data type has two types—`float` and `double`. The large values in these data types are represented in exponential form such as X10 or E or e.
8. The character constants include not only individual characters but also the various escape sequences to be used to display some special characters.
9. The Boolean variable is used to store only true or false in its variables. This is utilised in decision making in an application program.
10. An *assignment statement* changes the value of a variable. The equal sign = is used as an *assignment operator*.
11. The `String` class is a predefined class which helps in displaying string constants and can also be combined with other data types.
12. The arithmetic, relational and bitwise operators provide a mechanism to handle values in the respective data types.
13. The variable appearing on either side of an assignment operator may be replaced by the arithmetic assignment operator, which simplifies the writing of the expression.
14. The lifetime of the variables declared in a block provides the scope for the variables. There are sequences of blocks and nested blocks which provide different scopes for the declared variables.
15. The comments help the documentation of programs and are a good programming practice. It is inserted to explain any complex process of the program components. Java provides single and multiline comments.
16. The `Scanner` class is a predefined class that helps in reading values. This class has various methods to read different data types.

SHORT QUESTIONS

1. What is meant by case-sensitive? Give an example.
2. Explain the ways of compiling Java programs.
3. Write the compilations and execution commands of Java.
4. Write the uses of API. Brief about any two API classes.
5. Which package is the default for Java? Explain.
6. What are variables? Give examples.
7. List the rules for naming a variable in Java.
8. Write the primitive data types with the number of bytes occupied by each type in memory.
9. What is the reason for naming the fractional values as floating-point values? Give examples.
10. What is an escape sequence? Mention the list of escape sequences in Java.
11. What is a comment in Java? Explain its types and uses.

COMPREHENSIVE QUESTIONS

1. Write a simple Java program and explain its components.
2. Elaborate on the template of the Java application program. Give an example.
3. What is the `String` class? How it is used in programming? Give an example.
4. Discuss the various types of operators in Java.
5. Explain the bitwise operators with examples for each operator.
6. Explain the advantages of using assignment operators over assignment arithmetic operators.
7. What is the need for data conversion? Explain implicit and explicit conversions, with an example each.
8. What is the scope of a variable? Give the various forms of scope in Java.
9. How is input given to a Java program? Explain the input process with an example.

SOLVED PROGRAMS

1. Write a program that asks the user to enter two numbers, obtains the two numbers from the user, and prints the sum, product, difference and quotient of the two numbers.

```
import java.util.Scanner;
/*
  * To asks the user to enter two numbers,
  * get two numbers from the user, and print the
  * sum, product, difference, and quotient of the two numbers.
*/
public class number23 {
  public static void main(String[] args) {
     int num1, num2;
     Scanner inp= new Scanner(System.in);
     System.out.println("Enter two values");
     num1 =inp.nextInt();
     num2 = inp.nextInt();
     System.out.println("The values are
     "+num1 + " " +num2);
     System.out.println("The Sum of two
     values = "num1+num2));
     System.out.println("The Product of two values = "+(num1*num2));
     System.out.println("The Difference of two values = "+(num1-num2));
     System.out.println("The Quotient of two values = "+(num1/num2));
  }
}
```

Output

```
Enter two values
48
22
The values are 48 22
The Sum of two values = 70
The Product of two values = 1056
The Difference of two values = 26
The Quotient of two values = 2
```

2. Write a program that inputs the number of hours that an employee works and the employee's hourly wage. Then display the employee's gross pay.

```
import java.util.Scanner;
/*
  * To inputs the number of hours that an
  employee works and
  * the employee's hourly wage. Then display
  the employee's gross pay.
*/
public class wages {
  public static void main(String[] args) {
  int hours, wage;
  Scanner inp= new Scanner(System.in);
```

Output

```
Enter the number of hours
50
Enter the wage
65
The number of hours worked = 50
The wage = 65
The Gross pay = 3250
```

```
    System.out.println("Enter the number of hours");
    hours =inp.nextInt();
    System.out.println("Enter the wage");
    wage =inp.nextInt();
    System.out.println("The number of hours worked = "+hours);
    System.out.println("The wage = "+wage);
    System.out.println("The Gross pay = "+(hours * wage));
}}
```

3. Write a program to read the values of a, b and c and display the value of x where $x = \frac{a}{(b-c)}$.

```
import java.util.Scanner;
/*
* To read the values of a,b and c and
* display the value of x according to the given equation
*/
public class divionexp {
public static void main(String[] args) {
  int a,b,c,x;
  Scanner inp= new Scanner(System.in);
  System.out.println("Enter three values");
  a =inp.nextInt();
  b =inp.nextInt();
  c =inp.nextInt();
  System.out.println("a= "+a);
  System.out.println("b= "+b);
  System.out.println("c= "+c);
  System.out.println("x= "+(( a/(b+c))));
}}
```

Output

```
Enter three values
250
85
25
a= 250
b= 85
c= 25
x= 2
```

4. Write a program that generates the following output
10, 20, 19
Use an integer constant for the 10, an arithmetic assignment operator to generate the 20, and a decrement operator to generate the 19.

```
/*
* Generate the following output 10, 20, 19
*/
public class incdec {
  public static void main(String[] args) {
  int a=10;
  System.out.print(a);
  a+=10;
  System.out.print(" "+a);
  --a;
  System.out.print(" "+a);
}}
```

Output

```
10 20 19
```

PROGRAMMING EXERCISES

1. Write a program to prompt the user to input two integers and store the first number in num1 and the second number in num2.
2. Write a program to output the values of num1 and num2, indicating which is num1 and which is num2. For example, if num1 is 25 and num2 is 100, then the output is:

```
The value of num1 = 25 and the value
of num2 = 100.
```

3. Write a program that multiplies the value of num1 by 2, adds the value of num2 to it, and then stores the result in `newNum`. Then the program outputs the value of `newNum`.
4. Write a program that prompts the user to input the length and width of a rectangle and then prints the rectangle's area and perimeter.
5. Write a program that prompts the user to input a five-digit positive integer. The program then outputs the digits of the number, one digit per line without using a loop structure. For example, if the input is 12345, the output is:

   5
   4
   3
   2
   1

CHAPTER

3

Control Statements

Program execution in the code samples seen in the previous chapter was sequential in nature. This chapter shows how programmers can alter the order of execution of program statements or the control flow, using different conditional statements and looping structures. The conditional and looping structures provide groups of instructions which are executed sequentially. Conditional statements and loops are discussed in detail in this chapter. An example of a conditional statement is the if-then-else statement. First, the `if` statement is explained with true or false blocks, then the `if` statement is elaborated with an `else` part followed by `if-else-if` statements. More conditions are applied to the `if` control statement using logical operators. Multiple `if` statements are illustrated and the use of the `switch` statement to replace such statements is described. The importance of the two unary operators, the increment and decrement operators, is discussed. The loop statement and its types `while`, `do-while` and `for` are explained in detail. To enter and exit the loop, `break` and `continue` statements are described. These programming notions are explained with their structure, program flow and sample programs.

3.1 THE `if` STATEMENT

Programing steps do not always execute the instructions sequentially in the order in which they appear. Programmers may like the program flow to proceed in an alternative way. To change the work flow of the program, almost all the programming languages have a provision for branching condition structures. The `if` statement is a conditional statement that alters the program flow. The format of the `if` statement is

```
if (Boolean Expression)
{
}
```

In this `if` statement, first the Boolean expression is evaluated, the result is either *true* or *false*. If the result is *true* the instructions inside the curly braces will be executed, otherwise the program control skips the instructions inside the curly braces. The curly braces are optional if there is only a single statement, though it is better to provide curly braces for better code readability. **Program 3.1** works on the billing for a customer who purchases dress material from a retail shop. For every purchase of more than Rs 5000, the retailer permits a 10% discount.

Program 3.1

```
import java.util.Scanner;
public class IfTest {
   /**
       * Program to implement If statement for calculating Discount
       * for the purchase amount is more than 5000.
   */
   public static void main(String[] args) {
       int purchase;
   Scanner inp= new Scanner(System.in);
   System.out.println("Enter the amount purchased");
   purchase = inp.nextInt();
       if(purchase >=5000)
       {
           System.out.println("Purchase Amount =  "+purchase);
           System.out.println("Discount= "+purchase*.1);
           System.out.println("Amount to be Paid =  "+(purchase-(purchase*.1)));
       }}}
```

Output 3.1

```
Enter the amount purchased
  6000
Purchase Amount     = 6000
Discount            = 600.0
Amount to be Paid   = 5400.0
```

The program gets input using the predefined `Scanner` class. An object of the `Scanner` class is created and the method `nextInt()` is called to read an integer and assign it to purchase. The condition tests whether the purchase amount is greater than or equal to 5000. If it is true, the purchase amount, discount and the amount to be paid is displayed. If the condition fails, nothing is displayed by the program. While this program is correct and illustrates the usage of the `if` statement, generally conditional statements are not like the one seen in this program. This program does not show any output for amounts less than 5000 and that makes the user annoyed. A better way of handling this situation is given in the following section.

3.2 THE `if-else` STATEMENT

The `if-else` statement finds the alternatives between the true part and the false part based on the Boolean expression. The format of the `if-else` statement is

```
if (Boolean Expression)
{
    ….
    Block A
    ….
}
else
{
    ….
    Block B
    ….
}
```

In the `if-else` statement, the outcome of the Boolean expression is true or false. If the outcome is true one block of the code is executed, otherwise the second block is executed. **Program 3.2** tests a given number for odd or even numbers using the `if-else` statement.

Program 3.2

```
import java.util.Scanner;
public class OddEven {
    /**
        * Program to test whether the given integer is ODD or EVEN
        * Using if statement
    */
    public static void main(String[] args) {
        int number;
        Scanner inp= new Scanner(System.in);
        System.out.println("Enter a number to check for odd
        or even");
        number = inp.nextInt();
        if(number %2 ==0)
        {
            System.out.println("The Given number is EVEN");
        }
        else
        {
            System.out.println("The Given number is ODD");
        }
    }
}
```

Output 3.2

Run-1

```
Enter a number to
check for odd or
even
    21
TheGiven number is
ODD
```

Run-2

```
Enter a number to
check for odd or
even
    46
The Given number is
EVEN
```

The program reads a number using `Scanner` class. `If` tests whether the number is exactly divisible by 2 using the modulo operator to get the remainder. If the remainder is equal to zero then it is an even number otherwise the number is an odd number. This conditional statement has two paths out of which one path is chosen based on the true or false outcome after testing whether the number is odd or even. Conditional statements do not come with a single condition, logic that calls for more conditions will be handled in the following section.

3.3 NESTED `if` STATEMENTS

The conditional statements can be expanded by nesting an `if` statement inside the true part of the outer `if` statement and/or nesting another `if` statement inside the false part of the outer `if` statement. The format of a nested `if-else` statement is,

```
if (Boolean Expression-1)
{
    if (Boolean Expression-2)
    {
        Block 1
    }
}

else  {
    if (Boolean Expression-3)
    {
        Block 2
    }
}
```

In this `if` statement, Boolean expression-1 is evaluated and if found to be true the `if` statement in the block evaluates Boolean expression-2 and if that is found to be true, Block 1 is executed. If Boolean expression-1 fails, the program executes the `else` part and it contains the `if` with Boolean expression-3 and if that is true then Block 2 executed. In a textile company, the employees get a salary hike during every calendar year. The increase in the salary is based on four conditions. If the employee has more than 15 years of experience and the salary is more than Rs 8000, there is a Rs 1500 increase in the salary. If the employee has less than 15 years of experience and the salary is more than Rs 6000, there is Rs 1000 increase in the salary. **Program 3.3** executes the employee salary calculation based on the above conditions.

Program 3.3

```
import java.util.Scanner;
public class NestedIf {
    /**
        * The program illustrates the use of Nested if statement by
        * reading the experience and salary and calculates the new salary
    */
    public static void main(String[] args) {
        String empname;
        int exp;
        float salary;
        Scanner inp= new Scanner(System.in);
        System.out.println("Enter Employee Name ");
        empname = inp.nextLine();
        System.out.println("Enter Employee Experience ");
        exp = inp.nextInt();
        System.out.println("Enter Employee Salary ");
        salary = inp.nextFloat();
        if(exp>=15)
        {
            if(salary >=8000)
            {
                System.out.println("Employee Name
                ="+empname);
                System.out.println("Experience
                ="+exp);
                System.out.println("Salary =" +
                (salary+1500));
            }
        }
        else
        {
            if(salary >=6000)
            {
                System.out.println("Employee Name ="+empname);
                System.out.println("Experience    ="+exp);
                System.out.println("Salary =" + (salary+1000));
            } }} }
```

Output 3.3

```
Run-1
Enter Employee Name
    Mohan
Enter Employee Experience
    17
Enter Employee Salary
    9000
Employee Name    = Mohan
Experience       = 17
Salary           = 10500.0

Run-2
Enter Employee Name
    Natarajan
Enter Employee Experience
    12
Enter Employee Salary
    7000
Employee Name    = Natarajan
Experience       = 12
Salary           = 8000.0
```

The program reads name, experience and salary of the employee using the `Scanner` class. `If` tests the experience to see whether it is greater than 15 and if true it checks with another `if` for the salary greater than Rs 8000. If so, the salary is increased by Rs 1500. If the first conditional statement fails, the control flows to the `else` part and another `if` statement checks whether the salary is greater than Rs 6000 and if so the salary is enhanced by Rs 1000. The nested conditional statements can have many paths to decide on the true or false part but the above program has taken only the true part. The program may be expanded by providing the false path for each `if` statement.

3.4 THE `if-else-if` STATEMENT

The conditional statements can be expanded by nesting an `if` statement inside the false part of the outer `if` statement using a nested `if-else-if` statement. The students are classified as distinction, first, second, third class and unsuccessful based on the marks scored. Assume that a student who has secured more than 80 is declared as distinction, less than 80 but more than 60 is declared as first class, less than 60 but more than 50 is declared as second class, less than 50 but more than 40 is declared as third class and less than 40 is declared as unsuccessful. The format of nested `if-else` statement is

```
if (Boolean Expression-1)
{
    ....
    Block 1
}
else if (Boolean Expression-2)
{
    ....
    Block 2
}
else if (Boolean Expression-3)
{
    ....
    Block 3
}
.
.
.
else if (Boolean Expression-n)
{
    ....
    Block n
}
else
{
    ....
    Block for other Alternatives
}
```

The nested `if-else` statements show the Boolean expression-1 and if it true then Block 1 is executed. If it fails, the program checks for the `else if` with Boolean expression-2 and if it is true then Block 2 is executed. If it fails, the program checks for the `else if` with Boolean expression-3 and if it is true, Block 3 is executed. The checking continues till the last `else if` statement. The final `else` is optional and if it is provided it will take care of conditions not met by the earlier alternatives. The nested `if-else` statement will execute only one block of the entire structure. **Program 3.4** illustrates students' marks classification.

Program 3.4

```
import java.util.Scanner;
public class NestedIff {
   /**
      * Program to illustrate the use of
      * Nested If statement by reading the marks
      * of the student and classifying them as
      * distinction, first, second, third class
      * and unsuccessful.
   */
   public static void main(String[] args) {
   String name;
   int mark;
      Scanner inp= new Scanner(System.in);
      System.out.println("Enter Student Name \n");
      name = inp.nextLine();
      System.out.println("Enter Student Marks");
      mark = inp.nextInt();
      if(mark>=80)
      {
         System.out.println("Student Name
         ="+name);
         System.out.println("Student Mark
         ="+mark);
         System.out.println("Secured
         =DISTINCTION");
      }
      else if(mark>=60)
      {
         System.out.println("Student Name ="+name);
         System.out.println("Student Mark ="+mark);
         System.out.println("Secured =FIRST
         CLASS");
      }
      else if(mark >= 50)
      {
         System.out.println("Student Name ="+name);
         System.out.println("Student Marks
         ="+mark);
         System.out.println("Secured =SECOND
         CLASS");
      }
      else if(mark >= 40)
      {
         System.out.println("Student Name ="+name);
         System.out.println("Student Marks
         ="+mark);
         System.out.println("Secured =THIRD
         CLASS");
      }
      else if(mark < 40)
      {
         System.out.println("Student Name ="+name);
         System.out.println("Student Marks ="+mark);
         System.out.println("Secured = UNSUCCESSFUL");
      }  } }
```

Output 3.4

Run-1

```
Enter Student Name
   Daniel
Enter Student Marks
   92
Student Name  = Daniel
Student Marks = 92
Secured       = DISTINCTION
```

Run-2

```
Enter Student Name
   Anburaj  -
Enter Student Marks
   67
Student Name  = Anburaj
Student Marks = 67
Secured       = FIRST CLASS
```

Run-3

```
Enter Student Name
   Poovarasan
Enter Student Marks
   54
Student Name  = Poovarasan
Student Marks = 54
Secured       = SECOND CLASS
```

Run-4

```
Enter Student Name
   Ramkumar
Enter Student Marks
   47
Student Name  = Ramkumar
Student Marks = 47
Secured       = THIRD CLASS
```

Run-5

```
Enter Student Name
   Ramya
Enter Student Marks
   34
Student Name  = Ramya
Student Marks = 34
Secured       = UNSUCCESSFUL
```

The program reads the name and marks using the `Scanner` class. `If` tests the marks to see whether they are greater than 80; if so it displays the name, marks and secured distinction. The first `else if` structure again checks whether the marks are greater than 60 and less than 80 and then prints the details with 'First class'. The second `else if` structure checks the marks to see whether they are greater than 50 and less than 60 then prints the details with 'Second class'. The third `else if` structure checks the marks to see whether greater than 40 and less than 50 then prints the details with 'Third class'. The fourth `else if` structure checks whether the marks are less than 40 and displays the details with 'Unsuccessful' status. The `if-else-if` conditional statement has many paths to decide on true or false parts for finding the various classifications for the marks secured.

3.5 LOGICAL OPERATORS

In nested `if` statements, each `if` statement has a Boolean expression and in case both the `if` statements are true in Program 3.3, the details are calculated and displayed for the experience more than 15 years and the salary more than Rs 8000. But instead of having a separate Boolean expression for each `if` statement, they can be combined with logical operators. The logical operators are `&&` (AND), `||` (OR) and `!` (NOT). The function of each logical operator is given in the following tables.

`&&` (AND) operator

&&	**true**	**false**
true	true	false
false	false	false

If two Boolean expressions are available, they are combined with the `&&` logical operator. If the outcome of both Boolean expressions is true then the `if` condition becomes true; otherwise for the rest of the conditions the `if` condition is false.

`||` (OR) operator

||	**true**	**false**
true	true	true
false	true	false

If two Boolean expressions are available they are combined with the `||` logical operator. If the outcome of both Boolean expressions is false then the `if` condition becomes false; otherwise for the rest of the conditions the `if` condition is true.

`!` (NOT) operator

	!
true	false
false	true

Logical ! operator is used to reverse the logical state of its Boolean expression. If a condition is true then the Logical NOT operator will make the outcome of the condition false.

As mentioned above, the logical operators help the programmer to combine the Boolean expressions in a single `if` statement rather than having a separate `if` statement for each Boolean expression. **Program 3.5** has used logical operators.

Program 3.5

```
import java.util.Scanner;
public class LogicalOp {
   /**
      * The program illustrates the use of Logical Operator by
      * reading the experience and salary and calculates the new salary
   */
   public static void main(String[] args) {
      String empname;
      int exp;
      float salary;
      Scanner inp= new Scanner(System.in);
      System.out.println("Enter Employee Name ");
      empname = inp.nextLine();
      System.out.println("Enter Employee Experience ");
      exp = inp.nextInt();
      System.out.println("Enter Employee Salary ");
      salary = inp.nextFloat();
      if((exp>=15)&& (salary >=8000))
      {
         System.out.println("Employee Name   ="+empname);
         System.out.println("Experience      ="+exp);
         System.out.println("Salary          =" + (salary+1500));
      }
      else
      {
         if((exp<15)&&(salary >=6000))
         {
            System.out.println("Employee Name ="+empname);
            System.out.println("Experience     ="+exp);
            System.out.println("Salary         =" + (salary+1000));
         }
      }
   }
}
```

The program reads name, experience and salary of the employee using the `Scanner` class. `If` tests whether the experience is greater than 15 and the salary is greater than Rs 8000. If so, the salary is increased by Rs 1500. If the first conditional statement fails, the control flows to the second `if` statement which checks whether it is less than 15 and the salary is greater than Rs 6000; if so the salary is increased by Rs 1000. The output of Program 3.5 is the same as Program 3.3. These sections have compared numerical values with various formats of `if` statements. The next section checks whether the String objects are equal or not.

3.6 COMPARING STRING OBJECTS

String objects, introduced in Chapter 2, are compared here with two methods; the remaining methods are discussed in Chapter 7. Two strings are compared to see whether they are equal or not. The two methods are `equals()` and `compareTo` methods. The `equals()` method compares two strings by checking whether they contain equal number of characters, the same characters, in the same order and the same case; if so, they are equal. **Program 3.6** explains the use of `equals()` method.

Program 3.6

```
import java.util.Scanner;
public class Equals{
   /**
      * The program demonstrates the use of
      * equals() methods by comparing two strings
   */
   public static void main(String[] args) {
      String s1, s2, s3;
      Scanner inp= new Scanner(System.in);
      System.out.println("Enter First String ");
      s1 = inp.nextLine();
      System.out.println("Enter Second String ");
      s2 = inp.nextLine();
      System.out.println("Enter Third String ");
      s3= inp.nextLine();
      System.out.println("First String ="+s1);
      System.out.println("Second String ="+s2);
      System.out.println("Third String ="+s3);
      System.out.println(s1 + " and " +s2 +" are
      EQUAL="+s1.equals(s2));
      System.out.println(s1 + " and " +s3 +" are
      EQUAL="+s1.equals(s3));
      System.out.println(s2 + " and " +s3 +" are EQUAL="+s2.equals(s3));
   } }
```

Output 3.6

```
Enter First String
   Raguram
Enter Second String
   RAGURAM
Enter Third String
   Raguram
First String     = Raguram
Second String    = RAGURAM
Third String     = Raguram
Raguram and RAGURAM are
EQUAL=false
Raguram and Raguram are
EQUAL=true
RAGURAM and Raguram are
EQUAL=false
```

The first string `s1` and second string `s2` are equal if the case is ignored, but they are not equal so the `equals()` methods has returned False. The first string `s1` and third string `s3` are equal so the `equals()` method has returned True. The second string `s2` and third string `s3` are not equal so the `equals()` method has returned False.

Another approach is to use the `compareTo()` method which returns three values based on the arguments. If the strings are equal, `compareTo()` returns zero if the first string is greater than the second string as per the alphabetical order it returns a value greater than zero and if the first string is less than the second string as per the alphabetical order it return a value less than zero. **Program 3.7** describes the use of the `compareTo()` method.

Program 3.7

```
import java.util.Scanner;
public class Compare{
  /**
   * The program demonstrates the use of compareTo()methods
   * by comparing two strings
  */
  public static void main(String[] args) {
    String s1, s2, s3;
    Scanner inp= new Scanner(System.in);
    System.out.println("Enter First String ");
    s1 = inp.nextLine();
    System.out.println("Enter Second String ");
    s2 = inp.nextLine();
    System.out.println("Enter Third String ");
    s3= inp.nextLine();
    System.out.println("First String ="+s1);
    System.out.println("Second String ="+s2);
    System.out.println("Third String ="+s3);
    if(s1.compareTo(s1) ==0)
    System.out.println(s1 + " and " +s1 +" are EQUAL");
    else
    System.out.println(s1 + " and " +s1 +" are NOT EQUAL");
    if(s2.compareTo(s3) ==0)
    System.out.println(s2 + " and " +s3 +" are EQUAL");
    else
    System.out.println(s2 + " and" +s3 +" are NOT EQUAL");
    System.out.println(s1+" and "+s1+"="+s1.compareTo(s1));
    System.out.println(s1+" and "+s3+"="+s1.compareTo(s3));
    System.out.println(s3+" and "+s2+"="+s3.compareTo(s2));
    System.out.println("ZERO - BOTH STRINGS ARE EQUALS ");
    System.out.println("GREATER THAN ZERO - FIRST STRING IS GREATER THAN SECOND
    STRING");
    System.out.println("LESS THAN ZERO - FIRST STRING IS LESS THAN SECOND STRING");
  } }
```

Output 3.7

```
Enter First String
  java
Enter Second String
  pascal
Enter Third String
  fortran
First String    = java
Second String   = pascal
Third String    = fortran
java and java are EQUAL
pascal and fortran are
NOT EQUAL
java and java=0 java and
fortran=4 fortran and
pascal=-10
ZERO - BOTH STRINGS ARE
EQUALS
GREATER THAN ZERO -
FIRST STRING IS GREATER
THAN SECOND STRING
LESS  THAN  ZERO  -
FIRST STRING IS LESS
THAN SECOND STRING
```

The program received three strings and to prove the equality of strings, the string `s1` is compared with string `s1` and they are equal so the result is equal to 0 and the message displayed is `EQUAL`. The string `s2` is compared with string `s3`; since they are different, the message displayed is `NOT EQUAL`. To display the compared results the strings `s1` and `s1` are compared and the outcome is 0. The strings `s1` and `s3` are compared in the alphabetical order. The distance between *java* and *fortran* is 4 which is greater than zero. The strings `s2` and `s3` are compared in the alphabetical order and the distance between *fortran* and *pascal* is –10, which is less than zero. The conditional statements covered so far have another version if the true part or the false part has only one statement, as explained in the following section.

3.7 THE CONDITIONAL OPERATOR

A one-line code that works like an `if-else` statement is called a conditional operator or ternary operator. It can assign value to a Right Hand Side variable based on an expression's Boolean value. The general format of the ternary operator is,

```
result = testCondition ? value1 : value2;
```

If the test condition is true, assign the value of `value1` to `result`; otherwise, assign the value of `value2` to `result`. In Program 3.3, if the salary of an employee is greater than Rs 8000, his increment is Rs 1500 else it is Rs 1000 if the experience is ignored. This can be expressed as,

```
increment = salary>8000 ? 1500 : 1000;
salary = salary +increment;
```

If the salary is greater than Rs 8000, the outcome of the Boolean expression is true and Rs 1500 is assigned to the variable `increment`; otherwise Rs 1000 is assigned. The example has used the Boolean expression in the conditional operator. Boolean state can also be used in place of the Boolean expression. Apart from using a ternary operator to assign values to a variable, it can be used as follows,

```
String s = mark1 >= 40 ? "Pass" : "Fail";
```

If `mark1` is greater than or equal to 40 'Pass' is assigned to string `s`; otherwise 'Fail' is assigned. The same example can be used inside a display statement also.

```
System.out.println(mark1 >= 40 ? "Pass" : "Fail");
```

The line of code will display either Pass or Fail based on the value of `mark1`. A better way to handle multiple `if-else` statements is provided in the next section.

3.8 THE switch STATEMENT

In multiple `if` statements, for any number of conditions for a given value, only one `if` statement is executed. A better way to handle multiple `if` statements is provided by the `switch` statement. A `switch` statement allows a variable to be tested against a list of values. The outcome of the expression is tested for a value in each case. If the value is equal to a case then the statements in the case are executed till a `break` statement is reached and then control moves to the next line after the `switch` statement. The conditional values that cannot be handled will be taken care of by the default section. The general format of the `switch` statement is,

```
switch(expression)
{
   case value1 :
   {
      …
      …
      break;
   }
   case value2 :
   {
      …
      …
      break;
   }.
   .
   .
   default :
   {
      …
      …
   }
}
```

The `switch` statement can use only integers, characters, strings and enum. It can have any number of `case` statements. Each `case` is followed by an integer value. Each `case` should end with a `break` statement, otherwise the control flows to the remaining `case` structures till it reaches a `break`. A `switch` statement can have an optional default structure, which is the last structure after all the `case` structures. The purpose of the default structure is to perform a task when the other `case` structures are false. `Break` is not necessary inside the default structure.

In a marksheet, students are categorised based on the grades such as Distinction, First, Second, Third and Fail, as discussed in **Program 3.8**. By giving the grades, the following program lists the type of grade a student has scored.

Program 3.8

```
import java.util.Scanner;
public class Markswitch{
  /**
     * The program demonstrates the use of Switch statement
     * by getting the grades of the student
  */
  public static void main(String[] args) {
    String name;
    char grade;
    Scanner inp= new Scanner(System.in);
    System.out.println("Enter Student Name ");
    name = inp.nextLine();
    System.out.println("Enter a character: ");
    grade = inp.next().charAt(0);
    System.out.println("STUDENT NAME ="+name);
    System.out.print("GRADE ="); switch(grade)
    {
    case 'D':
        {
          System.out.println("DISTINCTION ");
          break;
        }
    case 'F':
        {
          System.out.println("FIRST ");
          break;
        }
    case 'S':
        {
          System.out.println("SECOND ");
          break;
        }
    case 'T':
        {
          System.out.println("THIRD ");
          break;
        }
    default :
        {
          System.out.println("FAIL ");
          break;
        }
    } }}
```

Output 3.8

Run 1

```
Enter Student Name
   Maheswari
Enter a character:
   D
STUDENT NAME = Maheswari
GRADE        = DISTINCTION
```

Run 2

```
Enter Student Name
   Ruban
Enter a character:
   X
STUDENT NAME = Ruban
GRADE        = FAIL
```

The program code receives name and grade, and tests the grade for different values. In *Run 1,* the grade is D and it matches with the first case structure hence it has displayed DISTINCTION. In *Run 2* the grade is X which does not match with any of the case structures so it is taken care of by the default structure to display FAIL. The following section discusses unary operators.

3.9 INCREMENT AND DECREMENT OPERATORS

Increment and decrement operators are another version of arithmetic operators. These operators are unary operators that work on a single operand. Increment operator is used to increment the value stored in a variable by 1. Decrement operator is used to decrement the value stored in a variable by 1. There are two types of increment and two types of decrement operators in Java. They are,

Increment operators

- Pre-increment (++ variable)
- Post-increment (variable ++)

Decrement operators

- Pre-decrement (–– variable)
- Post-decrement (variable ––)

3.9.1 Pre-increment Operator

The unary operator ++ is placed before the variable name. The value in the variable is incremented first and the value is used.

```
int x = 5;
int y;
++x;
y=++x;
```

The variable x is initialised with 5 and pre-incremented to become 6. Then the variable x is again pre-incremented and assigned to y. The value of both the variables is 7.

3.9.2 Post-increment Operator

The unary operator ++ is placed after the variable name. The value in the variable is used first and then the value is incremented.

```
int x = 5;
int y;
x++;
y=x++;
```

The variable x is initialised to 5 and post incremented to become 6. Then the value of the variable x is assigned to y and again post incremented. The value in x is 7 and value in y is 6 because before the value of x is post incremented, it is assigned to y.

3.9.3 Pre-decrement Operator

The unary operator –– is placed before the variable name. The value in the variable is decremented first and then the value is used.

```
n1 = 50;
n2 = --n1;
n3 = --n2;
n4 = --n1 + --n2;
```

The variable `n1` is initialised to 50, decremented and assigned to `n2`. The values of `n1` and `n2` are 49. The variable `n2` is decremented to 48 and assigned to `n3`. The last line adds the decremented values of `n1` from 49 to 48 and the value of `n2` from 48 to 47 gives the value 95 to `n4`.

3.9.4 Post-decrement Operator

The unary operator `--` is placed after the variable name. The value in the variable is used first and then the value is decremented.

```
n1 = 50;
n2 = n1--;
n3 = n2--;
n4 = n1-- + n2--;
```

The variable `n1` is initialised to 50, assigned to `n2` and decremented. The value of `n1` is 49 and `n2` is 50. The value 50 of `n2` is assigned to `n3` and decremented to 49. The last line adds the value 49 of `n1`, the value 49 of `n2` and gives the value 98 to `n4` and the values of `n1` and `n2` are decremented. To evaluate the expression, Java provides well defined rules of operator precedence. It defines how an expression is evaluated when it contains many operators. In an expression, if multiplication and subtraction operators are present, the multiplication is done first, followed by the subtraction. Table 3.1 provides the list of operators and their order of precedence from the highest to the least.

Table 3.1 Operator precedence

S. no.	Category	Operator	Associativity
1.	Postfix	() [] ++ --	Left to right
2.	Unary	+ ! - ++ -- ~	Right to left
3.	Multiplicative	* / %	Left to right
4.	Additive	+ -	Left to right
5.	Shift	<< >>	Left to right
6.	Left to right	< <= > >=	Left to right
7.	Equality	== !=	Left to right
8.	Bitwise AND	&	Left to right
9.	Bitwise OR	|	Left to right
10.	Bitwise XOR	^	Left to right
11.	Logical AND	&&	Left to right
12.	Logical OR	||	Left to right
13.	Conditional	?:	Right to left
14.	Assignment	= += -= *= /=	Right to left

An important programming statement loop is explained in the following section.

3.10 while LOOP

The amount received from a bank or ATM is counted from 1 to 10 or 20 depending on the amount. In a daily walk, after completing the initial round of the track counted as 1, continue walking and count every round. After each round, check whether 5 rounds have been completed or not. If 5 rounds have not been completed then continue walking otherwise finish walking. The above two processes make a loop of activity in terms of counting currencies or rounds in walking. Java provides three types of loops, such as

- `while` loop
- `do-while` loop
- `for` loop

This section discusses the `while` loop and the remaining loops will be discussed in subsequent sections. The `while` loop executes a set of statements or a single statement if the Boolean condition outcome is true. The general format is,

```
while (Boolean
Condition)
{
    ...
    ...
}
```

The Boolean condition is any valid expression or a Boolean state. If it is true, the group of statements is executed. The `while` loop continues as long as the Boolean condition outcome is true. If the condition fails, control moves to the next line of the `while` statement. The curly braces are optional if there is only one statement. If the outcome of the Boolean condition is false, the statements in the `while` loop are never executed. The `while` loop statement has three parts—initialisation, condition and updation. Before entering the `while` structure the loop variable is initialised. The Boolean condition makes the condition based on the loop variable and inside the loop, the loop variable is updated. Hence the order of the parts for a `while` loop is initialisation, condition and updating.

The usage of `while` is presented in **Program 3.9** that reads a number and displays its digits in reverse order.

Program 3.9

```
import java.util.Scanner;
public class whileDemo
{
    /**
      * The program demonstrates the use of while loop
      * by reversing the digits of a number
    */
    public static void main(String args[])
    {
        int n,d;
        Scanner inp= new Scanner(System.in);
        System.out.println("Enter a Five digit Number ");
        n = inp.nextInt();
        System.out.println("The Given Number is : "+n);
        System.out.print("The Reversed Number is : "); while(n!=0)
        { d=n%10;
            System.out.print(d); n/=10;
        } }}
```

Output 3.9

```
Enter a Five digit
Number
   12345
The Given Number:
   12345
TheReversed Number:
   54321
```

The program reads a five-digit number to `n` and verifies whether it is not equal to 0. The outcome is true and the control flows to the loop statements by assigning 5 to `d` using modulus operator. The digit in `d` is displayed and `n` is divided by 10 and assigned to `n` itself. The value of `n` is 12345. By dividing by 10 the fraction is ignored by the integer and 1234 is assigned to `n`. The `while` loop checks that the value of `n` is not equal to 0 hence the loop statements are executed by assigning 4 to `d`. Then 4 is displayed and `n` is divided by 10 and the value of `n` is 123. The loop continues by extracting a digit, displaying it and reducing the value of `n` till the value of `n` is equal to 0. Once `n` reaches 0 the loop terminates. Another version of the loop, which is the `do-while` loop, is presented in the next section.

3.11 do-while LOOP

The `do-while` loop executes a set of statements or a single statement even if the Boolean condition outcome is false. The general format is

```
do
{
    ...
    ...
}
while (Boolean Condition);
```

The control executes the loop statements and checks the Boolean condition. If it is true, the loop continues; otherwise, the next line of the `do-while` statement is executed. The `do-while` loop statement also has three parts. The sequence of execution is initialisation, updation and condition. Before entering the `do-while` structure the loop variable is initialised; inside the loop the loop variable is updated and the Boolean condition is based on the loop variable.

Program 3.10 finds the factors of a given number.

Program 3.10

```
import java.util.Scanner;
public class doWhile1 {
   /**
      * The program demonstrates the use of do-while loop
      * by displaying the factors of a given number
   */
   public static void main(String args[])
   {
      int n,d=2;
      Scanner inp= new Scanner(System.in);
      System.out.println("Enter a Number ");
      n = inp.nextInt();
      System.out.println("The Number is : "+n);
      System.out.println("The Factors are : ");
      do
      {
         if (n%d ==0)
         System.out.print(d +" ");
         ++d;
      } while(d<=n/2);
      System.out.print(n);
   }}
```

Output 3.10

```
Enter a Number
   144
The Number is   : 144
The Factors are :
2 3  4  6 8 9 12 16 18 24
36 48 72 144
```

The program reads a number to n and the control executes the loop statements. Whether the number is divisible by d is checked using the modulus operator. If d is a factor of the number n, then the factor d is displayed. Do-while checks if the value of d is less than n/2; if so, the loop statements are executed once again. The loop continues till all the factors are displayed. When d is not less than n/2 the loop terminates. The value n is also a factor, so it is also displayed. The next form of the loop, the for loop, is presented in the next section.

3.12 for LOOP

The general format of the for loop is,

```
for(initial-state; condition; updating)
{
    ...
    ...
}
```

The for loop initialises the loop variable and checks the condition; if it is true the loop statements are executed. After completing the loop the first time, the updating part is executed and the condition is checked. If it is true, the loop continues. If the condition fails, control executes the next line of the for statement. The for loop statement also has three parts. The sequence of execution is initialisation, condition and updation. The flow of execution is given in Fig. 3.6.

Program 3.11 checks whether the given number is a palindrome or not.

Program 3.11

```
import java.util.Scanner;
public class forDemo {
   /**
      * The program demonstrates the use of for loop
      * by checking a number is a Palindrome or not
   */
   public static void main(String[] args) {
   int n, number,revno=0, t=0;
   Scanner inp= new Scanner(System.in);
   System.out.println("Enter a Number ");
   number = inp.nextInt();
   for(n=number; n>0; n/=10)
   {
      t = n % 10;
      revno = revno * 10 + t;
   }
   if(number == revno)
      System.out.println(number + " is a PALINDROME");
   else
      System.out.println(number + " is NOT a PALINDROME");
   }}
```

Output 3.11

Run-1

```
Enter a Number
    12321
12321  is a PALINDROME
```

Run-2

```
Enter a Number
    12345
12345  is NOT a PALINDROME
```

The program reads a number and assigns it to `n` inside the `for` loop. Since `n` is 12321, which is greater than 0, the loop statements are executed by taking the Least Significant Digit (LSB) from the number using the modulus operator and assigning to `t`. The `n` is 12321 is mod by 10 to get 1 to `t`. The `revno` is 0, is multiplied with 10 is 0, added with 1 of `t` and the result is 1, is assigned to `revno`. The loop updates the value of `n` by dividing it by 10; now `n` is 1232 and the condition is true hence the loop continues. Again LSB 2 is extracted from `n` and assigned to `t`. The `revno` is 1 is multiplied with 10 that is 10 is added to the LSB 2 and `revno` is 12. Loop continues and terminates with 12321 in `revno`. The `if` statement checks `number` and `revno` for equality. If they are equal the number is a palindrome otherwise the number is not a palindrome. Nested loops are discussed in the following section.

3.13 NESTED LOOPS

One `if` statement inside another `if` statement is called a nested `if` statement. Similarly, one loop structure inside another loop structure is called a nested loop. In nested loops, the outer loop executes the inner loop repeatedly till the condition of the outer one is satisfied. A nested loop can be formed by having the same type of loop or involving one loop with another loop. In other words, a `for` loop can have another `for` loop in nesting or a `while` loop can have a `do-while` nested inside. In a nested loop, the outer loop changes its value only when the inner loop completes its execution. **Program 3.12** displays Floyd's triangle for the given number of rows.

Program 3.12

```
import java.util.Scanner;
class Floyds{
   /**
     * The program demonstrates the use of nested for loop
     * by printing Floyd's triangle
   */
   public static void main(String args[])
   {
      int r, n=1, i, j;
      Scanner inp = new Scanner(System.in);
      System.out.println("Enter number of Rows");
      r = inp.nextInt();
      System.out.println("~~~~~~~~~~~~~~~~");
      System.out.println("Floyd's Triangle");
      System.out.println("~~~~~~~~~~~~~~~~");
      for ( i= 1 ; i <= r ; i++ )
      {
         for ( j = 1 ; j <= i ; j++ )
         {
            System.out.print(n+" ");
            n++;
         }
         System.out.println();
      }
   }
}
```

Output 3.12

```
Enter number of Rows
7
~~~~~~~~~~~~~~~~
Floyd's Triangle
~~~~~~~~~~~~~~~~
1
2 3
4 5  6
7 8  9  10
11 12  13  14 15
16 17  18  19 20 21
22 23  24  25 26 27 28
```

The program receives the number of rows to be displayed and the outer loop is formed from 1 to the given number of rows. The inner loop runs from 1 to the first value 1, and displays the value of `n` as 1. The outer loop increments the `i` to 2 and the inner loop is executed again from 1 to 2 to display the `n` values 2 and 3 and terminates. The outer loop continues till the `n` is exhausted, to display the required number of rows of the Floyd's triangle. In some situations, the loop need not execute the loop statements completely or partially, and some of these situations are discussed in the following section.

3.14 break AND continue STATEMENTS

`break` and `continue` are part of the control structures. Both have different functionalities to be used inside the loop structure. Inside the loop, if `break` is encountered, the loop terminates and program control is transferred to the next statement following the loop. `break` is also used in the `switch` statement to terminate a case.

The loop is to be executed 50 times. Inside the loop, an integer is received and checked to determine whether it is 0 or not. If not 0, the value is added to the sum. If the value is 0 the loop is terminated by the `break` statement. There are two ways to come out of the loop. The first is by giving 0 to the input value and the second is that the loop terminates automatically after receiving the values 50 times.

Inside the loop, if `continue` is encountered, the remaining statements of the loop are skipped and the program execution proceeds with the next iteration. In a `for` loop statement, the `continue` proceeds with the update statement without executing the remaining loop statements. In `while` or `do-while`, the `continue` statement will transfer the control to the Boolean expression.

Program 3.13 adds the entered integers continuously and terminates when 0 is entered.

Program 3.13

```
import java.util.Scanner;
public class breakDemo {
   /**
      * The program demonstrates the use of break statement
      * by summing the values till the input is 0
   */
   public static void main(String[] args) {
      int x,y=1, sum=0;
      Scanner inp = new Scanner(System.in);
      do
      {
         System.out.println("Enter an Integer ");
         x= inp.nextInt();
         if(x==0)
            break;
         sum+=x;
         ++y;
      }
      while(y<=50);
      System.out.println("Sum of the number is : "+sum);
   }
}
```

Output 3.13

```
Enter an Integer
56
Enter an Integer
34
Enter an Integer
2
Enter an Integer
-5
Enter an Integer
-78
Enter an Integer
23
Enter an Integer
0
Sum of the numbers is:
32
```

Program 3.14 adds the positive numbers and neglects 0 and the negative values.

Program 3.14

```
import java.util.Scanner;
public class continueDemo {
   /**
      * The program demonstrates the use of continue statement
      * by summing the positive values given as input
   */
   public static void main(String[] args) {
      int i, x, sum=0;
   Scanner inp= new Scanner(System.in);
   for(i=0; i<10; i++)
   {
      System.out.println("Enter an Integer ");
      x= inp.nextInt();
      if(x<0)
         continue;
      sum+=x;
   }
   System.out.println("Sum of the positive numbers is :
   "+sum);
   }
}
```

Output 3.14

```
Enter an Integer
45
Enter an Integer
-45
Enter an Integer
55
Enter an Integer
-55
Enter an Integer
65
Enter an Integer
-65
Enter an Integer
35
Enter an Integer
-35
Enter an Integer
75
Enter an Integer
-25
Sum of the positive
numbers is: 275
```

The loop is executed 10 times for values of `i` from 0 to 9 and an integer value is received and tested to check whether it is less than zero. If it is, then the next integer value is received, otherwise the value is added to `sum`. At the end of the loop, the total of the all the positive values stored in `sum` is displayed.

Now that the three loops have been explained, the next section discusses which loop structure is better for a problem.

3.15 DECIDING WHICH LOOP TO USE

Each loop structure executes a set of statements when the condition is true. In a `while` loop structure, the loop statements are repeatedly executed until a condition is satisfied. If the condition is false the loop statements are never executed. Whether the condition is satisfied or not is decided by the loop variable which is either numeric or alphaumeric. This loop structure is good for situations where the number of times the loop is to be executed in not known in advance.

`do-while` also works based on the concept of the `while` loop, where the `while` will not execute the loop statements even once if the condition is not met. That's why a `while` loop is also called an entry condition loop. The `do-while` however will execute the loop statements at least once even if the condition is not met. Hence the `do-while` is called an exit condition loop. This loop is a good choice for getting inputs from the user and based on the value of the input, the loop is repeated.

`for` loop is a compact loop statement; all the parts of the loop are located in the beginning of the loop itself. The `for` loop executes statements a finite number of times. The loop variable counts the number of times the loop is executed. A `for` loop is good for situations where a loop is to be repeated for the specific number of times.

SUMMARY

1. `if-else` and `switch` are control statements that help in altering the sequence in which the program statements are executed.
2. `if-else` statement always has two parts: one is a true part and the other is a false part.
3. Logical operators help to combine many conditions in a single `if` statement.
4. Multilevel `if` statements help the program to have more conditions.
5. `switch` statement checks for multiple conditions and multiple branching statements.
6. There are three types of loop statements—`while`, `do-while`, and `for` statements.
7. A `do-while` statement always repeats its loop statements at least once even if the condition is not satisfied.
8. Both `while` statement and `for` statement repeat the loop statements zero times when the condition is not satisfied.
9. Nesting of loops helps in efficient programming.
10. A loop need not always be iterated to completion; program execution can leave the loop in the middle or execute only part of the loop statements based on conditions. In such a case, exit can be provided by the `break` and `continue` statements.

SHORT QUESTIONS

1. What is the need for conditional statements?
2. Mention the general structure of an `if` statement.
3. Why are the logical operators used in a conditional statement?
4. Write the two methods that are used to compare String objects.
5. Compare the functionalities of conditional statements and conditional operators.
6. List the advantages of using a `switch` statement instead of multiple conditional statements.
7. What is the difference between a pre-decrement and a post-decrement operation?
8. What is the essential difference between a `while` and a `do-while` loop?
9. What happens if the condition in a `while` loop is initially false?
10. Which is the better loop, `for` or `while`?
11. What are the advantages of using the `for` loop?
12. How does the `for` loop operate?
13. What is meant by a nested `for` loop?
14. What are the differences between `break` and `continue`?

COMPREHENSIVE QUESTIONS

1. What is a conditional statement? Explain its execution with an example.
2. What is the advantage of using an `if-else` statement over an `if` statement. Give an example.
3. Write the advantages of using multiple `if` statements over individual `if` statements. Give an example.
4. Discuss the execution of multiple `if` statements with an example.
5. What is a `switch` statement? Explain its execution with an example.
6. Explain briefly the process of comparing two string objects. Give an example.
7. Differentiate between post-increment operator and post-decrement operator.
8. Write the general format of the `while` statement and explain its execution.
9. Give the common format for the `do-while` statement and explain its implementation with an example.
10. Write the advantages of the `for` statement over other loop statements. Explain its execution with an example.
11. How do nested loops help in programming? Give an example.

SOLVED PROGRAMS

1. Write a program to display the multiples of 5 using a while loop statement.

```
public class whileDemo
{
  /**
   * The program demonstrates the use of while loop
   * by counting and displaying multiples of 5
   */
  public static void main(String args[])
  {
     int count=0;
     while(count <=50)
     {
        count +=5;
        System.out.println(count);
     }
  }
}
```

Output

```
5
10
15
20
25
30
35
40
45
50
```

2. Write a Java program to read two integer values and display the largest.

```
import java.util.Scanner;
public class sp01
{
  public static void main(String[] args) {
     int a , b;
     Scanner inp = new Scanner(System.in);
     System.out.print("Enter A Value: ");
     a = inp.nextInt();
     System.out.print("Enter B Value: ");
     b = inp.nextInt();
     if(a > b)
     System.out.println(" a is greater ");
     else
     System.out.println(" b is greater");
  }
}
```

Output

```
Enter A Value: 45
Enter B Value: 67
b is greater
```

3. Write a program to read the amount to be withdrawn from an ATM. If the limit is less than 40001, the customer can collect cash; otherwise the system should give an appropriate message.

```
import java.util.Scanner;
public class sp02
{
  public static void main( String[] args )
  {
     int a;
     Scanner inp = new Scanner( System.in );
     System.out.print( "Enter a Value: " );
     a = inp.nextInt();
     if ( a >= 100 && a<=40000 )
        System.out.println( "You can take a cash
        from ATM " );
     else if(a >40000 && a <=50000)
        System.out.println("You take cash from Bank Counter");
     else
        System.out.println("Your have reached the maximum limit for the week");
  }
}
```

Output

```
Run 1
Enter a Value: 30000
You can take cash from ATM
Run 2
Enter a Value: 55000
Your have reached the
maximum limit for the week
```

4. **Write a program to calculate the roots of a quadratic equation.**

```
import java.util.*;
class sp03
{
   public static void main (String[ ] args)
   {
      Scanner inp=new Scanner (System.in ) ;
      System.out.print("Enter the a,b,c of equation
      ax^2+bx+c=0:" ) ;
      double a=inp.nextDouble();
      double b=inp.nextDouble();
      double c=inp.nextDouble();
      double d=b*b-4.0*a*c ;
      double r1, r2;
      if(d >=0)
      {
         r1= (-b-Math.sqrt(d))/(2.0* a ) ;
         r2= (-b+Math.sqrt(d))/(2.0* a ) ;
         System.out.println( "Two real roots:"+r1+" "+r2);
      }
      else
         System.out.println("There are no real roots" );
   }
}
```

Output

```
Run 1
Enter the a,b,c of equation
ax^2+bx+c=0:2 3 4
There are no real roots
Run 2
Enter the a,b,c of equation
ax^2+bx+c=0:-1 -2 3
Two real roots:1.0 -3.0
```

5. **Write a program to find the Greatest Common Divisor of two given numbers.**

```
import java.util.Scanner;
public class gcd{
   public static void main (String [ ] arg )
   {
      int a ;
      int b ;
      Scanner inp = new Scanner(System.in);
      System.out.println("Enter value for a ");
      a=inp.nextInt();
      System.out.println("Enter value for b ");
      b=inp.nextInt();
      while(a!=b)
      {
         if(a>b)
         a=a-b ;
         else
         b=b-a ;
      }
      System.out.println("The GCD = "+a) ;
   }
}
```

Output

```
Enter value for a
128
Enter value for b
72
The GCD = 8
```

6. **Write a program to read a digit and display the number in a word.**

```
import java.util.Scanner;
public class NumberToWord {
   public static void main(String[] args) {
      int a;
      Scanner inp = new Scanner(System.in);
      System.out.print("Enter a number between 0-9:");
      a = inp.nextInt();
      if (a == 0) {
```

```
            System.out.println("Zero" );
        } else if (a== 1) {
            System.out.println( "One" );
        } else if (a== 2) {
            System.out.println( "Two" );
        } else if (a== 3) {
            System.out.println( "Three" );
        } else if (a== 4) {
            System.out.println( "Four" );
        } else if (a== 5) {
            System.out.println( "Five" );
        } else if (a== 6) {
            System.out.println( "Six" );
        } else if (a== 7) {
            System.out.println( "Seven" );
        } else if (a== 8) {
            System.out.println( "Eight" );
        } else if (a== 9) {System.out.println( "Nine" );
        }
    }
}
```

Output

```
Enter a number between 0-9: 5
Five
```

PROGRAMMING EXERCISES

1. Write a program that prompts the user to input a number. The program should then output the number and a message saying whether the number is positive, negative or zero.
2. Write a program that prompts the user to input an integer between 0 and 35. If the number is less than or equal to 9, the program should output the number; otherwise, it should output A for 10, B for 11, C for 12 … and Z for 35.
3. In a right angled triangle, the square of the length of one side is equal to the sum of the squares of the lengths of the other two sides. Write a program that prompts the user to enter the lengths of three sides of a triangle and then output a message indicating whether the triangle is a right triangle.
4. The name and age of two faculty members are entered through the keyboard. Write a program to display the name of the senior faculty.
5. A bank collects an interest of 6% for loans given up to Rs 7000, 8% for loans between Rs 7001 and Rs 10000 and 10% for loans above Rs 10000. Write a program to find the simple interest for one year, for a given amount according to the above interest rates.
6. The names and salaries of 3 persons are given as input. Write a program to display the name of the person earning the maximum salary.
7. The commission on a sales representative's sales is calculated as follows:
   (a) If sales Rs 1000, then there is no commission.
   (b) If Rs 1000 < sales Rs 5000, then commission = 10% of sales.
   (c) If sales > Rs 5000, then commission = 2000 + 8% of sales.

   Write a program to read in the sales amount and then compute the sales commission as per the above schedule.
8. The temperatures on the 7 days of a week at a hill station are given as input. Write a program to compute the average temperature for the week.
9. Write a program that converts an input number into Roman numerals. Print the number in Roman numerals. The decimal values of the Roman numerals are: M is 1000, D is 500, C is 100, L is 50, X is 10, V

is 5 and I is 1. If the given number is 3021, the program should display MMMXXI.

10. Write a program using the `while` statement, to generate all terms in the Fibonacci series that are less than 100.
11. Write a program using the `for` loop that will print both the uppercase and lowercase alphabet in sequence.
12. Write a program using a nested `for` loop that prints a 10*10 pattern of 0s.
13. Write a program using a `for` statement to count from 100 to 200 by 2s.
14. Write a program that functions like a calculator. The program should take as input two integers and the operation to be performed. It should then output the numbers, the operator and the result.
15. Write a program that reads a set of integers, and then finds and prints the sum of the even and odd integers.
16. Write a program that prompts the user to input a positive integer. It should then output a message indicating whether the number is a prime number or not.
17. Write a program that displays the number of even numbers in a series, the number of odd numbers in the series, the number of positive numbers, and the number of negative numbers. The program should then display the average of all the numbers.
18. Write a program that asks the user to enter a radius value and computes the volume of a sphere with that radius. The program should terminate when a non-positive value is entered. (Volume of the sphere = $4/3\ \pi\ r^3$)
19. Write a program that tests all the numbers from 1 to 100, displaying all those for which the sum of the cubes of the digits equals the number itself.
20. Write a program to calculate the average of `n` numbers, with the value of `n` entered by the user.

CHAPTER

4

Classes and Objects

Object-Oriented Programming is the dominant programming paradigm these days, having replaced the 'structured', that is, procedural-oriented programming techniques that were developed in the early 1970s. Most programmers working with the procedural style will not find it difficult to switch to the object-oriented style. The heart of Java is classes and objects. These are the basic building blocks of any Java program, as discussed in the earlier chapters. Every program in Java involves classes because the code for a program can appear only within a class definition. This chapter explores the details of how a class definition is put together, how to create your own classes, and how to use classes to solve computing problems.

4.1 CLASSES AND OBJECTS

Within the program, a programmer will write instructions to create objects. For the computer to be able to create an object, the programmer must provide a definition, called a *class*. A *class* is a kind of mould that dictates what *objects* can and cannot do. A *class* is a template or blueprint for how to build an *object*. A *class* is a prototype that defines state placeholders and behaviour which is common to all objects of its kind. An *object* is called an instance of a *class*. An *object* is an instance of exactly one *class*. Once a class is defined, it is possible to create many instances of the class, as the program requires. This section deals with the concept of classes and objects in the context of Java. A typical class can contain a data member, method, constructor, block, class and interface. The general format to declare a class is,

```
class <class_name>
{
    data member;
    method;
}
```

The `class` is a keyword and class_name can be any valid name. The members of the class are data members and methods. Data members represent the variables and the methods refer to the functionality. The following code segment contains a definition for a class named `Student`.

```
class Student
{
    String name;
    int rollno;
    int age;
}
```

The three lines from the start of the class definition define three instance variables `name` as String, `rollno` and `age` as integer. But this class has no methods. The class definition informs the compiler that a new data type has been created. But this definition is not going to occupy space in the memory, by which class definition is abstract. To make class definition a reality, the objects created will have to occupy space in the memory. Figure 4.1 shows a class diagram. A rectangle is generally used to represent a class, with its name appearing inside the rectangle.

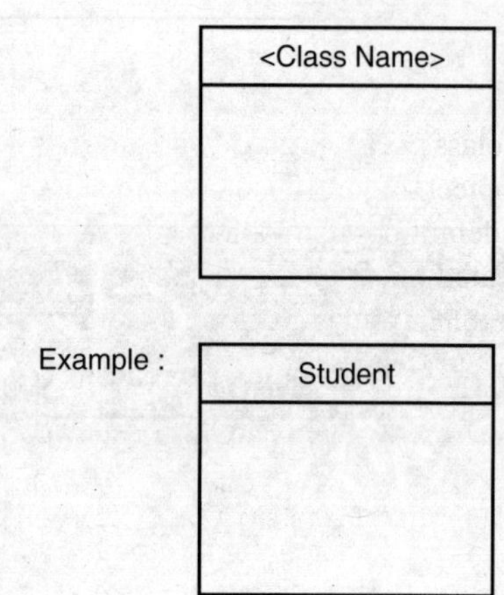

Fig. 4.1 Graphical representation of a class

An object is a collection of data along with the methods which work on that data. An object is a thing, both tangible and intangible. A program written in the object-oriented style will consist of interactive objects. The objects are the base for all programs and this is useful in two ways. One is that the objects allow one to encapsulate and structure a set of data. The other is to provide the objects a set of functions called *methods*, that act on the encapsulated data. Figure 4.2 shows a diagram to represent an object. A rectangle is used to represent an object and place the underlined name of the object inside the rectangle.

<Object_name>

Example: <s1>

Fig. 4.2 Graphical representation of an object

For example, in a two-wheeler shop, there will be bicycles and many other objects. Figure 4.3 shows two objects with the names `Splendor` and `Honda` and one `Customer` object with the name `Joseph`. An object name is followed by the class name. For example, `Splendor` is the object and `twowheeler` is the class name.

<Splendor : twowheeler >   <Honda : twowheeler >   <Joseph: Customer>

Fig. 4.3 Representation of objects with the class

The `new` operator is used to create an object of a class and associate the object with a variable. The syntax is as follows:

```
Class_Name object_Name = new Class_Name( );
```

The `Class_Name` refers to a defined class name, `object_Name` refers to the object which is user-defined, followed by an = symbol; then the `new` keyword allocates memory space for the class name and `Class_Name()` refers to the constructor which is used only once. Constructor is a method which will be called automatically during the creation of the object and will execute its functionality. For example, the class definition for `Date1` is as follows,

```
class Date1
{
   int day, month, year;
}
```

The class has defined `Date1` as a class name and data members are `day`, `month` and `year`.

```
Date1 birthday = new Date1();
```

The class `Date1` is used to create an object namely `birthday` and the `new` keyword allocates memory to the object. Figure 4.4 shows the object variable `birthday` which refers to the newly constructed object. The definition of an object must start with the class name and the object `birthday` has reference to the allocated memory for the data members. The object `birthday` has access to each of the data members `day`, `month` and `year`. A class can have many objects and each object has a unique set of data.

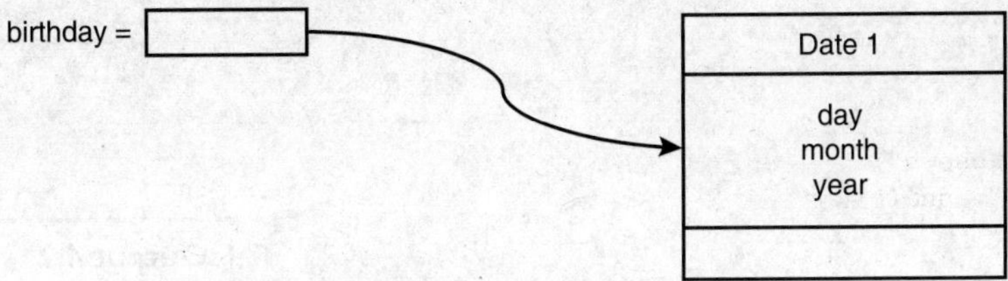

Fig. 4.4 Representation of object and class

The data members are accessed only with an object. The dot (.) operator is used to connect the object with its data members. The following statement initialises the `birthday` object.

```
birthday.day = 23;
birthday.month= 5;
birthday.year = 2017;
```

The object `birthday` and the data member `day` are connected by the dot operator and initialised with 23. Similarly, the remaining data members are initialised. The `Student` class is created and its data members are accessed in the following **Program 4.1**.

Program 4.1

```
class Student{
int id; String name;
public static void main(String args[]){
   Student s1=new Student();
   System.out.println(s1.id);
   System.out.println(s1.name);
   }
}
```

Output 4.1

```
0 null
```

In the above program, the class name is `Student`. The class definition has two variables: `id` as an integer type and `name` as String type. There is no method defined in the class. In the `main()` method the object for the `Student` class is created, namely `s1` by the `new` keyword. The `new` keyword allocates memory space for the object `s1`. There is no explicit constructor defined in the class, so the values for the data members are not initialised. Then, the values of variables are displayed by `s1.id` and `s1.name`, where `s1` is the object followed by the dot operator added with the variables `id` and `name`. Since the variables are not initialised with any values, it returns `0` and `null` as output. By default Java initialises integer variables with the `0` value and string as `null`. That's why the value for `id` is `0` and `name` is `null`. Java provides data hiding with the help of access specifiers such as `private`. These access specifiers allow the data members to be accessed only within the class and not be accessed from outside the class definition. The class definition has methods which manipulate the data, as is presented in **Program 4.2**.

Program 4.2

```
class Student
{
    private String name, city;
    private int age;
    public void getData1()
    {
        name="Anand";
        city="Vellore";
        age=23;
    }
    public void getData2()
    {   name="Joseph";
        city="Chennai";
        age=22;
    }
    public void printData()
    {
        System.out.println("Student name = "+name);
        System.out.println("Student city = "+city);
        System.out.println("Student age ="+age);
    }
}
class Cs
{
    public static void main(String args[])
    {
        Student s1=new Student();
        Student s2=new Student();
        s1.getData1();
        s1.printData();
        s2.getData2();
        s2.printData();
    }
}
```

Output 4.2

```
Student name = Anand
Student city = Vellore
Student age =23
Student name = Joseph
Student city = Chennai
Student age =22
```

The program has two classes, namely, `Student` and `Cs`. `Cs` refers to the `main()` class. The `Student` class has `name`, `city` and `age` as variables. The method `getData1()` and `getData2()` are used to initialise the values to the data members `name`, `city` and `age`. Then, the `printData()` method is used to display the values of the data members. In the `main` class `Cs` two objects are created for `Student` class `s1` and `s2`. The memory space for `s1` and `s2` objects are allocated by `new` keyword. The `s1` object invokes `getData1()` method and 'Anand' is assigned to name, 'Vellore' is assigned to `city` and '23' is assigned to `age`. Similarly, the `s2` object invokes `getData2()` method and 'Joseph' is assigned to name, 'Chennai' is assigned to `city` and '22' is assigned to `age`. Hence `s1` and `s2` objects have unique data as data members. A class can have any number of objects and each object has its own set of data. These data members are displayed using the `printData()` method. The methods `getData1()`, `getData2()` and `printData()` are accessed by the object and dot operator. In the above program, two objects are created, namely `s1` and `s2`, that can access these methods. Collectively, the methods and variables defined within a class are called members of the class. In most classes, the instance variables are acted upon and accessed by the methods defined for that class. It is the methods that determine how a class' data can be used. Therefore, methods are necessary for manipulating the data contained in the class. Methods are declared in the body of the class immediately after the declaration of variables. Methods can be seen as self-contained blocks of statements that are used to perform a task. The general form of declaring the method is:

```
accessspecifier data_type method_name(parameter_list)
{
   body of the method;
}
```

In the above method declaration, *access specifier* refers to private, public and protected, *data_type* refers to the type of data returned by the method, *method_name* refers to the name of the method, the *parameter_list* is always enclosed in a pair of parenthesis where it contains variable names and the types of values that the programmer wants to give method as input. The variables in the list should be separated by commas. For example,

```
public void input(int x, int y)
```

`public` is the access specifier, `void` is the return type, `input` is the method name and the *parameter_list* has two integer variables `x, y`.

A detailed description about methods is given later in this chapter. The following section explains the access specifiers used in a program.

4.2 MODIFIERS

Modifiers are keywords used to define the scope and behaviour of the classes, methods and variables. Class definitions have different access levels and this determines where an object of the class can be instantiated. All the variables and methods in a class are available to any code written for that class. There are four possible access specifiers: public, protected, private and default access. The *public* access refers to the data members and methods that can be freely accessed by the code from any other class. The *protected* access refers to the members that cannot be accessed by the code from any other class, except the class that inherits from this class and classes in the same package – which refers to a collection of classes – basically all the classes stored in the same directory. The *private* access means that the member will not be accessed by code in any other class, including classes that inherit from this one. Then there is the fourth possibility, the *default* access, which is used if there is no access specifier mentioned.

There are other modifiers which can be used in a program. The *static* modifier is used to create methods and variables, the *abstract* modifier is used to create abstract classes and methods, the *final* modifier for finalising the implementations of classes, methods and variables, the *synchronised* and *volatile* modifiers for threads and the *native* modifier for creating native methods. Table 4.1 shows the access to members permitted by each modifier.

Table 4.1 Access specifiers

Modifier	Used	Description
Public	Outer classes, interfaces, constructors, inner classes, methods and variables	Accessed by classes outside the package
Protected	Constructor, inner classes, methods and variables	Accessed by the same package or by any subclass outside of package
Private	Constructor, inner classes, methods and variables	Access only within class where they are declared
No modifier (Default)	Outer classes, inner classes, interface, constructor, method and variables	Access only within the package where they exist

It should be remembered that there cannot be more than one access modifier for a class, method or variable. All the modifiers are essentially optional, but a good programming style suggests that modifiers should be added. **Program 4.3** explains the use of access specifiers in an application.

Program 4.3

```
public class ModifierEx {
    private String name="Joseph";
    private int age=20;
    public void display()
    {
        System.out.println("Name :"+name);
        System.out.println("Age :"+age);
    }
    private void show()
    {
        System.out.println("Name :"+name);
        System.out.println("Age :"+age);
    }
}
class ModifierEx1
{
    public static void main(String args[])
    {
        ModifierEx m1=new ModifierEx();
        m1.display();
        //m1.show();
    }
}
```

Output 4.3

```
Name :Joseph
Age :20
```

The name of the class is `ModifierEx` and it has two variables and two methods. The data members `name` and `age` are declared and initialised with the values Joseph and 20 respectively. The two methods `display()` and `show()` print the values of the data members. The data members `name` and `age` are declared as private. All the instance variables are private by default. The `display()` method is public and hence it can be accessed from the `main()` method to display the data members; `show()` method is to display the data members but is defined as private, hence it can't be accessed from the `main()` method. The program has commented the invoking line `m1.show()` otherwise the compiler will give an error message. The methods used in this section have not used any parameters as arguments (which will be discussed in the following section).

4.3 PASSING ARGUMENTS

The previous section briefly explained the concept of class, object, access specifiers and their usage. This section explains the terms that describe how parameters are passed to a method. Before passing any arguments, there should be methods in a program. The methods defined for a class provide the actions that can be carried out on variables specified in the class definition. As with variables in a class definition, there are two types of methods, namely, *instance methods* and *class methods*. The programmer can execute class methods even when no objects of a class exist, whereas instance methods can be executed in relation to a particular object, so if no objects exist, there is no way to execute any of the instance methods defined in the class.

4.3.1 Defining Methods

A method is a self-contained block of code that has a name and set of properties that are reusable; the same method can be executed from many different places in a program, as required. Methods also serve to break up large and complex calculations that might involve many lines of code, into more manageable chunks. The programmer can execute a method by calling its name and the method may or may not return a value. Methods that do not return a value are invoked without assigning them to any variables. Methods that return a value have many uses, such as assigning to variables, being used in the evaluation of an expression and invoking within another method. As a whole, a method describes the behaviour of an object and is also a collection of statements that are grouped together to perform operations. In Java, a method is defined as follows:

```
access specifier returntype methodname(type1 arg1, type2 arg2, type3 arg3....)
{
    body of the method;
}
```

In the above illustration, *access specifier* refers to (the modifier) private, public and protected. The *returntype* refers to the type of value the method returns; it can be any primitive data type or class name, if the method returns a value. If the method does not return a value, the return type is void. *methodname* is a user-defined name like variable name. The parameter list appears between the parentheses (….) following the method name. The parameters have two components—one is the type of parameter and another is the name of the parameter. The parameters are passed from the invoking statement to the method. The number of arguments passed from the invoking statement should have a one-to-one mapping to the arguments in the method definition. The data types in the method call and method definition should have identical types and should be in the same order. For example,

```
public int display( int a, int b)
{
    // body of the method
}
```

public is the access specifier, `int` is the return type, `display` is the method name and inside the parenthesis `int` refers to the data type and `a, b` refer to the variables.

4.3.2 Returning Value from a Method

To return a value from a method when its execution is completed, use a `return` statement. For example,

```
return return_value; // Return a value from a method
```

In the above statement, `return` is the keyword, the `return_value` is the value returned by the method. After executing the `return` statement in a method, the program continues from the point where the method was called. The `return_value` that is returned by the method can be any expression that produces a value of the type specified for the return value in the declaration of the method. For example,

```
public int display( int a, int b)
{
    // body of the method
    return (a+b);
}
```

In the statement, `public` refers to the access specifier, `int` refers to the return type, `display()` is the name of the method and inside the parenthesis the `parameter_list` has `a, b` as integer variables. When the program is executed, the `display()` method is called and at the end it will produce the addition operation of the two integers `a, b` as return value. The `return_value` that is returned by the above example is an expression `(a+b)` that produces a value of integer type which matches the specified return type in the declaration of the method. Methods that return a value when declared with a return type other than void must always finish by executing a `return` statement. If a method does not return a value, use keyword `return` by itself to end execution of the method.

```
return; // Return from a method
```

For methods that do not return a value, falling through the closing brace enclosing the body of the method is equivalent to executing a `return` statement. **Program 4.4** illustrates how to define a method and the use of the `return` statement.

Program 4.4

```
class minimum
{
    public static void main(String[ ] args)
    {
        int num1 = 12, num2 = 10;
        System.out.println("The minimum of " + num1 + "
        and " + num2 + " is " + min(num1,num2));
    }
    public static int min(int x, int y)
    {
        int min;
        if (x < y)
        min = x;
        else
        min= y;
        return (min);
    }
}
```

Output 4.4

```
The minimum of 12 and 10 is
10.
```

The name of the class is `minimum` and it has two variables namely `num1` and `num2`. Then the variables are initialised with values 12 and 10 respectively. In the next line the `min()` method is called where the parameters inside the parenthesis are `num1, num2`. The definition for the `min()` method which handles the call needs to receive two integers and return one integer and hence it is declared as `public static int min(int x, int y)`. Where `public` is the access specifiers, `static` refers to the method is static, they use no instance variables and will usually take input from the parameters, perform actions on it, then return some result, `int` is the return type and inside the parenthesis, the parameter list consists of `int x, int y,` in order to receive and hold `num1` and `num2` values. Now the value of variable `x` is 12 and value of `y` is 10. Then the local variable `min` is declared as type integer. The `if` condition checks if `x` is smaller than `y.` If true, `x` value is assigned to `min` otherwise the condition moves to the `else` part and assigns `y` value to `min`. The value of `min` is returned to the `main()` method where it is called.

4.3.3 Parameters Vs Arguments

Parameter is the value passed to a method. Method body is a collection of statements that define what the method does. This section describes how parameters can be passed to a method. There are two ways to pass an argument to a method, *call by value* and *call by reference*. The term call by value refers to the method that gets just the value that the caller provides. In contrast, in call by reference the method gets the location of the variable that the caller provides. Thus, a method can modify the value stored in a variable that is passed by reference but not in one that is passed by value. Java always uses call by value by default. That means, the method gets a copy of all parameter values. In particular, the method cannot modify the contents of any parameter variables that are passed to it. For example, consider the following call:

```
double percent = 10;
joe.raiseSalary(percent);
```

No matter how the method is implemented, it is known that after the method call, the value of `percent` is still 10. Often programmers get confused between parameters and arguments. Both are alike but the perspective is somewhat different. Parameter is a variable defined by a method that receives value when the method is called. Parameters are always local to the method and don't have scope outside the method. Argument is a value that is passed to a method when it is called. For example,

```
public void sum(int x, int y)
{
    System.out.println(x+y);
}
public static void main(String[] args)
{
    Test b=new Test();
    b.sum(10,20);
}
```

In the above program `x,y` are variables of method `sum()` and they are referred to as parameters and the values 10 and 20 passed by `sum()` method are referred to as arguments. So, when the variables are declared in a method, they are called parameters and when values are passed to a method they are called arguments. A method can have multiple parameter variables which allows passing multiple arguments to the method. There are two different ways to pass an argument to a method. **Program 4.5** demonstrates the call by value technique.

Program 4.5

```
public class CallByValue
{
    public void display(int y)
    {
    y = 20;
    }
    public static void main(String args[])
    {
        CallByValue cbv = new CallByValue();
        int x = 10;
        cbv.display(x);
        System.out.println(x);
    }
}
```

Output 4.5

```
10
```

In Program 4.5, the class name is `CallByValue` and it has two methods, `display()` and `main()`. The `display()` method is defined as `public`, return type is `void`, `display` is the name of the method and `y` is a parameter. The value 20 is assigned to the parameter `y`. In the `main ()` method the object `cbv` for the defined class is created and the value 10 is passed as argument to the `display()` method. As a copy of `x` is passed, changing `y` does not change the value of `x` in `main()` method. Hence the value of `x` does not change, so the output is 10. **Program 4.6** also briefly explains the call by value technique.

Program 4.6

```
class byvalue
{
    int data=50;
    void change(int data)
    {
        data=data+100;
        //changes will be in the local variable only
    }
    public static void main(String args[])
    {
        byvalue op=new byvalue();
        System.out.println("before change "+op.data); op.change(500);
        System.out.println("after change "+op.data);
    }
}
```

Output 4.6

```
before change 50
after change 50
```

In Program 4.6, the class name is `byvalue`, the integer variable `data` is declared and initialised with value 50, the method `change()` is defined with integer variable `data`. The method `change()` adds 100 to the value of `data` which is 50 and assigns it to `data`. In `main()` method, the object `op` is created for the defined class. The next line prints the value before change, that is 50, through `op.data`. Then the value 500 is passed as an argument to the `change()` method using object `op`. The next statement prints the value of data after the change. A copy of the variable `data` is passed; this has the scope within the method which receives the copy of these variables. The changes made to the parameters inside the methods are not returned to the calling method. This ensures that the value of the variables in the calling method will remain unchanged after return from the called method. Hence the output before change and after change remains 50.

In *call by reference*, however, the reference (words address of an argument) is passed to a method. Any changes made inside the method will affect the argument's value. It manipulates objects by reference and hence all object variables are referenced. When the reference is passed to a method, the parameter that receives it will refer to the same object. Hence changes to the object inside the method will affect the object used as an argument. **Program 4.7** demonstrates the objects being passed by reference.

Program 4.7

```
class byreference
{
    int data=50;
    void change(byreference op)
    {
        op.data=op.data+100;
        //changes will be in the instance variable
    }
    public static void main(String args[])
    {
        byreference op=new byreference();
        System.out.println("before change "+op.data);
        op.change(op);//passing object
        System.out.println("after change "+op.data);
    }
}
```

Output 4.7

```
before change 50
after change 150
```

In Program 4.7, the class name is `byreference`; an integer variable `data` is declared and initialised to 50. The method name is `change()` and it holds object `op` as a parameter. The `change()` method sums the value 100 with the value of `op.data`, that is 50, and assigns it to the integer variable `data`. In `main()` method, the object `op` is created for the defined class. The next line prints the value of `data` before it is changed through `op.data`. Then the object `op` is passed to the `change()` method. The next statement prints the value of `data` after change through `op.data`. Since the object `op` is passed as a parameter to the method `change()`, the called method returns the value to the calling method. The changes to the object inside the method do affect the object used as an argument. Hence the output before change is 50 and after change is 150.

4.4 CONSTRUCTORS

When the programmer creates an object of a class, a special kind of method called a constructor is always invoked. If no constructors are defined for a class, the compiler supplies a default constructor in the class, which does nothing. The default constructor is also described as the no-argument constructor because it requires no arguments to be specified when it is called. The primary purpose of a constructor is to provide the means of initialising the instance variables uniquely for the object that is being created. If a user creates a `Person` object with the name John, then it enables to initialise the member holding the person's name to 'John'. This is precisely what a constructor can do. Any initialisation blocks should be defined in the constructor. A constructor has two special characteristics that differentiate it from other class methods. A constructor never returns a value, and must not specify a return type, not even of the type void. A constructor always has the same name as the class. Constructors in Java can also be seen as methods in a Class. Constructors have only one purpose; they are exclusively for creating an object of a class and initialising its instance variables. This instantiation includes memory allocation and member initialisation. The general form of creating a constructor is,

```
class Student
{
    String name;
    String dept;
    Student( ) //Constructor
    {
    name ="";
    dept="";
    }
}
```

In the above example, the class name is `student` and the data members are `name` and `dept`. Then there is a method, `Student()`, and it has a name similar to the class name so it has been called as a constructor. In most cases, the declaration of a constructor will involve a parameter list. If the constructor is not explicitly declared in the class, then the Java compiler will automatically generate and execute a constructor that has no arguments. Such a constructor is known as the default constructor. When the Java compiler generates and executes a default constructor, it will initialise the instance variables to their default values. If the programmer passes any parameter then it is referred to as a parameterised constructor. Each time a new object is created, at least one constructor will be invoked.

For example:

```
Student s=new Student(); //Default constructor invoked
Student s=new Student(name); //Parameterized constructor invoked
```

4.4.1 Default Constructor

As has been clearly discussed above, if the programmer doesn't define a constructor, then the compiler creates a default constructor. Default constructors do not contain any parameters. Default constructors are created only if there are no constructors defined. The default constructor does nothing, but it enables all variables that are not initialised in their declaration to assume default values as follows:

- Numeric data members are set to 0.
- Boolean data members are set to False.
- String are set to null.

The default constructor looks like,

```
public Rectangle()
{ }
```

In the statement, `public` is the access specifier and `Rectangle()` refers to the constructor. There is no parameter passed in the constructor so the compiler creates a default constructor and it does nothing. The objects created by the default constructor will have fields with their default values. It should be remembered that constructors are invoked only after the instance variables of a newly created object of the class have been assigned their default initial values and after their explicit initialisations are complete. **Program 4.8** describes the concept of default constructor.

Program 4.8

```
class Display
{
    int a=5; //initializer expression
    int b; //assigned default value
    Display()
    {
        a=5; //override default and initializer expression
    }
    void show()
    {
        System.out.println("Value of a : " +a);
        System.out.println("Value of b : " +b);
    }
}
class DefaultConstructor
{
    public static void main(String[] args)
    {
        Display data=new Display();
        data.show();
    }
}
```

Output 4.8

```
Value of a : 5
Value of b : 0
```

In Program 4.8, the class name is `Display`, the variables are `a, b` as integer type. The variable `a` is initialised with value 5 and the other variable `b` is not initialised. There is a constructor namely `Display()` with no parameters and inside the constructor definition, the variable `a` is assigned with the value 5. The method `show()` is of return type `void` and it prints the values of `a, b`. The `DefaultConstructor` is the name of the `main` class. Then an object `data` is created for the defined class. During the `data` object creation, no values are passed as arguments to the constructor `Display()`. On the execution of the statement, `Display data = new Display();` the constructor overrides the default value 5 and assigns the value 5 to `a`. When the `show()` method is called it prints the value of `a` as 5 and `b` does not have any value. So, the constructor itself assigns 0 value by assessing the datatype to be integer. Hence the value of `a` is 5 and `b` is 0 is obtained as output.

4.4.2 Parameterised Constructor

While default constructors do not have any parameters, it is however possible to have one or more parameters in a constructor. This type of constructor which has parameters is known as a parameterised constructor. Using a parameterised constructor, it is possible to initialise objects with different sets of values at the time of their creation. These different sets of initialisation values must be passed as arguments when the constructor is invoked. The parameter list can be specified in parentheses in the same way as the parameter list is specified in the method.

The general form of the parameterised constructor is,

```
PConstructor(datatype1 arg1, datatype2 arg2….)
{
    // give initial values to data members
}
```

The name of the constructor is `PConstructor` and `datatype1 arg1`.. and so on, are referred to as the parameter list. Generally, the parameterised constructor has no return type. Then it may take zero, one or more arguments and it is always called with the `new` operator. **Program 4.9** explicitly describes the parameterised constructor.

Program 4.9

```
class Rectangle
{
    int length;
    int breadth;
    //constructor to initialize length and breadth of rectangle
    Rectangle(int l,int b)
    {
        length = l;
        breadth= b;
    }
    int area()
    {
        return (length * breadth);
    }
}
//class to create rectangle objects and calculate area
class ParameterizedConstructor
{
    public static void main(String[] args)
    {
        Rectangle firstRect = new Rectangle(5,6);
        Rectangle secondRect = new Rectangle(7,8);
        System.out.println("Area of First Rectangle : "+firstRect.area());
        System.out.println("Area of Second Rectangle :"+secondRect.area());
    }
}
```

Output 4.9

```
Area of First Rectangle :
30
Area of Second Rectangle :
56
```

In Program 4.9, the class name is `Rectangle` and the variables are `length, breadth` as integer type. There is need for a constructor to initialise the variables. Hence the constructor `Rectangle()` is created and it contains two parameters `l, b` as integer. The method `area()` is declared to calculate the area of a rectangle where it returns the multiplied value of `length` and `breadth`. The name of the `main` class is `ParameterizedConstructor`. The objects `firstRect, secondRect` are created for the `Rectangle` class. During the `firstRect` object creation, the values 5, 6 are passed as arguments; similarly, when the `secondRect` object is created, the values 7, 8 are passed as arguments to the constructor `Rectangle()`. The specified values passed to this constructor are used to initialise instance variables `length` and `breadth` of an object. On the execution of the statement `Rectangle firstRect = new Rectangle (5, 6)`, the arguments 5 and 6 are passed to the parameters `l` and `b` of the `Rectangle` object's constructor which are then used to initialise `length` and `breadth` instance variables. It works similarly for the other object `secondRect`. Hence the output for the first pass is 30 and the second pass is 56.

The following section explains the scope of the variables.

4.4.3 Scope of Variables

Instance fields are visible to all the class's instance methods. Local variables, including parameter variables, are visible only to statements in the method where they are declared. A variable's name is visible only to statements inside the variable's scope. The location of a variable's declaration determines the variable's scope. So far, the chapters have discussed variables and methods declared in programs. This section talks about placing variables and methods in a class definition. The following are the list of locations.

Inside a method: Variables declared inside a method are known as local variables.

Inside a class, but not inside any method: Variables that are declared inside a class, but not inside any method are known as fields.

Inside the parentheses of a method header: Variables that are declared inside the parentheses of a method header are known as parameter variables.

The following list summarises the scope for each of these types of variables.

Local variable: A local variable's scope is the method in which it is declared; from the variable's declaration to the end of the method. Only statements in this area can access the variable.

Fields: One will define a field's scope as the entire class in which it is declared. A field can be accessed by the methods that are members of the same class as the field.

Parameter variables: A parameter variable's scope is the method in which it is declared. Only statements inside the method can access the parameter variable.

4.5 PACKAGES AND IMPORT STATEMENTS

Java allows programmers to group classes in a collection called a *package.* The standard Java library is distributed over a number of packages, including `java.lang`, `java.util`, `java.net`, and so on. Packages help to organise files within a program, as well as to collect objects into groups to improve the reusability of a code. Packages are used in Java in order to avoid name conflicts and to control access of class, interface and enumeration, and so on. It becomes easier to locate the related classes using a package. A package structure is a tree structure that maps to a folder/directory structure. It is also to be noted that,

- package names correspond to directory names,
- a dot is used between levels of a multilevel structure,
- searching for files starts at the root level of the structure during compiling or class-load at runtime,
- one can't use packages or directory structures without explicitly placing a class in a package via code,

- classes are always referenced from the root of the structure, and the *fully-qualified name* of the class contains the relative path elements to reach the class from the root point, separated by dot characters, and
- a class can use all classes from its own package and all *public* classes from other packages.

To assign a class to a package, use a `package` statement as *the first* non-blank, non-comment line of code. Packages are categorised into two forms:

(i) *Built-in package*: Existing Java package, for example `java.lang`, `java.util` and so on.
(ii) *User-defined-package*: Java package created by user to categorise classes and interfaces.

Table 4.2 shows a few of the standard Java packages.

Table 4.2 Java packages

Package	Description
`java.applet`	The classes necessary to create an applet
`java.awt`	Classes for the Abstract Windowing Toolkit; these classes are used in drawing images and creating graphical user interfaces
`java.io`	Classes that perform various types of input and output
`java.lang`	General classes for the Java language; this package is automatically imported
`java.net`	Classes for network communications
`java.security`	Classes that implement security features
`java.sql`	Classes for accessing databases using structured query language
`java.text`	Various classes for formatting text
`java.util`	Various utility classes
`javax.swing`	Classes for creating graphical user interfaces

The following are the steps to create a package in NetBeans.

1. Select `File` Menu → Click `New Project` → Select `Java` → Click `Java Application` → Click `Next` → Give Project Name as `Employee` → Click `Finish`.

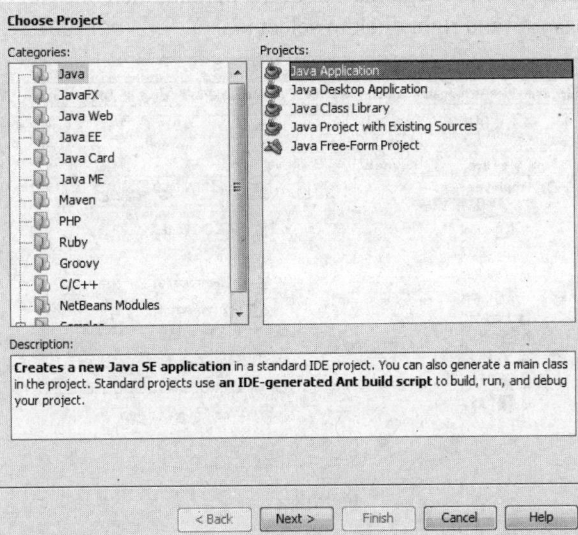

Name and Location
Project Name: Employee
Project Location: C:\Users\DENIS\Documents\NetBeansProjects Browse...
Project Folder: C:\Users\DENIS\Documents\NetBeansProjects\Employee
Use Dedicated Folder for Storing Libraries
Libraries Folder: Browse...
Different users and projects can share the same compilation libraries (see Help for details).
Create Main Class employee.Main
Set as Main Project

The File directory is shown below. Note that the package name is `Employee` (as the screenshot shows).

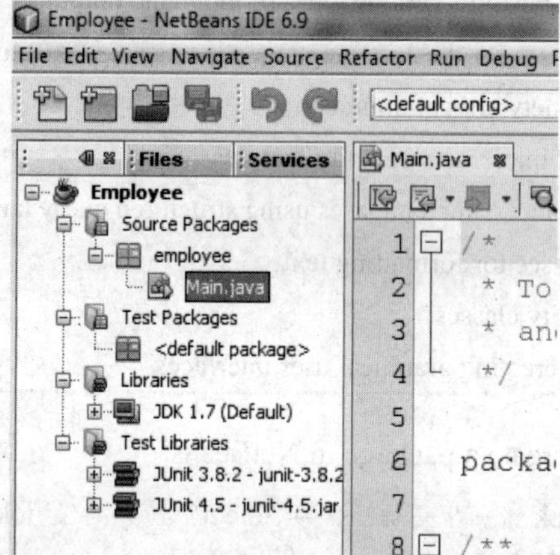

2. If one needs to create a new package instead of the default, then one can do so.
3. Select `Source Packages` and right click to select `New` à `Java Package`.

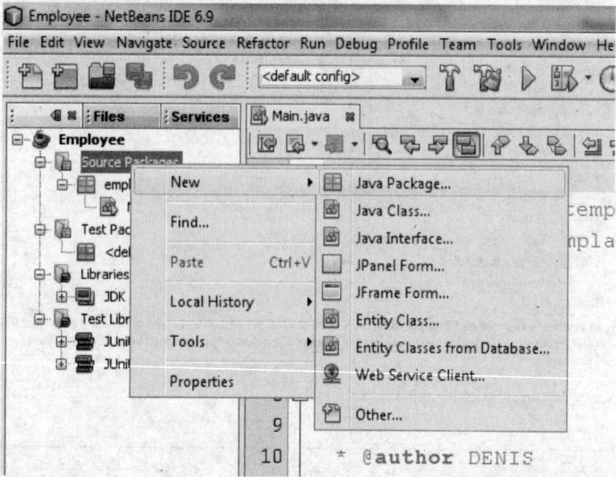

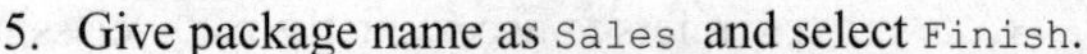

5. Give package name as `Sales` and select `Finish`.

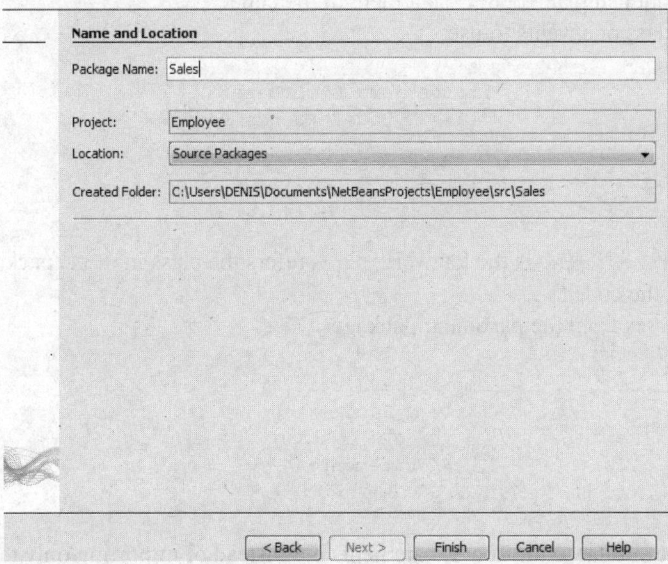

One can see the package created in the name of `Sales`. Then one can add Java files to the package.

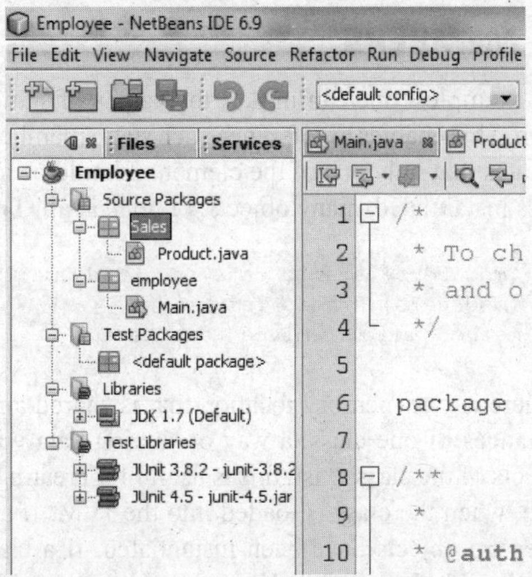

The keyword *import* is used to import built-in and user-defined packages into a Java source file. Then a class can refer to a class that is in another package, by directly using its name. There are three different ways to refer to a class that is present in a different package.

- Using fully qualified name (but, this is not a good practice).

```
class MyDate extends java.util.Date
{
    //statement;
}
```

Class name is `MyDate`, `extends` is the keyword, `java.util.Date` refers to accessing the `Date` class in `util` package without using an `import` statement in the code.

- Import only the class one wants to use.

```
import java.util.Date;
class MyDate extends Date
{
    //statement.
}
```

Class name is `MyDate`, `extends` is the keyword, `Date` refers the class in `util` package and the `import` statement is used in the code.

- Import all the classes from the particular package.

```
import java.util.*;
class MyDate extends Date
{
    //statement;
}
```

These statements are similar to the above statements but instead of importing only the `Date` class in the `util` package, * is used, where it refers to all the classes in the package.

4.6 STATIC CLASS MEMBERS

As discussed in some of the examples, one can import the names of static members of a class from a named package into a program. This enables to reference such static members by their simple unqualified names. The keyword *static* states that only one of the elements should be available at all times, whether there is one object of the class instantiated, many objects, or none at all. The general form is as follows:

```
[modifiers] static dataType fieldName;
[modifiers] static returnType
methodName(paramType ParamName )
```

If a data member is *static*, there is one memory location that is shared among all instances of a class. This allows the separate instances of one class, a way of sharing data with each other. That memory location exists even if no objects of the class exist; this is useful for creating constants. Any initialisation of this value occurs just once, when the class is loaded into the JVM. If a method is *static* and *public*, then it is available even when no objects have been instantiated. If a class has *static* fields, the user needs to have methods to work with those fields. It would make sense that those methods be static as well. Utility functions, like the random number and trigonometric functions in *Math* have to be part of a class, but the programmer wouldn't want to have to instantiate some special object just to generate a single random number or calculate a cosine. For more sophisticated random number generation, where repeatability of a sequence of random values might be desirable, there is a *Random* class. One limitation with this approach is that the method cannot access any of the other elements like data members or methods that are not *static*, since it is not guaranteed that they will exist when the method is called. Such an element is referenced using the name of the class, a dot, then the element name as follows:

```
double x = Math.random();
double y = Math.sqrt(x);
```

4.6.1 Static Variables and Methods

Methods and variables defined inside the class are called instance methods and instance variables, that is, a separate copy of them is created upon the creation of each new object. But in some cases, it is necessary to define a member that is common to all the objects and accessed without using a particular object. The member belongs to the class as a whole rather than to objects created from the class. Such members can be created by prefixing them with the keyword *static*. When a member is declared static, it can be accessed before any objects of its class are created and without reference to any object. The programmer can declare both methods and variables to be *static*. The most common example of a static member is `main()` method. The method `main()` is declared as static because it must be called before any objects exist. Instance variables declared as static are essentially good variables. When objects of its class are declared, no copy of a static variable is made. Instead, all instances of the class share the same static members. Since these members are associated with the class rather than individual objects, the static variables and static methods are often referred to as class variables and class methods in order to distinguish them from instance variables and instance methods. Once a method or variable is declared as static, there is no need to create the object for the class in order to access it. Just use the dot operator in between the name of the class and static member. The Java class library has several sets of static variables and methods. The concept of static members has added power and flexibility to the Java language. The format for declaring a static variable is as follows.

```
static dataType variableName;
```

In the statement, *static* refers to the keyword, `dataType` refers to the primitive data type and `variableName` refers to the name of the variable defined by the user. For example,

```
static int num;
```

where *static* is the keyword, `int` is the data type and `num` is the variable name. When the static variables are not initialised, they will be initialised to default values. While Boolean variables will be set to False, the numeric type variables will be set to zero. Any variable name that acts as a reference to an object of a class will be set to null. **Program 4.10** illustrates the value assignment to static variables.

Program 4.10

```
class sample
{
   static int i;
   static int j=2;
   static int k;
   static String s1;
   static String s2="Welcome";
   static Boolean flag;
}
class Staticdemo
{
   public static void main(String[] args)
   {  System.out.println(sample.i);
      System.out.println(sample.j);
      System.out.println(sample.k);
      System.out.println(sample.s1);
      System.out.println(sample.s2);
      System.out.println(sample.flag);
   }
}
```

Output 4.10

```
0
2
0 null
Welcome
False
```

In Program 4.10, the class name is `sample` and it has six static variables. They are static variable `i` as integer, static variable `j` as integer with initialised value 2, static variable `k` as integer, static variable `s1` as String type, static variable `s2` as String type with initial value 'Welcome' and static variable `flag` as Boolean. `Staticdemo` is the name of the main class. In the main class, the values of the declared variables are printed one by one, using the class name `sample` and a dot operator followed by the variable. There is no object created for the defined class since the variables are declared as static. During declaration, the initial values are provided to some of the static variables and will be printed as it is. The other static variables which are not initialised are set to the default values of their respective data type. Hence the output is `0 2 0 0 null Welcome` and `False`.

The format for declaring a static method is as follows.

```
static returntype methodname(parameters)
```

In the statement, `static` is the keyword, `returntype` refers to `int` or `void`, `methodname` () is the name of the method and inside the method there are `parameters`.

```
static void display(int a)
```

`static` is the keyword, `void` is the returntype, `display()` is the method and `a` is variable of type integer as a parameter. A static method can invoke only other static methods. Similarly, they can access only static data members. **Program 4.11** demonstrates the use of static variables and methods.

Program 4.11

```
class StaticMethod
{
    static int x=10;
    static void display(int x){
        System.out.println(x);
        System.out.println(StaticMethod.x);
    }
    public static void main(String[] args)
    {   display(37);
        System.out.println(x);
    }
}
```

Output 4.11

```
37
10
10
```

In Program 4.11 the class name is `StaticMethod`, a static variable `x` is integer with an initial value 10; there is a static method `display()` with return type `void` and variable integer `x` as parameter. The next statement prints the value of `x`. Then the value of `x` is printed with the help of the defined class name followed by the dot operator with the variable `x` at the end. In the `main()` method, the object for the class has not been created since the variable and method are static. The value 37 is passed as parameter to the method `display()`. The value 37 is assigned to the variable `x` as both are of static members. While printing, the value of `x` is 10 and when the method `display(0)` is called, it prints 37 as output.

4.7 METHOD OVERLOADING

Java enables the programmer to define several methods in a class with the same name, as long as each method has a unique set of parameters. Defining two or more methods with the same name in a class is called method overloading. If programmer has to perform only one operation, having methods with the same name increases the readability of the program. When an overloaded method is called, Java uses the data type and/or the number of arguments as its guides to determine which version of the overloaded method to actually call. Thus, overloaded methods will differ in the type or number of their parameters. While the overloaded methods have different return types, the return type alone is insufficient to distinguish between two versions of a method. When Java encounters a call to an overloaded method, it executes the version of the method whose parameters match the arguments used in the call. For example,

```
System.out.println("Hello Java");
System.out.println (59); //displays int
System.out.println(true); //displays Boolean
System.out.println(31.37); //displays double
System.out.println(); //no parameter
```

In the statements, all the methods have same name `println()` but each takes a different parameter list. The first takes a String, the second takes an int, third takes a Boolean, fourth takes a double and fifth takes no parameter at all. Thus, `println()` method is overloaded. **Program 4.12** illustrates the method overloading by changing the number of arguments.

Program 4.12

```
class Total{
void sum(int a, int b)
{
   System.out.println(a + b);}
   void sum(int a, int b, int c)
   {
      System.out.println(a + b + c);
   }
   public static void main(String args[]){
      Total obj=new Total();
      obj.sum(10,10,10);
      obj.sum(20,20);
   }
}
```

Output 4.12

```
30
50
```

In Program 4.12 the class name is *Total* and it has two methods named `sum()`. Since both methods have the same name they are called overloaded methods. The first `sum()` method has two arguments `a, b` of integer type and the second `sum()` method consists of three arguments `a, b, c` as integer types. The first `sum` method performs addition of two numbers and the second `sum` method performs addition of three numbers. In `main()` method an object for the class `Total` is created as `obj`. Then with the help of object `obj` the arguments are passed to the `sum()` method. The first call passes three integer values to the `sum()` method with three arguments. The second call passes two integer values to the `sum()` method with two arguments. The execution in an overloaded method depends on the number of arguments and the data type of the arguments passed to the methods. Thus, the first passing generates output 30 and the second time the output is 50. **Program 4.13** explicitly describes method overloading by changing the data type of the arguments.

Program 4.13

```
class Calculation
{
    void sum(int a, int b)
    {
        System.out.println(a + b);
    }
    void sum(double a, double b)
    {
        System.out.println(a + b);
    }
    public static void main(String args[])
    {
        Calculation obj=new Calculation();
        obj.sum(10.5,10.5);
        obj.sum(20,20);
    }
}
```

Output 4.13

```
21.0
50
```

In Program 4.13, the class name is `Calculation` and it has two overloaded methods named `sum()` where both have two parameters. The first `sum()` method holds `a, b` of integer type and the second `sum()` method holds `a, b` as double. In `main()` method, the object for the class is created as `obj`. Then for the `sum()` method, two double values have been assigned and it executes the method which holds double values as parameters. Similarly, in the next line two integer values are assigned and the method which holds two integers as parameters is executed. Hence the output for the first `sum` method is double value 21.0 and the second `sum` method is 50. **Program 4.14** illustrates the concept of method overloading with return value.

Program 4.14

```
class overloading
{
    int cal;
    float val;
    int add(int x, int y)
    {
        cal= x + y;
        return(cal);
    }
    int add(int z)
    {
        cal= z+10;
        return(cal);
    }
    float add(float x, float y)
    {
        val =x + y;
        return(val);
    }
}
class Maths
{
    public static void main(String args[])
    {
        overloading m=new overloading();
        System.out.println("10+10="+m.add(10,10));
        System.out.println("15+10="+m.add(15));
        System.out.println("1.5+1.5="+m.add(1.5f,1.5f));
    }
}
```

Output 4.14

```
10+10=20
15+10=25
1.5+1.5=3.0
```

In Program 4.14, the class name is `overloading` and it has two variables `cal` as integer, `val` as float. There are three different versions of the method `add()` in the defined class. The first `add()` method has return type `int`, variables `x, y` as integers in parameters and it sums the value of `x, y` assigns it to `cal` then returns the value of `cal`. The second `add()` method has return type `int`, variable `z` as integer in parameters and it sums the value of `z` with 10 assigns it to `cal`, then returns the value of `cal`. The third `add()` method has return type `float`, variables `x, y` as float in parameters and it sums the value of `x, y` assigns it to `val` then return the value of `val`. The name of the `main()` class is `Maths`. The object `m` for the class overloading is created. In the next statements the values 10, 10 have been passed as arguments to the `add()` method first, followed by value 15 then 1.5, 1.5. In the first pass, the `add()` method refers to the method which receives two integer values. The second pass refers to the `add()` method which can receive one integer value. The third pass refers to the `add()` method which receives two float values. Thus, the output of the first pass is 20,.second pass is 25 and third pass is 3.0.

4.8 CONSTRUCTOR OVERLOADIING

Constructor overloading is a technique in which a class can have any number of constructors that differ in parameter lists. The compiler differentiates these constructors by taking into account the number of parameters in the list and their type, enabling the programmer to create objects with desired functionality. **Program 4.15** explains the concept of overloaded constructors.

Program 4.15

```
class Box
{
   int height, depth, length;
   Box()
   {
      height=depth=length=10;
   }
   Box(int x, int y)
   {
      height=x;
      depth=y;
   }
   Box(int x, int y, int z)
   {
      height=x;
      depth=y;
      length=z;
   }
}
class BoxClass
{
   public static void main(String args[])
   {
      Box a= new Box();
      System.out.println("Depth of a: "+a.depth);
      Box b= new Box(10,15);
      System.out.println("Depth of b: "+b.depth);
      Box c= new Box(12,15,20);
      System.out.println("Depth of c: "+c.depth);
   }
}
```

Output 4.15

```
Depth of a: 10
Depth of b: 15
Depth of c: 15
```

In Program 4.15, the class `Box` contains three different variables `height`, `depth` and `length` as integers. It also has three constructors named `Box()`. The first constructor `Box()` is a default constructor since it does not have any parameters but it initialises the variables `length`, `height` and `depth` to the value 10. The second constructor `Box()` receives two integers `x, y` as parameters and assigns `x` value to `height`, `y` value to `depth`. The third constructor `Box()` receives three integers `x, y, z` as parameters and assigns `x` value to `height`, `y` value to `depth`, `z` value to `length`. In `main()` class `BoxClass` an object `a` for the defined class is created with no parameters passed and it will call the default constructor. The next statement prints the `depth` value. The object `b` is created for the `Box` class and the values 10, 15 are passed as arguments; it will call the constructor which has two integer values as parameters. Similarly, object `c` is created for the `Box` class and the values 12, 15, 20 are passed as arguments; it will call the constructor which holds three integers as parameters. Thus, the output of the program is 10, 15 and 15.

Even though there are similarities between methods and constructors, there are also some differences. These are given in Table 4.3.

Table 4.3 Differences between constructor and method

Constructor	Method
Constructor is used to initialise the state of an object.	Method is used to expose the behaviour of an object.
Constructor must not have a return type.	Method must have return type.
Constructor is invoked implicitly.	Method is invoked explicitly.
The Java compiler provides a default constructor if there is no constructor.	Method is not provided by the compiler in any case.
Constructor name must be the same as the class name.	Method name may or may not be the same as the class name.

4.9 METHODS RETURNING OBJECTS

A method can return any type of data, including class types that one creates. It can also return objects. But, in the method call, the returning value of the method must be assigned to the object of that type. **Program 4.16** shows how a method `getRectangleObject()` returns an object.

Program 4.16

```
class Rectangle {
   int length; int breadth;
   Rectangle(int l,int b) {
      length = l;
      breadth = b;
   }
   Rectangle getRectangleObject() {
      Rectangle rect = new Rectangle(10,20);
      return rect;
   }
}
class RetOb {
   public static void main(String args[]) {
      Rectangle ob1 = new Rectangle(50,50);
      Rectangle ob2;
      ob2 = ob1.getRectangleObject();
      System.out.println("ob1.length:" + ob1.length);
      System.out.println("ob1.breadth:"+ ob1.breadth);
      System.out.println("ob2.length:" + ob2.length);
      System.out.println("ob2.breadth:"+ ob2.breadth);
   }
}
```

Output 4.16

```
ob1.length : 50
ob1.breadth: 50
ob2.length : 10
ob2.breadth: 20
```

In Program 4.16, the programmer called a method `getRectangleObject()` and the method creates object `rect` of class `Rectangle` from which it has been called. All objects are dynamically allocated using new; one doesn't need to worry about an object going out-of-scope because the method in which it was created terminates. The object will continue to exist as long as there is a reference to it somewhere in the program. When there are no references to it, the object will be reclaimed the next time garbage collection takes place.

4.10 this REFERENCE VARIABLE

Java provides the keyword `this` that gives reference to the current object within the body of a method. It is used to resolve name conflicts. By referring to the current object, programmers will be able to access the instance variables of that object. In addition, the reference would allow the programmer to pass the current object as an argument to another method. The `this` keyword can be used anywhere the current object might appear. It can be used in the dot notation to refer to the object's instance variables, as an argument to a method, as the return value for the current method and so on. This is illustrated in the following examples.

```
t = this.x; // the x instance variable for this object
this. display(this);// call the display() method, defined in this class and passes
                      it to the current object.
return this; // returns the current object
```

Observe the following code,

```
Class Box
{
    int height, depth, length;
    Box(int height, int depth, int length)
    {
        this. height=height;
        this. depth=depth;
        this. length= length;
    }
}
```

In the code segment, the class `Box` contains three instance variables—`height`, `breadth` and `length`. The constructor of the class also contains three different local variables with the same names of instance variables. The compiler will not give any error. How do we differentiate these variables? The `this` keyword does this job. `this` will refer to the variables of its own class. It is acting as the object of the current class. **Program 4.17** illustrates the use of the keyword `this`.

Program 4.17

```
class Student{
    int id;
    String name;
    Student(int id, String name){
        this.id = id;
        this.name = name;
    }
    void display(){System.out.println(id+" "+name);}
    public static void main(String args[]){
        Student s1 = new Student(111,"Joseph");
        Student s2 = new Student(222,"Andrew");
        s1.display();
        s2.display();
    }
}
```

Output 4.17

```
111  Joseph
222  Andrew
```

In Program 4.17, the class `Student` has two variables `id` as integer and `name` as String. The constructor `Student` receives two parameters `id` and `name` and assigns them to the variables which are similar. To differentiate, the `this` keyword is used followed by the dot operator and the variable name. The `display()` method is used to print the values of `id` and `name`. In `main()` the objects `s1, s2` are created for the defined class then an integer value and String value are passed as arguments to the constructor `Student()`. The next two statements will print the values of the object by calling the `display()` method.

4.11 RECURSION

Recursion is the process of defining something in terms of itself. If it is related to Java programming, it is the process of a method calling itself to form a chain of execution. This process continues until some condition is satisfied. A method that calls itself is said to be recursive.

The recursive method is used when we require the output of the previous stage upon which the next stage of calculation is dependent. A classic example of recursion is the process of finding the factorial of a number. Factorial of the number *n* can be found by calculating the multiplication of all the numbers from 1 to *n*. If we want to develop the algorithm then following factors are to be considered.

n! = n * (n – 1)!
(n – 1)! = (n – 1) * (n – 2)!
(n – 2)! = (n – 2) * (n – 3)!
....
....

This process continues until the value of *n* becomes 0. And, as we know, the factorial of 0 is 1. So, this can be combined in the recursive method as shown in **Program 4.18**.

Program 4.18

```
// Finding factorial using recursion
class Factorial
{
   int fact(int n)
   {
      if(n==1)
      return 1; //statement1
   else
      return (n*fact(n-1));
   }
   public static void main(String args[])
   {
      Factorial f=new Factorial();
      System.out.print("Factorial of 4:");
      System.out.println(f.fact(4));
      System.out.print("Factorial of 5:");
      System.out.println(f.fact(5));
      System.out.print("Factorial of 6:");
      System.out.println(f.fact(6));
   }
}
```

Output 4.18

```
Factorial of 4:24
Factorial of 5:120
Factorial of 6:720
```

In the above example, the statement1 is called the return point of the method. This statement is executed as the last of the method. If statement1 is not given, the method will go infinitely (actually it is executed until the capacity of the stack ends). The recursion takes more time than that of the iterative algorithm method. But, many cases, it is simple and necessary to implement a method with recursion. The design of the algorithm depends upon the programmer.

4.12 NESTED AND INNER CLASSES

It is possible to define a class within another class; such classes are known as nested classes. The scope of a nested class is bounded by the scope of its enclosing class. Thus, if class B is defined within class A, then B is known to A, but not outside of A. A nested class has access to all the members, of the class in which it is nested. However, the enclosing class does not have access to the members of the nested class.

There are two types of nested classes—static and non-static. A static nested class is one which has the static modifier applied. Because it is static, it must access the members of its enclosing class through an object. That is, it cannot refer to the members of its enclosing class directly. Because of this restriction, static nested classes are rarely used. The most important type of nested class is the inner class.

An inner class is a non-static nested class. It has access to all of the variables and methods of its outer class and may refer to them directly in the same way that other non-static members of the outer class do. Thus, an inner class is fully within the scope of its enclosing class. Observe **Program 4.19**.

Program 4.19

```
//Demo of an inner class
class Outer //outer class
{
    int out_x;
    Outer(int x)
    {
        out_x=x;
    }
    void test()
    {
        Inner inner=new Inner();
        inner.display();
    }
    class Inner //Inner class
    {
        void display()
        {
            System.out.print("Value: out_x=");
            System.out.println(out_x);
        }
    }
}
class Innnerclass
{
    public static void main(String args[])
    {
        Outer outer=new Outer(15);
        outer.test();
    }
}
```

Output 4.19

```
Value: out_x=15
```

In the above program, two classes are defined—`Inner` and `Outer`. `Inner` class is defined outside the `Outer` class. So, we can create the object of the `Inner` class only inside the `Outer` class. That is, the `Inner` class is bounded by the scope of the `Outer` class. If we create the object of `Inner` class in the `Innerclass` then the complier will flash the error. Because `Inner` class cannot be accessed in `Innerclass`.

We have created an object of `Outer` class. Then by using it, we called the method 'test()' of it. Inside the 'test()' method, the object of `Inner` class is created. That object is used to call the method 'display()' of the `Inner` class. Inner class can access all the members of the outer class.

Remember, any number of classes can be nested inside the class. As class creates a new data type, it can also be created inside the method. **Program 4.20** shows the demonstration of creation of a class inside the method.

Program 4.20

```
class MethodClass
{
   public static void main(String args[])
   {
      class MyClass //A class inside main() method
      {
         int x;
         MyClass(int x) // Constructor
         {
            this.x=x;
         }
         void display() //method
         {
            System.out.print("Your Value:");
            System.out.println(x);
         }
      }
      MyClass m=new MyClass(63); //object
      m.display(); //method call
   }
}
```

Output 4.20

```
Your Value:63
```

In Program 4.20, the class `MyClass` is defined inside the main() method. So, we can create its object only inside main. It is bounded by the scope of main().

4.13 ABSTRACT CLASSES AND METHODS

In some situations, it may be required to define a super class that declares the structure of a given abstraction without providing a complete implementation of every method. That is, sometimes we will want to create a super class that only defines a generalised form that will be shared by all its subclasses and leaving it to each subclass to fill in the details. Such a class determines the nature of the methods that the subclasses must implement. This can be done by creating a class as an abstract.

We can indicate that a method must always be redefined in a subclass by making the overriding compulsory. This can be achieved by the preceding the keyword `abstract` in the method definition with the following form:

```
abstract datatype methodname(Parameters);
```

There is no method body present. Any class that contains one or more abstract methods must also be declared as abstract. To declare a class abstract, we have to write 'abstract' in front of keyword 'class' in the definition. For example;

```
abstract class White
{
    ..................
    abstract void paint();
    ..................
    ..................
}
```

We cannot create the objects of an abstract class. That is, an abstract class cannot be directly instantiated with the new operator. Such objects would be useless, because an abstract class is not fully defined. Also, we cannot declare abstract constructors, or abstract static methods. Any subclass of an abstract class must either implement all of the abstract methods in the super class, or be itself declared abstract.

Program 4.21 is an example of abstract class and methods.

Program 4.21

```
abstract class Maths
{
   int var1,var2,var3;
   abstract void calculate();
   void addition()
   {
      var3=var1 + var2;
      System.out.println("Adition:" +var3);
   }
}
class Arithmetic extends Maths
{
   Arithmetic(int x, int y)
   {
      var1=x;
      var2=y;
   }
   void calculate()
   {
      var3=var1-var2;
      System.out.println("Subtraction: " +var3);
   }
}
class AbstractClass
{
   public static void main(String args[])
   {
      Arithmetic a=new Arithmetic(30,18);
      a.calculate();
      a.addition();
   }
}
```

Output 4.21

```
Subtraction: 12
Adition:48
```

As class `Maths` is declared as abstract, we cannot create an object of this class. `Maths` class has its own concrete method named `addition`. This is acceptable. The overridden method `calculate` is declared abstract in the super class with empty implementation.

4.14 WRAPPER CLASSES

Each primitive data type in Java has a corresponding wrapper class. Wrapper classes are used to represent a primitive data type as an object. In other words, a wrapper class is used to convert a primitive data type into its equivalent class type. Wrapper classes belong to the `java.lang` package. These wrapper classes also define useful methods for manipulating both primitive data values and objects. Table 4.4 shows the wrapper classes of respective data types.

Table 4.4 Wrapper classes for the primitive data types

Primitive data types	Wrapper classes
Boolean	Boolean
Char	Character
Double	Double
Float	Float
Int	Integer
Long	Long
Short	Short
Byte	Byte

Wrapper classes for integers and floating-point numbers are called subclasses of the Number class in the java.lang package. **Program 4.22** illustrates the use of wrapper classes (primitive double to wrapper double and vice versa).

Program 4.22

```
import java.util.ArrayList;
public class TestWrapper
{
   public static void main(String[] args)
   {
      double dValue=345.876;
      double primResult=objNegate(dValue);
      System.out.println("Converting double into Double"+""+primResult);
      primResult=primNegate(dValue);
      System.out.println("Converting double
      into Double"+""+primResult);
      Double objValue=-23.567;
      Double objResult=primNegate(objValue);
      System.out.println("Converting double
      into Double"+""+objResult);
      objResult=objNegate(objValue);
      System.out.println("Converting double
      into Double"+""+objResult);
   }
   public static Double objNegate(Double n)
   {
      return n;
   }
   public static double primNegate(double n)
   {
      return -n;
   }
}
```

Output 4.22

```
Converting double into Double
345.876
Converting double into Double
-345.876
Converting double into Double
23.567
Converting double into Double
-23.567
```

Program 4.23 demonstrates the use of integer wrapper class and its methods.

Program 4.23

```
public class WrapperInt
{
   public static void main(String[] args)
   {
      Integer x= new Integer(141);
      byte b=x.byteValue();
      System.out.println("Byte value:"+b);
      int hash=x.hashCode();
      System.out.println("Hash code:"+hash);
      int val=Integer.parseInt("63");
      System.out.println("Parsed value:"+val);
      String s=x.toString();
      System.out.println("String value:"+s);
      Integer y=new Integer(Integer.valueOf("22"));
      System.out.println("Short value:"+y.shortValue());
      String bin=Integer.toBinaryString(59);
      String oct=Integer.toOctalString(59);
      String hex=Integer.toHexString(59);
      System.out.println("Binary of 59:"+bin);
      System.out.println("Octal of 59:"+oct);
      System.out.println("Hex of 59:"+hex);
   }
}
```

Output 4.23

```
Byte value:-115
Hash code:141
Parsed value:63
String value:141
Short value:22
Binary of 59:111011
Octal of 59:73
Hex of 59:3b
```

Program 4.24 demonstrates the use of the character wrapper class and its methods.

Program 4.24

```
public class WrapperChar
{
   public static void main(String[] args)
   {
      Character ch=new Character('X');
      System.out.println("Char value:");
      System.out.println(ch.charValue());
      if(Character.isDigit('0'))
      System.out.println("0 is a digit");
      if(Character.isLowerCase('R'))
      System.out.println("R is lower case");
   else
   {
      System.out.println("R is upper case");
      System.out.println("Lower case:");
      System.out.println(Character.toLowerCase('R'));
   }
   if(Character.isWhitespace(' '))
      System.out.println("Character is white space");
   }
}
```

Output 4.24

```
Char value: X
0 is a digit
R is upper case
Lower case: r
Character is white space
```

4.15 GENERICS

In general, data structures use the type object to store data of any type. It is easy to store any object of any type in a Collection of objects; however, when objects are to be retrieved, casting the objects to its original type is required. A wrong type-casting causes an error in the program. Thus, writing programs with suitable casting is cumbersome and carries a performance penalty for run-time type-checking. Generics allow parameterised types for storing and manipulation of the data in classes, interfaces and methods.

Generics are useful for creating new types based on a passed parameter type. The compiler uses some algorithms provided in the Java 1.5 version to create the new types. These algorithms also avoid casting to the original types during insertions of objects or retrieval of objects.

Generics, simply called parameterised types, can be defined as a mechanism by which a single piece of code can be used for different data types without mentioning a separate entity explicitly for each data type. The programmer can create generic methods, classes and interfaces by using parameterised types, and the type of data on which they work is specified as a parameter. With this concept, the programmer can reuse the code for different applications. Two main advantages of generics are the following:

- code reuse, and
- type-safety by avoiding explicit casting.

Generics also provide a facility for creating types that have type parameters. It also allows creating a single class that works on different types of data. For example, the following code declares a generic Queue class with a type parameter T. Depending on the parameters passed by the user, the compiler checks which function is to be called.

```
Public class Queue<T>
{
    T [] element;
    int size;
    public void insert(T x) {.........}
    public T delete() {...........}
}
```

The type parameter T is specified between angle brackets (< and >) after the class name. This parameter acts as a place holder. The element to be inserted in the queue is represented by x. The actual type, which is substituted in place of T, is supplied as parameter when the actual class is used in a program, when the type argument for T is specified as int then the code is of the form,

```
Queue<int> queue= new Queue<int>();
Queue.insert(6);
int x = queue.delete();
```

The Queue<int> type is called a constructed type. Here, every occurrence of T is replaced with the type argument int. In the above example class Queue<T> there is only one type parameter. In general, generics type declaration can include more than one type parameter.

After compilation of a generic type, the compiler produces intermediate language instructions and metadata. When an application creates an instance of a generic type, the compiler converts the intermediate language instructions and metadata to native code. During this process, it substitutes the actual types for type parameters. So, for the next call to same generic type, the compiler uses the same native code. Thus, the compiler maintains one copy of the native code for each generic type instantiation with a value type and shares it for all other reference types.

Generics provide a way to create and use type-safe data structures. Using generics, compile-time type safety resolves the type-casting problem. Examples using generics are ArrayList, Hashtable, HashMap, LinkedList, PriorityQueue, Queue, Stack, TreeMap, TreeSet and Vector. According to the programmers' need, generics can be recompiled with different types.

Consider the example below:

```
List numbers=new List();
```

Using generics, the above code can be written as,

```
List <Integer> numbers = new List <Integer> ();
```

The insertion of elements other than string type results in an error at compile time. This feature helps in fixing the bug at compile-time rather than having a run-time exception, as was the case in earlier versions of Java.

Another advantage of generics is that after the declaration of generics, no type-casting is required. For example, the following statement,

```
String s1= ((Integer) numbers.get(i).toString();
```

can be written as shown below:

```
String s1=numbers.get(i).toString();
```

Other advantages of generics include generalising existing methods, classes and interfaces. It is easier to understand than class methods parameterisation.

A major goal of generics is that it increases type-safety without type variation. Type-mismatch errors are caught at compile time rather than at run time and improves understandability of the code and APIs (Application Programming Interface). The generic feature makes Java a strongly typed language. That is, an error occurs during compile time itself, whenever a wrong type is used. **Program 4.25** shows the working of user defined Generic classes.

Program 4.25

```
class Test<T>
{
   // An object of type T is declared
   T obj;
   Test(T obj) { this.obj = obj; } // constructor
   public T getObject() { return this.obj; }
}
// Driver class to test above
class Main
{
   public static void main (String[] args)
   {
      // instance of Integer type
      Test <Integer> iObj = new Test<Integer>(15);
      System.out.println(iObj.getObject());
      // instance of String type
      Test <String> sObj = new Test<String>("Computer Science");
      System.out.println(sObj.getObject());
   }
}
```

Output 4.25

```
15
Computer Science
```

4.16 AUTOBOXING AND UNBOXING

Primitive types have built-in functionalities in the language. Primitive data-types are byte, short, int, float, double, char and Boolean. Java provides specialised classes corresponding to each of the primitive data types. These are called wrapper classes. Examples of wrapper classes are Integer, Character, Double and so on. Autoboxing and unboxing features avoid the manual conversion between primitive types and wrapper classes.

In earlier versions of Java, it is not possible to directly put primitives into collections and vice versa, and thus conversion between these types is necessary to store the elements in collections. The compiler does the job of conversion, such as integer to Integer and Boolean to Boolean.

The autoboxing and auto-unboxing features allow automatic conversion of primitive type to its associated wrapper type, called boxing, and the conversion of wrapper type to its associated primitive type, called unboxing.

```
Integer i=3; is an example of autoboxing
int k=i; is an example of unboxing
```

The main idea behind using autoboxing and auto-unboxing is to make it easier to convert between primitive data types and wrapper types.

Consider the following statement:

```
Boolean res=Boolean.TRUE && Boolean.False;
```

This would have generated the following error previously as

```
Operator && cannot be applied to java.lang.Boolean.
```

With Java 1.5, Booleans are automatically converted to Booleans before the && operator is applied.

```
Boolean res = Boolean.TRUE && Boolean. FALSE;
```

Program 4.26 illustrates the concept of autoboxing and unboxing.

Program 4.26

```
import java.io.*;
class GFG
{
   public static void main (String[] args)
   {
      // creating an Integer Object
      // with value 10.
      Integer i = new Integer(10);
      // unboxing the Object
      int i1 = i;
      System.out.println("Value of i: " + i);
      System.out.println("Value of i1: " + i1);
      //Autoboxing of char
      Character gfg = 'a';
      // Auto-unboxing of Character
      char ch = gfg;
      System.out.println("Value of ch: " + ch);
      System.out.println("Value of gfg: " + gfg);
   }
}
```

Output 4.26

```
Value of i: 10
Value of i1: 10
Value of ch: a
Value of gfg: a
```

Program 4.27 shows how compilers do autoboxing and unboxing with collections in Java using generics.

Program 4.27

```
import java.io.*;
import java.util.*;
class BoxingEx
{
    public static void main (String[] args)
    {
        List<Integer> list = new ArrayList<Integer>();
        for (int i = 0; i < 10; i++)
        list.add(i);
    }
}
```

In the above program, a list of elements of Integer type is created. Then, int primitive type values are added instead of Integer Object and the code successfully compiled. It does not generate a compile time error as the Java compiler creates an Integer wrapper Object from primitive int i and adds it to the list.

4.17 METADATA (ANNOTATIONS)

The purpose of the metadata facility is to add annotations to code that do not alter its semantics, but provide additional information that can be used by a compiler. It embeds annotations into a program, which can be processed by various programming tools. These tools generate the Java source code as specified by an annotation. That means, the programmer specifies an action in the source code and the tool actually provides the source code. This style of programming is often referred to as declarative programming. One of the main advantages of such an approach is that it reduces the amount of repetitious code that a programmer must write.

In Java 1.5, the metadata feature provides the ability to associate additional data alongside Java Classes, Interfaces, methods and fields. One of the primary reasons for adding metadata to the Java platform is to enable development and run-time tools to have a common infrastructure, and so reduce the effort required for programming and deployment.

This feature also avoids writing boilerplate code that is inserted repeatedly, into many different programs. The @ symbol is used to tell the compiler to fetch the code from somewhere else, and insert it under many circumstances by enabling tools to generate it from annotations in the source code. Also, it eliminates the need for maintaining 'side files' that must be kept up-to-date with changes in the source files; instead, the information can be maintained in the source file. The annotation type declaration is itself sometimes annotated. Such annotations are called meta-annotations.

Java 1.5 introduces a new tag, called @override, with which the programmer can explicitly state the intention to override a method of the super-class. If the super-class contains no such method, then the compiler generates an error.

```
public @ Overrides String toString()
{
    return value+ "of" +x;
}
```

SUMMARY

1. A class is a blueprint or a template for creating different objects, which defines its properties and behaviour. Java class objects exhibit the properties and behaviour defined by its class. A class can contain variables and methods to describe the behaviour of an object.
2. An object is an instance of a class. An object is created through the `new` operator with the class name and the constructor.
3. Constructor is a method which has a name similar to the class name and it is used to give initial values to the instance variables.
4. Method overloading is a feature that allows a class to have two or more methods having the same name but with different argument lists.
5. Constructor overloading is a mechanism that allows a class to have more than one constructor with different argument lists.
6. When a member is declared as static, it can be accessed before any objects of its class are created and without reference to any object.
7. A package organises a set of related classes and interfaces. The importance of packages in a program is to group the classes to provide reusability.
8. The keyword `this` is a reference variable that refers to the current object. It can be used to refer to the current class instance variable, and invoke or initiate the current class constructor. It can be passed as an argument in the method call.
9. The autoboxing and auto-unboxing features allow automatic conversion of primitive type to its associated wrapper type, called boxing, and the conversion of wrapper type to its associated primitive type, called unboxing.
10. A wrapper class is used to convert a primitive data type into its equivalent class type.

SHORT QUESTIONS

1. What is a class?
2. Mention the general format of a class.
3. Define constructor.
4. What are methods and how are they defined?
5. What are the different types of access modifiers (access specifiers)?
6. Why do we create an object of a class?
7. What is an object and how do you allocate memory to it?
8. What are the types of constructors?
9. Define method and constructor overloading.
10. What is the advantage of using the `this` keyword?
11. What are static member classes?
12. State the importance of packages.
13. What is autoboxing and unboxing?
14. What is the purpose of metadata (annotations)?

COMPREHENSIVE QUESTIONS

1. How do we pass arguments to a method? Give an example.
2. Explain the difference between arguments and parameters.
3. Explain the concept of call by value and call by reference.
4. What is the purpose of constructors? Explain the types of constructors.
5. Discuss the concept of method overloading.
6. Explain the usage of Java packages.
7. Explain the concept of returning the objects from method.
8. Explain the importance of packages and import statements.
9. Explain the difference between constructors and methods.
10. Bring out the purpose of abstract classes and methods.

11. Write a program to find the factorial of a given number using recursion.
12. Explain constructor overloading.
13. Discuss the concept of wrapper classes.

SOLVED PROGRAMS

1. Program to illustrate the constructor and its types.

```
import java.util.Scanner;
class student
{
  String name;
  int regno;
  int marks1,marks2,marks3;
  student()
  {
     name="Joe";
     regno=12345;
     marks1=75;
     marks2=65;
     marks3=78;
  }
  student(String n, int r, int m1,int m2,int m3)
  {
     name=n;
     regno=r;
     marks1=m1;
     marks2=m2;
     marks3=m3;
  }
  student(student s)
  {
     name=s.name;
     regno=s.regno;
     marks1=s.marks1;
     marks2=s.marks2;
     marks3=s.marks3;
  }
  void display()
  {
     System.out.println(name + "\t" +regno+ "\t" +marks1+ "\t" +marks2+ "\t" +
     marks3);
  }
}
Class studentdemo
{
  public static void main(String arg[])
  {
     String name;
     int reg,m1,m2,m3;
     Scanner s=new Scanner(System.in);
     System.out.println("Enter Name: ");
     name=s.nextLine();
     System.out.println("Enter Register No: ");
     reg=s.nextInt();
     System.out.println("Enter Mark 1: ");
     m1=s.nextInt();
```

Output

```
Enter Name: Sam
Enter Register No:
504
Enter Mark 1:
98
Enter Mark 2:
95
Enter Mark 3:
80
name   regno mark1  mark2  mark3
Joe    12345 75     65     78
Sam    504   98     95     80
Joe    12345 75     65     78
```

```
        System.out.println("Enter Mark 2: ");
        m2=s.nextInt();
        System.out.println("Enter Mark 3: ");
        m3=s.nextInt();
        System.out.println("name\tregno\tmark1\tmark2\tmark3");
        student s1=new student();
        student s2=new student(name,reg,m1,m2,m3);
        student s3=new student(s1);
        s1.display();
        s2.display();
        s3.display();
    }
}
```

2. Program to demonstrate method overloading.

```
import java.util.Scanner;
class add
{
  void display(int a, int b)
  {
     int c=a+b;
     int d=a-b;
     int e=a*b;
     int f=a/b;
     System.out.println("Integer Value
     :\n");
     System.out.println("The Addition of "
     + a + " & " + b + " is " + c);
     System.out.println("The Subtraction
     of " + a + " & " + b + " is " + d);
     System.out.println("The Multiplication
     of " + a + " & " + b + " is " + e);
     System.out.println("The Division of "
     + a + " & " + b + " is " + f);
  }
  void display(double a, double b)
  {
     double c=a+b;
     double d=a-b;
     double e=a*b;
     double f=a/b;
     System.out.println("\nDouble Value
     :\n");
     System.out.println("The Addition of "
     + a + " & " + b + " is " + c);
     System.out.println("The Subtraction
     of " + a + " & " + b + " is " + d);
     System.out.println("The Multiplication of " + a + " & " + b + " is " + e);
     System.out.println("The Division of " + a + " & " + b + " is " + f);
  }
}
Class add_demo
{
  public static void main(String arg[])
  {
     int a,b;
     double x,y;
```

Output

```
Enter Integer Values for A:
2
Enter Integer Values for B:
4
Enter Float Values for A:
6
Enter Float Values for B:
2.3
Integer Value :
The Addition of 2 & 4 is 6
The Subtraction of 2 & 4 is -2
The Multiplication of 2 & 4 is 8
The Division of 2 & 4 is 0
Double Value :
The Addition of 6.0 & 2.3 is 8.3
The Subtraction of 6.0 & 2.3 is
3.7
The Multiplication of 6.0 & 2.3
is 13.799999999999999
The Division of 6.0 & 2.3 is
2.608695652173913
```

```
        add obj=new add();
        Scanner s=new Scanner(System.in);
        System.out.println("Enter Integer Values for A: ");
        a=s.nextInt();
        System.out.println("Enter Integer Values for B: ");
        b=s.nextInt();
        System.out.println("Enter Float Values for A: ");
        x=s.nextDouble();
        System.out.println("Enter Float Values for B: ");
        y=s.nextDouble();
        obj.display(a,b);
        obj.display(x,y);
    }
}
```

3. Program to show the method that returns an array of objects.

```
import java.io.*;
import java.util.Scanner;
class Student
{
    long Regno;
    String Name;
    String Dept;
    long Shift;
    Student(long Id, String N, String Br, long sh)
    {
        Regno = Id; Name = N;
        Dept = Br; Shift = sh;
    }
    void display()
    {
        System.out.println(Regno + "\t" + Name + "\t" + Dept + "\t" + Shift);
    }
}
class StudentDeatils
{
    public static void main(String args[])
    throws IOException
    {
        Scanner s1 = new Scanner(System.in);
        System.out.println("Enter the
        numbers of students:");
        int n = s1.nextInt();
        Student[ ] S = new Student[n];
        for (int i = 0; i < n; i++)
        {
            System.out.println("Enter the
            Details of Student no: " + (i + 1));
            System.out.println("Register
            Number: ");
            long No = s1.nextLong(); System.
            out.println("Name: ");
            String Nm = s1.next();
            System.out.println("Department : ");
            String Br = s1.next();
            System.out.println("Shift : ");
            longsh = s1.nextLong();
```

Output

```
Enter the numbers of students: 2
Enter the Details of Student no: 1
Register Number: 504
Name: Prabu
Department : MSC
Shift : 2
Enter the Details of Student no: 2
Register Number: 506
Name: John
Department: MSC
Shift :2
Regno Name  Dept  Shift
504   Prabu MSC   2
506   John  MSC   2
```

```
            S[i] = new Student(No, Nm, Br, sh);
        }
        System.out.println("\nRegno" + "\tName" + "\tDept" + "\tShift");
        for (int i = 0; i < n; i++)
        { S[i].display();
        }
    }
}
```

PROGRAMMING EXERCISES

1. Write a Java program that performs call by value and call by reference.
2. Write a Java program that gives an example for `this` operator and the use of `this` keyword.
3. Write a Java program that gives a demonstration of static variables and methods.
4. Write a Java program that demonstrates the difference between method overloading and overriding.
5. Write a Java program that demonstrates the difference between method overloading and constructor overloading.
6. Write a Java program that illustrates the usage of classes and objects in applications.
7. Write a program that calculates and prints the product of three integers.
8. Write an application that displays the numbers 1 to 5 on the same line, with each pair of adjacent numbers separated by one space. Write the application using the following techniques:
   (a) use one System.out.println statement
   (b) use four System.out.print statements
   (c) use one System.out.print statement.
9. Write an application that inputs three integers from the user and displays the sum, average, product, smallest and largest of the numbers.
10. Write an application that reads two integers, determines whether the first is a multiple of the second and print the result. [**Hint:** use the remainder operator.]
11. Create class SavingsAccount. Use a static variable annualInterestRate to store the annual interest rate for all account holders. Each object of the class contains a private instance variable savingsBalance indicating the amount the saver currently has on deposit. Provide method calculateMonthlyInterest to calculate the monthly interest by multiplying the savingsBalance by annualInterestRate divided by 12, this interest should be added to savingsBalance. Provide a static method modifyInterestRate that sets the annualInterestRate to a new value. Write a program to test class SavingsAccount. Instantiate two savingsAccount objects, saver1 and saver2, with balances of \$2000.00 and \$3000.00, respectively. Set annualInterestRate to 5%, then calculate the monthly interest and print the new balances for both savers. Then set the annualInterestRate to 5%, calculate the next month's interest and print the new balances for both savers.
12. Write a Java program to illustrate different access specifiers.
13. Write a Java program to implement the types of methods and constructors.
14. Write a Java program to illustrate the functionality of returning objects from methods.

CHAPTER

5

Arrays

An array is a collection of similar data types such as integer, float, characters, objects, and so on. Large groups of data can be accessed and processed easily with the help of arrays. Java provides one dimensional, two dimensional, three dimensional and multi-dimensional arrays. This chapter explains array declaration and usage. It also explains how to pass and return arrays in methods and to pass arrays of objects to methods. The final section deals with two and multi-dimensional arrays.

5.1 INTRODUCTION TO ARRAYS

The programs presented in the previous chapters have used simple data types in which only a few variables are declared and used. To handle large collections of the same type of data, the program should declare variables first and then store data in them. For example, if the marks of the students, in a class with minimum 50 students, are to be stored, then 50 variables need to be declared. Figure 5.1 depicts how these 50 variables are declared and accessed.

marks1	marks2	marks3		marks49	marks50
			……		

Fig. 5.1 Memory allocation for 50 students' marks

For reading, calculating and displaying these values, all the variables must be accessed individually. If these values are to be summed up, all the variables must be added, like marks1 + marks2 + marks3 … + marks50, which is a cumbersome process. Also, it takes more number of lines of code for these processes. Arrays are an elegant way to handle this situation. An array is a user defined data type, and it groups the same data type together. All the 50 students' marks will be grouped in a single array `marks`. Fifty locations can be declared to store all the 50 marks and accessed using a single name. Each location of the array is accessed through indexes. The indexes for the `marks` are from 0 to 49. The first student's marks restored in `marks[0]`, the second student's marks restored in `marks[1]` and the fiftieth student's marks restored in `marks[49]`. To declare an array, three attributes are needed—name, data type and the size. The name is to identify the array, the data type is to define the type of data to store in the array and the size fixes the maximum number of values the array can store. An array is declared using the following syntax,

```
dataType [] nameOfTheArray = new dataType [size]
or dataTypenameOfTheArray[] = new dataType [size]
```

The `dataType` of the array can be any simple data type, the empty `[]` informs the compiler that the variable is an array, `nameOfTheArray` is any valid variable name, `new` allocates memory for the array name and `[size]` fixes the number of locations to be allocated for the array. To store the marks of the students the declaration is,

```
int [] marks = new int[50];
```

The name of the array is `marks`, the type of the array is integer and the size allocated is 50 locations. The memory allocation for the array `marks` is given in Fig. 5.2.

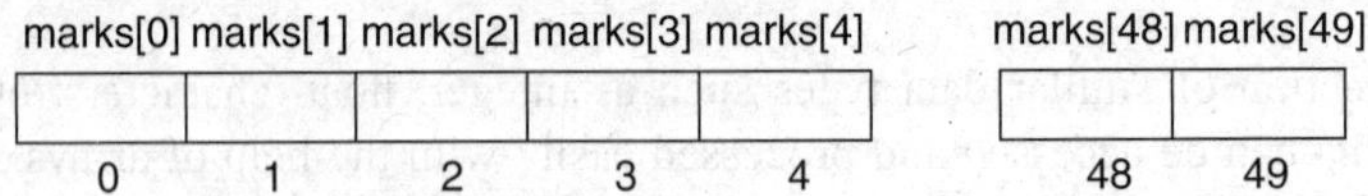

Fig. 5.2 Memory allocation for an array of size 50

The array indexes are from 0 to 49 and the array locations are accessed using `marks[0]`, `marks[1]`.. `marks[49]`. Since all the locations are referred to by a single name, the values can be stored and retrieved more easily than when storing in individual variables. The scores will be stored for 50 students in this array `marks`. The following statement assigns scores to the first student,

```
marks[0] = 79;
```

The integer constant 79 is stored in the array `marks` using the index 0. The scores of all the students can be assigned to the `marks` array in this manner, but that will take more time and that is not the purpose of the array. There are other simpler means of assignment which you will come across in the course of the chapter. Accessing them is made very easy with the help of a loop structure. The values for the array can be read as follows:

```
Scanner inp = new Scanner(System.in);
for(int i=0;i<50; i++)
{
    System.out.println("Enter a value for the array");
    marks[i]=inp.nextInt();
}
```

The `for` loop assigns 0 to the loop variable and it is used as the index for the array `marks`. The value for the array `marks[0]` is assigned using `Scanner` class. The first time, is 0. The loop variable `i` is incremented to 1, since the condition is true and the loop continues to read the second value and assigns it to `marks[1]`. The loop continues till the loop variable is 49 to read for the last student's marks in `marks[49]` and then terminates. **Program 5.1** illustrates the use of the array for storing marks of the students.

Program 5.1

```
import java.util.Scanner;
public class Array1 {
  /**
    * To read and display values for the array
   */
   public static void main(String[] args) {
   int [] marks = new int[5];
   int i;
   Scanner inp = new Scanner(System.in);
   for(i=0;i<5; i++)
   {
      System.out.println("Enter the marks ");
      marks[i]=inp.nextInt();
   }
      System.out.println("The Students marks are ");
      for(i=0;i<5; i++)
      {
         System.out.println(marks[i]);
      }  }}
```

Output 5.1

```
Enter the marks 78
Enter the marks 89
Enter the marks 67
Enter the marks 45
Enter the marks 34
The Students marks are
78
89
67
45
34
```

The program is simple and only reads marks and displays. The array is declared with size of 5 instead of 50 so that the loop is short, otherwise the loop will be executed 50 times. The loop condition is fixed to be less than 5, and can be changed to,

```
for(i=0;i<marks.length; i++)
```

The array is an object in Java and has only one instance variable length. When the array is declared, the array size is assigned to the length of the array. Hence the array size 5 is assigned to `length` instance variable. The `length` instance variable helps the programmer to not have to remember the size of the array. The array can be initialised as follows,

```
double [] height = {1.52, 1.61, 1.58, 1.72, 1.68. 1.70};
```

The heights of the students are initialised to an array by declaring the type as double followed by empty `[]` and the name of the array is `height`. The values on the right hand side are 6 double values that represent the height in metres and are separated by commas and enclosed within curly braces. The size of the array is to be 6 based on the number of assigned values. In the above statement initialisation is done using a single line. In Program 5.1, the array is declared and the values are read and initialised. Array initialisation is optional. Java automatically initialises the array based on its type. For example, in the array `height,` after declaration all its locations are initialised with 0.0. The next section shows how arrays are used in various problems.

5.2 PROCESSING ARRAY CONTENTS

An array is a data structure used to solve many programming problems. Operations like traversing, inserting, deleting and searching are performed on arrays. A single array's values can be sorted in ascending or descending order with a few algorithms. Two arrays can be merged into a single array. **Program 5.2** reads the values of the array and displays them in a pyramid structure.

Program 5.2

```
import java.util.Scanner;
public class ArrayDisplay {
    /**
     * To read array values and displaying them in a triangular structure
    */
    public static void main(String[] args) {
        int [] val = new int[10];
        int i, j,k, x, mid,mid1, lo, up;
        Scanner inp = new Scanner(System.in);
        System.out.println("Enter odd number from 5 to 10 ");
        x = inp.nextInt();
        for(i=0;i<x; i++)
        {
            System.out.println("Enter the
            values for the array ");
            val[i]=inp.nextInt();
        }
        System.out.println("\nTHE GIVEN
        VALUES ARE \n");
        mid = x/2;
        lo = mid;
        up = mid;
        mid1= mid;
        for(k=0; k<=mid;k++)
        {
            for(j=mid1;j>=0; j--)
            {
                System.out.print("        ");
            }
            for(i=lo;i<=up; i++)
            {
                System.out.print(val[i]+"        ");
            }
            lo--;
            up++;
            mid1--;
            System.out.println();
 }  } }
```

Output 5.2

```
Enter odd number from 5 to 10
5
Enter the values for the array 1
Enter the values for the array 2
Enter the values for the array 3
Enter the values for the array 4
Enter the values for the array 5
THE GIVEN VALUES ARE
               3
            2  3  4
         1  2  3  4  5
```

The above program receives values between 5 and 10 in terms of odd numbers to display values in a triangular structure. The array values are read to the array. The `mid` of the array is calculated by dividing the array size by 2. This value is assigned to the variables `lo` and `up` to display the array values from the mid index. There are three loops; the first loop is executed for 0 to mid value times, and in the sample output the number is 5 hence the `mid` value is 2, and the first loop is running for 0 to 2 times to finalise the number of rows. The second loop is to set the tab for the display; from the sample output the `mid` value is 3, so the display is to be set for 3 tabs and next time the loop is decremented for two tabs. The third loop displays the value as 3, then the values on either side of the `mid` are accessed by setting the range by decrementing the `mid` and assigning to `lo`. Similarly, the `mid` is incremented and assigned to `up` and the next time the loop displays three values for the third loop. Hence the first loop is executed for `mid` times; second loop is for setting the tab and third is to display the values from the mid-point and progress on either side.

An array is used in numerous applications and helps in handling data in an efficient manner. **Program 5.3** declares two arrays, one array is for storing input values; the program takes each value from the first array and finds the summation of the values and stores it to the corresponding index of the second array.

Program 5.3

```
import java.util.Scanner;
public class ArraySum {
   /**
      * To read values of an array and calculate the sum of values.
   */
   public static void main(String[] args) {
      int [] sum = new int[20];
      int [] sum1 = new int[20];
      int i, j,x;
      Scanner inp = new Scanner(System.in);
      System.out.println("Enter size of the
      array");
      x = inp.nextInt();
      for(i=0;i<x; i++)
      {
         System.out.println("Enter the
         values for the array ");
         sum[i]=inp.nextInt();
      }
      for(i=0; i<x;i++)
      {
         for(j=1;j<=sum[i]; j++)
         {
            sum1[i] +=j;
         }
      }
      System.out.println("GIVEN VALUES        SUMMED VALUES");
      for(i=0; i<x;i++)
      {
         System.out.println( "\n "+ sum[i]+" "+ sum1[i] );
      }
   }
}
```

Output 5.3

```
Enter size of the array
5
Enter the values for the array
12
Enter the values for the array
23
Enter the values for the array
34
Enter the values for the array
45
Enter the values for the array
56
GIVEN VALUES    SUMMED VALUES
      12              78
      23              276
      34              595
      45              1035
      56              1596
```

Two arrays are initialised in the program, the size of the array is read and values are read for the array `sum`. The first loop provides index values of the array from 0 to the size of the array. The second loop sums the values from 1 to the value of the first index of the array in `sum1`. The arrays are initialised during the declaration of the array, so the `sum1` array values are already initialised to 0. Each index value of `sum` is added and placed in the corresponding index of the `sum1` array. The number and its sum values stored in the array are displayed. The next section elaborates on passing arrays as arguments to a method.

5.3 PASSING ARRAYS AS ARGUMENTS TO METHODS

Repeated code fragments are efficiently handled by methods in all programming languages. First they reduce the code length and help in adding execution efficiency. In the case of one dimensional arrays, if two arrays are to be added, the two arrays are first to be read, added and stored in a third array and finally all three arrays are to be displayed. In this program, array values are to be read twice and the array values are to be displayed thrice. By doing so, the program length is expanded. If suitable methods are utilised for this program, the reading of array values is done once and displaying the array will also be done once. To achieve this code reduction and increased program efficiency, the arrays are passed as arguments to the methods. This problem is illustrated in **Program 5.4**.

Program 5.4

```
import java.util.Scanner;
public class ArraySum1 {
    /**
        * To read two arrays values, add the corresponding index values and stores
        * it another array and displaying three arrays
    */
    public static void readarray(int[] x)
    {
        int i,n;
        Scanner inp = new Scanner(System.in);
        for(i=0;i<x.length; i++)
        {
            System.out.println("Enter the
            values for the array ");
            x[i]=inp.nextInt();
        }
    }
    public static void printarray(int[] x)
    {
        int i;
        for(i=0; i<x.length;i++)
        {
            System.out.print( x[i]+"     ");
        }
        System.out.println();
    }
    public static void main(String[] args) {
        int [] a = new int[10];
        int [] b = new int[10];
        int [] c = new int[10];
        int i, j;
        readarray(a);
        readarray(b);
        for(i=0;i<a.length; i++)
        {
            c[i] = a[i] + b[i];
        }
        System.out.println("First Array Values are ");
        printarray(a);
        System.out.println("Second Array Values are ");
        printarray(b);
        System.out.println("Sum Array Values are ");
        printarray(c);
    }
}
```

Output 5.4

```
Enter the values for the array 1
Enter the values for the array 2
Enter the values for the array 3
Enter the values for the array 4
Enter the values for the array 5
Enter the values for the array 6
Enter the values for the array 7
Enter the values for the array 8
Enter the values for the array 9
Enter the values for the array 10
Enter the values for the array 19
Enter the values for the array 18
Enter the values for the array 17
Enter the values for the array 16
Enter the values for the array 15
Enter the values for the array 14
Enter the values for the array 13
Enter the values for the array 12
Enter the values for the array 11
Enter the values for the array 10
First Array Values are
1  2  3  4  5  6  7  8  9  10
Second Array Values are
19 18  17  16  15  14  13  12  11  10
Sum Array Values are
20  20  20  20  20  20  20  20  20  20
```

A method that is declared as static is called a class method. A class method is called with the class name with a dot operator. A class method is always invoked without reference to a particular object. Non-static methods referenced with objects of the class with a dot operator, are called instance methods. The class method is declared in a class and accessed in another class using the class name.

Program 5.4 declared two static methods `readarray()` and `printarray()`. But, in this program the static methods are not used outside the class `ArraySum1`. Since it is part of the definition of the class, there is no need for referencing the static method with the class name. The three arrays are declared and values for the two arrays are read through the static method `readarray()`. Each index of the two arrays is added and stored in the corresponding index of the third array using the loop structure. Finally all the array values are displayed using the static method `printarray()`. The programs used in this section have explained the concepts of declaration, passing arrays as arguments and processing arrays. The operations and algorithm-based problems are discussed in the next section.

5.4 RETURNING ARRAYS FROM METHODS

A method must be able to receive parameters from other program segments and process the data; the result will be displayed or sent back. An elegant way to send back values from a method is provided by the `return` statement. Simple data types and user defined data types are handled by the `return` statement. The returned value from the method is assigned to another variable of the same type or used in an expression or used to display the value in the called program or method. **Program 5.5** returns a double type value from the method as the batting average of a cricketer. A batsman's scores in various games are given as input and the batting average of the player is calculated.

Program 5.5

```
import java.util.Scanner;
public class ValueReturn {
    /**
        * Reads an array and passes to the methods.
        * Calculates the batting average and returns
    */
    public static void readarray(int[] b, int s1)
    {
        int i,n;
        Scanner inp = new Scanner(System.in);
        for(i=0;i<s1; i++)
        {
            System.out.println("Enter the score for the "+(i+1) +" ODI");
            b[i]=inp.nextInt();
        }
    }
    public static double battingavg(int[] b, int s1)
    {
        int i,total=0;
        double avg=0.0;
        for(i=0; i<s1;i++)
        {
            total += b[i];
        }
        avg = total/s1;
        return avg;
    }
```

```
    public static void printarray(int[] b, int s1)
    {
        int i;
        for(i=0; i<s1;i++)
        {
            System.out.println( "Match :
            "+(i+1)+ "     "+b[i]);
        }
        System.out.println();
    }
    public static void main(String[] args) {
        int [] score = new int[10];
        int s,i;
        double a;
        Scanner inp = new Scanner(System.in);
        System.out.println("Enter the size of
        the array");
        s=inp.nextInt();
        readarray(score,s);
        a=battingavg(score,s);
        System.out.println("Batting
        performance of the Batsman");
        System.out.
        println("---------------------------
        ------------");
        printarray(score,s);
        System.out.println("---------------
        -----------------------");
        System.out.println("Batting Average "+a);
        System.out.println("--------------------------------------");
    }
}
```

Output 5.5

```
Enter the size of the array
8
Enter the score for the 1 ODI12
Enter the score for the 2 ODI45
Enter the score for the 3 ODI82
Enter the score for the 4 ODI106
Enter the score for the 5 ODI2
Enter the score for the 6 ODI31
Enter the score for the 7 ODI0
Enter the score for the 8 ODI67
Batting performance of the Batsman
-----------------------------------
Match : 1    12
Match : 2    45
Match : 3    82
Match : 4    106
Match : 5    2
Match : 6    31
Match : 7    0
Match : 8    67
-----------------------------------
Batting Average 43.0
-----------------------------------
```

The program declares and reads the scores of the player using the method `readarray()`. The `battingavg()` method is called with the array and its size. The method computes the total by adding each score of the match. The batting average is calculated by dividing the total by the number of matches. The method `battingavg()` returns double type value. The returned batting average value is assigned to a double type variable `a`. The `printarray()` method displays the score in each match and the batting average.

Program 5.6 returns an array from a method. An integer array passes as argument to a method and the array values are placed in two arrays, according to whether they are odd or even values.

Program 5.6

```
import java.util.Scanner;
public class OddEvenArray {
    /**
        * Reads an array values, passes it to the method.
        * Method creates two arrays based on odd or even values.
    */
    public static void readarray(int[] x, int s1)
    {
        int i,n;
        Scanner inp = new Scanner(System.in);
        for(i=0;i<s1; i++)
```

```
    {
        System.out.println("Enter the values for the array ");
        x[i]=inp.nextInt();
    }
  }
  public static int[] Odd(int[] a, int s1)
  {
    int i,j, count=0;
    for(i=0; i<s1; i++)
    {
        if(a[i]%2!=0)
        count++;
    }
    int o[] = new int[count];
    j=0;
    for(i=0; i<s1; i++)
    {
        if(a[i]%2!=0)
        {
            o[j]=a[i];
        }
        return o;
    }
    ++j;
  }
  public static int[] Even(int[] a, int s1)
  {
    int i,j, count=0;
    for(i=0; i<s1; i++)
    {
        if(a[i]%2==0) count++;
    }
    int e[] = new int[count];
    j=0;
    for(i=0; i<s1; i++)
    {
        if(a[i]%2==0)
        {
            e[j]=a[i];
            ++j;
        }
    }
    return e;
  }
  public static void printarray(int[] x)
  {
    int i;
    for(i=0; i<x.length;i++)
    {
        System.out.print( x[i]+"     ");
    }
    System.out.println();
  }
```

Output 5.6

```
Enter the size of the array
20
Enter the values for the array 7
Enter the values for the array 3
Enter the values for the array 5
Enter the values for the array 9
Enter the values for the array 6
Enter the values for the array 4
Enter the values for the array 1
Enter the values for the array 8
Enter the values for the array 2
Enter the values for the array 99
Enter the values for the array 77
Enter the values for the array 22
Enter the values for the array 33
Enter the values for the array 11
Enter the values for the array 12
Enter the values for the array 56
Enter the values for the array 89
Enter the values for the array 47
Enter the values for the array 28
Enter the values for the array 94
Array Before Separation
7  3  5  9  6  4  1  8  2
99  77  22  33  11  12  56
89  47  28  94
ODD values Array
7  3  5  9  1  99  77  33
11  89  47
EVEN values Array
6  4  8  2  22  12  56  28  94
```

```
    public static void main(String[] args) {
        int [] num = new int[20];
        int [] od = new int[10];
        int [] ev = new int[10];
        int s,x, i;
        Scanner inp = new Scanner(System.in);
        System.out.println("Enter the size of the array");
        s=inp.nextInt();
        readarray(num,s);
        System.out.println("\nArray Before Separation ");
        printarray(num);
        od=Odd(num,s);
        ev=Even(num,s);
        System.out.println("\nODD values Array ");
        printarray(od);
        System.out.println("\nEVEN values Array ");
        printarray(ev);
    }
}
```

Array size is read and passed to the method for reading values. Before the values are separated into two arrays, the received array values are displayed. The array is passed to the method `Odd()` where the values are tested for odd numbers; if so, a count is taken of how many values of the array are odd values. A new array is declared based on the count value as its size. Again, the array values are tested for odd; if odd, they are assigned to the new array. The new array is returned from the method and assigned to the another similar type array in the `main()` method. The `Odd()` method returns an array to the invoking statement, this is facilitated by the return type `int[]`of the method. The array is then passed to the method `Even()` where the values are tested for even; if so, a count is taken of how many values of the array are even values. A new array is declared based on the count value as its size. Again, the array values are tested for even; if even, they are assigned to the new array. The new array is returned from the method and assigned to another array. Similar to the `Odd()` method this `Even()` method also has return type `int[]`. The odd value array and even value array are displayed by the `printarray()` method.

5.5 STRING ARRAYS

The String class (introduced in Chapter 2) has a group of characters that are stored in a String Object. The String class was used to create objects and store string constants. This section declares the String array in the following manner.

```
String states[] = new String[29];
```

The String class created an array of objects and the memory is allocated for 29 `states`. The string values for `states` are read using the loop.

```
Scanner inp = new Scanner(System.in);
for(i=0; i<states.length; i++)
states[i]=inp.nextLine();
```

The `Scanner` class creates an object and reads the string constant to the String object using the loop structure. The string constants read for the String object states are displayed using the following loop.

```
for(i=0; i<states.length; i++)
System.out.println(states[i]);
```

There is another way to display the values of the string constant which is,

```
for(String element : states)
System.out.println(element);
```

In Java 5, a new type of `for-each` loop is added that can go through each element of the array without using the array index. This type of `for` is called a `for-each` loop or *enhanced for* loop. This new `for-each` loop can be used with arrays and arrays of objects.

The general format of the `for-each` loop is,

```
for(arrayType variable : arrayName)
{
   Statements;
}
```

The `arrayType` is any simple data type or array, `variable` is any valid name and `arrayName` is an already declared array name which is looped through by the `for` statement. The last code segment can be read as – for each element in `states` do the following. The element must be the type of the array used in the *enhanced for* loop. The `for` loop takes each element of the String array `states[]` and displays the values. Each time the loop takes successive elements of the array and prints them on the screen. Also, the loop continues to display the string constants to the end of the string length. The advantage of using the above type of loop structure eliminates the use of the loop variable, condition and increment constructs. **Program 5.7** combines the code segments explained in this section.

Program 5.7

```
import java.util.Scanner;
public class StringArray {
   /**
      * Declares a String array and reads String
      * constants.
      * The String constants are displayed in
      * two ways.
*/
   public static void main(String[] args) {
      String states[] = new String[5];
      int i;
      Scanner inp = new Scanner(System.in);
      for(i=0; i<states.length; i++)
      {
         System.out.println("Enter State Name");
         states[i]=inp.nextLine();
      }
      System.out.println("\n State Name ");
      for(i=0; i<states.length; i++)
      System.out.println(states[i]);
      System.out.println("\n Enhanced for - State Name");
      for(String element : states)
      System.out.println(element);
   }
}
```

Output 5.7

```
Enter State Name Assam
Enter State Name Bihar
Enter State Name Karnataka
Enter State Name Kerala
Enter State Name Tamilnadu

State Name
Assam
Bihar
Karnataka
Kerala
Tamilnadu

Enhanced for - State Name
Assam
Bihar
Karnataka
Kerala
Tamilnadu
```

Searching is another important operation performed in arrays. For example, this search operation is performed for a word in a dictionary, for a contact in the mobile, a particular chapter in a book, and so on. A list of names is read in to a string array. A name is read and searched in the string array. The outcome of **Program 5.8** will be that the searched string is either present or not present in the array.

Program 5.8

```
import java.util.Scanner;
public class StringFind {
   /**
     * Declares a String array and reads string constants.
     * Reads a string to check the presence of a string in String array.
   */
   public static void main(String[] args) {
     int i;
     String names[] = new String[7];
     boolean present = false;
     String loc = "";
     Scanner inp = new Scanner(System.in);
     for(i=0; i<names.length; i++)
     {
        System.out.println("Enter a Name ");
        names[i]=inp.nextLine();
     }
     System.out.println("\nEnter Name to be
     searched ");
     loc = inp.nextLine();
     for(String element : names)
     {
        if(element.equals(loc))
        present = true;
     }
     System.out.println("Name List ");
     System.out.println("--------------");
     for(String value : names)
     System.out.println(value);
     if(present)
        System.out.println("\nThe string " +
        loc + " is present in the string array ");
     else
        System.out.println("\nThe string " + loc + " is NOT present in the string
        array ");
   }
}
```

Output 5.8

```
Enter a Name Harsitha
Enter a Name Karthika
Enter a Name Karishma
Enter a Name Vignesh
Enter a Name Senthil
Enter a Name Kumaran
Enter a Name Mano

Enter Name to be searched
Vignesh
Name List
-------------
Harsitha
Karishma
Karthika
Vignesh
Senthil
Kumaran
Mano

The string Vignesh is
present in the string array
```

Program 5.8 first reads the names into the array using `Scanner` class. Then, the name to be searched in the array is read and the *enhanced for* loop is used to locate the name in the string array. The array values are iterated to check for the equality with the elements using `equals()` method. If they are equal, the Boolean variable present is set to true; otherwise the loop continues till the end of the loop. Once the loop is terminated, the value of the Boolean variable present is checked for true or false; if it is true, it reflects that the given name is present in the array otherwise the name is not present in the array. The next section will explain how user defined objects are stored in the array.

5.6 ARRAYS OF OBJECTS

Chapter 4 provided a complete idea of classes and objects. This section combines both arrays and objects. Arrays are capable of storing objects. Storing objects in arrays has already been shown in Section 5.6 where the pre-defined String class objects are stored in the array. But String is a reference type variable which is not suitable for explaining an array of objects. To explain an array of objects, an employee class is defined as follows,

```
class employee {
    String name, empno, dept, desg;
    double salary;
}
```

The class `employee` contains one double instance variable to hold the employee salary and four instance variables `name, empno, dept, desg` as String objects for storing employee name, employee number, department and designation. The company has more employees, and to store their data an array of `employee` is defined as follows,

```
employee [] earr = new employee[10];
```

The definition has created arrays of ten employees' object reference. But it has not allocated memory for these ten `employee` objects. The memory allocation is to be done using the employee class constructors. The `earr` array contains ten memory locations where the references of ten employee objects are to be stored. If `earr` array is accessed to store values for the employee details, the compiler will report a run time error (which will be discussed in Chapter 8). To allocate memory to the objects of the employee class, the constructor is used and references are assigned to the `earr` array. Since it involves many objects, a loop is used to allocate memory and assign references to the array as follows,

```
for(i=0; i<10: i++)
    earr[i] = new employee();
```

The loop has created ten `employee` objects and their references are assigned to the `earr` array elements. This class is used in **Program 5.9** to read values for the array objects and list the employees' details.

Program 5.9

```
import java.util.Scanner;
/**
   * Defines a class employee with instance variables and methods.
*/
class employee
{
   String name, empno, dept, desg;
   double salary;
   Scanner inp = new Scanner(System.in);
   void reademp()
   {
      System.out.println("Enter the employee Name ");
      name=inp.nextLine();
      System.out.println("Enter the employee Number ");
      empno=inp.nextLine();
      System.out.println("Enter the employee Department ");
```

```
        dept=inp.nextLine();
        System.out.println("Enter the employee Designation ");
        desg=inp.nextLine();
        System.out.println("Enter the employee Salary ");
        salary=inp.nextDouble();
    }
    void displayemp()
    {
        System.out.println(name +"      " + empno +"    " + dept + "    " +desg + "
        " + salary);
    }
}
public class emparray {
    /**
     * Declares array of employee objects, read values and
     * list the employee based on their department.
    */
    public static void main(String[] args) {
        employeeearr[] = new employee[10];
        int i,n;
        Scanner inp = new Scanner(System.in);
        for(i=0; i<earr.length; i++)
        {
            earr[i]= new employee();
        }
        System.out.println("\nEnter Number of employee ");
        n = inp.nextInt();
        for(i=0; i<n; i++)
        earr[i].reademp();
        System.out.println("--------------------------------------------------------");
        System.out.println("Name        Number  Department Designation Salary ");
        System.out.println("--------------------------------------------------------");
        for(i=0; i<n; i++)
        earr[i].displayemp();
        System.out.println("--------------------------------------------------------");
    }
}
```

Output 5.9

```
Enter Number of employee
2
Enter the employee Name Natrajan
Enter the employee Number MAR2301
Enter the employee Department Marketing
Enter the employee Designation Manager
Enter the employee Salary 36750.25
Enter the employee Name Manoharan
Enter the employee Number SAL3425
Enter the employee Department Sales
Enter the employee Designation Executive
Enter the employee Salary 45650.25
------------------------------------------------------
Name       Number    Department  Designation  Salary
------------------------------------------------------
Natrajan   MAR2301   Marketing   Manager      36750.25
Manoharan  SAL3425   Sales       Executive    45650.25
------------------------------------------------------
```

The employee class is defined with five instance variables and two methods. The instance variables are to hold the name of the employee, his number, department, designation and salary. The reademp() method reads the values for the variables and displayemp() method displays the employee details. The emparray class declared an array of ten objects for the employee class. The loop allocates memory for each object and assigns its reference to the earr array. The loop calls the reademp() method based on the value for number of employees. In a similar manner, the displayemp() method is called to display the values of the employee object. In this way any type of objects can be defined and used in array objects.

5.7 TWO DIMENSIONAL ARRAYS

Thus far we have considered only one dimensional arrays for basic data types, Strings and objects. Arrays discussed have stored only similar data items in a single line of elements. But data representation is also needed for tables such as students' marks in a class. Each cell of the array can hold a value and work like a variable. A one dimensional array uses a single subscript and two dimensional arrays use two subscripts, one for the row and another for the column. A table is needed to store the data of five students in a class with five subjects. To store marks, the row represents the students and columns represent the marks in each subject (Fig. 5.3).

	Mark 1	Mark 2	Mark 3	Mark 4	Mark 5
Student 1	89	92	79	94	87
Student 2	45	65	54	42	53
Student 3	65	68	71	58	55
Student 4	34	42	47	43	50
Student 5	12	56	42	49	65

Fig. 5.3 Two dimensional array representation for students' marks

To store marks, the two dimensional array is declared as,

```
int [][] marks = new int[5][5]
```

The statement declares the array variable marks of type integer, creates the array with five students elements, each of which is an array of 5 elements to store marks. The two dimensional array representation is provided in Fig. 5.4. The students are represented by the rows and the marks are represented by the columns. The indexes for students are between 0 and 4, and each student's marks indexes are between 0 and 4. To reference the 2nd student and his 4th subject, the index for the student index is 1 and mark index is 3 (index starts from 0).

Right index determines column values

Left index determines row values

	0	1	2	3	4
0	[0][0]	[0][1]	[0][2]	[0][3]	[0][4]
1	[1][0]	[1][1]	[1][2]	[1][3]	[1][4]
2	[2][0]	[2][1]	[2][2]	[2][3]	[2][4]
3	[3][0]	[3][1]	[3][2]	[3][3]	[3][4]
4	[4][0]	[4][1]	[4][2]	[4][3]	[4][4]

Fig. 5.4 Two dimensional array index representation

In a class, student marks are to be totalled after the examination, to find the total marks for each student and the pass percentage in each subject. **Program 5.10** calculates the students' total marks and the subject-wise total to determine the percentage.

Program 5.10

```
import java.util.Scanner;
public class TwoDim {
   /**
      * Declares a two dimensional array and reads students marks.
      * Calculates the students total marks and subject wise total.
*/
   public static void main(String[] args) {
      int marks[][] = new int[5][5];
      int i,j,n;
      Scanner inp = new Scanner(System.in);
      System.out.println("\nEnter Number of
      Students ");
      n = inp.nextInt();
      for(i=0; i<marks.length-1; i++)
      for(j=0; j<marks.length-1; j++)
      {
         System.out.println("Enter the " +
         (i+1) +" Student's marks");
         marks[i][j]=inp.nextInt();
      }
      for(i=0; i<marks.length-1; i++)
      {
         marks[i][4]=0;
         for(j=0; j<marks.length-1; j++)
         marks[i][4]+=marks[i][j];
      }
      for(i=0; i<marks.length-1; i++)
      {
         marks[4][i]=0;
         for(j=0; j<marks.length-1; j++)
         marks[4][i]+=marks[i][j];
      }
      marks[4][4]=0;
      for(i=0; i<marks.length-1; i++)
      {
         marks[4][4]+=marks[4][i];
      }
      System.out.println("\nSub-1  Sub-2  Sub-3  Sub-4  Total ");
      System.out.println("---------------------------------------");
      for (int[] a : marks)
      {
         for (int y : a)
         {
            System.out.print(" "+y + "\t");
         }
         System.out.println("\n");
      }
      System.out.println("---------------------------------------");
   }
}
```

Output 5.10

```
Enter the 1 Student's marks 45
Enter the 1 Student's marks 46
Enter the 1 Student's marks 47
Enter the 1 Student's marks 48
Enter the 2 Student's marks 56
Enter the 2 Student's marks 57
Enter the 2 Student's marks 58
Enter the 2 Student's marks 59
Enter the 3 Student's marks 23
Enter the 3 Student's marks 24
Enter the 3 Student's marks 25
Enter the 3 Student's marks 26
Enter the 4 Student's marks 89
Enter the 4 Student's marks 90
Enter the 4 Student's marks 91
Enter the 4 Student's marks 92

Sub-1 Sub-2 Sub-3 Sub-4 Total
------------------------------
45    46    47    48    186
56    57    58    59    230
23    24    25    26    98
89    90    91    92    362
186   230   98    362   876
------------------------------
```

The above program has declared a two dimensional array with five rows and five columns. Each row represents a student's marks and each column represents the marks in each subject. The data is received for each student using two for loops. Each loop is terminated before storing the last value in each row and column. Because the student total and the subject total will be stored in these locations, that is, the 4th column is the last where each student's total will be stored and the 4th row is the last where each subject total will be stored. There are two sets of for loops being used in this program. The first set is the `for` loop which calculates the total of each student and stores it in the last column. Before the start of the second loop, the column locations are initialised. The second set of the `for` loop calculates the subject total and stores it in the last row. Before the start of the second loop the row locations are initialised. The 4th row and 4th column are initialised to store all subject totals.

Students' information is displayed with their total marks, the subject total and total of all subjects. This is displayed with two `for-each` loops. The two dimensional array is an array of arrays.

5.8 ARRAYS WITH THREE OR MORE DIMENSIONS

A two dimensional array is called an array of arrays. Three dimensional arrays are called array of array of arrays. Java provides, in the same way, multi-dimensional arrays that can be defined and manipulated. In Program 5.10 marks were stored for the entire class. If the students' marks are to be stored for the entire school, with a fixed number of students and a fixed number of subjects, three dimensional arrays can be used. The declaration for the three dimensional array is,

```
intSchoolmarks [][][] = new int[][][];
```

The `Schoolmarks` array has three dimensions, one for each class in a school; the second is to store the students in a class and the third is to store the marks in each subject. The three dimensional array declaration is similar to that of two dimensional arrays. The array declaration of `Schoolmarks` can be thought of as the innermost loop that makes a one dimensional array to store marks of the subject; the second innermost loop contains the two dimensional array of each student's marks and the outmost loop contains a three dimensional array for the entire school. The marks for the three dimensional array is initialised as follows,

```
for(i=0; i<5; i++)
{
    for(j=0; j<50; j++)
    {
        for(k=0; k<5; k++)
        {
            arr[i][j][k] = 0;
        }
    }
}
```

There is a need for three loops and each loop variable takes a separate dimension. In this manner multi-dimensional arrays are declared and manipulated. Is it possible to declare a multi-dimensional array for any number of dimensions? Basically, Java has no limits for defining multi-dimensional arrays. The dimensions of a multi-dimensional array may be restricted by the memory size available for programming.

SUMMARY

1. Collection of similar data types is called array.
2. Data values in an array are called array elements.
3. Each individual element in an array is accessed by its index.
4. Array elements can be values of basic data types or objects.
5. An array can include only elements of the same data type.
6. A Java array is a reference data type.
7. Array is created with the `new` operator.
8. An array can have multiple indices.
9. While passing an array to a method, only a reference to the array is passed. A copy of the array is not created.
10. The reference to an array passed to a method uses the call-by-value scheme.
11. The array passed to a method returns a simple data type or array.
12. In a string array, stored characters are processed as in other simple-type arrays.
13. The arrays are also used to store objects; each object is referenced using the index of the array and each member of the object can be accessed.
14. Table type data are stored in two dimensional arrays and handled with two loops, one for the first dimension row and the second loop for the second dimension column.
15. Java allows declaring and use of multi-dimensional arrays.

SHORT QUESTIONS

1. What is an array?
2. What are the differences between a simple data types and arrays?
3. How is memory allocated for an array?
4. What is the subscript of the first element of an array?
5. How can one declare an array p containing 50 float elements followed by 50 integer elements?
6. What is the purpose of initialising an array?
7. Is it possible to declare and initialise an array? If so how?
8. What is a `for each` loop?
9. What is the other name of a two dimensional array?
10. What is the maximum number of dimensions that an array in Java may have?

COMPREHENSIVE QUESTIONS

1. Briefly explain array declaration and initialisation.
2. Explain with suitable examples, how arrays simplify programming.
3. Explain how the loop structure helps in processing array elements.
4. Describe the process of passing an array to a method. Give an example.
5. Elaborate how a method returns an array. Give an example.
6. Compare the declaration, usage and storage of arrays and String arrays. Give examples.
7. Give the general format of the `for each` loop statement and explain it with an example.
8. Write the advantages of using arrays of objects. Give an example.
9. Write down a situation where the two dimensional array can be used. Give an example.
10. How are two dimensional arrays stored in memory? Explain.
11. Where can you apply multi-dimensional arrays like three dimensional arrays? Give an example.

SOLVED PROGRAMS

1. Write a program to read an array and insert a value in a specified index.

```
import java.util.Scanner;
public class ArrayInsert {
   /**
   * Reads an array values, a value to be inserted and index where the value to be
     inserted.
   * The program inserts the value in the index of the array and displays it.
   */
   public static void readarray(int[] x, int s1)
   {
      int i,n;
      Scanner inp = new Scanner(System.in);
      for(i=0;i<s1; i++)
      {
         System.out.println("Enter the values for the array ");
         x[i]=inp.nextInt();
      }
   }
   public static void insert(int[] a, int x1, int s1, int i)
   {
      int j;
      for(j=s1-1; j>=i;j--)
      {
         a[j+1] = a[j];
      }
      a[i]=x1;
   }
   public static void printarray(int[] x,
   int s1)
   {
      int i;
      for(i=0; i<s1;i++)
      {
         System.out.print( x[i]+" ");
      }
      System.out.println();
   }
   public static void main(String[] args)
   {
      int [] arr = new int[10];
      int s,x, i;
      Scanner inp = new Scanner(System.in);
      System.out.println("Enter the size of the array");
      s=inp.nextInt();
      readarray(arr,s);
      System.out.println("Enter the value to be inserted");
      x=inp.nextInt();
      System.out.println("Enter the index where the value to be inserted ");
      i=inp.nextInt();
      System.out.println("\nArray Before Insertion ");
      printarray(arr,s);
      insert(arr,x,s,i);
      System.out.println("\nArray After Insertion ");
      printarray(arr,++s);
```

Output

```
Enter the size of the array 7
Enter the values for the array 2
Enter the values for the array 4
Enter the values for the array 6
Enter the values for the array 8
Enter the values for the array 10
Enter the values for the array 12
Enter the values for the array 14
Enter the value to be inserted 5
Enter the index where the value to
be inserted 2
Array Before Insertion
2 4 6 8 10 12 14
Array After Insertion
2 4 5 6 8 10 12 14
```

```
    }
}
```

2. Write a program to read an array and delete a value in a specified index.

```
import java.util.Scanner;
public class ArrayDelete {
  /**
   * Reads an array values and an index to be removed.
   * The program removes the value from the array and displays it
  */
  public static void readarray(int[] x, int s1)
  {
     int i,n;
     Scanner inp = new Scanner(System.in);
     for(i=0;i<s1; i++)
     {
        System.out.println("Enter the values for the array ");
        x[i]=inp.nextInt();
     }
  }
  public static void delete(int[] a, int s1, int i)
  {
     int j;
     for(j=i; j<s1;j++)
     {
        a[j] = a[j+1];
     }
  }
  public static void printarray(int[] x,
  int s1)
  {
     int i;
     for(i=0; i<s1;i++)
     {
        System.out.print( x[i]+" ");
     }
     System.out.println();
  }
  public static void main(String[] args)
  {
     int [] arr = new int[10];
     int s,i;
     Scanner inp = new Scanner(System.in);
     System.out.println("Enter the size of the array");
     s=inp.nextInt();
     readarray(arr,s);
     System.out.println("Enter the index where the value to be deleted ");
     i=inp.nextInt();
     System.out.println("\nArray Before Deletion ");
     printarray(arr,s);
     delete(arr,s,i);
     System.out.println("\nArray After Deletion ");
     printarray(arr,--s);
  }
}
```

Output

```
Enter the size of the array 8
Enter the values for the array 34
Enter the values for the array -45
Enter the values for the array 56
Enter the values for the array -12
Enter the values for the array 78
Enter the values for the array -41
Enter the values for the array 90
Enter the values for the array -3
Enter the index where the value to
be deleted 2
Array Before Deletion
34 -45 56 -12 78 -41 90 -3
Array After Deletion
34 -45 -12 78 -41 90 -3
```

3. Write a program to sort the given set of numbers using bubble sort.

```
import java.util.Scanner;
/*
  * Program to sort the given set of numbers
  * using Bubble sort.
*/
public class bubbleSort {
  public static void main(String[] args) {
     double [] arr = new double[10];
     double temp;
     int size,i,j;
     Scanner inp= new Scanner(System.in);
     System.out.println("Enter the size of the array ");
     size = inp.nextInt();
     for(i=0;i<size;i++)
     {
        System.out.println("Enter a
        Double value");
        arr[i]=inp.nextDouble();
     }
     System.out.println("Bubble Sorting ");
     System.out.
     println("***************");
     System.out.println("The Array
     values Before Sorting ");
     for(i=0;i<size;i++)
     System.out.print(arr[i]+ " ");
     for(i=0;i<size-1;i++)
     for(j=i+1;j<size;j++)
     if (arr[i]>= arr[j])
     {
        temp=arr[i];
        arr[i]=arr[j];
        arr[j]=temp;
     }
     System.out.println("\n\nThe Array values After Sorting ");
     for(i=0;i<size;i++)
     System.out.print(arr[i]+" ");
  }
}
```

Output

```
Enter the size of the array 5
Enter a Double value 120.50
Enter a Double value -350.60
Enter a Double value 680.90
Enter a Double value -455.25
Enter a Double value 560.75
Bubble Sorting
***************
The Array values are Before Sorting
120.5 -350.6 680.9 -455.25 560.75
The Array values are After Sorting
-455.25 -350.6 120.5 560.75 680.9
```

4. Write a program to receive a set of values and find the maximum and the minimum of the array.

```
import java.util.Scanner;
/*
  * Program to receive a set of values and
  * find the maximum and the minim of the array.
*/
public class minimumMaximun {
  public static void main(String[] args) {
     double [] arr = new double[10];
     double min, max;
     int i;
     int size;
     Scanner inp= new Scanner(System.in);
     System.out.println("Enter the size of the array ");
     size = inp.nextInt();
```

```
        for(i=0;i<size;i++)
        {
           System.out.println("Enter a Double value");
           arr[i]=inp.nextDouble();
        }
        System.out.println("The Array values
");
        for(i=0;i<size;i++)
        System.out.print(arr[i]+ " ");
        min = max = arr[0];
        for(i=1;i<size;i++)
        {
           if ( arr[i] < min)
           min=arr[i];
           if (arr[i] >max)
           max=arr[i];
        }
        System.out.println("\nThe Array
        Minimum value is = " +min);
        System.out.println("The Array Maximun value is = " +max);
     }
  }
```

Output

```
Enter the size of the array 5
Enter a Double value 12.34
Enter a Double value 500.45
Enter a Double value 1.75
Enter a Double value 986.35
Enter a Double value 45.32
The Array values
12.34 500.45 1.75 986.35 45.32
The Array Minimum value is = 1.75
The Array Maximum value is =
986.35
```

5. **Write a program to find out the mean, variance and standard deviation of the given set of numbers.**

```
import java.util.Scanner;
/*
  * Program to find out the mean, variance
  * and standard deviation of the given set of numbers.
*/
public class meanAvgSD {
  public static void main(String[] args) {
     double [] arr = new double[10];
     int size, i;
     double sum=0.0,mean, var,sd;
     Scanner inp= new
     Scanner(System.in);
     System.out.println("Enter the
     size of the array ");
     size = inp.nextInt();
     for(i=0;i<size;i++)
     {
        System.out.println("Enter a
        Double value");
        arr[i]=inp.nextDouble();
     }
     System.out.println("The Array
     values ");
     for(i=0;i<size;i++)
     System.out.print(arr[i]+ " ");
     for(i=0;i<size;i++)
     sum+=arr[i];
     mean = sum/size;
     sum=0.0;
     for(i=0;i<size;i++)
     sum+=(arr[i]-mean)*(arr[i]-mean);
     var = sum/size;
     sd=Math.sqrt(var);
```

Output

```
Enter the size of the array 7
Enter a Double value 12.50
Enter a Double value 34.78
Enter a Double value 14.60
Enter a Double value 30.75
Enter a Double value 25.57
Enter a Double value 22.89
Enter a Double value 29.34
The Array values
12.5 34.78 14.6 30.75 25.57 22.89 29.34
The Arithmetic Mean = 24.347142857142853
The Variance = 59.10713469387756
The Standard Deviations =
7.688116459437745
```

```
        System.out.println("\nThe Arithmetic Mean = " +mean);
        System.out.println("The Variance = " +var);
        System.out.println("The Standard Deviations = " +sd);
    }
}
```

PROGRAMMING EXERCISES

1. Write a program to read in a number and print it out digit by digit as a series of words. 752 should be printed as 'Seven Five Two'.
2. Write a program that reads in short strings and displays the characters in all possible permutations.
3. Write a program to read in grades and display the top five.
4. Write a program that declares an array for 50 elements of type integer. Initialise and display the first 25 elements of the array with the square of the index and the remaining with three times the index value.
5. Write a program that reads an array of students' test scores in the range 0–100. It should then determine the number of students having scores in each of the following ranges:
   0–10, 11–20, 21–30, 31–40, 41–50, 51–60, 61–70, 71–80, 81–90 and 91–100. Display the score ranges and the number of students in that range.
6. The mathematics teacher conducted a True/ False test. The students' test answers are stored in a two dimensional array. The correct answers to the test are in the form:
   10010110011111010101
   The answer to question 1 is True, the answer to question 2 is False, and so on. The exam has 20 questions, and the class has more than 50 students. The answers are stored in a one dimensional array and it is checked for correctness for each student represented by a row of the two dimensional array. Each correct answer is awarded two points and each wrong answer gets –1 point. Write a program that processes the test data. The output displays each student's answer, test score and test grade. Assume the following grade scale: 90%–100% : O; 80%–89.99% : A; 70%–79.99% : B; 60%–69.99% : C; and 0%–59.99% : D.
7. In a class, the maximum number of students is 50. Write a program that reads students' test scores, stores them in an array and outputs the following:
   (a) Class average.
   (b) List of all students with test scores below the class average.
   (c) List of all students with test scores above the class average.
8. Write a program that reads a set of positive integers in an array and displays how many times a particular number appears in the array.
9. Write a program that prompts the user to input two numbers, first and diff. The program then creates a one dimensional array of 20 elements and initialises them with the arithmetic sequence. For example, if first =11 and diff = 4, the arithmetic sequence is: 11 15 19 23 27 31 35 39 43 47 51 55 59 63 67 71 75 79 83 87.
10. Write a program to read two integer arrays, sort them in order and merge the first array with the second array by taking the first element of the first array and the first element of the second array and placing the least value among these two in the result array. Display the source and resultant arrays.
11. Write a program to read a two dimensional array of size 10 by 10. Sort the values in each row and display.

CHAPTER

6

String Handling

Strings are extensively used as a data type and it allows the programmer to handle words, sentences, phone numbers, or even just usual numbers. Fundamentally, a String is an object that represents a sequence of character values.

6.1 STRING CLASS

The `String` class is a standard class that comes with Java and it is specifically designed for creating and processing Strings. An array of characters also works in the same way as a Java String. For example, in the statements given below, the data type is `char` with an array namely `ch` being initialised and the values stored as 'javastring'. Then an object for `String` class `s` is created and `ch` has been passed as argument.

```
char[] ch={'j','a','v','a','s','t','r','i','n','g'};
String s=new String (ch);
```

The above two lines can be rewritten as `String s="javastring"`. Therefore, it is clear that String consists of an array of characters. This chapter briefly explains the different String operations, methods and tokenizer in Strings. Java `String` class provides a lot of methods to perform operations on Strings such as `compare()`, `concat()`, `equals()`, `split()`, `length()`, `replace()`, `compareTo()`, `intern()`, `substring()`, and so on. The `String` class implements *Serialisable*, *Comparable* and *CharSequence* interfaces.

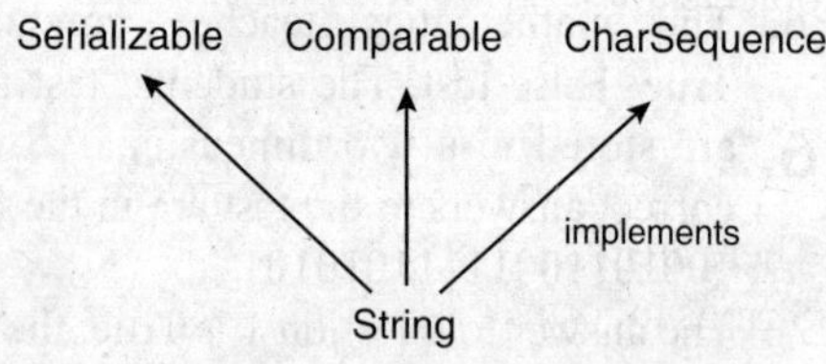

Fig. 6.1 `String` class

Every time the `println()` method is used in a program a *String literal* has been passed as argument. A *String literal* is a sequence of characters between double quotes. For example,

```
"This is a string literal".
```

Some characters can't be entered from the keyboard, for example, including a new line character by pressing the Enter key moves the cursor to a new line, and it is not possible to use an escape sequence simply in a program. Therein comes the usage of String literals. For example, the statement

```
System.out.println(" This is \n a string constant!");
```

produces the output,

```
This is
a string constant!
```

because \n is interpreted as a new line character. A double quote character as it is in a String literal is used to indicate where a String literal begins and ends. String objects are said to be immutable. Immutable means unmodifiable or unchangeable. Once the object for String is created its data or state remains unchanged; however, a new String object can be created. **Program 6.1** explains the concept of immutability.

Program 6.1

```
class Testimmutablestring
{
    public static void main(String args[])
    {
        String s="Abdul";
        s.concat(" Kalam");
        System.out.println(s);
    }
}
```

Output 6.1

```
Abdul
```

In Program 6.1, the class name is Testimmutablestring. In main(), String variable s is declared and initialised with the value 'Abdul'. The concat() method generally appends the String at the end. The statement s.concat() concatenates the value of the object s to the value of argument 'Kalam'. While the program is executed the String object s prints 'Abdul' output instead of 'AbdulKalam'. This is because in the first case the String object s holds a value so when the same object is used for some other operation it won't hold the new data; rather, it refers to the old one. The reason behind this is that String objects are immutable. Hence the output is Abdul.

6.2 STRING CONCATENATION

There are many operations that can be performed on Strings. This section deals with joining two or more Strings to form a new String. This is called *String concatenation.* There are two ways to join two Strings.

- By the + (String concatenation) operator
- By the concat() method

String concatenation by + operator

The simplest use of this is to join two Strings together as follows.

```
String s= "welcome to" + "string handling";
```

This joins the two Strings on the right of the assignment and stores the result in the String variable s. The + operation generates a completely new String object that is separate from the two original String objects that are operands and a reference to this new object is stored in s. So, if s is displayed, the output will be 'welcome to string handling'. The + operator can also be used for arithmetic addition, but the condition is that if either of the operands for the + operator is a String object or literal, then the compiler interprets the operation as String concatenation and converts the operand that is not a String object to a String. For example, the following statements concatenate Strings referenced by String variables.

```
String date="28th";
String month="February";
String lastday=date+month;
```

First, the `date` variable is declared as a String and initialised with the value 28th. The variable `month` is declared as a String and initialised to February. In the last statement, the String variable `lastday` is declared and the date value is concatenated with the month value using the + operator and assigned to `lastday`. The + operator concatenates the String values since both are declared as Strings. There is no surprise that the output will be '28th February'. The String concatenation operator (+) is used largely to append Strings. **Program 6.2** illustrates the joining of two Strings using the + operator.

Program 6.2

```
class StringConcatenation
{
    public static void main(String args[])
    {
        String s="Abdul"+" Kalam";
        System.out.println(s);
    }
}
```

Output 6.2

```
AbdulKalam
```

In Program 6.2, the class name is `StringConcatenation`. In `main()`, a String variable `s` is declared and initialised with two Strings separated by the + operator. The String object `s` is instantiated as 'Abdul' then followed by the + operator, then the string 'Kalam'. The String concatenation operator (+) produces a new String by appending the second operand onto the end of the first operand. Hence the output is 'AbdulKalam'. The String concatenation operator can concatenate not only Strings but primitive values also. **Program 6.3** explains the same where it concatenates numeric values and String values.

Program 6.3

```
class StringConcatenation
{
    public static void main(String args[])
    {
        String s=50+30+"Joe"+40+40;
        System.out.println(s);
    }
}
```

Output 6.3

```
80Joe4040
```

In Program 6.3, the class name is `StringConcatenation`. In `main()`, a String variable `s` is declared and initialised with four numeric values and a String value. The String object `s` is instantiated with a value 50 followed by the + operator then the value 30, then the + operator and the next String 'Joe' followed by the + operator then the value 40, the next + operator and at the end, a numeric value 40. The String concatenation operator (+) produces a new String by appending the operands onto the end of the preceding operands successively. As the first two operands are numeric values, the arithmetic operation is performed to give the value 80, concatenated with String value 'Joe', then the other two numeric values are concatenated without performing any operation. Hence the output is 80Joe4040.

String concatenation by `concat()` method

The `concat()` method concatenates the particular String to the end of the present String. The syntax for the method is,

```
public String concat(String another)
```

In the statement, `public` is the access specifier, `String` is the returntype, `concat()` is the method name and it has a String variable `another` as a parameter. **Program 6.4** illustrates the use of String `concat()` method.

Program 6.4

```
class StringConcatenation
{
   public static void main(String args[])
   {
      String s1="Abdul ";
      String s2="Kalam";
      String s3=s1.concat(s2);
      System.out.println(s3);
   }
}
```

Output 6.4

```
Abdul Kalam
```

In Program 6.4, the class `StringConcatenation` has three String objects—`s1`, `s2` and `s3`. The String object `s1` holds 'Abdul' and `s2` holds 'Kalam'. The String object `s3` has been set to hold the data that is now `s1` concatenated with `s2`. Thus, the output of the program is 'Abdul Kalam'.

6.3 COMPARING STRINGS

Various techniques are used to compare values stored in variables of the primitive types, for equality. For example, *authentication* (by `equals()` method), *sorting* (by `compareTo()` method), *reference matching* (by == operator), and so on. Basically, there are three ways in Java to compare Strings.

- By `equals()` method
- By == operator
- By `compareTo()` method

String compare by `equals()` method

The String `equals()` method compares the unique contents of the String. It compares values of Strings for parity or equality. String class provides two methods.

- *public Boolean equals(Object another)* compares this String to the particular object.
- *public Boolean equalsIgnoreCase(String another)* compares this String to another String, ignoring case.

Program 6.5 explains the concept of comparing Strings with the equal method.

Program 6.5

```
class Stringcomparison
{
    public static void main(String args[])
    {
        String s1="Abdul";
        String s2="Abdul";
        String s3=new String("Abdul");
        String s4="Andre";
        System.out.println(s1.equals(s2));
        System.out.println(s1.equals(s3));
        System.out.println(s1.equals(s4));
    }
}
```

Output 6.5

```
True
True
False
```

In Program 6.5, the class name is `Stringcomparison`. There are four String objects—`s1`, `s2`, `s3` and `s4`. The String object `s1` is assigned with a value 'Abdul', `s2` is assigned with a value 'Abdul', `s3` holds 'Abdul' passed from the `String()` constructor and `s4` is assigned with a value 'Andre'. When the stored values are compared with each other it will return either True or False. If equal, the return value will be True else it will be False. Thus, comparing `s1` with `s2` returns True, comparing `s1` with `s3` returns True and comparing `s1` with `s4` returns False as the output.

String compare by == operator

The == operator checks whether the two String variables refer to the same String. If it references separate Strings then the expression has the value False. The result is true only if both the Strings are the same. **Program 6.6** illustrates comparing Strings with the == operator.

Program 6.6

```
class Stringcomparison
{
    public static void main(String args[])
    {
        String s1="Sachin";
        String s2="Sachin";
        String s3= "Dhoni";
        System.out.println(s1==s2);
        System.out.println(s1==s3);
    }
}
```

Output 6.6

```
True
False
```

In Program 6.6, the class `Stringcomparison` has three String objects—`s1`, `s2`, and `s3`. The objects `s1` and `s2` are assigned with the value 'Sachin' whereas the object `s3` is assigned with the value 'Dhoni'. In the first case `s1` is compared with `s2` and it returns True because both the objects refer to the same instance. Then `s1` is compared with `s3` and the value returned is False because `s3` holds different data.

String compare by `compareTo()` method

The String `compareTo()` method compares values lexicographically and returns an integer value that indicates whether the first String is less than, equal to or greater than the second String. For example, `s1` and `s2` are two String variables and they can be compared as follows.

```
s1 == s2 : 0
s1 > s2 : positive value
s1 < s2 : negative value
```

The first statement checks if both the Strings are equal; if true returns 0. The second statement checks whether s1 is greater than s2, if true returns a positive value and the third statement checks whether s2 is greater than s1, else returns a negative value. **Program 6.7** illustrates the comparison of Strings using `compareTo()` method.

Program 6.7

```
class Test
{
    public static void main(String args[])
    {
        String s1="Sachin";
        String s2="Sachin";
        String s3="Ratan";
        System.out.println(s1.compareTo(s2));//0
        System.out.println(s1. compareTo(s3));//1(because s1>s3)
        System.out.println(s3.compareTo(s1)); //-1(because s3 < s1 )
    }
}
```

Output 6.7

```
0
1
-1
```

In Program 6.7, the class `Test` consists of three objects namely, `s1, s2, s3` and the values stored in those objects are 'Sachin', 'Sachin' and 'Ratan' respectively. When s1 is compared to s2, the length of the two values are same so it returns 0 as output. On comparing s1 with s3, the output is 1 because s1 is greater than s3 in length. Finally, s3 is compared to s1 and it returns –1 because s3 is smaller than s1 String.

6.4 SUBSTRING

A branch or piece of a String is called a *substring*. A substring can also be defined as a compartment of another String. In case of a substring, *startIndex* is inclusive, that is, complete or broad; and *endIndex* is exclusive, that is, limited or restricted. Typically, the index always starts from 0. A substring can be retrieved from the given String object by one of the two methods.

- `public String substring(int startIndex)`

This method returns a new String object containing the substring of the given String from a particular startIndex.

- `public String substring(int startIndex, int endIndex)`

This method returns a new String object containing the substring of the given String from the specified startIndex to endIndex.

The following code explains the startIndex and endIndex.

```
String s="hello";
System.out.println(s.substring(0,2));
```

In the above statement, the substring argument, 0 points to `h` but 2 points to `e`. Thus, the output will be 'he'. **Program 6.8** explicitly illustrates the formation of substrings.

Program 6.8

```
public class TestSubstring
{
   public static void main(String args[])
   {
      String s="SachinTendulkar";
      System.out.println(s.substring(6));//Tendulkar
      System.out.println(s.substring(0,6));//Sachin
   }
}
```

Output 6.8

```
Tendulkar
Sachin
```

In Program 6.8, the class `TestSubstring` has `s` as a String object. The String object `s` is assigned with the value 'SachinTendulkar'. The method `s.substring(6)` returns 'Tendulkar' since the condition value is after the sixth character. The next method `s.substring(0,6)` returns 'Sachin' because the `startIndex` is 0 and the `endIndex` is 6.

6.5 STRING CLASS METHODS

The String class provides various valuable methods to carry out manipulations or operations on a sequence of char values. **Table 6.1** depicts the different String class methods.

Table 6.1 String class methods

No.	Method	Description
1	char charAt(int index)	Returns char value for the particular index
2	int length()	Returns the String length
3	static String format(String format, Object... args)	Returns the formatted String
4	static String format(Locale l, String format, Object... args)	Returns the formatted String with given locale
5	String substring(int beginIndex)	Returns the substring for the given begin index
6	String substring(int beginIndex, int endIndex)	Returns substring for the given begin index and end index
7	Boolean contains(CharSequence s)	Returns True or False after matching the sequence of char values
8	static String join(CharSequence delimiter, CharSequence... elements)	Returns a joined String

(Continued)

Table 6.1 (Continued)

No.	Method	Description
9	static String join(CharSequence delimiter, Iterable<? extends CharSequence> elements)	Returns a joined String
10	Boolean equals(Object another)	Checks the equality of the String with the object
11	Boolean isEmpty()	Checks if the String is empty
12	String concat(String str)	Concatenates the specified String
13	String replace(char old, char new)	Replaces all occurrences of the specified char value
14	String replace(CharSequence old, CharSequence new)	Replaces all occurrences of the specified charsequence
15	static String equalsIgnoreCase(String another)	Compares another String; it doesn't check case
16	String[] split(String regex)	Returns split String matching the regex
17	String[] split(String regex, int limit)	Returns split String matching the regex and limit
18	String intern()	Returns the interned String
19	int indexOf(int ch)	Returns the specified char value index
20	int indexOf(int ch, int fromIndex)	Returns the specified char value index starting with the given index
21	int indexOf(String substring)	Returns the specified substring index
22	int indexOf(String substring, int fromIndex)	Returns the specified substring index starting with the given index
23	String toLowerCase()	Returns the String in lowercase
24	String toLowerCase(Locale l)	Returns the String in lowercase using specified locale
25	String toUpperCase()	Returns the String in uppercase
26	String toUpperCase(Locale l)	Returns the String in uppercase using specified locale
27	String trim()	Removes beginning and ending spaces of this String
28	static String valueOf(int value)	Converts the given type into String; it is overloaded

6.6 OTHER STRING CLASS METHODS

The String class provides several of methods to force on Strings. By using these methods, it is possible to perform operations on Strings such as trimming, concatenating, converting, comparing, replacing Strings, and so on. The important methods of String class are briefly shown below.

`toUpperCase()` and `toLowerCase()` method

The java String `toUpperCase()` method converts the Strings into uppercase letter and String `toLowerCase()` method into lowercase letter.

Syntax:

```
String toLowerCase()
String toUpperCase()
```

Example:

```
String s=" Sachin";
System.out.println(s.toUpperCase());//SACHIN
System.out.println(s.toLowerCase());//sachin
System.out.println(s); //Sachin(no change in original)
```

The initial value of the String object `s` is 'Sachin'. After the execution of `s.toUppercase()` method, the value of `s` will be 'SACHIN'. The `s.Lowercase()` method converts the upper case value 'SACHIN' to 'sachin'. While printing the value of the object `s` it remains the same, that is, 'Sachin'.

`trim()` method

The String `trim()` method eliminates white spaces before and after a String. It is used to remove the leading and trailing white spaces from the String. It does not remove the spaces in between the characters of the String.

Syntax:

```
String trim()
```

Example:

```
String s="Sachin";
System.out.println(s);// Sachin
System.out.println(s.trim());//Sachin
```

Initially the object `s` of String type is assigned with a value 'Sachin' where there are whitespaces before the first character *S*. While printing `s` it displays the same which is initialised. When `trim()` method is applied to the String object `s` it removes the white spaces. Hence, the output will be 'Sachin'.

`startsWith()` and `endsWith()` method

The method `startsWith()` determines whether a given String starts with a specified String or not. Conversely, `endsWith()` determines whether a given String ends with a specified String or not.

Syntax:

```
Boolean startsWith(String s)
Boolean endsWith(String s)
Boolean startsWith(String s, int startIndex)
```

In the above syntax, `s` is the String to be checked and `startIndex` is the index from which the comparison is to be made. Similarly, `endsWith` is the index in which the String ends.

Example:

```
String s="Sachin";
System.out.println(s.startsWith("Sa"));//true
System.out.println(s.endsWith("n"));//true
```

The initial value of the String object `s` is assigned with the value 'Sachin'. The argument passed to the method `startsWith()` is 'Sa' refers to the index from which the comparison will be made. Similarly, the `endsWith()` has argument 'n' where it will check for the String whose end value is n.

`charAt()` method

The String `charAt()` method returns a character at the specified index, or in other words this method extracts a single character from the String.

Syntax:

```
char charAt(int index)
```

It extracts the character from the invoking String from the position specified by the index. For example:

```
String s="Sachin";
System.out.println(s.charAt(0));//S
System.out.println(s.charAt(3));//h
```

The initial value of String object `s` is 'Sachin'. The `charAt()` method has 0 as the argument so it will return the first character of the String, that is, 'S'. The next `charAt()` method has 3 as argument and hence it will return the character present at the third position in the String 'Sachin', that is 'h'.

`length()` method

The String `length()` method returns the length of the String, that is, the total number of characters in the String.

Syntax:

```
int length()
```

Example:

```
String s="Sachin";
System.out.println(s.length());//6
```

The initial value of the String object `s` is 'Sachin'. The `length()` method is applied to the object `s`. This will print the value 6 which is the length of the String `s` value that is 'Sachin'.

`intern()` method

A group of Strings, initially empty, is maintained privately by the class `String`. When the intern method is invoked, if the pool already contains a String equal to this String object as determined by the `equals(-Object)` method, then the String from the pool is returned. Otherwise, this String object is added to the pool and a reference to this String object is returned.

Syntax:

```
intern()
```

Example:

```
String s=new String("Sachin");
String s2=s.intern();
System.out.println(s2);//Sachin
```

In the statements, the object `s` is created for the String class and through the `String()` constructor the argument 'Sachin' has been passed. Then the object `s2` is created for the defined class. The `intern ()` method is applied to the value of the String object `s`. While printing `s2`, it displays the value of object `s` that is 'Sachin'.

`valueOf()` method

The string `valueOf()` method coverts a given type such as int, long, float, double, Boolean, char and char array into String.

Syntax:

```
valueOf()
```

Example:

```
int a=10;
String s=String.valueOf(a);
System.out.println(s+10); //1010
```

The integer variable a is assigned with value 10. An object `s` has been created for the String class and it is assigned a value using the `valueOf()` method where the parameter is `a`. While printing the value of `s` with the + operator then the value 10, it prints 1010.

`replace()` method

The String `replace()` method replaces all occurrences of the first sequence of character with the second sequence of character.

Syntax:

```
String replace(char original, char replacement)
```

`Original` is the character to be replaced and `replacement` is the new character exchanged instead of that.

Example:

```
String s1="Java is a platform. Java is purely object oriented.";
String replaceString=s1.replace("Java","Kava");
System.out.println(replaceString);
```

Output:

```
Kava is a platform. Kava is purely object oriented.
```

From the output it is evident that 'Java' Strings are replaced by 'Kava' in two occurrences.

6.7 `StringBuffer` CLASS

The `String` and `StringBuffer` classes are defined in the 'java.lang' package. `StringBuffer` class is used to create a mutable, that is, a modifiable String. The `StringBuffer` class in Java is the same as the `String` class except it can be changed. It represents growable and writeable character sequences. It is possible to insert the characters anywhere inside the `StringBuffer`. `StringBuffer` will automatically grow to make room for such additions and often has more pre-allocated characters than are actually needed. `StringBuffer` class is thread-safe, that is multiple threads cannot access it simultaneously. So, it is safe and will result in an order. `StringBuffer` class defines three important constructors.

```
StringBuffer()
StringBuffer(String str)
StringBuffer(int Size)
```

The first form which is the default constructor creates an empty String buffer with the initial capacity of 16 characters. The second form creates a String buffer with the specified String. The third form creates an empty String buffer with the specified size as length. An object of the StringBuffer class can be constructed as follows.

```
StringBuffer sb=new StringBuffer();
```

In the statement, `StringBuffer` is the class name and `sb` is the object of the defined class. `StringBuffer()` is the constructor with no arguments. There are some important methods of StringBuffer classes and they are listed below.

`public synchronized StringBuffer append(String s)`
It is used to append the specified String with the String. The `append()` method is overloaded like `append(char)`, `append(Boolean)`, `append(int)`, `append(float)`, `append(double)`, and so on.

`public synchronized StringBuffer insert(int offset, String s)`
This method is used to insert the specified String within the String at the specified position. The `insert()` method is overloaded like `insert(int, char)`, `insert(int, Boolean)`, `insert(int, int)`, `insert(int, float)`, `insert(int, double)`, and so on.

`public synchronized StringBuffer replace(int startIndex, int endIndex, String str)`
This method is used to replace the String from the specified `startIndex` to the `endIndex`.

`public synchronized StringBuffer delete(int startIndex, int endIndex)`
This is used to delete the String from the specified `startIndex` to the `endIndex`.

`public synchronized StringBuffer reverse()` is used to reverse the String.

`public int capacity()` is used to return the current capacity.

`public void ensureCapacity(int minimumCapacity)` is used to ensure the capacity at least equal to the given minimum.

`public char charAt(int index)` is used to return the character at the specified position.

`public int length()` is used to return the length of the String, that is, the total number of characters.

`public String substring(int beginIndex)` is used to return the substring from the specified `beginIndex`.

`public String substring(int beginIndex, int endIndex)` is used to return the substring from the specified `beginIndex` to the endIndex.

A String that can be customised or altered is known as a mutable String. `StringBuffer` and `StringBuilder` classes are used for creating mutable Strings. The following section briefly explains the use of each method in the `StringBuffer` class.

append()

The `append()` method concatenates the given argument with the String.

Syntax:

```
StringBuffer append(String str)
StringBuffer append(int num)
StringBuffer append(Object obj)
```

Example:

```
class A
{
    public static void main(String args[])
    {
        StringBuffer sb=new StringBuffer("Java ");
        sb.append("Book");//now original string is changed
        System.out.println(sb);//prints Java Book
    }
}
```

In the code segment, the class name is `A`. In `main()`, the object `sb` is created for the `StringBuffer` class and the `StringBuffer()` constructor has 'Java' as argument. The object `sb` will have the value 'Java'. The next statement `append()` method has 'Book' as argument and it has access to `sb`. While printing `sb` the output will be 'Java Book'.

insert()

The `insert()` method inserts the given String, character or object into another String.

Syntax:

```
StringBuffer insert(int index, String str)
StringBuffer insert(int index, char ch)
StringBuffer insert(int index, Object ob)
```

'index' specifies the position at which the String will be inserted. For example:

```
class InsertEx
{
    public static void main(String args[])
    {
        StringBuffer sb=new StringBuffer("Hello ");
        sb.insert(1,"Java");
        //now original string is changed
        System.out.println(sb);//prints Hjavaello
    }
}
```

The class name is `InsertEx`, object `sb` is created for the defined class where the `StringBuffer()` constructor has value 'Hello' as argument. The statement `sb.insert(1, "Java")` indicates that, in the position 1 in the value of `sb` that is 'Hello', a new String value is inserted that is 'Java'. Hence the ouput is `HJavaello`.

delete()

The `delete()` method of `StringBuffer` class deletes the String from the specified `beginIndex` to `endIndex`. This method is used to delete a single character or a sequence of characters from the `StringBuffer`.

Syntax:

```
StringBuffer delete(int startIndex, int endIndex)
StringBuffer deleteCharAt(int loc)
```

The `delete()` method deletes a sequence of characters from the invoking object. The `startIndex` specifies the index of the first character to remove, and `endIndex` specifies an index one past the last character to remove. Thus, the substring deleted runs from `startIndex` to `endIndex-1`. The resulting `StringBuffer` object is returned. The `deleteCharAt()` method deletes the character at the index specified by 'loc'. It returns the resulting `StringBuffer` object.

Example 1:

```
class A
{
    public static void main(String args[])
    {
        StringBuffer sb=new StringBuffer("Hello");
        sb.delete(1,3);
        System.out.println(sb);//prints Hlo
    }
}
```

Initially `sb` object has the value 'Hello'. The `delete(1,3)` method removes the characters (of `sb`) from position 1 to 3. Hence the output is `Hlo`.

Example 2:

```
StringBuffer sb=new StringBuffer("Programming")
sb.delete(4,7) // sb will be "Progming"
sb.deleteCharAt(0);// sb will be "rogming"
```

Initially `sb` object has the value 'Programming'. The `delete(4,7)` method removes the characters from position 4 to 7 which results in 'Progming'. The `deleteCharAt(0)` method removes the value of the 0th position in the `sb` value. Hence the output is 'rogming'.

reverse()

The `reverse()` method of `StringBuffer` class reverses the current String of characters.

Syntax:

```
StringBuffer reverse()
```

This method returns the reversed object upon which it is called. Example 1:

```
StringBuffer s=new StringBuffer("Yellow");
s.reverse(); // s will be "wolleY"
```

Initially `s` object has the value 'Yellow'. The `reverse()` reverses the value of the `s` object. Hence the output is 'wolleY'. Example 2:

```
class Reverse
{
    public static void main(String args[])
    {
        StringBuffer sb=new StringBuffer("Hello");
        sb.reverse();
        System.out.println(sb);//prints olleH
    }
}
```

The name of the class is `Reverse`. In `main()` the object `sb` is created for the defined class and the `StringBuffer()` constructor has the value 'Hello' as argument.

The `reverse()` method reverses the characters in the object `sb`, which is 'Hello'. While printing the value of `sb` it prints 'olleH' as output.

capacity()

The `capacity()` method of `StringBuffer` class returns the current capacity of the buffer. The default capacity of the buffer is 16. If the number of characters increases from its current capacity, it increases the capacity by (oldcapacity*2) + 2. For example if the current capacity is 16, it will be (16*2) + 2 = 34.

Syntax:

```
int capacity()
```

Example:

```
class A
{
    public static void main(String args[])
    {
        StringBuffer sb=new StringBuffer();
        System.out.println(sb.capacity());
        //default 16 sb.append("Hello");
        System.out.println(sb.capacity());//now 16
        sb.append("java is my favourite language");
        System.out.println(sb.capacity()); //34
    }
}
```

The name of the class is `A`. In `main()`, the object `sb` is created for the defined class and the `StringBuffer()` constructor has no arguments. While printing the capacity of the object `sb` the value is 16. Through the `append()` the value of the `sb` object is appended with the value 'Hello'. When appending the value the first time to the object, the capacity remains at the default, that is, 16. Then the next `append()` method appends the String value 'java is my favourite language' to object `sb`. Since there is an increase in characters, `sb` capacity increases which results in the change in capacity value, that is, 34.

ensureCapacity()

The `ensureCapacity()` method of `StringBuffer` class ensures that the given capacity is the minimum to the current capacity. If it is greater than the current capacity, it increases the capacity by (oldcapacity*2)+2. For example if current capacity is 16, it will be (16*2) + 2 = 34. It is useful to know in advance that a large number of small Strings will be appended to a `StringBuffer`.

Syntax:

```
void ensureCapacity(int capacity)
```

`'capacity'` specifies the size of the buffer.

Example :

```
StringBuffersb=newStringBuffer(10);
sb.ensureCapacity(20);
```

`StringBuffer` refers to the class, `sb` is the object and `StringBuffer()` constructor has a value 10 as the argument. The value 10 specifies the size of the buffer. The method `ensureCapacity(20)` represents the information that will be appending of String values to the buffer.

6.8 StringBuilder CLASS

`StringBuilder` class is used to create mutable or modifiable Strings. The `StringBuilder` class is the same as the `StringBuffer` class except that it is non-synchronised. It has been available since JDK 1.5. There are three important constructors of `StringBuilder` class, which are as follows.

```
StringBuilder()
StringBuilder(String str)
StringBuilder(int length)
```

The first form of the default constructor creates an empty StringBuilder with an initial size of 16. The second form of the `StringBuilder` class creates a `StringBuilder` with the specified String. The third form of the constructor creates an empty `StringBuilder` with the specified capacity as length. Table 6.2 represents the methods of the `StringBuilder` class

Table 6.2 Methods of StringBuilder class

S. no.	Method	Description
1	public StringBuilder append(String s)	used to append the specified String with this String.
2	public StringBuilder insert(int offset, String s)	used to insert the specified String with this String at the specified position.
3	public StringBuilder replace(int startIndex, int endIndex, String str)	used to replace the String from specified startIndex and endIndex.
4	public StringBuilder delete(int startIndex, int endIndex)	used to delete the String from specified startIndex and endIndex.
5	public StringBuilder reverse()	used to reverse the String.
6	public int capacity()	used to return the current capacity.
7	public void ensureCapacity(int minimumCapacity)	used to ensure the capacity at least equal to the given minimum.
8	public char charAt(int index)	used to return the character at the specified position.
9	public int length()	used to return the length of the String, that is, total number of characters.
10	public String substring(int beginIndex)	used to return the substring from the specified beginIndex.
11	public String substring(int beginIndex, int endIndex)	used to return the substring from the specified beginIndex and endIndex.

The following statements explain the append method of `StringBuilder` class.

append()

The StringBuilder `append()` method concatenates the given argument with the String.

Example:

```
class A
{
    public static void main(String args[])
    {
        StringBuilder sb=new StringBuilder("Hello ");
        sb.append("Java");//now original string is changed
        System.out.println(sb);//prints Hello Java
    }
}
```

In the code segment, the class name is `A`. In `main()` the object `s` is created for the `StringBuilder` class and the `StringBuilder()` constructor has 'Hello' as argument. The object `sb` will have the value 'Hello'. In the next statement, the `append()` method for `sb` is called and it has 'Java' as argument. While printing *sb* the output will be 'Hello Java'. Similarly, all the other methods that are explained in the section `StringBuffer` class are used in the `StringBuilder` class. The only thing that is needed is to replace the keyword `StringBuffer` by `StringBuilder` in all the methods.

There are various differences between String and StringBuffer. The differences between String and StringBuffer are tabled below:

Table 6.3 Differences between `String` and `StringBuffer` class

S. no.	String	StringBuffer
1	String class is immutable.	StringBuffer class is mutable.
2	String is slow and consumes more memory when concatenating too many Strings because it creates a new instance every time.	StringBuffer is fast and consumes less memory when concatenating Strings.
3	String class overrides the equals() method of Object class. So it is possible to compare the contents of two Strings by equals() method.	StringBuffer class doesn't override the equals() method of Object class.

There are many differences between the `StringBuffer` and `StringBuilder` class. These are listed here:

Table 6.4 Differences between `StringBuffer` and `StringBuilder` class

S. no.	StringBuffer	StringBuilder
1	StringBuffer is *synchronised*, that is, thread safe. It means two threads can't call the methods of StringBuffer simultaneously.	StringBuilder is *non-synchronised*, that is, not thread safe. It means two threads can call the methods of StringBuilder simultaneously.
2	StringBuffer is *less efficient* than StringBuilder.	StringBuilder is *more efficient* than StringBuffer.

6.9 StringTokenizer CLASS

The `StringTokenizer` class allows breaking a String into tokens. It provides a simple means to break up a large String that contains delimited text. The idea is that a String tokenizer object attaches to a String. When constructing the tokenizer object, there is need to specify which characters are the delimiters. For example,

```
StringTokenizer t = new StringTokenizer(line, "|");
```

`StringTokenizer` is the class name, `t` is the object for the defined class and the `StringTokenizer ()` constructor has line and '|' as parameters. There can be multiple delimiters specified in the String. For example, to set up a String tokenizer that would let one search for any delimiter in the set

```
" \t\n\r"
```

use the following:

```
StringTokenizer t = new StringTokenizer(line," \t\n\r");
```

These four delimiters are used as the defaults in constructing a String tokenizer like this:

```
StringTokenizer t = new StringTokenizer(line);
```

Once a String tokenizer is constructed, it is possible to use its methods to quickly extract the tokens from the String. The `nextToken` method returns the next unread token. The `hasMoreTokens` method returns true if more tokens are available. The following section describes the constructors in `StringTokenizer` class.

Constructors of StringTokenizer class

There are three constructors defined in the `StringTokenizer` class. Table 6.5 presents the constructors of the `StringTokenizer` class.

Table 6.5 Constructors of StringTokenizer class

S. no.	Constructor	Description
1	StringTokenizer(String str)	creates StringTokenizer with the particular String.
2	StringTokenizer(String str, String delim)	creates StringTokenizer with the particular String and delimeter.
3	StringTokenizer(String str, String delim, Boolean returnValue)	creates StringTokenizer with the particular String, delimeter and returnValue. If return value is True, delimiter characters are considered to be tokens. If it is False, delimiter characters provide to separate tokens.

StringTokenizer class methods

There are six useful methods of `StringTokenizer` class. Table 6.6 lists the methods of `StringTokenizer` class.

Table 6.6 Methods of StringTokenizer class

S. no.	Methods	Description
1	Boolean hasMoreTokens()	returns True if more tokens exist.
2	String nextToken()	constructs a String tokenizer with the default delimiter set " \t\n\r". Returns the next token; throws a `NoSuchElementException` if there are no more tokens.
3	String nextToken(String delim)	returns the next token after switching to the new delimiter set. The new delimiter set is subsequently used.
4	int countTokens()	returns the number of tokens still in the String.

Program 6.9 explains the `StringTokenizer` class that tokenizes a String 'Welcome to String Handling Concept' on the basis of whitespace.

Program 6.9

```
import java.util.StringTokenizer;
public class TokenizerEx
{
   public static void main(String args[])
   {
      StringTokenizer st = new StringTokenizer("Welcome to
      String Handling Concept "," ");
      while (st.hasMoreTokens())
      { System.out.println(st.nextToken());
      }
   }
}
```

Output 6.9

```
Welcome
to
String
Handling
Concept
```

In Program 6.9 the first statement imports the `StringTokenizer` class that resides in the *util* package. The name of the class is `TokenizerEx`. In `main()`, an object `st` has been created for the defined class, and the argument value 'Welcome to String Handling Concept' is passed to the `StringTokenizer()` constructor. The object intern holds the value of the argument of the constructor. The method `hasMoreTokens()` checks for the presence of tokens in the object `st` in a loop; if true, returns to the loop for continuing the execution, else the execution is terminated. The `nextToken()` constructs a String tokenizer with the default delimiter set, that is the white spaces. Then it returns to the next token. Thus, the tokens are printed on a new line and the output is obtained. **Program 6.10** shows how to specify a delimiter for a StringTokenizer object. The default delimiters are `\t` character (tab), `\n` character (new line), `\r` character (carriage return) and `\f` character (form feed).

Program 6.10

```
import java.util.StringTokenizer;
class StringTokenizerDelimiter
{
    public static void main(String[] args)
    {
        //1. Using StringTokenizer constructor
        StringTokenizer st1 = new
        StringTokenizer("Java|StringTokenizer|Concept", "|");
        //iterate through tokens while(st1.hasMoreTokens())
        System.out.println(st1.nextToken());
        //2. Using nextToken() method
        //default after this method call
        StringTokenizer st2 = new
        StringTokenizer("Java|objectoriented|Programming");
        //iterate through tokens while(st2.hasMoreTokens())
        System.out.println(st2.nextToken("|"));
    }
}
```

Output 6.10

```
Java
StringTokenizer
Concept
Java
objectoriented
Programming
```

There are two ways to specify a delimiter for a `StringTokenizer` object. The first one is at the time of creation, by specifying in the `StringTokenizer` constructor. Then, to specify it in the `nextToken()` method. In Program 6.10, the first statement imports the `StringTokenizer` class that resides in the util package. The name of the class is `StringTokenizerDelimiter`. In `main()`, an object `st1` has been created for the defined class and the argument value 'Java|StringTokenizer|Concept', '|' is passed to the `StringTokenizer()` constructor where the | symbol refers to the delimiter. The object in turn holds the value of the argument of the constructor. The `hasMoreTokens()` iterates through tokens, checks for the presence of tokens in the object `st1`; if True, returns to the loop for continuing the execution, else the execution is terminated. The `nextToken()` constructs a String tokenizer with the default delimiter set, that is |. Then it returns to the next token. Then an another object `st2` has been created for the defined class and the argument value 'Java|objectoriented|Programming' is passed to the `StringTokenizer()` constructor where | symbol refers to the delimiter and at the end of the statement '|' is missing when comparing to the `st1` object creation. The object in turn holds the value of the argument of the constructor. The `hasMoreTokens()` iterates through tokens, checks for the presence of tokens in the object `st1`; if True, returns to the loop for continuing the execution else the execution is terminated. The `nextToken("|")` construct holds the delimiter as argument and according to that it will return the tokens. Both the methods produce the same result but the passing is different.

SUMMARY

1. A `string` represents a group of characters. `String` is an immutable object which means it is constant and cannot be changed once it has been created.
2. `String` class provides many methods to perform operations on Strings, such as `compare()`, `concat()`, `equals()`, `split()`, `length()`, `replace()`, `compareTo()`, `intern()`, `substring()`, and so on.
3. The `String` class implements `Serializable`, `Comparable` and `CharSequence` interfaces.
4. `StringBuffer` class is a thread-safe, mutable sequence of characters. It contains a particular sequence of characters, but the length and content of the sequence can be changed through certain method calls. They are safe for use by multiple threads.

5. `StringBuilder` class is used to create mutable Strings. The `StringBuilder` class is the same as `StringBuffer` class except that it is non-synchronised. `StringBuffer` will automatically grow to make room to insert the characters anywhere inside.

6. The `StringTokenizer` class allows breaking a String into tokens. This class is a legacy class that is retained for compatibility reasons although its use is discouraged in new code. Its methods do not distinguish between identifiers, numbers and quoted Strings.

SHORT QUESTIONS

1. Define `String`.
2. Why is `String` class called immutable? Justify.
3. Which package contains the `String` class?
4. Which method is helpful for character replacement in a String?
5. State the purpose of `startsWith()` and `endsWith()` method.
6. How does `compareTo()` differ from `equals()` method?
7. What is the use of `substring()` and `replace` methods?
8. Define `StringBuffer` class.
9. '`StringBuffer` class is mutable'. Comment on this statement.
10. Write a short note on `insert()` and `reverse()` methods in `StringBuffer` class.
11. What is the objective of the `StringBuilder` class?
12. What is the use of the `StringTokenizer` class?

COMPREHENSIVE QUESTIONS

1. Explain the ways in which a String can be constructed.
2. Explain the different String handling functions in Java.
3. Discuss the features of the `StringBuffer` class with an example.
4. Explain the different ways of creating a `StringBuffer` object.
5. Discuss `append ()` and `insert ()` methods of the `StringBuffer` class.
6. What are the `StringBuffer` operations and methods? Explain with an example.
7. Differentiate between `String` and `StringBuffer` class.
8. Differentiate `StringBuffer` from `StringBuilder` class.
9. Explain the functionality of the `StringTokenizer` class with an example.
10. Write a program to implement the String handling mechanism.

SOLVED PROGRAMS

1. Program that checks whether a given string is a palindrome or not.

```
import java.io.*;
class Palind
{
  public static void main(String args[ ])throws IOException
  {
     BufferedReader br=new BufferedReader(new InputStreamReader(System.in));
     System.out.println("Enter the string to check for palindrome:");
     String s1=br.readLine();
     StringBuffer sb=new StringBuffer();
```

```
        sb.append(s1);
        sb.reverse();
        String s2=sb.toString();
        if(s1.equals(s2))
           System.out.println("palindrome");
        else
           System.out.println("not palindrome");
     }
  }
```

Output

```
Enter the string to check for
palindrome: malayalam
Palindrome
```

2. **Program for sorting a given list of names in ascending order.**

```
import java.io.*;
class Test
{
   int len,i,j;
   String arr[ ];
   Test(int n)
   {
      len=n;
      arr=new String[n];
   }
   String[ ] getArray()throws IOException
   {
      BufferedReader br=new BufferedReader (new InputStreamReader(System.in));
      System.out.println ("Enter the strings U want to sort");
      for (int i=0;i<len;i++)
         arr[i]=br.readLine();
         return arr;
   }
   String[ ] check()throws ArrayIndexOutOfBoundsException
   {
      for (i=0;i<len-1;i++)
      {
         for(int j=i+1;j<len;j++)
         {
            if ((arr[i].compareTo(arr[j]))>0)
            {
               String s1=arr[i];
               arr[i]=arr[j];
               arr[j]=s1;
            }
         }
      }
      return arr;
   }
   void display()throws ArrayIndexOutOfBoundsException
   {
      System.out.println ("Sorted list is---");
      for (i=0;i<len;i++)
         System.out.println(arr[i]);
   }
} //end of the Test class
class Ascend
{
   public static void main(String args[ ])throws IOException
   {
      Test obj1=new Test(4);
```

Output

```
Enter the strings U want to sort
Java Programming
Welcome to string Handling
Hello java
Sorted list is---
Java Programming
Hello java
Welcome to string Handling
```

```
        obj1.getArray();
        obj1.check();
        obj1.display();
    }
}
```

3. Program that reads a line of integers and then displays each integer and the sum of all integers using `StringTokenizer` class.

```
import java.lang.*;
import java.util.*;
class tokendemo
{
    public static void main(String args[ ])
    {
        String s="10,20,30,40,50";
        int sum=0;
        StringTokenizer a=new
        StringTokenizer(s,",",false);
        System.out.println("integers are ");
        while(a.hasMoreTokens())
        {
            int b=Integer.parseInt(a.nextToken());
            sum=sum+b;
        }
        System.out.println(" "+b);
    }
    System.out.println("sum of integers is "+sum);
}
```

Output

```
integers are
10
20
30
40
50
sum of integers is 150
```

PROGRAMMING EXERCISES

1. Write a program to get the character at the given index within the String.
2. Write a program using any five String handling functions.
3. Write a program to compare two Strings.
4. Write a program to compare two Strings while ignoring case differences.
5. Write a program to concatenate a given String to the end of another String.
6. Write a program to test if a given String contains the specified sequence of char values.
7. Write a program to compare a given String to the specified character sequence.
8. Write a program to compare a given String to the specified String buffer.
9. Write a program to create a new String object with the contents of a character array.
10. Write a program to check whether a given String ends with the contents of another String.
11. Write a program to check whether two String objects contain the same data.
12. Write a program to compare a given String to another String, ignoring case considerations.
13. Write a program to print the current date and time in the specified format.
14. Write a program to get the contents of a given String as a byte array.
15. Write a program to get the contents of a given String as a character array.
16. Write a program to get the canonical representation of the String object.
17. Write a program to get the last index of a String within a String.
18. Write a program to get the length of a given String.

19. Write a program to find out whether a region in the current String matches a region in another String.
21. Write a program to replace all the 'd' characters with 'f' characters. .
22. Write a program to replace each substring of a given String that matches the given regular expression with the given replacement.
23. Write a program to check whether a given String starts with the contents of another String.
24. Write a program to get a substring of a given String between two specified positions.
25. Write a program to convert all the characters in a String to lowercase.
26. Write a program to convert all the characters in a String to uppercase.
27. Write a program to trim any leading or trailing whitespace from a given String.
28. Write a program to illustrate the `StringBuffer` class.
29. Write a program using `StringBuilder` class methods.
30. Write a program to retrieve tokens using `StringTokenizer` class.

CHAPTER

7

Inheritance

In this chapter, classes and objects will be handled in terms of working to achieve code reusability through inheritance. *Inheritance* is the mechanism for instances of the subclass to access the superclass variables and methods. It is the practice where one object obtains the properties of another object. With the help of inheritance, the information can be managed in a hierarchical order. The method which overrides its superclass methods, the overridden method, can be called upon through the *super* keyword. *Polymorphism* is the capability to associate many meanings to one method name. The use of polymorphism in OOP comes into play when a base class reference is used to refer to a subclass object. *Abstraction* facilitates in making a class abstract in OOP. It assists in reducing the complications and also improves the maintainability of the system. These OOP features and their development will be discussed.

7.1 BASICS OF INHERITANCE

Inheritance is the process by which one object can obtain the properties of another object. This is significant as all Java classes are arranged in a hierarchical classification. For instance,

The hierarchal classification of `Food` is given in Fig. 7.1. A `Delicious Apple` is part of `Fruit` class, which in turn is under the larger class `Food`. Therefore, the `food` is known as the Base or Superclass, `Fruit` is known as the subclass which derives the properties from the Base class of `Food`.

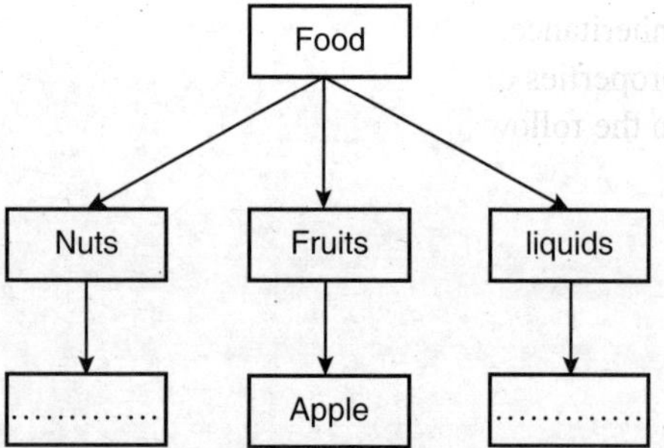

Fig. 7.1 Hierarchical order of `food`

Superclass is an elevated class that supplies its attributes and methods to the ladder of subclasses. *Subclass* is an object class that is derived from a superclass from which it inherits the base set of properties and methods. In general, *inheritance* is the process of developing a new class from an existing class. An existing class is called a base class, or superclass, or parent class. The new class is called subclass, or derived class, or child class. Inheritance permits the subclasses to use the base class properties and methods.

Inheritance involves a *superclass* and a *subclass*. The *superclass* is the general class and the *subclass* is a specialised class. The subclass is an extended version of the superclass. The subclass inherits fields and methods from the superclass without any of them being rewritten. Furthermore, new fields and methods can be added to the subclass to make it more specialised than the superclass. When one object is a specialised version of another object, there is an *'is a' relationship* between them. For example, a grasshopper *is an* insect. Here are a few other examples of an 'is a' relationship.

- A car *is a* vehicle.
- A flower *is a* plant.
- A rectangle *is a* shape.

When an 'is a' relationship exists between objects, it means that the specialised object has all of the characteristics of the general object, and additional characteristics that make it special. In OOP, *inheritance* is used to create an 'is a' relationship among classes. This allows extending the capabilities of a class by creating another class that is a specialised version of it.

For an example, let us see how inheritance can be used in the context of 'is a' relationship. Figure 7.2 shows the Unified Modeling Language (UML) diagram for the `Payment` and `Cheque` classes, which are designed to hold variables and methods in the context of 'is a' relationship.

The UML diagram to represent the classes consists of three parts in the box. The first part represents the class name, the middle part consists of a list of variables or member variables and the third part, the list of methods. By default, the variables are private and are represented with a – in the beginning of the variables, the methods are public and are represented with a + in the beginning of the methods. To connect the base class from the subclass, a triangle shaped arrow symbol is used in UML. This symbol represents the `extends` keyword in java.

Let's see how the `extends` keyword is used to achieve inheritance. The `extends` keyword is used to inherit the properties of a class. The syntax of `extends` keyword is given in the following example.

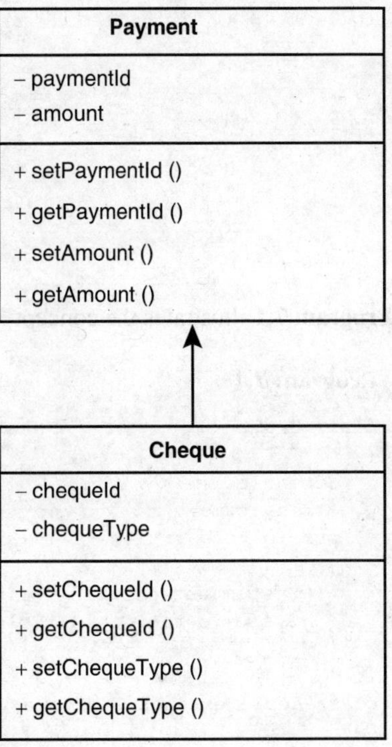

Fig. 7.2 'is a' Relationship between `Payment` and `Cheque` classes

```
public class Fruit
{
    ...
}
public class Apple extends Fruit
{
    ...
}
public class Orange extends Fruit
{
    ...
}
```

Now, based on the above example, in OO terms, the following are true:

- `Fruit` is a superclass of `Apple` subclass.

`Fruit` is a superclass of `Orange` subclass. `Apple` and `Orange` are the `subclass`es which are deriving the member variables and methods of `Fruit` superclass using `extends` keyword. The program structure of inheritance for `Fruit`, `Apple` and `Orange` class is given below:

```
class Fruit
{
    //variables or properties
    //Methods
}
class Apple extends Fruit
{
    //variables or properties
    //Methods
}
class Orange extends Fruit
{
    //variables or properties
    //Methods
}
```

Program 7.1 illustrates the concept of inheritance.

Program 7.1

```
class Fruit
{
    String color;
    String name;
    public void fruitdetails(String name,String color)
    {
        System.out.println("Name of the fruit:="+name);
        System.out.println("Color of the fruit:="+color);
    }
}
class Apple extends Fruit
{
    String benefit="Good for Heart";
    public void printdetail()
    {
        System.out.println("Health benefit:="+benefit);
    }
}
public class FruitExample
{
    public static void main(String[] args)
    {
        Apple obj=new Apple();
        obj.fruitdetails("Ooty Apple", "red yellow");
        obj.printdetail();
    }
}
```

Output 7.1

```
Name of the fruit:=Ooty Apple
Color of the fruit:=red yellow
Health benefit:=Good for Heart
```

Program 7.1 demonstrates that two classes are created, namely `Fruit` and `Apple`. `Fruit` is the superclass which consists of two variables namely `name`, `color` and the method `fruitdetails()` defined in the class. `Apple` is the subclass that derives the variables and methods of the `Fruit` superclass using `extends` keyword and has its own method `printdetail()`. In the `main()` method, an object is created for the subclass `Apple`. The object is capable of accessing the superclass properties and methods. When the object `obj` invokes the superclass method `fruitdetails( )` using the dot operator, the two parameter values of `name` and `color` have been passed. Then `Apple` class method `printdetail()` is invoked. Finally, it will display the fruit details as shown in the output.

7.2 INHERITING AND OVERRIDING SUPERCLASS METHODS

This section is about inheritance of methods, and overriding of the methods of the superclass using the keyword *super* for invoking the overridden methods. When defining methods in the subclass, there is a need to use any one the three following scenarios:

(i) The first scenario is as simple as *inheriting the methods of the superclass*; now all methods defined in the superclass are automatically inherited by the subclass.
(ii) *Defining new methods in the subclass*; when the methods of the superclass are not enough to provide the functionalities, then defining of new methods in the subclass is the best way.
(iii) *Overriding* the methods which are defined in the superclass. Defining a method in a subclass, the method name and its arguments are of the same type as of a superclass method. Now the subclass method will override the superclass method. In this scenario, when the method is invoked by the subclass object, only the subclass method will be executed (superclass method is overridden).

The first scenario of inheriting the superclass methods and the second scenario of defining the new methods in the subclass are explained in **Program 7.2**.

Program 7.2

```
//Vehicle is a superclass and Car is a subclass.
//Simple Inheritance: A Car is a Vehicle
class Vehicle
{
   String brandname;
   double price;
   public void PrintVehicleDetails()
   {
      System.out.println("Vehicle Details");
      System.out.println(" Brand of Vehicle:"+brandname);
      System.out.println(" Price of Vehicle:"+price);
   }
}
class Car extends Vehicle
{
   String fueltype;
   String color;
   public void PrintCarDetails()
   {
      System.out.println("Car Details");
      System.out.println("Car fueltype:"+fueltype);
      System.out.println("Car Color:"+color);
   }
}
public class SimpleInheritance
{
   public static void main(String[] args)
   {
      Car obj=new Car();
      obj.brandname="BMW";
      obj.price=3999999.0;
      obj.fueltype="petrol";
      obj.color="Red";
      obj.PrintVehicleDetails();
      obj.PrintCarDetails();
   }
}
```

Output 7.2

```
Vehicle Details
Brand of Vehicle:BMW
Price of Vehicle:3999999.0
Car Details
Car fueltype:petrol
Car Color:Red
```

Program 7.2 illustrated the first scenario, that is, *inheriting the methods of the superclass* `vehicle` in the subclass of `Car` by using `extends` keyword. The superclass `Vehicle` has two data members and `PrintVehicleDetails()` method. The second scenario of defining the *new methods in the subclass* are carried out in the `Car` subclass and it has `PrintCarDetails()` as the new method. By creating object `obj` for subclass `Car` invoking the data members and methods of both the classes using the dot operator, the data members `brandname`, `price`, `fueltype` and `color` are initialised using the `obj` object with the dot operator. Then the superclass and subclass methods are invoked by the object and the details are displayed.

The method name of the superclass and subclass are not the same. So, there is no possibility of overriding the methods of the superclass in the subclass. Overriding takes place when the method in the superclass and subclass are the same in the context of name, arguments and its type of data. If there are overridden methods between superclass and subclass, then the following section explains how to override the method of superclass in the subclass.

7.2.1 Overriding the Superclass Method

Inheriting the method enables the programmer to define and use methods repeatedly in the subclasses without having to define the methods again in the subclass. However, there are some occasions when the program needs an object to present the same method available in both superclass and subclass but the methods have different behaviour. This is done by defining a method in the subclass that has the same name, same arguments and same return type as a method in the superclass. That means, the superclass method is overridden by the subclass, and this is called overriding. This concept is illustrated in **Program 7.3.**

Program 7.3

```
//Code to illustrate overriding method of the Vehicle superclass
class Vehicle
{
   public void PrintDetails()
   {
      System.out.println("Vehicle Details");
   }
}
class Car extends Vehicle
{
   String fueltype;
   String color;
   public void PrintDetails()
   {
      System.out.println("Car Details");
      System.out.println("Car fueltype:"+fueltype);
      System.out.println("Car Color:"+color);
   }
}
public class OverridingMethods
{
   public static void main(String[] args)
   {
      Car obj=new Car();
      obj.fueltype="petrol";
      obj.color="Red";
      obj.PrintDetails();
   }
}
```

Output 7.3

```
Car Details
Car fueltype:petrol
Car Color:Red
```

Program 7.3 is essentially the same as Program 7.2, except that the `Vehicle` and `Car` classes have taken to overriding the methods. Thereby, the same method name and signature is used to define the methods in `Vehicle` and `Car` classes. The method `PrintDetails()` is defined in `Vehicle` class that is the superclass of `Car`. The subclass `Car` has the same method `PrintDetails()` as the superclass but the behaviour is different from the superclass. The superclass method definition is given as,

```
public void PrintDetails()
{
    System.out.println("Vehicle Details");
}
```

The subclass method definition is given as,

```
public void PrintDetails()
{
    System.out.println("Car Details");
    System.out.println("Car fueltype:"+fueltype);
    System.out.println("Car Color:"+color);
}
```

While creating an object for the subclass, the object `obj` invokes only the subclass method `PrintDetails()`, because of overriding the superclass method `PrintDetails()`. Both class methods have the same method name and signature. The method in the superclass is overridden by the subclass method.

```
Car obj=new Car();
obj.fueltype="petrol";
obj.color="Red";
obj.PrintDetails();
```

Only the `PrintDetails()` method of subclass `Car` is invoked by the object and the output shows that it does not print the value of the superclass method `PrintDetails()`.

Overriding takes place only when two methods declared in two different classes have the *same method name, arguments and return type.*

Program 7.4 also illustrates the concept of overriding method as follows.

Program 7.4

```
class company
{
    String sector;
    String name;
    String headoffice;
    public void printcompany()
    {
        System.out.println("Company Details");
    }
}
```

```
class Branch extends company
{
    String bname;
    String place;
    public void printcompany()
    {
        System.out.println("Company Name:"+name);
        System.out.println("Sector:"+sector);
        System.out.println("Company Headoffice:"+headoffice);
    }
    public void printbranch()
    {
        System.out.println("Branch name:"+bname);
        System.out.println("Place of Branch:"+place);
    }
}
public class MethodOverriding2
{
    public static void main(String[] args)
    {
        Branch b=new Branch();
        b.name="Wipro";
        b.sector="IT and Services";
        b.headoffice="Bangalore";
        b.bname="Chennai TechPark";
        b.place="solinganallur";
        b.printcompany();
        b.printbranch();
    }
}
```

Output 7.4

```
Company Name:Wipro
Sector:IT and
Services Company
Headoffice:Bangalore Branch
name:Chennai TechPark
PlaceofBranch:Solinganallur
```

Program 7.4 contains `company` as the base class and `Branch` as the subclass. Each class has the same method name called `printcompany()`. But the method's behaviour for the classes is different. Note that the object `b` invokes the superclass method `printcompany()` but this method has been overridden by the subclass method. Only the subclass method's details are displayed in the output.

In some situations, there is a need to invoke the overridden method of the superclass, and this can be done with the help of the keyword *super*. The general form to invoke an overridden method is given below.

```
super.methodname(args);
```

As was the case in the previous program, the `super.PrintDetails()` statement has been included inside the subclass method definition. Through this, the superclass method is executed when the subclass method is invoked by the object. **Program 7.5** demonstrates the invoking of the overridden method in the superclass `Vehicle` using *super* keyword inside the subclass method.

Program 7.5

```
class Vehicle
{
    public void PrintDetails()
    {
        System.out.println("Vehicle Details");
    }
}
```

```
class Car extends Vehicle
{
   String fueltype;
   String color;
   public void PrintDetails()
   {  super.PrintDetails();
      System.out.println("Car Details");
      System.out.println("Car fueltype:"+fueltype);
      System.out.println("Car Color:"+color);
   }
}
public class OverridingMethods
{
   public static void main(String[] args)
   {
      Car obj=new Car();
      obj.fueltype="petrol";
      obj.color="Red";
      obj.PrintDetails();
   }
}
```

Output 7.5

```
Vehicle Details
Car Details
Car fueltype:petrol
Car Color:Red

Vehicle Details
Car Details
Car fueltype:petrol
Car Color:Red
```

Program 7.5 is similar to Program 7.3, but in this program, the super method is not overridden by the subclass; instead the superclass method has been invoked in the subclass method `PrintDetails()` using `super.PrintDetails()`. The details of both superclass and subclass method are displayed in the output.

Program 7.6 is similar to Program 7.4. This is another example of invoking the methods of the superclass, using the keyword, *super*.

Program 7.6

```
class company
{
   String sector;
   String name;
   String headoffice;
   public void printcompany()
   {
      System.out.println("*****Company Details*****");
   }
}
class Branch extends company
{
   String bname;
   String place;
   public void printcompany()
   {  super.printcompany();
      System.out.println("Company Name:"+name);
      System.out.println("Sector:"+sector);
      System.out.println("Company Headoffice:"+headoffice);
   }
   public void printbranch()
   {
      System.out.println("Branch name:"+bname);
      System.out.println("Place of Branch:"+place);
   }
}
```

```
public class overridesuper2
{
    public static void main(String[] args)
    {
        Branch b=new Branch();
        b.name="Wipro";
        b.sector="IT and Services";
        b.headoffice="Bangalore";
        b.bname="Chennai TechPark ";
        b.place="solinganallur";
        b.printcompany();
        b.printbranch();
    }
}
```

Output 7.6

```
*****Company Details*****
Company Name:Wipro Sector:IT
and Services
Company Headoffice:Bangalore
Branch name:Chennai TechPark
PlaceofBranch:solinganallur
```

Program 7.6 illustrates how the overriding method `printcompany()` of superclass company is invoked by subclass `Branch` using the *super* keyword. The *super* keyword is not only used to invoke the overridden method of the superclass and also used to invoke the superclass constructor in the derived class. The following section illustrates this concept of calling a superclass constructor.

7.3 CALLING SUPERCLASS CONSTRUCTOR

The state and behaviour of a class are defined not only by that class but also by its superclass. Therefore, in order to initialise an object of a class, it is necessary to execute the constructor of its superclass. The proper way of initialising subclass constructors in the subclass, is to first invoke the superclass constructor. For instance,

```
class x
{
    x(int i )
    {…}
}
class y extends x
{
    y( )
    {…}
}
```

Here, `x` is the superclass of `y`, so the constructor of `x` is `x(int i)`, and it should be invoked before the constructor of `y` is invoked. Hence, the superclass constructor can be invoked by using the *super* keyword inside the subclass constructor of `y` which has the following form:

```
super(i);
```

Then the above code for subclass is changed to the following form:

```
class y extends x
{
    y( )
    {
        super(i);
    }
}
```

This has been illustrated in **Program 7.7**.

Program 7.7

```
//Code to illustrate super()
class superclass
{
   String s="Hello";
   public superclass()
   {
      System.out.println("Superclass method:"+s);
   }
}
class subclass extends superclass
{
   String s1="Inheritance";
   public subclass()
   {
      super();
      System.out.println("Subclass method:"+s1);
   }
}
public class SimpleInheritance
{
   public static void main(String[] args)
   {
      subclass obj=new subclass();
   }
}
```

Output 7.7

```
Superclass method: Hello
Subclass method: Inheritance
```

Program 7.7 demonstrates that the subclass constructor named as `subclass()` has been defined in subclass; within the subclass constructor, the superclass constructor has been invoked using `super()` method.

Note that the constructor method cannot be invoked using the dot operator, that means `super.superclass()` is not possible. Instead `super()` can be used to invoke the superclass constructor. While creating object `obj` for the subclass, it automatically invokes the subclass constructor with the superclass constructor. **Program 7.8** illustrates the same concept.

Program 7.8

```
class college
{
   String name="Arts and Science College";
   String status="Autonomous";
   public college()
   {
      System.out.println("Name of college:"+name);
      System.out.println("Status of college:"+status);
   }
}
```

```
class department extends college
{
    String dname;
    public department(String dname)
    {
        super();
        System.out.println("Department name:"+dname);
    }
}
public class superconstructordemo
{
    public static void main(String[] args)
    {
        department d=new department("Computer Science");
    }
}
```

Output 7.8

```
Name of college:Arts and
Science College
Status of college:Autonomous
Department name:Computer.Science
```

Program 7.8 demonstrates how the `super()` method has been used inside the subclass constructor `department()` to invoke the superclass constructor `college()`, because the object is created only for the subclass and can invoke the constructor of this class. In the next section, the overloading of methods is performed in the context of polymorphism.

7.4 POLYMORPHISM

Polymorphism is the perception of executing a *single action in different ways*. Polymorphism is derived from Greek words: *poly* and *morphs*. The word 'poly' means many and 'morphs' means forms. Polymorphism means many forms.

There are two types of polymorphism in Java—compile time polymorphism and runtime polymorphism. It can be carried out by using method overloading and method overriding concept. Method overriding is resolved at compile time by invoking those methods within the subclass using *super* keyword, as has been discussed in the previous section. This section will discuss the overloading and overriding methods using static and dynamic binding.

Overloading method

In method overloading, one or more methods have the same name but different parameters as arguments for the methods. That means, the method name is the same but number of signatures or arguments, return type, type of arguments, and order of arguments are different. Overloaded methods can appear within the same class. In the context of inheritance, a method in the subclass can overload a method of the superclass or another method of the same class. Overloading methods can be invoked in one of two ways:

- static binding,
- dynamic binding.

Static binding

The general structure of overloading methods between superclass and subclass is given below.

```
class X
{ public void method1(String a){}}
class Y extends X
{ public void method1(int a){}
public int method1(int a, int b){}}
```

The above structure shows that if class `X` is the superclass and class `Y` is the subclass, a method named as `method1(int)` in class `Y` can overload a method named as `method1(String)` in class `X`, or another method named `method1(int , int)` in class `Y`. Overloading a method can be used inside the class as well as in the inherited class. This concept is illustrated in **Program 7.9**.

Program 7.9

```
//Overloading concept with static binding
//Superclass
class shapes
{
   int a, r;
   double area;
   public void calculate()
   {
      System.out.println("Area of circle and square");
   }
}
class circle extends shapes
{
   final double pi = 3.14;
   circle(int r)
   {
      this.r = r;
   }
   public void calculate(int r)
   {
      area = pi * r * r;
      System.out.println("Area of circle:=" + area);
   }
}
class square extends shapes
{
   square(int a)
   {
      this.a = a;
   }
   public void calculate(int a)
   {
      area = a * a;
      System.out.println("Area of square:=" + area);
   }
}
public class OverloadingExample
{
   public static void main(String[] args)
   {
      circle obj = new circle(3);
      obj.calculate();
      obj.calculate(obj.r);
      square s = new square(4);
      s.calculate(s.a);
   }
}
```

Output 7.9

```
Area of circle and square
Area of circle:=28.259999999999998
Area of square:=16.0
```

Program 7.9 contains three classes—`shapes`, `circle` and `square`. `Shapes` is the superclass and consists of three datamembers(`a,r,area`) and one method(`calculate()`). The `circle` class is the subclass of `shapes` which has one data member, one constructor and an overloaded method of shapes called `calculate(int)`. Similarly, `square` is the subclass of `shapes` which has one constructor and one overloaded method of the superclass. First the object `obj` of `circle` class invokes the method `calculate()` of the superclass. Then the same object invokes the overloaded method `calculate(r)` of its own class. Finally, the `square` class object invokes its overloaded method `calculate(a)`. In this program, the type of the object is determined at compile time, and this is known as *static binding*. If there is any *private, final* or *static* method or variable in a class, then overloading the method is known as static binding. The class circle has one final variable called `pi`. Thus, the program is an example of static binding.

Runtime polymorphism or dynamic binding

Runtime polymorphism or *Dynamic Method Dispatch* is a process in which, a call to an overridden method is resolved at runtime rather than at compile-time. In this process, an overridden method is called through the reference variable of a superclass. The determination of the method to be called is based on the object being referred by the reference variable. This concept is illustrated in **Program 7.10.**

Program 7.10

```
// Illustration of run time polymorphism
//Superclass
class shapes
{
    int r=3;
    double area;
    public void calculate()
    {
        System.out.println("Area of circle:");
    }
}
class circle extends shapes
{
    final double pi = 3.14;
    public void calculate()
    {
        area = pi * r * r;
        System.out.println("Area of circle:=" + area);
    }
}
public class OverloadingExample
{
    public static void main(String[] args)
    {
        shapes obj = new circle();
        obj.calculate();
    }
}
```

Output 7.10

```
Area of circle:=28.259999999999998
```

In Program 7.10, two classes are created—`shapes` and `circle`. `Circle` class extends `shapes` class and overrides its `calculate()` method. The `calculate()` method is called by the reference variable of Parent class. Since it refers to the subclass object and the subclass method overrides the Parent class method, the subclass method is invoked at runtime. It is clearly illustrated that the instance of `shapes obj` is referenced by the subclass of `circle` because the compiler does not know the exact object to be invoked. The method is dynamically determined during run time and not at compile time; this is known as *runtime polymorphism* or *dynamic binding*.

Overloading vs overriding

There is a distinction between overloading a method and overriding a method. When a method has the same name as one or more other methods, but a different parameter list, then it is a case of overloading. Although overloaded methods have the same name, they have different signatures. When a method overrides another method, they both have the same signature. Both overloading and overriding can take place in an inheritance relationship. Overloaded methods can appear within the same class or a method in a subclass can overload a method in the superclass.

Overriding, on the other hand, can take place only in an inheritance relationship. A method cannot override another method in the same class. The distinction between overloading and overriding is important because it can affect the accessibility of superclass methods in a subclass. When a subclass overloads a superclass method, both methods can be called with a subclass object. However, when a subclass overrides a superclass method, only the subclass's version of the method can be called with a subclass object. In the following section, different types of subclasses that inherit from top level classes are explained.

7.5 CLASSES THAT INHERIT FROM DIFFERENT CLASSES

A class can inherit the properties and methods from various classes like one superclass for subclass, or more than one subclass for a superclass, or nested subclasses for a superclass. Java provides various types of inheritance such as,

- single inheritance,
- multilevel inheritance,
- hierarchical inheritance.

Unlike C++, Java does not support multiple inheritance. Multiple inheritance leads to ambiguous problems. Instead of multiple inheritance, Java uses interfaces to implement multiple inheritance.

7.5.1 Single Inheritance

The properties and methods of a base class are derived by a subclass, and this is called single inheritance. For instance, in Fig. 7.3, Class A is the base class and Class B is the subclass.

The general form of single inheritance is given below.

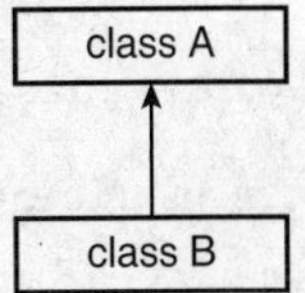

Fig. 7.3 Single inheritance

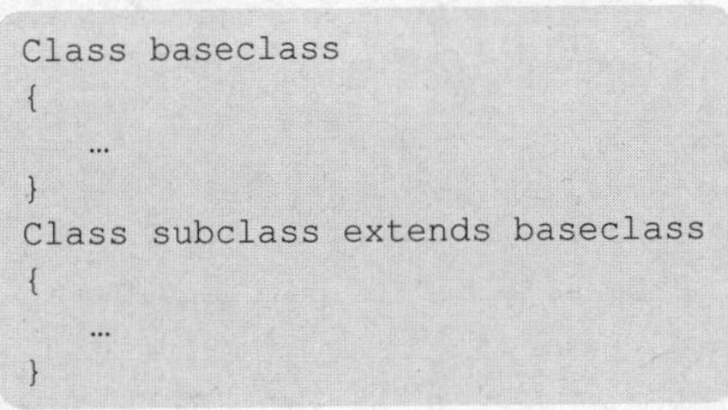

```
Class baseclass
{
    ...
}
Class subclass extends baseclass
{
    ...
}
```

The above structure consists of two classes, namely baseclass and subclass. To derive the data members and methods of the baseclass, a subclass uses the *extends* keyword in the class declaration statement.

Program 7.11 illustrates single inheritance. A subclass derives the members of the base class.

Program 7.11

```
// Single inheritance Example
//Base Class
class payment
{  private int paymentId;
   private double amount;
   public int getPaymentId()
   {
      return paymentId;
   }
   public void setPaymentId(int paymentId)
   {
      this.paymentId = paymentId;
   }
   public double getAmount()
   {
      return amount;
   }
   public void setAmount(double amount)
   {
      this.amount = amount;
   }
}
//Subclass cheque used extends keyword to get base class properties
class Cheque extends payment
{
   private String ChequeType;
   public String getChequeType()
   {
      return ChequeType;
   }
   public void setChequeType(String chequeType)
   {
      ChequeType = chequeType;
   }
}
//Main Class to invoke methods using objects
public class SingleInheritance
{
   public static void main(String[] args)
   {
      Cheque c1=new Cheque();
      c1.setPaymentId(15);
      c1.setAmount(2600);
      c1.setChequeType("ICICI");
      System.out.println("Payment Id:"+c1.getPaymentId());
      System.out.println("Payment Amount:"+c1.getAmount());
      System.out.println("Payment Cheque Type:"+c1.getChequeType());
   }
}
```

Output 7.11

```
Payment Id:15
Payment Amount:2600.0
Payment Cheque Type:ICICI
```

Program 7.11 illustrates how single inheritance is implemented in Java. Here the base class is `Payment` and the subclass `Cheque` derives the properties and methods of `Payment` class using `extends` keyword. Single inheritance must contain a base class and only one subclass to derive the base class properties. In the `main()` method, object `c1` is created for subclass `Cheque`, `c1` object invokes the base class methods `setPaymentId()` and `setAmount()` and value for those methods is passed. Then `c1` invokes the subclass method `setChequeType()` and the value for that method is passed. Finally `getPaymentId()`, `getAmount()` and `getChequeType()` methods are called by `c1` object and the values are printed as shown in the output.

7.5.2 Multilevel Inheritance

Here, the base class is derived by the subclass and the derived class inherited by another subclass one after another. It is a ladder or hierarchy of single level inheritance. This means if class `A` is extended by class `B` and then class `C` further extends class `B`, then the whole structure is termed as multilevel inheritance (Fig. 7.4).

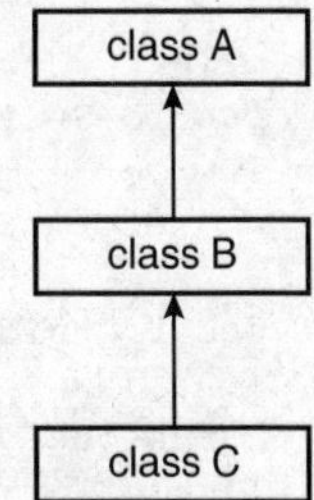

Fig. 7.4 Multilevel inheritance

Multiple classes are involved in inheritance, but one class extends only one class. The lowermost subclass can make use of all its superclass members.

The general form of multilevel inheritance is given below.

```
class baseclass
{
    ...
}
class subclass1 extends baseclass
{
    ...
}
class subclass2 extends subclass1
{
    ...
}
```

The above structure contains a base class and two subclasses. The `subclass1` derives the data members and methods of `baseclass`. The `subclass2` derives the data members and methods of `subclass1`. By this, `subclass2` derives both `baseclass` and `subclass1` data members and methods.

Program 7.12 illustrates multilevel inheritance.

Program 7.12

```
// Multilevel inheritance
//Base Class
class payment
{
   private int paymentId;
   private double amount;
   public int getPaymentId()
   {
      return paymentId;
   }
   public void setPaymentId(int paymentId)
   {
      this.paymentId = paymentId;
   }
```

```
    public double getAmount()
    {
        return amount;
    }
    public void setAmount(double amount)
    {
        this.amount = amount;
    }
}
//Subclass from base class
class Cheque extends payment
{
    private String ChequeType;
    public String getChequeType()
    {
        return ChequeType;
    }
    public void setChequeType(String chequeType)
    {
        ChequeType = chequeType;
    }
}
//inheriting from subclass cheque
class CreditCard extends Cheque
{
    private String CreditCardType;
    public String getCreditCardType()
    {
        return CreditCardType;
    }
    public void setCreditCardType(String creditCardType)
    {
        CreditCardType = creditCardType;
    }
}
public class multilevel
{
    public static void main(String[] args)
    {
        CreditCard c1=new CreditCard();
        c1.setPaymentId(15); //base class method
        c1.setAmount(2600); //base class method
        c1.setChequeType("ICICI"); // Subclass method
        c1.setCreditCardType("VISA"); // subclass from another sub method
        System.out.println("Payment Id:"+c1.getPaymentId());
        System.out.println("Payment Amount:"+c1.getAmount());
        System.out.println("Payment Cheque Type:"+c1.getChequeType());
        System.out.println("Payment Credit card Type:"+c1.getCreditCardType());
    }
}
```

Output 7.12

```
Payment Id:15
Payment Amount:2600.0
Payment Cheque Type:ICICI
Payment Credit card Type:VISA
```

In Program 7.12, `CreditCard` is the subclass of `Cheque`, in turn `Cheque` is the subclass of `Payment`. Here the multilevel architecture is maintained. `Payment` base class is derived by `Cheque` subclass and this again is derived by `CreditCard` class. By creating an object for `CreditCard` class, the object invokes the methods of the top level classes of `Cheque` and `Payment`.

7.5.3 Hierarchical Inheritance

The superclass properties and methods can be inherited by multiple subclasses. That means many subclasses can derive the properties of one base class. Figure 7.5 illustrates this concept. The father is the base class and his three children are the subclasses. The children have the characteristic of their father. So, they are inheriting the father's properties and behaviour.

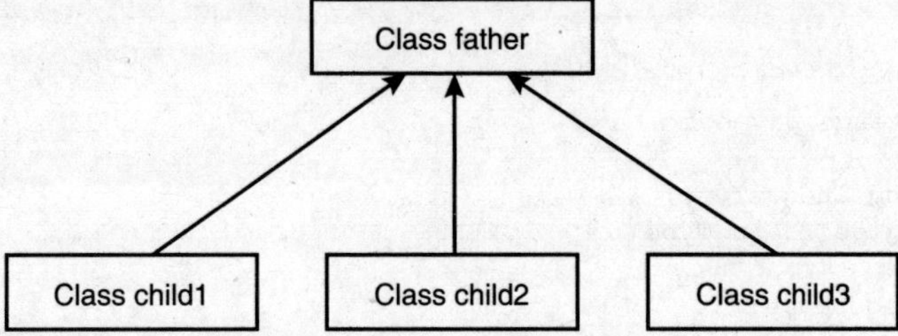

Fig. 7.5 Hierarchical inheritance

The general form of hierarchical inheritance is given below.

```
class baseclass
{
    ...
}
class subclass1 extends baseclass
{
    ...
}
class subclass2 extends baseclass
{
    ...
}
class subclass3 extends baseclass
{
    ...
}
```

The structure shows that one base class is derived by three subclasses.

Program 7.13 illustrates hierarchical inheritance.

Program 7.13

```
// Hierarchical inheritance
//Base Class
class payment
{
   private int paymentId;
   private double amount;
   public int getPaymentId()
   {
      return paymentId;
   }
   public void setPaymentId(int paymentId)
   {
      this.paymentId = paymentId;
   }
```

```
    public double getAmount()
    {
        return amount;
    }
    public void setAmount(double amount)
    {
        this.amount = amount;
    }
}
//Subclass
class Cheque extends payment
{
    private String ChequeType;
    public String getChequeType()
    {
        return ChequeType;
    }
    public void setChequeType(String chequeType)
    {
        ChequeType = chequeType;
    }
}
//Another sub calss for same base class
class CreditCard extends payment
{
    private String CreditCardType;
    public String getCreditCardType()
    {
        return CreditCardType;
    }
    public void setCreditCardType(String
creditCardType)
    {
        CreditCardType = creditCardType;
    }
}
public class Hierarchical
{
    public static void main(String[] args)
    {
        Cheque c1=new Cheque();
        c1.setPaymentId(2);
        c1.setAmount(5000);
        c1.setChequeType("ICICI");
        System.out.println("Cheque Id:"+c1.getPaymentId());
        System.out.println("Cheque Amount:"+c1.getAmount());
        System.out.println("Cheque Type:"+c1.getChequeType());
        CreditCard c=new CreditCard();
        c.setPaymentId(1);
        c.setAmount(26000);
        c.setCreditCardType("VISA");
        System.out.println("Creditcard Id:"+c.getPaymentId());
        System.out.println("Creditcard Amount:"+c.getAmount());
        System.out.println("Credit card Type:"+c.getCreditCardType());
    }
}
```

Output 7.13

```
Cheque Id:2
Cheque Amount:5000.0
Cheque Type:ICICI
Creditcard Id:1
Creditcard Amount:26000.0
Credit card Type:VISA
```

Program 7.13 illustrates the hierarchical way of inheriting the properties and methods of the base class `Payment` that are used by two subclasses `Cheque` and `CreditCard`. Both `Cheque` and `CreditCard` classes access the methods of superclass `Payment`. The combination of any two of the three types of inheritance discussed in this chapter can be used to provide a hybrid type of inheritance.

Note that multiple inheritance is not supported by Java. Instead, multiple inheritance can be achieved by an interface. There are situations where there is a need to hide some method details of the base class that are inherited by the subclasses. This hiding can be achieved by *abstraction*. The next section discusses abstract class and abstract methods usage in detail.

7.6 ABSTRACT CLASSES

Abstraction is a process *of hiding the implementation details* and showing only the functionality to the user, that is, it hides the internal details from the user. Abstraction agrees to focus on what the object does instead of how it does it. Abstract methods are usually declared when two or more subclasses are expected to do a similar job in different ways through different implementations. These subclasses extend the same abstract class and provide different implementations for the abstract methods. Abstract classes are used to define generic types of behaviour for the class hierarchy, and use its subclasses to provide implementation details of the abstract class.

There are two ways to achieve abstraction in Java,

- abstract class,
- interface.

A class stated with the `abstract` keyword, is known as an abstract class in Java. It can have abstract and non-abstract methods (method with body). Simply stated, an abstract class is a class with a missing method body. The missing bodies are supplied by subclasses that extend the abstract class. A method that is declared as abstract and does not have an implementation is known as an abstract method. The abstract class cannot be instantiated, that means, an object of the abstract class cannot be created. Creating subclasses to the abstract classes can instantiate and invoke the methods of the abstract class. An abstract class may or may not have abstract methods. A method of an abstract class that is declared without any implementation of method body is called abstract method. For example, a class `Person` is an important component of many programs. Perhaps the author of class `Person` intended that `Person` objects must have addresses, but the author did not wish to code the address part. An abstract class can state exactly the author's wishes. **Program 7.14** illustrates abstract classes and abstract methods.

Program 7.14

```
abstract class Person // note the keyword abstract
{
   private String name;
   public Person(String n)
   {
      name = n;
   }
   public String getName()
   {
      return name;
   }
   public abstract String getAddress(); // method will be written later
}
```

```
class PersonAddress extends Person
{
   private String address;
   public PersonAddress(String the_name, String the_addr)
   {
      super(the_name); // this gives the_name to Person's constructor
      address = the_addr;
   }
   public String getAddress()
   {
      return address;
   }
}
class PersonWithInt extends Person
{
   private int address;
   public PersonWithInt(String the_name, int
   the_addr)
   {  super(the_name);
      address = the_addr;
   }
   public String getAddress()
   {
      return " " + address;
   } // make the int into a string
}
public class abstractexample
{
   public static void main(String[] args)
   {
      PersonAddress a=new PersonAddress("Jose", "chennai");
      PersonWithInt p=new PersonWithInt("Joel", 277);
      System.out.println(p.getName());
      System.out.println(p.getAddress());
      System.out.println(a.getName());
      System.out.println(a.getAddress());
   }
}
```

Output 7.14

```
Joel
277
Jose chennai

Joel
277
Jose chennai
```

Program 7.14 has demonstrated the abstract class and method. The program contains `Person` as the base class. This class is inherited by `PersonAddress` and `PersonWithInt` subclasses. The method `getAd dress()` of `Person` class is declared as abstract; the implementation is given by its subclasses. `PersonAddress` class invokes the `Person` class constructor using `super()` method within its constructor. Similarly `PersonWithInt` class inherits the `Person` class and invokes the `Person` class constructor using `super()` method within its constructor. Creating objects for `PersonAddress` and `PersonWithInt` subclasses invokes the constructor and `getAddress()` method. Since `Person` is the abstract class, the object cannot be created for this class.

Program 7.15 illustrates the same concept of abstract class and abstract method in `Bike` as an abstract class that contains only one abstract method `getDetails()`. Its implementation is provided by the `pulsar` class.

Program 7.15

```
//abstract class and abstract method
abstract class Bike
{
   abstract void getDetails(); // no implementation
}
class pulsar extends Bike
{
   void getDetails()
   {
      System.out.println("Pulsar Black");
      System.out.println(" Rs.75000");
   }
   public static void main(String args[])
   {
      Bike obj = new pulsar();
      obj.getDetails();
   }
}
```

Output 7.15

```
Pulsar Black
Rs.75000
```

Program 7.15 demonstrates that the abstract class `Bike` contains only one abstract method `getDetails()`, thus the method is not defined by the `Bike` class. The class `pulsar` inherits the abstract class of `Bike` using *extends* keyword and the abstract method `getDetails()` is defined by the inherited class `pulsar`. Then, creating an object for `Bike` class invokes the method.

The scope of the variables and methods in one class that can be accessed by other classes can be determined by Access Specifiers or Modifiers. Different types of Modifiers are available in Java. In the following section, final modifier is explained with an example. The remaining modifiers will be discussed in the next chapter.

7.7 FINAL CLASS

A class that is declared with the `final` modifier cannot be inherited by other classes. This means that such a class cannot have any subclass. Also, the methods in such a class cannot be overridden. Sometimes there is a need to define a class in such a way that the methods implemented by that class cannot be overridden. Such a class is declared with the `final` modifier. The `abstract` and `final` modifiers are not used simultaneously. The general form of final class is as follows.

```
final class classname
{
   ...
}
```

A class is declared with `final` keyword as in the general form. If the class is declared with `final`, this class cannot be derived by the subclasses. **Program 7.16** illustrates this concept.

Program 7.16

```
final class UGcourse
{
   String name;
   void display(String name)
   {
      System.out.println("UG Department:"+name);
   }}
```

```
class PGcourse extends UGcourse //Error cannot inherit from final class
{
    void display()
    {  System.out.println("MCA,M.Sc");
    }
}
public class Departments
{
    public static void main(String[] args)
    {
        PGcourse p=new PGcourse();
        p.display();
    }
}
```

Output 7.16

```
Exception in thread "main"
java.lang.VerifyError:
Cannot inherit from final
class
```

Program 7.16 demonstrates that the final class `UGcourse` cannot be inherited by the subclass `PGcourse`. While declaring the `PGcourse` with `extends` keyword, the program shows an error message. Creating object for subclass `PGcourse` and invokes the method `display()`. While executing the program, it throws the exception `java.lang.VerifyError` as shown in the output.

The base class cannot be declared as `final` whereas `final` methods can be defined in the class. The subclass may be declared as `final` class and it can inherit the base class properties and `final` methods. **Program 7.17** illustrates this.

Program 7.17

```
class UGcourse
{
    String name;
    final void display(String name)
    {
        System.out.println("UG Department:"+name);
    }
}
final class PGcourse extends UGcourse
{
    void display()
    {  System.out.println("MCA,M.Sc");
    }
}
public class Departments
{
    public static void main(String[] args)
    {
        PGcourse p=new PGcourse();
        p.display("B.Sc CS");
        p.display();
    }
}
```

Output 7.17

```
UG Department:B.Sc CS
MCA,M.Sc
```

Program 7.17 demonstrates that the subclass `PGcourse` is declared as `final` class. Now this class can derive the properties and methods of base class `UGcourse`. The base class `UGcourse` contains `final` method `display(name)`. Creating object `p` for subclass `PGcourse` can invoke the `final` method of the base class as well as its own method `display()`.

SUMMARY

1. Code reusability is incorporated via inheritance and its types. Inheritance is the process of creating a new class from an existing class. An existing class is called a base or super or parent class. The new class is called subclass or derived or child class.
2. It is possible to create two or more methods that have the same name but different parameter lists, and this is referred to as method overloading. This is known as polymorphism.
3. Polymorphism is the ability to take many forms. A method is overridden when a subclass contains a method with the same name, return type and parameter.
4. The `super` keyword is used to access a member of the `superclass`, from the subclass; super can only be used within a derived class constructor method.
5. An abstract class is used to declare the methods not the implementation, and the implementation of the method should be defined in the derived class.
6. When the methods of a class cannot be overridden by other classes then the `final` modifier is used to declare the class and this class cannot be inherited by the subclasses.

SHORT QUESTIONS

1. What is meant by inheritance?
2. Why is multiple inheritance not allowed in Java?
3. What is the purpose of `super` keyword?
4. Define polymorphism.
5. Why is the `super()` method used?
6. Define abstract class.
7. Why cannot abstract class be instantiated?
8. What is meant by abstract methods?
9. What are the two general forms of the `super` keyword?
10. Why is the `final` modifier used for class declaration?

COMPREHENSIVE QUESTIONS

1. Briefly describe the concepts of inheritance.
2. Explain the importance of inheritance.
3. Briefly explain the types of inheritances with suitable examples.
4. Differentiate abstract class and normal Java class.
5. Explain polymorphism with an example.
6. Differentiate between overloading and overriding.
7. Write down the types of inheritance.
8. Describe the concept of abstract class with an example.
9. Elucidate the use of abstract class.
10. Explain the importance of `final` class with an example.

SOLVED PROGRAMS

1. Multilevel inheritance.

```
import java.util.Scanner;
class Company
{
   String cname;
   String ceo;
   String founder;
```

```
public void getDetails()
    {
        Scanner sc=new Scanner(System.in);
        System.out.println("Enter Company Name:");
        cname=sc.next();
        System.out.println("Enter CEO Name:");
        ceo=sc.next();
        System.out.println("Enter Founder Name:");
        founder=sc.next();
    }
}
class Company1 extends Company
{
    String sector;
    public void getSector()
    {
        Scanner sc=new Scanner(System.in);
        System.out.println("Enter Sector:");
        sector=sc.next();
    }
}
class Company2 extends Company1
{
    /***Company2 extends the class of
    Company1*/
    public void Printc2Details() {
        System.out.println("Sector:"+sector);
        System.out.println("Company Name:"+cname);
        System.out.println("CEO of the Company:"+ceo);
        System.out.println("Founder of Company:"+founder);
    }
}
public class Multilevelinheritance {
    public static void main(String[] args) {
        Company2 c1=new Company2();
        c1.getSector();
        c1.getDetails();
        c1.Printc2Details();
    }
}
```

Output

```
Enter Sector:
Information technology
Enter Company Name:
google
Enter CEO Name:
sundarpichai
Enter Founder Name:
larrypage
Sector:Information
Company Name:google
CEO of the Company:sundarpichai
Founder of Company:larrypage
```

2. **Overriding super class method** display().

```
class A {
    int i;
    void display() {
        System.out.println(i);
    }
}
class B extends A {
    int j;
    void display() {
        System.out.println(j);
    }
}
class inheritance_demo {
    public static void main(String args[])
    {
```

```
        B obj = new B();
        obj.i=1;
        obj.j=2;
        obj.display();
    }
}
```

Output

```
2
```

3. Using super keyword to access a member of the base class.

```
class A1 {
  int i;
}
class B1 extends A1 {
  int j;
  void display() {
      super.i = j + 1;
      System.out.println(j + " " + i);
  }
}
class inheritance {
  public static void main(String args[])
  {
      B1 obj = new B1();
      obj.i=1;
      obj.j=2;
      obj.display();
  }
}
```

Output

```
2 3
```

4. Using super keyword to access a data member of a base class.

```
class A2 {
  public int i;
  private int j;
}
class B2 extends A2 {
  void display() {
      super.j = super.i + 1;
      System.out.println(super.i + " " + super.j);
  }
}
class inheritance {
  public static void main(String args[])
  {
      B2 obj = new B2();
      obj.i=1;
      obj.j=2;
      obj.display();
  }
}
```

Output

```
Exception in thread "main" java.lang.RuntimeException: Uncompilable source code -
j has private access in A
```

5. Illustrating dynamic dispatch in polymorphism.

```
class A3 {
  int i;
```

```
    public void display() {
        System.out.println(i);
    }
}
class B3 extends A3 {
    int j;
    public void display() {
        System.out.println(j);
    }
}
public class Dynamicdispatch {
    public static void main(String args[])
    {
        B3 obj2 = new B3();
        obj2.i = 1;
        obj2.j = 2;
        A3 r=new A3();
        r = obj2; //the object obj2 assigned to r object of A3
        r.display();
    }
}
```

Output

```
2
```

6. Demonstrating the overloading of methods.

```
class overload {
    int x;
    void add(int a) {
        x = a + 1;
    }
    void add(int a, int b){
        x = a + b + 2;
    }
}
public class overloading {
    public static void main(String args[])
    {
        overload obj = new overload();
        obj.add(6);
        System.out.println(obj.x);
        obj.add(6,7);
        System.out.println(obj.x);
    }
}
```

Output

```
7
15
```

7. Multilevel inheritance for student marks.

```
class student
{
    int rollno;
    String name;
    student(int r, String n)
    {
        rollno = r;
        name = n;
    }
    void dispdatas()
    {
        System.out.println("Rollno = " + rollno);
        System.out.println("Name = " + name);
```

```
    }
}
class marks extends student
{
    int total;
    marks(int r, String n, int t)
    {
        super(r,n);
        total = t;
    }
    void dispdatam()
    {
        dispdatas();
        System.out.println("Total = " + total);
    }
}
class percentage extends marks
{
    int per;
    percentage(int r, String n, int t, int p)
    {
        super(r,n,t);
        per = p;
    }
    void dispdatap()
    {
        dispdatam();
        System.out.println("Percentage = " + per);
    }
}
class Multilevel
{
    public static void main(String args[])
    {
        percentage stu = new percentage(507, "Joel", 450, 90); //call constructor
        percentage stu.dispdatap();
        stu.dispdatap();
    }
}
```

Output

```
Rollno = 507
Name = Joel
Total = 450
Percentage = 90
```

8. Overloading and overriding the methods for Loan and PersonalLoan classes.

```
public class OverloadingOverridingTest {
    public static void main(String[] args) {
        // Example of method overloading in Java
        Loan cheapLoan = Loan.createLoan("HSBC");
        Loan veryCheapLoan = Loan.createLoan("Citibank");
        // Example of method overriding in Java
        Loan personalLoan = new PersonalLoan();
        personalLoan.toString();
        System.out.println("loan by citi bank");
    }
}
class Loan {
    private double interestRate;
    private String customer;
    private String lender;
```

```
    public static Loan createLoan(String lender)
    {
       Loan loan = new Loan();
       loan.lender = lender;
       return loan;
    }
    public static Loan createLoan(String lender, double interestRate)
    {
       Loan loan = new Loan();
       loan.lender = lender;
       loan.interestRate =interestRate;
       return loan;
    }
    public String toString() {
       return "This is Loan by Citibank";
    }
 }
 class PersonalLoan extends Loan {
    public String toString() {
       return "This is Personal Loan by Citibank";
    }
 }
```

Output

```
loan by citi bank
```

PROGRAMMING EXERCISES

1. Define a class called `Department` with data members `department name`, `HoD name` and methods `Constructor` and `PrintDepartmentDetails()`. Then, define another class named StaffMember that extends the class Department and which contains data members `staff name`, `staff qualification` and methods `Constructor`, `PrintStaffDetails()`. Create objects for the class `Department` and invoke the methods and run it.
2. Design a class to represent `bank account details` as base class and bank process as the subclass. The `bankdetails` class contains the data members such as name of the account holder, account number, type of account, balance and the methods are `getdetails()` and `printdetails`. And then create `bankprocess` class which is the subclass of `bankdetails` class which contains `amount` as datamember and methods are `deposit()` and `withdraw()` and then return balance. Finally create an object for the subclass and test it.
3. Implement the concept of overriding for the following: Create the base class called `shapes` which contains `calculate()` method, and create derived classes called `Rectangle` and `Triangle` which contain its constructor and `calculate()` method to find the area of its shape.
4. Implement the concept of abstract for the following: Create a base class as `Conversion` defined with datamember `amount` and the abstract method `MoneyConversion()`. Then create two subclasses named as `Rupee todollar` and `RupeetoEuro`, then implement the abstract method `MoneyConversion()` in these classes. Finally create an object for the subclasses and test it.
5. Implement the concept of overloading for the following: Create the base class `Person` with datamember as `name`, `age` and the method `persondetails()` with two parameters, name and age. Then create subclass `Address` with datamember as `address` and the `persondetails` with three parameters, name, age and address. Finally,

create an object for the subclass `Address` to invoke the overloaded method of `Person` and `Address` classes and test it.

6. Define the classes `Vehicle` as base class then create `two_wheeler` and `four_wheeler` as the subclasses. Finally, create an object for the subclasses, invoke the methods and execute it.
7. Implement multilevel inheritance for the following classes. `Grandfather` is the base class and `Father` is the subclass of `Grandfather` and `Son` is the subclass of `Father`. The data members and methods will be defined by you.
8. Create `Employee` as the base class with its constructor and create `Regular_Employee` subclass for `Employee` class with its constructor. Within the subclass constructor, invoke the constructor of base class using `super()`. Likewise create another subclass for `Employee` called `Contract_Employee` with its constructor. The data members and methods will be defined by you.
9. Create the abstract base class `Student` with basic details of students as data members and abstract method of `marks()`. Then create two subclasses called `CIA` and `Semester` classes. These two subclasses should implement the `marks()` method. Then create objects for each subclass to invoke its methods and test it.
10. Create `sport` class as the base class containing constructor and `favoritesports()` method. Derive this class in `person1` class and invoke the superclass constructor using `super()`. Similarly create another subclass `person2`. And then create an object to invoke the methods of the subclasses and test it.

CHAPTER

8

Interface and Package

This chapter explains the concept of interfaces, packages and various types of access specifiers or modifiers. An *interface* is used to solve the problem of multiple inheritance by declaring the abstract methods in the interface and implementing these methods in the inherited classes. A *package* is used to group the classes and interfaces. Common functionality of classes is grouped together in one package and accesses the package classes in another package. To inherit the class from another class is done by providing restriction on accessibility of the classes. This can be achieved by using various types of modifiers.

8.1 BASICS OF INTERFACE

An interface is a collection of abstract methods. A class implements an interface, thereby inheriting the abstract methods of the interface. Interfaces are used to declare methods and variables without the implementation of the method's behaviour. The class makes use of the interface by implementing the methods of the interface. The features of interfaces are,

- interface cannot be instantiated,
- an interface does not contain any constructors,
- all of the methods in an interface are abstract.

Relationship between classes and interface

An interface is similar to a class, but there are important differences.

- Methods are declared in an interface. Implementation of the method should not be provided by an interface.
- The methods in an interface should always public.
- The variables in an interface should be constant. The constant variables are inherited by the class that implements this interface.

The behaviour of the method is defined in the class that *implements* the interface. Different classes may provide different implementation codes for the methods declared in the interface. The method's return type should be public and the variables declaration should be constant. The general structure of an interface is as follows:

```
interface interface_name
{
   final Variable1=value;
   public return-type methodname(parameter-list);
}
```

Note that in the above structure, all the variables are declared using the keyword `final` that denotes that variables are constants. The methods are always public and there is no implementation of the method. Every variable given in an interface is final, public and static. All methods in an interface are public and abstract. The class which implements the behaviour of the interface should have the following syntax:

```
class class_name implements interface_name
{
    public return-type methodname(parameter-list)
    {
        .
    }
        .
}
```

The `implements` keyword is used to implement the interface methods in the inherited class. The interface method's behaviour is defined inside the inherited class. **Program 8.1** shows how the interface is created and how the inherited class implements the interface. The program calculates the temperature in fahrenheit and celsius.

Program 8.1

```
//Calculating Temperature in Fahrenheit and celsius
interface Temperaturemethods
{
   //Method Declaration
   public double FahrenheitToCelsius(double degree);
   public double CelsiusToFahrenheit(double degree);
}
//inheriting class implements the interface
class TemperatureDefinition implements Temperaturemethods
{
   double degree;
   //interface method Definition or implementation
   public double FahrenheitToCelsius(double degree)
{
      return (degree - 32 * 5 / 9);
   }
   //interface method Definition or implementation
   public double CelsiusToFahrenheit(double degree)
   {
      return (degree * 9 / 5 + 32);
   }
}
public class Temperature
{
   public static void main(String args[])
   {
      TemperatureDefinition t = new TemperatureDefinition();
      t.degree = 54;
      System.out.println("FahrenheitToCelsius:"+t.FahrenheitToCelsius(t.degree));
      System.out.println("CelsiusToFahrenheit:"+t.CelsiusToFahrenheit(t.degree));
   }
}
```

Output 8.1

```
Fahrenheit To Celsius:37.0
Celsius To Fahrenheit:129.2
```

In Program 8.1, the interface is `TemperatureMethods` which consists of two methods declarations as `FahrenheitToCelsius(double)` and `CelsiusToFahrenheit(double)`. Note that only method declaration is given because an interface does not have method definition. The method definition is given by the inherited class `TemperatureDefinition`. The interface `TemperatureMethods` is inherited by the class called `TemperatureDefinition` using `implements` keyword which implements the interface methods. By creating object `t` for `TemperatureDefinition` class, the methods are invoked by passing `degree` value as argument. Finally, the outputs are printed.

8.2 MULTIPLE INTERFACES

Multiple inheritance cannot be achieved by class inheritance. Instead, multiple inheritance can be realised through implementing multiple interfaces. Multiple interfaces can be implemented by the inherited class by using comma separation for each interface. If one class needs to implement more than one interface, then the following syntax shows how multiple interfaces are implemented in the class.

```
interface A
{
   ...
}
interface B
{
   ...
}
class Sample implements A,B
{
   ...
}
```

Program 8.2 shows multiple interfaces and the implementation of methods in the inheriting class. The problem is to convert the temperature into fahrenheit and celsius and also to display the `Annualhumidity` of some cities in India. To solve this problem, two interfaces are declared with final variables and public methods.

Program 8.2

```
//multiple interfaces AnnualHumidity and Temperature
interface AnnualHumidity
{
   //interface variables
   final double avghumidity_chennai=70;
   final double avghumidity_bengaluru=65;
   final double avghumidity_Hyderabad=56;
   final double avghumidity_thiruvananthapuram=78;
}
interface Temperature
{
   //interface method declaration
   public double FahrenheitToCelsius(double degree);
   public double CelsiusToFahrenheit(double degree);
}
```

```
class WeatherDetails implements AnnualHumidity,Temperature
{
    double degree;
    //interface methods implementation
    public double FahrenheitToCelsius(double degree)
    {
        return (degree - 32 * 5 / 9);
    }
    public double CelsiusToFahrenheit(double degree)
    {
        return (degree * 9 / 5 + 32);
    }
    public void print_humidity()
    {
        //interface final variables access
        System.out.println("Humidity level in Chennai:"+avghumidity_chennai);
        System.out.println("Humidity level in Bengaluru:"+avghumidity_bengaluru);
        System.out.println("Humidity level in Hyderabad:"+avghumidity_Hyderabad);
        System.out.println("Humidity level in Trivandrum:"+
        avghumidity_thiruvananthapuram);
    }
}
public class MultipleinterfaceExample
{
    public static void main(String[] args)
    {
        WeatherDetails w=new WeatherDetails();
        w.degree=54;
        w.print_humidity();
        System.out.println("Fahrenheit To Celsius:"+w.FahrenheitToCelsius(w.
        degree));
        System.out.println("Celsius To Fahrenheit:"+w.CelsiusToFahrenheit(w.
        degree));
    }
}
```

Output 8.2

```
Humidity level in
Chennai:70.0
Humidity level in
Bengaluru:65.0
Humidity level in
Hyderabad:56.0
Humidity level in
Trivandrum:78.0
Fahrenheit To Celsius:37.0
Celsius To Fahrenheit:129.2
```

Program 8.2 illustrates multiple interfaces. The first interface `AnnualHumidity` contains list final variables. The second interface `Temperature` consists of two method declarations for temperature conversion. The class `WeatherDetails` implements the two interface methods and prints the details of annual humidities. Similar to multiple interfaces, multiple inheritances are possible with the help of interfaces, which is explained in the following section.

8.3 MULTIPLE INHERITANCE USING INTERFACE

Multiple inheritance is defined as two or more base classes being inherited by a single subclass. In Java, this cannot be done for the reason that it may lead to ambiguous (uncertain) results. This means that if two base classes contain the same method name and signature but the definition is different, when the subclass inherits two of the base classes, there may be a conflict regarding which base class method is invoked. This type of inheritance is not achieved directly in Java. Instead, this can be achieved via interfaces in three ways.

- A class implements multiple interfaces.
- An interface extends multiple interfaces.
- A class extends another class and implements an interface.

Figure 8.1 depicts the first and second types of multiple inheritance. The diagram shows that the first type of multiple interfaces is inherited by the class using *implements* keyword and this has been demonstrated in Program 8.2. The second type is where multiple interfaces are inherited by another interface using *extends* keyword as in class inheritance.

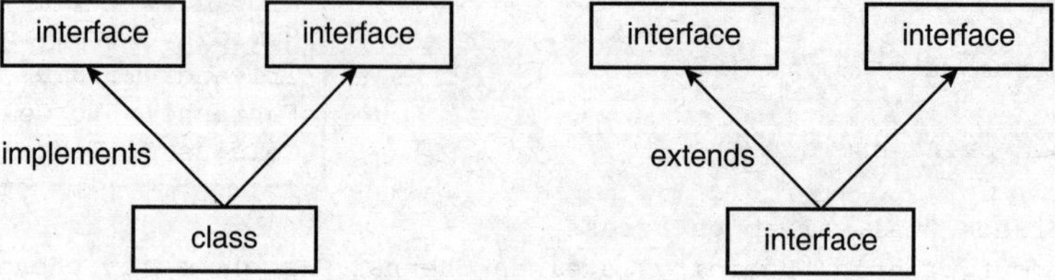

Fig. 8.1 Multiple inheritances in Java

In the third type of multiple inheritance, a class has to extend one class and implement an interface which has the following general structure.

```
class A
{
    ..
}
interface B
{
    ..
}
class Sample extends A implements B
{
    ..
}
```

The structure illustrates that a class sample can extend the class `A`, as well as implement an interface `B`. **Program 8.3** illustrates the third type of multiple inheritance. The program is defined with `Exam` interface and `Student` and `Result` classes. `Student` is the base class, `Result` class inherits the `Student` class as well as implements the `Exam` interface.

Program 8.3

```
//multiple inheritance interface Exam
{
   public void display();
}
class Student
{
   String name;
   int roll_no,mark1,mark2;
   Student(String n, int r, int m1, int m2)
   {  name=n;
      roll_no=r;
      mark1=m1;
      mark2=m2;
   }
```

```
    void display()
    {
        System.out.println ("Name of Student: "+name);
        System.out.println ("Roll No. of Student: "+roll_no);
        System.out.println ("Marks of Subject 1: "+mark1);
        System.out.println ("Marks of Subject 2: "+mark2);
    }
}
class Result extends Student implements Exam
{
    Result(String n, int r, int m1, int m2)
    {
        super(n,r,m1,m2);
    }
    public void display()
    {
        super.display();
        int total=(mark1+mark2);
        float percent=total*100/200;
        System.out.println ("Percentage: "+percent+"%");
    }
}
public class Multipleinheritance
{
    public static void main(String args[])
    {
        Result R = new Result("Ram",12,93,84);
        R.display();
    }
}
```

Output 8.3

```
Name of Student: Ram
Roll No. of Student: 12
Marks of Subject 1: 93
Marks of Subject 2: 84
Percentage: 88.0%
```

Program 8.3 is an example of multiple inheritance. The `Result` class inherits the properties and methods from `Student` base class. `Student` class contains one method named `Display()` and this method is defined by the `Student` class itself. `Result` class also inherits the interface `Exam`. The `Exam` interface contains the same `Display()` method as `Student` class but has no method definition given in the interface the `Result` subclass, which implements the interface method of `Display()`. Inside the implementation of `Display()` method, it invokes the `Student` class `Display()` method using `super.Display()` and its own definition of calculating total and percentage, using the properties of `Student` class. Here the ambiguity problem is overcome since the interface method `Display()` can be defined where the actual class inherits the interface. So, `Student` base class method and interface method are not in conflict. While creating an object for `Result` subclass, both superclass and subclass methods are invoked.

8.4 MULTILEVEL INTERFACE

A class can be directly inherited from the superclass using the keyword *extends.* In the same way, one interface can be inherited by another interface using the same *extends* keyword. As in multilevel inheritance, multilevel interface can be defined and implemented by the inherited class. The following is the general form of interface inheritance.

```
interface name1
{
    ................
}
interface name2 extends name1
{
    ..............
}
interface name3 extends name2
{
    ..............
}
```

Interface `name1` is derived by `name2` interface, and the interface `name3` derives the interface `name2`. The interfaces are inherited one by one from the previous one. **Program 8.4** illustrates interface inheritance. One interface being inherited by other interfaces is known as interface inheritance.

In this program, `AnnualHumidity` is the base interface which contains final variables. The `Temperature` is the sub-interface which extends the base interface `AnnualHumudity`.

Program 8.4

```
//interface inheritance
interface AnnualHumidity
{
   //interface variables
   final double avghumidity_chennai=70;
   final double avghumidity_bengaluru=65;
   final double avghumidity_Hyderabad=56;
   final double avghumidity_thiruvananthapuram=78;
}
interface Temperature extends AnnualHumidity
{
   //interface method declaration
   public double FahrenheitToCelsius(double degree);
   public double CelsiusToFahrenheit(double degree);
}
class WeatherDetails implements Temperature
{
   double degree;
   public double FahrenheitToCelsius(double degree)
   {
      return (degree - 32 * 5 / 9);
   }
   public double CelsiusToFahrenheit(double degree)
   {
      return (degree * 9 / 5 + 32);
   }
   public void print_humidity()
   {
      System.out.println("Humidity level in Chennai:"+avghumidity_chennai);
      System.out.println("Humidity level in Bengaluru:"+avghumidity_bengaluru);
      System.out.println("Humidity level in Hyderabad:"+avghumidity_Hyderabad);
      System.out.println("Humidity level in Trivandrum:"+
      avghumidity_thiruvananthapuram);
   }
}
```

Output 8.4

```
Humidity level in
Chennai:70.0
Humidity level in
Bengaluru:65.0
Humidity level in
Hyderabad:56.0
Humidity level in
Trivandrum:78.0
Fahrenheit To Celsius:37.0
Celsius To Fahrenheit:129.2
```

```
public class MultipleinterfaceExample
{
    public static void main(String[] args)
    {
        WeatherDetails w=new WeatherDetails();
        w.degree=54;
        w.print_humidity();
        System.out.println("Fahrenheit To Celsius:"+w.FahrenheitToCelsius(w. degree));
        System.out.println("Celsius To Fahrenheit:"+
        w.CelsiusToFahrenheit(w.degree));
    }
}
```

In Program 8.4, the interface of `Temperature` is inheriting from the interface of `Annualhumidity` using `extends` keyword. The `Weatherdetails` class does not need to implement the `AnnualHumidity` interface. While implementing `Temperature` interface in the `WeatherDetails` class, the variables of the `AnnualHumidity` interface are inherited automatically.

Creating an object for the `WeatherDetails` class and invoking the methods will print the details and temperature as given in the output.

Difference between abstract class and interface

Both abstract class and interface are used to achieve abstraction of OOP where one can declare the abstract methods. Abstract class and interface cannot be instantiated. But there are many differences between abstract class and interface (Table 8.1).

Table 8.1 Differences between abstract class and interface

	Abstract class	Interface
1	Abstract class can have both abstract and non-abstract methods.	Interface can have only abstract methods.
2	Abstract class does not support multiple inheritance.	Interface supports multiple inheritance.
3	Abstract class can have final, non-final, static and non-static variables.	Interface has only static and final variables.
4	Abstract class can have static methods, main method and constructor.	Interface cannot have static methods, main method or constructor.
5	Abstract class can provide the implementation of an interface.	Interface can't provide the implementation of an abstract class.
6	The *abstract* keyword is used to declare abstract class.	The *interface* keyword is used to declare interface.
7	Example: `public abstract class Shape{ public abstract void draw(); }`	Example: `public interface Drawable{ void draw(); }`

In the following section we will discuss the types of packages and how to create a user-defined package for classes and interfaces.

8.5 PACKAGES

A major feature of OOP is the ability to reuse the code which has already been created. One way of achieving this is by extending the classes and implementing the interfaces. That is, inheritance and interfaces, which have been already discussed. These two ways of reusing the code is limited to the program. If there is a need to repeatedly use classes from other programs without copying the code into the programs, then reusing the code from other package classes can be accomplished by packages. A **Java package** is a group of related types of classes, interfaces and subpackages.

Benefits of a Java package

A Java package is used to categorise the classes and interfaces so that they can be easily maintained, it provides access protection and removes naming collisions.

- The classes in the packages of other programs can be easily accessed.
- If two classes are in two different packages, they can have the same name; they may be referred by their fully qualified name, comprising the package name and class name.
- Packages provide a way to hide classes, thus preventing other programs or packages from accessing classes that are meant for internal use only.
- Packages are also used to separate the design from coding. First design classes and their relationships are defined, and then this will implement the code needed for the methods, without affecting the design.

The package can be divided into two types—built-in package and user-defined package. There are many built-in packages such as `java, lang, awt, javax, swing, net, io, util, sql` and so on. For instance, consider,

```
import java.lang.*;
```

In the above statement, `java` is the base or core package and `lang` is a subpackage. The `*` symbol denotes the built-in classes, methods and data members available within the subpackage of `lang`. `import` is the keyword to retrieve all the built-in classes and methods of `lang` package to be used in the program. Figure 8.2 illustrates the hierarchy of pre-defined packages and their subpackages.

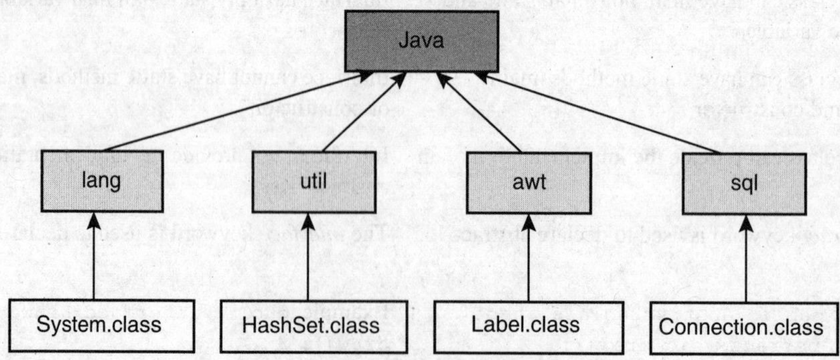

Fig. 8.2 Built-in package hierarchy

A set of packages are arranged in a hierarchical order. For example, from Fig. 8.2, consider the entry,

```
java.util.HashSet;
```

This statement can be used in the program by importing them using the `import` keyword. It is given as,

```
import java.util.HashSet;
```

The pre-defined packages are accessed directly by using the `import` statement at the start of every program.

User-defined package

The types of classes are created using inheritance, interface, polymorphism and abstract class. Using the concept of packages, these classes can be grouped together by categories for ease of access and uncertainties are avoided. The basic way of creating a user-defined package between classes has been discussed in Chapter 4 (Classes and Objects). In this chapter, creating the user-defined java package, accessing one package from another package and interface will be demonstrated.

8.5.1 Creating Packages

If the class or interface is created inside a package, then the declaration of the particular package name should be used. To create a package, first declare the name of the package using `package` keyword followed by the package name. Then the class is defined as just a normal class. The general form of package declaration is,

```
package package_name1;
public class firstclass
{
    …(class definition)
}
```

Here the package name is `package_name1`. The class `firstclass` is considered a part of this package. Now the class `firstclass.java` file is located in the directory `package_name1`. Creating a user-defined package involves the following steps:

Any name can be assigned to the name of the package. The name should satisfy the Java naming rules. According to naming convention, the package name begins with lowercase letters. For example, if two of the classes like `Temperature` and `Humidity` are created and grouped into the package called `weatherdetails` then these classes should consist of the following statement at the beginning of each class. For instance, first, class `Humidity` is created in the `weatherdetails` package and then another class named as `Temperature` is created in the same `weatherdetails` package.

```
package weatherdetails;
public class Humidity
{…}
package weatherdetails;
public class Temperature
{…}
```

Subpackage

Java also supports the concept of package hierarchy. This is done by specifying multiple names in a package statement, separated by dots. For example,

```
package package_name1.package_name2;
```

This approach is used to group related classes into a package and group the related packages into a larger package. Thus, the package inside a package is called a *subpackage*. It should be created to categorise the package further. Let's take an example. Sun Microsystems has defined a package named `java` that contains many classes like `System`, `String`, `Reader`, `Writer`, `Socket` and so on. These classes represent a particular group, for example, `Reader` and `Writer` classes are for Input/Output operation, and so on. So, Sun has subcategorised the Java package into subpackages such as `lang`, `net`, `io` , and put the Input/ Output related classes in the `io` package, and so on. The following example illustrates the subpackages.

- Pre-defined subpackage : `java.lang.*;`
- User-defined subpackage: `pack.sample.subpack;`

8.5.2 Accessing a Package from Another Package

There are three ways to access a package from outside the package.

(i) `import package.*;` // imports all the classes in the package.
(ii) `import package.classname;` // imports the particular class.
(iii) Fully qualified name: instead of using the import statement, fully qualified name of the class has been given in the place.

Example: `class A extends java.util.Scanner`

(i) Using packagename.*

Using `package.*`, all the classes and interfaces of this package will be accessible, but not the subpackages. The import keyword is used to make the classes and interface of another package accessible to the current package. The following example illustrates this.

Example

```
// A.java
package pack1;
public class A
{
    public void msg(){System.out.println("Hello");}
}
```

```
Output : Hello
```

Class A is created within the package pack1.

```
// B.java
package pack2;
import pack1.*;
class B
{
    public static void main(String args[])
    {
        A obj = new A();
        obj.msg();
    }
}
```

Class B is created within the package pack2. The first type of importing (import pack1.*) package has been used in class B to invoke the class A from package pack1.

(ii) Using packagename.classname

The second approach is using import package.classname. Only the declared classes of this package will be accessible. The following example shows that class A is created in the pack1 package. Class B is created in the pack2 package.

Example

```
//A.java
package pack1;
public class A
{  public void msg(){System.out.println("Hello");}
}
```

```
Output :Hello
```

```
//B.java
package pack2;
import pack1.A;
class B
{
   public static void main(String args[])
   {
      A obj = new A();
      obj.msg();
   }
}
```

The class A is imported in pack2 of class B using import pack1.A statement.

(iii) Using fully qualified name

The fully qualified class name of the package will be specified in-line without using the *import* keyword. Now there is no need to import. But it is necessary to use the fully qualified name every time one accesses the class or interface. It is generally used when two packages have the same class name, for example, java.util and java.sql packages contain the Date class. In the following example, class A is created in pack1 package and class B is in pack2 package.

Example

```
// A.java
package pack1;
public class A
{  public void msg(){System.out.println("Hello");}
}
```

```
Output: Hello
```

```
// B.java
package pack2;
class B
{
   public static void main(String args[])
   {
      pack1.A obj = new pack1.A();//using fully qualified name obj.msg();
   }
}
```

In the above example, class A is invoked in class B using fully qualified class name object creation. That is, through the statement,

```
pack1.A obj=new pack1.A();
```

8.6 CREATE AND ACCESS PACKAGES IN NETBEANS IDE

In this section, the procedure for creating and using a user-defined package `weatherdetails` will be discussed in detail with appropriate examples.

Steps to create package and classes in NetBeans IDE are given below.

1. Go to `File->new project`, a `New Project` dialog box will open.
2. Choose `Java` under `Categories` and `Java Application` under `Projects`, then click `Next`.

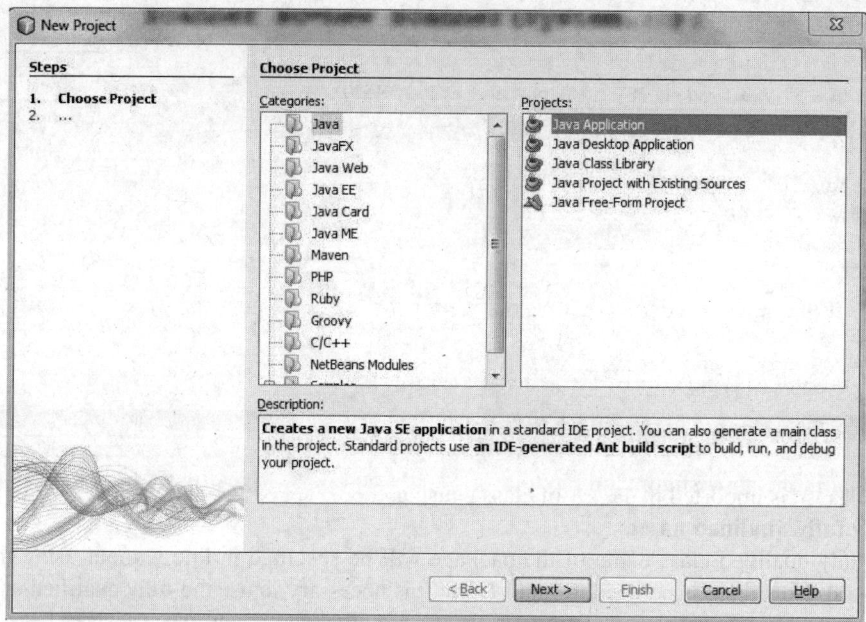

3. Give a name for the project (`Weatherdetails` in this case) and the location is chosen and displayed either by default or browsing to the desired location.

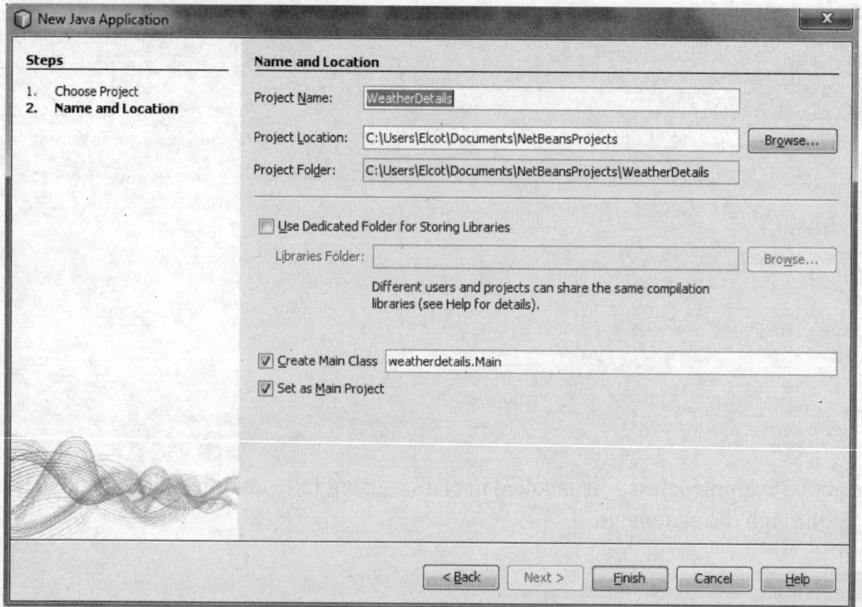

4. Click the `Finish` button.
5. Now the `main` class is created with the package name `weatherdetails` and will appear on the screen as shown in the following image.

```
package weatherdetails;

public class Main {

    /**
     * @param args the command line arguments
     */
    public static void main(String[] args) {
        // TODO code application logic here
    }

}
```

Note that in the above figure, on the left of Project window category, the project named WeatherDetails has opened. See that the user-defined package is automatically created with the project name (as package name `weatherdetails` in this case) with lowercase letters.

Suppose one more class is created in another package called `forecast`, to create another package in the same project, the steps are given below.

1. Right click on the `Source packages`, choose `New-> Java Package`

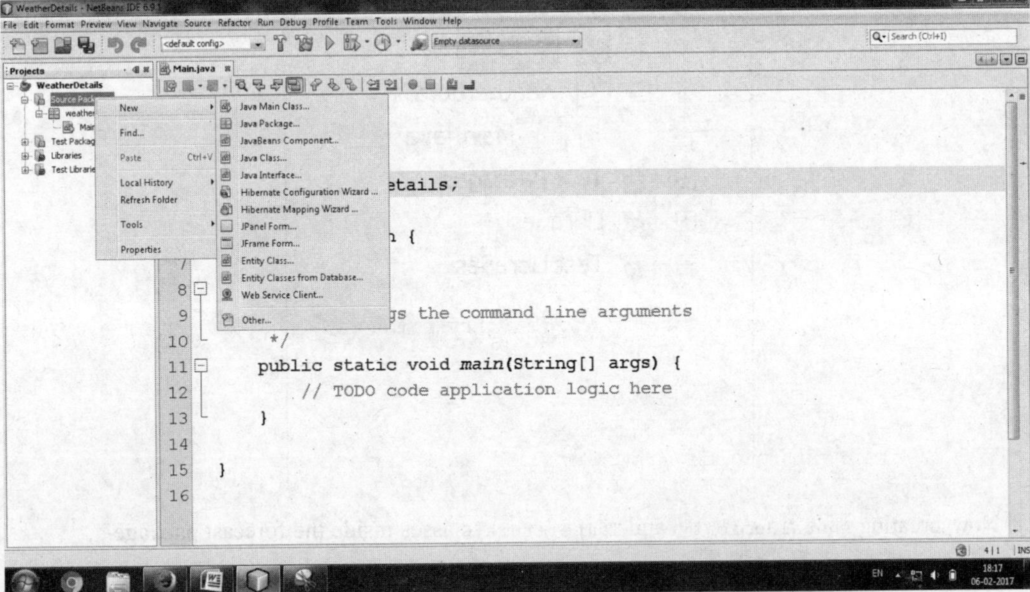

2. A dialog box will open. Type the name of the new package, as shown in the following image.

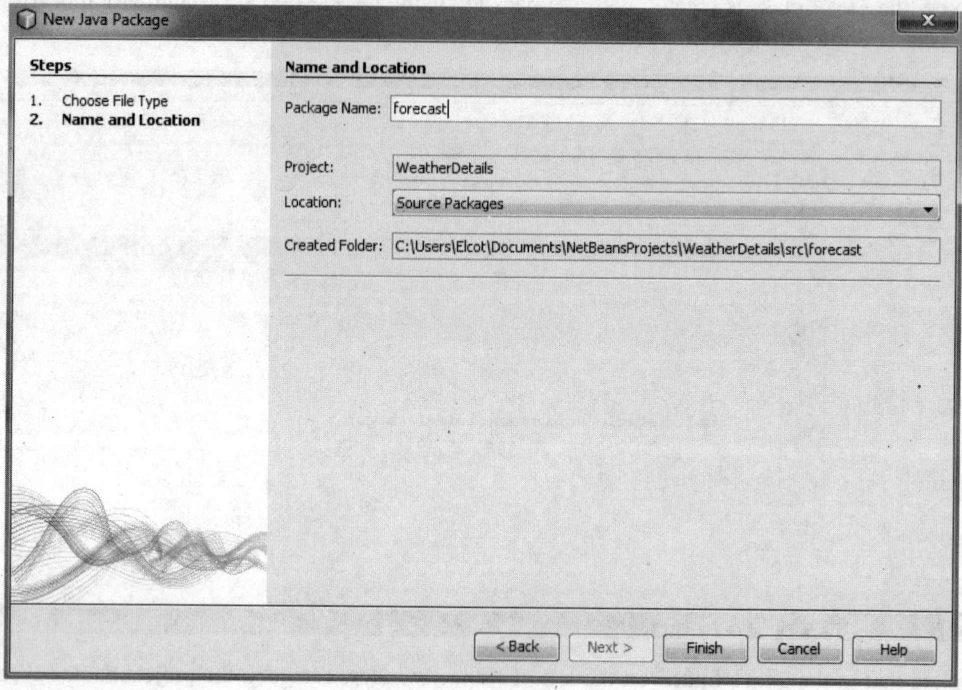

3. Click the `Finish` button.
4. A new package `forecast` has been created under `Source packages` as shown below.

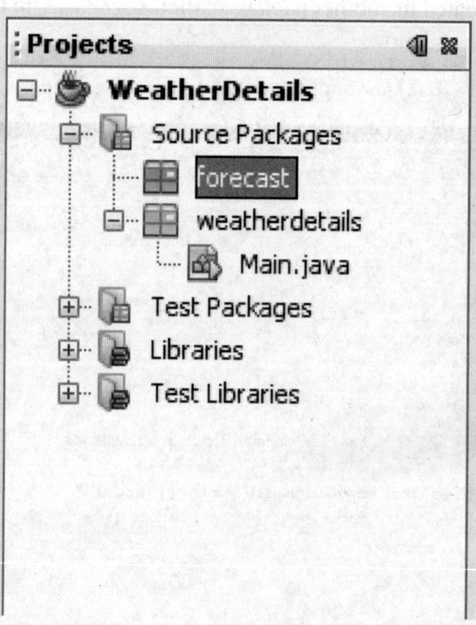

Now, creating `AnnualHumidity` and `Temperature` classes inside the forecast package.

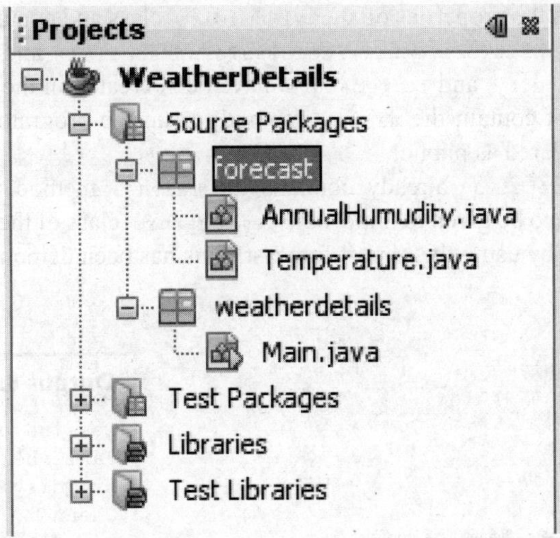

Program 8.5 lists the code for `AnnualHumudity` class.

Program 8.5

```
//AnnualHumudity.java
package forecast; //package declaration
public class AnnualHumidity // class definition
{
   double avghumidity_chennai=70;
   double avghumidity_bengaluru=65;
   double avghumidity_hyderabad=56;
   double avghumidity_thiruvananthapuram=78;
}
```

This class contains data members as the average humidity of four cities.

Next, `Temperature` class is created in the same package `forecast`, the code for which is given in **Program 8.6.**

Program 8.6

```
package forecast; //package declaration
public class Temperature extends AnnualHumidity
{
   double degree;
   public double FahrenheitToCelsius(double degree) {
      return (degree - 32 * 5 / 9);
   }
   public double CelsiusToFahrenheit(double degree) {
      return (degree * 9 / 5 + 32);
   }
   public void print_humidity() {
      System.out.println("Humidity level in Chennai:"+avghumidity_chennai);
      System.out.println("Humidity level in Bengaluru:"+avghumidity_bengaluru);
      System.out.println("Humidity level in Hyderabad:"+avghumidity_hyderabad);
      System.out.println("Humidity level in Thiruvananthapuram:"+avghumidity_
      thiruvananthapuram);
   }
}
```

`Temperature` class derives the properties of `AnnualHumidity` class and contains three methods defined in the class, namely `FahrenheitToCelsius()`, `CelsiusToFahrenheit()` and `print_humidity()`.

Two classes `AnnualHumidity` and `Temperature` have been created in the `forecast` package. Note that the two classes do not contain the `main()` method to run the program and both the classes are created separately and declared as public.

The package `weatherdetails` already contains the `main()` method in the `Main.java` class. Temperature statement has to be given to import the `Temperature` class of the `forecast` package in the `weatherdetails` package by using the import forecast. This has been demonstrated in **Program 8.7.**

Program 8.7

```
package weatherdetails;
import forecast.Temperature;
public class Main
{
    public static void main(String[] args)
    {
        Temperature t=new Temperature();
        System.out.println("Celsius to
        Fahrenheit:"+t. CelsiusToFahrenheit(29));
        System.out. println("Fahrenheit to
        Celsius:"+t. FahrenheitToCelsius(45));
        t.print_humidity();
    }
}
```

Output 8.7

```
Celsius to Fahrenheit:82.4
Fahrenheit to Celsius:28.0
Humidity level in
Chennai:70.0
Humidity level in
Bengaluru:65.0
Humidity level in
Hyderabad:56.0
Humidity level in
Thiruvananthapuram:78.0
```

The following figure shows the NetBeans window which shows the `Main.java` class and the output.

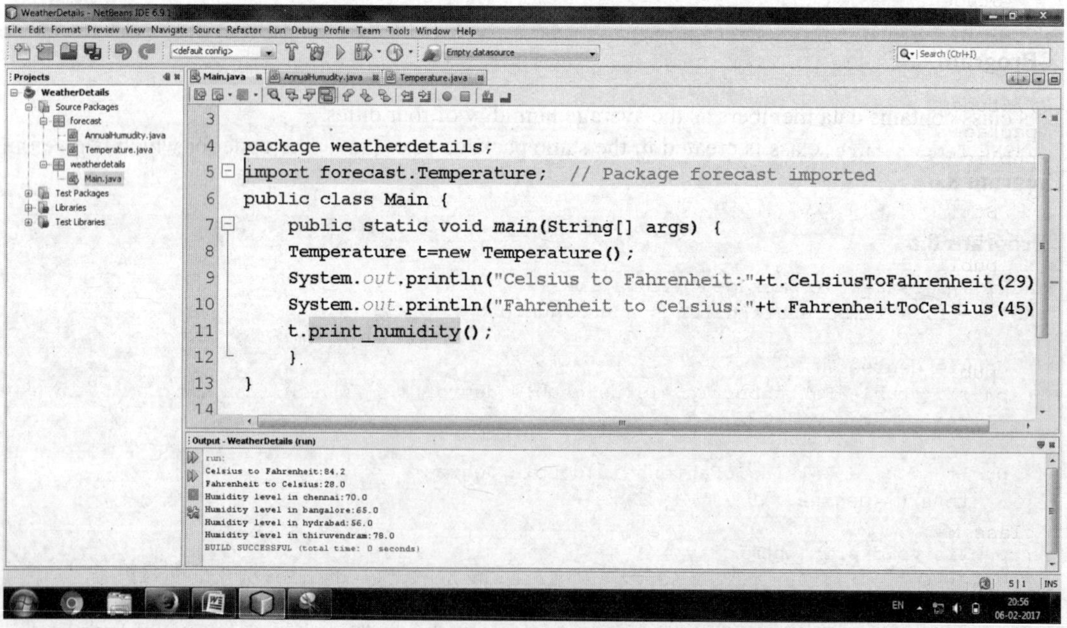

```
package weatherdetails;
import forecast.Temperature;  // Package forecast imported
public class Main {
    public static void main(String[] args) {
    Temperature t=new Temperature();
    System.out.println("Celsius to Fahrenheit:"+t.CelsiusToFahrenheit(29)
    System.out.println("Fahrenheit to Celsius:"+t.FahrenheitToCelsius(45)
    t.print_humidity();
    }
}
```

```
run:
Celsius to Fahrenheit:84.2
Fahrenheit to Celsius:28.0
Humidity level in chennai:70.0
Humidity level in bangalore:65.0
Humidity level in hydrabad:56.0
Humidity level in thiruvendram:78.0
BUILD SUCCESSFUL (total time: 0 seconds)
```

Multiple packages with identical class names

When there is a requirement to create multiple packages that contain classes with the same name in different packages, there is a problem of ambiguity in reference to the particular class in which these classes are accessed. This can be solved by referencing the classes which contains the same class name in a different package using the fully qualified class name in the object creation statement. For instance,

- Package `pack1` contains `Student` class.
- Package `pack2` contains `Student` class.
- In Package `pack3`, these `Student` classes are to be accessed. But in using the normal way of creating an object for this class,

```
Student s1= new Student();
```

the statement throws an error message like the reference to `Student` class is ambiguous, because of the same class name. The compiler gets confused regarding which `Student` class is to be invoked. To solve this problem, the fully qualified package with its class name is given during object creation. For instance,

```
pack1.Student s1=new pack1.Student();
pack2.Student s2=new pack2.Student();
```

Now, it is clear that the statement of object for each student class with its package name is given in the object intialisation. **Program 8.8** demonstrates this concept.

(a) Create `Student.java` file in the package `pack1`. Marks is another non-public class within the `Student` class.

Program 8.8

```
//Student.java
package pack1;
public class Student
{
   String name;
   String department;
   public Student(String na,String de)
   {  name=na;
      department=de;
   }
   public void display()
   {
      System.out.println("Name of the student:"+name);
      System.out.println("Name of the Department:"+department);
   }
}
class Marks
{
   int total;
   void displaymark()
   {
      System.out.println("Total marks:"+total);
   }
}
```

(b) Create `Teacher.java` file in the same package `pack1`.

```
//Teacher.java
package pack1;
public class Teacher
{
    String name;
    String department;
    public Teacher(String na,String de)
    {   name=na;
        department=de;
    }
    public void display()
    {
        System.out.println("Name of the staff:"+name);
        System.out.println("Name of the Department:"+department);
    }
}
```

(c) Create another package called `pack2`. And then create `Student.java` file package `pack2`.

```
Student.java
package pack2;
public class Student
{
    String name;
    String department;
    public Student(String na,String de)
    {   name=na;
        department=de;
    }
    public void display()
    {
        System.out.println("Name of the student:"+name);
        System.out.println("Name of the Department:"+department);
    }
}
```

Output 8.8

```
Name of the student:Joel
Name of the Department:Computer Science
Name of the student:farhan
Name of the Department:Computer Science
Name of the staff:Ajay
Name of the Department:Computer science
Name of the course:B.Sc
Duration of the course:3 yrs
```

(d) Create `Course.java` in the package `pack2`.

```
//Course.java
package pack2;
public class Course
{
    String cname;
    String duration;
    public Course(String na,String de)
    {   cname=na;
        duration=de;
    }
    public void display()
    {
        System.out.println("Name of the course:"+cname);
        System.out.println("Duration of the course:"+duration);
    }
}
```

(e) Create another package called `pack3`. Create the `main` method class `PrintDetails.java` in Package `pack3`.

```
//PrintDetails.java
package pack3;
import pack1.*;
import pack2.*;
public class Printdetails
{
    public static void main(String args[])
    {
        //Student s1=new student(); reference to student is ambiguous
        pack1.Students2=newpack1.Student("Joel","Computer Science");
        s2.display();
        //s2.displaymarks(); class marks not public
        pack2.Student s3=new pack2.Student("farhan"," Computer Science ");
        s3.display();
        Teacher t1=new Teacher("Ajay","Computer science");
        t1.display();
        Course c1=new Course("B.Sc","3 yrs");
        c1.display();
    }}
```

Program 8.8 demonstrates that multiple packages are imported with the same class name. The package `pack3` has been created and then the class `PrintDetails` created which contains the `main()` method to run the program. The packages `pack1` and `pack2` which have been created already contain their own classes. Package `pack1` contains `Student` and `Teacher` class whereas `pack2` contains the `Course` and `Student` class. These two packages have been imported using `import` keyword with an asterisk (*) which denotes that all the classes in that package are imported. Also, these packages contain the same class known as `Student`. While creating an object for `Student` class, an exception is thrown that the reference to student is ambiguous. To solve this issue, the fully qualified name is used in the object initialisation statement. And then methods of other package classes are invoked in the `PrintDetails` class. In the next section, we look at how static import is used.

8.7 STATIC IMPORT AND PACKAGE CLASS

The static import feature facilitates the programmer to access any static member of a class directly. There is no need to qualify it by its class name. The advantage of static import is that less coding is required if accessing any static member of a class frequently. The disadvantage of static import is, if overusing the static import feature, that it makes the program unreadable and unmanageable. **Program 8.9** illustrates this concept.

Program 8.9

```
import static java.lang.System.*;
class StaticImportExample
{
    public static void main(String args[])
    {
        out.println("Hello");//no need of System.
        out out.println("Java");
    }
}
```

Output 8.9

```
Hello
Java
```

Program 8.9 illustrates the static import of the pre-defined class `System`. This `System` class is available in the `java.lang` package. Since the `System` class is imported as static, it is not necessary to use the `System` class again and again in the input and output statements.

Difference between import and static import

Import allows the Java programmer to access classes of a package without package qualification whereas the static import feature allows access to the static members of a class without the class qualification. The import provides accessibility to classes and interfaces whereas static import provides accessibility to static members of the class.

Package class

The package class provides methods to get information about the specifications and implementation of a package. It provides methods such as `getName()`, `getImplementationTitle()`, `getImplementation-Vendor()`, `getImplementationVersion()` and so on.

In **Program 8.10**, the details of `java.lang` package are printed, by invoking the methods of the `package` class.

Program 8.10

```
class PackageInfo
{
    public static void main(String args[])
    {
        Package p=Package.getPackage("java.lang");
        System.out.println("package name: "+
        p.getName());
        System.out.println("Specification Title: "+
        p.getSpecificationTitle());
        System.out.println("Specification Vendor: "+
        p.getSpecificationVendor());
        System.out.println("Specification Version: "+
        p.getSpecificationVersion());
        System.out.println("Implementation Title: "+
        p.getImplementationTitle());
        System.out.println("Implementation Vendor: "+
        p.getImplementationVendor());
        System.out.println("Implementation Version: "+p.getImplementationVersion());
        System.out.println("Is sealed: "+p.isSealed());
    }
}
```

Output 8.10

```
package name: java.lang
Specification Title: Java
Platform API Specification
Specification Vendor:
Sun Microsystems, Inc.
Specification Version: 1.6
Implementation Title:
Java Runtime Environment
Implementation Vendor:
Sun Microsystems, Inc.
Implementation Version:
1.6.0_06
Is sealed: false
```

8.8 ACCESS SPECIFIERS

Modifiers are keywords that are added to class definition to change their meaning. Java language has a wide variety of modifiers, including the following:

- Java access modifiers, and
- non-access modifiers.

Java access modifiers

Java provides a number of access modifiers to set access levels for classes, variables, methods and constructors. The four access levels are:

- Visible to the package, the default. No modifiers are needed.

- Visible to the class only (private).
- Visible to the world (public).
- Visible to the package and all subclasses (protected).

Default access modifier—no keyword

The default access modifier does not explicitly declare an access modifier for a class, field, method and so on. A variable or method declared without any access modifier is available to any other class in the same package. For example, variables and methods can be declared without any modifiers.

```
String name = "Hello java";
boolean isDigit()
{
   return true;
}
```

The variable name does not have any access specifier like `private`, `protected` and `public`. The method `isDigit()` doesn't contain any access specifier. If there are no modifiers declared for the data member and method, then these variables and methods are visible to all the classes available in the same package. The package will be discussed in the next chapter.

Private access specifier—private

Methods, variables and constructors that are declared private can only be accessed within the declared class itself. Private access modifier is the most restrictive access level. Classes and interfaces cannot be private. If public methods are present in the class, variables that are declared private can be accessed from outside the class. Using the private modifier is the main way that an object encapsulates itself and hides data from the outside world. For example, the following class uses private access control:

```
public class Circle
{
   private int r;
   public double getArea()
   {
      return (3.14*r*r);
   }
   public void setArea(int r)
   {
      this.r = r;
   }
}
```

Here, the `r` variable of the `Circle` class is private, so there's no way for other classes to retrieve or set its value directly. To make this variable available to the outside world, we defined two public methods: `getArea()`, which returns the value of the circle with radius `r` variable, and `setArea(int)`, which sets its value.

Public access modifier—public

A class, method, constructor, interface, and so on, can be declared public and accessed from any other class. Therefore, fields, methods, blocks declared inside a public class can be accessed from any class belonging to the Java universe.

However, if the public class is trying to access a different package, then the public class must be imported. Because of class inheritance, all public methods and variables of a class are inherited by its subclasses. For example, the following function uses public access control:

```
public class Details
{
    public void getdata()
    {   System.out.println("hello");
    }
}
```

The class `Details` and method `getdata()` are declared as public. Therefore, any class is able to access this class from anywhere in the application.

Protected access modifier—protected

Variables, methods and constructors that are declared as protected in a superclass can be accessed only by the subclasses in other packages or any class that forms a part of the protected member's class. The protected access modifier cannot be applied to class and interfaces. Methods and fields can be declared as protected, provided these are not in an interface. Protected access modifier provides to the subclass to use the super class method or variable, while preventing a non-related class from trying to use it. For example, the following parent class uses protected access control, to allow its child class to override the *Matchcommentator()* method:

```
class Cricket
{
    protected String Matchcommentator(String sp)
    {
        // method definition
    }
}
class LiveCricket
{
    String Matchcommentator(String sp)
    {
        // method definition
    }
}
```

Here, if defining *Matchcommentator()* method as private, then it would not be accessible from any other class other than *Cricket*. If defining it as public, then it would become accessible by all, the outside world. But the intention is to expose this method to its subclass only, which is reason to have a *protected* modifier.

Access control for inheritance

The following rules are enforced for the subclass methods:

- Methods declared public in a superclass must also be public in all subclasses.
- Methods declared protected in a superclass must either be protected or public in subclasses; they cannot be private.
- Methods declared private are not inherited at all, so there is no rule for them.

Java non-access modifiers

Java provides a number of non-access modifiers to achieve many other functionalities.

static: The `static` modifier for creating class methods and variables. This has been demonstrated in Chapter, Classes and Objects.
final: The `final` modifier for finalising the implementations of classes, methods and variables. That means the subclass cannot access the final class. This has been discussed in Chapter 7 on Inheritance.
abstract: The `abstract` modifier for creating abstract classes and methods. This has been discussed in the chapter on Inheritance.
synchronised: The `synchronized` and `volatile` modifiers, which are used for threads. This will be discussed in Chapter 10 on Multithreading.

SUMMARY

1. An interface is a group of constants, member variables and public method declarations that are defined by the derived classes. Through interfaces, multiple inheritance is achieved in three ways.
2. The three ways are, by implementing more than two interfaces in a class or when an interface is implemented and a class is derived by another class or when more than two interfaces are extended by another interface.
3. A package is a group of related classes and interfaces. According to the functionalities of the class, classes are grouped into multiple packages.
4. Multiple packages can have the same class names. They can be referenced or accessed through fully qualified class names of the particular package. There are three ways for accessing the package classes using the import keyword.
5. A class can access a hidden member variable through its superclass. The accessibility of the hidden member variables outside the scope of the class can be restricted by access specifiers or modifiers.
6. Some of the modifiers like private, protected, public, and so on, provide accessibility to the member variables and methods in the class.

SHORT QUESTIONS

1. What is meant by an interface?
2. Distinguish between interface and inheritance.
3. When is it necessary to extend an interface?
4. When is it necessary to implement an interface?
5. What is meant by multiple interfaces?
6. What are the three ways to develop multiple inheritance?
7. Define a package.
8. How can one access packages?
9. What is meant by static import?
10. What is the use of access specifiers?

COMPREHENSIVE QUESTIONS

1. Discuss interfaces in detail, with examples.
2. Briefly describe the features of an interface.
3. How is an interface defined? Give an example.
4. How are multiple inheritances achieved in interfaces? Explain with an example.
5. Write a program to illustrate multiple interfaces.
6. How do you create a package in Netbeans IDE?
7. Explain the types of packages, with examples.

8. How are packages accessed from another package? Explain with an example.
9. How are multiple packages with identical class names accessed? Explain with an example.
10. Explain static import with an example.

SOLVED PROGRAMS

1. Two interfaces `Food` and `Vitamins` are implemented by a class `FoodUse`. `FoodDetails` class is used to create object for the class `FoodUse` and invoked the methods of the class.

```
interface food
{
   public void vegetables(String name);
   public void fruit(String name);
   public void nuts(String name);
}
interface vitamins
{
   public void vitaminsinfood(String name, String food);
}
class FoodUse implements food, vitamins
{
   public void vegetables(String name) {
      System.out.println("Vegetable
      name:"+name);
   }
   public void fruit(String name) {
      System.out.println("Fruit name:"+name);
   }
   public void nuts(String name) {
      System.out.println("Nuts name:"+name);
   }
   public void vitaminsinfood(String name,String food) {
      System.out.println("Vitamin in: "+food+" "+ name);
   }
}
public class FoodDetails {
   public static void main(String[] args) {
      FoodUse f=new FoodUse();
      f.vegetables("Beans");
      f.vitaminsinfood("A and C","Beans");
      f.fruit("Apple");
      f.vitaminsinfood("A, B1, B2,C","Apple");
      f.nuts("Groundnut");
      f.vitaminsinfood("A & E","Groundnut");
   }
}
```

Output

```
Vegetable name:Beans
Vitamin in: Beans A and C
Fruit name:Apple
Vitamin in: Apple A, B1, B2, C
Nuts name:Groundnut
Vitamin in: Groundnut A & E
```

2. Interface `Area` is implemented by `rectangle` and `circle` class to find an area.

```
interface Area
{
   final static float pi=3.14F;
   float compute(float x,float y);
}
class rectangle implements Area
{
```

```
  public float compute(float x,float y)
  {
     return(pi*x*y);
  }
}
class circle implements Area
{
  public float compute(float x,float y)
  {
     return(pi*x*x);
  }
}
public class interfacedemo
{
  public static void main(String a[])
  {
     rectangle rect=new rectangle();
     circle cir=new circle();
     Area A;
     A=rect;
     System.out.println("Area of rectangle="+A.compute(10,20)); A=cir;
     System.out.println("Area of circle="+A.compute(30,0));
  }
}
```

Output

```
Area of rectangle=628.0
Area of circle=2826.0002
```

3. In the first package `pkg`, `arith.java` class is created then another package `package1` is created with `Arithmeticmain.java` class. The `arith` class methods of `pkg` package are invoked by the `Arithmeticmain` class of `package1` package.

```
//pkg
//arith.java
package pkg;
public class arith {
  public int rp, ip;
  public arith() {
     rp = 0;
     ip = 0;
  }
  public arith(int rp, int rip) {
     this.rp = rp;
     this.ip = rip;
  }
  public void add(arith a1, arith a2) {
     rp = a1.rp + a2.rp;
     ip = a1.ip + a2.ip;
  }
  public void sub(arith a1, arith a2) {
     rp = a1.rp - a2.rp;
     ip = a1.ip - a2.ip;
  }
}
//package1
//Arithmeticmain.java
import java.util.Scanner;
import pkg.arith;
public class Arithmeticmain {
  public static void main(String args[])
```

```
    {
        int rp, ip;
        Scanner sc = new Scanner(System.in);
        System.out.println("Enter real part and imaginary part of 1st complex no :");
        String am = sc.next();
        rp=Integer.parseInt(am);
        String ap=sc.next();
        ip= Integer.parseInt(ap);
        arith a1=new arith(rp,ip);
        System.out.println("Enter real part and
        imaginary part of 2nd complex no");
        String rm=sc.next();
        rp=Integer.parseInt(rm);
        String im=sc.next();
        ip= Integer.parseInt(im);
        arith a2=new arith(rp,ip);
        arith a3=new arith();
        System.out.println("a1="+a1.rp + "+" +a1.
        ip +"i");
        System.out.println("a2="+a2.rp + "+"+a2.ip + "i");
        a3.add(a1,a2);
        System.out.println("Added value:"+a3.rp +"+"+a3.ip +"i");
        a3.sub(a1,a2);
        System.out.println("Subtacted value :" + a3.rp + "-" + a3.ip + "i");
    }
}
```

Output

```
Enter real part and imaginary
part of 1st complex no :
10 5
Enter real part and imaginary
part of 2nd complex no:
3 6
a1=10+5i
a2=3+6i
Added value:13+11i
Subtracted value :7-1i
```

PROGRAMMING EXERCISES

1. Write a Java program to implement the concept of creating packages and importing classes from a user defined package `P1`. In `P1` package, `Student` class is to be created. Import this class to another package `P2` in `Studentmain` class.
2. Write a program to demonstrate the use of extending interfaces, for which `student` and `marks` are two interfaces which are extended by another interface called `department`. Create a class to implement these interfaces and test it.
3. Create an interface `currency` that contains two methods `moneyconversion()` and `countrycurrency()` methods. Create a class `currecyconversion` to implement the currency interface and its methods. In the `main` method class create an object for the class to invoke the methods of the interface and test it.
4. Create two interfaces namely `permutation` and `combination` and then create another interface named `NPRnNCR` that extends the two interfaces. Then create a class to implement the methods of the interfaces.

   Finally within `main()` method create an object for the class to invoke the methods of the interfaces and test it.
5. Create a package `p1` and define `Employee` and `Regular_empsalary` classes. Create another package `p2` and define `Employee` and `Contract_empsalary` classes. Import these two package classes of `p1` and `p2` to another package `p3` class `Empdetails` and test it. Note that the two packages `p1` and `p2` have the same class `Employee`.
6. Create a base class `Family` with protected datamembers and public methods. Inherit the `Family` class in `Relationship` subclass. Create an object for the subclass and test it.
7. Create a package `biodata` which consists of two interfaces namely `Schooling`, `college` and a class `Student` that implements these interfaces. Access the `Student` class in another package `pack1` in a class `Department` and test it.

CHAPTER

9

Exception Handling

When a program is developed and executed for the first time, it will most probably have mistakes. While some of them may only result in the generation of wrong output, others may cause unexpected termination of the execution of the program. Some serious mistakes may even cause a system crash. The errors involved in a program may either be compilation-time errors or run-time errors. The compilation errors are the syntax errors and they are caught during the compilation stage itself. The errors that occur during the execution of a program are known as run-time errors. An exception is an abnormal condition that is caused by a run-time error in the program.

9.1 INTRODUCTION

Exception handling in Java is the mechanism to handle run-time errors so that the usual flow of the application can be maintained. Exceptions are events that occur during the execution of programs, such as divide by zero, array access out of bound, and so on, that interrupt the normal flow of instructions. It is an object which is thrown at run-time. For example,

```
statement 1;
statement 2;
statement 3;
statement 4;
statement 5;//exception occurs statement 6;
statement 7;
statement 8;
statement 9;
statement 10;
```

Assume that there are 10 statements in a program and an exception occurs at Statement 5. The rest of the code will not be executed, that is, statements 6 to 10 will not run. If the concept of exception handling is applied to the above case, the rest of the statements will be executed. That is the purpose of using exception handling in Java. This chapter explains how exceptions can be thrown, propagated, caught and handled.

In Java, exceptions are objects. When an exception is thrown it is treated as throwing an object. All the types of exceptions are subclasses of the built-in abstract class `java.lang.Throwable`. `Throwable` serves as the base class for an entire family of classes declared in `java.lang` that a program can instantiate and throw. There are two subclasses that partition exceptions into two distinct categories, they are *exception* and *error*. Exceptions are thrown to signal abnormal conditions that can often be handled by some catcher. Errors are usually thrown for more serious problems, such as `OutOfMemoryError`, that may not be so easy to handle. In general, when a programmer writes a code, it should throw only exceptions, not errors. Errors are usually thrown by the methods of the Java API or by the Java virtual machine itself. To create an own class of throwable objects, the need is to declare it as a subclass of some member of the `Throwable` class. But the `Throwable` classes defined should extend the class `Exception`. The decision on whether to use an existing exception class from `java.lang` or to create one's own depends upon the situation. For example, if a program method is invoked with an invalid argument, it will throw an `IllegalArgumentException`, a subclass of `RuntimeException` in `java.lang`. However, when the programmer wants to convey more information about the abnormal condition, then a class from java.lang will allow it. Typically, the class of the exception object itself indicates the type of abnormal condition that was encountered. For example, if a thrown exception object has the class `IllegalArgumentException`, it indicates if someone passes an illegal argument to a method. Figure 9.1 shows the classes related to exceptions.

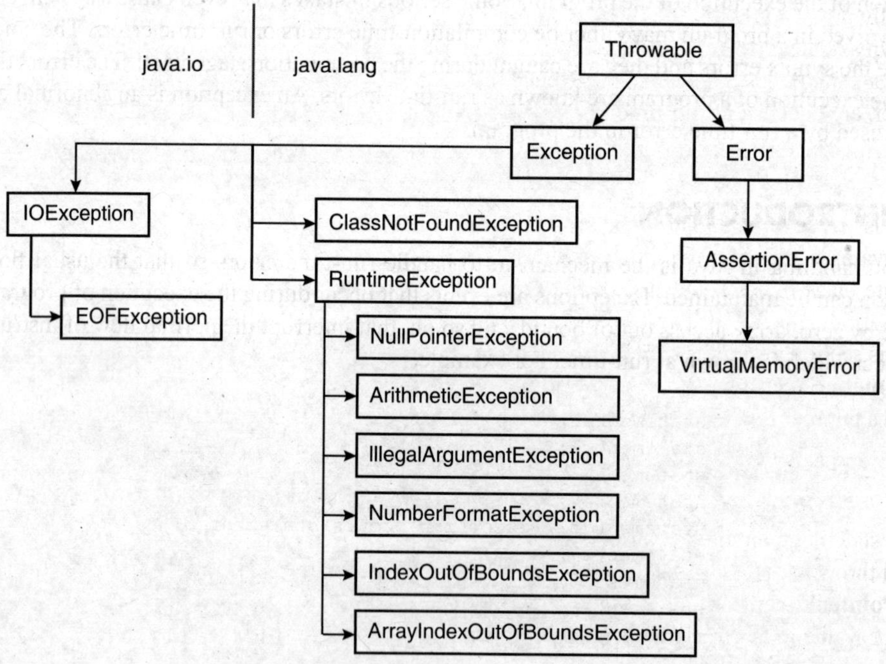

Fig. 9.1 Types of exceptions and errors

Based on the severity of the error, there are two types of exceptions—checked and unchecked. According to Sun Microsystems there are three types of exceptions:

- checked exception,
- unchecked exception, and
- error.

Before going into a brief description, it is important to know the difference between checked and unchecked exceptions. Java defines some special exceptions that a program cannot ignore when (they are) thrown. Such an exception is called a checked exception, because the compiler will complain if the method in which it can occur does not deal with it explicitly. Checked exceptions thus force the code in which they can occur to take explicit action to deal with them, resulting in programs that are robust that are able to handle error situations appropriately. The classes that extend the `Throwable` class except `Run-time Exception` and `Error` are known as checked exceptions. For example, `IOException`, `SQLException` and `ClassNotFoundException`. Hence, checked exceptions are checked during compile-time. Unchecked exceptions are exceptions typically relating to unanticipated errors such as programming errors, for example, ArithmeticException and an IllegalArgumentException. The difference from the checked exceptions is that the compiler does not check whether unchecked exceptions can be thrown. This means that a method does not have to deal with unchecked exceptions but it must face the consequences if the program is terminated due to an unchecked exception. The finest solution for handling such situations is to correct the cause of the errors in the program so that it does not occur during program execution. For example, selection statements or assertions can be used to check the conditions that a method imposes on its actual parameters before calling the method. Since the compiler ignores unchecked exceptions and a method is not forced to handle them, such exceptions are usually not specified in the throws clause of a method. The classes that extend run-time exception are known as unchecked exceptions, for example, `ArithmeticException`, `NullPointerException`, and `ArrayIndexOutOfBoundsException`. Hence, unchecked exceptions are not checked at compile-time, but rather, are checked at run-time.

Error

- Error is irrecoverable. The subclass `AssertionError` of the `java.lang.Error` class is used by the Java assertion facility. Other subclasses of the `java.lang.Error` class define exceptions that indicate class linkage, that is linkage error, for thread is `ThreadDeath` and for virtual machine is `VirtualMachineError`. These are invariably never explicitly caught and are usually irrecoverable.

This section describes some of the common scenarios where exceptions may occur.

- **ArithmeticException**

When a number is divided by zero, the exception `ArithmeticException` will be raised. For example,

```
int num=50/0;//ArithmeticException
```

In the statement, an integer variable `num` is declared and the value of 50 divided by 0 is assigned to it. It will throw `ArithmeticException`.

- **NullPointerException**

A `null` value in any variable in an operation may result in a `NullPointerException`. For example,

```
String s=null;
System.out.println(s.length());
//NullPointerException
```

In the statement, a String variable `s` is declared and the value `null` is initialised. Printing the length of the value that resides in `s` will throw a `NullPointerException`.

- **NumberFormatException**

The wrong formatting of any value results in `NumberFormatException`. For example,

```
String s="xyz";
int i=Integer.parseInt(s);//NumberFormatException
```

A String variable `s` has characters 'xyz'. Converting this variable into digits will produce `NumberFormatException`.

- **ArrayIndexOutOfBoundsException**

  If a programmer inserts a value in the wrong index, it would result in an `ArrayIndexOutOfBoundsException`. For example,

```
int a[]=new int[5];
a[10]=50; //ArrayIndexOutOfBoundsException
```

An array `a` has been declared with a size five. Inserting a value into the tenth position of the defined array will result in an `ArrayIndexOutOfBoundsException`. Exception handling in Java is accomplished by five keywords. They are *try, catch, throw, throws* and *finally*.

9.2 try AND catch BLOCK

During the execution of a program, various conditions can occur that cause an unexpected and abnormal termination of the program. To better understand the problem of not using exception handling in a program, see **Program 9.1**.

Program 9.1

```
public class uncaught{
   public static void main(String args[])
   {
      int data=50/0;//may throw exception
      System.out.println ("Execution is completed");
   }
}
```

Output 9.1

```
Exception in thread main
java.lang.
ArithmeticException:/ by
zero
```

In Program 9.1 the name of the class is `uncaught`. In `main()` method, an integer variable `i` is declared and the value of 50 divided by 0 is assigned to it. Since the condition is abnormal, the program throws an `ArithmeticException` and the statement 'Execution is completed' is not printed. It is clear that the code after the exception is not executed. There can be 100 lines of code after the exception. So, all code after the exception needs special attention, in order to be executed. To avoid a program that terminates unexpectedly, Java allows the programmer to handle exceptions by means of a suitable construct called `try-catch` block.

try block

A `try` block consists of a block with the keyword `try` in front. A `try` block contains arbitrary code where the statements may raise exceptions. A `catch` block is associated with a `try` block. A `catch` block constitutes an exception handler. An exception will be thrown as a result of executing the code in the `try` block and this exception can be caught and handled in an associated `catch` block. The block notation, braces {} are required for the `try` and `catch` blocks, even if a block only contains a single statement. A `try` block should be followed by either `catch` or `finally` block.

`catch` block

A catch block is a group of statements, enclosed in braces {} that are used to handle a specific exception that has been thrown. A `catch` block should be placed immediately after the `try` block. When an exception occurs in a `try` block, program control is transferred to the suitable `catch` block. The transfer of control is unconditional, that is, the control will not return to the statement after the throw point in the try block. A `catch` block is specified by the keyword `catch` followed by a single argument within parenthesis ( ). The argument type in a `catch` clause is from the `Throwable` class or one of its subclasses. Java initialises the argument to refer to the caught object. The general syntax for `try-catch` is,

```
try
{
    //code that may throw exception
}
catch (ExceptionType1 e)
{
    //exception handler for ExceptionType1
}
catch (ExceptionType2 e)
{
    //exception handler for ExceptionType2
}
```

The keyword `try` is used to preface a block of code that is likely to cause an error condition and throw an exception. The `catch` block catches the exception thrown by the `try` block and handles it appropriately. The catch block is added immediately after the `try` block. The `ExceptionType` is the type of exception that has occurred and `e` is the object. Figure 9.2 shows the exception handling mechanism using `try-catch`.

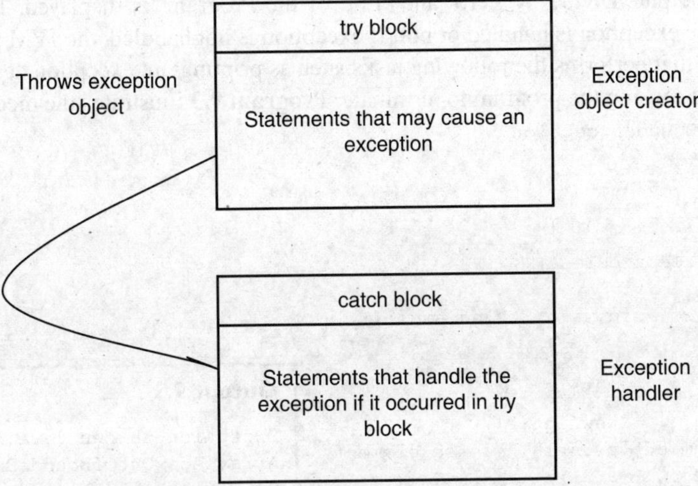

Fig. 9.2 Exception handling mechanism using `try-catch`

Program 9.2 explains the usage of `try-catch` statements.

Program 9.2

```
class trycatch
{
   public static void main(String args[])
   {
      int x=50;
      int y=0;
      int z;
      try
      {
         z = x/y;
         System.out.println("z = "+z);
      }
      catch(ArithmeticException e)
      {  System.out.println(e);
         System.out.println("Divide by Zero");
      }
      System.out.println("End of the Program");
   }
}
```

Output 9.2

```
java.lang.
ArithmeticException: / by
zero
Divide by Zero
End of the Program
```

In Program 9.2, the class name is `trycatch` and it has three integer variables `x, y, z`. The variable `x` is initialised to value 50 and `y` is initialised to value 0. Inside the `try` statement, an attempt of divide by zero is made, where the `x` value is divided by the value of `y` and the result will be assigned to `z`. It creates an exception object of type `ArithmeticException` and throws it out. The statement after the exception will not be executed and the value of `z` will not be displayed. The control will directly get transferred to the `catch` statement. Catch block catches the exception and puts in the object `e`. While printing the value of `e` it prints the description of the exception. Then, the subsequent lines are executed, as the output 'Divide by Zero' and 'End of the Program' is displayed. The JVM initially checks whether the exception is handled or not. If exception is not handled, the JVM provides a default exception handler that performs the following tasks such as printing out exception description, printing the stack trace and causing the program to terminate. **Program 9.3** illustrates the mechanism to handle `ArrayIndexOutOfBoundsException`.

Program 9.3

```
import java.io.*;
public class ExceptionTest
{
   public static void main(String args[])
   {
      try
      {
         int a[ ] = new int[2];
         System.out.println("Access element
         three :" + a[3]);
      }
      catch(ArrayIndexOutOfBoundsException e)
      {
         System.out.println("Exception thrown :" + e);
      }
      System.out.println("Out of the block");}
}
```

Output 9.3

```
Exception thrown java.lang.
ArrayIndexOutOfBoundsException: 3
Out of the block
```

In Program 9.3, the class name is `ExceptionTest`. In `main ()` the `try` and `catch` block is used. Inside `try` an integer array with name `a` is declared and the size of the array is 2. The next statement tries to print the value of the third position of the array `a`. The problem arises there since the size of the array is less; thus, the exception is thrown. The `catch` block catches the exception that is `ArrayIndexOutBoundsException` and puts it in the object `e`. While printing the value of `e` it prints the description of the exception.

Displaying the description of the message

The class `Throwable` provides the following common methods to query the exception so that it can be used along with the `Exception` class object.

`String getMessage()`—returns the detailed message of the exception.
`void printStackTrace()`—prints the stack trace on the standard error stream.
The stack trace comprises the method invocation sequence on the run time stack when the exception was thrown. It gives the same output as when exception occurred, but the program is not terminated.
`String toString()`—returns a short description of the exception which typically comprises the class name of the exception together with the string returned by the `getMessage()` method.

Program 9.4 shows the methods of displaying the description of exception.

Program 9.4

```
class trycatch
{
    public static void main(String args[])
    {
        int x=50;
        int y=0;
        int z;
        try
        {
            z = x/y;
        }
        catch(ArithmeticException e)
        {   System.out.println(e.getMessage());
            System.out.println(e.printStackTrace());
            System.out.println(e.toString());
            System.out.println(e);
        }
        System.out.println("End of the Program");
    }
}
```

Output 9.4

```
/ by zero java.lang.
ArithmeticException: / by
zero at trycatch.
main(trycatch.java:10)
java.lang.
ArithmeticException: / by
zero
java.lang.
ArithmeticException: / by
zero
End of the Program
```

In Program 9.4, the class name is `trycatch` and it has three integer variables `x, y, z`. The variable `x` is initialised to value 50 and `y` is initialised to value 0. Inside the `try` statement, an attempt to divide by zero is made, where the `x` value is divided by the value of `y` and the result will be assigned to `z`. It creates an exception object of type `ArithmeticException` and throws it out. The statement after the exception will not be executed and the value of `z` will not be displayed. The control will directly get transferred to the `catch` statement. The `catch` block catches the exception and puts it in the object `e`. While printing the value of `e` with the help of `getMessage()` method, it prints `/by zero`, the `printStackTrace()` method gives a detailed message, the `toString()` method prints `java.lang.ArithmeticException: / by zero` and the object `e` also displays the same message.

9.3 MULTIPLE catch BLOCKS

In some cases, more than one exception may occur in a single program. To handle this type of situation, two or more `catch` statements can be used in a program. Each `catch` will catch a different type of exception. When an exception is thrown, each statement is inspected in order and the first one whose type matches that of the exception is executed. After one `catch` statement executes, the others are bypassed and the execution continues after the `try/catch` block. To perform different tasks at the occurrence of different exceptions, use a multi-catch block. **Program 9.5** illustrates the types of exceptions with multiple `catch` associated with a single `try`.

Program 9.5

```
import java.util.Scanner;
class MultipleCatch
{
   public static void main(String args[])
   {
      int a, b, c;
      Scanner inp= new Scanner(System.in);
      System.out.println("Enter the Number :");
      a= inp.nextInt();
      try
      {
         c=50/a;// statement1
         System.out.println("Division: "+c);
         int d[ ]= {1,2,3};
         d[10]=150;// statement2
      }
      catch(ArithmeticException e)
      {
         System.out.println("Divide By Zero");
      }
      catch(ArrayIndexOutOfBoundsException e)
      {
         System.out.println("Array Index wrong");
      }
      System.out.println("Execution completed");
   }
}
```

Output 9.5

```
Run 1
Enter the Number :
0
Divide By Zero Execution
completed Run 2
Enter the Number :
5
Division: 10
Array Index wrong
Execution completed
```

In Program 9.5, the class name is `MultipleCatch`. The code written in the `try` block will cause either 'divide by zero' or 'array index out of bounds'. If any one of these exceptions occur, it will be caught in the appropriate catch statement and action will be taken. Depending upon the type of exception object thrown, only one of the catch statements will be executed. If the exception throw does not match with the exception object written in the `catch` block, the program will be terminated. In the program, there are three integer variables—`a, b, c`. Using the scanner, the input for the variable `a` is taken from the keyboard. If the value of the input is 0 then the divide by zero exception will occur at statement 1 else array index out of bounds will occur at statement 2. Then the exceptions are caught by the appropriate `catch` clause.

9.4 NESTED try

The `try` statement can be nested. The `try` block within a `try` block is known as a `nested try` block in Java. The `nested try` block is used in circumstances where a part of a block may cause one error and the entire block itself may cause another error. In such cases, exception handlers have to be nested. Each time a `try` statement is entered, the context of that exception is pushed on the stack. If an inner `try` statement does not have a catch handler for a particular exception, the stack is unwound and the next `try` statement's catch handlers are inspected for a match of exception. This continues until one of the `catch` statements succeeds or until all the `nested try` statements are exhausted. If no `catch` statement matches, then the Java run-time system will handle the exception. The general syntax for nested try is,

```
....
try
{
    statement 1;
    statement 2;
    try
    {
        statement 1;
        statement 2;
    }
    catch(Exception e)
    {
    }
}
catch(Exception e)
{
}
....
```

Program 9.6 illustrates the use of `nested try` blocks.

Program 9.6

```
import java.util.Scanner;
class NestedTry
{
    public static void main(String args[ ])
    {
        int x,y,z;
        Scanner inp= new Scanner(System.in);
        System.out.println("Enter the Number :");
        x= inp.nextInt();
        try
        {
            z=50/x; //statement1
            System.out.println("Division: "+z);
            try
            {
                int a=100/(x-1); // statement2
                int array[]={20};
                array[10]=50; //statement3
            }
            catch(ArrayIndexOutOfBoundsException e)
            {
                System.out.println("Array Index wrong");
            }
        }
        catch(ArithmeticException e)
        {
            System.out.println("Divide By Zero");
        }
        System.out.println("Execution completed");
    }
}
```

Output 9.6

```
Run 1
Enter the Number :
0
Divide By Zero
Execution completed
Run 2
Enter the Number :
1
Division: 50
Divide By Zero
Execution completed
Run 3
Enter the Number :
2
Division: 25
Array Index wrong
Execution completed
```

In Program 9.6, the class name is `NestedTry` and it has two nested `try` statements in each other. Using the scanner, the input for the variable `x` is taken from the keyboard. When the value of `x` is input as 0, statement 1 will cause an exception 'Divide by Zero'. So, the program control will directly transfer to `catch` statement 2 to take action. When the value of `x` is input as 1, the outer `try` will work properly. In the inner `try`, the statement 2 will cause the exception of 'Divide by Zero'. In this case, the program control will get directly transferred to the inner try's `catch` block that is `catch` clause1. But the exception object will not match. So, it will check for the outer try's `catch` clause. Now, the match is found. That's why the output on Run2 is displayed. In the third case, when the input is any number other than 0 and 1, statement 3 will cause an exception 'ArrayIndexOutOfBounds'. This will be caught by inner try's `catch` clause. The outer try's clause will catch all the exception occurred inside it. If the exception of 'ArrayIndexOutOfBounds has occurred in the outer `try` then this will not be caught by the inner try's `catch` clause.

9.5 finally BLOCK

The final step in setting up an exception handler is providing a mechanism for cleaning up the program before control is passed to a different part of the program. This can be achieved by enclosing the clean-up logic within the `finally` block. The `finally` block is a block of code written after `try/catch`. The code within the `finally` block is always executed whether an exception is thrown or not. This can be useful for closing a file, closing connections and freeing up any other resources that might have been allocated at the beginning of the method. The `finally` clause is optional. But there is only one `finally` block per `try` block. The `try-catch-finally` construct can be created as follows.

```
try
{
    .............
}
catch(....)
{
    .............
}
finally
{
    .............. 
}
```

The `try-finally` can be created as follows.

```
try
{
    ..............
}
finally
{
    ..............
}
```

Program 9.7 illustrates the use of `finally` block.

Program 9.7

```
class FinallyClause
{
   public static void main(String args[])
   {
      try
      {
         //int val=0; //statement1
         //int m=100/val; //statement2
         int [ ]x=new int[-5]; //statement3
         System.out.println("No output Displayed");
      }
      catch(ArithmeticException e)
      {
         System.out.println("Exception : "+e);
      }
      finally
      {
         System.out.println("End of the program");
      }
   }
}
```

Output 9.7

```
End of the program
Exception in thread "main"
java.lang.
NegativeArraySizeException
at FinallyClause.
main(FinallyClause.java:11)
Java Result: 1
```

In Program 9.7, the class name is `FinallyClause`. Inside the `try` block, an array `x` has been declared and a negative size is passed as argument. Thus, the exception of 'negative array size' has occurred at statement3. But the `catch` statement will not catch it since only `ArithmeticException` is mentioned. Thus, the program will be terminated. Although before its termination and printing the stack trace, the `finally` block is executed. If the comment lines are removed from statement1 and statement2, the output will be:

```
Exception : java.lang.ArithmeticException: / by zero
End of the program
```

The exception of 'Divide by zero' will occur at statement2. This will be caught by the `catch` clause. So, the `catch` block is executed first and then the `finally` block is executed. That is, the `try-catch-finally` are executed in sequence. If a `finally` block is associated with only one `try`, the `finally` block will be executed upon conclusion of the `try`.

9.6 THE `throw` STATEMENT

An exception can be caught only if it is thrown. Exceptions can be thrown by the Java run-time system for the code that has been written. This can also be achieved by using the `throw` statement. The `throw` keyword is used to explicitly throw an exception followed by a single argument. The argument must be an object instantiated from the `Throwable` class or its subclass. The general form of the `throw` statement is:

```
throw <Exception object>
```

In the statement, `throw` is the keyword and `Exception object` is the object of type `Throwable`. In a specific case where an instance of 'Exception object' is to be thrown, it takes the following form:

```
throw new <Exception object>
```

Usually the above statement is used to pass a string argument along with the exceptional object, so that the string can be displayed when the exception is handled. For example,

```
throw new IndexOutOfBoundsException ("Index out of range");
```

In the statement, `throw` is the keyword, `new` allocates memory space for the exception and `IndexOutOfBoundsException` is the exception method. **Program 9.8** demonstrates the use of the `throw` statement.

Program 9.8

```
class ThrowEx
{
    static void validate(int age)
    {
        if(age<18)
            throw new ArithmeticException("not
            valid");
        else
            System.out.println("welcome to vote");
    }
    public static void main(String args[])
    {
        validate(13);
        System.out.println("End of the Program.");
    }
}
```

Output 9.8

```
Exception in thread
"main" java.lang.
ArithmeticException: not
valid
at ThrowEx.
validate(ThrowEx.java:4)
at ThrowEx.main(ThrowEx.
java:9)
```

In Program 9.8, the class name is `ThrowEx`. The static method `validate ()` with return type `void` has been created and the integer variable `age` is passed as argument. The method definition checks if `age` is less than 18. If so, the exception is thrown as the `ArithmeticException` otherwise a message 'welcome to vote' is printed. In the `main()` method, the value 13 is passed as an argument to the `validate()` method. The condition is checked and thus the `ArithmeticException` is thrown.

9.7 EXCEPTION PROPAGATION

If an exception is not caught and handled where it is thrown, the control is passed to the method that has invoked the method where the exception was thrown. The propagation continues until the exception is caught or the control passes to the `main` method, which terminates the program and produces an error message. It is the `throw` statements that start the chain of method terminations. An exception is first thrown from the top of the stack and if it is not caught, it drops down the call stack to the previous method. If not caught there, the exception again drops down to the previous method and so on until it is caught or until it reaches the very bottom of the call stack. This is called `exception propagation`. **Program 9.9** explains the concept of exception propagation.

Program 9.9

```
import java.io.*;
class ExceptionPropagation{
    public static void main(String[ ] args) throws Exception
    {
        BufferedReader br = new BufferedReader(new InputStreamReader(System.in));
        System.out.println("Insert a number:");
        int c = Integer.parseInt(br.
        readLine());
        first(c);
    }
    private static void first(int a) throws
    Exception
    {
        second(a);
    }
    private static void second(int b)
    throws Exception {
        Exception propagate = new
        Exception("The value is too small");
        if (b < 10)
        throw propagate;
        System.out.println("OK");
    }
}
```

Output 9.9

```
Insert a number:
5
Exception in thread "main" java.lang.
Exception: The value is too small.
at ExceptionPropagation.
second(ExceptionPropagation.java:13)
at ExceptionPropagation.
first(ExceptionPropagation.java:10)
at ExceptionPropagation.
main(ExceptionPropagation.java:7)
Java Result: 1
```

In Program 9.9, the class name is `ExceptionPropagation`. The value for the integer variable `c` is read from the keyboard with the help of `BufferedReader` and the value is type casted, then passed as an argument to the `first()` method. Then the argument of `first()` method is passed to `second()` as a chain. The object `propagates` has been created for the exception class and the message 'The value is too small' is passed as argument to the constructor `Exception ()`. If the program reads a value less than 10, for example 5, an exception is thrown and the above messages printed. In order to allow the chain of terminations started by the `second` method to propagate to the `main` method, it is necessary that all methods that are part of the termination chain have in their header the `throws` clause with the list of involved exceptions: in this case, only `Exception`.

9.8 `throws` CLAUSE

If a method is capable of causing an exception that it does not handle, it must specify this behaviour so that callers of the method protect themselves against that exception. The `throws` keyword is used to declare an exception. A `throws` clause lists the types of exceptions that a method might throw. This is necessary for all exceptions, except those of type `Error` or `Run-time Exception` or any other subclasses. All other exceptions that a method can throw must be declared in the `throws` clause. If not, a compile time error will occur. A general form of writing a `throws` clause is as follows.

```
data-type method-name(parameter-list)throws exception-list
{
    //method code
}
```

In the statement, the `data-type` refers to the primitive data types, `method-name` is the name of the method and `throws` is the keyword. The `exception-list` is the list of exceptions that the method might throw, separated by commas. For many classes and methods, it is necessary to throw the exception by the method that is using it. For example, while using `DataInputStream` it is necessary to throw the `IOException` as well as for many methods of multithreading it is necessary to throw `InterruptedException`. For example, when the following code is compiled:

```
class ThrowsDemo
{
    public static void main(String args[])
    {
        throw new ClassNotFoundException();
    }
}
```

the output will be,

```
Exception in thread "main" java.lang.
Run-timeException: Uncompilable source code
- unreported exception java.lang.
ClassNotFoundException; must be caught or declared to be thrown at ThrowsDemo.
main(ThrowsDemo.java:8)
Java Result: 1
```

The solution for the above example is to enclose the statement containing `throw` in a `try-catch` block or use `throws` clause as given below.

```
class ThrowsDemo
{
    public static void main(String args[]) throws
    ClassNotFoundException
    {
        throw new ClassNotFoundException();
    }
}
```

The output will be as follows,

```
Exception in thread "main" java.lang.
ClassNotFoundException
at ThrowsDemo.main(ThrowsDemo.java:8)
Java Result: 1
```

The `main()` method will throw the mentioned exception by itself, because the `ClassNotFoundException` is neither of type `error` nor `Run-timeException`. So, it can be thrown using the `throws` clause. Before the exception has occurred, the other exceptions such as divide by zero, array index out of bounds or negative array size exception cannot be written in the `throws` clause as they are of type `Run-timeException`.

There are many differences between `throw` and `throws` keywords. In Table 9.1, a list of differences between `throw` and `throws` are given.

Table 9.1 Differences between `throw` and `throws`

S. no.	throw	throws
1	`throw` keyword is used to explicitly throw an exception.	`throws` keyword is used to declare an exception.
2	Checked exception cannot be propagated using throw only.	Checked exception can be propagated with throws.
3	`throw` is followed by an instance.	`throws` is followed by class.
4	`throw` is used within the method.	`throws` is used with the method signature.
5	Cannot throw multiple exceptions.	Can declare multiple exceptions, for example, `public void method() throws IOException, SQLException`.

There are many differences between `final`, `finally` and `finalize`. Table 9.2 shows a list of differences between `final`, `finally` and `finalize`.

Table 9.2 Differences between `final`, `finally` and `finalize`

S. no.	Final	Finally	Finalize
1	`Final` is used to apply restrictions on class, method and variable. Final class can't be inherited, overridden and final variable value can't be changed.	`Finally` is used to place important code and it will be executed whether the exception is handled or not.	`Finalize` is used to perform clean up processing before the object is garbage collected.
2	`Final` is a keyword.	`Finally` is a block.	`Finalize` is a method.

9.9 CUSTOM EXCEPTION

Java has defined a lot of exception and error classes for different conditions. However, many times there are conditions where the programmer wants to create his/her own exception types to handle situations specific to the applications. This is often referred to as *custom exception* or *user-defined exception*. Java custom exceptions are used to customise the exception according to the need. With the help of custom exception, it is possible to have one's own exception and message. This is quite easy to do. The first step is to define a subclass of `Exception` which is a subclass of `Throwable`, but the subclasses don't need to implement anything. It is their existence in the type system that allows using them as exceptions. The `Exception` class does not define any methods of its own. It inherits all the methods provided by class `Throwable`. **Program 9.10** explains the concept of creating one's own exceptions.

Program 9.10

```
class NegativeOutputException extends Exception
{
    private int det;
    NegativeOutputException(int a)
    {
        det=a;
    }
    public String toString()
    {
        return "NegativeOutputException("+det+")";
    }
}
```

```
class OwnException
{
    public static void main(String args[])
    {
        int x=Integer.parseInt(args[0]);
        int y=Integer.parseInt(args[1]);
        int z;
        try{
            z=x*y;
            if (z<0)// statement1
            throw new NegativeOutputException(z);
            System.out.println("Output :"+z);
        }
        catch(NegativeOutputException e)
        {
            System.out.println("Caught : "+e);
        }
    }}
```

Output 9.10

```
java OwnException 4 8
Output : 32
java OwnException 4 -3
Caught :
NegativeOutputException[-12]
java OwnException -4 -3
Output : 12
```

In Program 9.10, there are two classes—`NegativeOutputException` and `OwnException`. In order to create own exception, the exception class is inherited from `java.lang.Exception`. The defined exception is `NegativeOutputException`. An integer variable `det` is declared and it is of type private. The constructor `NegativeOutputException ()` holds an integer variable `a` as argument and the value `a` is assigned to `det`. The method `toString()` has been overridden to print the custom message with exception class. In `main` class, three integer variables `x, y, z` are declared and for `x, y` the values can be passed as arguments and all the variables are type casted. The condition for the exception defined is that exception will occur when the result of the expression is negative. It is defined in statement1. The input has taken from the command line. The first argument is passed to `x` and the second to `y`. The first and third time when both the arguments are positive/negative, the result is positive so the output is displayed properly. But when any one of the arguments is negative the result is also negative. Then statement1 will be true. The exception is thrown using the `throw` clause. This exception is caught by the `catch` clause. If the programmer does not catch it using `catch,` a compile time error will occur.

Program 9.11 explains the creation of a user defined exception according to the requirements.

Program 9.11

```
import java.util.Scanner;
class ExceptionHandling
{
    public static void main(String[] args)
    {
        Scanner sc = new Scanner (System.in);
        System.out.println("Enter Your Age");
        int age = sc.nextInt();
        try
        {
            if(age < 0)
            {
                throw new Exception();
            }
        }
        catch(Exception ex)
        {  System.out.println(ex);
        //Prints exception description
        }
    }}
```

Output 9.11

```
Enter Your Age
` -5
java.lang.Exception
```

In Program 9.11 the class name is `ExceptionHandling`. The input for the integer variable `age` is read from the keyboard using the `Scanner` class and it is type casted. Inside the `try` block, the condition is checked to see whether `age` value is less than 0. When the programmer enters a negative value, it throws an exception and prints the exception description. The displayed description will not give a clear idea of the problem. So, it is better to make this program more user friendly. Program 9.11 can be modified so that it can indicate why the exception has occurred. To do this, create one subclass to Exception class and override the `toString ()` method as follows.

```
//Defining our own exception by extending Exception class
class AgeIsNegativeException extends Exception
{
    String errorMessage;
    public AgeIsNegativeException(String errorMessage)
    {
        this.errorMessage = errorMessage;
    }
//Modifying toString() method to display customized error message @Override
    public String toString()
    {
        return errorMessage;
    }
}
```

The class name is `AgeIsNegativeException`. Then, to create one's own exception, the class should extend the `Exception` class which is in `Throwable` class. A String variable `errorMessage` is declared and it has been passed as an argument to the constructor `AgeIsNegativeException()` which is public. The value of the string object `errorMessage` is assigned to the same variable using this keyword. Then `toString()` method is overridden to display the customised error message. The exception defined here is called a user defined exception or a customised exception. The next thing to do is to add a `throw` statement to this customised exception when the programmer enters a negative value. **Program 9.12** explains a complete user defined exception used in a program.

Program 9.12

```
import java.util.Scanner;
public class ExceptionHandling
{
    public static void main(String[] args)
    {
        Scanner sc = new Scanner(System.in);
        System.out.println("Enter Your Age");
        int age = sc.nextInt();
        try
        {
            if(age < 0)
            {
                throw new AgeIsNegativeException("Age cannot be negative");
            }
        }
        catch(AgeIsNegativeException ex)
        { System.out.println(ex);
        }
    }
}
```

In Program 9.12, the class name is `ExceptionHandling`. The input for the integer variable `age` is read from the keyboard using the `Scanner` class and it is type casted. Inside the `try` block, the condition is checked to determine whether the `age` value is less than 0. When the programmer enters a negative value the `throw` keyword throws an exception; `new` is the keyword which allocates memory space for the exception object and the constructor `AgeIsNegativeException()` has passed argument 'Age cannot be negative'. The `catch` block catches the exception thrown by the `throw` keyword in the `try` block and puts it in the object `ex`. Thus, the object `ex` prints 'Age cannot be negative' whenever a negative value is input. This helps the programmer understand easily why the error has occurred.

9.10 BUILT-IN EXCEPTIONS

Java has a lot of built-in exceptions. The list of unchecked exceptions or the exception classes which extend from `Run-timeException` are presented in Table 9.3.

Table 9.3 Unchecked exceptions

Exception	Description
`ArithmeticException`	Arithmetic error, such as divide-by-zero.
`ArrayIndexOutOfBoundsException`	Array index is out-of-bounds.
`ArrayStoreException`	Assignment to an array element of an incompatible type.
`ClassCastException`	Invalid typecasting.
`IllegalArgumentException`	Illegal argument used to invoke a method.
`IllegalMonitorStateException`	Illegal monitor operation, such as waiting on an unlocked thread.
`IllegalStateException`	Environment or application is in incorrect state.
`IllegalThreadStateException`	Requested operation not compatible with current thread state.
`IndexOutOfBoundsException`	Some type of index is out-of-bounds.
`NegativeArraySizeException`	Array created with a negative size.
`NullPointerException`	Invalid use of a null reference.
`NumberFormatException`	Invalid conversion of a string to a numeric format.
`SecurityException`	Attempt to violate security.
`StringIndexOutOfBounds`	Attempt to index outside the bounds of a string.
`UnsupportedOperationException`	Unsupported operation was encountered.

Table 9.4 shows the list of checked exceptions.

Table 9.4 Checked exceptions

Checked exceptions	Description
`ClassNotFoundException`	Class not found.
`CloneNotSupportedException`	Attempt to clone an object that does not implement the cloneable interface.
`IllegalAccessException`	Access to a class is denied.
`InstantiationException`	Attempt to create an object of an abstract class or interface.
`InterruptedException`	One thread has been interrupted by another thread.
`NoSuchFieldException`	A requested field does not exist.
`NoSuchMethodException`	A requested method does not exist.

SUMMARY

1. An exception is an event which occurs during the execution of a program, that disrupts the normal flow of the program's instructions. When an error occurs within a method, the method creates an object and hands it off to the run-time system.
2. `try` and `catch` are keywords that represent the handling of exceptions due to data or coding errors during program execution. A `try` block is the block of code in which exceptions occur. A `catch` block catches and handles `try` block exceptions.
3. Exception handlers can be nested within one another. A `try`, `catch` or a `finally` block can in turn contain another set of the `try- catch- finally` sequence.
4. `finally` block is used to execute important code such as closing a connection, stream and so on. It is always executed, whether the exception is handled or not, and it is written after the `try` or `catch` block.
5. An exception can be caught only if it is thrown. Exceptions can be thrown by the Java run-time system for the code that has been written. This can be achieved also by using the `throw` statement.
6. The `throws` keyword is used to declare an exception. A `throws` clause lists the types of exceptions that a method might throw. This is necessary for all exceptions, except those of type `Error` or `Run-time Exception` or any other subclasses.
7. Java custom exceptions are used to customise the exception according to the need. Due to this, it is possible to have one's own exception and message.

SHORT QUESTIONS

1. What is an exception? Give an example.
2. List the two distinct advantages of user-defined exception handling mechanisms.
3. How does the `try....catch` mechanism handle an exception?
4. What is the main use of `finally` block?
5. How is the `throw` statement used?
6. Differentiate `throws` from `throw` keyword.
7. Why do we need custom exceptions?
8. List the various keywords to manage errors.
9. Mention any five built-in exceptions.
10. Why should we throw an exception early?
11. What are checked and unchecked exceptions?
12. Differentiate between errors and exceptions.

COMPREHENSIVE QUESTIONS

1. Explain the mechanism of custom exception handling.
2. Discuss the features of exception handling mechanism with an example.
3. Explain multiple `catch` block with an example.
4. What is the difference between `final`, `finally` and `finalize()` in Java?
5. Discuss the Java error handling mechanism.
6. What is the difference between run-time (unchecked) exceptions and checked exceptions?
7. What is the implication of catching all the exceptions with the type 'Exception'?
8. What is exception handling? Briefly explain the exception types.
9. How can one manage errors in Java? Explain.
10. Explain the various built-in exceptions available in Java.
11. Write an example to show how the different types of exceptions are handled.
12. Give an account of nested `try` and `catch` blocks.

SOLVED PROGRAMS

1. Program to handle StringIndexOutOfBounds Exception.

```
import java.lang.*;
class StringIndexOut
{
  public static void main (String args[])
  {
    String a,b; char c; a="abc"; try{
    b=a.substring(2,5);
    System.out.println(b);
    c=a.charAt(9);
    System.out.println(c);
  }
  catch (Exception t)
  {
    System.out.println("The
    exception is"+t);
  }
  System.out.println("Exception Handling"); }
}
```

Output

```
The exception is java.lang.
StringIndexOutOfBoundsException:
String index out of range: 5
Exception Handling
```

2. Program to illustrate Arithmetic Exception.

```
class ArithmeticExcep
{
  public static void main (String args[])
  {
    int a,b,c,d,e,f;
    a=25;b=4;c=0;d=3;
    e=a/b;
    System.out.println(e);
    e=a/c;
    System.out.println(e);
    e=a/d;
    System.out.println(e);
    System.out.println("Exception Handling");
  }
}
```

Output

```
6
Exception in thread "main"
java.lang.ArithmeticException:
/ by zero
at ArithmeticExcep.
main(ArithmeticExcep.java:10)
Java Result: 1
```

3. Program to illustrate a proper way of handling exceptions.

```
class Test1
{
  int count = 0;
  void A() throws Exception
  {
    try
    {
      count++;
      try
      {
        count++;
        try
        {
          count++;
          throw new Exception();
        }
        catch(Exception ex)
        {
          count++;
          throw new Exception();
        }
      }
      catch(Exception ex)
      {
        count++;
      }
    }
    catch(Exception ex)
    {
      count++;
    }
  }
  void display()
  {
    System.out.println(count);
  }
  public static void main(String[] args) throws Exception
  {
    Table 1 obj = new Test1();
    obj.A();
    obj.display();
  }
}
```

Output

```
5
```

4. Program to illustrate the handling of string exceptions.

```
class StringExc
{
  String str = "a";
  void A()
  {
    try
    {
      str +="b"; B();
    }
    catch (Exception e)
```

```
        {
            str += "c";
        }
    }
    void B() throws Exception
    {
        try
        {
            str += "d"; C();
        }
        catch(Exception e)
        {
            throw new Exception();
        }
        finally
        {
            str += "e";
        }
        str += "f";
    }
    void C() throws Exception
    {
        throw new Exception();
    }
    void display()
    {   System.out.println(str);
    }
    public static void main(String[] args)
    {
        StringExc object = new StringExc();
        object.A();
        object.display();
    }
}
```

Output

```
Abdec
```

5. Program to illustrate the handling of ArrayIndexOutOfBounds exceptions.

```
class ArrayIndex
{
    public static void main(String[] args)
    {
        try
        {
            int a[]= {1, 2, 3, 4};
            for (int i = 1; i <= 4; i++)
            {
                System.out.
                println ("a["
                + i + "]=" +
                a[i] + "\n");
            }
        }
        catch (Exception e)
        {
            System.out.println ("error = " + e);
        }
    }
}
```

Output

```
a[1]=2
a[2]=3
a[3]=4
error = java.lang.ArrayIndexOutOfBoundsException: 4
```

PROGRAMMING EXERCISES

1. Write a class `Temperature` that converts temperature between fahrenheit (F) and celsius (C). The formulae for conversion between the two units are:
   - fahrenheit = (9.0 * celsius) / 5.0 + 32.0
   - celsius = (fahrenheit – 32.0) * 5.0 / 9.0

   The program should throw an exception of the type `NumberFormatException` if the number of degrees is not a legal floating-point number. The program should check the data from the command line and give suitable feedback.
2. Write a class `Area` that calculates the area of a rectangle, using the following formula: area = length * breadth. The program reads the length (L) and the breadth (B) from the command line. The program should throw a `NumberFormatException` if the sides are not legal values. The program should check the information read from the command line and give suitable feedback.
3. Write a program to implement a `try` and `catch` block.
4. Write a program to implement multiple `catch` clause.
5. Write a program to illustrate the `throws` clause.
6. Write a program to implement the `Arithmetic Exception`.
7. Write a program to implement `ArrayIndexOutOfBoundsException`.
8. Write a program to illustrate the default error handling mechanism.
9. Write a program to illustrate the user defined error handling mechanism.
10. Write a program to handle `ClassCastException`.
11. Read 20 marks and store in an array. Define your own exception in the name `WrongMarkException`. `Throw` and `catch` this type of exception when marks are <0 or marks are >100.
12. Capture all exceptions in a program and print out error messages that describe the type of error that occurred.

CHAPTER

10

Multithreading

Everyone knows about the ability of the human body to do many tasks simultaneously, such as hearing, talking, digesting food and many more. Likewise, a computer with a single processor can create an illusion of concurrent execution of multiple tasks such as playing music, downloading from the internet, sending pages to a printer, copying files from portable drives while typing on the word processor; it is not actually concurrent execution but it switches between processes. However, computers with multiple CPUs have started coming into the market, which actually execute more than one task at a time. Not only does the computer carry out multiple tasks concurrently, almost all modern applications and operating systems perform more than one task at a time. Who wants an application that can perform one task at a time or does them one by one? Sometimes it is better to do more than one task at a time, instead of doing one task very well. A word processing application such as MS Word can do two or more tasks at a time, for instance, while formatting the content it can perform a grammar check simultaneously.

10.1 INTRODUCTION

All modern programmers need to develop applications that can perform many tasks concurrently. Multithreading enables the developer to develop such dynamic applications. All modern computer programming languages support the concept of multithreading. Before getting deeper into the concept, let's understand what actually is a process and what is a thread. A *process* is a program in execution. If a program or a *process* is subdivided into smaller tasks or jobs, each such task is called a *thread*. A single process or a program may have many threads that can run simultaneously and do different tasks at a time. It is done to utilise the CPU time well. The process of running more than one thread concurrently is known as multithreading. Threads are lightweight sub-processes; each thread runs its own independent execution path and shares common memory space. If one thread triggers an exception, it doesn't affect the other threads that are executing concurrently. Table 10.1 differentiates between multithreading, multiprocessing and multitasking.

Table 10.1 Comparison of multitasking, multithreading, multiprocessing

Multitasking	Multithreading	Multiprocessing
• Capacity to run more than one process concurrently in a single CPU environment.	• A single process that contains more than one thread (sub-pro- cesses) running simultaneously is called multithreading.	• It is much like multitasking done with more than one CPU.
• Multitasking may be process-based or thread-based.	• It is a thread-based multitasking.	• It is a process-based multitasking.

Need for threads in programming

- To implement parallel processing.
- To decrease the response time of the application.
- To utilise the CPU idle time.
- To set priority to the tasks.
- To increase the processing speed.

Since we know what multithreading is, we will discuss how threads are supported in Java.

10.2 THREADS IN JAVA

In a single-threaded environment, an exception or I/O request triggered in one thread can cause the entire program to stop or halt. But in a multithreaded environment, one thread can be halted without stopping other threads of the program. In Java, multithreading is achieved using a *thread class* and a *runnable interface*. If the program needs to create a thread, it should either extend the `Thread` class or implement the `Runnable` interface. The `Thread` class provides many methods to manipulate threads. The constructors and methods that are used throughout this chapter are described in Tables 10.2 and 10.3.

Constructors and methods

`Thread` class in `java.lang` package provides many useful constructors and methods that are used for creating and working with threads. Table 10.2 shows the important constructors used in thread creation.

Table 10.2 Constructors in a `Thread` class

S. no.	Constructors of a `Thread` class
1.	`Thread()`
2.	`Thread(String n)`
3.	`Thread(Runnable r)`
4.	`Thread(Runnable r, String n)`

The first type of constructor `Thread()` creates a thread without any parameters, so no values can be passed using this constructor. The second form of the constructor `Thread(String n)` has one string type variable `n` to pass the name for the thread while creating an object. The third form of constructor `Thread(Runnable r)` passes the object of the class that created the thread by implementing the `Runnable` interface. By passing the object to the `Thread` class, the object of the `Thread` class will be used to manipulate the thread. The final form of the thread constructor is used to pass an object of a `Runnable` interface and its name. The third and last forms of the constructor look more or less same; if only `Runnable` object is specified, the third form of the constructor is considered otherwise the fourth form of constructor will be considered.

The important methods possessed by the `Thread` class are given in Table 10.3.

There is a difference in the results of `suspend()` and `sleep()` methods. If a thread is set to sleep for some seconds, it will automatically resume its execution after the sleep time is over, from where it left its execution before the `sleep()` method was invoked. If a thread is suspended using the `suspend()` method, it will not resume its operation automatically as in the `sleep()` method. The suspended thread will wait for the `resume()` method to be invoked to resume its operation from where it left off.

Table 10.3 Methods in a `Thread` class

S. no.	Methods	Description
1.	run()	This method implements the behaviour of a thread.
2.	start()	Starts the execution of a thread by invoking the `run()` method. Once the thread is started, it cannot be restarted again. An attempt to do so will throw an `illegalTheadStateException`.
3.	sleep(long millisec- onds)	Stops the execution of a thread for a specified period of time in milliseconds. (1000 milliseconds is equivalent to 1 second)
4.	join(long milliseconds)	It makes the thread to wait for the specified milliseconds and starts its execution after that.
5.	isAlive()	Checks whether the thread is alive or not. If not, returns False.
6.	yield()	Temporarily pauses the currently executing thread to allow other threads to execute.
7.	suspend()	Suspends the thread.
8.	resume()	Resumes the thread that was suspended.
9.	stop()	Stops the thread from execution.
10.	getPriority()	Returns the current priority of a thread.
11.	setPriority(int priority)	Sets the priority for a thread.
12.	getName()	Returns the name of a thread.
13.	setName(String name)	Sets the name for a thread.
14.	interrupt()	Interrupts the thread.
15.	isInterrupted()	Checks whether the thread has been interrupted or not.
16.	public Thread current- Thread()	Returns the reference of the currently executing thread.

Main thread

Whenever a Java program starts its execution, a default thread of that program automatically starts execution simultaneously. So, what is the default thread? In Java, the execution of a program starts from the class that has the `main()` function. The class that has a `main()` function is also called the *main thread* or default thread. All other threads are called *child threads*. The child threads are instantiated and manipulated in the main thread of a program. As a thread, the main thread can also be controlled using a `Thread` object. To manipulate a main thread, the following method is used:

```
static Thread currentThread()
```

The `currentThread()` method returns the reference of a thread in which it is invoked. Once the reference of a thread is received, it can be controlled. **Program 10.1** demonstrates the manipulation of a main thread.

Program 10.1

```
public class MThread
{
    public static void main(String[] args)
    {
        Thread mt=Thread.currentThread();
        System.out.println("DEFAULT NAME OF THE
        CURRENT THREAD IS: "+mt);
        mt.setName("MOTHER THREAD");
        System.out.println("AFTER SETTING THE NAME
        OF THE CURRENT THREAD : "+mt);
        String name=mt.getName();
        try
        {
            System.out.println(name+" is started its
            execution");
            for(int i=1;i<=10;i++)
            {
                System.out.println("Multithreading in
                JAVA");
                Thread.sleep(2000);
            }
            System.out.println(name+" is completed
            its execution");
        }
        catch(Exception e){System.out.println("An
        Exception has been occurred: "+e);}
    }
}
```

Output 10.1

```
DEFAULT NAME OF THE
CURRENT THREAD IS:
Thread[main,5,main]
AFTER SETTING THE
NAME OF THE CURRENT
THREAD : Thread[MOTHER
THREAD,5,main]
MOTHER THREAD is
started its execution
Multithreading in JAVA
Multithreading in JAVA
Multithreading in JAVA
Multithreading in JAVA
Multithreading in JAVA
Multithreading in JAVA
Multithreading in JAVA
Multithreading in JAVA
Multithreading in JAVA
Multithreading in JAVA
MOTHER THREAD is completed
its execution
```

In Program 10.1, a main thread is referred by invoking the method `currentThread()` and the reference of a current thread (*here current thread is a main thread*) is assigned to the thread object `mt`. Before setting the name for a current thread, the `println()` method displays the following message 'Thread[main,5,main]'. The first `main` is the name of the current thread, 5 is its priority and the second main is the name of the thread group.

The name for the thread can be changed at any time; to change the name of a current thread, the `setName()` method of a `Thread` class is called with MOTHER THREAD as a parameter. In the very next statement, the changed name of the current thread is then retrieved using `getName()` method and stored in a string type variable `name`. The changed name of the thread is then displayed.

The `try...catch` block is used to handle the `InterrruptedException`, because the `sleep()` method called inside the `try...catch` block may cause the thread to pause for a certain amount of time. Inside the `try...catch` block, the `for` loop has been declared to print a string 'Multithreading in JAVA' 10 times. After printing the string, the thread will be paused for 2 seconds. This is achieved using `sleep(2000)` method of the `Thread` class. So, in each iteration of the `for` loop, the string is displayed and the thread is paused for 2 seconds, after which it resumes its execution. It is repeated until `i` reaches 10. In this section, a thread is introduced with the main thread and in Section 10.4 the life cycle of a thread is illustrated using two threads, the main thread and one child thread.

10.3 THREAD CREATION

Java is a multi-thread programming language; its multithreading capability is supported by the built-in libraries which enable the programmer to develop applications that can support parallel processing. In Java, a thread can be created by the following two ways, using which, any class can become a thread.

- By implementing the `Runnable` interface.
- By extending the `Thread` class.

10.3.1 Creating a Thread by Implementing `Runnable` Interface

The simplest way of creating a thread is by implementing a `Runnable` interface. At a time, any number of threads can be created in a program using a `Runnable` interface. The following basic steps will help to develop a thread by implementing Runnable interface.

STEP 1: As a first step, the thread should be created through implementing a `Runnable` interface. The format for creating a thread is given below:

Syntax:

```
public class class_name implements Runnable
{
}
```

Example,

```
public class RT implements Runnable
{
}
```

where `RT` is the name of the class that is going to become a thread by implementing a `Runnable` interface.

STEP 2: Define a `run()` method inside the thread. The `run()` method can be used only after implementing the `Runnable` interface. Just like other ordinary methods, the `run()` method can also access other classes and methods, declare variables. The actual code that represents the functionality of a thread is introduced by a `run()` method and it is also the entry point for that thread. The syntax is given below:

Syntax:

```
public void run()
{
    Code for a thread
}
```

Example,

```
public void run()
{
    for(int i=1;i<=10i++)
    {
        System.out.println(i" * 6 =" +i * 6);
    }
}
```

STEP 3: Place the `run()` method inside the class which implements a `Runnable` interface.
Example,

```
public class RT implements Runnable
{
    public void run()
    {
        for (int i=1;i<=10i++)
        {
            System.out.println(i" * 6 =" +i * 6);
        }
    }
}
```

STEP 4: Next is to instantiate a `Thread` class inside the `main()` method and use that object to execute a thread. It has the following steps:

- Create an object for the class that implements the `Runnable` interface.
- Pass the object as a parameter using one of the thread constructors given below, while creating a thread object.

The instantiation can be done using any one of the following two thread constructors.

1. `Thread(Runnable r)`
2. `Thread(Runnable r, String n)`

where `r` is the object of a class that implements `Runnable` interface and `n` is the name given for the newly created thread. The following examples exhibit the use of constructors in creating Thread objects.

Example 1: Using the first constructor

```
public class Firstthread
{
    public static void main(String[] args)
    {
        RT r=new RT();
        Thread t=new Thread(r); //passing the instance of Runnable
        t.start();
    }
}
```

Example 2: Using the second constructor

```
public class Firstthread
{
    public static void main(String[] args)
    {
        RT r=new RT();
        Thread t=new Thread(r,DEMO); //passing the instance of Runnable with name
        t.start();
    }
}
```

Example 3: Explicitly passing the object creation as parameter

```
public class Firstthread
{
    public static void main(String[] args)
    {
        Thread t=new Thread(new RT());
        t.start();
    }
}
```

Program 10.2 has been developed using the above steps to generate a multiplication table for the number 6.

Program 10.2

```
class RT implements Runnable
{
    public void run()
    {
        System.out.println("Thread started its execution");
        for(int i=1;i<=10;i++)
        {
            System.out.println(i+" * 6 = "+i*6);
        }
        System.out.println("Thread completed its execution");
    }
}
public class Firstthread
{
    public static void main(String[] args)
    {
        RT r=new RT();
        Thread t=new Thread(r);
        t.start();
    }
}
```

Output 10.2

```
Thread started
its execution
1 * 6 = 6
2 * 6 = 12
3 * 6 = 18
4 * 6 = 24
5 * 6 = 30
6 * 6 = 36
7 * 6 = 42
8 * 6 = 48
9 * 6 = 54
10 * 6 = 60
Thread completed
its execution
```

In Program 10.2, a class `RT` has become a thread by implementing a `Runnable` interface. A particular behaviour of a class is defined in the methods of that class. Likewise, the behaviour or business logic of the thread is defined in the `run()` method. Whatever the thread is expected to perform must be placed inside the `run()` method. Here, the `run()` method is expected to generate the multiplication table of 6, up to 10 times. Inside the `main()` thread or class, an instantiation takes place. First the object `r` for the class `RT` which implements the `Runnable` interface is created and passed as a parameter to the thread constructor while creating object `t` for the `Thread` class. With thread object `t` a `start()` method is invoked which in turn calls the `run()` method of `RT` class. As soon as it is called, the multiplication table is generated and displayed. **Program 10.3** demonstrates executing a thread by directly calling `run()` method or through the `start()` method.

Program 10.3

```
class first implements Runnable
{
   public void run()
   {
      try
      {
         for(int i=1;i<=5;i++)
         { Thread.sleep(1000);
            System.out.println(i);
         }
      }
      catch(Exception e){System.out.println("An
      Exception has been occurred: "+e);}
   }
}
public class STRunnable
{
   public static void main(String[] args)
   {
      first f1=new first();
      Thread t1=new Thread(f1);
      Thread t2=new Thread(new first());
      /*
         t1.start();
         t2.start();
      */
      t1.run();
      t2.run();
   }
}
```

Output 10.3

```
Run - 1 directly calling
run() method
1
2
3
4
5
1
2
3
4
5
Run - 2 calling run()
method through start()
method
1
1
2
2
3
3
4
4
5
5
```

In Program 10.3, two threads are created—`main` and `first` thread. The `main` thread is the default thread or mother thread and the *first* thread is a child thread. The *first* thread is created by implementing a `Runnable` interface. The entire operation of the *first* thread is contained within the `run()` method. The `run()` method of the *first* thread prints the numbers from 1 to 5 through a `for` loop. The entire code is written inside the `try...catch` block to handle the interrupted exception caused by the `sleep()` method. In each iteration, the thread is put in the sleep stage and it resumes after 1 second and prints another number and again gets back to sleep for 1 second. This cycle will go on until the `i` value of the `for` loop reaches the MAX limit 5. Once it reaches the maximum limit of the loop, the program will be terminated. In the *main* thread, two objects `t1`, `t2` are created. Using these two objects, the `run()` method and `start()` method are called one after the other. The output shows the difference of calling the `run()` method and `start()` method. In *Run-1,* the `run()` method of the *first* thread is called using objects `t1` and `t2` one after the other. It produces the result just like calling the methods; no parallel processing is achieved. So, the result is displayed in a sequential order. In *Run-2*, the objects `t1` and `t2` call `run()` through the `start()` method of a `Thread` class, so the results are displayed in parallel. To see the change in output, just remove the comments before the statements and execute again. In **Program 10.4**, two threads have been created by implementing `Runnable` interface namely `Th1` and `Th2`. The first thread `Th1` will produce the area of circle results and the second thread `Th2` will generate the square values through looping.

Program 10.4

```
class Th1 implements Runnable
{
    public void run()
    {
        try
        {
            System.out.println("First Thread started its execution");
            for(int i=1;i<=6;i++)
            {
                if(i==4)
                {
                    System.out.println("First Thread is
                    sleeping...");
                    Thread.sleep(10000);
                    System.out.println("First Thread
                    resumed its execution");
                }
                System.out.println("Area of circle
                for the radius value:" + i +" is " +
                3.14*(i*i));
            }
        }
        catch(Exception e)
        {
            System.out.println("An Exception has
            occurred
            ="+e);
        }
    }
}
class Th2 implements Runnable
{
    public void run()
    {
        try
        {
            System.out.println("Second Thread started
            its execution...");
            for(int i=1;i<=5;i++)
            {
                System.out.println("The Square value
                of "+ i +"
                is "+ Math.pow(i, i));
            }
            System.out.println("Second Thread
            completed its execution");
        }
        catch(Exception e)
        {
            System.out.println("An Exception has been occurred ="+e);
        }
    }
}
```

Output 10.4

```
First Thread started its
execution
Area of circle for the
radius value:1 is 3.14
Area of circle for the
radius value:2 is 12.56
Area of circle for the
radius value:3 is 28.26
First Thread is
sleeping... Second Thread
started its execution...
The Square value of 1 is
1.0
The Square value of 2 is
4.0
The Square value of 3 is
27.0
The Square value of 4 is
256.0
The Square value of 5 is
3125.0
Second Thread completed
its execution
First_Thread resumed its
execution
Area of circle for the
radius value:4 is 50.24
Area of circle for the
radius value:5 is 78.5
Area of circle for the
radius value:6 is 113.04
```

```
public class RTdemo
{
    public static void main(String[] args)
    {
        Th1 t1=new Th1();
        Th2 t2=new Th2();
        Thread tc1=new Thread(t1);
        Thread tc2=new Thread(t2);
        tc1.start();
        tc2.start();
    }
}
```

Both threads are created with `Runnable` interfaces. So, each thread should pass its object through the thread constructor to start its execution. Because the `start()` method belongs to `Thread` class, a thread created by implementing `Runnable` interface cannot start its execution without the `Thread` class. First thread `Th1` computes the area of the circle for each iteration value in the `for` loop; this is the actual operation of a thread and the code for this operation is placed inside the `run()` method. The `run()` method shall be invoked through the `start()` method of a `Thread` class. When the `i` value reaches 4, the sleep (10000) method shall be invoked and the thread will be sent to the waiting state or non-runnable state for 10 seconds (1000 milliseconds equivalent to 1 second). After the sleep time is over, the first thread resumes its execution from where it left off before sleep. The second thread starts its execution while the first thread is in sleep for 10 seconds, and completes its execution. Inside the `run()` method of the second thread, a square value for each iteration of the `for` loop is calculated. This depicts the way to develop a thread using a `Runnable` interface. The next section exhibits how the thread can be created using the `Thread` class.

10.3.2 Creating a Thread by Extending the `Thread` Class

The second way to create a thread is by extending a `Thread` class. The class which extends the `Thread` class will become a subclass. The `Thread` class is contained in the package `java.lang.Thread`. The `Thread` class also inherits other classes and interfaces. The inheritance of `Thread` class is given below:

```
public class Thread extends object implements Runnable
```

From creation to execution, thread creation has the following steps:

STEP 1: Create a class by extending a `Thread` class, then this class will become a thread. The syntax for creating a thread by extending a `Thread` class is given below:

Syntax:

```
class class_name extends Thread
{
}
```

Example,

```
class Demo extends Thread
{
}
```

STEP 2: Override the `run()` method of a `Thread` class and place it inside the class which extends the `Thread` class as follows:

Syntax:

```
public void run()
{
    code for the thread
}
```

Example,

```
class Demo extends Thread
{
    public void run()
    {
        for(int i=1;i<=5;i++)
        {
            System.out.println("Multi-threading");
        }
    }
}
```

STEP 3: Create an object for the thread inside the `main()` method. One thing should be noted is that any number of objects can be created for a given thread. The syntax for creating an object is given below:

Syntax:

```
class_name object = new class_name();
```

Example,

```
public class Firstthread
{
    public static void main(String[] args)
    {
        Demo t=new Demo();
    }
}
```

STEP 4: Invoke the `start()` method through the object of the `Thread` class to execute the `run()` method of a thread.

Syntax:

```
public void start()
```

Example,

```
public class Firstthread
{
    public static void main(String[] args)
    {
        Demo t1=new Demo();
        Demo t2=new Demo();
        t1.start();
        t2.start();
    }
}
```

Program 10.5 creates a thread that prints a string for a specified period of time, using the above mentioned steps.

Program 10.5

```
class Demo extends Thread
{
   public void run()
   {
      System.out.println("Thread started its execution");
      for(int i=1;i<=5;i++)
      {
         System.out.println("Multi-threading");
      }
      System.out.printIn("Thread completed its
      execution");
   }
}
public class Firstthread
{
   public static void main(String[] args)
   {
      Demo t1=new Demo();
      Demo t2=new Demo();
      t1.start();
      t2.start();
   }
}
```

Output 10.5

```
Thread started its
execution
Multi-threading
Multi-threading
Multi-threading
Multi-threading
Multi-threading
Thread completed its
execution
Thread started its
execution
Multi-threading
Multi-threading
Multi-threading
Multi-threading
Multi-threading
Thread completed its
execution
```

Here, the name of the `Thread` class is `Demo` and it is created by extending a `Thread` class. The code that represents the functionality of a thread is given in the `run()` method. As already mentioned, just like other methods, a `run()` method can also access other methods and classes. The `run()` method can be invoked by the object of this class. If so, it doesn't employ the multithreading concept and it produces results just like other methods defined in the class. The `start()` method of the `Thread` class helps to execute the `run()` method in a multithreaded way. A single thread may have any number of objects and each object has its own execution path. To execute a thread, create an object of a class that extends the `Thread` class in a main thread and call the `start()` method with that object. Here two objects are created for a Demo thread, namely, `t1, t2` and each object triggers the `start()` method to send a call to the `run()` method of the Demo thread. As soon as a `run()` method is called, it displays the message `Multi-threading` for 5 times, twice.

In **Program 10.6**, two threads namely `thread1` and `thread2` are created by extending `Thread` class. `Thread1` will generate the multiplication table of 5 and `Thread2` will generate the multiplication table of 2.

Program 10.6

```
class Thread1 extends Thread
{
   public void run()
   {
      try
      {
         System.out.println("First Thread started its execution");
```

```
            for(int i=1;i<=10;i++)
            {
                if(i==6)
                {
                    System.out.println("First Thread is sleeping...");
                    Thread.sleep(20000);
                    System.out.println("First Thread resumed its execution");
                }
                System.out.println(i +" * 5 =" + i * 5);
            }
        }
        catch(Exception e)
        {
            System.out.println("An Exception has been
            occurred ="+e);
        }
    }
}
class Thread2 extends Thread
{
    public void run()
    {
        try
        {
            System.out.println("Second Thread started
            its execution...");
            for(int i=1;i<=10;i++)
            {
                System.out.println(i +" * 2 =" + i * 2);
            }
            System.out.println("Second Thread
            completed its execution");
        }
        catch(Exception e)
        {
            System.out.println("An Exception has been
            occurred ="+e);
        }
    }
}
public class Tdemo
{
    public static void main(String[] args)
    {
        Thread1 t1=new Thread1();
        Thread2 t2=new Thread2();
        t1.start();
        t2.start();
    }
}
```

Output 10.6

```
First Thread started its
execution
1 * 5 =5
2 * 5 =10
3 * 5 =15
4 * 5 =20
5 * 5 =25
First Thread is sleeping...
Second Thread started its
execution...
1 * 2 =2
2 * 2 =4
3 * 2 =6
4 * 2 =8
5 * 2 =10
6 * 2 =12
7 * 2 =14
8 * 2 =16
9 * 2 =18
10 * 2 =20
Second Thread completed its
execution
First Thread resumed its
execution
6 * 5 =30
7 * 5 =35
8 * 5 =40
9 * 5 =45
10 * 5 =50
```

The first thread, `Thread1` is created by extending the `Thread` class. `Thread1` overrides the `run()` method which represents the actual code of a thread. Inside a `run()` method of the first thread, a `for` loop has been declared for generating the multiplication table of 5. Once the value of the variable `i` reaches 6, the `sleep()` method of the `Thread` class will be invoked for 20 seconds (1000 milliseconds is equivalent to 1 second) and it will be sent to the waiting state. During the sleeping time of the first thread, the second thread starts its execution. After the sleep time is over, the first thread resumes its execution and completes the remaining portion. The second thread, `Thread2` is created by extending the `Thread` class. The second thread also overrides the `run()` method. Inside the `run()` method of the second thread, a `for` loop is declared for generating the multiplication table of 2. Unlike the first thread, the second thread completes its execution without sleep. One thing that must be noted is that the second thread can start its execution only after calling the `sleep()` method in the first thread. If the sleep time is changed, the execution of the second thread may change little bit. A `try... catch` block is used inside the `run()` method of the first thread to handle the interrupted exception. Even though the `run()` method represents the actual logic of a thread, without the `start()` method of a `Thread` class, a thread cannot start execution. The objects of the first and second thread will invoke the execution through the `run()` method by calling the `start()` method. **Program 10.7** demonstrates how an exception that occurs in one thread will not affect the execution of other threads.

Program 10.7

```
class MT extends Thread
{
    public void run()
    {
      float t=15/0;
      System.out.println(t);
    }
}
class FIB extends Thread
{
    public void run()
    {
      System.out.println("second thread:Fibonacci
      series started its execution");
      int f=0, s=1 ,t, i, MAX=10;
      System.out.println(f+"\n"+s);
      for(i=2;i<MAX;i++)
      {
          try
          {
              if(i==7)
              {
                  System.out.println("The second
                  thread is sleeping for 10
                  seconds......");
                  Thread.sleep (10000);
                  System.out.println("The second
                  thread resumed its execution");
              }
          }
          catch(Exception e){System.out.println("An
          Exception has occurred = "+e);}
          t=f+s;
          System.out.println(t);
          f=s;
          s=t;
      }
    }
}
```

Output 10.7

```
Exception in thread
"Thread-0" java.lang.
ArithmeticException: / by
zero
at MT.run(ThreadE. java:17)
second thread:Fibonacci
series started its
execution
0
1
1
2
3
5
8
The second thread
is sleeping for 10
seconds......
The second thread resumed
its execution
13
21
34
```

```
public class ThreadE
{
    public static void main(String[] args)
    {
        MT m1=new MT();
        m1.start();
        FIB f1=new FIB();
        f1.start();
    }
}
```

In this program, three threads have been created, namely, `MT`, `FIB` and the main thread `ThreadE`. Inside the `run()` method of the first thread `MT`, code has been added to trigger an exception due to division by zero. The second thread `FIB` is created to genérate the Fibonacci series, where the maximum limit to generate the series is set to 10 in the variable `MAX` and the two initial values of the series are given as constants and displayed first. The remaining series will be displayed through looping. When the `i` value of the `for` loop reaches 7, the thread sleeps for 10 seconds, resumes after 10 seconds and completes its balance task. The objects `m1`, `f1` for the `MT` and `FIB` threads are created in the main thread. First the `MT` thread is called through its object `m1` and its execution starts but ends in an exception. The second thread is called using the object `f1` and its execution is started, even though the first thread ended in an exception; that doesn't affect the execution of the second thread `FIB`. Hence the second thread finished its execution without any interruption. However, this will not work in a single-threaded program as the exception will cause the entire program to stop.

10.3.3 Thread Class vs Runnable Interface

The `Thread` class and `Runnable` interface, both are used for creating a thread in Java. But there is a marked difference in the way they are implemented and the results they produce. Table 10.4 shows a comparison between the two.

Table 10.4 Thread class vs Runnable interface

Thread class	Runnable interface
Once a class extends a `Thread` class to create a thread, it cannot extend other classes after that, because Java does not support multiple inheritance.	The class which implements a `Runnable` interface to create a thread has more space for inheriting other classes. So, it allows multiple inheritance.
Each access has its own object. So, for each access a separate object should be created.	It shares the same object across multiple accesses.
Multiple object creation consumes more memory.	Sharing the same object reduces memory overheads.
The code is tightly coupled.	The code is loosely coupled.

10.3.4 Choosing a Method for Thread Creation

- If the class needs to inherit more than one class, it is better to create a thread by implementing the `Runnable` interface.
- If the programmer wants to pass `Runnable` to any other thread or thread pool, then `Runnable` interface is a good choice.

- If the thread is going to use only `run()`, implement it with the `Runnable` interface. This is because the `Thread` class not only overrides the `run()` method, it overrides all the methods in the `Thread` class.
- If the programmer needs to reuse the `run()`, it is better to opt for the `Runnable` interface.

Program 10.8 demonstrates the difference in the use of the `Thread` class and `Runnable` interface for thread creation.

Program 10.8

```
class TRunnable implements Runnable
{
    int n = 0;
    public void run()
    {
        n++;
        System.out.println("Through Runnable Interface: " + n);
    }
}
class TThreadClass extends Thread
{
    int n = 0;
    public void run()
    {
        n++;
        System.out.println("Through Extending Thread class: " + n);
    }
}
public class TCvsRI
{
    public static void main(String[] args) throws
    InterruptedException
    {
        //Multiple threads share the same object.
        TRunnable run = new TRunnable();
        Thread RI1 = new Thread(run);
        RI1.start();
        Thread.sleep(1000);
        Thread RI2 = new Thread(run);
        RI2.start();
        Thread.sleep(1000);
        Thread RI3 = new Thread(run);
        RI3.start();
        //Creating new instance for every thread access. TThreadClass tc1 = new
        TThreadClass();
        tc1.start();
        Thread.sleep(1000);
        TThreadClass tc2 = new TThreadClass();
        tc2.start();
        Thread.sleep(1000);
        TThreadClass tc3 = new TThreadClass();
        tc3.start();
    }
}
```

Output 10.8

```
Through Runnable Interface:
1
Through Runnable Interface:
2
Through Runnable Interface:
3
Through Extending Thread
class: 1
Through Extending Thread
class: 1
Through Extending Thread
class: 1
```

Using the `Runnable` interface, only one object `run` of a class `TRunnable` is created and shared by several threads such as `RI1`, `RI2` and `RI3`. So, the counter value is increased for every thread access.

While using the `Thread` class, separate objects `tc1`, `tc2` and `tc3` need to be created for every class instance and each has a separate counter, so the value remains the same and there is no increase in the value of the counter. In the next section, the life cycle of a thread will be discussed.

10.4 LIFE CYCLE OF A THREAD

As a sub-process, a thread also has its own life cycle stages. Every thread should go through these life cycle stages until it is destroyed. According to the specifications of Sun Java, there are only four states in the life cycle of a thread in Java, namely *new, runnable, non-runnable* and *terminated.* So, there is no *running* state in a thread as per the specifications of Sun Java. The life cycle of a thread is controlled by the JVM (Java Virtual Machine) in Java.

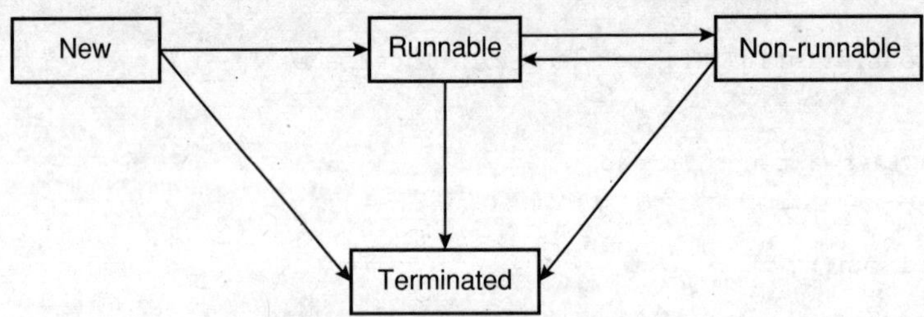

Fig. 10.1 Life cycle of a thread

In Fig. 10.1 the thread enters the life cycle, through the *new* state and when it is starts executing, it enters into the *runnable* state. During execution, a thread can be sent to the *non-runnable* state when it is paused using `sleep()` method or suspended for an I/O operation. A thread can move from a non-runnable to a runnable state when the sleep time is over or when it has completed its task. A thread can be terminated from the new, runnable or non-runnable states when it calls the `stop()` method or completes its execution.

Program 10.9 demonstrates the life cycle of a thread with two threads, one is a main thread and another is a child thread that is created by extending a `Thread` class.

Program 10.9

```
class chThread extends Thread
{
    public void run()
    {
        try
        {
            System.out.println("Thread started its execution");
            for(int i=1;i<=10;i++)
            {
                if(i==5)
                {
                    System.out.println("Thread is paused for 10 seconds");
                    Thread.sleep(10000); // Enters Non-runnable state
                    System.out.println("Thread resumed its execution");
                }
```

```
            System.out.println(i+i);
            // returns to Runnable state
          }
          System.out.println("Completed its
          execution.");
          // thread terminated
        }
        catch(Exception e){System.out.println("An
        Exception has occurred: "+e);}
    }
}
public class ThreadLC
{
    public static void main(String[] args)
    {
        chThread t=new chThread(); // Enters into
        the New state
        t.setName("CHILD THREAD");
        System.out.println("DEFAULT NAME OF THE
        CHILD THREAD IS: "+t);
        String name=t.getName();
        System.out.println("AFTER SETTING THE NAME
        OF THE CHILD THREAD : "+name);
        t.start(); // Enters into the runnable
        state
    }
}
```

Output 10.9

```
DEFAULT NAME OF THE CHILD
THREAD IS: Thread[CHILD
THREAD,5,main]
AFTER SETTING THE NAME OF
THE CHILD THREAD : CHILD
THREAD
Thread started its
execution
2
4
6
8
Thread is paused for 10
seconds
Thread resumed its
execution
10
12
14
16
18
20
Completed its execution.
```

In Program 10.9, the thread object is created with the statement `chThread t = new chThread();` it enters into the new stage or the 'born' stage. In the new stage, only the object is created with memory and the thread is still in an inactive state. Once the thread object `t` invokes the method `start()` with the statement `t.start()`, then the thread enters into the *runnable* state and the very first job it does after entering is to start its execution with a call of `run()` method. From the runnable stage, a thread may be sent to the *non-runnable* stage or blocked stage when the thread object `t` calls the `sleep()` method with the statement `t.sleep()`. During the non-runnable stage, a thread will become inactive.

When either sleep() or wait() method is called or is blocked for I/O, the thread will become non-runnable. A thread may return from the non-runnable stage once the sleep time is over. A thread may be terminated or destroyed when the thread object `t` invokes the `stop()` from any of the life cycle stages or dies when `run()` method exists.

10.5 JOINING A THREAD

A `sleep()` method makes a thread wait for some specified seconds in a non-runnable state to send the currently running thread to a waiting state, for other threads to complete their task. But how does one thread know whether another thread has finished its task or whether to make the current thread wait until other threads finish their task. In Java, one thread can know the execution status of other threads by using two different methods `isAlive()` and `join()`. Table 10.5 shows the difference between these two methods.

Table 10.5 Comparison of `isAlive()` and `join()` methods

`isAlive()` method	`join()` method
• It returns either *True* or *False*. • *True* when a thread upon which it is called is still running. • *False* when a thread upon which it is called has finished execution.	• It is used more frequently than `isAlive()` method. • Unlike `isAlive()` method, this method waits for the current thread for a defined period of time until the specified thread finishes its execution.

In **Program 10.10**, two threads are created by extending the `Thread` class, namely `th1` and `th2`. The first thread `th1` will display the message `Multithreaded programming` for a specified time period. Like the first thread, a second will also produce the message `Single threaded programming` for a specified period of time. The method `isAlive()` is used to know the execution status of both threads.

Program 10.10

```
class th1 extends Thread
{
    public void run()
    {
        try
        {
            for(int i=1;i<=5;i++)
            {
                if(i==3)
                {
                    System.out.println("1st thread will sleep for 5 seconds");
                    Thread.sleep(5000);
                    System.out.println("1st thread resumed its execution");
                }
                System.out.println("Multithreaded programming");
            }
        }
        catch(Exception e)
        {
            System.out.println("An Exception has occurred ="+e);
        }
    }
}
class th2 extends Thread
{
    public void run()
    {
        try
        {
            for(int i=1;i<=5;i++)
            {
                if(i==3)
                {
                    System.out.println("2nd thread will sleep for 15 seconds");
                    Thread.sleep(15000);
                    System.out.println("2nd thread resumed its execution");
                }
```

```
            System.out.println("Single threaded programming");
        }
      }
      catch(Exception e)
      {
         System.out.println("An Exception has occurred ="+e);
      }
   }
}
public class ISALIVE
{
   public static void main(String[] args)
   {
      th1 t1=new th1();
      th2 t2=new th2();
      if(t1.isAlive())
      {
         System.out.println(t1.isAlive() +" First
         thread is executing");
      }
      else
      {
         System.out.println(t1.isAlive()+" First
         thread is waiting or finished execution");
      }
      t1.start();
      if(t1.isAlive())
      {
         System.out.println(t1.isAlive() +" First
         thread is executing");
      }
      else
      {
         System.out.println(t1.isAlive()+" First
         thread is waiting or finished execution");
      }
      if(t2.isAlive())
      {
         System.out.println(t2.isAlive()+" Second
         thread is executing");
      }
      else
      {
         System.out.println(t2.isAlive()+" Second
         thread is waiting or finished execution");
      }
      t2.start();
      if(t2.isAlive())
      {
         System.out.println(t2.isAlive()+" Second thread is executing");
      }
      else
      {
         System.out.println(t2.isAlive()+" Second thread is waiting or finished
         execution");
      }
   }
}
```

Output 10.10

```
false First thread is
waiting or finished
execution
true First thread is
executing
false Second thread
is waiting or finished
execution
true Second thread is
executing
Multithreaded programming
Multithreaded programming
1st thread will sleep for 5
seconds
Single threaded programming
Single threaded programming
2nd thread will sleep for
15 seconds
1st thread resumed its
execution
Multithreaded programming
Multithreaded programming
Multithreaded programming
2nd thread resumed its
execution
Single threaded programming
Single threaded programming
Single threaded programming
```

The order of execution of the threads may vary from system to system or time to time, based on which the scheduling policy is implemented to dispatch the thread to the processor. Here, two threads have been created by extending the `Thread` class, namely `th1` and `th2`. The first thread `th1` will display a string 'Multithreaded programming' for a specified number of times through looping. Likewise, the second thread `th2` will also output the string 'Single threaded programming' for a specified number of times through looping. Objects for these threads have been declared in `Main()` thread `t1(th1` thread) and `t2(th2` thread). Before starting the first thread `th1`, it is checked by `isAlive()` method to verify whether the thread is alive or not, with an `if .. else` ladder. As the first thread has not been started, it will display `false First thread is waiting or finished execution`. After invoking `start()` method through `t1` object, it will display `true First thread is executing`. Once again `isAlive()` is applied for the second thread `th2` before invoking the `start()` method through its object. It will display `false Second thread is waiting or finished execution.` Once the `start()` method is invoked through an object, it will display `true Second thread is executing`. The first thread will display a string twice before going to sleep for 5 seconds. Once the first thread gets into the waiting state for 5 seconds, the second thread will start its execution and display its string twice. And then the second thread also sleeps for 5 seconds. Once the sleep time of both threads is over one by one, they will finish their remaining executions.

Program 10.11 has been developed without a `join()` method. The program is the same as Program

Program 10.11

```
class th1 extends Thread
{
   public void run()
   {
      try
      {
         for(int i=1;i<=5;i++)
         {
            if(i==3)
            {
               System.out.println("1st thread
               will sleep for 5 seconds");
               Thread.sleep(5000);
               System.out.println("1st thread
               resumed its execution");
            }
            System.out.println("Multithreaded
            programming");
         }
         System.out.println("1st thread has
         finished its execution");
      }
      catch(Exception e)
      {
         System.out.println("An Exception has
         been occurred ="+e);
      }
   }
}
```

Output 10.11

```
Multithreaded programming
Multithreaded programming
1st thread will sleep for 5
seconds
Single threaded programming
Single threaded programming
Single threaded programming
Single threaded programming
Single threaded programming
1st thread resumed its
execution
Multithreaded programming
Multithreaded programming
Multithreaded programming
1st thread has finished its
execution
```

```
class th2 extends Thread
{
   public void run()
   {
      for(int i=1;i<=5;i++)
      {
         System.out.println("Single threaded programming");
      }
   }
}
public class WOJOIN
{
   public static void main(String[] args)
   {
      th1 t1=new th1();
      th2 t2=new th2();
      t1.start();
      t2.start();
   }
}
```

The objects `t1` and `t2` are created for threads `th1` and `th2` respectively. Both threads are started through their objects one after the other. Soon after the first thread started its execution through `run()` method, it displays a string for a specified number of times until the iterative value reaches 3, when `sleep()` is invoked. Soon after the `sleep()` method is invoked, the first thread will be sent for the waiting stage for 5 seconds. During the waiting time, the second thread `th2` will initiate its execution. The second thread finishes its execution without stopping anywhere. Once the sleep time of the first thread is over, it will resume and finish its remaining execution. **Program10.12** is just like the previous one, but developed with the `join()` method.

Program 10.12

```
class th1 extends Thread
{
   public void run()
   {
      try
      {
         for(int i=1;i<=5;i++)
         {
            if(i==3)
            {
               System.out.println("1st thread will sleep for 5 seconds");
               Thread.sleep(5000);
               System.out.println("1st thread resumed its execution");
            }
            System.out.println("Multithreaded programming");
         }
         System.out.println("1st thread has finished its execution");
      }
      catch(Exception e)
      {
         System.out.println("An Exception has occurred ="+e);
      }
   }
}
```

```
class th2 extends Thread
{
    public void run()
    {
        System.out.println("2nd thread started its execution");
        for(int i=1;i<=5;i++)
        {
            System.out.println("Single threaded
            programming");
        }
        System.out.println("2nd thread finished its
        execution");
    }
}
public class JOINT
{
    public static void main(String[] args)
    {
        th1 t1=new th1();
        th2 t2=new th2();t1.start();
        try
        {
            t1.join(6000);
        }
        catch(Exception e){System.out.println("An
        exception has been occurred"+e);}
        t2.start();
    }
}
```

Output 10.12

```
Multithreaded programming
Multithreaded programming
1st thread will sleep for 5
seconds
1st thread resumed its
execution
Multithreaded programming
Multithreaded programming
Multithreaded programming
1st thread has finished its
execution
2nd thread started its
execution
Single threaded programming
Single threaded programming
Single threaded programming
Single threaded programming
Single threaded programming
2nd thread finished its
execution
```

The objects `t1` and `t2` are created for threads `th1` and `th2` respectively. The first thread `th1` is started through its object `t1` by calling the `start()` method. Soon after starting the first thread, a string 'Multithread programming' is displayed twice and then the `if` condition is checked with iterative value == 3. If the condition is true, `sleep()` is invoked for 6000 milliseconds (6 seconds), so the execution of the first thread is stopped for 6 seconds. The second thread `th2` will not start its execution, because the `join()` method is invoked through the object `t1` of the first thread `th1`. The `join()` lets the first thread complete its execution for the specified time. Soon after that, the second thread initiates its execution. Let's compare the outputs of Programs 10.6 and 10.7 to realise the difference of implementing `join()`. Table 10.6 compares the outputs of Programs 10.6 and 10.7.

Table 10.6 Comparison of the outputs of Programs 10.6 and 10.7

Program 10.6 (*without* `join()` *method*)	**Program 10.7 (*using* `join()` *method*)**
Multithreaded programming	Multithreaded programming
Multithreaded programming	Multithreaded programming
1st thread will sleep for 5 seconds	1st thread will sleep for 5 seconds
Single threaded programming	1st thread resumed its execution
Single threaded programming	Multithreaded programming
Single threaded programming	Multithreaded programming
Single threaded programming	Multithreaded programming

(Continued)

Table 10.6 *(Continued)*

Program 10.6 (*without* `join()` *method*)	**`Program 10.7` (*using* `join()` *method*)**
Single threaded programming	1st thread has finished its execution
1st thread resumed its execution	2nd thread started its execution
Multithreaded programming	Single threaded programming
Multithreaded programming	Single threaded programming
Multithreaded programming	Single threaded programming
1st thread has finished its execution	Single threaded programming
	Single threaded programming
	2nd thread finished its execution
On the left hand side, in the output of Program 10.6, the first thread started its execution and displayed a string twice and then went into a waiting state for 5 seconds. Soon after that the second thread started and finished its execution. After the sleep time is over the first thread resumes its execution.	The first thread started its execution (just like in Program 10.6) and displayed a string twice and went into a waiting state for 5 seconds. Here the difference is, instead of starting the second thread, the first thread resumes its execution after sleep time is over, because of the `join()` method. After the execution of the first thread, the second thread actually starts its execution for the first time and finishes it without stopping.

The next section discusses scheduler in detail.

10.6 THREAD SCHEDULER AND PRIORITY

Scheduling a thread is one of the jobs of a JVM (Java Virtual Machine). It is difficult to determine which thread in a runnable state will be chosen for execution. A preemptive scheduling or a time slice scheduling policy is primarily used by the thread scheduler to choose threads from runnable states for execution. At a time, only one thread in a process will be executed.

Table 10.7 **Comparison of scheduling policies**

Preemptive scheduling policy	**Time slice scheduling policy**
A higher priority thread will be executed first, until it is moved to a non-runnable state or until another higher priority thread comes into existence.	A thread is chosen based on a round robin scheme. A thread is allowed to execute only for a fixed period of time. After that it must be moved to a non-runnable state. The thread scheduler then decides which thread is the next to be moved to runnable state, based on some factors.

The operating system is used to assign priority for a process to be allocated to the processor. The process which has the highest priority will be scheduled first to the processor by the process scheduler. Like a process, a thread can also be assigned priority using the `setPriority()` method. The `Thread` class provides three constants such as `MAX_PRIORITY`, `MIN_PRIORITY` and `NORM_PRIORITY` to specify the priorities for the threads. Normally, priorities are represented from 1 to 10. `MIN_PRIORITY` has a default value of 1 and `MAX_PRIORITY` has 10, `NORM_PRIORITY` has a thread priority of 5.

The thread scheduler first chooses the thread that has the highest priority. The lowest priority thread will be suspended when the higher priority thread newly arrives or wakes up from sleep. If a thread is set at `MIN_PRIORITY` even though it is started first with `start()` method, the higher priority thread is scheduled first, pushing `MIN_PRIORITY` to next. For instance, thread A is set priority of `MIN_PRIORITY` and thread B is set a priority of `MAX_PRIORITY`. Even though the thread A is invoked by the `start()` method first, it will not be executed. Instead of executing thread A, the JVM chooses the thread B which has `MAX_ PRIORITY`. So, thread A will start its execution only after all the higher priority threads have been executed. In **Program 10.13,** two threads have been created. `MT` is the first thread which generates the multiplication table of 6 and `FIB` is the second thread which generates the Fibonacci series. Both threads are created by extending the `Thread` class. Priorities will be set for both threads through their objects in the main thread.

Program 10.13

```
class MT extends Thread
{
   public void run()
   {
      System.out.println("first thread:Multiplication table started its
      execution");
      for(int i=1;i<=10;i++)
      {
         System.out.println(i+" * 6 ="+(i*6));
      }
   }
}
class FIB extends Thread
{
   public void run()
   {
      System.out.println("second thread:
      Fibonacci series started its execution");
      int f=0, s=1 ,t,i,MAX=10;
      System.out.println(f+"\n"+s);
      for(i=2;i<MAX;i++)
      { t=f+s;
         System.out.println(t);
         f=s;
         s=t;
      }
   }
}
public class PThread
{
   public static void main(String[] args)
   {
      MT m=new MT();
      m.setPriority(Thread.MIN_PRIORITY);
      System.out.println("The priority value of
      a first thread is: "+m.getPriority());
      m.start();
      FIB f=new FIB();
      f.setPriority(Thread.MAX_PRIORITY);
      System.out.println("The priority value of a second thread is: "+f.
      getPriority());
      f.start();
   }
}
```

Output 10.13

```
The priority value of a
first thread is: 1
The priority value of a
second thread is: 10 second
thread: Fibonacci series
started its execution
0
1
1
2
3
5
8
13
21
34
first thread: Multiplication
table started its execution
1 * 6 =6
2 * 6 =12
3 * 6 =18
4 * 6 =24
5 * 6 =30
6 * 6 =36
7 * 6 =42
8 * 6 =48
9 * 6 =54
10 * 6 =60
```

The first thread `MT` is created to generate a multiplication table of 6 and the second thread `FIB` is created for generating a Fibonacci series. In the `run()` method of the first thread, a `for` loop is declared with the maximum iterative value of 10 to generate a multiplication table. In the `run()` method of the second thread, a `for` loop is declared with the maximum iterative value of 15 to generate a Fibonacci series. Objects for starting both threads have been declared in main threads `m` and `f` respectively. `MIN_PRIORITY` has been set for the first thread and the `start()` method invoked in the beginning itself. For the second thread `MAX_PRIORITY` has been set and the `start()` method invoked for execution. Even though the first thread invoked a `start()` method, the JVM will not allow this thread to proceed further for execution, because it has a minimum priority. So, the JVM will select a second thread which has a maximum priority for execution. Only after completing the execution of the second thread will the first thread be allowed to run. If the priority of the threads is changed or removed, the output may vary. The same **Program 10.14** is used here to demonstrate the behaviour when the `MAX_PRIORITY` thread wakes up from sleep; the currently running thread which has `MIN_PRIORITY` will be suspended. The `MAX_PRIORITY` thread will proceed its execution from where it has left off.

Program 10.14

```
class MT extends Thread
{
   public void run()
   {
      System.out.println("first thread:
      Multiplication table started its execution");
      for(int i=1;i<=10;i++)
      {
         try
         { Thread.sleep(2000);
         }
         catch(Exception e){System.out.println("An
         Exception has occurred = "+e);}
         System.out.println(i+" * 6 ="+(i*6));
      }
   }
}
class FIB extends Thread
{
   public void run()
   {
      System.out.println("second thread: Fibonacci
      series started its execution");
      int f=0, s=1 ,t,i,MAX=15;
      System.out.println(f+"\n"+s);
      for(i=2;i<MAX;i++)
      {
         try
         {
            if(i==7)
            { Thread.sleep(5000);
            }
         }
         catch(Exception e){System.out.println("An
         Exception has occurred = "+e);}
         t=f+s;
         System.out.println(t);
```

Output 10.14

```
The priority value of a
first thread is: 1
The priority value of a
second thread is: 10 second
thread: Fibonacci series
started its execution
0
1
1
2
3
5
8
first thread: Multiplication
table started its execution
1 * 6 =6
2 * 6 =12
13
21
34
55
89
144
233
377
3 * 6 =18
4 * 6 =24
5 * 6 =30
6 * 6 =36
7 * 6 =42
8 * 6 =48
9 * 6 =54
10 * 6 =60
```

```
            f=s;
            s=t;
        }
    }
}
public class PThread2
{
    public static void main(String[ ] args)
    {
        MT m=new MT();
        m.setPriority(Thread.MIN_PRIORITY);
        System.out.println("The priority value of a first thread is: "+m.
        getPriority());
        m.start();
        FIB f=new FIB();
        f.setPriority(Thread.MAX_PRIORITY);
        System.out.println("The priority value of a second thread is: "+f.
        getPriority());
        f.start();
    }
}
```

`MIN_PRIORITY` has been set for the first thread and it has invoked the `start()` method in the beginning itself. For the second thread, `MAX_PRIORITY` has been set and the thread has invoked the `start()` method for execution. Even though the first thread invoked a `start()` method, the JVM will not allow this thread to proceed further for execution because of its minimum priority. So, the JVM will select a second thread which has the maximum priority for execution. Soon after the second thread started its execution, the `sleep()` method is invoked for 5 seconds when the value of *i* reaches 7. Once the second thread enters into the waiting state, the first thread which has a `MIN_PRIORITY` will start execution; here the sleep time is set for 2 seconds for each iteration. Before the execution of the first thread is completed, the second thread can take over the execution when the sleep time is over. In this way, the `MAX_PRIORITY` thread takes over the execution from the `MIN_PRIORITY` thread. The first thread will complete its execution after the second thread completes its remaining execution.

10.7 THREAD SYNCHRONISATION

There may be a situation where more than one thread tries to write to the same document simultaneously. If so, the data in that document will be overwritten. The reason behind this chaos is that there is no control over the shared resource by all the threads. The process of controlling the access of shared resources by more than one thread is called *synchronisation*. Synchronisation helps to ensure that the resource is accessed by only one thread at a time and preserves consistency of the resources during multiple accesses.

A semaphore or monitor is a key to synchronisation. The monitor is an object that is used as a mutually exclusive lock or *mutex*. Only one thread at a time can hold a monitor. All other threads attempting a shared resource are suspended until the resource is released. The synchronisation is very difficult to implement in other programming languages such as C or C++. It expects to use the operating system primitives to implement synchronisation in the program whereas Java provides language level support for synchronisation. Java implements synchronisation using the following statement:

```
synchronized(object)
{
    // block of code
}
```

The *object* is the one which is going to be synchronised. **Program 10.15** is developed without synchronisation in order to demonstrate the importance of synchronisation.

Program 10.15

```
class MT
{
    void printMT(int n)
    {//method not synchronized
    for(int i=1;i<=5;i++)
    {
        System.out.println(n*i);
        try
        {
            Thread.sleep(400);
            }catch(Exception e){System.out.println(e);}
        }
    }
}
class FThread extends Thread
{
    MT t;
    FThread(MT t)
    {
        this.t=t;
    }
    public void run()
    10
    {
        t.printMT(10);
    }
}
class SThread extends Thread
{
    MT t;
    SThread(MT t)
    {
        this.t=t;
    }
    public void run()
    {
        t.printMT(25);
    }
}
class SynThread
{
    public static void main(String args[])
    {
        MT M = new MT();
        FThread t1=new FThread(M);
        SThread t2=new SThread(M);
        t1.start();
        t2.start();
    }
}
```

Output 10.15

```
25
20
50
30
75
40
100
125
50
```

In Program 10.15, two threads `SThread` and `FThread` are created by extending a `Thread` class. A general class `MT` is created with single method `printMT()`, which multiplies the given value five times. An object for a class `MT` is declared in both the threads. Each thread has its own constructor and the object of class MT created in that thread is passed as a parameter. The run() methods of both threads call the printMT() with constant values 10 and 25 respectively as a parameter. An object M is created for the class MT and passed as parameter to constructors of SThread and FTthread while creating an object. Objects t1 and t2 are declared for the threads SThread and FThread. Object t1 of FThread calls start() to execute its run() and then object t2 of SThread calls the start() method to execute its run() method. Both threads invoke the printMT() method of MT class in their run() method. When two threads try to access the same method, the result of each thread would get scrambled because there is no restriction of access employed. To solve this problem, the method that is accessed by the threads will be set as synchronised. **Program 10.16** modifies Program 10.15 with synchronisation.

Program 10.16

```
class MT
{
    synchronized void printMT(int n)
    {//method synchronized for(int i=1;i<=5;i++)
        { System.out.println(n*i);
           try
           { Thread.sleep(400);
           }catch(Exception e){System.out.println(e);}
        }
    }
}
class FThread extends Thread
{
    MT t;
    FThread(MT t)
    {
        this.t=t;
    }
    public void run()
    {
        t.printMT(10);
    }
}
class SThread extends Thread
{
    MT t;
    SThread(MT t)
    {
        this.t=t;
    }
    public void run()
    {
        t.printMT(25);
    }
}
class SynThread2
{
    public static void main(String args[])
    {
        MT M = new MT();
        FThread t1=new FThread(M);
        SThread t2=new SThread(M);
        t1.start();
        t2.start();
    }
}
```

Output 10.16

```
10
20
30
40
50
25
50
75
100
125
```

Program 10.16 is modified from Program 10.15. Here, the method `printMT()` of `MT` class is a shareable resource among threads. This time, the `printMT()` method is prefixed with `synchronized` keyword which makes the method such that it can be shared by only one thread at a time. Only after it is released by the first thread can the next thread acquire it. The object `t1` of the thread `FThread` calls the `start()` method which in turn triggers the `run()` method of the class. Likewise the object `t2` of a thread `SThread` calls `start()` which in turn calls the `run()` method of the class. The object `t1` acquires the shared resource method `printMT()`, so the object `t2` must wait until the `t1` finishes its task. Soon after the task is finished by object of `FThread`, the object `t2` can acquire the shared resource method and finish its task. By employing synchronisation, threads can share the resource in a defined manner without affecting the result of other threads. So, object `t1` first prints multiplication values and then object `t2` displays its results.

So far learned about how to create shared resource that can be used by more than one thread in a synchronised manner. The next section explains the thread communication.

10.8 INTER-THREAD COMMUNICATION

Inter-thread communication is a way to allow synchronised threads to exchange information or interact with each other and this is the only way to handle the producer–consumer problem in thread communication. When the threads are interacting with each other without using the methods defined by an object class, the resulting data will be scrambled.

The following methods are used to implement thread communication in Java.

- `wait()`
- `notify()`
- `notifyAll()`

The above three methods should be called only within the synchronised context and because these methods are related to locking an object, they are defined in the object's class, not in the `Thread` class.

wait()

Makes the current thread release the monitor and waits until either of the following things happens:

- Another thread calls the `notify()` or `notifyAll()` method.
- The specified time is intervened or is over.

The current thread which owns the monitor should be called from the synchronised method, otherwise it will throw an exception.

Table 10.8 `wait()` method

S. no.	Method	Description
1.	`public final void wait()`	Waits until object is notified.
2.	`Public final void wait(long timeout)`	Waits for the specified amount of time.

notify()

It notifies a single thread that was put in a waiting state by invoking a `wait()` method.

```
public final void notify()
```

notifyall()

Wakes up all the threads that are waiting in the monitor. The thread which has the highest priority will run first.

```
public final void notifyAll()
```

Difference between wait() and sleep() methods

Table 10.9 differentiates between the wait() and sleep() methods.

Table 10.9 Differences between wait() and sleep() methods.

wait() method	sleep() method
It releases the lock	It doesn't release the lock
Is contained in the object class	It is contained in the Thread class
It is a non-static method	It is a static method
Wakes up with notify() or notifyAll() methods	Wakes after the sleep time is complete

Program 10.17 implements a joint account for a husband and wife, to demonstrate the producer and consumer problem, without the methods for handling the inter-thread communication.

Program 10.17

```
import java.io.*;
class Jacc
{
    int damount=0;
    int wamount;
    synchronized void withdraw(int a)
    {
        this.wamount=a;
        System.out.println("trying to withdraw Rs."+this.wamount);
        if(this.damount<a)
        {
            System.out.println("Available balance is "+this.damount);
            System.out.println("Less balance; waiting for deposit...");
            System.out.println("Enter the amount to deposit:");
            try
            {
                wait();
            }catch(Exception e){System.out.println("An Exception has occurred:"+e);}
            this.damount-=a;
            System.out.println("withdrawal completed..."+"Balance amount = "+this.
            damount);
        }
    }
    synchronized void deposit(int a)
    {
        System.out.println("going to deposit...");
        this.damount=a;
        System.out.println("deposited amount = "+this.damount);
        notifyAll();
    }
}
```

```
class WThread extends Thread
{
   Jacc t;
   WThread(Jacc t)
   {
      this.t=t;
   }
   public void run()
   {
      t.withdraw(5000);
   }
}
class DThread extends Thread
{
   Jacc t;
   DThread(Jacc t) throws IOException
   {
      this.t=t;
   }
   public void run()
   {
      t.deposit(15000);
   }
}
class ITCWO
{
   public static void main(String args[]) throws IOException
   {
      Jacc c=new Jacc();
      WThread w=new WThread(c);
      DThread d=new DThread(c);
      w.start();
      d.start();
   }
}
```

Output 10.17

```
trying to withdraw Rs.5000
Available balance is 0
Less balance; waiting for
deposit...
Enter the amount to
deposit:
going to deposit...
deposited amount = 15000
withdrawal completed...
Balance amount = 10000
```

The class `Jacc` is declared with two sharable resource methods `withdraw()` and `deposit()` prefixed with `synchronized`. That means these methods can be accessed by only one thread at a time. The `withdraw()` method receives the amount to be withdrawn through its parameter and uses an `if` structure to check whether the given amount is greater than the available amount. If so, it triggers the `wait()` method; it doesn't do anything until it is notified by some other method of the class. The `deposit()` method of a `Jacc` class is also a synchronised one and the amount to be deposited is passed as a parameter when this is called. As soon as it receives the amount, it stores it in the class variable `damount` and triggers the `notify()` method which in turn wakes up the `withdraw()` method and makes it continue its execution from where it left off before calling the `wait()` method. After the required amount is deposited, the amount is debited and the balance amount is then displayed to the user.

The next section explains how to control the thread during its execution.

10.9 THREAD CONTROL

Having control over the execution of a thread is sometimes useful. When the operation of a thread is not required it can be stopped or suspended instead of letting the thread to go on to finish its task completely.

For example, a thread is created to receive the current date of the system; if the user doesn't want the current date then that thread can be suspended and it can be resumed later on when the need arises. Java provides an efficient way to control the execution of a thread using the following methods of a `Thread` class.

- `public void suspend()`
- `public void resume()`
- `public void stop()`

suspend()

The `suspend()` method is used to halt the currently running thread until it is resumed using the `resume()` method. Unlike `sleep()`, the `suspend()` method can't just resume operation after a time period. It expects a `resume()` method to be called.

resume()

This method causes the suspended thread which was suspended using the `suspend()` method to resume. It lets the thread start its operations from where it left off before the `suspend()` method was invoked.

stop()

A thread is alive during the suspend and resume operations. But when the thread object invokes the `stop()` method, it is stopped once and for all. Once the `stop()` method is called, it is not possible to get back the thread during run time.

Program 10.18 implements the `suspend, resume, stop` methods which control the execution of a program.

Program 10.18

```
import java.io.*;
class First extends Thread
{
   public void run()
   {
      for(int i=1;i<=10;i++)
      {
         if(i==5)
         try
         {
            System.out.println("Thread is sleeping for 5 seconds....");
            Thread.sleep(5000);
            System.out.println("Thread woke up from SLEEP");
         }
         catch (InterruptedException ex){ System.out. print(ex); }
         System.out.println(i+" * 4 ="+i*4);
      }
      System.out.println("THREAD FINISHED");
   }
}
```

```
public class ThreadSR
{
   public static void main(String[] args) throws
   IOException
   {
      First f=new First();
      f.start();
      System.out.println("Thread is suspended");
      f.suspend();
      System.out.println("RESUME: Enter 1, STOP:
      Enter any number: ");
      InputStreamReader r=new
      InputStreamReader(System. in);
      BufferedReader br=new BufferedReader(r);
      String ch=br.readLine();
      int c=Integer.parseInt(ch);
      if(c==1)
      {
         System.out.println("Thread resumed from
         suspended state");
         f.resume();
      }
      else
      {
         System.out.println("Thread has been
         stopped: NOTE Thread once stopped will
         never resume execution");
         f.stop();
      }
   }
}
```

Output 10.18

```
Run-1
Thread is suspended
RESUME: Enter 1, STOP:
Enter any number:
250
Thread has been stopped:
NOTE Thread once stopped
will never resume execution
Run-2
Thread is suspended
RESUME: Enter 1, STOP:
Enter any number:
1
Thread resumed from
suspended state
1 * 4 =4
2 * 4 =8
3 * 4 =12
4 * 4 =16
Thread is sleeping for 5
seconds....
Thread woke up from SLEEP
5 * 4 =20
6 * 4 =24
7 * 4 =28
8 * 4 =32
9 * 4 =36
10 * 4 =40
THREAD FINISHED
```

A thread named `First` is created by extending a `Thread` class. In the `run()` method of the `First` thread, a `for` loop is declared to generate the multiplication table for 4. The `if` control structure which is inside the `for` loop checks the `i` value in each iteration; when the `i` value reaches 5, the thread will be put to sleep for 5 seconds after which it wakes up and finishes its remaining task. In the main class `ThreadSR`, an object `f` is created for the class `first` which extends the `Thread` class. Soon after the creation of an object, the `start()` method is called which in turn calls the `run()` method of the class. The next statement `f.suspend()` is invoked; this tells the JVM to suspend the thread which was started. As soon as it is triggered, the thread is put in a suspended state and waits for the `resume()` method to be called with the same object. From here, two choices are asked from the user using `InputStreamReader` and `BufferedReader`. Choice 1 is to resume the operation and another one is to stop the thread; the operation for the choice is employed using the `if` control structure. If the user enters the value 1, the first `if` block is executed and the `resume()` method is called to make the thread continue its execution. If the user enters any other number, the `else` block is executed and `stop()` method is invoked to terminate the thread once and for all. In this way, the `resume()`, `start()` and `suspend()` methods control the execution of a thread.

So far, we have learned about controlling the execution of a thread. The concept of a pool of threads is introduced in the next section.

10.10 THREAD POOL

A thread pool represents a group of threads just like workers in a factory. In a thread pool, a fixed number of threads are created. If a worker in a factory completes a task, another task can be allocated. Likewise, if a thread completes its allocated task, another task can be allocated. In this way, a thread may be used several times. The thread pool concept is mostly used in servlets and JSP to develop thread pools for handling each client request separately. `Java.util.concurrent` class provides the necessary class and methods for implementing a thread pool.

Each thread in a thread pool has the following life cycle:

- listen for a new task to be allocated,
- complete the task, and
- return to the thread pool for getting the next task.

In Java, a thread can be created in two ways—the first one is through the `Thread` class and the second through the `Runnable` interface. Once a thread is created and terminated, it can't be reused again by using the `Thread` class. Using a `Runnable` interface, a pool of threads is created and used again and again, instead of creating individual threads many times.

Program 10.19 implements the thread pool concept to calculate the odd or even number through three threads.

Program 10.19

```
import java.io.*;
import java.util.concurrent.*;
class OE implements Runnable
{
   public int n;
   public OE (int n)
   {
      this.n=n;
   }
   public void run()
   {
      System.out.println(Thread.currentThread().getName());
      for(int i=1;i<=n;i++)
      {
         if(i%2==0)
         {
            System.out.println(i+" is an even number");
         }
         else
         {
            System.out.println(i+" is an odd number");
         }
      }
   }
}
public class ThreadP
{
   public static void main(String[] args) throws IOException
   {
      ExecutorService ex = Executors. newFixedThreadPool(5);//creating a pool of 5 threads
```

Output 10.19

```
5
pool-1-thread-1
1 is an odd number
2 is an even number
3 is an odd number
4 is an even number
5 is an odd number
6
pool-1-thread-2
1 is an odd number
2 is an even number
3 is an odd number
4 is an even number
5 is an odd number
6 is an even number
3
pool-1-thread-3
1 is an odd number
2 is an even number
3 is an odd number
```

```
        for (int i = 1; i <= 5; i++)
        {
            InputStreamReader r=new
            InputStreamReader(System. in);
            BufferedReader in=new
            BufferedReader(r);
            String v=in.readLine();
            int n=Integer.parseInt(v);
            Runnable worker = new OE(n);
            ex.execute(worker);
        }
        ex.shutdown();
        while (!ex.isTerminated()) { } System.out.
        println("Finished all
        threads");
    }
}
```

```
4
pool-1-thread-4
1 is an odd number
2 is an even number
3 is an odd number
4 is an even number
8
pool-1-thread-5
1 is an odd number
2 is an even number
3 is an odd number
4 is an even number
5 is an odd number
6 is an even number
7 is an odd number
8 is an even number
Finished all threads
```

In this program, only one thread has been created with the `Runnable` interface to implement a thread pool. The thread `OE` is created to check whether a given number is odd or even, through a `for` loop and its iterative value is set through a constructor. In the main thread, a thread pool is created with 5 fixed threads. Through an `ExecutorService` object, a thread pool is created. A `for` loop is used to iterate through the number of threads one by one. `Runnable` object `worker` is passed with `OE` constructor values and `n` value for finding odd and even number verification. The `ExecuterService` object `ex` invokes `execute()` with parameter value `worker` to run each thread in a thread pool. Every time the `for` loop is executed, each thread gets executed.

10.11 THREAD GROUP

It groups the various threads into one convenient group. Through an object of a *thread group*, all the threads belonging to that group can be manipulated. In a thread group, threads can be added or removed at any time. In Java, a thread group can be created by using `java.lang.ThreadGroup` class. The `java. lang.ThreadGroup` provides important constructors and methods to implement a thread group. Before placing more than one thread in a thread group, a thread group should be created first. The following code snippet demonstrates how the thread group is created with one of the constructors in Table 10.10.

```
ThreadGroup tg=new ThreadGroup("Arithmetic");
```

In the above code snippet, `Arithmetic` is a name of a ThreadGroup and `tg` is an object of a ThreadGroup. Table 10.10 describes the two constructors used to create a thread group.

Table 10.10 Constructors in a ThreadGroup

S. no.	Constructor	Description
1.	`ThreadGroup(String n)`	Generates a thread group with a specified name. Parameter `n is used to specify the name for a thread group.`
2.	`ThreadGroup(ThreadGroup p, String n)`	Generates a thread group with a specified parent group and name.

Table 10.11 describes the various methods to manipulate the thread group.

Table 10.11 Methods in ThreadGroup

S. no.	Method	Description
1.	`activeCount()`	Returns the number of threads executing the current thread in this thread group.
2.	`activeGroupCount()`	Returns the number of active groups in this thread group.
3.	`destroy()`	Destroys a thread group.
4.	`getName()`	Returns the name of the thread group.
5.	`ThreadGroup getParent()`	Returns the parent of the thread group.
6.	`interrupt()`	Interrupts all threads in this thread group.

In **Program 10.20**, the thread group concept is implemented with four threads. These four threads are meant to perform arithmetic operations. Through the ThreadGroup object, these four threads are manipulated.

Program 10.20

```
import java.io.*;
import java.lang.ThreadGroup.*;
class A implements Runnable
{
   int a, b;
   public A(int a, int b)
   {
      this.a=a;
      this.b=b;
   }
   public void run()
   {
      int r=a+b;
      System.out.println("Addition value is ="+r);
   }
}
class S implements Runnable
{
   int a,b;
   public S(int a, int b)
   {
      this.a=a;
      this.b=b;
   }
   public void run()
   {
      int r=a-b;
      System.out.println("Subtraction value is ="+r);
   }
}
class D implements Runnable
{
   double a, b;
   public D(double a, double b)
   {
      this.a=a;
      this.b=b;
   }
```

```
    public void run()
    {
        double r=a/b;
        System.out.println("Division value is ="+r);
    }
}
class M implements Runnable
{
    int a,b;
    public M(int a, int b)
    {
        this.a = a;
        this.b = b;
    }
    public void run()
    {
        int r=a*b;
        System.out.println("Multiplication value
        is ="+r);
    }
}
public class TGroup
{
    public static void main(String[] args)
    throws IOException
    {
        ThreadGroup tg=new
        ThreadGroup("Arithmetic");
        A a=new A(10,2);
        S s=new S(25,5);
        D d=new D(75,25);
        M m=new M(15,5);
        Thread t1=new Thread(tg,a,"ONE");
        Thread t2=new Thread(tg,s,"TWO");
        Thread t3=new Thread(tg,d,"THREE");
        Thread t4=new Thread(tg,m,"FOUR");
        t1.start();
        t2.start();
        t3.start();
        t4.start();
        System.out.println("ThreadGroup Name is "+tg.getName());
        System.out.println("Number of Threads in the ThreadGroup are "+tg.
        activeCount());
        // tg.suspend();
        // tg.resume();
        // tg.stop();
    }
}
```

Output 10.20

```
Run-1
ThreadGroup Name is Arithmetic
Number of Threads in the
ThreadGroup are 4
Addition value is =12
Subtraction value is =20
Division value is =3.0
Multiplication value is =75
Run-2 (uncomment a tg.suspend()
it will produce following
result and wait for resume)
ThreadGroup Name is Arithmetic
Number of Threads in the
ThreadGroup are 4
Run-3 (uncomment a tg.suspend()
and tg.resume() it will produce
following result)
ThreadGroup Name is Arithmetic
Number of Threads in the
ThreadGroup are 4
Multiplication value is =75
Division value is =3.0
Subtraction value is =20
Addition value is =12
Run-3 (uncomment a tg.stop()
and it will produce following
result)
ThreadGroup Name is Arithmetic
Number of Threads in the
ThreadGroup are 4
// further execution will be
stopped once and for all
```

Four threads, namely, `A`, `S`, `D` and `M` have been created by implementing a `Runnable` interface. The ThreadGroup named 'Arithmetic' is created in the main thread using the statement,

```
ThreadGroup tg=new ThreadGroup("Arithmetic");
```

All the four threads will be added to the `Arithmetic ThreadGroup` one by one, using the statement `Thread t1=new Thread(tg,a,"ONE");` here `tg` is an object of `ThreadGroup`, an object of a runnable interface and `ONE` is a name for that thread in a `ThreadGroup`. After that, all the threads will be started one by one with their respective `Thread` class object. Using `ThreadGroup` object `tg`, all the threads in a `ThreadGroup` can be controlled using `tg.suspend()`, `tg.resume()`, `tg.stop()`. If `tg.suspend()` is invoked, it suspends all the threads contained in a thread group and waits for `resume()` to be invoked. If `tg.resume()` is invoked, it resumes all the threads contained in a thread group that were previously suspended using the `tg.suspend()` method. When the `tg.stop()` method is invoked, it stops or destroys all the threads from further execution.

10.12 DAEMON THREAD

Java daemon thread is a service provider thread and it mostly runs in the background. It serves the user threads. When user threads are no longer running, a daemon thread is destroyed by the JVM automatically, as the daemon thread is executed only for providing service for the user threads. As soon as the last user thread finishes its execution, the JVM will automatically destroy the daemon thread. These types of threads are low priority threads. The `java.lang.Thread` class provides methods to handle daemon threads. Table 10.12 describes the methods used to handle daemon threads.

Table 10.12 Methods to handle daemon threads

S. no.	Method	Description
1.	`public void setDaemon(boolean status)`	Sets the current thread as a daemon thread.
2.	`public boolean isDaemon()`	Checks whether the given thread is a daemon thread or not.

Program 10.21 demonstrates how to set a user thread as a daemon thread and to check which one is a daemon thread and which one is a user thread.

Program 10.21

```
class dThread extends Thread
{
   public void run()
   {
      if(Thread.currentThread().isDaemon())
      {
         System.out.print(Thread.currentThread().getName());
         System.out.println(" IS A DAEMON THREAD");
      }
      else
      {
         System.out.print(Thread.currentThread(). getName());
         System.out.println(" IS A USER THREAD");
      }
   }
}
public class DaeThread
{
   public static void main(String[] args)
   {
      dThread dt1=new dThread();
      dThread dt2=new dThread();
      dt1.setDaemon(true);
      dt1.start();
      dt2.start();
   }
}
```

Output 10.21

```
Thread-0 IS A DAEMON THREAD
Thread-1 IS A USER THREAD
```

`dThread` is created by extending the `Thread` class to check whether the current thread is a daemon or user thread. Two objects are created for the `dThread` in a main thread, namely `dt1` and `dt2`. `dt1` will be set as a daemon thread by using `setDaemon()` method and then it invokes `start()` method. `dt2` is a user level thread. If a user thread is stopped with the `stop()` method, the daemon will not be executed. When both threads invoke the `start()` method, the result will be displayed, indicating whether the current thread is a daemon or user thread.

SUMMARY

1. A process is a program in execution. If a program or a process is subdivided into smaller tasks or jobs, each such task is called a thread.
2. A process of running more than one thread concurrently is known as multithreading.
3. According to the specifications of Sun Java, there are only four states in the life cycle of a thread in Java—*new, runnable, non-runnable* and *terminated.*
4. A thread can be created by either of the following two ways: through the `Runnable` interface or through extending the `Thread` class.
5. A preemptive scheduling or time slice scheduling policy is primarily used by the thread scheduler to choose a thread from the runnable state for execution.
6. In Java, one thread can know the execution status of other threads by using two different methods, `isAlive()` and `join()`.
7. A thread can be assigned a priority using `setPriority()` method. The `Thread` class provides three constants, namely `MAX_PRIORITY`, `MIN_PRIORITY` and `NORM_PRIORITY` to specify the priority for threads.
8. A thread pool represents a group of threads, just like workers in a factory. In a thread pool, a fixed number of threads are created. If a thread completes its allocated task, another task can be allocated. In this way, a thread may be used several times.
9. `ThreadGroup` groups the various threads in one convenient group. Through an object of a thread group, all the threads belonging to that group can be manipulated.
10. A Java daemon thread is a service provider thread and it mostly runs in the background. It serves the user threads.

SHORT QUESTIONS

1. Differentiate between process and thread.
2. Compare multitasking, multiprocessing and multithreading.
3. What are the ways to create a thread in Java?
4. Write a code snippet for declaring and starting a thread using `Thread` class.
5. Write a brief note on thread scheduler.
6. Differentiate between thread group and thread pool.
7. What is the purpose of a daemon thread?
8. Compare the `isAlive()` and `join()` methods.
9. How will you set the priority for a thread?
10. What is a thread pool?

MEDIUM QUESTIONS

1. Illustrate the life cycle of a thread, with a neat diagram.
2. Tabulate the methods available in the `Thread` class.

3. Describe the constructors and various methods available to manipulate threads in a thread group.
4. Create a thread by implementing `Runnable` interface.
5. Create a thread by extending the `Thread` class.
6. Using a program, explain the `isAlive()` and `join()` methods.
7. Write a program with and one without using `isAlive()` and `join()` methods and compare the results.
8. Briefly explain the thread group in Java.
9. Using a program, explain the thread pool concept.
10. Which is the most useful when developing more than one thread in a single program, using a thread group or a thread pool? Justify your answer.

SOLVED PROGRAMS

1. Naming a Thread using setName() and getName() methods and displays it while running a thread.

```
class demo implements Runnable
{
  public void run()
  {
    for(int i=1;i<=10;i++)
    {
      try
      {
        Thread.sleep(2000);
      } catch (InterruptedException ex) {
        System.out.println("Exception occurrred: "+ex);}
      System.out.println("World of JAVA");
    }
  }
}
public class TNaming
{
  public static void main(String[] args)
  {
    demo d=new demo();
    Thread t1=new Thread(d);
    t1.setName("APPLE Thread:");
    System.out.println(t1.getName()+" is running");
    t1.start();
  }
}
```

Output

```
APPLE Thread: is running
World of JAVA
World of JAVA
World of JAVA
World of JAVA
World of JAVA
World of JAVA
World of JAVA
World of JAVA
World of JAVA
World of JAVA
```

2. Interrupting a Thread while in a sleeping or waiting.

```
import java.util.Scanner;
class FT extends Thread
{
  public void run()
  {
    int r, n = 1;
    Scanner in = new Scanner(System.in);
    System.out.println("Enter the number of rows: ");
    r = in.nextInt();
```

```
        System.out.println("1st FLOYD'S TRIANGLE");
        for ( int i = 1 ; i <= r ; i++ )
        {
           for ( int j = 1 ; j <= i ; j++ )
           {
              try
              {
                 System.out.print(n+" ");
                 n++;
                 Thread.sleep(2000);
              }  catch (InterruptedException ex) { System.out.println("An Exception
                 has been occurred"+ex); }
           }
           System.out.println();
        }
     }
  }
  class FT2 extends Thread
  {
     public void run()
     {
        int n = 1;
        Scanner in = new Scanner(System.in);
        System.out.println("Enter the number of
        rows: ");
        int r = in.nextInt();
        System.out.println("2nd FLOYD'S TRIANGLE");
        for ( int i = 1 ; i <= r ; i++ )
        {
           for ( int j = 1 ; j <= i ; j++ )
           {
              try
              {
                 System.out.print(n+" ");
                 n++;
                 Thread.sleep(1000);
              }  catch (InterruptedException ex) { System.out.println("An Exception
                 has been occurred: "+ex); }
           }
           System.out.println();
        }
     }
  }
  public class Inthread
  {
     public static void main(String[] args)
     {
        FT f=new FT();
        f.start();
        f.interrupt();
        FT2 f1=new FT2();
        f1.start();
     }
  }
```

Output

```
Enter the number of rows:
Enter the number of rows:
3
1st FLOYD'S TRIANGLE
1 An Exception has been
occurredjava.lang.
InterruptedException: sleep
interrupted
2 3
4 5  6
5
2nd FLOYD'S TRIANGLE
1
2 3
4 5  6
7 8  9  10
11 12  13  14 15
```

3. Converting Binary to Decimal and Decimal to Binary.

```
class binary extends Thread
{
  int n;
  public void set(int n)
  {
     this.n=n;
  }
  public void run()
  {
     int b[] = new int[25];
     int in = 0;
     System.out.print("Binary equivalent of "+this.n+" is ");
     while(n > 0){
        b[in++] = n%2;
        n = n/2;
     }
     for(int i = in-1;i >= 0;i--)
     {
        System.out.print(b[i]);
     }
  }
}
class decimal extends Thread
{
  int n;
  public void set(int n)
  {
     this.n=n;
  }
  public void run()
  {
     String decimal = Integer.toString(n);

     System.out.println("Decimal Value is : " + decimal);
  }
}
public class DTB
{
  public static void main(String args[])
  {
     binary dtb = new binary();
     Scanner in = new Scanner(System.in);
     System.out.println("Enter DECIMAL value: ");
     int d = in.nextInt();
     dtb.set(d);
     dtb.start();
     decimal btd=new decimal();
     Scanner scan = new Scanner(System.in);
     System.out.println("\nEnter BINARY value :");
     int num = Integer.parseInt(scan.nextLine(), 2);
     btd.set(num);
     btd.start();
  }
}
```

Output

```
Enter DECIMAL value:
89
Binary equivalent of
89 is 1011001
Enter BINARY value :
11100
Decimal Value is :
28
```

PROGRAMMING EXERCISES

1. Create two threads by extending the `Thread` class. Use the first thread for calculating the Fixed Deposit and second thread for calculating Recurring Deposit. Declare objects for both threads in the main thread and execute them.
2. Modify Problem (1) through assigning the minimum priority for the first thread and maximum priority for the second thread. Declare objects for both threads in the main thread and execute them.
3. Define three threads for calculating the mean, median and mode of given `n` numbers. Set a sleep time for each of these threads. For the first thread, set sleep time for 1000, for the second thread 5000, and for the third thread 10000. Test the threads by creating objects in the main thread.
4. Modify Problem (3) by implementing `suspend()` and `resume()` methods. Test the threads by creating objects in the main thread.
5. Create a thread group with two threads. The first thread is for converting kilometres to miles and the second thread for converting fahrenheit to celsius. Supply different values through the constructors of the thread and test it with their objects.
6. Develop threads by implementing a `Runnable` interface to calculate the sin and cos values of a given number.
7. Create a thread pool of 5 threads for calculating age using the current date and DOB. Get the current date through `java.util.Date` and supply the DOB for each thread in a thread pool, through the keyboard. Execute the thread pool.
8. Develop a thread by implementing a `Runnable` interface to generate a list of odd and even numbers through looping. The maximum limit for the loop should be given from the main class through constructors. Test the thread with different objects and values.
9. Develop a thread by extending the `Thread` class to display a string `HELLO WORLD` 15 times. Set a sleep timer for 25 seconds after reaching the eighth time. Before completing the sleep time, interrupt a thread in between and make it continue the remaining task.
10. Develop a thread to differentiate between the `SLEEP`, `SUSPEND` and `RESUME` operations.

CHAPTER

11

Files and I/O Streams

Files are the most important mechanism for storing data permanently on mass storage devices. Storing the data ensures that it is not lost when the machine is switched off. Files can contain data in a binary format that can be interpreted by programs, but not easily by humans. It also includes alphanumeric characters, codified in a standard way using ASCII or Unicode and directly readable by a human as in text files. Text files are normally organised in a sequence of lines, each containing a sequence of characters and ending with a special character, usually the newline character. Each file is characterised by a name and a directory in which the file is placed. The most important operations on files are: creation, reading from, writing to, renaming and deleting. To do all these operations on a file, the input has to read from the keyboard using I/O streams. This chapter briefly explains file handling techniques and the streams.

11.1 THE `File` CLASS

To execute reading and writing operations on a file, the first and foremost thing to do is to open the file before the operations and to close it after completing the action on it. *Opening a file* means, to indicate to the operating system that the programmer wants to operate on a file from within a Java program and the operating system verifies whether the operation is possible and allowed. There are two ways of opening a file: opening for reading and opening for writing, which cause different behaviours of the operating system. For example, two files may be opened at the same time by two applications for reading, but not for writing; or a file on a disk may be opened for reading, but not for writing. In many programming languages, opening a file for writing implies actually creating a new file. *Closing a file* means, to indicate to the operating system that the file that was previously opened is not being used anymore by the program. Closing a file also has the effect of ensuring that the data written on the file is effectively transferred to the hard disk.

Exceptions

File operations can typically cause unexpected situations that the program is not capable of handling. For example, a programmer trying to open a file for reading specifies a filename that does not exist. Such situations are called exceptions. It will be classified according to the type of inconvenience that has been caused and it must be handled by the program by inserting suitable Java code. The methods that make use of the statements that can generate an exception must declare as follows. For example, the methods for opening a file for reading can generate an exception of type `IOException`. Therefore, any method that calls such methods must declare explicitly that it can itself generate an exception of that type. The type of exception that a method can generate is specified in the `throws` clause, which must be added to the method declaration before the body of the method. For example:

```
public static void main(String [ ] args) throws IOException
{
   //body
}
```

The `File` class is defined in `java.io` package and it is used in various stream related activities. So, it is necessary to study this first. The `File` class deals directly with files and the file system. That is, it does not specify how information is retrieved from or stored in files; it describes the properties of that file. It does not actually change the contents of the file. A file object is used to obtain or manipulate the information associated with a disk file. That is, it can obtain the permissions, time, date, directory path, and can be used to navigate subdirectory hierarchies. Files are a primary source and destination for data within many Java programs. Although there are some strict restrictions on their use within applets for security reasons, files are still a central resource for storing constant and shared information. A directory in Java is treated simply as a File with one additional property. The following constructors can be used to create File objects:

```
File (String dirPath)
File (String dirPath, String filename)
File (File dirObj, String filename)
```

In the statements **dirPath** is the path name of the file, **filename** is the name of the file, whereas **dirObj** is a File object that specifies a directory. File `class` defines many methods that obtain the standard properties of a File object. These are listed below in Table 11.1.

Table 11.1 Methods of file class

Method	Purpose
`String getName()`	Returns only the name of the file
`String getPath()`	Returns the whole path of the file
`String getAbsolutePath()`	Returns the absolute path of the file
`String getParent()`	Returns the name of the parent directory of the file
`boolean exists()`	Returns true if the filename exists
`boolean canWrite()`	Returns true if the file is writable
`boolean canRead()`	Returns true if the file is readable
`boolean isDirectory()`	Returns true if it is a directory
`boolean isFile()`	Returns true if it is a file / not directory
`boolean isAbsolute()`	Returns true if the file is absolute
`long lastModified()`	Returns the no. of milliseconds elapsed from last modified time
`int length()`	Returns the total number of bytes of the file
`boolean delete()`	Deletes the file and returns true on successful deletion
`boolean renameTo(File newName)`	Renames the file name to newName
`boolean deleteOnExit()`	Deletes the file after program completion
`boolean isHidden()`	Returns true if the file is hidden
`boolean setReadOnly()`	Returns if the file is read only

Program 11.1 demonstrates some of the methods of File class.

Program 11.1

```
// File class operations
import java.io.File;
class FileClass
{
   public static void main(String args[])
   {
      File f = new File("C:\\Users\\Documents\\shc. txt");
      System.out.println("isFile:" +f.isFile());
      System.out.println("Name:"+f.getName());
      System.out.println("Size: "+f.length());
      System.out.println("Path:"+f.getPath());
      System.out.println("Parent:"+f.getParent());
      System.out.println("Hidden:"+f.isHidden());
   }
}
```

Output 11.1

```
isFile:true
Name:shc.txt
Size:26
Path: "C:\\Users\\
Documents\\shc.txt"
Parent: "C:\\Users\\
Documents\\shc.txt"
Hidden:false
```

Writing text files

To write strings of text on a file do the following:

1. Open the file for writing by creating an object of the class `FileWriter` associated to the name of the file and creating an object of the class `PrintWriter` associated to the `FileWriter` object created.
2. Write text on the file by using the `print` and `println` methods of the `PrintWriter` object.
3. Close the file when you have finished writing to it.

The Java statements that realise the three phases described above are:

// Opening the file for writing (creation of the file)

```
FileWriter f = new FileWriter("test.txt");
PrintWriter out = new PrintWriter(f);
```

// Writing text on the file

```
out.println("some text to write to the file");
```

//Closing the output channel and the file

```
out.close();
f.close();
```

The invocation of the constructor of the class `FileWriter` has the effect of creating a file that is ready to be written on. If the file already exists, all its contents are erased first. To append text to an already existing file without erasing the previous contents of the file, use the constructor with the signature `FileWriter(String, boolean)`, specifying the value true for the second argument. **Program 11.2** creates a text file called `shc.txt` and writes on it the string 'Welcome to File Handling'.

Program 11.2

```
import java.io.*;
public class WritingOnFile {
    public static void main(String[ ] args) throws IOException {
        // opening the file for writing
        FileWriter f = new FileWriter("shc.txt");
        // creation of the object for writing
        PrintWriter out = new PrintWriter(f);
        // writing text on the file
        out.println("Welcome to File Handling");
        // closing the output channel and the file
        out.close();
        f.close();
    }
}
```

Output 11.2

```
shc.txt
Welcome to File Handling
```

Reading from a text file

To read strings of text from a file, do the following.

1. Open the file for reading by creating an object of the class `FileReader` and an object of the class `BufferedReader` associated to the `FileReader` object just created.
2. Read the lines of text from the file by using the `readLine` method of the `BufferedReader` object.
3. Close the file when you have finished reading from it.

The Java statements that realise the three phases described above are:

//opening the file for reading

```
FileReader f = new FileReader("test.txt");
BufferedReader in = new BufferedReader(f);
```

//reading a line of text from the file

```
String line = in.readLine();
```

// closing the file

```
f.close();
```

If the file that the programmer wants to open for reading does not exist, then an exception of type `FileNotFoundException` is raised when the object `FileReader` is created. After the file is opened, start reading from its first line. Then, each time the method `readLine` is invoked, the input is advanced to the next line, so that each invocation of `readLine` will read the next line of text in the file. **Program 11.3** opens a text file called `shc.txt`, reads from it a line of text and prints in on the console.

Program 11.3

```
import java.io.*;
class ReadingFromFile {
    public static void main(String[ ] args) throws IOException {
        // opening the file for reading
        FileReader f = new FileReader("shc.txt");
        // creation of the object for reading
        BufferedReader in = new BufferedReader(f);
        // reading a line of text from the file
        String line = in.readLine();
        System.out.println(line);
        System.out.println(line);
        // closing the file
        f.close();
    }
}
```

Output 11.3

```
Welcome to File Handling
```

Renaming and deleting a file

To delete a file, that is, to remove it completely from the mass storage device, the method `delete` is invoked on an object of type `File` created with the name of the file to delete.

```
File f1 = new File ("shc.txt");
Boolean b = f1.delete();
// if b is true, then the file has been deleted successfully
```

The constructor of the class `File` does not generate an exception if the file does not exist. The result of the deletion operation is returned by the `delete` method. To rename a file, invoke the method `renameTo()` on two objects of type `File` that represent respectively the file to rename and the new name to give to the file.

```
File f1 = new File ("oldname.txt");
File f2 = new File ("newname.txt");
Boolean b = f1.renameTo(f2);
// if b is true, then the file has been renamed successfully
```

The file `oldname.txt`, if it exists, is renamed to the file `newname.txt`. If there already exists a file named `newname.txt`, then it is overwritten. The result of the renaming operation is returned by the `renameTo()` method. The operations for reading from input streams and writing to output streams are standardised, that is, they do not depend on the particular stream being used. This means that the programmer can use the same Java statements to read strings from a keyboard, from a file or from the internet. Such operations make use of the classes of the Streams. This is described in the next section.

11.2 STREAMS

Input and output are the most commonly used operations in any program. Reading data from the keyboard and writing data on to the monitor form the basic input and output operations. It is essential for a programmer to know how to read the data from files and write data to files. Java uses streams to handle data input and output. In general, a *stream* is referred to as a flow. In the case of programming, it is the flow of data. A *stream* is an ordered sequence of bytes that has an input stream or an output stream. File processing input refers to the flow of data inside the program and output means flow of data out of the program. This input may come from the keyboard, mouse, memory, disk file or any another program. Similarly, the program output may go to the console, printer, memory, disk file, network or any another program. The `java.io` package defines various classes and methods for reading and writing files and handling streams. This section describes the input and output streams provided in Java. Figure 11.1 illustrates the data flow in a Java program.

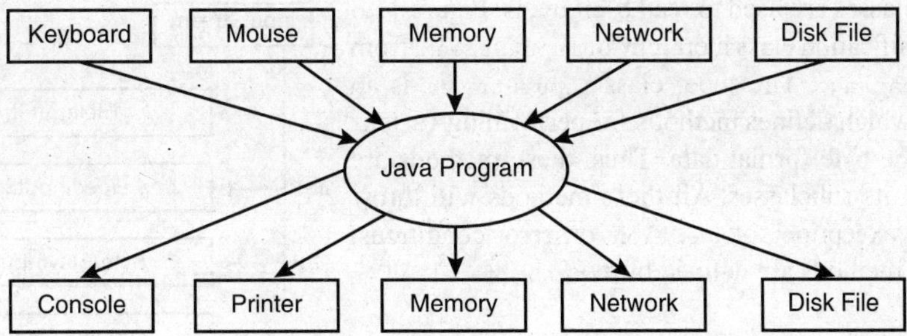

Fig. 11.1 Data flow of a Java program

Java uses the concept of streams to represent the ordered sequence of data. The stream presents a uniform, easy to use, object-oriented interface between the program and the I/O devices. The process of sending data from one device to another has made streams in Java an influential tool for information processing. The stream can be used to filter the data along the lines of streams so that it is possible to obtain the data in the desired format. For example, a programmer can use one stream to obtain data in the binary format and then another stream in series to convert it to integers. As the name suggests, an input stream reads data from the source and sends it to the program. Similarly, an output stream takes data from the program and sends it to the destination.

Java stream classes

Java's stream-based I/O is built upon abstract classes from `java.io.package` that are `InputStream`, `OutputStream`, `Reader`, and `Writer`. They are used to create several concrete stream subclasses. Although the programs perform I/O operations through concrete stream subclasses, the top level classes define the basic functionality common to all stream classes. These classes may be categorised into two types based on the data type on which they operate:

- byte streams, and
- character streams.

Figure 11.2 shows the categories of the Java stream classes.

The byte stream classes provide support for handling I/O operations on bytes or any binary objects whereas character stream classes provide support for managing I/O operations on characters or strings. These two types can further be classified based on their purpose.

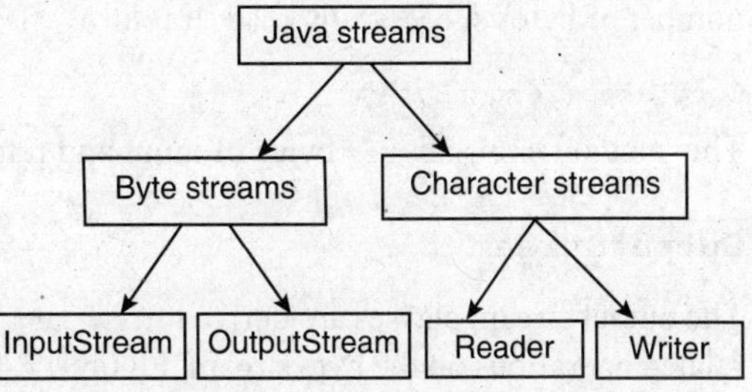

Fig. 11.2 Classification of Java stream classes

11.3 THE BYTE STREAMS

Byte streams are used in a program to read and write 8-bit bytes. These classes have been designed to provide functional features for creating and manipulating streams and files for reading and writing bytes or binary objects. There are two main byte stream classes, `InputStream` and `OutputStream`.

InputStream

Input Stream classes are used to read 8-bit bytes. Figure 11.3 shows the classification class hierarchy of `InputStream` from the `java.io.package`. The super class `InputStream` is an abstract class which defines methods for performing various functions on the byte format data. Thus, these methods are available to all its subclasses. All these methods will throw the unchecked exception `IOException` on error conditions. The following methods are defined by `InputStream`.

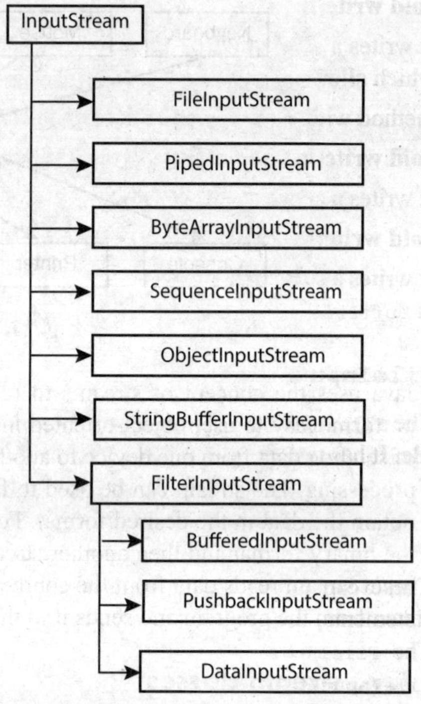

Fig. 11.3 `InputStream` class hierarchy

`int available()`

It returns the number of bytes of input currently available for reading from the stream.

`void close()`

It closes the input stream. If there is an attempt to read further, it will generate an `IOException`.

`int read()`

It returns an integer representation of the next available byte of input. It returns the value -1 when the end of the file is encountered.

`int read(byte buffer[ ])`

It attempts to read up to `buffer.length` bytes into byte array `buffer` and returns the actual number of bytes that were successfully read. It returns –1 when the end of the file is encountered.

`int read(byte buffer[ ], int offset, int nBytes)`

It attempts to read up to `nBytes` bytes into 'buffer' starting at 'buffer[offset]' position and returns the number of bytes successfully read. It returns –1 when the end of the file is encountered.

`long skip(long nBytes)`

This method skips `nBytes` bytes of input and returns the number of bytes actually ignored.

OutputStream

The output stream classes are derived from `OutputStream` class which is used for performing all output related operations on the byte stream. Figure 11.4 shows the class hierarchy of the `OutputStream`, which includes various methods that are designed to perform different tasks related to output of the data. The following methods are defined by `OutputStream`. All of the methods in this class return a void value and throw an `IOException` in the case of errors.

void close()

This closes the output stream. An attempt to read further will generate an `IOException`.

void flush()

This method finalises the output state so that any buffers are cleared. That is, it flushes the output buffers.

void write(int b)

It writes a single byte to an `OutputStream`. The parameter is an `int`, which allows to call `write ()`

method with expressions not having to cast it back to byte.

void write(byte buffer[ ])

It writes a complete array of bytes 'buffer' to an output stream.

void write(byte buffer[ ], int offset, int nBytes)

It writes a sub-range of `nBytes` bytes from the array buffer, beginning at `buffer[offset]`.

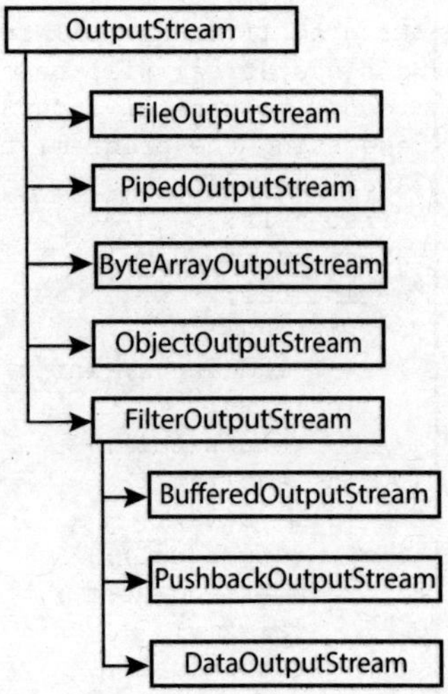

Fig. 11.4 The `OutputStream` class hierarchy

`FileInputStream`

The `FileInputStream` class creates an `InputStream` by which the programmer can read bytes from a file. It has two common constructors:

```
FileInputStream (String filepath)
FileInputStream (File fileObj)
```

These can throw a `FileNotFoundException` when the file name or its path is incorrect. In the statements, `filepath` is the full path name of a file and `fileObj` is a file object that describes the file. The `FileInputStream` overrides all methods defined above. **Program 11.4** illustrates the use of `FileInputStream` class.

Program 11.4

```
//Reading file using FileInputStream
import java.io.InputStream;
import java.io.FileInputStream;
class FileInput
{
   public static void main (String args [])
   throws Exception
   {
      InputStream f=new FileInputStream("Maths.java");
      int size =f.available();
      System.out.println("Available:"+ size +"bytes");
      System.out.println("First half:");
      for(int i=0;i<size/2;i++)
      System.out.print((char) f.read());
      size=f.available();
      System.out.println("Now Available:"+ size);
      System.out.println("Second half:");
      for(int i=0;i<size;i++)
      System.out.print((char)f.read());
      f.close();
   }}
```

Output 11.4

```
Program 11.4 uses FileInputStream to read from the Maths.java file. The object
of InputStream will be created for this file. In the program available() and
read() methods of InputStream are used to perform input operations on the file. On
executing the program, the following output is displayed.
Available:741bytes
First half:
class overloading{
  int cal;
  float val;
  int add(int x, int y)
  {cal=x+y;
     return(cal);}
  int add(int z)
  {cal= z+10;
     return(cal);}
     float add(float x, float y){
     val=x+y;
     return(val);
  }
}
clNow Available:371
Second half:
ass Maths{
  public static void main(String args[])
  {
     overloading m=new overloading();
     System.out.println("10+10="+m. add(10,10));
  System.out.println("15+10="+m. add(15));
  System.out.println("1.5+1.5="+m. add(1.5f,1.5f));
  }
}
```

FileOutputStream

The class `FileOutputStream` creates an `OutputStream` that allows us to write bytes to a file. Its most commonly used constructors are:

```
FileOutputStream(String filePath)
FileOutputStream(File fileObj)
FileOutputStream(String filePath, Boolean append)
FileOutputStream(File fileObj, Boolean append)
```

All these can throw a `FileNotFoundException` or a `SecurityException`. `filePath` is the full path name of a file and `fileObj` is a file object that describes the file. If the value of the Boolean variable `append` is true, the file is opened in appending mode. The creation of a `FileOutputStream` is not dependent on whether the file already exists. `FileOutputStream` will create the file before opening it for output when the object is created. Any attempt to open a Read only file, will throw an IOException. All the methods of `OutputStream` are available for use in `FileOutputStream`. **Program 11.5** illustrates the use of `FileOutputStream`.

Program 11.5

```
import java.io.OutputStream;
import java.io.FileOutputStream;
class FileOutput
{
   public static void main(String args[ ]) throws Exception
   {
      String str="Java is purely"+"Object Oriented
      Programming";
      byte buf[ ] = str.getBytes();//statement1
      OutputStream f1 = new FileOutputStream("shc. txt");
      for(int i=0;i<buf.length; i += 2)
      f1.write(buf[i]);
      f1.close();
      OutputStream f2 = new FileOutputStream("file. txt");
      f2.write(buf);
      f2.close();
      OutputStream f3=new FileOutputStream("cs.txt");
      f3.write(buf,buf.length-buf.length/4,buf.length/4);
      f3.close();
   }
}
```

Output 11.5

```
Contents of "shc.txt":
Jv sprl0jc retdPormig
Contents of "file.txt":
Java is purelyObject
Oriented Programmimg
Contents of "cs.txt":
Rogramming
```

Observe Statement1 in Program 11.5. It is used to convert the character or string type data into byte format because the programmer is using the output stream with byte oriented stream facilities.

ByteArrayInputStream

The `ByteArrayInputStream` is an implementation of an input stream that uses a byte array as the source data. This class has two constructors, each of which requires a byte array to provide the data source:

```
ByteArrayInputStream(byte array[ ])
ByteArrayInputStream(byte array[ ], int start, int nBytes)
```

In the statement, `array` is the input source of data. The second constructor creates an InputStream from a subset of byte array that begins with the character at the index specified by `start` and is `nBytes` long. **Program 11.6** illustrates the use of `ByteArrayInputStream`.

Program 11.6

```
// Demonstrating ByteArrayInputStream.
import java.io.ByteArrayInputStream;
class ByteArrayInput
{
   public static void main(String args[]) throws Exception
   {
      String str="Object oriented concept in c++ and
      Java are same of different";
      byte b[ ] = str.getBytes();
      ByteArrayInputStream str1=new ByteArrayInputStream(b);
      ByteArrayInputStream str2=new ByteArrayInputStream(b,6,6);
```

```
        int size=str1.available();
        System.out.println("contents of str1:");
        for(int i=0;i<size;i++)
        System.out.print((char) str1.read());
        System.out.println("\n\nContent of str2:");
        size=str2.available();
        for(int i=0;i<size;i++)
        System.out.print((char) str2.read());
    }
}
```

Output 11.6

```
contents of str1:
Object oriented concept in
c++ and Java are same of
different
Content of str2: Orien
```

ByteArrayOutputStream

The `ByteArrayOutputStream` is an implementation of an output stream that uses a byte array as the destination type. The `ByteArrayOutputStream` contains two protected integer members named `buf` and `count` to store the data. It also has two constructors which are shown below:

```
ByteArrayOutputStream()
ByteArrayOutputStream(int nBytes)
```

In the first form a buffer of 32 bytes is created and in the second a buffer is created with a size equal to that specified by `nBytes`. The buffer is held in the protected `buf` field of `ByteArrayOutputStream`. The buffer size will be increased automatically, if needed. The number of bytes held by the buffer is contained in the protected `count` field of `ByteArrayOutputStream`. **Program 11.7** demonstrates the use `ByteArrayOutputStream`.

Program 11.7

```
import java.io.ByteArrayOutputStream;
import java.io.OutputStream;
import java.io.FileOutputStream;
class ByteArrayOutput
{
   public static void main(String args[]) throws Exception
   {
      ByteArrayOutputStream f=new ByteArrayOutputStream();
      String str="Java is Object Oriented";
      byte buf[]=str.getBytes();
      f.write(buf);
      System.out.println("String format:");
      System.out.println(f.toString());
      System.out.println("Array format:");
      byte b[]= f.toByteArray();
      for(int i=0;i<b.length;i++)
      System.out.print((char)b[i]);
      System.out.println("\n TO FileOutputStream():-");
      OutputStream f2= new FileOutputStream("shc.txt");
      f.writeTo(f2);
      f2.close();
   }
}
```

Output 11.7

```
String format:
Java is Object Oriented
Array format:
Java is Object Oriented
TO FileOutputStream():-
```

In Program 11.7, the `writeTo()` method is used. It is the method of `ByteArrayOutputStream` which is used to write the contents of invoking string to another `OutputStream`. The `FileInputStream` is used to read the contents of the file '`shc.txt`'.

11.4 FILTERED BYTE STREAMS

Filtered streams provide the basic ability to create input and output streams for filtering input and output in a number of ways. These filtered streams lie between input and output streams to perform some optional processing on the data they transfer. The filtered streams can be combined to perform a series of filtering operations such as buffering, character extraction and raw data translation, and so on. The filtered byte streams are `FilterInputStream` and `FilterOutputStream`. Their constructors are shown below:

```
FilterOutputStream(OutputStream os)
FilterInputStream(InputStream is)
```

The methods provided in these classes are identical to those in `InputStream` and `OutputStream`.

Buffered byte streams

The buffered streams extend a filtered stream class by attaching a memory buffer to the I/O Streams. This buffer allows Java to do I/O operations on more than a byte at a time, hence enhancing the performance. Because of the availability of the buffer, skipping, marking and resetting operations on the stream is possible. The buffered byte stream classes are `BufferedInputStream` and `BufferedOutputStream`.

The pushbackInputStream also implements buffered stream classes.

BufferedInputStream

The `BufferedInputStream` class allows us to encapsulate any `InputStream` into a buffered stream and achieve improvement in performance. The `BufferedInputStream` has two constructors:

```
BufferedInputStream(InputStream is)
BufferedInputStream(InputStream is, int bufSize)
```

The first form creates a buffered stream using a default buffer size. In the second, `bufSize` specifies the size of the buffer. An optimal buffer size is generally dependent on the host operating system, the amount of memory available and how the machine is configured. Generally, the size is around 8,192 bytes and attaching even a rather small buffer to an I/O stream is always a good idea. That way, the low- level system can read blocks of data from the disk or network and store the result in the buffer. Thus, even a programmer reading the data a byte at a time out of the `InputStream`, will be manipulating fast memory over 99.9% of the time. Buffering an input stream also provides the required facilities to support movement on both directions in the stream of the available buffer. All other operations that a `BufferedInputStream` provides are the same as `InputStream`.

BufferedOutputStream

The functionality of `BufferedOutputStream` is similar to any `OutputStream` with the exception of an added `flush()` method that is used to ensure that data buffers are physically written to the actual output device. A `BufferedOutputStream` is used to improve performance by reducing the number of times the system actually writes data. It needs to call a `flush()` method to cause any data that is in the buffer to get written. Buffering output does not provide additional functionality. Buffers for output in Java are present to increase performance. There are two different constructors of `BufferedOutputStream`:

```
BufferedOutputSream(OutputStream os)
BufferedOutputStream(OutputSream os, int bufSize)
```

The first form creates a buffered stream using a buffer of 512 bytes and in the second form the size of the buffer is passed in `bufSize`.

PushbackInputStream

`PushbackInputStream` is used on an input stream to allow a byte to be read and then returned, that is, 'pushed back' to the stream. It has the following constructors:

```
PushbackInputStream(InputStream is)
PushbackInputStream(Inputstream is, int nBytes)
```

The first form creates a stream object that allows returning one byte to the input stream. The second form creates a stream that has a pushback buffer `nBytes` long. Using this, multiple bytes can be returned to the input stream. `PushbackInputStream` provides one of its own method `unread()` as shown below:

```
void unread(int ch)
void unread(byte buffer[ ])
void unread(byte buffer, int offset, int nChars)
```

The first form of `unread()` pushes back the low-order byte of `ch`. This will be the next byte returned by a subsequent call to `read()` method. The second form returns the bytes in `buffer` and the third form pushes back `nChars` bytes beginning at `offset` from `buffer`. If there is an attempt to return a byte when the pushback buffer is full, an `IOException` will be thrown. **Program 11.8** illustrates the `unread()` method.

Program 11.8

```
//Demonstrating the unread() method
import java.io.ByteArrayInputStream;
import java.io.PushbackInputStream;
class Pushback
{
   public static void main (String args[])throws
Exception
   {
      String str="The pushback is used on input
      stream "+"to allow a byte to be read";
      byte buf []= str.getBytes();
      ByteArrayInputStream in =new
      ByteArrayInputStream(buf);
      PushbackInputStream f= new
      PushbackInputStream(in);
      int var;
      while(f.available ()!=0)
      { var=f.read();
         if (var=='e')
         f.unread('#');
         System.out.print((char)var);
      }
   }
}
```

Output 11.8

```
The# pushback is use#d on
input stre#am to allow a
byte# to be# re#ad.
```

Program 11.8 uses the PushbackInputStream to add a '#' sign after all occurrences of character 'e'.

SequenceInputStream

The `SequenceInputStream` class allows the concatenation of multiple `InputStreams`. The construction of a `SequenceInputStream` is different from any other `InputStream`. A `SequenceInputStream` constructor uses a pair of `InputStreams` as its argument:

```
SequenceInputStream(InputStream second)
```

Program 11.9 demonstrates the use of `SequenceInputStream` which concatenates the contents of two files using `InputStream`. For example, consider contents of file `file1.txt` to be 'The SequenceInputStream class defines' and the contents of file `file2.txt` to be 'to concatenate multiple InputStreams'.

Program 11.9

```
//Demonstrating SequenceInputStream
import java.io.InputStream;
import java.io.FileInputStream;
import java.io.SequenceInputStream;
class SequenceInput
{
   public static void main (String args [])throws
   Exception
   {
      InputStream fir =new FileInputStream ("file1.txt");
      InputStream sec=new FileInputStream("file2.txt");
      InputStream s=new SequenceInputStream(fir, sec);
      int x=fir.available() , y=sec.available();
      int z=x+y;
      System.out.print("Concatenated contents:");
      while(z-->0)
      System.out.print((char) s.read());
   }
}
```

Output 11.9

```
Concatenated contents:
The SequenceInputStream
class defines to
concatenate multiple
InputStreams
```

PrintStream

The `PrintStream` class provides all of the formatting capabilities that have been used from the System file handle, System.out. It contains two constructors:

```
PrintStream (OutputStream os)
PrintStream(OutputStream os, boolean newline)
```

In the statements, the Boolean value `newline` controls whether Java flushes the output stream every time a new-line (\n) character is output. If the value of `newline` is True, flushing automatically takes place. If it is False, flushing will not be automatic. The first constructor does not flush automatically. `PrintStream` objects support the `print()` and `println()` methods for all types, including Object. If an argument is not a primitive type then the `PrintStream` methods will call the objects `toString()` method and then print the result on the console. **Program 11.10** demonstrates the use of `PrintStream` for outputting data.

Program 11.10

```
//Demonstrating PrintStream;
import java.io.PrintStream;
class PrintStreams
{
   public static void main (String args[])
   {
      PrintStream p =new PrintStream(System.out);
      p.println("Dear students'");
      p.print("Kindly study well");
      p.println("PrintStream class");
   }
}
```

Output 11.10

```
Dear students' Kindly study
wellPrintStream class
```

DataInputStream

The `Scanner` class from `java.util` package is used to read input from the keyboard. The `DataInputStream` serves the same purpose. It is used to take the data input from the keyboard. The following constructor is used to create an object of `DataInputStream` :

```
DataInputStream(InputStream is)
```

The `readLine()` method of `DataInputStream` class returns the string which has been read through the keyboard. **Program 11.11** demonstrates the use of `DataInputStream`.

Program 11.11

```
//Demonstrating DataInputStream;
import java.io.DataInputStream;
class DataInputs
{
   public static void main (String args[]) throws Exception
   {
      DataInputStream d=new DataInputStream (System.in);
      System.out.print("Enter any String:");
      String in=d. readLine();
      System.out.println("The string is :"+in);
      System.out.println("Enter two numbers:");
      int x=Integer.parseInt(d.readLine());
      int y =Integer.parseInt(d.readLine());
      System.out.println("Addition :" +(x+y));
   }
}
```

Output 11.11

```
Enter any String:
DataInputStream
The string is :
DataInputStream
Enter two numbers:
5
5
Addition: 10
```

11.5 THE RandomAccessFile CLASS

`RandomAccessFile` class from `java.io` package allows the programmer to create a file that can be used for reading and writing the data with random-access. This means that it is possible to jump to any position inside the file for accessing the data. This is done with the file pointer of the file. This class contains two constructors:

```
RandomAccessFile(File obj, String access)
RandomAccessFile(String filename, String access)
```

Both constructors throw unchecked `FileNotException` when the file name or path name is wrong. In the first form, `obj` is the name of the file to open as a file object. In the second form, the name of the file is passed in `filename`. For both constructors, `access` determines what type of file access is permitted for that file. The possible values for access are listed here, along with what they signify:

'r' : file can be read, but not written.
'rw' : file is opened in read–write mode. The existing file can be updated using this.
'rws' : file is opened for read–write operations and every change to the file's data or metadata will be immediately written to the disk file.
'rwd' : file is opened for read–write operations and every change to the file's data will be immediately written to the disk file.

The method `seek( )` of `RandomAccessFile` is used to set or change the current position of the file pointer within the file. Its general form is:

```
void seek(long pos)
```

This method throws `IOException`. In the statement, long integer value specifies the new position (in bytes) of the file pointer from the beginning of the file. When calling the `seek()` method, the next read or write operation will occur at this new file position. `RandomAccessFile` have methods for reading and writing the data in the file. These are:

```
int read()
void write(byte buf[ ])
```

These work in the same way as `read ()` and `write ()` methods of `InputStream` and `OutputStream` classes respectively. **Program 11.12** demonstrates the use of all these methods.

Program 11.12

```
//using Random AccessFile
import java.io.RandomAccessFile;
class RandomAccess
{
   public static void main(String args[ ]) throws Exception
   {
      RandomAccessFile f=new RandomAccessFile ("file. txt","rw");
      String s="The RandomAccessFile have methods"+"for reading and writing"+"the
      data in the file and it provide more efficiency \nas well as accuracy of
      data";
      byte[ ] buf=s.getBytes();
      Long len;
      f.write(buf);
      f.seek(0);
      len=f.length();
      System.out.println("Contents of file:");
```

```
        while(len>0)
        {
            System.out.print((char) f.read());
            len=len-1;
        }
        System.out.println("\nsize of file:"+f.
        length());
        System.out.println("\nAfter change:
        contents of file:");
        f.seek(82);
        buf="less".getBytes();
        f.write(buf);
        f.seek(0);
        len=f.length();
        while(len>0)
        {
            System.out.print((char) f.read());
            len=len-1;
        }
    }
}
```

Output 11.12

```
Contents of file:
The RandomAccessFile have
methods for reading and
writing the data in the
file and it provide more
efficiency as well as
accuracy of data
size of file:136

After change: contents of
file:
The RandomAccessFile have
methods for reading and
writing the data in the
file and ilessovide more
efficiency as well as
accuracy of data
```

In Program 11.12, a random access file is created and written with the data. Then using the `seek()` method, the file pointer is moved to the 82nd byte in the file. The characters in that position are replaced by the new string using the `write` method.

11.6 THE CHARACTER STREAMS

When Java was first introduced, character streams were not part of it. They were added later in Java 1.1 since one of the main purposes of Java was to support the 'Write once, run anywhere' methodology, and it was necessary to include direct I/O support for characters. These streams can be used to read and write 16-bit Unicode characters. Like byte streams, they are classified into two categories that are Reader and Writer.

Reader

The `Reader` class is designed to stream the data in the form of characters. `Reader` is the abstract base class which has several subclasses under it (Fig. 11.5). `Reader` class contains methods that are identical to those in `InputStream` class, except that the `Reader` class methods are designed to handle characters only. The following are some useful methods of `Reader`.

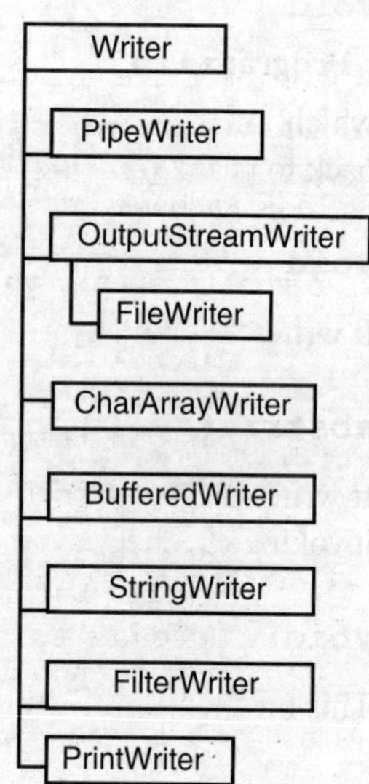

Fig. 11.5 The `Reader` class hierarchy

`abstract void close()`

It closes the input source of data. Any attempt to read further will generate an IOException.

`int read()`

It returns an integer representation of the next available character from the invoking character input stream. It returns –1 when the end of the stream is encountered.

int read(char buffer[ ])

It attempts to read up to `buffer.length` characters into `buffer` and returns the actual number of characters that were successfully read. It returns –1 when the end of the stream is encountered.

long skip(long nChars)

This method skips over `nChars` characters in reading, and returns the numbers of characters actually skipped by it.

Writer

Like output streams, the writer streams classes are designed to perform operations on output data. But write stream classes use only the character type data. `Writer` is an abstract base class which is acting as the base for all the classes handling the character stream output data. The hierarchy of writer classes is shown in Fig. 11.6. `Writer` also defines methods which are identical to those in OutputStream. All the methods in this class return a void value and throw an `IOException` in the case of errors. These methods are listed below.

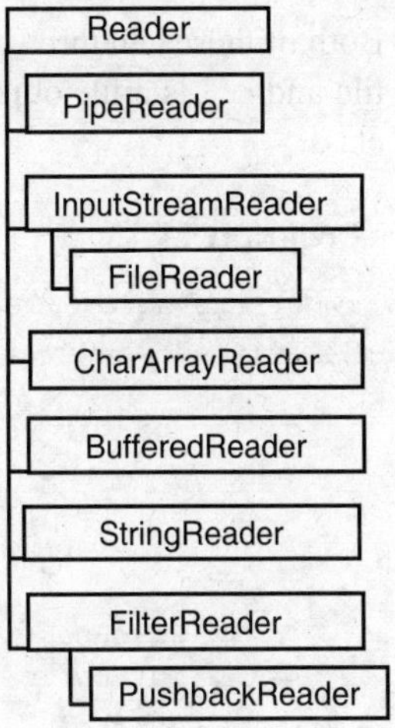

Fig. 11.6 The `Writer` class hierarchy

abstract void close()

It closes the output character stream. Any attempt to write further will generate an `IOException`.

abstract void flush()

It finalises the output state so that any buffers used, are cleared. That is, it flushes out the output buffers.

void write(int ch)

It writes a single character to the invoking character output stream. The parameter is an int variable which allows calling the `write()` method with expression without any compulsion for casting them back to char.

void write(char buffer[ ])

It writes a complete array of characters to the invoking character output stream.

abstract void write(char buffer[ ], int offset, int nChars)

It writes a sub-range of `nChars` characters from the array `buffer`, beginning at `buffer[offset]` to the invoking character output stream.

void write(String str)

This method writes string `str` to the invoking character output stream.

`void write(String str, int offset, int nChars)`

It writes a sub-range of `nChars` characters from the string `str` beginning at the specified `offset`.

`FileReader` class

The `FileReader` class creates a `Reader` object so that it can be used to read the contents of a file. The data processing is in terms of characters only. It has two constructors, shown below:

```
FileReader(String path)
FileReader(File obj)
```

Both of these can throw a `FileNotFoundException`. In the constructors, `path` is the full path name of a file and `obj` is a file object that describes the file. **Program 11.13** demonstrates the use of `FileReader` class.

Program 11.13

```
import java.io.File;
class FileReader
{
   public static void main(String args[]) throws Exception
   {
      File f=new File("FileReader.java");
      if(f.exists())
      {
         FileReader fr=new FileReader (f);
         int ch;
         while((ch=fr.read())!=-1)
         System.out.print((char) ch);
         fr.close();
      }
   }
   private FileReader(File f)
   {
      throw new UnsupportedOperationException("Not yet implemented");
   }
   private int read()
   {


      throw new UnsupportedOperationException("Not yet implemented");
   }
   private void close()
   {
      throw new UnsupportedOperationException("Not yet implemented");
   }
}
```

Output 11.13

```
Output will be the contents
of this file itself.
The second constructor is
used to create the object
of FileReader class
```

`FileWriter` class

The `FileWriter` creates a `Writer` which is used to write into a file by a character stream. It contains four different constructors, shown below:

```
FileWriter(String path)
FileWriter (String path, boolean append)
FileWriter (File obj)
FileWriter (File obj, boolean append)
```

All these four can throw an `IOException` on error. In the statements, `path` is the full path name of a file, and `obj` is a file object that describes the file. If the Boolean value `append` is true, then the output is appended to the end of the file. Creation of a `FileWriter` is not dependent on the file already being in existence. `FileWriter` will create the file before opening it for output when creating the object. If an attempt is made to open a read-only file, an IOException will be thrown. **Program 11.14** illustrates the use of `FileWriter`.

Program 11.14

```
//Demonstrating FileWriter.
import java.io.FileWriter;
class FileWrite
{
   public static void main(String args[]) throws Exception
   {
      String str="FileWriter is used"+ "print the values.";
      char buf[]=str.toCharArray();
      int len=buf.length;
      FileWriter f1= new FileWriter("file1.txt");
      for(int i=0;i<len;i+=2)
      f1.write(buf[i]);
      f1.close();
      FileWriter f2=new FileWriter("file2.txt");
      f2.write(buf);
      f2.close();
      FileWriter f3=new FileWriter("file3.txt");
      f3.write(buf,buf.length-buf.length/4,buf.length/4);
      f3.close();
   }
}
```

Output 11.14

```
Demonstrating FileWriter
class and methods.
FileWriter is used"+ "print
the values.
```

CharArrayReader

The `CharArrayReader` is an implementation of an input stream that uses a character array as the source. This character stream class is the counterpart of `ByteArrayInputStream`. This class has two constructors, both of them require a character array as the data source.

```
CharArrayReader(char array[ ])
CharArrayReader(char array[ ], int start, int nChars)
```

In the statements, `array` is the input data source for stream. The second constructor creates a `Reader` from a subset of the character array that begins with the character at the index specified by the value of start and is 'nChars' long. **Program 11.15** illustrates the use of `CharArrayReader`.

Program 11.15

```
import java.io.CharArrayReader;
import java.io.IOException;
public class CharArrayReaderDemo {
   public static void main(String args[]) throws IOException {
      char c[ ] = {'J','a','v','a','.',' ','W','o','r','l','d','!'};
      CharArrayReader chARedOne = new CharArrayReader(c);
      CharArrayReader chARedTwo = new CharArrayReader(c, 0, 5);
      int i;
      while((i = chARedOne.read()) != -1)
      {
         System.out.print((char)i);
      }
      System.out.println();
      while((i = chARedTwo.read()) != -1)
      {
         System.out.print((char)i);
      }
   }
}
```

Output 11.15

```
Java. World! Java.
```

CharArrayWriter

It is an implementation of a character output stream that uses a character array as the destination. `CharArrayWriter` class has two constructors:

```
CharArrayWriter()
CharArrayWriter(int nChars)
```

In the first form, a buffer with a default size is created and in the second, a buffer is created with a size equal to that specified by `nChars`. The `CharArrayWriter` class contains two protected variable fields. The first is the `buf` field which contains the buffer. The buffer size will be increased automatically, if needed. The second is the `count` field which contains the number of characters held by the buffer. **Program 11.16** demonstrates the use of `CharArrayWriter`.

Program 11.16

```
import java.io.CharArrayWriter;
class CharArrayWriterDemo {
   public static void main(String[ ] args)
   {
      CharArrayWriter chw = null;
      try{
         // create character array writer
         chw = new CharArrayWriter();
         String str = "Java Programming!!";
         // write string to writer
         chw.write(str);
         // get array of character from the writer
         char[ ] ch = chw.toCharArray();
```

```
        // for each character in character array
        for (char c : ch)
        {
            // print character
            System.out.println(c);
        }
    }
    catch(Exception e){
    // for any error e.printStackTrace();
    }finally{
        // releases all system resources from writer
if(chw!=null)
        chw.close();
    }
  }
}
```

Output 11.16

```
J
a
v
a
P
r
o
g
r
a
m
m
i
n
g
!
```

Buffered character streams

`BufferedReader`

A `BufferedReader` improves performance by buffering the input. It contains two constructors.

```
BufferedReader(Reader is)
BufferedReader(Reader is, int bufSize)
```

The first form creates a buffered character stream using a default buffer size. In the second, the size of the buffer is passed in `bufSize`. As in the byte-oriented streams, buffering an input character stream also provides the foundation required to support backward movement in the stream within the available buffer. All operations of buffered streams are the same as those in a general stream.

`BufferedWriter`

A `BufferedWriter` is a `Writer` that adds a `flush()` method that can be used to ensure that data buffers are physically written to the actual character output stream. Using a `BufferedWriter` can increase performance by reducing the number of times data is actually physically written to the output stream. A `BufferedWriter` has two constructors.

```
BufferedWriter(Writer os)
BufferedWriter(Writer os, int bufSize)
```

The first form creates a buffered character stream using a buffer with a default size. In the second, the size of the buffer is passed in the value `bufSize`.

`PushbackReader`

This is a character oriented counterpart of the byte oriented stream `PushbackInputStream`. It allows one or more characters to be returned to the input stream. This also allows looking ahead in the input stream. It contains two constructors:

```
PushbackReader(Reader is)
PushbackReader(Reader is, int bufSize)
```

The first form creates a buffered stream that allows one character to be pushed back to the stream. In the second form, the size of the pushback buffer is passed in the value `bufSize`. `PushbackReader` also provides `unread()`, which returns one or more characters to the invoking character input stream. It has the three different forms shown below.

```
void unread(int ch)
void unread(char buffer[ ])
void unread(char buffer[ ], int offset, int nChars)
```

The first form pushes back the character passed in `ch`. This will be the next character returned by a subsequent call to `read()`. The second form returns the characters in the array `buffer`. The third form pushes back `nChars` characters beginning at `offset` from `buffer`. An IOException will be thrown on an attempt to return a character when the pushback buffer is full. **Program 11.17** demonstrates the `PushbackReader`.

Program 11.17

```
import java.io.FileReader;
import java.io.IOException;
import java.io.PushbackReader;
class PushbackReaderExample {
   public static void main(String[] args) throws IOException {
      //Create Reader instance
      FileReader reader = new FileReader("shc.txt");
      //Create PushBackReader instance with setting 10 as unread
      PushbackReader pushbackReader = new
      PushbackReader(reader,10);
      int c = pushbackReader.read();
      while (c != -1){
         //Converting to character System.out.print((char)c);
         c= pushbackReader.read();
      }
      //Closing the file io reader.close();
   }
}
```

Output 11.17

```
Java is Object Oriented
```

`Printwriter`

`PrintWriter` is a character-oriented version of the `PrintStream` class. It provides the formatted output methods `print()` and `println()`. It has the following four constructors.

```
PrintWriter(OutputStream os)
PrintWriter(OutputStream os, boolean newline)
PrintWriter(Writer os)
PrintWriter(Writer os, boolean newline)
```

Here `newline` controls whether Java flushes the output stream every time `println()` is called. If `newline` is True, flushing automatically takes place. If False, flushing will not be automatic. The first and third constructors do not automatically flush. The `PrintWriter` object supports the `print( )` and `println( )` methods for all primitive types, including objects. If an argument is not a primitive type, the `PrintWriter` methods will call the object's `toString( )` method and then print the result on the console. **Program 11.18** illustrates the use of `PrintWriter` class.

Program 11.18

```
//Demonstrating PrintWriter
import java.io.PrintWriter;
class PrintWrite
{
    public static void main( String args[ ])
    {
        PrintWriter p= new PrintWriter(System.out, true);
        p.println("Welcome");
        p.print("This program demonstrates the use of");
        p.println("PrintWriter class");
    }
}
```

Output 11.18

```
Welcome
This program demonstrates
the use of PrintWriter
class
```

`InputStreamReader`

This is also a character oriented version of `DataInputStream` used for reading data from the keyboard. It contains the following constructor.

```
InputStreamReader(InputStream is)
```

The `read( )` method of `Reader` can be used to read the data from keyboard. The method `readLine( )` of class `BufferedReader` can also be used to read a string from the keyboard by constructing the object from `BufferedReader` as:

```
BufferedReader br=new BufferedReader(new InputStreamReader(System.in));
```

Program 11.19 illustrates the use of `InputStreamReader` class.

Program 11.19

```
// Demonstrating InputStreamReader
import java.io.InputStreamReader;
import java.io.BufferedReader;
class InputStreams
{
    public static void main(String args[ ]) throws
    Exception
    {
        BufferedReader d= new BufferedReader(new
        InputStreamReader(System.in));
        System.out.print("Enter any string :");
        String in=d.readLine();
        System.out.println("Your string : "+in);
        System.out.println("Enter two numbers: ");
        int x = Integer.parseInt(d.readLine());
        int y = Integer.parseInt(d.readLine());
        System.out.println("Multiplication : "+(x*y));
    }
}
```

Output 11.19

```
Enter any string :End of
the chapter
The string : End of the
chapter
Enter two numbers:
20
20
Multiplication : 400
```

SUMMARY

1. A stream can be defined as a sequence of data.
2. The `File` class is one of the important classes defined in the `java.io` package and is used in various stream related activities. A `File` object is used to obtain or manipulate the information associated with a disk file.
3. Stream classes are categorised into two types – byte streams and character streams – based on the data type on which they operate.
4. There are two kinds of byte streams—InputStream and OutputStream. InputStream is used to read data from a source and OutputStream is used for writing data to a destination.
5. Character streams are classified into two types, `Reader` and `Writer`.
6. The filtered stream provides the basic ability to create input and output streams for filtering input and output in a number of ways. These filtered streams lie between input and output streams to perform some optional processing on the data they transfer.
7. The `RandomAccessFile` class from the `java.io` package allows the creation of files that can be used for reading and writing the data with random-access. This means that it is possible to jump to any position inside the file for accessing the data.

SHORT QUESTIONS

1. What is a stream?
2. What is a file stream?
3. Define byte stream.
4. Define character stream.
5. What is input stream?
6. What is output stream?
7. Distinguish between input stream and output stream.
8. Distinguish between byte stream and character stream classes.
9. Name some input and output stream classes.
10. Define the purpose of a file.
11. Mention the types of byte streams.
12. What are the various types of character streams?
13. How can a programmer read file content using a byte array?
14. How can a programmer read file content line by line in Java?
15. How can a programmer store and read objects from a file in Java?

COMPREHENSIVE QUESTIONS

1. What do you mean by a stream? Explain any three input and output stream classes.
2. Discuss the Java InputStream.
3. Explain the Java OutputStream in detail.
4. Explain the concept of I/O stream classes in detail.
5. Explain filtered byte streams with an example.
6. Discuss the use of `PrintStream` class.
7. Explain the concept of RandomAccessfile class.
8. What are the categories of character stream classes? Explain.
9. Differentiate `FileReader` from `FileWriter`.
10. What is the difference between `CharArray-Reader` and `CharArrayWriter`?

SOLVED PROGRAMS

1. Program to print the file information.

```
import java.io.File;
import java.io.IOException;
public class FileInfo {
  public static void main(String[] args)
  {
     String fileName = args[0];
     File fn = new File(fileName);
     try {
        fn.createNewFile();
     } catch (IOException e)
     {
     }
     System.out.println("Name: " + fn.getName());
     // Check if the file exists using exists()
     method if (fn.exists())
     {
        System.out.println(fileName + " does
        exist.");
     }
     if (fn.canRead())
     {
        System.out.println(fileName + " is
        readable.");
     }
     System.out.println(fileName + " is " +
     fn.length() + " bytes long.");
     System.out.println(fileName + " is last modifed at " + new java.util.Date(fn.
     lastModified())) ;
     if (fn.canWrite())
     {
        System.out.println(fileName + " is writable.");
     }
     else{
        System.out.println(fileName + " is not writable.");
     }
  }
}
```

Output

```
Name: dummy
dummy does exist.
dummy is readable.
dummy is 0 bytes long.
dummy is last modifed at Wed
Feb 08 20:58:30 IST 2017
dummy is writable.
```

```
Empty file
this is a new empty file
```

2. Program to print the directory information.

```
import java.io.File;
public class DirectoryInfo {
  public static void main(String[] args)
  {
     System.out.println("Creating temp directory...");
     String fileName = "temp";
     File fn = new File(fileName);
     fn.mkdir();
     // Create sub directories under the temp directory File subdir1 = new
     File(fn, "subdir1");
     subdir1.mkdir();
     File subdir2 = new File(fn, "subdir2");
     subdir2.mkdir();
```

```
        // Check if it is a file or directory using isFile() method
        System.out.println(fileName + " is a " + (fn.isFile()? "file."
        :"directory."));
        if (fn.isDirectory())
        {
           String content[] = fn.list();
           System.out.println("The content of this
           directory:");
           for (int i = 0; i <content.length;
           i++)
           {
              System.out.println(content[i]);
           }
        }
        // Delete a directory
        System.out.println(fileName +
        (fn.exists()? " exists": " does not exist"));
        System.out.println("Deleting temp directory...");
        fn.delete();
    }
  }
```

Output

```
Creating temp directory...
temp is a directory.
The content of this
directory:
subdir1 subdir2
temp exists
Deleting temp directory...
```

3. **Program to illustrate RandomAccessFileHandling.**

```
import java.io.IOException;
import java.io.RandomAccessFile;
public class RandomAccessFileHandling {
  public static void main(String[] args)
  {
     try {
        RandomAccessFileraf = new RandomAccessFile("test.txt", "rw");
        raf.writeInt(10);
        raf.writeInt(43);
        raf.writeInt(88);
        raf.writeInt(455);
        // change the 3rd integer from 88 to 99 raf.seek((3 - 1) * 4);
        raf.writeInt(99);
        raf.seek(0);
        // go to the first integer int i = raf.
        readInt();
        while (i != -1)
        {
           System.out.println(i);
           i = raf.readInt();
        }
        raf.close();
     } catch (IOException e)
     {
     }
  }
}
```

Output

```
10
43
99
455
BUILD SUCCESSFUL (total
time: 0 seconds)
```

4. **Program to illustrate the use of FileInput and FileOutput stream.**

```
import java.io.*;
public class FileInputOutputStream {
  public static void main(String[] args) throws IOException {
     File inputFile = new File("infile.txt");
     File outputFile = new File("outfile.txt");
     FileInputStream in = new FileInputStream(inputFile);
```

```
        FileOutputStream out = new FileOutputStream(outputFile);
        int c;
        while ((c = in.read()) != -1){
            System.out.println(c);
            out.write(c);
        }
        System.out.println("FileInputStream is used
        to read a file and
        FileOutPutStream is used for writing.");
        in.close();
        out.close();
    }
}
```

Output

```
Welcome to File handling
FileInputStream is
used to read a file and
FileOutPutStream is used
for writing.
```

5. Program to take string input from the keyboard.

```
import java.io.*;
class CharRead
{
    public static void main(String[] args) throws IOException
    {
        String text;
        InputStreamReader isr = new InputStreamReader(System.in);
        BufferedReader br = new BufferedReader(isr);
        text = br.readLine();
        System.out.println(text);
    }
}
```

Output

```
File Handling
File Handling
```

PROGRAMMING EXERCISES

1. Write a program to illustrate the use of the `FileWriter` class.
2. Write a program to illustrate the use of the `FileReader` class.
3. Write a program to illustrate `RandomAccessFile`.
4. Write a program to read and display a string using `BufferedReader` class.
5. Write a program to implement the `PrintStream` class.
6. Write a program to implement the `PrintWriter` class.
7. Write a program to read a character from a file and display it to standard output and also check for end of file.
8. Write a program that reads a number from the keyboard and displays its equivalent ASCII character.
9. Write a program that takes an input from a text file and replaces a '#' (single space) by a '*' and replaces every new line with '/' and stores the output to another file.
10. Write a program to read one byte at a time from a file and copy it into another file immediately.
11. Write a program using all file operation in file handling.

FURTHER READING

1. https://docs.oracle.com/javase/tutorial/essential/io/index.html
2. https://personales.unican.es/corcuerp/java/Labs/LAB_20.htm#Homework

CHAPTER

12

Applets

The programs discussed so far are console-based. This chapter introduces programmers to the world of Windows-based programs through applets. An *applet* is a small Windows-based program that is embedded in the browser and works on the client side. This Windows-based programming approach provides the developer with much more flexibility to develop interactive applications. Console-based applications are less effective and this is an outdated approach only used in programming development practice. An applet is a panel that allows interaction with a Java program and it does not provide an approach for developing standalone applications, but the combination of applet and Abstract Windowing Toolkit (AWT) allows the developer to develop standalone Windows-based desktop applications. Unlike console-based programs which interact through Input/Output classes, an applet needs the AWT for interaction with the user by way of some Graphical User Interface (GUI) components such as Textboxes, buttons, checkboxes, and so on. Applets are displayed in a window and expect an AWT to perform I/O operations. An applet provides the developer an event-driven approach, whereby the execution flow of the program is decided by user actions such as a mouse-click or a key press. There are two types of applets available, AWT-based applets and the second one is Swing-based applets or JApplet. Even though the Swing-based applet is widely used to develop Java based GUI applications, The AWT-based applet is used for developing simple window-based applications. This chapter explains the AWT-based applet that was introduced in the first version of Java. In the next section, the basics of an Applet will be discussed.

12.1 APPLET FUNDAMENTALS

The AWT-based applets directly inherit the `Applet` class and override all its member functions. Before using the applet in a program, two important packages need to be included in the program—`java.applet` and `java.awt`.

The `java.awt` package is also needed by an applet program to output its results, since it is not executed on a console screen. A typical Java program uses the command prompt for execution, but Applets are executed by web browsers or the *appletviewer* provided by the SDK.

To become an applet, a Java class should extend the `Applet` class before using its properties. A `main()` method is not defined in the applet to start its execution as in the case of console-based Java programs. Input/Output operations are also handled differently by applets; rather than getting the input through the console screen, it gets its input by explicitly specifying in methods or by passing as parameters. An applet doesn't output its results through the `Sysem.out.println()` method in a console screen. It outputs its results through the AWT method `drawString()` in X, Y coordinate positions on the Window.

After it is successfully developed and compiled, the applet program can be executed in two ways. In the first method, a separate HTML file is created and the class name of an applet is specified in the APPLET tag. Using the second method, an APPLET tag is specified in the comments before the declaration of a public class. After all parts of the Applet program are declared, the applet program can be executed by a Java enabled web browser or appletviewer.

A typical applet program looks like this:

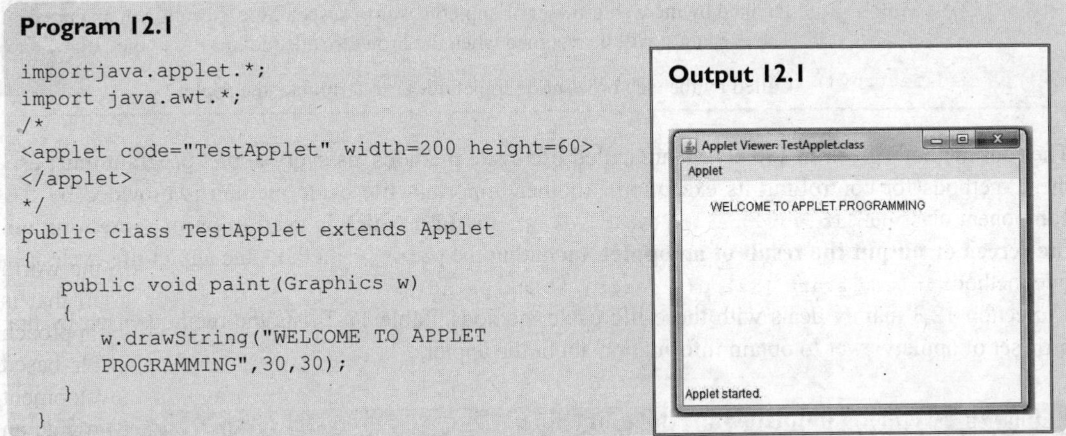

Program 12.1

```
importjava.applet.*;
import java.awt.*;
/*
<applet code="TestApplet" width=200 height=60>
</applet>
*/
public class TestApplet extends Applet
{
   public void paint(Graphics w)
   {
      w.drawString("WELCOME TO APPLET
      PROGRAMMING",30,30);
   }
}
```

Output 12.1

In **Program 12.1**, a class `TestApplet` becomes an applet by extending an `Applet` class. As mentioned earlier, two important packages `java.applet` and `java.awt` should be included in the program, otherwise the Java compiler cannot recognise `TestApplet` as an `Applet` class. The applet class `TestApplet` contains `paint()` method of `awt.component` class to paint itself on the window and the `Graphics` object `w` is passed as parameter. Inside the `paint()` method (described in the next section), `drawstring()` (described in the next section) method of the `Graphics` class is invoked and it draws the string 'WELCOME TO APPLET PROGRAMMING' on the window at X and Y position, where the values for X and Y are 30, 30. The applet is designed to work with a browser; so it needs to be specified in the APPLET tag of HTML. In the above example, the class file of the `TestApplet` program is specified in the APPLET tag which in turn is declared inside the comments. The APPLET tag creates a window with width 200 and height 60. In the next section, the Applet class and its methods are discussed.

12.2 `Applet` CLASS

The Java program which extends the `java.applet.Applet` class becomes an applet program. The `Applet` class offers support for applet execution. The methods provided by the base `Applet` class helps the developer to perform various operations in an applet program, such as obtaining applet parameters, getting the network location of the HTML file that contains the applet, printing a status message in the browser, fetching an image and audio, playing an audio, and so on.

In addition to this, an interface is provided by the `Applet` class that will be used by the Java-enabled web browser or applet viewer to get information about the applet such as author name, version and copyright of an applet, and to manage the execution, such as the starting and stopping of an applet. The applet also extends the *panel* of AWT class which in turn extends container, and container extends the component. This hierarchical inheritance of `Applet` and `AWT` classes gives room for Window-based activities. The following table describes the frequently used methods in the `Applet` class.

Table 12.1 Life cycle methods of an Applet

S. no.	Method	Description
1.	`void init()`	It is the first method that is invoked when an applet program starts execution.
2.	`void start()`	It is called by the web browser or appletviewer to start or resume execution. It is called soon after the `init()` method.
3.	`void stop()`	Invoked by the web browser or appletviewer to suspend the execution of an applet. The execution will be resumed when the browser calls the `start()` method.
4.	`void destroy()`	Called by the web browser or appletviewer to terminate the applet.

The four methods given in Table 12.1 are called life cycle methods, as every applet program must use these methods for controlling its execution. Another important life cycle method is provided by the component class `public void paint (Graphics g)` **method which is used to paint something on the screen or output the result of an applet**. Including the `paint()` method, the applet life cycle has five methods `init()`, `start()`, `stop()`, `destroy()` and `paint()`.

Section 12.3 mainly deals with these life cycle methods. Table 12.2 lists the methods used by the browser or appletviewer to obtain information about the applet.

Table 12.2 Methods supplying information to the browser or appletviewer

S. no.	Methods	Description
1.	`String getAppletInfo()`	Invoked by the browser or appletviewer to receive a string that describes the applet.
2.	`URL getCodeBase()`	Returns the URL.
3.	`URL getDocumentBase()`	Returns the URL of the HTML doc.
4.	`booleanisActive()`	True if the applet has started and False if the applet has stopped.
5.	`void showStatus(String m)`	Displays the string `m` in the status windows of the browser or appletviewer.
6.	`String getParameter(String PN)`	Returns the parameter.
7.	`AppletContextgetAppletContext()`	Returns the applet context.

Table 12.3 provides the various methods for handling audio clips and images.

Table 12.3 Methods for handling audio clips and images

S. no.	Methods	Description
1.	`AudioClipgetAudioClip(URL url)`	Retrieves the audio clip found at the location mentioned in the *url*.
2.	`AudioClipgetAudioClip(URL url, String clipName)`	Retrieves the audio clip having the name *clipName* found at the location mentioned in *url*.

(Continued)

Table 12.3 *(Continued)*

S. no.	Methods	Description
3.	`void play(URL url)`	The audio clip will be played if the audio clip is found at the location mentioned in the *url.*
4.	`void play(URL url, String clipName)`	The audio clip will be played, if the audio clip is found at the location mentioned in *url* and having the name *clipName.*
5.	`Image getImage(URL url)`	Retrieves the image found at the location specified in *url.*
6.	`Image getImage(URL url, String imageName)`	Retrieves the image having the name *imageName* found at the location specified in the *url*.

The methods described in Table 12.4 will be used throughout this chapter.

Table 12.4 Methods in `AWT` and `Graphics` class

S. no.	Methods	Description
1.	`public void paint(Graphics g)`	Paints on the window.
2.	`public void update(Graphics g)`	Updates the contents on the window.
3.	`public void repaint()`	It is triggered when the window is moved or resized.
4.	`public void drawString(String s, int x, int y)`	Draws a string which is given in *s* at x, y coordinates of the screen.
5.	`setSize()`	Sets the dimensions of a component.
6.	`getSize()`	Returns the current size of a component.
7.	`setFont()`	Sets the font.
8.	`getFont()`	Gets the current font.
9.	`setBackground()`	Sets the background colour.
10.	`setforeground()`	Sets the foreground colour.

In the next section the life cycle of an applet is discussed.

12.3 APPLET LIFE CYCLE

The life cycle of an applet program has four stages – *initialised*, *started*, *stopped* and *destroyed* – and these stages are implemented with the corresponding methods from the `Applet` class, namely `init()`, `start()`, `stop()` and `destroy()` methods. One more method, `paint()`, is provided by the component class and it is used to draw something on the window. The life cycle starts when the Java-enabled web browser or an appletviewer executes the applet program. All the life cycle methods are called automatically during execution or can be manually overridden by the user to perform specific actions. The console-based programs have the `main()` method to start and control its execution, but an applet, doesn't have *main()* method to start its execution, instead the web browser or appletviewer takes care of executing the life cycle methods. Using the life cycle methods, the developer can control the behaviour of an applet. Figure 12.1 depicts the flow of life cycle methods.

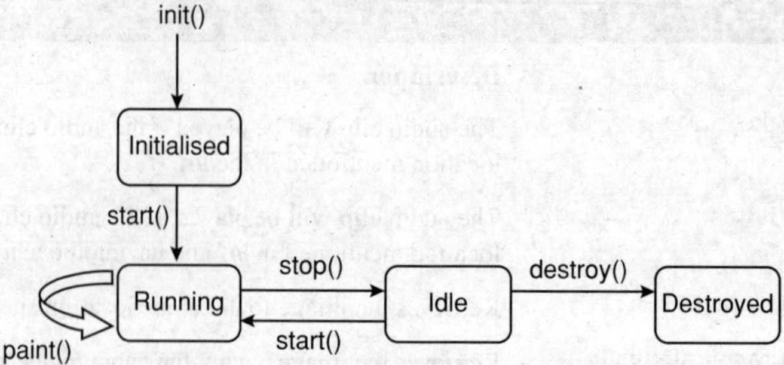

Fig. 12.1 Life cycle of an Applet

Stage1: The first stage is handled by the `init()` method and it is invoked automatically when the applet is loaded for the first time or executed by the appletviewer. It is called only once during the life cycle of an applet. The code segment placed inside the `init()` method is executed only once. This method is mostly used for initialisation purposes. Various parameters can be passed or set in this stage of the life cycle.

Stage 2: The second stage is handled by `start()`. When the web browser or appletviewer loads and initialises the applet, the JVM automatically invokes the `start()` method. It can also be called when an applet resumes execution from the idle stage. Unlike the `init()` method, this method is called many times during the life cycle. Whenever the user moves to another web page, the web browser stops the execution of an applet through invoking `stop()` and when the user returns to the web page that contains the applet, the browser resumes its execution using the `start()` method. So this method is used in conjunction with the `stop()` method. As mentioned earlier, all the life cycle methods can be overridden by the developer and called manually. Likewise, the `start()` method can be overridden by the developer to add some specific actions such as starting animation, triggering other thread execution.

Stage 3: The `stop()` method represents the third stage of the applet life cycle. It is called automatically by the web browser, to suspend execution when the user moves from the web page which contains the applet to the next web page, for saving system resources. The execution can be resumed by a call to `start()` and this is also called automatically when the user returns to the web page. Similar to the `start()` method, `stop()` too can be called more than once.

Stage 4: Whenever the user closes the browser or appletviewer, the `destroy()` method is invoked automatically to close the applet. Unlike the `stop()` method, once the `destroy()` method is invoked to terminate the applet, it can never be resumed again. Like the `init()`, it is called only once during the life cycle.

It is not always necessary to override all the life cycle methods to create an applet. As already mentioned, it can be called automatically by the web browser or appletviewer. The use of these life cycle methods mainly depends on what type of applet program is going to being developed. At the minimum level, `init()` is mostly overridden. This discussion would be incomplete without the `paint()` method. Even though the `paint()` method doesn't represent any stages in the life cycle of an applet, it is often called to draw something on the window or to display an output just like `System. out.println()` is used to display the output in console-based programs. Like the `paint()` method, sometimes `repaint()` and `update()` methods are also used to display content in a window. The next section helps the developer to develop an applet program in a step-by-step manner.

12.4 STEPS FOR DEVELOPING AN APPLET PROGRAM

To develop an applet program, the following steps should be followed.

STEP 1: Import the required package.
STEP 2: Develop a class which extends an `Applet` class.
STEP 3: Compile the applet program.
STEP 4: Write HTML code and include the `Applet` class.
STEP 5: Run the program.

The steps are briefly explained below:

STEP 1: Import the required package. The following packages need to be included in the program before developing an applet program.

```
importjava.applet.Applet;
importjava.awt.Graphics;
```

The `Applet` class provides very important methods that represent the life cycle of an applet program. The `Graphics` class of `awt` provides methods for handling graphical elements in the applet. These two packages are frequently used in developing an applet program.

STEP 2: Develop a class which extends an `Applet` class. In Java, every program is written inside the class which has `main()` method. To become an applet, this class should extend an `Applet` class and use all its methods. For example,

```
importjava.applet.Applet.*;
importjava.awt.Graphics.*;
public class Demo extends Applet
{
   publicvoid paint(Graphics g)
   {
      g.drawString("Welcome to APPLET ",100,100);
   }
}
```

The above program includes two important packages `java.applet.Applet` and `java.awt.Graphics` and all their methods. Without these packages, the Java compiler can't recognise the program as an applet-based program. The name of the class is `Demo` and it should be declared as *public* because its object will be created by the Java plug-in of the web browser. The `Demo` class must extend the `Applet` class to become an applet program; otherwise it is just an ordinary class.

Inside the `Demo` class, the `paint()` method of `Component` class is declared with `Graphics` object `g` as a parameter and is used to paint something on the screen. Inside this, the `drawString()` method of the `Graphics` class is called. The `drawString()` method actually passes the contents to the `paint()` method to display them on the screen. Whatever is present in the `drawString()` method will be drawn on the screen. In this program, it passes the string 'Welcome to APPLET' to the `paint()` method, to be displayed in the x-coordinate and y-coordinate position of the screen. To draw something on the window, the upper leftmost corner is always taken as the starting point. Every applet has its own area on the screen known as canvas, where it creates a display. The Java coordinate system has the origin (0, 0) in the upper-left corner. The x-coordinate increases horizontally to the right and the y-coordinate increases vertically downwards. Positive x and y axis will be taken. The values of (x, y) are in pixels.

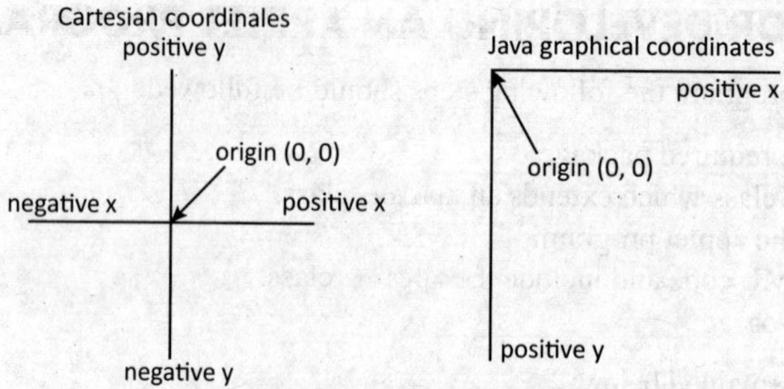

Fig. 12.2 Graphical coordinates of an applet

In Fig. 12.2, the origin (0,0) is the top-leftmost corner of the screen from where the shapes are drawn. The syntax of the `drawString()` method is given below with the respective code from the above program. Syntax:

```
voiddrawString(String s, int x, int y)
```

The first parameter *String s* represents what to draw on the screen and *int x, int y* tells where to draw the string given in String `s` variable. Code from the above program,

```
voiddrawString("Welcome to APPLET", 100, 100)
```

The above code draws the string 'Welcome to APPLET' in the 100th x-coordinate position and 100th y-coordinate position.

STEP 3: Compile the applet program. An applet program is just another program that extends the `Applet` class and produces its output on the window screen, instead of the console-screen. The usual way of compiling the Java program is followed and it produces the `.classfile` in the name of the class which in turn is used inside the applet tag or HTML file.

```
javac Demo.java
```

The above command produces the `Demo.class` file which contains the byte format of the code. The source file, that is, `Demo.java` file should be recompiled after any changes are made, to reflect the changes.

STEP 4: Write HTML code and include the `Applet` class. An applet program is meant to be embedded within a web page and to be used at the client side of the network. To be embedded, the applet program must be included in the HTML code either explicitly or implicitly. In an implicit approach, the applet program is going to be viewed using an applet viewer, and the applet program should use the <APPLET> tag. Using an explicit approach, a separate HTML file is created and class file of the applet program is referred. This HTML file which contains a reference to the `Applet` class can be viewed using the Java-enabled web browser. Before embedding the applet's class file into the web page using HTML, it is better to know the background of HTML. Covering HTML in full detail is beyond the scope of this book, but a brief introduction has been given in the following section.

12.4.1 Anatomy of HTML

A web site consists of more than one web page and each page is developed using Hyper Text Markup Language (HTML). A typical HTML or Web page has the following structure:

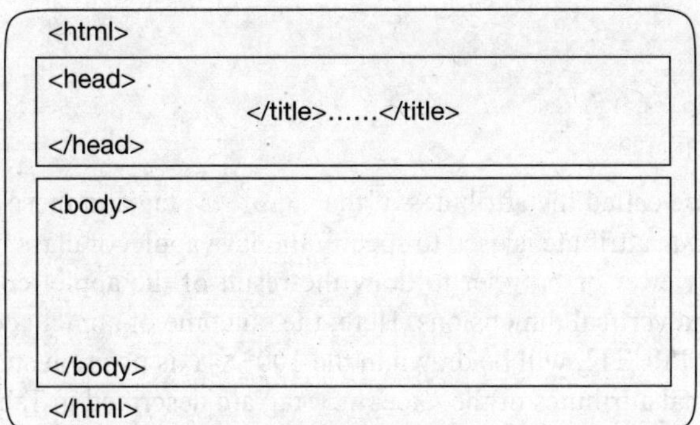

Fig. 12.3 Structure of HTML page

In Fig. 12.3, the HTML page has been divided into two sections—*head* and *body*. Each line in the HTML page is called an element and this element is presented in the opening and closing (*on* and *off tags* or *start* and *end tags*) tags as given below:

```
<tag-name>..........</tag-name>
```

For example,

```
<html> ..............</html>
```

The opening tag is `<html>` and the closing tag is `</html>`; every tag must be enclosed within these. The HTML page has the following three sections:

- Root ------ `<html>` ..... `</html>`
- Head ------- `<head>`......`</head>`
- Body ------ `<body>`.......`</body>`

The *root section* includes all other tags. Every web page should start and end with opening and closing tags of the Root element, that is, `<html></html>`. The *head section* represents the meta data and it has one additional title tag which displays the title of the page in the browser window. The *body section* has the contents which are going to be displayed in the browser. The HTML tag which is used to embed an applet program into the web page is `<applet>`. This `<applet>` tag can be specified implicitly in the applet program itself or by explicitly creating a separate HTML file.

12.4.2 Implicit Way

In the implicit way, the `<applet>` tag is specified just before the applet class declaration in between the opening and closing comments. The syntax of `<applet>` is:

```
/*
<applet code= "Demo.class" width= 100 height= 100>
</applet>
*/
```

where,

Opening tag ----- `<applet>`
Closing tag ----- `</applet>`

code, *width* and *height* are called the attributes of the `<applet>` tag and these are frequently used with the `<applet>` tag. The *code* attribute is used to specify the Java applet or class file. The *width* and *height* attributes tell the appletviewer or browser to draw the result of the applet code specified in the *code* attribute in horizontal and vertical dimensions. Here, the outcome of applet code `Demo.class`, which is the string 'Welcome to APPLET', will be drawn in the 100th x-axis position and 100th y-axis position of the window. Other optional attributes of the `<applet>` tag are described in Table 12.5.

Table 12.5 Attributes of `<applet>` tag

S. no.	Attributes	Value	Description
1	`align`	left, right, top, bottom, middle	Aligns the applet
2	`alt`	text	Used to specify the alternative text for an applet
3	`name`	name	Naming the given applet
4	`hspace`	pixels	Indicates the horizontal space around an applet
5	`vspace`	pixels	Indicates the vertical space around an applet

Now the stage has been set for embedding the Java applet code into the web page. The Applet class developed in the STEP 2 is now going to be embedded using the `<applet>` tag as given below:

```
import java.applet.*;
import java.awt.*;
/*
<applet code= "Demo.class" width=100 height=100>
</applet>
*/ importjava.applet.Applet.*;
importjava.awt.Graphics.*;
public class Demo extends Applet
{
    public void paint(Graphics g)
    {
        g.drawString("Welcome to APPLET",100,100);
    }
}
```

The complete applet program which is eligible to be embedded in the web page is given above. The applet program has the following three sections,

- packages to be imported,
- `<applet>` tag for embedding, and
- Java applet code.

12.4.3 Explicit Way

In the explicit way a separate HTML file is created, specifying the same `<applet>` tag inside the body tag. Before developing the HTML file, the Java applet class should be compiled successfully and kept ready because the `<applet>` tag expects the class file of the Java applet. Now the program is separated into two, the first one is the *Java Applet* and the second one is the *HTML file* which has a reference to the Java applet. The typical HTML file structure is given below. The HTML file should be saved with an extension `.html` and syntax for saving the HTML files is `filename.html`. For the Java applet developed in *STEP 2,* the separate HTML file is created as given below:

```
html>
<head>
</head>
<body>
<title>APPLET PAGE</title>
<applet code= "Demo.class" width = 300
height = 300>
</applet>
</body>
</html>
<
```

The `<applet>` specifies the executable version of `Demo.java` inside the HTML file.

STEP 5: Run the program

The applet program can be executed in two ways, using:

- HTML File
- appletviewer

To run an applet using an HTML file, first create an applet and compile it, after that create an HTML file and specify the applet code inside the body tag. When the html file is double-clicked, it is executed through the default browser. The same HTML file is viewed using the appletviewer as:

```
appletviewer demo.html
```

The appletviewer is needed to run the applet program which is going to be embedded in an explicit way. First, the program is compiled as given below,

```
javac Demo.java
```

To run the applet program, the code is typed as given below to invoke the appletviewer. The Java applet should be specified with a `.java` extension, because the applet program doesn't have a `main()` function to run with the usual run command.

```
appletviewerDemo.java
```

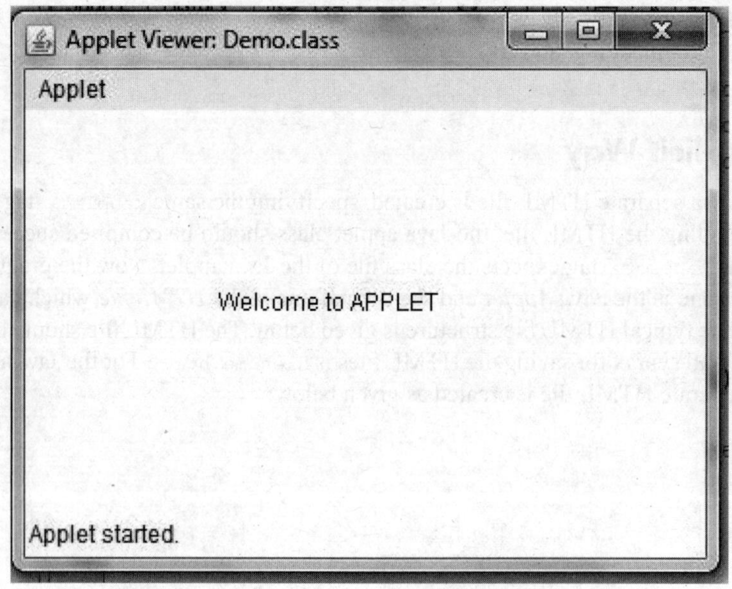

The `drawString("Welcome to APPLET",100,100)` method draws the string 'Welcome to APPLET' in the applet window in the position defined by the x and y-coordinates.

Program 12.2 modifies Program 12.1 and sets the background and foreground colours, and applies the colour for the string to be displayed.

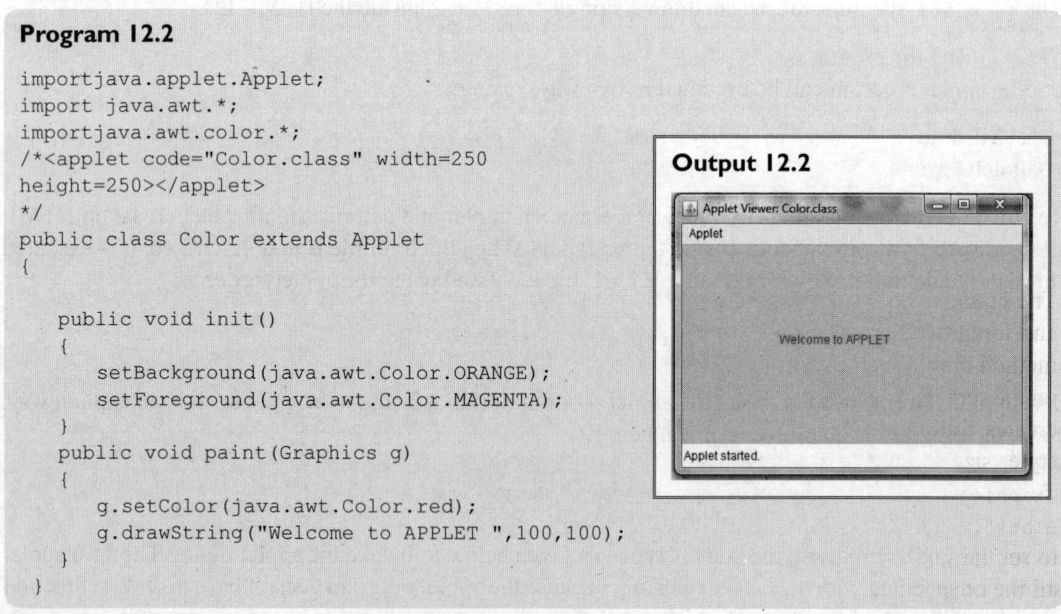

Program 12.2

```
importjava.applet.Applet;
import java.awt.*;
importjava.awt.color.*;
/*<applet code="Color.class" width=250
height=250></applet>
*/
public class Color extends Applet
{

   public void init()
   {
      setBackground(java.awt.Color.ORANGE);
      setForeground(java.awt.Color.MAGENTA);
   }
   public void paint(Graphics g)
   {
      g.setColor(java.awt.Color.red);
      g.drawString("Welcome to APPLET ",100,100);
   }
}
```

Output 12.2

In Program 12.2, the `Demo` class became an applet by extending the `Applet` class. Inside the Demo class, the `init()` method is declared, which is one of the life cycle methods of an applet. The `init()` method contains two display methods—`component` class `setBackground()` and `setForeground()`. The `setBackground()` method has a parameter `java.awt.Color.ORANGE` which sets the background colour of this applet in ORANGE during the loading. The `setForeground()` method has a parameter `java.awt.Color.MAGENTA`, which sets the foreground colour of the applet in MAGENTA during the loading. The `paint()` method has an object `g` of the `Graphics` class and it is used to draw a string on the screen by invoking the `drawString()` method, and sets the colour for the font in red using the `setColor()` method. The colour name is specified as a parameter in the `setColor()` method. **Program 12.3** demonstrates how to set font style and draw more than one string at a time.

Program 12.3

```
importjava.applet.Applet;
import java.awt.*;
importjava.awt.color.*;
/*<applet code="Color2.class" width=250 height=250></applet>*/
public class Color2 extends Applet
{
   public void init()
   {
      setBackground(java.awt.Color.CYAN);
      setForeground(java.awt.Color.MAGENTA);
   }
   public void paint(Graphics g)
   {
      Font f=new Font("Serif",Font.BOLD,14);
      g.setColor(java.awt.Color.BLACK);
      g.setFont(f);
      g.drawString("OOP IN JAVA ",100,100);
      Font d=new Font("Cooper Black",Font.
ITALIC,14);
      g.setColor(java.awt.Color.BLUE);
      g.setFont(d);
      g.drawString("* Class and Objects",120,120);
      g.drawString("* Inheritance",120,140);
      g.drawString("* Polymorphism",120,160);
   }

}
```

Output 12.3

Applet Viewer: Color2.class
Applet

OOP IN JAVA
* Class and Objects
* Inheritance
* Polymorphism

Applet started.

The class `Color2` becomes an applet by extending an applet. In the `init()` method, the background and foreground colours are set using `setBackground()` and `setForeground()` methods. The `paint()` method draws the four strings, 'OOP IN JAVA', 'Class and Objects,' 'Inheritance' and 'Polymorphism' on the screen, using `drawString()` method. The statement `Font f=new Font("Serif",Font.BOLD,14)` creates font object `f` and this object is passed as parameter in `setFont()` method to set the font style, size for the first string, 'OOP IN JAVA'. The `setColor()` method is also invoked using the `Graphics` object `g` to set font colour BLACK for that string. The statement `Font d=new Font("Cooper Black",Font.ITALIC,14)` creates a font object `d` and it is passed as parameter in `setFont()` method to set the font style, size for the remaining strings. The `setColor()` method sets the colour BLUE for all the other strings. The first `drawString("OOP IN JAVA ",100,100)` method draws the string in the position where the x, y coordinates are 100,100. The second statement, `g.drawString("* Class and Objects",120,120)` draws a string in the 120th x-coordinate position and 120th y-coordinate position. Likewise, all other `drawString()` methods draw their strings in the respective x and y-coordinate positions. We have discussed how to draw the string and apply font colour and style. In the next section, we shall discuss how data is passed in the applet program.

12.5 PASSING VALUES THROUGH PARAMETERS

Java applets allow the user to pass parameters to the applet with the help of <PARAM> tag. The <PARAM> tag has following two attributes:

- NAME – specifies the name of the parameter
- VALUE – assigns the value to the given parameter

The <PARAM> tag must be placed inside the <APPLET>...</APPLET> tag. An <APPLET> tag can have more than one <PARAM> tags. Each parameter is identified using its `NAME` attribute and data for the named attribute is assigned using `formatting` attribute. Using the `getParameter()` method, the value assigned in the VALUE attribute of <PARAM> tag can be retrieved. The syntax of the <PARAM> tag is given below:

```
<APPLET>
<PARAM NAME = parameter1 name VALUE=
parameter1_value>
<PARAM NAME = parameter2 name VALUE=
parameter2_value>
.
.
.
<PARAM NAME = parametern name VALUE=
parametern_value>
</APPLET>
```

Example,

```
<APPLET>
<PARAM NAME = age VALUE= 17>
</APPLET>
```

The name of the parameter is **age** and the value for the **age** parameter is 17.

Program 12.4 passes one string type parameter to the applet program. Run these programs in the command prompt with the appletviewer.

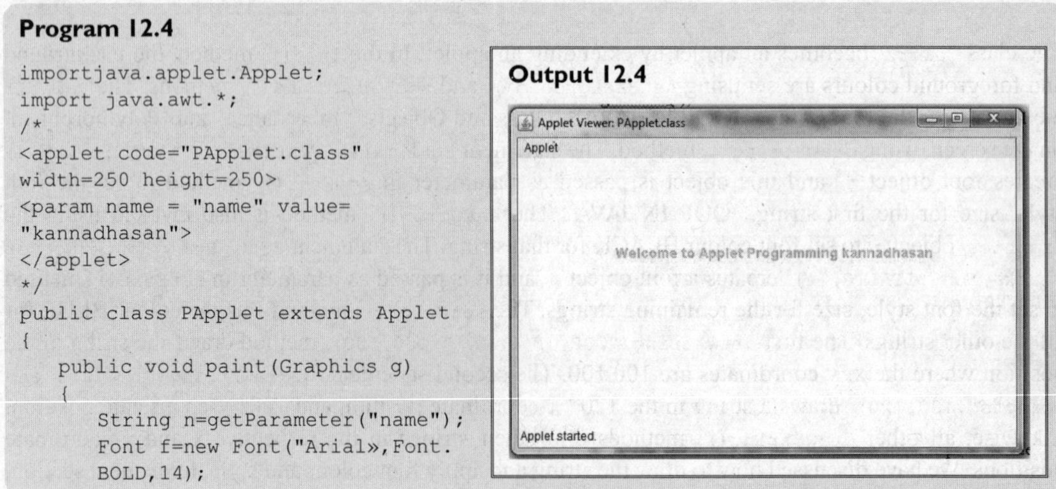

Program 12.4

```
importjava.applet.Applet;
import java.awt.*;
/*
<applet code="PApplet.class"
width=250 height=250>
<param name = "name" value=
"kannadhasan">
</applet>
*/
public class PApplet extends Applet
{
   public void paint(Graphics g)
   {
      String n=getParameter("name");
      Font f=new Font("Arial»,Font.
      BOLD,14);
```

Output 12.4

```
      g.setColor(java.awt.Color.GREEN);
      g.setFont(f);

      g.drawString("Welcome to Applet Programming "+n,100,100);
   }
}
```

Program 12.5 demonstrates how to pass more than one parameter at a time.

Program 12.5

```
import java.applet.Applet;
import java.awt.*;
/*
<applet code="multiparam.class" width=250 height=250>
<param name = "regno" value= "BP161501">
<param name = "name" value= "Janaki">
<param name = "deg" value= "MSc(ST)">
</applet>
*/
public class multiparam extends Applet
{
   String r, n, d;
   public void init()
   {
      r=getParameter("regno");
      n=getParameter("name");
      d=getParameter("deg");
   }
   public void paint(Graphics g)
   {
      Font re=new Font("Elephant",Font.BOLD,14);
      g.setColor(java.awt.Color.RED);
      g.setFont(re);
      g.drawString(r,100,100);
      Font na=new Font("Aharoni",Font.BOLD,16);
      g.setColor(java.awt.Color.GREEN);
      g.setFont(na);
      g.drawString(n,100,120);

      Font de=new Font("Times New Roman",Font.BOLD,18);
      g.setColor(java.awt.Color.BLUE);
      g.setFont(de);
      g.drawString(d,100,140);
   }
}
```

Output 12.5

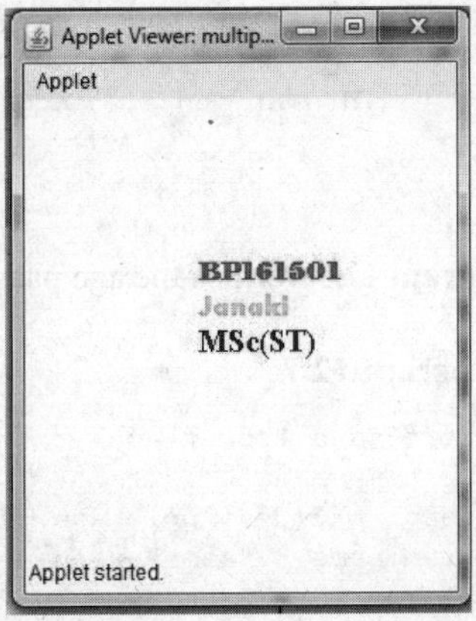

Applet Viewer: multip...
Applet

BP161501
Janaki
MSc(ST)

Applet started.

Program 12.6 passes two integer type parameters and performs an addition operation.

Program 12.6

```
import java.applet.Applet;
import java.awt.*;
/*
<applet code="Appletage.class" width=250 height=250>
```

```
<param name = a value= 8>
<param name = b value= 12>
</applet>
*/
public class Appletage extends Applet
{
   String n1,n2,r;
   inta,b,result;
   public void init()
   {
      n1=getParameter("a");
      a=Integer.parseInt(n1);
      n2=getParameter("b");
      b=Integer.parseInt(n2);
      result=a+b;
      r=String.valueOf(result);
   }
   public void paint(Graphics g)
   {
      Font na=new Font("Aharoni»,Font.
BOLD,16);
      g.setColor(java.awt.Color.GREEN);
      g.setFont(na);
      g.drawString(r,110,100);
   }
}
```

Output 12.6

Applet Viewer: Applet...

Applet

20

Applet started.

Program 12.7 verifies the age passed as a parameter, to determine eligibility to vote.

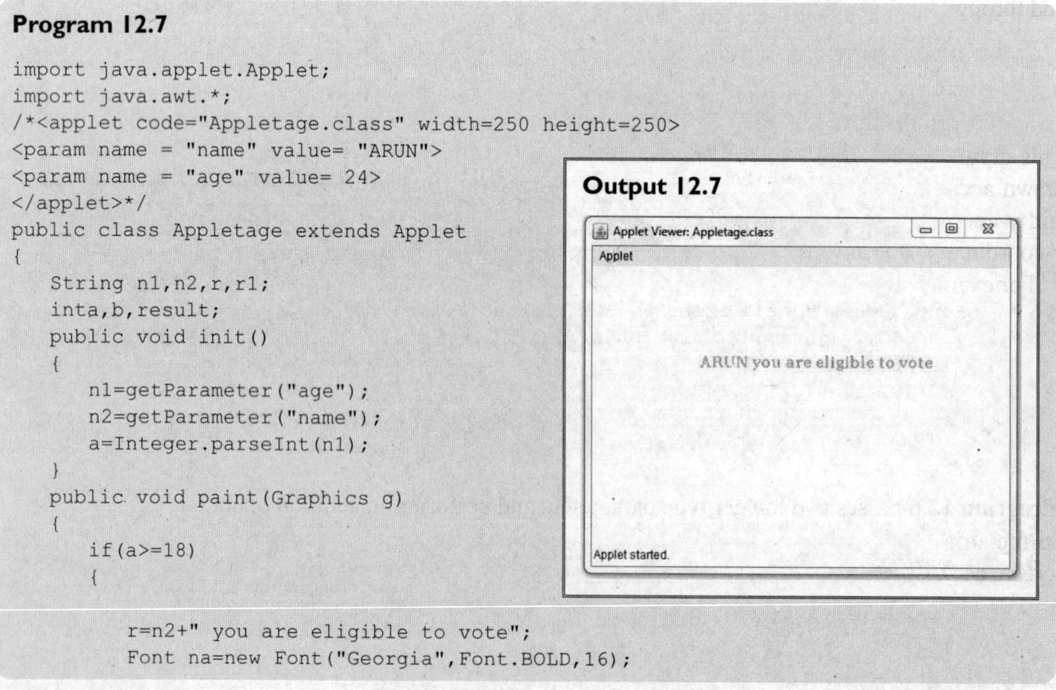

Program 12.7

```
import java.applet.Applet;
import java.awt.*;
/*<applet code="Appletage.class" width=250 height=250>
<param name = "name" value= "ARUN">
<param name = "age" value= 24>
</applet>*/
public class Appletage extends Applet
{
   String n1,n2,r,r1;
   inta,b,result;
   public void init()
   {
      n1=getParameter("age");
      n2=getParameter("name");
      a=Integer.parseInt(n1);
   }
   public void paint(Graphics g)
   {
      if(a>=18)
      {
         r=n2+" you are eligible to vote";
         Font na=new Font("Georgia",Font.BOLD,16);
```

Output 12.7

```
        g.setColor(java.awt.Color.GREEN);
        g.setFont(na);
        g.drawString(r,110,100);
      }
    else
    {
        r1=n2+" you are NOT eligible
        to vote";
        Font na2=new
        Font("Georgia",Font.BOLD,16);
        g.setColor(java.awt.Color.
        RED);
        g.setFont(na2);
        g.drawString(r1,110,100);
    }
  }
}
```

Output 12.7

Applet Viewer: Appletage.class

Applet

ARUN you are NOT eligible to vote

Applet started.

The next section explains how graphics are handled in applets.

12.6 GRAPHICS IN AN APPLET

The `java.awt.Graphics` package provides methods to draw various shapes such as *lines*, *rectangles*, *polygons* and *ovals* on the screen using x, y coordinates. The values for x and y are specified in pixels. This is mostly used in developing applets for use in gaming and animation, and similar applications. The methods provided by the `Graphics` class are explained and these methods are invoked inside `paint()` and through `Graphics` objects.

```
drawString(String str, int x, int y)
```

This draws on the screen, the given string specified in the string type variable *str*. The string will be drawn according to the existing colour and font. The position on the screen will be defined by the x and y-coordinates, where the x-coordinate specifies the position of the left end of the string and the y-coordinate is the baseline of the string. The baseline is a horizontal line on which the string is placed.

For example,

```
drawString(String str, int x, int y)
Values for parameters,
String str = "JAVA Programming"
int x = 50 int y= 100
drawString("JAVA Programming", 50,100)
```

So the string 'JAVA Programming' will be drawn on the 50th x-axis and 100th y-axis position on the screen, as shown below.

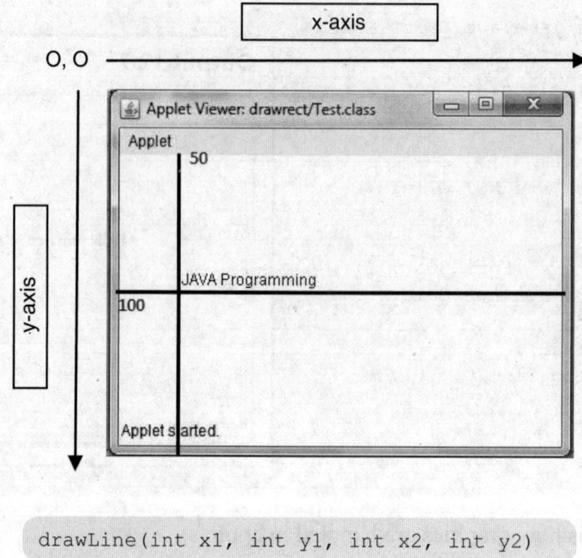


```
drawLine(int x1, int y1, int x2, int y2)
```

This draws a line from the starting point (x1, y1) to the ending point (x2, y2). The line is drawn as if with a pen that hangs one pixel to the right and one pixel down from the (x, y) point where the pen is located. For example, if `g` refers to an object of type Graphics, then the command `g.drawLine(x,y,x,y)`, which corresponds to putting the pen down at a point, draws the single pixel located at the point (x, y).

For example,

```
drawLine(int x1, int y1, int x2, int y2)
```

Values for the parameters,

x1 = 20 y1 = 20 x2 = 100 y2 = 100

```
drawLine(20, 20, 100,100)
```

The line is drawn from the starting point (20,20) till the ending point (100,100) as shown below.

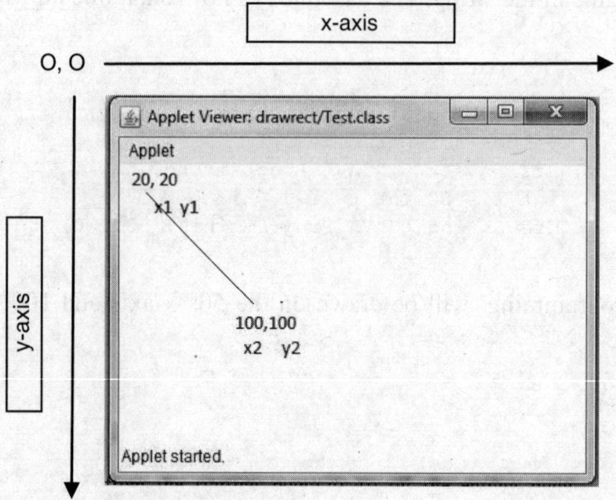

```
drawRect(int x, int y, int w, int h)
```

This method is used to draw a rectangle shape on the screen at the point defined by the x and y-coordinates. The width and height of the rectangle is specified in the integer type variables `w` and `h`. If width equals height, then the rectangle is a square. If the width or the height is negative, then nothing is drawn. The rectangle is drawn with the same pen that is used for `drawLine()`. This means that the actual width of the rectangle as drawn is width+1, and similarly for the height. There is an extra pixel along the right edge and the bottom edge. For example, if you want to draw a rectangle around the edges of the component, you can say `g.drawRect(0, 0, getSize().width-1, getSize().height-1);`, where `g` is a graphics context for the component.

For example, the statement

```
drawRect(100, 100, 150, 100)
```

The above statement draws a rectangle starting at x and y-axis position (100,100) with the width 150 pixels and height 100 pixels. The result of the statement is given below.

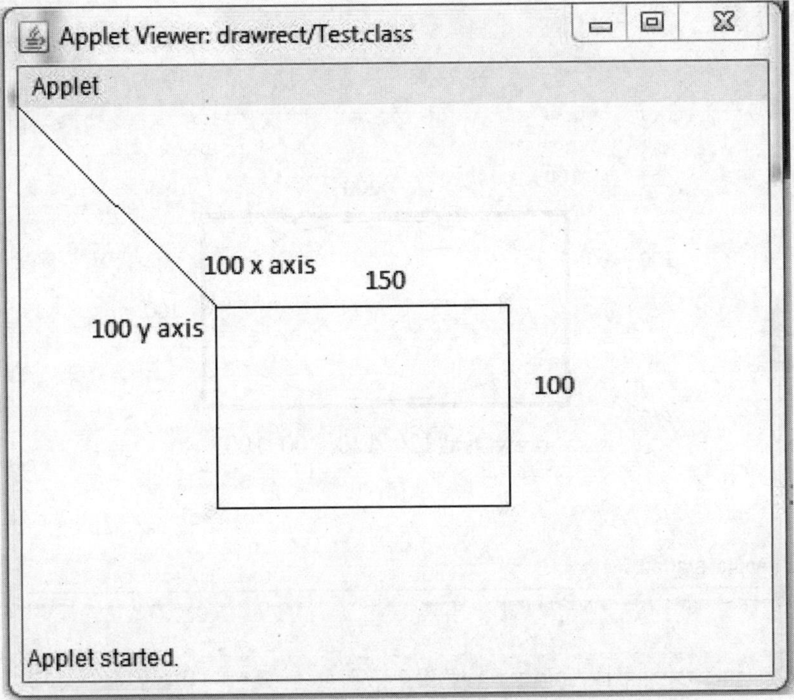


```
drawOval(int x, int y, int width, int height)
```

This draws a circle or an oval that fits inside the rectangle specified by x, y, width and height arguments. If the values of width and height are the same, then the oval becomes a circle.

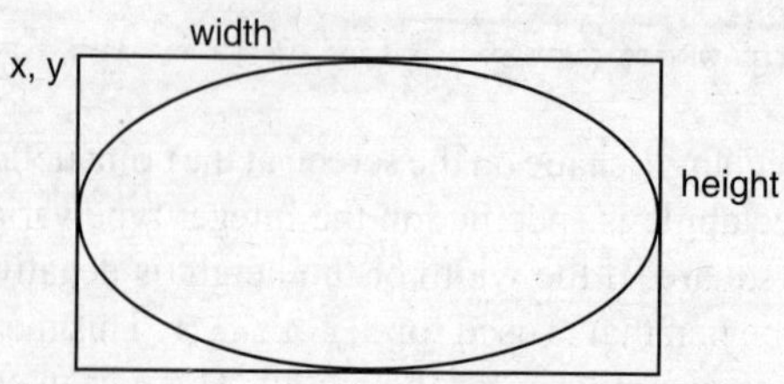

For example,

```
drawOval(100, 100, 200, 100);
```

where the x and y-axis value is 120, width is 200 pixels and height is 100 pixels. The oval is drawn as given below.

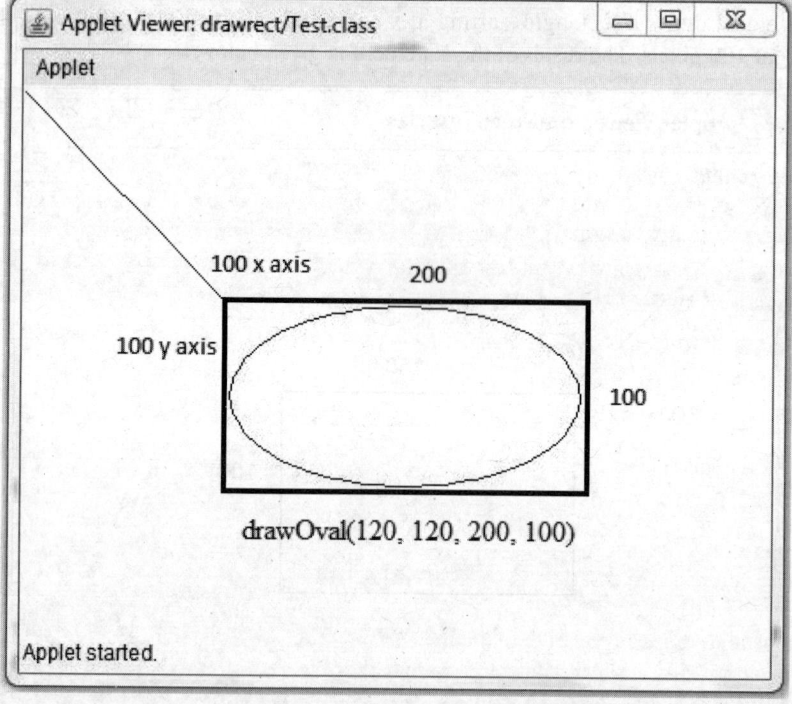


```
drawRoundRect(int x, int y, int width, int height, intxdiam, intydiam)
```

This draws the outline of a rectangle with rounded corners. The basic rectangle is specified by x, y, width, and height, but the corners are rounded. The degree of rounding is given by `xdiam` and `ydiam`. `Xdiam` is the diameter of the rounding arc at the x-axis and ydiam is the diameter of the rounding arc at the y-axis. The corners are arcs of an ellipse with horizontal diameter `xdiam` and vertical diameter `ydiam`.

For example,

```
drawRoundRect(100, 100, 150, 100, 26, 19)
```

where the values of x and y axes are 100. The width and height of the rounded rectangle are 150 and 100 respectively. 26 and 19 represent the diameter of the x and y-axis corner of the rounded rectangle.

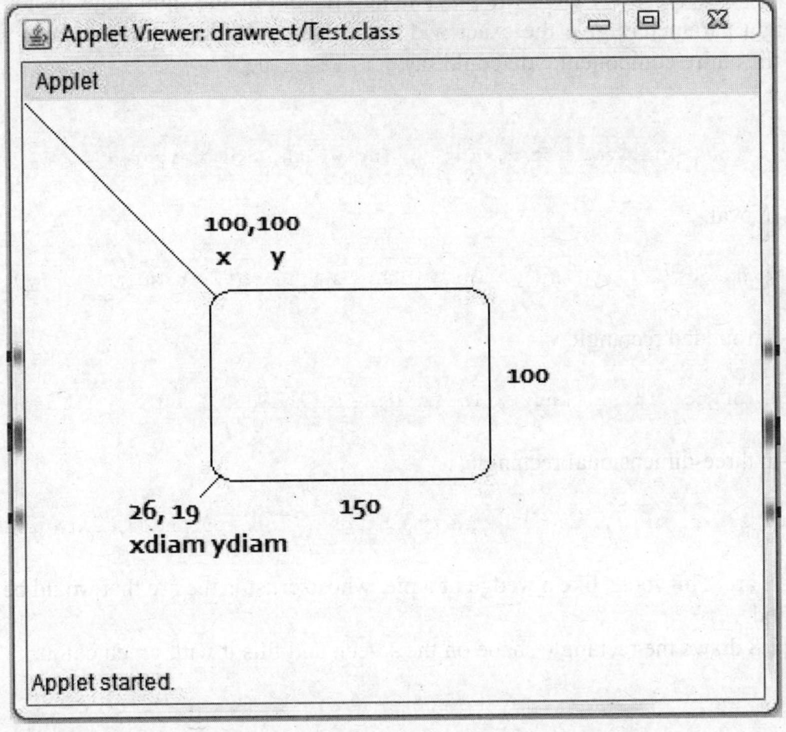


```
draw3DRect(int x, int y, int width, int height, boolean raised)
```

This method is used to draw a rectangle that can have a three dimensional effect. The basic rectangle is drawn using the parameters `x, y, width` and `height`. The *raised* parameter tells whether the rectangle should be raised from the screen or pushed into it. The 3D effect is achieved by using brighter and darker versions of the drawing colour for different edges of the rectangle. The documentation recommends setting the drawing colour equal to the background colour before using this method. The effect won't work well for some colours.

```
drawArc(int x, int y, int width, int height, intstartAngle, intarcAngle)
```

This draws part of the oval or arc that can fit inside the rectangle specified by parameters *x*, *y*, width and height. The drawn part is an arc that extends arcAngle degrees from a starting angle at startAngle degrees. Angles are measured with 0 degrees at the 3 o'clock position (the positive direction of the horizontal axis). Positive angles are measured counterclockwise from zero, and negative angles are measured clockwise. To get an arc of a circle, make sure that width is equal to the height.

```
fillRect(int x, int y, int width, int height)
```

This draws a filled-in rectangle. This fills in the interior of the rectangle that would be drawn by `drawRect(x,y,width,height)`. The extra pixel along the bottom and right edges is not included. The width and height parameters give the exact width and height of the rectangle. For example, if you want to fill in the entire component, you could say `g.fillRect(0, 0, getSize().width, getSize().height);`

```
fillOval(int x, int y, int width, int height)
```

draws a filled-in oval.

```
fillRoundRect(int x, int y, int width, int height, intxdiam, intydiam)
```

draws a filled-in rounded rectangle.

```
fill3DRect(int x, int y, int width, int height, boolean raised)
```

draws a filled-in three-dimensional rectangle.

```
fillArc(int x, int y, int width, int height, intstartAngle, intarcAngle)
```

draws a filled-in arc. This looks like a wedge of a pie, whose crust is the arc that would be drawn by the `drawArc` method.

Program 12.8 draws the rectangle shape on the screen and fills it with green colour.

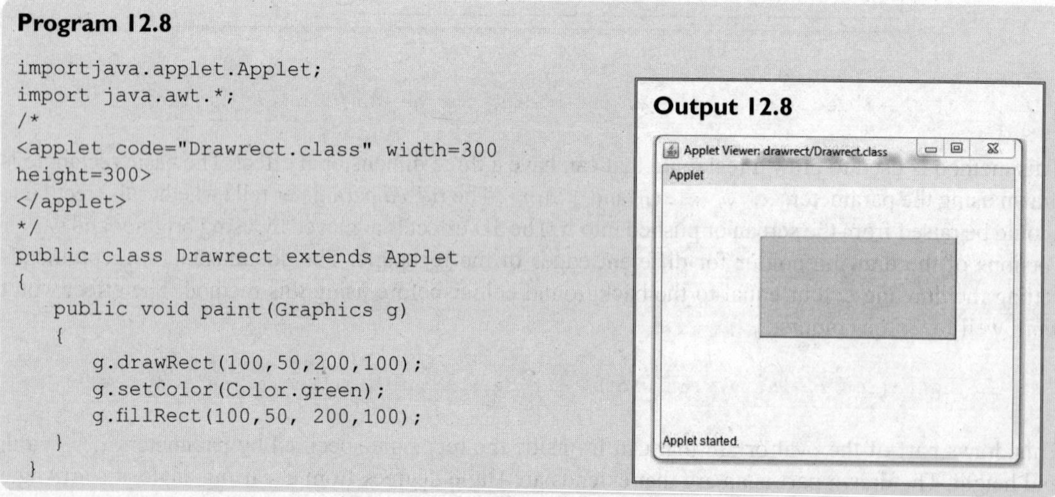

Program 12.8

```
importjava.applet.Applet;
import java.awt.*;
/*
<applet code="Drawrect.class" width=300
height=300>
</applet>
*/
public class Drawrect extends Applet
{
   public void paint(Graphics g)
   {
      g.drawRect(100,50,200,100);
      g.setColor(Color.green);
      g.fillRect(100,50, 200,100);
   }
}
```

Output 12.8

Program 12.9 draws three ovals and fills them in with different colours.

Program 12.9

```
import java.applet.Applet;
import java.awt.*;
/*
<applet code="Drawoval.class" width=300
height=300>
</applet>
*/
public class Drawoval extends Applet
{
   public void paint(Graphics g)
   {
      g.drawOval(100,100,75,50);
      g.setColor(Color.magenta);
      g.fillOval(100,100,75,50);
      g.drawOval(100,160,75,50);
      g.setColor(Color.cyan);
      g.fillOval(100,160,75,50);
      g.drawOval(100,220,75,50);
      g.setColor(Color.pink);
      g.fillOval(100,220,75,50);
   }
 }
```

Output 12.9

Applet Viewer: drawrect/Drawoval.class

Applet

Applet started.

Program 12.10 draws different types of shapes in colours with a caption for each shape.

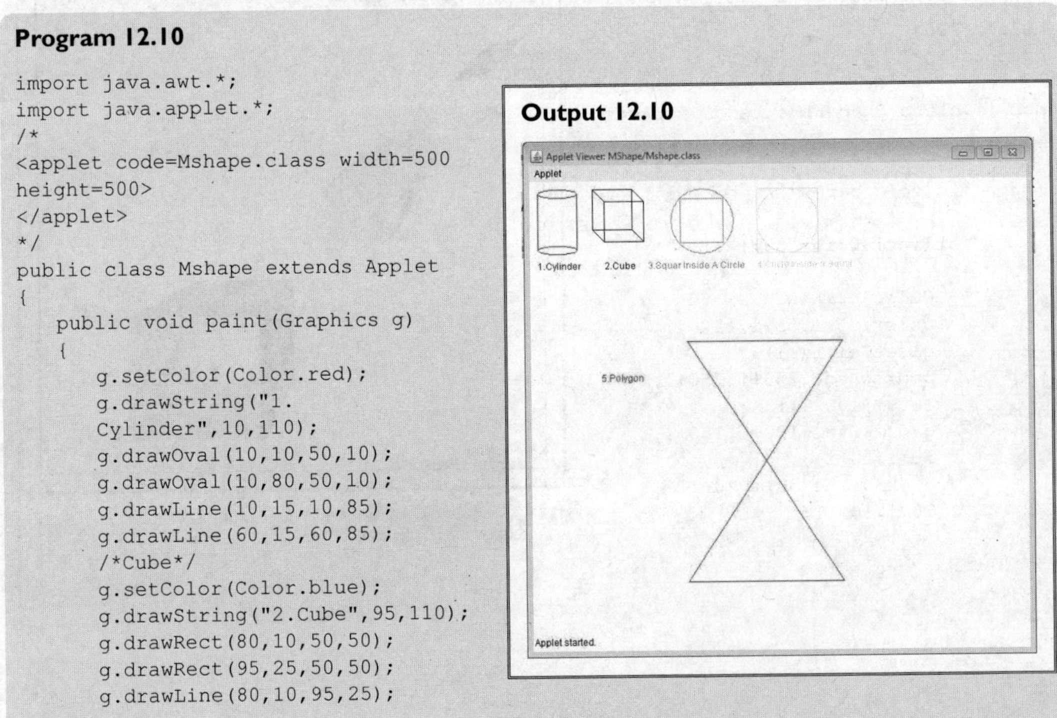

Program 12.10

```
import java.awt.*;
import java.applet.*;
/*
<applet code=Mshape.class width=500
height=500>
</applet>
*/
public class Mshape extends Applet
{
   public void paint(Graphics g)
   {
      g.setColor(Color.red);
      g.drawString("1.
      Cylinder",10,110);
      g.drawOval(10,10,50,10);
      g.drawOval(10,80,50,10);
      g.drawLine(10,15,10,85);
      g.drawLine(60,15,60,85);
      /*Cube*/
      g.setColor(Color.blue);
      g.drawString("2.Cube",95,110);
      g.drawRect(80,10,50,50);
      g.drawRect(95,25,50,50);
      g.drawLine(80,10,95,25);
```

```
        g.drawLine(130,10,145,25);
        g.drawLine(80,60,95,75);
        g.drawLine(130,60,145,75);
        /*Squar Inside A Circle*/
        g.setColor(Color.green);
        g.drawString("3.Square Inside A Circle",150,110);
        g.drawOval(180,10,80,80);
        g.drawRect(192,22,55,55);
        /*Circle Inside a Squar*/
        g.setColor(Color.yellow);
        g.drawString("4.Circle Inside a Square",290,110);
        g.drawRect(290,10,80,80);
        g.drawOval(290,10,80,80);
        /*Polygon*/ g.setColor(Color.MAGENTA);
        g.drawString("5.Polygon",90,250);
        int a[]={200,400,200,400};
        int b[]={200,500,500,200};
        g.drawPolygon(a,b,4);
    }
}
```

Program 12.11 draws shapes using a loop to generate a hollow shape.

Program 12.11

```
import java.awt.*;
import java.applet.*;
/*
<applet code="ShapeFL" width=200
height=200>
</applet>
*/
public class ShapeFL extends Applet
{

   public void paint(Graphics g)
   {
      for(inti=0;i<=250;i++)
      {
         Color c1=new
         Color(35-i,55-i,110-i);
         g.setColor(c1);
         g.drawRect(250+i,250+i,
         100+i,100+i);
         g.drawOval(100+i,100+i,
         50+i,50+i);
         g.drawLine(50+i,20+i,
         10+i,10+i);
      }
   }
}
```

Output 12.11

Applet Viewer: MShape/ShapeFL.class
Applet
Applet started.

12.7 EVENT HANDLING

As described in the beginning of this chapter, applet programs are based on an event-driven approach. Unlike console-based programs which interact with the user through commands, the applet uses GUI components. When the user interacts with a GUI application such as an applet through components like buttons, an event is triggered when the button is clicked, to perform some operation. As a GUI based application, applets cannot be written without event-handling. Java supports event-handling through the packages `java.util`, `java.awt` and `java.awt.event`.

Delegation-event model

In Java, the event-handling mechanism is implemented through the *delegation-event model*. This model provides a consistent and standard approach to produce and process events. The logic of this model is quite simple: the *source* generates an event which will be handled by the respective *listener*; here the listener waits until it receives an event from the source. Once the event is received, the listener processes it and returns. The main feature of the delegation-event model is that it separates the UI logic that generates an event from the application logic that processes the event. In the delegation-event model, a source must register with the respective listener before producing an event. Only a registered listener can receive the notification from the concerned source. The delegation-event model has the following components to produce and process the events:

- event source,
- event listener, and
- event class.

Before getting into the concept, it is important to understand what an event actually is. An event is the change of state of an object. It is generated by one of the GUI components. In a GUI environment, the interaction takes place when the *user clicks a button* or *selects an item from a menu* or *moves the mouse* or *enters any key from the keyboard*. Events occur not only by direct interaction with one or more GUI components, but also when the counting time expires or software/hardware fails or some operation is completed. Fundamentally, there are two types of events in GUI applications—*semantic events* and *low-level events*. Semantic events are produced by GUI components such as buttons, textboxes, combo boxes, check boxes or radio buttons. Low-level events are generated by hardware components such as the *keyboard* and *mouse*.

Event source

An event source is an ordinary GUI component which is capable of producing events, such as a button, TextField, menu, and so on. In Java, an object is created for each such source which in turn triggers an event.

Event listener

Listeners are interfaces which are specially designed to handle the events generated by the GUI components or controls. Each GUI component has its own listener. For example, button control has an `ActionListener` interface to handle an event produced by clicking the button control. Not only does a listener handle a particular kind of controls, but some listeners handle more than one component, such as the `ActionListener` which handles not only button but also `TextField`, `List` and `Menu`. Table 12.6 shows event sources and corresponding event classes and listeners.

Table 12.6 Event sources and the corresponding event classes and listeners

Event source	Event class	Event listener
Menu, Button, TextField	ActionEvent	ActionListener
Checkbox, Choice, List	ItemEvent	ItemListener
TextField	TextEvent	TextListener
Scrollbar	AdjustmentEvent	AdjustmentListener
Frame	WindowEvent	WindowListener
Mouse	MouseEvent	MouseListener and MouseMotionListener
Mouse wheel	MouseWheelEvent	MouseWheelListener
Keyboard	KeyEvent	KeyListener
All the components	FocusEvent	FocusListener
All the component	ComponentEvent	ComponentListener
Container	ContainerEvent	ContainerListener

Event classes

Most GUI components or controls generate an event that can be handled by its unique event class. Event classes are defined for all GUI components. For instance, an event generated when the button control is clicked, is handled by the `ActionEvent` class. The class `AWTEvent`, defined within the `java.awt` package, is a subclass of `EventObject`. It is the superclass of all AWT-based events used by the delegation-event model. Let's learn about event class and event listener in depth.

`ActionEvent` class and `ActionListener` interface

`ActionEvent` class

The `ActionEvent` is generated when the user clicks a button or an item in a menu or double-clicks an item in a list. The `ActionEvent` has the following constants and constructors:

Constants in `ActionEvent` *class*

- `ALT_MASK`
- `CTRL_MASK`
- `META_MASK and SHIFT_MASK`
- `ACTION_PERFORMED`

These constants are used to identify the modifiers related to the action event.

Constructors of `ActionEvent` *class*

- `ActionEvent(Object src, int type, String cmd)`
- `ActionEvent(Object src, int type, String cmd, int modifiers)`
- `ActionEvent(Object src, int type, String cmd, long when, int modifiers)`

Here, `src` refers to the source object (an object created for a GUI component) that generated this event. The type of event is specified in `type` parameter and its command string is `cmd`. The parameter `modifiers` specifies what type of modifier key was pressed during event generation.

Methods in an ActionEvent class

- `String getActionCommand( )`
- `int getModifiers( )`
- `long getWhen( )`

The String `getActionCommand( )` method helps to bring the name or label of the `ActionEvent` object (GUI Component object). When the button control is pressed, this method returns the label of that button. The int `getModifiers()` returns the type of modifier pressed during the event generation. The long `getWhen()` method returns the time at which the event was generated.

`ActionListener` interface

This listener interface provides the following method that can be used with an event source such as a button. It waits for the event to be generated by the corresponding GUI component and triggers the corresponding action for that event. The method has the following form:

```
void actionPerformed(ActionEvent ae)
```

`ItemEvent` class and `ItemListener` interface

`ItemEvent` class

This is triggered when the user selects or deselects the checkable items or an item in the list control is clicked.

Constants in `ItemEvent` *class*

- `SELECTED`
- `DESELECTED`

These constants are used to identify the selected or deselected items in the check box or list controls.

Constructors of `ItemEvent` *class*

- `ItemEvent(ItemSelectable src, int type, Object entry, int state)`

Here, `src` refers to the item of the check box or list box that generated this event. Type of event is specified in `type` parameter. The `entry` parameter marks the specific item which generated this event. The current state of the item is in `state` parameter.

Methods in an `ItemEvent` *class*

- `Object getItem()`
- `ItemSelectable getItemSelectable()`
- `int getStateChange()`

The `getItem()` method refers to the item that is changed. `getItemSelectabel()` method refers to the `ItemSelectable` object that is generated this event. Method `getStateChange()` returns the state change, that is, `SELECTED` or `DESELECTED` for this event.

`ItemListener` interface

This interface defines the following method that can be invoked when the user changes state of a selectable item whether in check box or list. It has the following general form:

```
void itemStateChanged(ItemEvent ie )
```

`TextEvent` class and `TextListener` interface

`TextEvent` class

This is generated when the user enters text in the `TextField` or `TextArea` control. `TextEvent` class has only one constant value `TEXT_VALUE_CHANGED`.

Constructors of TextEvent class

- `TextEvent(Object src, int type)`

Here, `src` refers to the GUI object that generated this event. Type of event is specified in `type` parameter.

`TextListener` interface

This defines the following method that can be used to invoke the corresponding action when the text entered in `TextArea` or `TextField` is changed. The method has the following general form:

```
void textValueChanged(TextEvent te)
```

`AdjustmentEvent` class and `AdjustmentListener` interface

`AdjustmentEvent` class

It is triggered by the scroll bar control. It has the following constants and constructors to manipulate the scroll bar function.

Constants in `AdjustmentEvent` *class*

- `BLOCK_DECREMENT` click inside the scroll bar to decrease its value.
- `BLOCK_INCREMENT` click inside the scroll bar to increase its value.
- `TRACK` drag the slider.
- `UNIT_DECREMENT` click the button at the end of the scroll bar to decrease its value.
- `UNIT_INCREMENT` click the button at the end of the scroll bar to increase its value.
- `ADJUSTMENT_VALUE_CHANGED` indicates that a change has occurred.

Constructors of `AdjustmentEvent` *class*

- `AdjustmentEvent(Adjustable src, int id, int type, int val)`

Here, `src` refers to the GUI object that is generated this event. The event `id` and type of adjustment is specified in the parameter `type` and its value in `val`.

Methods in an `AdjustmentEvent` *class*

- `Adjustable getAdjustable( )` returns the object that generated this event.
- `int getAdjustmentType( )` returns the type of adjustment event.
- `int getValue( )` returns the amount of adjustment.

`AdjustmentListener` **interface**

This interface defines the following method that is invoked when an adjustment event occurs. The general form is:

```
void adjustmentValueChanged(AdjustmentEvent ae)
```

`WindowEvent` and `WindowListener` interface

`WindowEvent`

`WindowEvent` is a subclass of `ComponentEvent` class. It has ten events and ten different types of constants that can be used to identify the events.

Constants in WindowEvent class

- `WINDOW_ACTIVATED` window was activated.
- `WINDOW_CLOSED` window has been closed.
- `WINDOW_CLOSING` user requested that the window be closed.
- `WINDOW_DEACTIVATED` window was deactivated.
- `WINDOW_DEICONIFIED` window was de-iconified.
- `WINDOW_GAINED_FOCUS` window gained input focus.
- `WINDOW_ICONIFIED` window was iconified.
- `WINDOW_LOST_FOCUS` window lost input focus.
- `WINDOW_OPENED` window was opened.
- `WINDOW_STATE_CHANGED` state of the window changed.

Constructors of WindowEvent class

- `WindowEvent(Window src, int type)`
- `WindowEvent(Window src, int type, Window other)`
- `WindowEvent(Window src, int type, int fromState, int toState)`
- `WindowEvent(Window src, int type, Window other, int fromState, int toState)`

Here, `src` is a reference to the object that generated this event. The type of the event is `type`, `other` specifies the opposite window and `fromState` refers to the prior state of the window. `toState` marks the new state of the window.

Methods in `WindowEvent` *class*

- `Window getWindow()` returns an object that generated an event.
- `Window getOppositeWindow( )` returns the opposite window.
- `int getOldState()` returns the old state of the window.
- `int getNewState()` returns the new state of the window.

`WindowListener` **interface**

This interface defines the following methods to operate the window.

- `void windowActivated(WindowEvent we)` triggered when window is activated.
- `void windowClosed(WindowEvent we)` invoked when the user requests to close the window.
- `void windowClosing(WindowEvent we)` triggered when the window is being closed.

- `void windowDeactivated(WindowEvent we)` invoked to deactivate the window.
- `void windowDeiconified(WindowEvent we)` used de-iconify the window.
- `void windowIconified(WindowEvent we)` called to iconify the window.
- `void windowOpened(WindowEvent we)` triggered to open the window.

`MouseEvent` class and `MouseListener` interface

`MouseEvent` class

`MouseEvent` class is the subclass of `InputEvent` class. This class has seven different mouse events and seven constants to identify them.

Constants in `MouseEvent` *class*

- `MOUSE_CLICKED` the mouse is clicked by the user.
- `MOUSE_DRAGGED` the mouse is dragged by the user.
- `MOUSE_ENTERED` the mouse entered a component.
- `MOUSE_EXITED` the mouse exited from a component.
- `MOUSE_MOVED` the mouse moved.
- `MOUSE_PRESSED` the mouse was pressed.
- `MOUSE_RELEASED` the mouse was released.
- `MOUSE_WHEEL` the mouse wheel was moved.

Constructors of `MouseEvent` *class*

- `MouseEvent(Component src, int type, long when, int modifiers, int x, int y, int clicks, boolean triggersPopup)`

Here, `src` is a reference to the component that generated the event. The type of the event is specified by `type`. The time when the mouse event was triggered is passed on in `when`. The `modifiers` argument indicates which modifiers were pressed when a mouse event occurred. The coordinates of the mouse are passed in `x` and `y`. The click count is passed in `clicks`. The `triggersPopup` flag indicates if this event causes a pop-up menu to appear on this platform.

Methods in `WindowEvent` *class*

- `int getX( )`
- `int getY( )`
- `Point getPoint( )`
- `void translatePoint(int x, int y)`
- `int getClickCount( )`
- `boolean isPopupTrigger( )`
- `int getButton( )`
- `Point getLocationOnScreen( )`
- `int getXOnScreen( )`
- `int getYOnScreen( )`

`getX()` and `getY()` methods return the x and y-coordinate positions of the mouse while in the component during the occurrence of an event. The `getPoint()` method returns the x and y-coordinate positions in integer variables `x` and `y`. The `translatePoint(int x, int y)` method changes the location of the event. `getClickCount()` returns the number of mouse clicks. The appearance of the pop-up menu is checked through the `isPopupTrigger()` method. The `getButton()` method returns the value that indicates the button that triggered an event.

`MouseListener` interface

The `MouseListener` interface defines the following five methods to manipulate mouse motion.

- `void mouseClicked(MouseEvent me)`
- `void mouseEntered(MouseEvent me)`
- `void mouseExited(MouseEvent me)`
- `void mousePressed(MouseEvent me)`
- `void mouseReleased(MouseEvent me)`

When the mouse is pressed and released at the same time, `mouseClicked()` is invoked. When the mouse enters the component and when it leaves, the `mouseEntered()` and `mouseExited()` methods are called respectively. When the mouse is pressed and released individually, the `mousePressed()` and `mouseReleased()` method are triggered respectively. Two more methods are defined in the `MouseMotionListener` interface for handling mouse dragging and moving operations.

`MouseMotionListener` Interface

This interface defines the following two methods to handle the functionality of dragging and moving the mouse. Their general forms are,

```
void mouseDragged(MouseEvent me)
void mouseMoved(MouseEvent me)
```

`MouseWheelEvent` class and `MouseWheelListener` interface

`MouseWheelEvent` class

This is a sub-class of `MouseEvent`. It contains the events for manipulating the mouse wheel. This event is less utilised because it is triggered only by a mouse wheel, and not all mouse units have a wheel.

Constants in `MouseWheelEvent` *class*

- `WHEEL_BLOCK_SCROLL` a page-up or page-down scroll event occurred.
- `WHEEL_UNIT_SCROLL` a line-up or line-down scroll event occurred.

Constructors of `MouseWheelEvent` *class*

- `MouseWheelEvent(Component src, int type, long when, int modifiers, int x, int y, int clicks, boolean triggersPopup, int scrollHow, int amount, int count)`

Here, `src` is a reference to the component that generated the event. The type of the event is specified by `type`. The time at which the mouse event was triggered, is passed in `when`. The `modifiers` argument indicates which modifiers were pressed when a mouse event occurred. The coordinates of the mouse are passed in `x` and `y`. The click count is passed in `clicks`. The `triggersPopup` flag indicates if this event causes a pop-up menu to appear on this platform. The `scrollHow` should have a value either `WHEEL_UNIT_SCROLL` or `WHEEL_BLOCK_SCROLL`. The number of units to scroll is passed in `amount`. The `count` parameter indicates the number of rotations the wheel moved.

Methods in `MouseWheelEvent` *class*

- `int getWheelRotation( )` returns the number of mouse wheel rotations.
- `int getScrollType( )` returns the `WHEEL_UNIT_SCROLL` or `WHEEL_BLOCK_ SCROLL`.
- `int getScrollAmount( )` returns the number of units of scrolling.

`MouseWheelListener` **interface**

This interface defines a single method that can be called when the mouse wheel is moved. It has the following form:

```
void mouseWheelMoved(MouseWheelEvent mwe)
```

`KeyEvent` class and `KeyListener` interface

`KeyEvent` **class**

`KeyEvent` is a subclass of `InputEvent` and is generated when a key is pressed on the keyboard. There are three types of key events in this class and these are identified by the following constants.

Constants in `KeyEvent` *class*

- KEY_PRESSED
- KEY_RELEASED
- KEY_TYPED

The `KEY_PRESSED` and `KEY_RELEASED` events are called when a keyboard key is pressed and released. `KEY_TYPED` event is triggered only when the keyboard key pressed can produce a character, such as the key `A`.

Constructors of `KeyEvent` *class*

- `KeyEvent(Component src, int type, long when, int modifiers, int code, char ch)`

Here, `src`, *type, when* and *modifiers* mean the same as in earlier mouse events. The parameter `code` is used to pass the virtual key code such as `VK_LEFT` or `VK_RIGHT`. The character equivalent is specified in the parameter of *ch,* if no character equivalent is available `CHAR_UNDEFINED` is mentioned in `ch` parameter. For `KEY_TYPED` events, the code will contain `VK_UNDEFINED`.

Methods in `KeyEvent` *class*

- `char getKeyChar( )` returns the character equivalent of the VK.
- `int getKeyCode( )` returns the key code.

`KeyListener` **interface**

Three types of methods have been defined in this interface to handle keyboard events. The methods have the following general form:

- `void keyPressed(KeyEvent ke)`
- `void keyReleased(KeyEvent ke)`
- `void keyTyped(KeyEvent ke)`

If the user presses a key that doesn't generate any character, such as SHIFT, only two methods keyPressed() and keyReleased() are executed respectively. If the user presses a key that can produce a character, such as M, all the above three methods are executed in the following order—keyPressed(), keyTyped() and keyReleased().

FocusEvent class and FocusListener interface

FocusEvent class

It is generated when a GUI component gains or loses focus. It has two constants to identify the gaining or losing of focus, FOCUS_GAINED and FOCUS_LOST.

Constructors of FocusEvent *class*

- FocusEvent(Component src, int type)
- FocusEvent(Component src, int type, boolean temporaryFlag)
- FocusEvent(Component src, int type, boolean temporaryFlag, Component other)

Here, src is a reference to the component that generated the event. The type of the event is specified by type. The temporaryFlag will be set to True if the focus event is temporary. Otherwise, it is set to False. The parameter other refers to the component that either gains focus or loses focus.

Methods in FocusEvent *class*

- boolean isTemporary( ) - indicates that this focus is temporary.

FocusListener interface

The FocusListener interface has two methods—one is for gaining focus and the other for losing focus. It has the following general form,

- void focusGained(FocusEvent fe) called when the component gains input focus.
- void focusLost(FocusEvent fe) invoked when the component loses its focus.

ComponentEvent class and ComponentListener interface

ComponentEvent class

This class can be used for almost all types of GUI components. It is generated when the component's size, position and visibility are changed. There are four types of events contained in this class— HIDDEN, MOVED, RESIZED and SHOWN. Four different constants are defined to identify each of these events.

Constants in ComponentEvent *class*

- COMPONENT_HIDDEN component was hidden.
- COMPONENT_MOVED component was moved.
- COMPONENT_RESIZED component was resized.
- COMPONENT_SHOWN component became visible.

Constructors of ComponentEvent *class*

- ComponentEvent(Component src, int type)

Here, src is a reference to the component that generated the event. The type of the event is specified by type.

Methods in `ComponentEvent` *class*

- `Component getComponent()` returns the component that generated this event.

`ComponentListener` **interface**

This interface provides four different methods to handle the `HIDDEN`, `MOVED`, `RESIZED` and `SHOWN` operations on a particular component.

- `void componentResized(ComponentEvent ce)`
- `void componentMoved(ComponentEvent ce)`
- `void componentShown(ComponentEvent ce)`
- `void componentHidden(ComponentEvent ce)`

`ContainerEvent` class and `ContainerListener` interface

`ContainerEvent` **class**

This event is invoked when a component is added or removed from the container and it has two specific events, that is, adding and removing a component. There are two different constants defined in this class to identify these two operations.

Constants in `ContainerEvent` *class*

- `COMPONENT_ADDED` component is added to the container.
- `COMPONENT_REMOVED` component is removed from the container.

Constructors of `ContainerEvent` *class*

- `ContainerEvent(Component src, int type, Component comp)`

Here, `src` is a reference to the component that generated the event. The type of the event is specified by `type`. The argument `comp` refers to the component that was either added to the container or removed from the container.

Methods in `ContainerEvent` *class*

- `Container getContainer( )` refers to the container that generated this event.
- `Component getChild( )` refers to the component that was added or removed.

`ContainerListener` **interface**

This interface has the following two methods to handle adding and removing components to or from the container.

- `void componentAdded(ContainerEvent ce)`
- `void componentRemoved(ContainerEvent ce)`

The first method is called when a component is added to the container; likewise, the second method is invoked to remove a component from the container.

12.7.1 Handling Mouse Events

The delegation-event model is implemented in developing applet programs that can respond to mouse events. As usual, to become an applet the program should extend the `Applet` class. The `MouseListener` and MouseMotionListener interfaces should also be implemented in order to make use of the available methods. The following mouse events handling methods are used from the MouseListener interface.

- void mouseClicked()
- void mouseEntered()
- void mouseExited()
- void mousePressed()
- void mouseReleased()

Two more mouse events handling methods mouseMoved() and mouseDragged() are implemented from the *MouseMotionListener* interface (**Program 12.2**).

Program 12.12

```
import java.awt.*;
import java.awt.event.*;
import java.applet.*;
/*
<applet code="ME" width=500 height=200>
</applet>
*/
public class ME extends Applet implements MouseListener,MouseMotionListener
{
   String t=»»;
   int x=20,y=50;
   public void init()
   {
      addMouseListener(this);
      addMouseMotionListener(this);
   }
   public void
   mouseClicked(MouseEvent me)
   {
      t="MOUSE IS CLICKED";
      setForeground(Color.pink);
      repaint();
   }
   public void
   mouseEntered(MouseEvent me)
   {
      t="MOUSE IS ENTERED";
      repaint();
   }
   public void
   mouseExited(MouseEvent me)
   {
      t="MOUSE EXITED";
      setForeground(Color.gray);
      repaint();
   }
   public void mousePressed(MouseEvent me)
   {
      t="MOUSE IS PRESSED";
      setForeground(Color.blue);
      repaint();
   }
```

Output 12.12

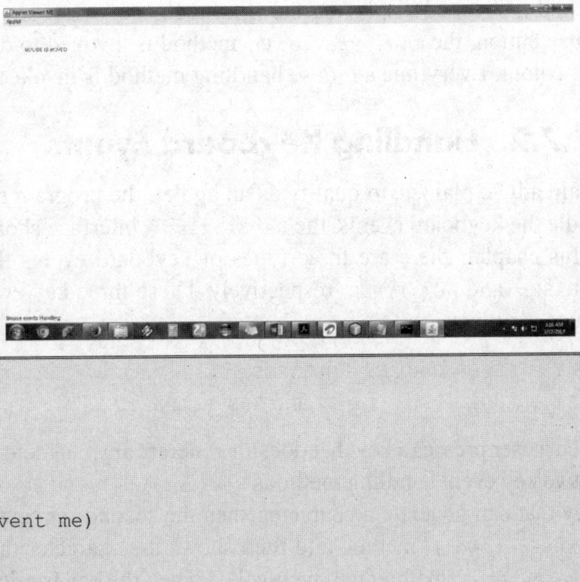

```
    public void mouseMoved(MouseEvent me)
    {
        t="MOUSE IS MOVED";
        setForeground(Color.red);
        repaint();
    }
    public void mouseDragged(MouseEvent me)
    {
        t="MOUSE IS DRAGGED";
        setForeground(Color.green);
        repaint();
    }
    public void mouseReleased(MouseEvent me)
    {
        t="MOUSE IS RELEASED";
        setForeground(Color.magenta);
        repaint();
    }
    public void paint(Graphics g)
    {
        g.drawString(t,50,60);
        showStatus("Mouse events Handling");
    }
}
```

As soon as the applet is loaded, the status message displayed in the applet window states `Mouse events handling`. Inside `init()` method, the applet registers itself as a listener for mouse events. This is done by using `addMouseListener()` and `addMouseMotionListener()`. All the seven mouse handling events are invoked. When the user moves the cursor over the applet window, it displays the message `MOUSE IS MOVED`, in red colour. When the mouse is moved out of the applet window area the `mouseExited()` method is invoked displaying the message `MOUSE EXITED`, in grey colour. When the user presses the mouse button, the `mousePressed()` method is invoked to display the message `MOUSE IS PRESSED`, in blue colour. Everytime a mouse handling method is invoked, the applet window is repainted.

12.7.2 Handling Keyboard Events

As already explained, to qualify as an applet, the program should extend the `Applet` class. In order to handle the keyboard events, the `KeyListener` interface should also implemented. As mentioned earlier in this chapter, there are three types of keyboard events that can be generated—`KEY_PRESSED`, `KEY_RELEASED` and `KEY_TYPED` respectively. These three key events can be generated in the following two sequence orders:

- `KEY_PRESSED` and `KEY_RELEASED`
- `KEY_PRESSED`, `KEY_TYPED` and `KEY_RELEASED`

When a user presses a key that doesn't generate any characters, the first sequence is implemented. It calls the two key event handling methods `keyPressed()` and `keyReleased()` respectively. If the user presses a key that can generate a character, then the second sequence of key events is implemented. It invokes the `keyPressed()` method and then shows the character through `keyTyped()` method and finally the `keyReleased()` method will be invoked when the key is released. **Program 12.13** demonstrates the key events discussed above.

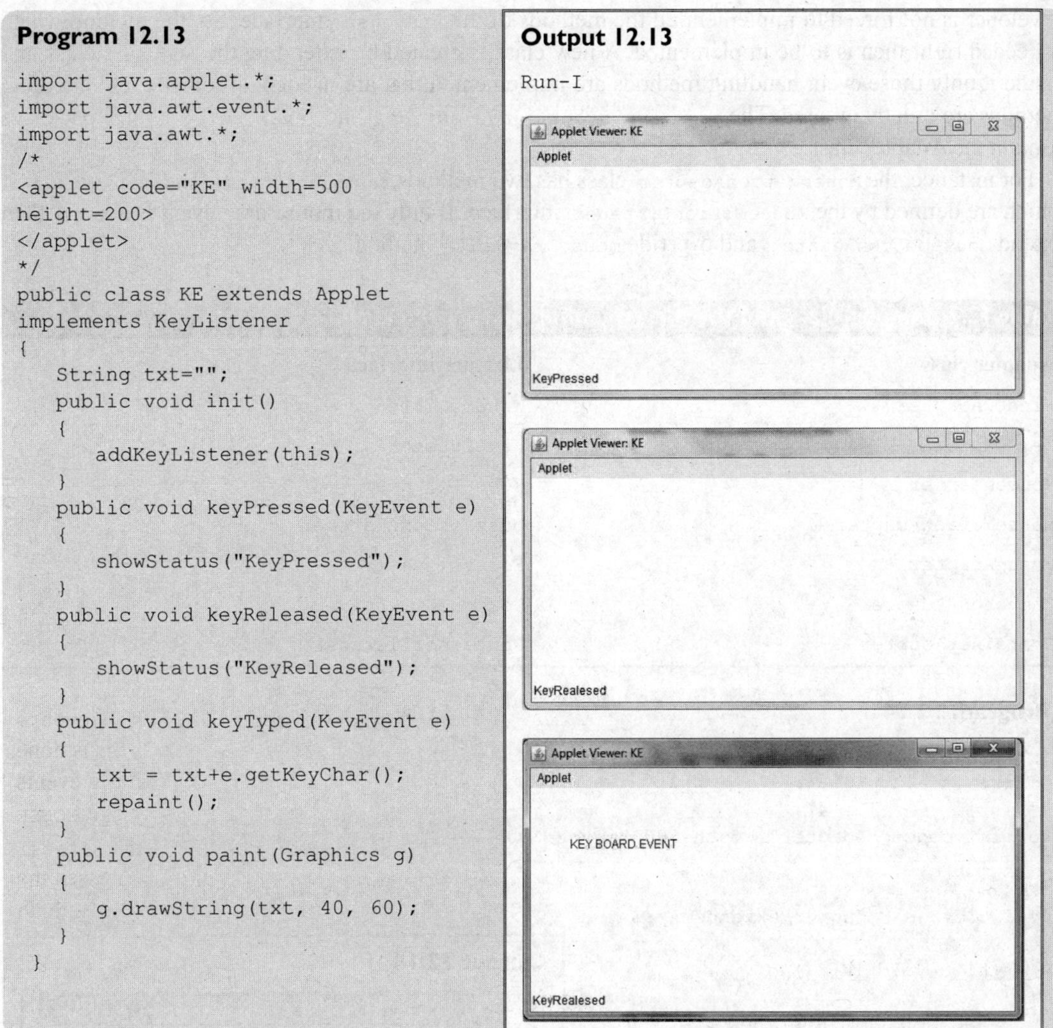

Program 12.13

```
import java.applet.*;
import java.awt.event.*;
import java.awt.*;
/*
<applet code="KE" width=500
height=200>
</applet>
*/
public class KE extends Applet
implements KeyListener
{
   String txt="";
   public void init()
   {
      addKeyListener(this);
   }
   public void keyPressed(KeyEvent e)
   {
      showStatus("KeyPressed");
   }
   public void keyReleased(KeyEvent e)
   {
      showStatus("KeyReleased");
   }
   public void keyTyped(KeyEvent e)
   {
      txt = txt+e.getKeyChar();
      repaint();
   }
   public void paint(Graphics g)
   {
      g.drawString(txt, 40, 60);
   }
 }
```

Output 12.13

Run-I

When the applet is loaded, the `init()` method sets the `addKeyListener()` method. All the three key event handling methods are implemented through their respective methods. When the user presses a key, a `keyPressed()` method is invoked and it show the status message as `KeyPressed`; when the same key is released the `keyReleased()` method is called and the message `KeyReleased` is shown in the status bar. If the user presses a key that can produce a character then both `keyPressed()` and `keyReleased()` methods are invoked. While pressing and releasing the key, one more key event handling method is also called after the `keyPressed()` method, namely the `keyTyped()` method, which is invoked only when the pressed key can generate any character; the corresponding character is displayed in the applet window.

12.7.3 Adapter Class

While using the `Listener` interface to handle events, all the methods in that interface should be implemented, even though some methods may not be needed in a particular situation, otherwise it will trigger an error. This can be avoided by using the `Adapter` class. By inheriting the `Adapter` class, the developer is not forced to implement all the methods of the `Listener` interface. So, the method which is needed right then is to be implemented. A new class is created by extending the `Adapter` class and inside it only those event handling methods are implemented that are needed; all other event handling methods are quietly ignored. The `java.awt.event`, `java.awt.dnd` and `javax.swing.event` packages contain the Adapter class.

For instance, the `MouseMotionAdapter` class has two methods, `mouseDragged()` and `mouseMoved()`, which are defined by the `MouseMotionListener` interface. If only the mouse drag event is needed, then extend `MouseMotionAdapter` and override `mouseDragged()` method.

Table 12.7 Adapter class and the corresponding listener interface

Adapter class	Listener interface
WindowAdapter	WindowListener
KeyAdapter	KeyListener
MouseAdapter	MouseListener
MouseMotionAdapter M	ouseMotionListener
FocusAdapter	FocusListener
ComponentAdapter	ComponentListener
ContainerAdapter	ContainerListener

Program 12.14

```
import java.awt.event.*;
import java.applet.*;
/*
<applet code="MAdapter" width=500 height=100>
</applet>
*/
public class MAdapter extends Applet
{
   public void init()
   {
      addMouseListener(new
      MC(this));
      addMouseMotionListener(new
      MD(this));
   }
}
class MC extends MouseAdapter
{
   MAdapter ma;
   public MC(MAdapter ma)
   {
      this.ma = ma;
   }
   public void
   mouseClicked(MouseEvent me)
   {
      ma.showStatus("MOUSE IS CLICKED");
   }
}
```

Output 12.14

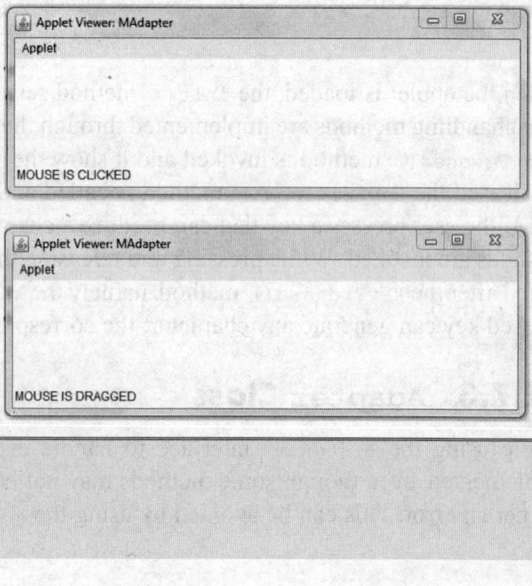

Applet Viewer: MAdapter
Applet
MOUSE IS CLICKED

Applet Viewer: MAdapter
Applet
MOUSE IS DRAGGED

```
class MD extends MouseMotionAdapter
{
   MAdapter ma;
   public MD(MAdapter ma)
   {
      this.ma = ma;
   }
   public void mouseDragged(MouseEvent me)
   {
      ma.showStatus("MOUSE IS DRAGGED");
   }
}
```

Here, two new classes `MC` and `MD` are created. `MC` class extends `MouseAdapter` corresponding to the `MouseListener` interface. The `MouseListener` interface has the following mouse event handling methods:

- `void mouseClicked(MouseEvent me)`
- `void mouseEntered(MouseEvent me)`
- `void mouseExited(MouseEvent me)`
- `void mousePressed(MouseEvent me)`
- `void mouseReleased(MouseEvent me)`

If only the `MouseListener` interface is used to handle the mouse event, all these methods should be implemented, whether needed or not. By using the corresponding adapter class `MouseAdapter` mentioned in Table 12.7, only the mouse event handling method which is/are needed is implemented, instead of implementing all the methods. Here in the `MC` class only `mouseClicked()` method from `MouseListener` interface is used; all other methods are silently ignored. Likewise, the `MD` class is declared by extending `MouseMotionAdapter` corresponding to the `MouseMotionListener`. If `MouseMotionListener` is used to handle the events then all the methods of this interface should be implemented. By using the corresponding adapter class `MouseMotionAdapter`, the above state can be avoided by using only the methods that are needed. In the MD class only the `mouseDragged()` is implemented; all other methods are avoided.

12.7.4 `inner` class

An `inner` class is a class that is declared inside another class. We will discuss how the `inner` class is used to improve the event handling in applets. A class that is defined inside another class can have access to all the members of the outer class. **Program 12.15** is developed in the regular way to handle mouse events and **Program 12.16** shows how Program 12.15 can be improved using the inner class concept.

Without using the inner class concept

Program 12.15

```
import java.awt.event.*;
import java.applet.*;
/*
<applet code="MAInner" width=500 height=100>
</applet>
*/
```

```
public class MAInner extends Applet
{
   public void init()
   {
      addMouseListener(new MC(this));
   }
}
class MC extends MouseAdapter
{
   MAInner ma;
   public MC(MAInner ma)
   {
      this.ma = ma;
   }
   public void
   mouseClicked(MouseEvent me)
   {
      ma.showStatus("MOUSE IS
      CLICKED");
   }
 }
```

Output 12.15

Applet Viewer: MAInner

Applet

MOUSE IS CLICKED

Using the inner class concept

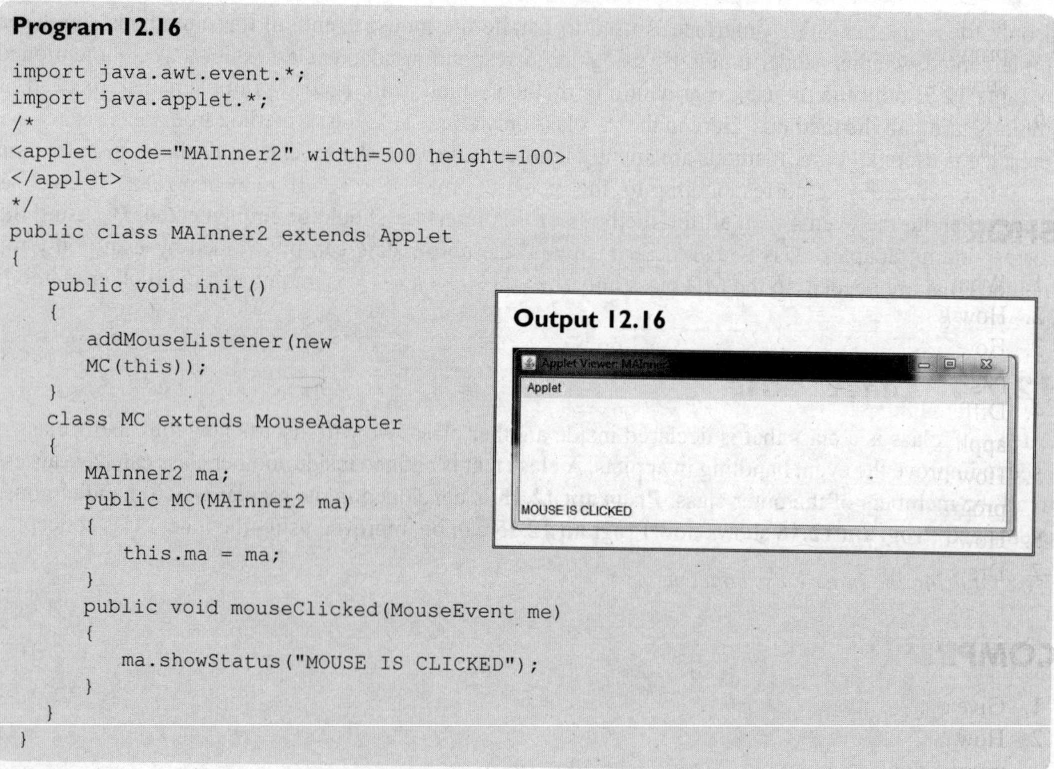

Program 12.16

```
import java.awt.event.*;
import java.applet.*;
/*
<applet code="MAInner2" width=500 height=100>
</applet>
*/
public class MAInner2 extends Applet
{
   public void init()
   {
      addMouseListener(new
      MC(this));
   }
   class MC extends MouseAdapter
   {
      MAInner2 ma;
      public MC(MAInner2 ma)
      {
         this.ma = ma;
      }
      public void mouseClicked(MouseEvent me)
      {
         ma.showStatus("MOUSE IS CLICKED");
      }
   }
}
```

Output 12.16

Here, `MAInner2` is top-level class which extends an `Applet` class and `MC` is an inner class which is defined inside the `MAInner2` class, so it has access to all the members of the top-level class. Therefore, the `mouseClicked()` method can call the `showStatus()` method directly. It no longer needs to do this via a stored reference to the applet. Thus, it is no longer necessary to pass `MC()` a reference to the invoking object.

SUMMARY

1. An applet is a small window-based program that is embedded into the browser and works on the client side.
2. There are two types of applets available—AWT-based applets and swing-based applets or JApplets.
3. To become an applet, a Java class should extend the `Applet` class before using its properties.
4. There is no `main()` method defined in the applet to start its execution as in the case of console-based Java programs.
5. The Java program which extends the `java.applet.Applet` class becomes an applet program. The `Applet` class offers varied support for an applet execution.
6. The life cycle of an applet program has four stages—*initialised*, *started*, *stopped* and *destroyed,* and these stages are implemented with the corresponding methods from the `Applet` class `init()`, `start()`, `stop()` and `destroy()` methods.
7. The life cycle starts when the Java-enabled web browser or an appletviewer executes the applet program.
8. All the life cycle methods are called automatically during execution or can be manually overridden by the user to perform some specific actions.
9. Java applets allow the user to pass parameters to the applet with the help of the `<PARAM>` tag.
10. The `<PARAM>` tag must be placed inside the `<APPLET>…</APPLET>` tag.

SHORT QUESTIONS

1. What is an applet in Java?
2. How will you initialise an applet?
3. How do you embed an applet into the web page?
4. Differentiate between applets and applications.
5. How are parameters passed in an applet program?
6. How do you run an applet program?
7. Draw the life cycle of an applet program.
8. List the methods that control the behaviour of an applet.
9. How can we draw the following shapes in an applet?
   (a) Rectangle
   (b) Oval
   (c) Rounded rectangle
10. Differentiate between `paint()` and `update()`.

COMPREHENSIVE QUESTIONS

1. Give a brief note on applets.
2. How are parameters handled by an applet program? Explain with an example.
3. Illustrate the life cycle of an applet program with a neat diagram.
4. Explain with an example, the steps involved in developing an applet program.

5. Describe how parameters are retrieved from the applets.
6. Describe the methods that represent each stage in the life cycle of a Java applet.
7. Tabulate the methods which supply information about the applet to the web browser or applet viewer.
8. Give a brief note on the ways to embed an applet in the HTML file.
9. Tabulate the methods provided by the `component` class.
10. Write a simple applet program which draws a string on the screen. Explain the structure of that program and how it works.

SOLVED PROGRAMS

1. Program 1 draws a smiley face of the human with different colours.

```
import java.awt.*;
importjava.applet.*;
/*
<applet code="SMILEY.class" width=300
height=300>
</applet>
*/
public class SMILEY extends Applet{
  public void paint(Graphics g){
      Font f = new Font("Century School
      Book", Font.BOLD,25);
      g.setFont(f);
      g.drawString("SMILE PLEASE", 50, 30);
      g.setColor(Color.LIGHT_GRAY);
      g.drawOval(60, 60, 200, 200);
      g.setColor(Color.GREEN);
      g.fillOval(90, 120, 50, 20);
      g.setColor(Color.orange);
      g.fillOval(190, 120, 50, 20);
      g.drawLine(165, 125, 165, 175);
      g.drawArc(110, 130, 95, 95, 0, -180);
  }
}
```

Output

2. Program 2 draws the snow man with different colours.

```
import java.awt.*;
importjava.applet.*;
/*
<applet code="SMan.class" width=300 height=300>
</applet>
*/
public class SMan extends Applet
{
  public void paint (Graphics g)
  {

      finalint M = 150;
      finalint T = 50;
      setBackground (Color.GREEN);
      g.setColor (Color.DARK_GRAY);
      g.fillRect (1, 175, 300, 50) ;
      g.setColor (Color.white);
      g.fillOval (M - 20, T, 40, 40);
```

Output

```
        g.fillOval (M - 35, T + 35, 70, 50);
        g.fillOval (M - 50, T + 80, 100, 60);
        g.setColor (Color.black);
        g.fillOval (M - 10, T + 10, 5, 5);
        g.fillOval (M + 5, T + 10, 5, 5);
        g.drawArc (M - 10, T + 20, 20, 10, 190, 160);
        g.drawLine (M - 25, T + 60, M - 50, T + 40);
        g.drawLine (M + 25, T + 60, M + 55, T + 60);
        g.drawLine (M - 20, T + 5, M + 20, T + 5);
        g.fillRect (M - 15, T - 20, 30, 25);
    }
}
```

3. Program 3 draws a house using rectangle and triangle shapes.

```
import java.awt.*;
importjava.applet.*;
/*
<applet code=HApplet.class width=500
height=500>
</applet>
*/
public class HApplet extends Applet
{
   public void paint(Graphics g)
   {
      g.setColor(Color.magenta);
      intxs[] = { 100,160,220} ;
      intys[] = { 100,50,100} ;
      Polygon poly=new Polygon(xs,ys,3);
      g.fillPolygon(poly);
      g.setColor(Color.cyan);
      g.fillRect(100,100,120,120);
      g.setColor(Color.white);
      g.fillRect(145,160,30,60);
      g.setColor(Color.yellow);
      g.fillOval(240,30,50,50);
      g.setColor(Color.black);
      g.fillRect(120,55,10,30);
   }
}
```

Output

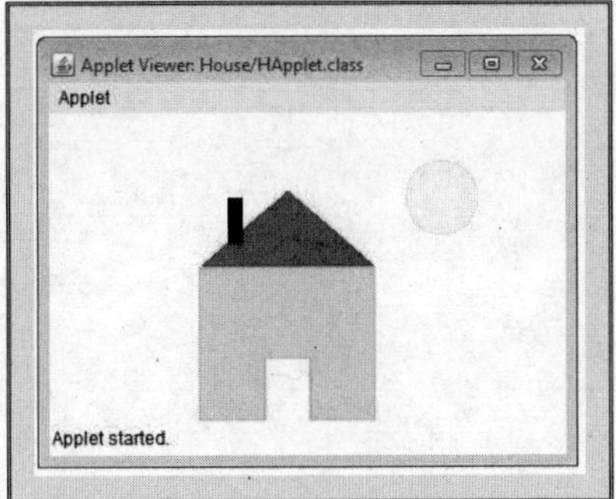

PROGRAMMING EXERCISES

1. Write a program to draw a sunflower with different colours.
2. Write a program to pass the radius to the applet using parameters and display the area of circle on the screen with different font style and colour.
3. Draw three hexagons in red, green and blue.
4. Write an applet program to receive a name through a parameter and display it with a greeting message.
5. Draw a big circle, and inside it draw all other shapes and fill each shape with different colours.
6. Develop an applet program to display the following list of data in different font styles and colours.

   FRUITS
   Banana
   Apple
   Orange
   Cherry

7. Draw a circle and divide it into four quarters and fill in each quarter with a different colour.
8. Draw a rounded rectangle and draw a circle inside it. Display the drawn shape in a web browser.
9. Develop an applet program to perform the following:
   (a) Pass and retrieve two integer type values.
   (b) Perform all arithmetic operations on the values.
   (c) Display the results with different colours and fonts.
10. Develop an applet program to draw an arc with different colours.

CHAPTER

13

GUI Applications – Part 1

This chapter provides the various user interface components to develop Window-based applications which provide a high end Graphical User Interface (GUI) environment to the user for easy interaction with the application. Java provides a predefined set of graphical components to design the GUI application with the help of the AWT (Abstract Window Toolkit) package. AWT is used to develop system-dependent Window applications. Independent Windows applications can be developed using the Swing package. This chapter also discusses the components of Swing packages to develop GUI applications.

13.1 GRAPHICAL USER INTERFACE

The Graphical User Interface (GUI) of an application can include a variety of components such as buttons, checkboxes, text fields, scrollbars, menus and dialog boxes. A user can interact with the GUI application through these components. Java provides an AWT package which enables programmers to create GUI Applications. This package comes with built-in classes, interfaces and methods that help to implement Window-based functions. All of these classes and methods are available under a special package called `java.awt`. AWT supports both standard and applet Windows. The AWT classes are hierarchically arranged inside the AWT package (Fig. 13.1).

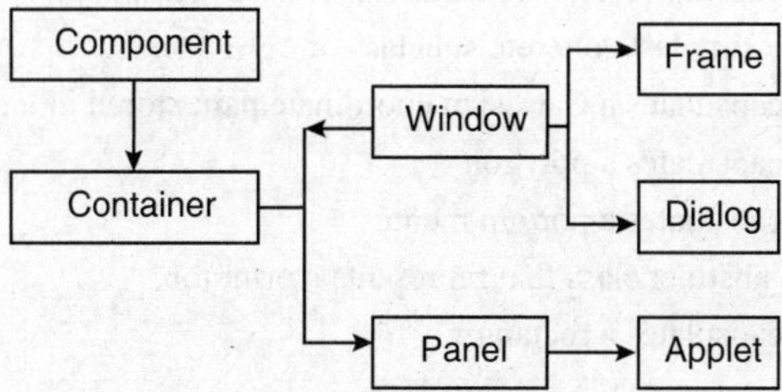

Fig. 13.1 Hierarchy of AWT classes

The key concepts of AWT class hierarchy are:

- **Component** class is an abstract class for all the classes of GUI elements. This is responsible for effectively rendering the components on the monitor and handling various events such as mouse and keyboard events in the GUI application.
- **Container** class contains an AWT component for managing the layout and placing the AWT components within it. A container can be nested within another container. Container class can be implemented in two ways. Two such objects are the Window object and Panel object.

- A **Window** object is recognised as top-level Window with no Border and menu bar. It is used to define the layout of the Window. The Window is created directly but derived from its subclass called *Frame*.
- A **Panel** is another type of container object that is a base class of `Applet`. A panel represents a window space on which the GUI components are displayed. It is also a normal Window having no Border or menu bar. A panel can be nested within another Panel.
- The **Frame** object recognises Window space with a Border and menu bar. It supports all the Window events such as open, close, activate and deactivate.

This chapter helps to develop GUI-based applications using components, container, Window, Panel and Frame which are provided by `java.awt` package.

Classes available under `java.awt` package are given in Table 13.1 (referenced from *JavaTM: The Complete Reference*, 9e, Herbert Schildt, Oracle Press, 2014).

Table 13.1 AWT classes

Class	Description
`GraphicsEnvironment`	Describes the collection of available font and `GraphicsDevice` objects.
`GridBagConstraints`	Defines different constraints relating to the `GridBagLayout` class.
`GridBagLayout`	Grid bag layout displays components subject to the constraints specified by `GridBagConstraints`.
`GridLayout`	The grid layout manager. Grid layout shows components in a two dimensional grid.
`Image`	Summarises graphical images.
`Insets`	Encapsulates the Borders of a container.
`List`	Creates a list from which the user can choose. Similar to the standard Windows list box.
`Label`	Creates a Label that displays a string.
`MediaTracker`	Manages media objects.
`Menu`	Creates a pull-down menu.
`MenuBar`	Creates a menu bar.
`MenuComponent`	An abstract class implemented by various menu classes.
`MenuItem`	Creates a menu item.
`MenuShortcut`	Encapsulates a keyboard shortcut for a menu item.
`Panel`	The simplest concrete subclass of `Container`.
`Point`	Encapsulates a Cartesian coordinate pair, stored in `x` and `y`.
`Polygon`	Encapsulates a polygon.
`PopupMenu`	Encapsulates a pop-up menu.
`PrintJob`	An abstract class that represents a print job.
`Rectangle`	Encapsulates a rectangle.
`Scrollbar`	Creates a scrollbar control.
`ScrollPane`	A container that provides horizontal and/or vertical scroll bars for another component.
`SystemColor`	Contains the colours of GUI widgets such as Windows, scroll bars, text and others.
`TextArea`	Creates a multiline edit control.
`TextComponent`	A superclass for `TextArea` and `TextField`.
`TextField`	Creates a single-line edit control.
`Toolkit`	Abstract class implemented by the AWT.
`Window`	Creates a Window with no Frame, no menu bar and no title.

In the next section we will discuss how to create an AWT Window object with the help of the Frame subclass of `Window`. Window is a base component where all the components are placed within the Window.

13.2 CREATING WINDOWS

The AWT describes the Windows according to the class hierarchy, to facilitate adding functionality and specificity with each stage. The two important Windows are those derived from the `Panel` class, which is often used by applets and those derived from the `Frame` class, which creates a standard Window. Much of the functionality of these Windows is derived from their parent classes. A picture of the class hierarchies relating to these two classes (Fig. 13.2), is fundamental to their understanding.

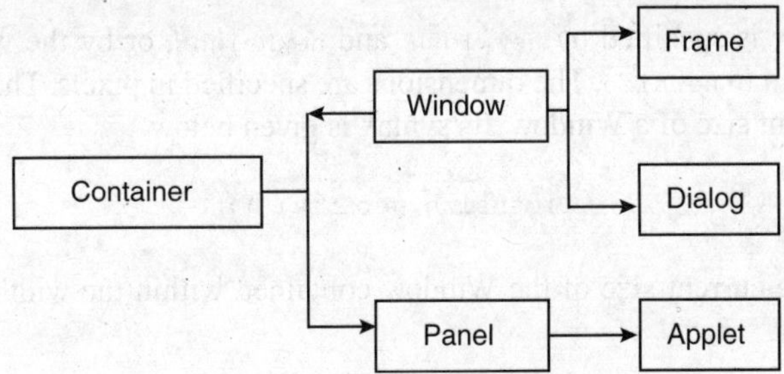

Fig. 13.2 Class hierarchy for Window and Panel

Window

The `Window` class creates a top-level Window that is not controlled within any other object. The `Window` sits directly on the desktop. Generally, programmers cannot create Window objects directly. Instead, it will be used by a subclass of `Window` called `Frame` which is described next.

13.2.1 Frame

`Frame` is the general consideration of a Window. This is a subclass of `Window` and has a title bar, menu bar, Borders, and resizing corners. A Frame can be used in application development in two ways.

- If creating a frame object from within an applet, it includes a warning message to the user, such as 'Java Applet Window', that an applet Window has been created. This message warns users that the Window they see was started by an applet and not by software running on their computer.
- When a Frame Window is created by a program rather than an applet, a normal Window is created.

Basics of Frame windows

The type of Window that will be created is derived most often from Frame. A programmer uses this to create child Windows inside the applets, and top-level or child Windows for applications. As mentioned, Frame creates a standard Window. Here are two forms of Frame's constructors:

```
Frame( )
Frame(String title)
```

The first form creates a standard Window that does not contain a title. The second form creates a Window with the title specified as the parameter. Note that the size of the Window is not specified yet. The size of the Window is set after it has been created. There are several methods that will be used when working with Frame Windows. They are observed in the following subsection.

Setting window dimensions

The `setSize()` method is used to set the dimensions of the Window. Its syntax is given below.

```
void setSize(int newwidth, int newheight)
void setSize(Dimension newsize)
```

The size of the Window is specified by `newwidth` and `newheight`, or by the width and height of the `Dimension` object passed to `newsize`. The dimensions are specified in pixels. The `getSize()` method is used to obtain the current size of a Window. Its syntax is given below:

```
Dimension getSize( );
```

This method returns the current size of the Window contained within the width and height fields of a dimension object.

Window: hide and show

After a Frame Window has been created, it will not be visible until the `setVisible( )` method is called. Its syntax is given below.

```
void setVisible(boolean visibleFlag)
```

The component is visible if the argument to this method is True. Otherwise, it is hidden.

Setting window's title

The title of the Window has been changed in a Frame Window using `setTitle()` method, which has the general form given below.

```
void setTitle(String newTitle)
```

Here, `newTitle` is the new title for the Window.

Closing a Frame window

If a Frame Window is used, the program must remove the Window from the screen when it is closed, by calling `setVisible(false)`. To catch a Window-close event, invoke the `WindowClosing( )` method of the `WindowListener` interface. **Program 13.1** illustrates this technique.

Program 13.1

```
// Demonstration of Creating Window using Frame class.
import java.awt.*;
public class WindowExample extends Frame{
    public void paint(Graphics g) {
        g.drawString("Hello", 10, 40);
    }
    public static void main(String[] args)
    {
        WindowExample appwin = new
        WindowExample();
        appwin.setSize(new Dimension(200,
        100));
        appwin.setTitle("An AWT-Based
        Application");
        appwin.setVisible(true);
    }
}
```

Output 13.1

An AWT-Based Application

Hello

Program 13.1 shows how to create a Window using the Frame class. First, the `WindowExample` class extends the Frame class. Then an object is created for the class. First the Window size should be specified using the `setSize()` method, next the title for Window is set using the `setTitle()` method and finally, to view the Window, invoke the `setVisible()` to be True. Then `paint()` is used to place the contents in the Window. In this program, the text is just displays by calling the `drawstring()` method. The output clearly shows the size of Window and its title and it displays the text 'Hello' inside the Window. In the next section, we discuss the second type of creating a Window called Panel, which is used for creating a Window with no Border and menu bar.

13.2.2 Panel

`Panel` is the simplest container class. It provides space in which an application can attach any other component like a button, Label, text field, and so on. It inherits the `Container` class. Unlike the `Frame` class, `Panel` does not have a title bar. AWT Panel class is declared with the following syntax.

```
public class Panel extends Container implements Accessible
```

The frequently used methods in the panel class are listed in Table 13.2.

Table 13.2 Panel class methods

Method	Description
`setBounds(int x, int y, int width, int height)`	Moves and resizes this component. The new location of the top-left corner is specified by x and y, and the new size is specified by width and height.
`setBackground(Color c)`	Sets the background colour of this component. The background colour affects each component differently.

Program 13.2 demonstrates how to create a Window using the Panel class.

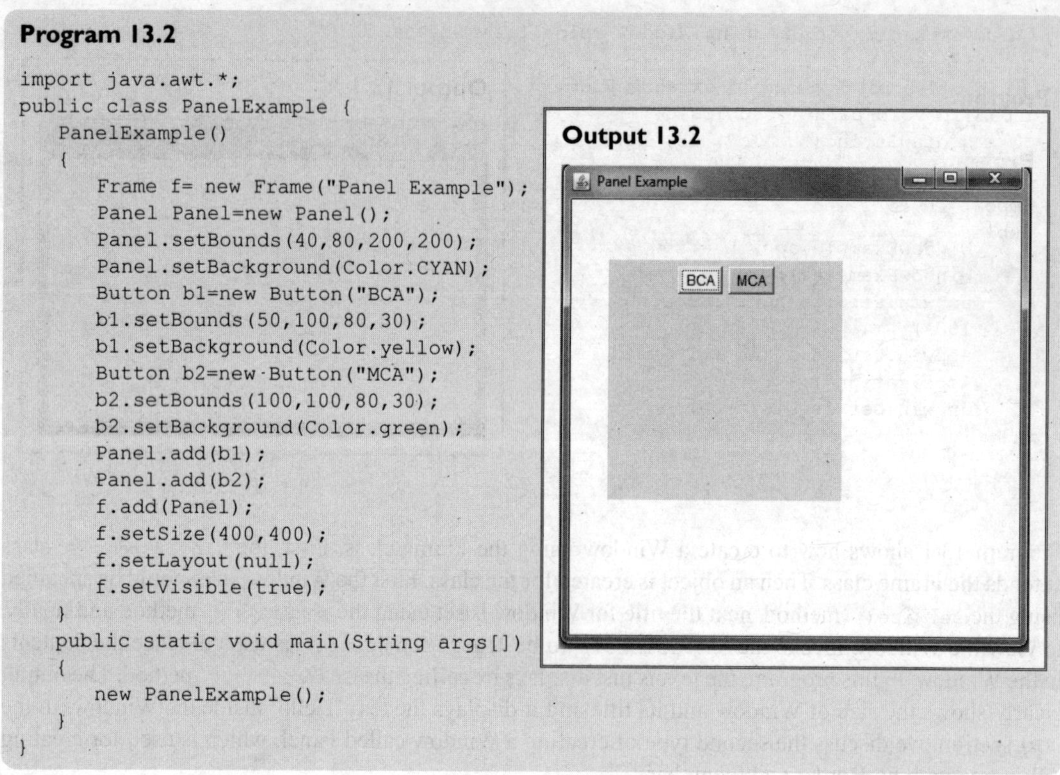

Program 13.2

```
import java.awt.*;
public class PanelExample {
   PanelExample()
   {
      Frame f= new Frame("Panel Example");
      Panel Panel=new Panel();
      Panel.setBounds(40,80,200,200);
      Panel.setBackground(Color.CYAN);
      Button b1=new Button("BCA");
      b1.setBounds(50,100,80,30);
      b1.setBackground(Color.yellow);
      Button b2=new Button("MCA");
      b2.setBounds(100,100,80,30);
      b2.setBackground(Color.green);
      Panel.add(b1);
      Panel.add(b2);
      f.add(Panel);
      f.setSize(400,400);
      f.setLayout(null);
      f.setVisible(true);
   }
   public static void main(String args[])
   {
      new PanelExample();
   }
}
```

Output 13.2

Program 13.2 illustrates the concept of creating a Window using the Panel class. First the object is created for the frame class and title of Window is given in the object creation of the frame class itself, because Panel does not support the title bar. Inside the frame class, a Panel object is created and bounds are set for the Panel using `setBounds()` method with top-left, height and width passed as parameters. Then the Panel background is set using the `setBackground()` method with colour value passed as a parameter. And then two user interface component of buttons are created with names `BCA` and `MCA`. Finally, `Panel` is added to the `Frame` Window and Frame set to be visible using the `setVisible(true)` method. The program output is as shown above. In the next section we discuss another method of creating a Window using the `Dialog` class which is a subclass of the `Window` class.

13.3 DIALOG BOXES

The `Dialog` control represents a top level Window with a Border and a title. This is used for taking some form of input from the user. It inherits the `Window` class.

- Compared with `Frame`, it does not have Maximize and Minimize buttons in the title bar of the Window and has a close button.

Frame vs Dialog

`Frame` and `Dialog` both inherit the `Window` class. `Frame` has Maximize and Minimize buttons, unlike `Dialog` control.

The AWT `Dialog` class is declared with the following syntax.

```
public class Dialog extends Window
```

Program 13.3 illustrates the use of this dialog control.

Program 13.3

```
import java.awt.*;
public class dialogExample {
    private static Dialog d;
    dialogExample() {
        Frame f= new Frame();
        d = new Dialog(f,"Dialog Demo",true);
        d.setLayout( new FlowLayout() );
        Button b = new Button ("OK");
        d.add( new Label ("Dialog example
        Button"));
        d.add(b);
        d.setSize(300,300);
        d.setVisible(true);
    }
    public static void main(String args[])
    {
        new dialogExample();
    }
}
```

Output 13.3

Dialog Demo

Dialog example Button OK

Program 13.3 demonstrates that `Dialog` control is used to create the Window instead of `Frame`. Dialog control is placed inside the `Frame` class. A `Dialog` object is created and its methods are invoked. The `add()` method is used to place any component within the dialog Window. `setSize()` method is used to set the size of the dialog Window in the context of height and width, and then `setVisible(true)` method is invoked to make the dialog Window visible to the user. From the output, we see that the output dialog Window does not have Maximize and Minimize buttons on the title bar of the Window.

13.3.1 FileDialog

Java provides a pre-defined dialog box that helps the user to specify a file. To create a file dialog box, instantiate an object of type `FileDialog`. This is the basis for a file dialog box to be displayed. Generally, this is the standard file dialog box provided by the operating system. `FileDialog` offers the following constructors:

```
FileDialog(Frame parent, String boxname) FileDialog(Frame
parent, String boxname, int how) FileDialog(Frame parent)
```

Here, `parent` is the owner of the dialog box, and `boxname` is the name displayed in the box's title bar. If `boxname` is omitted, the title of the dialog box is empty. If `how` is `FileDialog.LOAD`, then the box is selecting a file for reading. If `how` is `FileDialog.SAVE`, the box is selecting a file for writing. The third constructor creates a dialog box for selecting a file for reading. **Program 13.4** demonstrates this.

Program 13.4

```
import java.awt.*;
class FileDialogDemo {
    public static void
    main(String args[]) {
        Frame f = new
        Frame("File Dialog
        Demo");
        f.setVisible(true);
        f.setSize(100, 100);
        FileDialog fd = new
        FileDialog(f, "File
        Dialog");
        fd.setVisible(true);
    }
}
```

Output 13.4

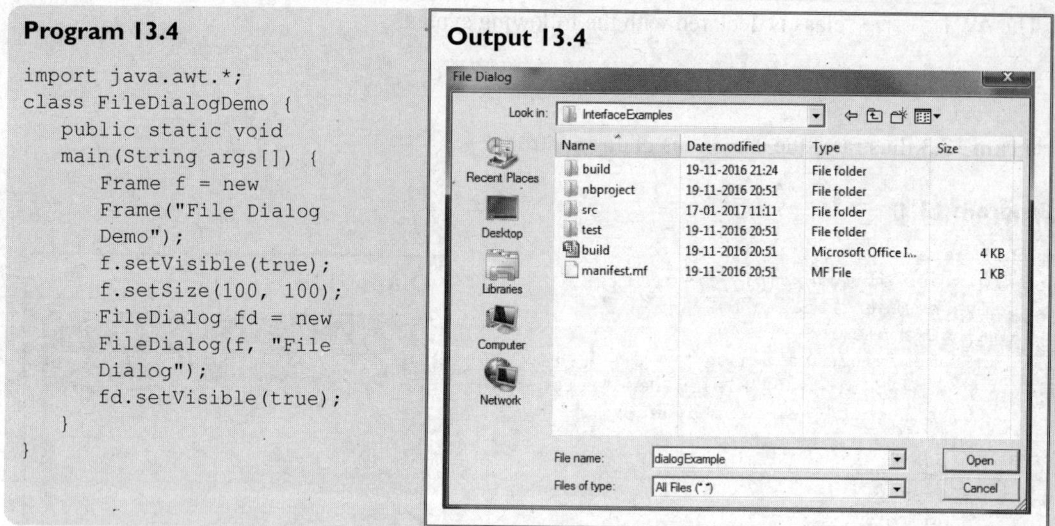

Program 13.4 illustrates opening of the file dialog Window using `FileDialog` class of the AWT package. Note that the output Window shows an option to open a file from the current directory or folder. If the second type of constructor is used with `FileDialog(f,"File Dialog", FileDialog.SAVE)`, then instead of the open option in the dialog Window, the save dialog Window will be displayed. In Program 13.3, with help of dialog object `d`, one of the Container methods `setLayout()` is invoked. This layout concept will be discussed in greater detail in the next section.

13.4 LAYOUT MANAGERS

The layout managers are used to place the components in some particular order. `LayoutManager` is an interface that is implemented by all the classes of layout managers.

The `Container` object has a layout manager associated with it. The layout manager is an instance of any class that implements the `LayoutManager` interface. The layout manager is located by the `setLayout( )` method. If there is no method to call by `setLayout()`, then the default layout manager is used. When the container is resized, the layout manager is used to position each of the components within it. The `setLayout()` method has the following syntax:

```
void setLayout(LayoutManager obj)
```

The following are classes that are represented by the layout managers:

```
java.awt.BorderLayout
java.awt.FlowLayout
java.awt.GridLayout
java.awt.CardLayout
java.awt.GridBagLayout
```

13.4.1 BorderLayout

The `BorderLayout` is used to arrange the components in five sections—north, south, east, west and centre. Each section or area holds one component only. It is the default layout of a Frame or Window. `BorderLayout` provides five constants for each section:

```
public static final int NORTH
public static final int SOUTH
public static final int EAST
public static final int WEST
public static final int CENTER
```

Constructors of `BorderLayout` class

- `BorderLayout()`: creates a Border layout but with no gaps between the components.
- `BorderLayout(int hgap, int vgap)`: creates a Border layout with the given horizontal and vertical gaps between the components.

Program 13.5 illustrates the use of `BorderLayout` class.

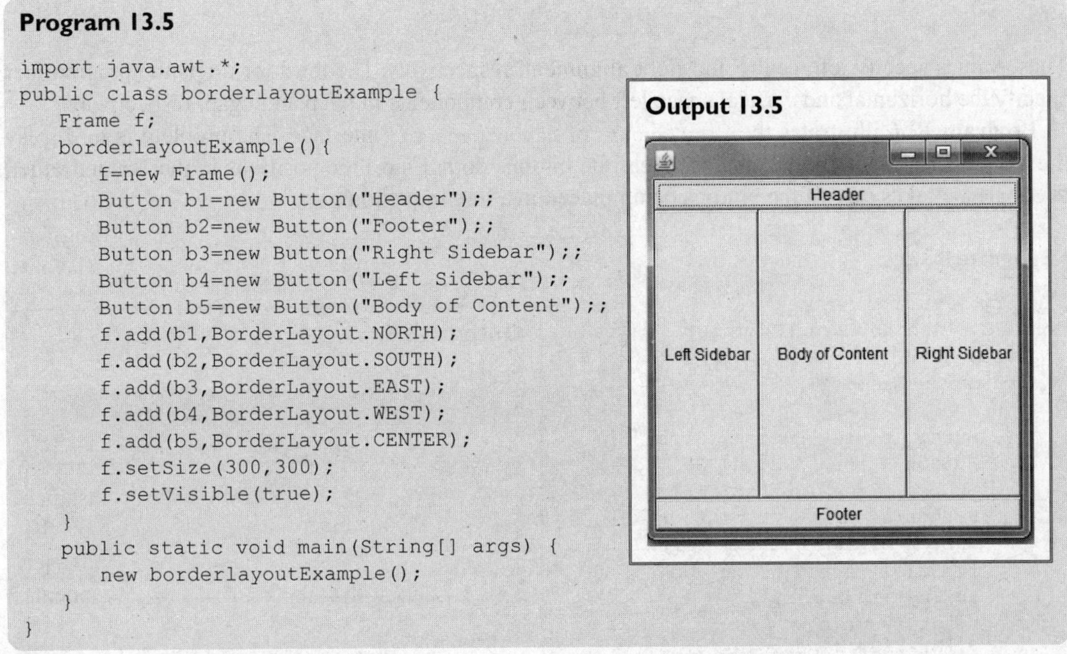

Program 13.5

```
import java.awt.*;
public class borderlayoutExample {
    Frame f;
    borderlayoutExample(){
        f=new Frame();
        Button b1=new Button("Header");;
        Button b2=new Button("Footer");;
        Button b3=new Button("Right Sidebar");;
        Button b4=new Button("Left Sidebar");;
        Button b5=new Button("Body of Content");;
        f.add(b1,BorderLayout.NORTH);
        f.add(b2,BorderLayout.SOUTH);
        f.add(b3,BorderLayout.EAST);
        f.add(b4,BorderLayout.WEST);
        f.add(b5,BorderLayout.CENTER);
        f.setSize(300,300);
        f.setVisible(true);
    }
    public static void main(String[] args) {
        new borderlayoutExample();
    }
}
```

Output 13.5

Program 13.5 demonstrates the `BorderLayout` of `LayoutManagers`. There are five buttons added into the frame, arranged in five regions based on `BorderLayout` bounds. `BorderLayout` has the regions of NORTH, SOUTH, EAST, WEST and CENTRE. Then the size of the Window is set using the `setSize()` method. Finally, by setting the `setVisible(true)` method, the output is viewed as shown.

13.4.2 `FlowLayout`

`FlowLayout` is the default `LayoutManager` class. The `FlowLayout` is used to organise the components in a line, one after another, in a flow. It is the default layout of an applet or Panel. This is the layout manager that we have already used in the Dialog example of Program 13.3. `FlowLayout` implements a simple layout style which is similar to how words flow in a text editor. Components are laid out from the upper left corner, left to right, and top to bottom. When no more components fit on a line, the next one appears on the next line. A small space is left between two components, above and below, as well as left and right. Here are the constructors for `FlowLayout`:

`FlowLayout()`: Create a flow layout with centre alignment with default 5 unit horizontal and vertical gap.

`FlowLayout(int align)`: Create a flow layout with the given alignment with default 5 unit horizontal and vertical gap.

`FlowLayout(int align, int hgap, int vgap)`: create a flow layout with the given alignment, the given horizontal and vertical gap.

The first form creates the default layout, which centres components and leaves five pixels of space between each component. The second form is for defining how each line is aligned.

Valid values for `FlowLayout` field are as follows:

```
FlowLayout. LEFT
FlowLayout.CENTER
FlowLayout.RIGHT
FlowLayout.LEADING
FlowLayout.TRAILING
```

These values specify left, centre and right alignment, respectively. The third form lets the programmer specify the horizontal and vertical space left between components in hgap and vgap, respectively.

Program 13.6 illustrates the `FlowLayout` of `LayoutManager` interface. The problem is to display the five buttons in the frame Window. Here the buttons do not have the positions in the Frame; rather, `FlowLayout` takes care of the buttons being placed in a line sequentially.

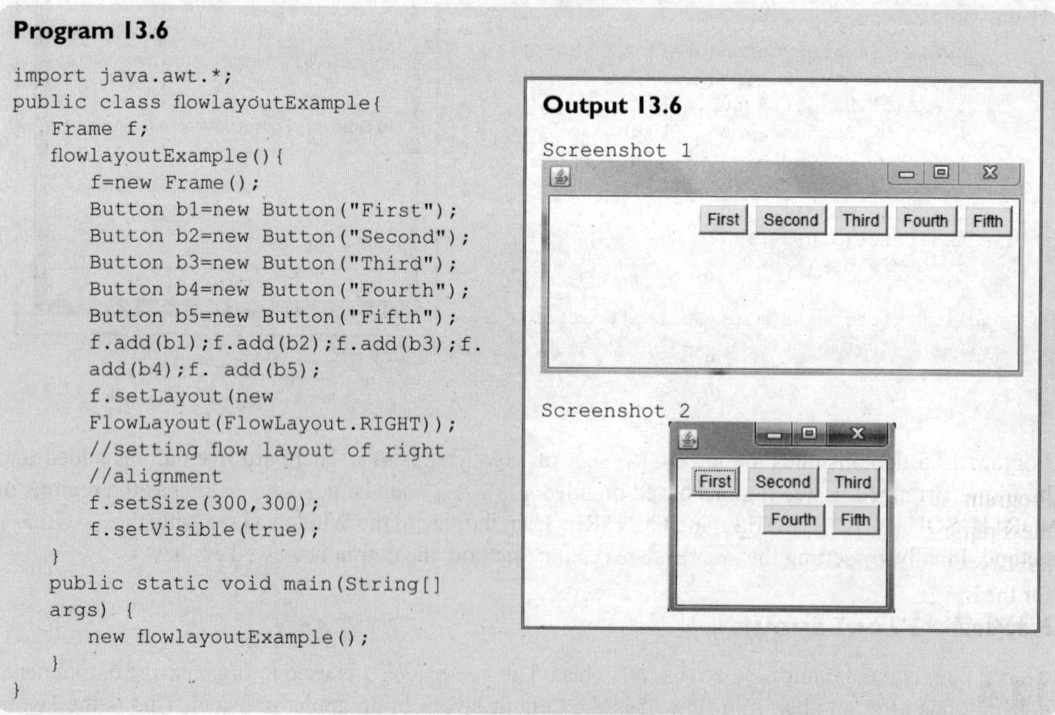

Program 13.6

```
import java.awt.*;
public class flowlayoutExample{
   Frame f;
   flowlayoutExample(){
       f=new Frame();
       Button b1=new Button("First");
       Button b2=new Button("Second");
       Button b3=new Button("Third");
       Button b4=new Button("Fourth");
       Button b5=new Button("Fifth");
       f.add(b1);f.add(b2);f.add(b3);f.
       add(b4);f. add(b5);
       f.setLayout(new
       FlowLayout(FlowLayout.RIGHT));
       //setting flow layout of right
       //alignment
       f.setSize(300,300);
       f.setVisible(true);
   }
   public static void main(String[]
   args) {
       new flowlayoutExample();
   }
}
```


In Program 13.6, `setLayout( )` is invoked after adding the button components into the `Frame` class object. Within this `setLayout()` method, the `FlowLayout` position is defined. Here it has been set as `FlowLayout.RIGHT`. The output Screenshot 1 shows the buttons arranged in a line from the right side of the Window. Screenshot 2 shows that when resizing the Window, the buttons are automatically rearranged with the help of `FlowLayout` class.

13.4.3 GridLayout

The `GridLayout` is used to arrange the components in rectangular grid. One component is displayed in each rectangle. Here, the constructors of `GridLayout` class are:

`GridLayout()`: Creates a grid layout with one column per component in a row.

`GridLayout(int rows, int columns)`: Creates a grid layout with the given rows and columns but no gaps between the components.

`GridLayout(int rows, int columns, int hgap, int vgap)`: Creates a grid layout with the given rows and columns along with given horizontal and vertical gaps.

Program 13.7 demonstrates `GridLayout` class of `LayoutManager` class.

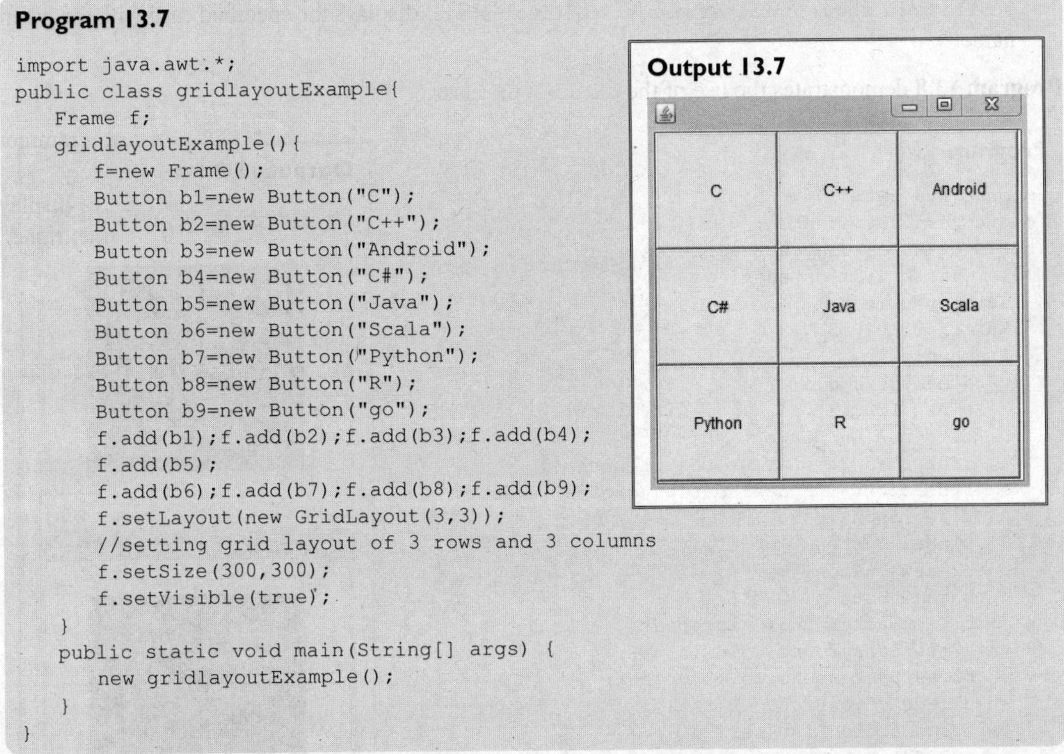

Program 13.7

```
import java.awt.*;
public class gridlayoutExample{
    Frame f;
    gridlayoutExample(){
        f=new Frame();
        Button b1=new Button("C");
        Button b2=new Button("C++");
        Button b3=new Button("Android");
        Button b4=new Button("C#");
        Button b5=new Button("Java");
        Button b6=new Button("Scala");
        Button b7=new Button("Python");
        Button b8=new Button("R");
        Button b9=new Button("go");
        f.add(b1);f.add(b2);f.add(b3);f.add(b4);
        f.add(b5);
        f.add(b6);f.add(b7);f.add(b8);f.add(b9);
        f.setLayout(new GridLayout(3,3));
        //setting grid layout of 3 rows and 3 columns
        f.setSize(300,300);
        f.setVisible(true);
    }
    public static void main(String[] args) {
        new gridlayoutExample();
    }
}
```

Output 13.7

Program 13.7 shows that initially the frame object is created and then nine buttons are added into the Frame object. The buttons are named after different programming languages. Then, using the `setLayout()` method, `GridLayout( )` method is passed as argument with a three by three value passed for the `GridLayout` method, which means that the Frame Window is divided into 3 by 3 rectangle areas or regions. The program output is displayed as in the given output Window.

13.4.4 CardLayout

This layout organises the components within a container in the same way as a stack of cards are arranged in a deck, hence the name. Each component is like a card. Each card may contain one or more controls.

`CardLayout` class handles the components in such a manner that only one component is visible at a time. The constructors in this `LayoutManager` are given below.

`CardLayout():` Creates a card layout with horizontal and vertical gap as zero.

`CardLayout(int hgap, int vgap):` creates a card layout with the given horizontal and vertical gap.

The methods available in the `CardLayout` class are given below.

`public void next(Container parent):` displays the next card of the given container.

`public void previous(Container parent):` displays the previous card of the given container.

`public void first(Container parent):` displays the first card of the given container.

`public void last(Container parent):` displays the last card of the given container.

`public void show(Container parent, String name):` displays the specified card with the given name.

Program 13.8 demonstrates the use of the `CardLayout` class.

Program 13.8

```
import java.awt.*;
import java.awt.event.*;
public class cardlayoutExample extends Frame
implements ActionListener{
   CardLayout card;
   Button b1,b2,b3;
   Frame c;
   cardlayoutExample(){
      c=new Frame();
      card=new CardLayout(40,30);
      //created CardLayout object with 40
      //horizontal space and 30 vertical space
      c.setLayout(card);
      b1=new Button("Apple");
      b2=new Button("Boy");
      b3=new Button("Cat");
      b1.setBackground(Color.red);
      b2.setBackground(Color.blue);
      b3.setBackground(Color.green);
      b1.addActionListener(this);
      b2.addActionListener(this);
      b3.addActionListener(this);
      c.add("a",b1);
      c.add("b",b2);
      c.add("c",b3);
      c.setSize(400,400);
      c.setVisible(true);
   }
   public void actionPerformed(ActionEvent e) {
      card.next(c);
   }
   public static void main(String[] args) {
      cardlayoutExample cl=new
cardlayoutExample();
   }
}
```

Output 13.8

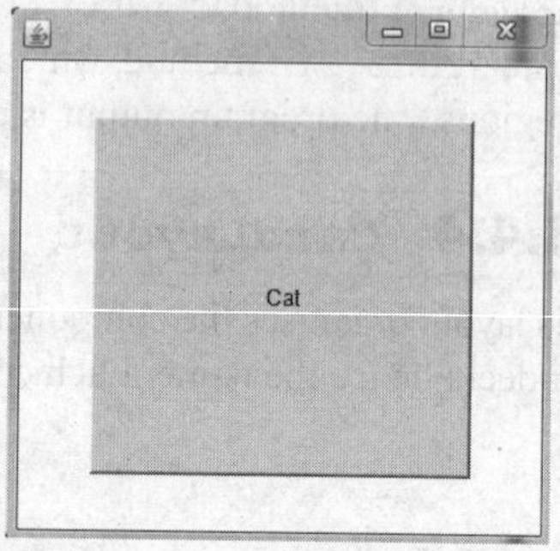

Program 13.8 illustrates the `CardLayout` implementation. In this program, first an object is created for the frame class. Then an object for the CardLayout class is created with parameter values passed to the constructor as (40,30), to provide space in the horizontal and vertical gap between the card and the frame Window. Three buttons are created and added into the card layout. Here, a new task is included which causes some action on a button click. This can be done by implementing an `ActionListener` interface and implementing the `actionPerformed(ActionEvent event)` method in the class. Within this method, the `next( )` method is invoked. Then, by invoking `addListener(this)` with each button object, the `actionPerformed( )` method is called. By assigning True to `setVisible( )`, all the components and Frame objects are ready to be displayed. The program output Window is displayed above. Initially the red `Apple` button is displayed. This button invokes `next( )` method to display the blue `Boy` button.

Other event handling classes and methods will be discussed in Chapter 14.

Different component classes and their user interface design with functionalities of each component are discussed in the next section.

13.5 AWT COMPONENT CLASSES

The AWT Package provides the following types of controls for user interface design:

- labels,
- text fields,
- buttons,
- check boxes,
- radio buttons,
- choice lists,
- lists,
- scroll bars, and
- menu bars and menu items.

These controls are subclasses of the `Component` class.

The `Component` class methods are used on adding and removing controls in a Window. First create an instance of the desired control and then add it to a Window by calling the `add( )` method, which is defined by the `Container` class. The `add( )` method has several forms, and the one that is used for adding components into the Window is:

```
Component add(Component obj)
```

Here, `obj` is an instance of the control that the user wants to add. A reference to `obj` is returned. Once a control has been added, it will automatically be visible whenever its parent Window is displayed. To remove a control from a Window when the control is no longer needed, call `remove( )`. This method is also defined by the `Container` class.

It has this general form:

```
void remove(Component obj)
```

Here, `obj` is a reference to the control that needs to be removed. All controls can be removed by calling the `removeAll( )` method.

13.5.1 Responding to Controls

Except for labels, which are passive controls, all controls generate events when they are accessed by the user. For example, when the user clicks on a push button, an event is generated that identifies the push button. The basic controls used to develop graphical user interaction applications are discussed below.

`Label` control

The object of `Label` class is a component for placing text in a container. It is used to display a single line of read only text. The text can be changed by an application but a user cannot edit it directly. AWT `Label` class declaration is given as follows.

```
public class Label extends Component implements Accessible
```

Program 13.9 demonstrates the use of the `Label` class.

Program 13.9

```
import java.awt.*;
class labelExample{
    public static void main(String args[]){
        Frame f1= new Frame("Label:Example");
        Label l1,l2;
        l1=new Label("JAVA.");
        l1.setBounds(50,100, 100,30);
        l2=new Label("Programming");
        l2.setBounds(50,150, 100,30);
        f1.add(l1);
        f1.add(l2);
        f1.setSize(400,400);
        f1.setLayout(null);
        f1.setVisible(true);

    }
}
```

Output 13.9

Label:Example

JAVA

Programming

Program 13.9 illustrates the basic component of the AWT label. Initially, the object is created for the frame class. The label class instance l1 and l2 is created and initialised with 'JAVA' and 'Programming' respectively. By adding these instances l1 and l2 using the `add( )` method of the frame class. Then set the size of the Window, layout and visibility of the Window using the `setSize( )` and `setLayout( )` methods. Finally, by executing the program, the output is obtained.

`Textfield` control

The object of a `TextField` class is a text component that allows the editing of a single line of text. It inherits the `TextComponent` class. The AWT `TextField` class declaration is given below:

- `public class TextField extends TextComponent`

Program 13.10 illustrates the use of `TextField` component class.

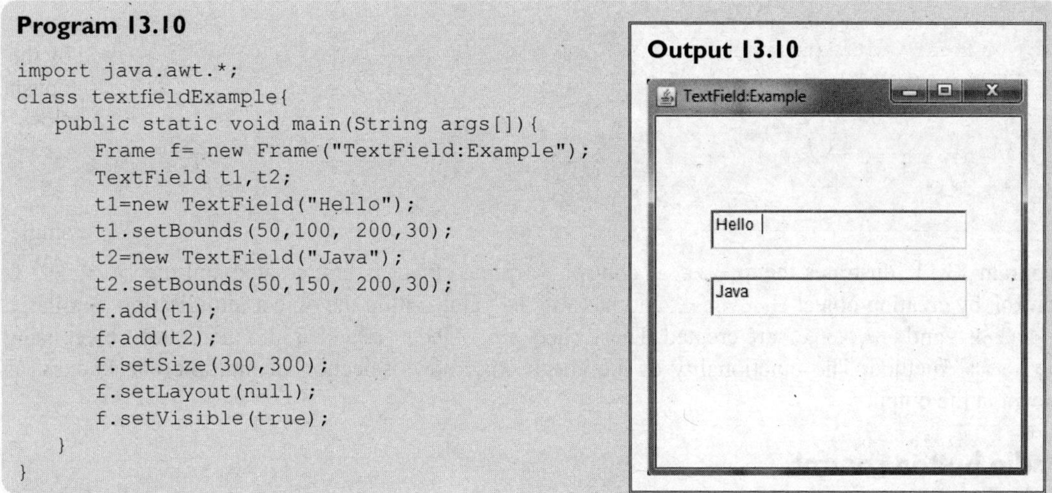

Program 13.10

```
import java.awt.*;
class textfieldExample{
    public static void main(String args[]){
        Frame f= new Frame("TextField:Example");
        TextField t1,t2;
        t1=new TextField("Hello");
        t1.setBounds(50,100, 200,30);
        t2=new TextField("Java");
        t2.setBounds(50,150, 200,30);
        f.add(t1);
        f.add(t2);
        f.setSize(300,300);
        f.setLayout(null);
        f.setVisible(true);
    }
}
```

Output 13.10

Program 13.10 demonstrates the `TextField` component class of AWT. This component is created using the `TextField` class. Two text field objects are created in the program, namely `t1` and `t2`. Default text values 'Hello' and 'Java' have been passed to `t1` and `t2` object which hold the given value that the user can edit. Finally, `t1` and `t2` objects are added into the Frame object. The output is as shown.

`Checkbox` control

The `Checkbox` class is used to create a checkbox. It is used to turn an option on (True) or off (False). Clicking on a checkbox changes its state from 'on' to 'off' or from 'off'" to 'on'. The AWT `Checkbox` class declaration is as given below.

```
public class Checkbox extends Component implements ItemSelectable, Accessible
```

Program 13.11 illustrates the use of the `CheckBox` control component class.

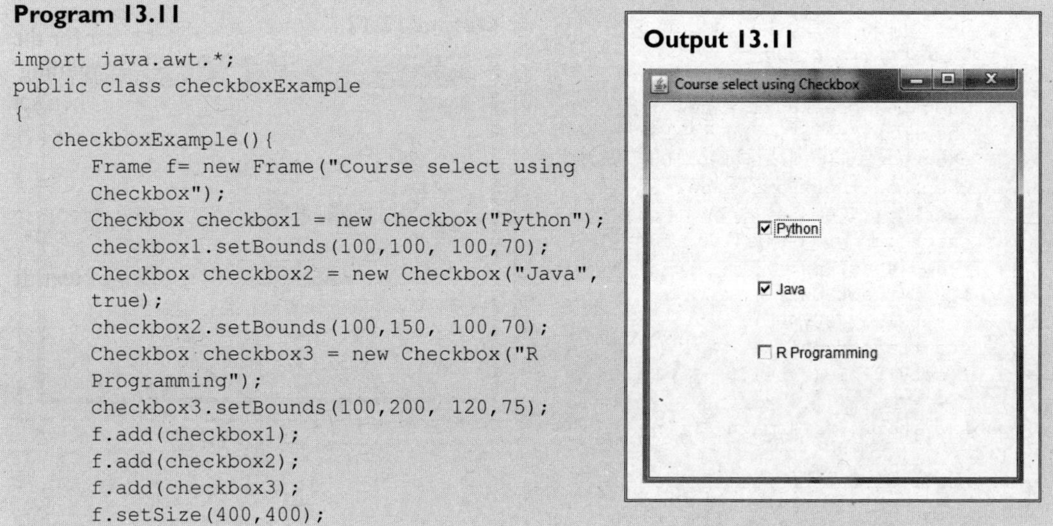

Program 13.11

```
import java.awt.*;
public class checkboxExample
{
    checkboxExample(){
        Frame f= new Frame("Course select using
        Checkbox");
        Checkbox checkbox1 = new Checkbox("Python");
        checkbox1.setBounds(100,100, 100,70);
        Checkbox checkbox2 = new Checkbox("Java",
        true);
        checkbox2.setBounds(100,150, 100,70);
        Checkbox checkbox3 = new Checkbox("R
        Programming");
        checkbox3.setBounds(100,200, 120,75);
        f.add(checkbox1);
        f.add(checkbox2);
        f.add(checkbox3);
        f.setSize(400,400);
```

Output 13.11

```
        f.setLayout(null);
        f.setVisible(true);
    }
    public static void main(String args[])
    {
        new checkboxExample();
    }
}
```

Program 13.11 illustrates the `CheckBox` control. A frame object is first created and then a `CheckBox` control, by creating object `checkbox1` and passing the value within the object initialisation. Similarly, `checkbox2` and `checkbox3` are created. These checkbox objects are added into the Frame object using the `add()` method. The functionality of the check box allows selection of multiple checkboxes, as shown in the output.

Radio button control

There is no direct control class for creating radio buttons in AWT, but the `CheckboxGroup` enables you to create them. `CheckboxGroup` class is used to group together a set of checkboxes, where only one check box button at a time is allowed to be in the 'on' state and the remaining check box buttons are in the 'off' state. This acts like a radio button. It inherits the object class. The AWT `CheckboxGroup` class declaration is given below.

```
public class CheckboxGroup extends Object implements Serializable
```

Program 13.12 illustrates the `CheckBoxGroup` component class which act as a radio button control.

Program 13.12

```
import java.awt.*;
public class radiobuttonExample
{
    radiobuttonExample(){
        Frame f= new Frame("Gender
        Selection using Radio button");
        CheckboxGroup cbg = new
        CheckboxGroup();
        Checkbox checkBox1 = new
        Checkbox("Male", cbg, false);
        checkBox1.setBounds(100,100, 50,50);
        Checkbox checkBox2 = new
        Checkbox("Female", cbg, true);
        checkBox2.setBounds(100,150, 70,50);
        f.add(checkBox1);
        f.add(checkBox2);
        f.setSize(400,400);
        f.setLayout(null);
        f.setVisible(true);
    }
    public static void main(String args[])
    {
        new radiobuttonExample();
    }
}
```

Output 13.12

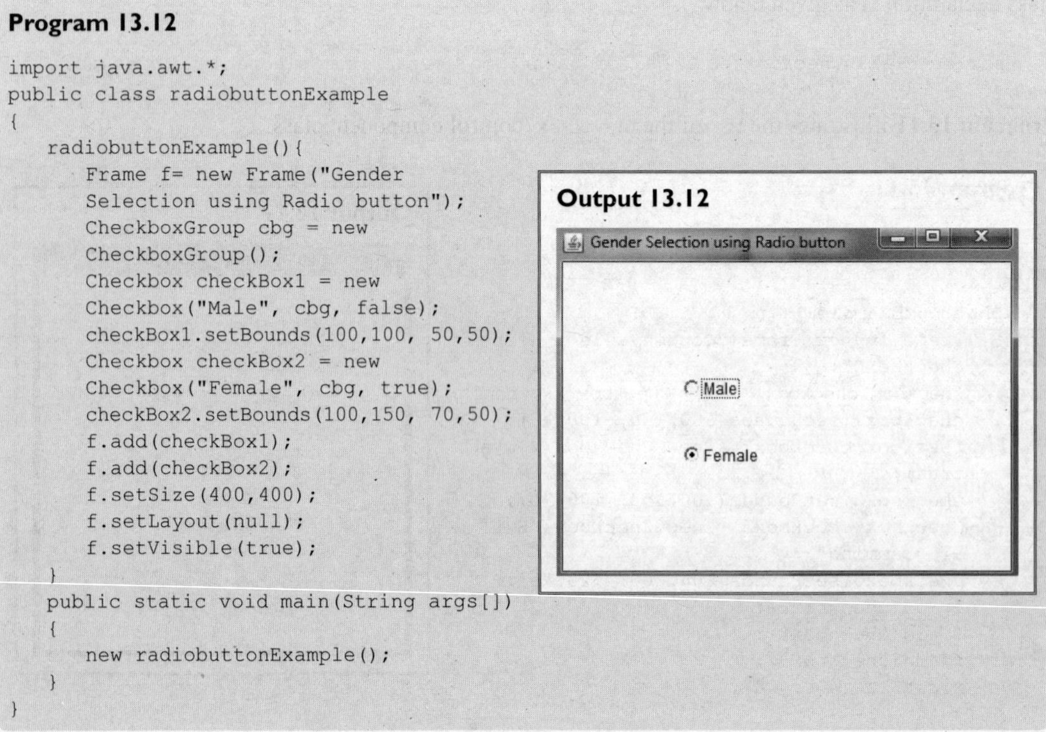

Program 13.12 demonstrates radio button control. A radio button is created using the `CheckBoxGroup` component. An object of the `CheckBoxGroup` class is created and then is passed to `CheckBox` class objects to assign the values. The radio button appears as a circular selection area automatically whereas in the previous example, the selection area appears as square checkboxes. The same type of object is being used here, just with different settings. Two check boxes are created and the values are initialised as male and female. Only one of them may be selected at a time, as seen in the output.

In the next section, Swing's basic controls will be discussed with examples.

13.6 SWING COMPONENT CLASSES

Java Swing is another way of creating the Graphical User Interface components for Window-based applications. It is built on top of the AWT Package and written entirely in Java. Unlike AWT, swing provides platform-independent lightweight components for developing GUI applications. The swing package offers classes for Java Swing API such as `JFrame`, `JPanel`, `JButton`, `JTextField`, `JTextArea`, `JRadioButton`, `JCheckbox`, `JMenu`, `JColorChooser` and so on. Figure 13.3 shows the hierarchy of the Java swing component classes.

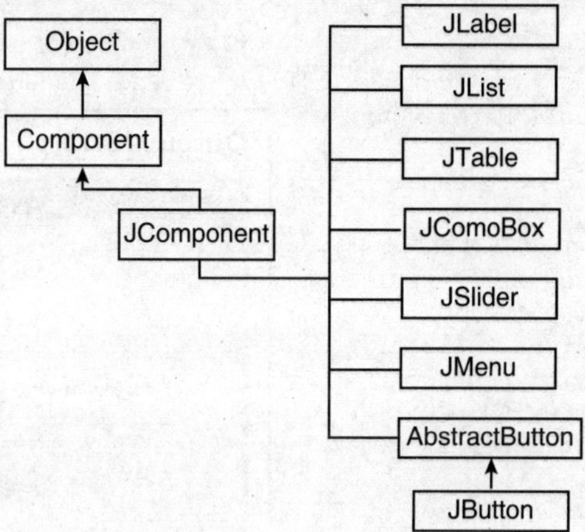

Fig. 13.3 Java `Swing` component classes

The differences between the AWT package and the swing package are listed in Table.13.3.

Table 13.3 **`AWT` package vs `swing` package**

Java AWT	Java Swing
AWT components are platform-dependent.	Swing components are platform-independent.
AWT components are heavyweight.	Swing components are lightweight.
AWT does not support pluggable look and feel.	Swing supports pluggable look and feel.
AWT offers less components compared to swing.	Swing offers more powerful components such as tables, lists, scrollpanes, colorchooser, tabbedpane, and so on.

13.6.1 Creating Swing Program Using `JFrame`

To work with GUI applications, an important task is to create the Window. In AWT, the Window is created using `Frame` and `Panel` class. In swing, the Window is created using `JFrame` class and `JPanel` class.

There are two ways to create a Frame:

- By creating the object of `JFrame` class (association).
- By extending `JFrame` class (inheritance).

For writing the code of swing inside the `main()`, constructor or any other method, let's see a simple swing example in **Program 13.13**, to create a button, Label, textfield which are specific to a swing component using `JButton`, `JLabel` and `JTextField` classes and add it on the `JFrame` object inside the `main()` method.

Program 13.13

```
import javax.swing.*;
public class simpleSwingExample {
    JFrame f;
    simpleSwingExample(){
        f=new JFrame("Simple Swing Example");//creating instance of JFrame
        JLabel l=new JLabel("Enter your
        name:");
        //creating instance of JLabel
        l.setBounds(50,100, 100,30);
        JTextField t=new JTextField("jose");
        //creating instance of JTextField
        t.setBounds(200,100,100,40);
        JButton b=new JButton("click");//
        creating instance of JButton
        b.setBounds(130,150,100, 40);
        f.add(l); //adding label in JFrame
        f.add(t);
        //adding textfield in JFrame
        f.add(b);//adding button in JFrame
        f.setSize(400,500);
        //400 width and 500 height
        f.setLayout(null);
        //using no layout managers
        f.setVisible(true);//making the Frame visible
    }
    public static void main(String[] args) {
        new simpleSwingExample();
    }
}
```

Output 13.13

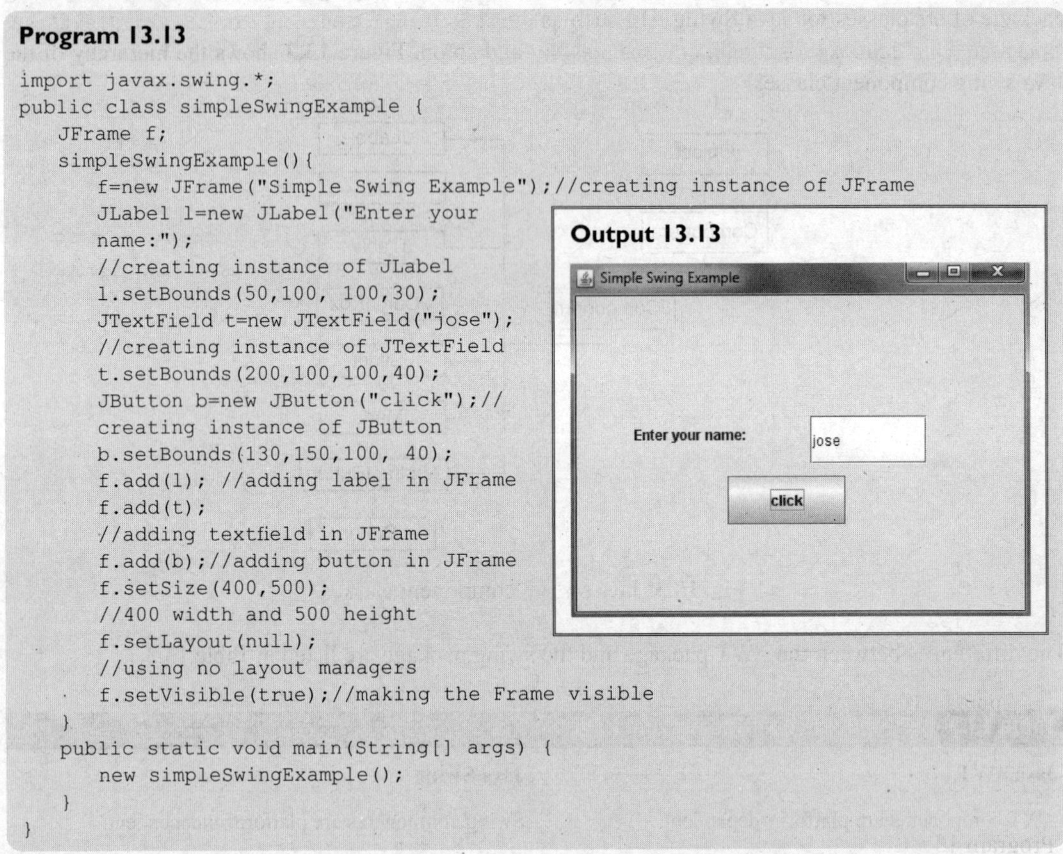

Program 13.13 illustrates the basic components of the swing package. The program contains `JLabel`, `JTextField` and `JButton` controls. Initially an object is created for each of these three components with the necessary parameters and supporting methods. `Frame` class `JFrame` is used in swing which holds all the components inside the Window. `add()` is used to include the `JLabel`, `JTextField` and `JButton` controls into the `JFrame` object. The program on execution will display the Window as shown in the output.

13.6.2 Creating Swing Program Using `JPanel`

The `JPanel` is the simplest container class which provides space for an application to add any other component in the output Window. It inherits the `JComponents` class. `JPanel` is used to group the components into multiple Panels, which means more than one Panel class can be added into the Window. (`JFrame` however cannot have multiple `JFrame` instances). Unlike `JFrame` class, `JPanel` class does not have a title bar. The `JPanel` program is demonstrated in **Program 13.14.**

Program 13.14

```
import java.awt.Color;
import javax.swing.*;
public class JPanelexample {
   JFrame f;
   JPanelexample(){
      f=new JFrame("Simple JPanel Example");//
      creating instance of JFrame
      JPanel Panel1=new JPanel();//creating instance of JPanel
      Panel1.setBounds(40,80,100,100);
      Panel1.setBackground(Color.CYAN);
      JLabel l=new JLabel("Enter your name:");
      l.setBounds(50,100, 100,30);
      JTextField t=new JTextField("joe");
      t.setBounds(200,100,100,80);
      JPanel Panel2=new JPanel();
      //creating instance of JPanel
      Panel2.setBounds(140,80,100,100);
      Panel2.setBackground(Color.LIGHT_GRAY);
      JButton b=new JButton("click");
      //creating instance of JButton
       b.setBounds(130,150,100, 40);
      Panel1.add(l);
      Panel1.add(t);
      Panel2.add(b);//adding button in JPanel
      f.add(Panel1);
      //adding JPanel into JFrame
      f.add(Panel2);
      f.setSize(400,300);
      f.setLayout(null);
      f.setVisible(true);
   }
   public static void main(String[] args) {
      new JPanelexample();
   }
}
```

Output 13.14

Simple JPanel Example

Enter your name:

joe

click

Program 13.14 is similar to Program 13.13, but here the `JLabel`, `JTextField` controls are not directly added using the `JFrame` object. Instead, the `JPanel` class is used here which is used to group the components in a container and more than one container can be used in the program. Here the `JLabel` and `JTextField` components are added into `Panel1` object and the `JButton` component is added using the `Panel2` object. To differentiate between `Panel1` and `Panel2`, `AWT Color` is given as the background. Finally, the Panel objects are added into the `JFrame` object to display the components in the output Window.

13.6.3 Creating Swing Programs Using `JApplet`

Applets are the second type of programs that normally use swing. Swing applets are similar to AWT applets, but with minor differences—a swing applet extends `JApplet` rather than `Applet`. `JApplet` is derived from `Applet`, therefore, it includes all the functionality available in `Applet`. `JApplet` is a toplevel swing container, which means that it is *not* derived from `JComponent`. All components are added to the `JApplet` content pane in the same way that components are added to the `JFrame` content pane.

Swing applets use the same four life-cycle methods as described in Chapter 12, namely `init()`, `start()`, `stop()`, and `destroy()`. Therefore, the need is to override only those methods that are required by the applet. Painting accomplished by swing is different from that in AWT, and a swing applet does not normally override the `paint()` method. All interaction with components in a swing applet must take place on the event dispatching thread.

Program 13.15 demonstrates the `JApplet` in Swing. Note that the program is run in the `AppletViewer`.

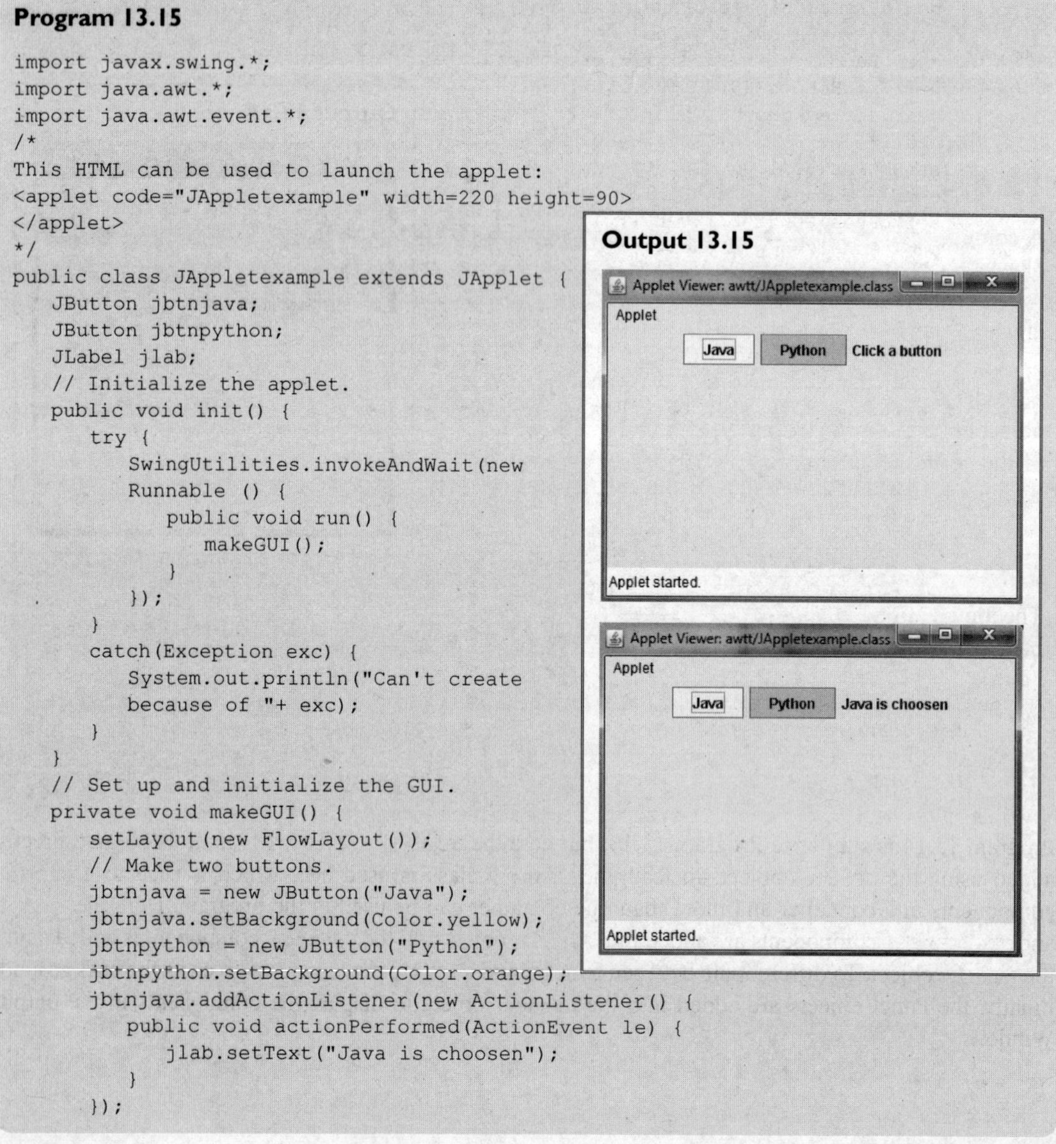

Program 13.15

```
import javax.swing.*;
import java.awt.*;
import java.awt.event.*;
/*
This HTML can be used to launch the applet:
<applet code="JAppletexample" width=220 height=90>
</applet>
*/
public class JAppletexample extends JApplet {
   JButton jbtnjava;
   JButton jbtnpython;
   JLabel jlab;
   // Initialize the applet.
   public void init() {
      try {
         SwingUtilities.invokeAndWait(new
         Runnable () {
            public void run() {
               makeGUI();
            }
         });
      }
      catch(Exception exc) {
         System.out.println("Can't create
         because of "+ exc);
      }
   }
   // Set up and initialize the GUI.
   private void makeGUI() {
      setLayout(new FlowLayout());
      // Make two buttons.
      jbtnjava = new JButton("Java");
      jbtnjava.setBackground(Color.yellow);
      jbtnpython = new JButton("Python");
      jbtnpython.setBackground(Color.orange);
      jbtnjava.addActionListener(new ActionListener() {
         public void actionPerformed(ActionEvent le) {
            jlab.setText("Java is choosen");
         }
      });
```

Output 13.15

```
        jbtnpython.addActionListener(new ActionListener() {
            public void actionPerformed(ActionEvent le) {
                jlab.setText("pyhton is choosen");
            }
        });
        add(jbtnjava);
        add(jbtnpython);
        jlab = new JLabel("Click a button");
        add(jlab);
    }
}
```

Program 13.15 shows that the `JApplet` class is used to create the content Panel for placing the swing components. Here, the swing `JButton` and `Jlabel` are placed inside the `JApplet` Window. Note that there is no `paint` method used in this program. Instead, the `makeGUI()` method is used to invoke the functionality of the swing components. When the button is pressed, it will invoke `actionPerformed(ActionEvent e)` and set the Label value. Finally the swing button and Label components are added into the JApplet Window using the `add()` method. On executing the program, the output is displayed in the `AppletViewer` Window as shown.

13.6.4 Border Control

A component can appear with several different styles of Borders around it. Sometimes it is helpful to place a Border around a component or a group of components, as it results in a more organised display. A `Border` object specifies the details of a Border. The `BorderFactory` class is used to create border objects.

A component derived from `JComponent` inherits a method named as `setBorder`, which is used to add a Border to the component. The `setBorder()` method accepts a `Border` object as argument. A `Border` object holds detailed information about the look of the Border. The `BorderFactory` class, which is part of the `javax.swing` package, is used to create Borders. Methods available in the Border Control of Swing are listed below.

```
createEmptyBorder(int top, int left, int bottom, int right)
```

The arguments passed into top, left, bottom, and right specify in pixels the size of the Border's top, left, bottom and right edges. The method returns a reference to a border object.

```
createLineBorder(Color color, int thickness)
```

The arguments passed into `color` and `thickness` specify the colour of the line and the size of the line in pixels. The method returns a reference to a `Border` object.

```
createTitledBorder(String title)
```

The argument passed into `title` is the text to be displayed as the Border's title. The method returns a reference to a `Border` object.

Program 13.16 demonstrates how to create Borders for `Panel` class using `BorderFactory` class with the help of `createLineBorder()` method.

Program13.16

```
import java.awt.*;
import javax.swing.BorderFactory;
import javax.swing.JPanel;
public class PanelExample {
    PanelExample()
    {
        Frame f= new Frame("Panel Example");
        JPanel Panel=new JPanel();
        Panel.setBounds(40,80,200,200);
        Panel.setBorder(BorderFactory.
        createLineBorder(Color.RED, 5));
        Panel.setBackground(Color.CYAN);
        Button b1=new Button("BCA");
        b1.setBounds(50,100,80,30);
        b1.setBackground(Color.yellow);
        Button b2=new Button("MCA");
        b2.setBounds(100,100,80,30);
        b2.setBackground(Color.green);
        Panel.add(b1);
        Panel.add(b2);
        f.add(Panel);
        f.setSize(400,400);
        f.setLayout(null);
        f.setVisible(true);
    }
    public static void main(String args[])
    {
        new PanelExample();
    }
}
```

Output 13.16

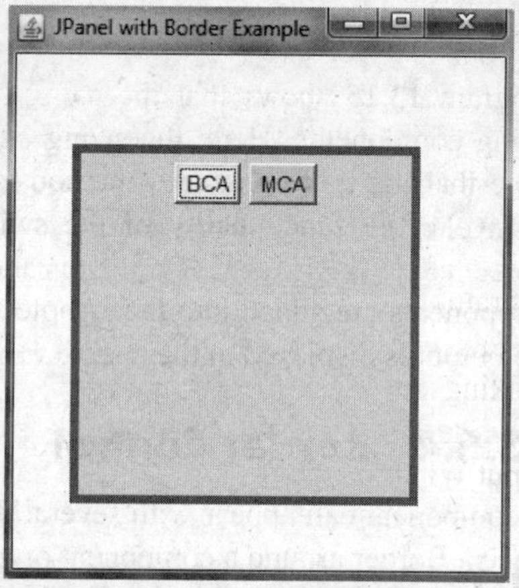

JPanel with Border Example

BCA MCA

Program 13.16 illustrates the use of the `Border` class to display the Border for Windows like `Panel` and `Frame`. This program is created to show the Border for a `JPanel` Window. It is done by invoking the `setBorder()` method of the `BorderFactory` class. This `BorderFactory` class invokes `createLineBorder` to set the colour of the Panel.

Program 13.17 demonstrates how to create Borders for the `Panel` class using `BorderFactory` class with the help of `createTitledBorder()` method.

Program 13.17

```
import java.awt.*;
import javax.swing.BorderFactory;
import javax.swing.JPanel;
public class PanelExample {
    PanelExample()
    {
        Frame f= new Frame("JPanel with Border
        Example");
        JPanel Panel=new JPanel();
        Panel.setBounds(40,80,200,200);
        Panel.setBorder(BorderFactory. createTitledBorder("Courses"));
        Button b1=new Button("BCA");
        b1.setBounds(50,100,80,30);
```

```
        b1.setBackground(Color.yellow);
        Button b2=new Button("MCA");
        b2.setBounds(100,100,80,30);
        b2.setBackground(Color.green);
        Panel.add(b1);
        Panel.add(b2);
        f.add(Panel);
        f.setSize(400,400);
        f.setLayout(null);
        f.setVisible(true);
    }
    public static void main(String args[])
    {
        new PanelExample();
    }
}
```

Output 13.17

JPanel with Border Example

Courses

BCA MCA

Program 13.17 illustrates the use of `Border` class to display the border for `Panel` Window using the `createTitledBorder()` method. This program creates the Border for a `JPanel` Window by invoking the `setBorder()` method of `BorderFactory` class. This `BorderFactory` class invokes `createTitledBorder()` method to set the Border colour with the title of the Panel as shown in the output Window.

13.7 SIMPLE APPLICATIONS USING AWT CONTROLS

In Section 13.5, various AWT controls have been explained with simple example programs. Based on AWT controls, the user can create simple desktop applications using AWT controls. The first application to be explained here is the arithmetic calculator. To construct an arithmetic calculator, the user has to design the application using Label, TextField and Button controls of AWT and to perform the ActionEvent when the button is clicked. **Program 13.18** demonstrates a simple arithmetic calculator using AWT controls.

Program 13.18

```
import java.awt.*;
import java.awt.event.*;
class simplecalculator implements ActionListener {
    Frame f1 = new Frame();
    Label l1 = new Label("FirstNumber");
    Label l2 = new Label("SecondNumber");
    Label l3 = new Label("Result");
    TextField t1 = new TextField();
    TextField t2 = new TextField();
    TextField t3 = new TextField();
    Button b1 = new Button("Add+");
    Button b2 = new Button("Sub-");
    Button b3 = new Button("Mul*");
    Button b4 = new Button("Div/");
    Button b5 = new Button("Cancel");
    simplecalculator() {
```

```
        //Giving Coordinates
        l1.setBounds(40, 100, 100, 15);
        l2.setBounds(40, 140, 100, 15);
        l3.setBounds(40, 180, 100, 15);
        t1.setBounds(200, 100, 100, 15);
        t2.setBounds(200, 140, 100, 15);
        t3.setBounds(200, 180, 100, 15);
        b1.setBounds(50, 250, 45, 15);
        b2.setBounds(110, 250, 45, 15);
        b3.setBounds(170, 250, 45, 15);
        b4.setBounds(230, 250, 45, 15);
        b5.setBounds(290, 250, 45, 15);
        //Adding components to the Frame
        f1.add(l1);
        f1.add(l2);
        f1.add(l3);
        f1.add(t1);
        f1.add(t2);
        f1.add(t3);
        f1.add(b1);
        f1.add(b2);
        f1.add(b3);
        f1.add(b4);
        f1.add(b5);
        b1.addActionListener(this);
        b2.addActionListener(this);
        b3.addActionListener(this);
        b4.addActionListener(this);
        b5.addActionListener(this);
        f1.setLayout(null);
        f1.setVisible(true);
        f1.setSize(400, 350);
    }
    public void
    actionPerformed(ActionEvent e) {
        int n1 = Integer.parseInt(t1.getText());
        int n2 = Integer.parseInt(t2.getText());
        if (e.getSource() == b1) {
            t3.setText(String.valueOf(n1 + n2));
        }
        if (e.getSource() == b2) {
            t3.setText(String.valueOf(n1 - n2));
        }
        if (e.getSource() == b3) {
            t3.setText(String.valueOf(n1 * n2));
        }
        if (e.getSource() == b4) {
            t3.setText(String.valueOf(n1 / n2));
        }
        if (e.getSource() == b5) {
            System.exit(0);
        }
    }
    public static void main(String... s) {
        new simplecalculator();
    }
}
```

Output 13.18

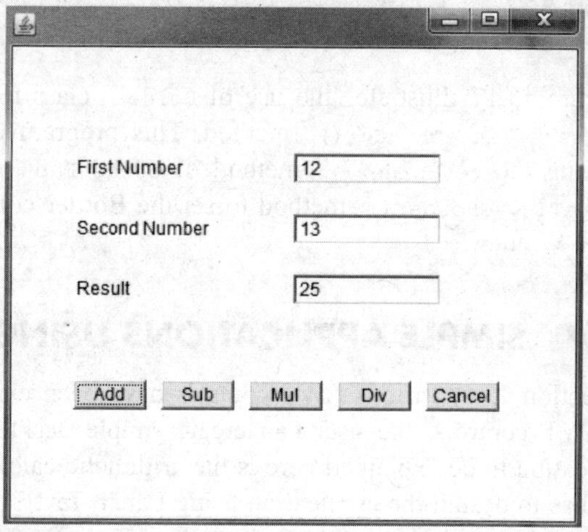

Program 13.18 illustrates performing an arithmetic calculation for the two given numbers. To design this application, three `Label`, `TextFields` and five `Button` controls of AWT have been used. After creating the AWT controls, the `setBounds()` method are used to define the position of the controls in the frame Window. Next, all the AWT controls are added into the `Frame` Window using the `add()` method. Finally, the logic of the program is performed, such as addition, subtraction operations using `actionPerformed()` method. By executing the program, the output is obtained as shown.

The next application is to calculate the factorial of a given number using AWT controls with Applet. **Program 13.19** illustrates finding the factorial of a given number using applet with AWT.

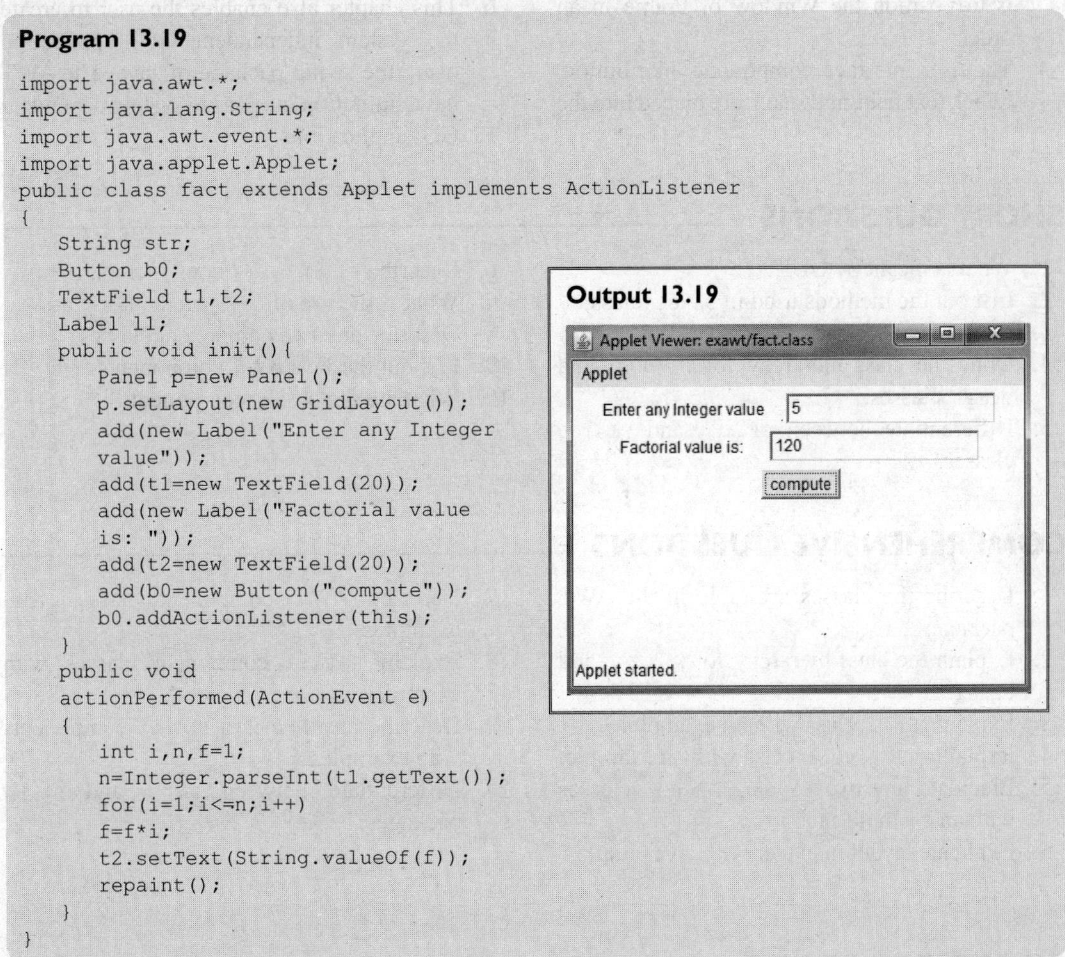

Program 13.19

```
import java.awt.*;
import java.lang.String;
import java.awt.event.*;
import java.applet.Applet;
public class fact extends Applet implements ActionListener
{
    String str;
    Button b0;
    TextField t1,t2;
    Label l1;
    public void init(){
        Panel p=new Panel();
        p.setLayout(new GridLayout());
        add(new Label("Enter any Integer
        value"));
        add(t1=new TextField(20));
        add(new Label("Factorial value
        is: "));
        add(t2=new TextField(20));
        add(b0=new Button("compute"));
        b0.addActionListener(this);
    }
    public void
    actionPerformed(ActionEvent e)
    {
        int i,n,f=1;
        n=Integer.parseInt(t1.getText());
        for(i=1;i<=n;i++)
        f=f*i;
        t2.setText(String.valueOf(f));
        repaint();
    }
}
```

Output 13.19

Program 13.19 contains two `TextFields`, `Labels` and one `Button` control. `TextField t1` will get any integer value as input and by clicking the `Button` compute, the factorial value is calculated using `actionPerformed()` method and the value is shown in the `TextField t2`.

SUMMARY

1. This chapter enables the programmer to design and code Windows-based applications or desktop applications using various components of the AWT package which is provided with many Graphical User Interface component classes and its methods.

2. Initially, the user can create the Window using Frame class, Panel class and Dialog. The user can also apply the layouts for Window using Layout Manager Classes provided by the AWT package.
3. GridLayout, CardLayout and FlowLayout of LayoutManager classes has been discussed. The purpose of this LayoutManager classes is to position the Window or Frame in an order.
4. The user interface components like button, Label, text field, and so on, are placed into the Frame or Panel class to get the appearance of a windows application.
5. Border control is used to provide Borders to Frame or Panel Windows. There are two ways for the Border to be set for the Window using BorderFactory class and its methods such as `createLineBorder()` and `createTitledBorder()`.
6. This chapter also enables the user to create the system independent GUI application using the swing package of Java. The AWT has a limitation in creating system dependent GUI applications.

SHORT QUESTIONS

1. What is meant by GUI?
2. List out the methods used in `Panel` class.
3. Define `Frame` class.
4. Draw the class hierarchy for `Window` and `Panel` classes.
5. Differentiate between `Frame` and `Dialog` classes.
6. Describe `FileDialog` constructors.
7. What is the use of `LayoutManager` class?
8. Describe any two component classes.
9. List out the Java AWT components.
10. What are the `Swing` components?

COMPREHENSIVE QUESTIONS

1. Describe the classes available in the AWT package.
2. Explain the class hierarchy for `Window` and `Panel`.
3. Explain `Panel` class with an example.
4. Explain `FileDialog` class with an example.
5. Elucidate any two `LayoutManager` classes with an example each.
6. Explicate layout manager with an example.
7. Describe AWT component classes with examples.
8. Explain `Swing` component classes with examples.
9. Describe any five java `Swing` components with examples.
10. Differentiate between `AWT` and `Swing` packages.

SOLVED PROGRAMS

1. Demonstration of LayoutManagers and Color classes.

```
import java.awt.*;
import java.applet.Applet;
public class Mixed1 extends Applet
{
  Panel noPanel, soPanel, coPanel, tocPanel, bocPanel;
  Button one1, two2, three3, four4, five5, six6;
  Label bottom1, lbl11, lbl21, lbl31;
  public void init()
```

```
{
    noPanel = new Panel();
    noPanel.setBackground(Color.blue);
    one1 = new Button("One");
    two2 = new Button("Two");
    three3 = new Button("Three");
    noPanel.setLayout (new FlowLayout(FlowLayout.CENTER));
    noPanel.add(one);
    noPanel.add(two);
    noPanel.add(three);
    soPanel = new Panel();
    soPanel.
    setBackground(Color.
    yellow);
    bottom1 = new Label("This
    is South");
    soPanel.setLayout (new
    FlowLayout(FlowLayout.
    CENTER));
    soPanel.add (bottom1);
    coPanel = new Panel();
    tocPanel = new Panel();
    tocPanel.
    setBackground(Color.gray);
    bocPanel = new Panel();
    bocPanel.
    setBackground(Color.green);
    lbl11 = new Label("One");
    lbl21 = new Label("Two");
    lbl31 = new Label("Three");
    four4 = new Button("Four");
    five5 = new Button("Five");
    six6 = new Button("Six");
    tocPanel.setLayout (new GridLayout(1, 3, 5, 5));
    tocPanel.add(lbl11);
    tocPanel.add(lbl21);
    tocPanel.add(lbl31);
    bocPanel.setLayout (new GridLayout(3, 1, 5, 5));
    bocPanel.add(four4);
    bocPanel.add(five5);
    bocPanel.add(six6);
    coPanel.setLayout(new GridLayout(2, 1));
    coPanel.add(tcPanel);
    coPanel.add(bcPanel);
    this.setLayout (new BorderLayout());
    add(noPanel, BorderLayout.NORTH);
    add(soPanel, BorderLayout.SOUTH);
    add(coPanel, BorderLayout.CENTER);
  }
}
```

Output

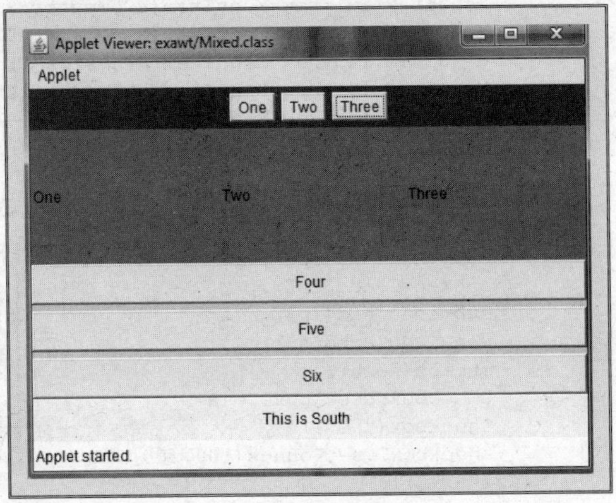

Applet Viewer: exawt/Mixed.class
Applet
One Two Three
One Two Three
Four
Five
Six
This is South
Applet started.

2. List of courses using checkbox and menu.

```
import java.awt.Checkbox;
import java.awt.Frame;
import java.awt.Label;
import java.awt.Menu;
import java.awt.MenuBar;
```

```
import java.awt.MenuItem;
import java.awt.event.ItemListener;
public class MenuandCheck {
  MenuandCheck(){
      Frame f= new Frame("Menu, MenuItem Example");
      MenuBar mb=new MenuBar();
      Menu menu=new Menu(«Colleges»);
      Menu submenu1=new Menu(«Govt Science College»);
      Menu submenu2=new Menu(«Govt Arts College»);
      MenuItem iu1=new MenuItem(«Computer Science»);
      MenuItem iu2=new MenuItem("Chemistry");
      MenuItem iu3=new MenuItem("Physics");
      MenuItem ip1=new MenuItem("Bio-Chemistry");
      MenuItem ip2=new MenuItem("Maths");
      MenuItem ip3=new MenuItem("Commerce");
      submenu1.add(iu1);
      submenu1.add(iu2);
      submenu1.add(iu3);
      submenu1.add(ip1);
      submenu1.add(ip2);
      submenu1.add(ip3);
      menu.add(submenu1);
      mb.add(menu);
      Checkbox checkbox1 = new
      Checkbox("UG");
      checkbox1.setBounds(100,100,
      100,70);
      Checkbox checkbox2 = new
      Checkbox("PG", true);
      checkbox2.setBounds(100,150,
      100,70);
      Checkbox checkbox3 = new
      Checkbox("M.phil");
      checkbox3.setBounds(100,200,
      120,75);
      f.add(checkbox1);
      f.add(checkbox2);
      f.add(checkbox3);
      f.setMenuBar(mb);
      f.setSize(400,400);
      f.setLayout(null);
      f.setVisible(true);
  }
  public static void main(String[] args) {
      new MenuandCheck();
  }
```

Output

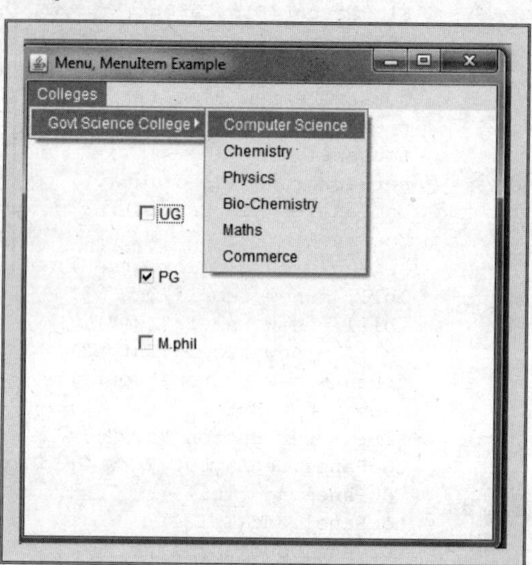

3. Finding the fibonacci of a given number using applet with AWT.

```
import java.awt.*;
import java.awt.event.*;
import java.applet.Applet;
public class fibonacci extends Applet implements ActionListener {
  String str;
  Button b0;
  TextField t1, t2;
  public void init() {
     Panel p = new Panel();
```

```
        p.setLayout(new GridLayout());
        add(new Label(«Enter any Integer value»));
        add(t1 = new TextField(20));
        add(new Label(«Fibonacci value is: «));
        add(t2 = new TextField(20));
        add(b0 = new Button(«compute»));
        b0.addActionListener(this);
    }
    public void actionPerformed(ActionEvent e)
  {
        int i, n, f0 = 1, f1 = 1, f2 = 0;
        n = Integer.parseInt(t1.getText());
        for (i = 2; i < n; i++) {
            f2 = f0 + f1;
            f0 = f1;
            f1 = f2;
        }
        t2.setText(String.valueOf(f2));
        repaint();
    }
  }
```

Output

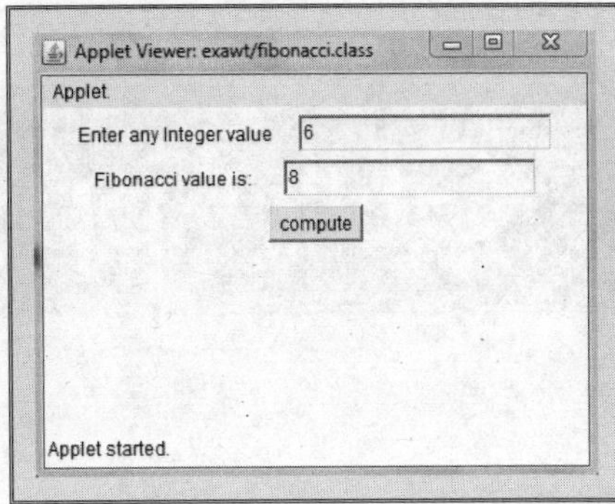

PROGRAMMING EXERCISES

1. Create a Window application to display three Labels, namely Amazon, Snapdeal and Flipkart and a corresponding textfield control for each Label to give a favourite item's details.
2. Create a login application with username and password Labels with textfields and place.
3. Create a Window application to set the titled Border for the course registration form.
4. Create a Window application having a button that acts as a deck of cards with four suits, namely, clubs, diamonds, hearts and spades, by performing the action, change the colour of the card and name of the card on a button click using `CardLayout` class.
5. Create a Window application to display the list of UG courses, in `GridLayout` form.
6. Create a Window application to calculate the factorial of a given number (n) and also to give the first n terms of the Fibonacci sequence. Create a textfield to take the number (n) as a user input for these operations. To perform the calculation, create two buttons namely `factorial` and `Fibonacci`. Create another textfield to display the results.
7. Create a Window application for electricity bill calculation using swing class controls. Create three Labels – number of units, cost per unit and total amount – and its text-fields, then create a button to perform the calculation.

CHAPTER

14

GUI Applications – Part 2

Chapter 13 discussed the concepts of creating windows, dialog control, various Layout Manager classes and some of the basic GUI based components of the AWT package as well as Swing components for creating GUI based applications. This chapter takes that discussion forward and deals with event handling on components, demonstrating more components on AWT, Swing classes and working with graphics elements such as Font, Image and Colour.

14.1 EVENT HANDLING

Event handling is an action that takes place often in GUI programming. This approach is based on the event delegation model. This representation provides a mechanism to process the events. The source such as a button fires an event and sends it to one or more *listeners.* The listener waits until it receives an appropriate event. Once it receives such an event, the listener ensures that the corresponding event-handling method is executed.

Consider an example to realise the source, event and listener. When a user clicks a button, an event is generated. Here, the button is the source. The event is represented as an object of class `java.awt.event. ActionEvent`. The listeners receive the click event from the button component, by calling the following method available in the `java.awt.Button` class.

```
addActionListener(ActionListener a){}
```

Similarly the `java.awt.event` package provides many other `Event` classes and `Listener` interfaces for event handling. Some of them are listed in Table 14.1.

Table 14.1 Event handling classes and its listener interfaces

Event handling classes	Listeners interface
ActionEvent	ActionListener
ItemEvent	ItemListener
AdjustmentEvent	AdjustmentListener
MouseEvent	MouseListener and MouseMotionListener
MouseWheelEvent	MouseWheelListener

(*Continued*)

Table 14.1 *(Continued)*

Event handling classes	Listeners interface
KeyEvent	KeyListener
TextEvent	TextListener
WindowEvent	WindowListener
ComponentEvent	ComponentListener
ContainerEvent	ContainerListener
FocusEvent	FocusListener

Registering listeners on methods

Registering the components with the `Listener` interface, many classes provide the registration methods that are listed below.

```
Button    : addActionListener(ActionListener a);
MenuItem  : addActionListener(ActionListener a)
TextField : addActionListener(ActionListener a)
            addTextListener(TextListener a)
TextArea  : addTextListener(TextListener a)
Checkbox  : addItemListener(ItemListener a)
Choice    : addItemListener(ItemListener a)
List      : addActionListener(ActionListener a)
            addItemListener(ItemListener a)
```

In Chapter 12 (Applets), various types of mouse and keyboard events have been discussed. Event handling classes such as ActionEvent, ItemEvent, TextEvent and AdjustmentEvent along with the AWT components will be discussed in this chapter, with example programs.

14.2 OTHER AWT COMPONENTS

So far, basic AWT component classes of `Button`, `Label`, `Text field`, `Checkbox` and `Radio button` were created using the `java.awt` package. Other components of the AWT package are:

- `TextArea,`
- `Choice(combo box),`
- `List,`
- `Scrollbar,` and
- `MenuItem` and `Menu`

`TextArea` control

The object of a `TextArea` class is a multi-line text box that displays text. This allows the editing of multiple lines of text and inherits the `TextComponent` class. `TextArea` class declaration is given in the following form.

```
public class TextArea extends TextComponent
```

Program 14.1 illustrates the use of `TextArea` component class to enter the permanent address in the text area field.

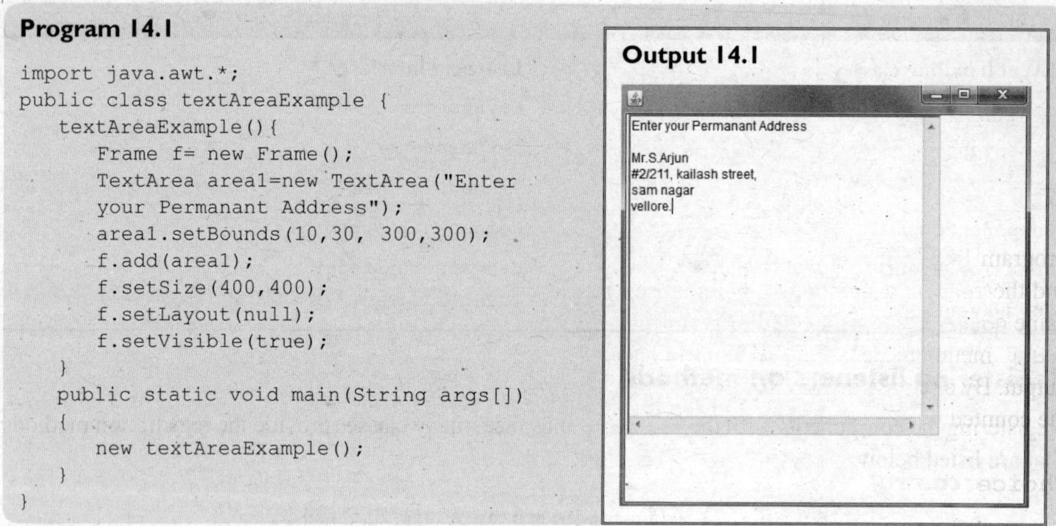

Program 14.1

```
import java.awt.*;
public class textAreaExample {
    textAreaExample(){
        Frame f= new Frame();
        TextArea area1=new TextArea("Enter
        your Permanant Address");
        area1.setBounds(10,30, 300,300);
        f.add(area1);
        f.setSize(400,400);
        f.setLayout(null);
        f.setVisible(true);
    }
    public static void main(String args[])
    {
        new textAreaExample();
    }
}
```

Output 14.1

Program 14.1 demonstrates the use of the `TextArea` component class. Here, a `Frame` object is created first and then the constructor of the `TextArea` component invoked by setting the bounds using the `setBounds( )` method. Finally the `TextArea` object is added into the `Frame` class using the `add( )` method and invoking the `setSize( )`, `setVisible(true)` methods to display the frame window to the user view. The output window is as shown.

Program 14.2 demonstrates event handling using `ActionListener` class for `TextArea`. The aim of the program is to count the words and characters in the given multiline text value in the `TextArea` field.

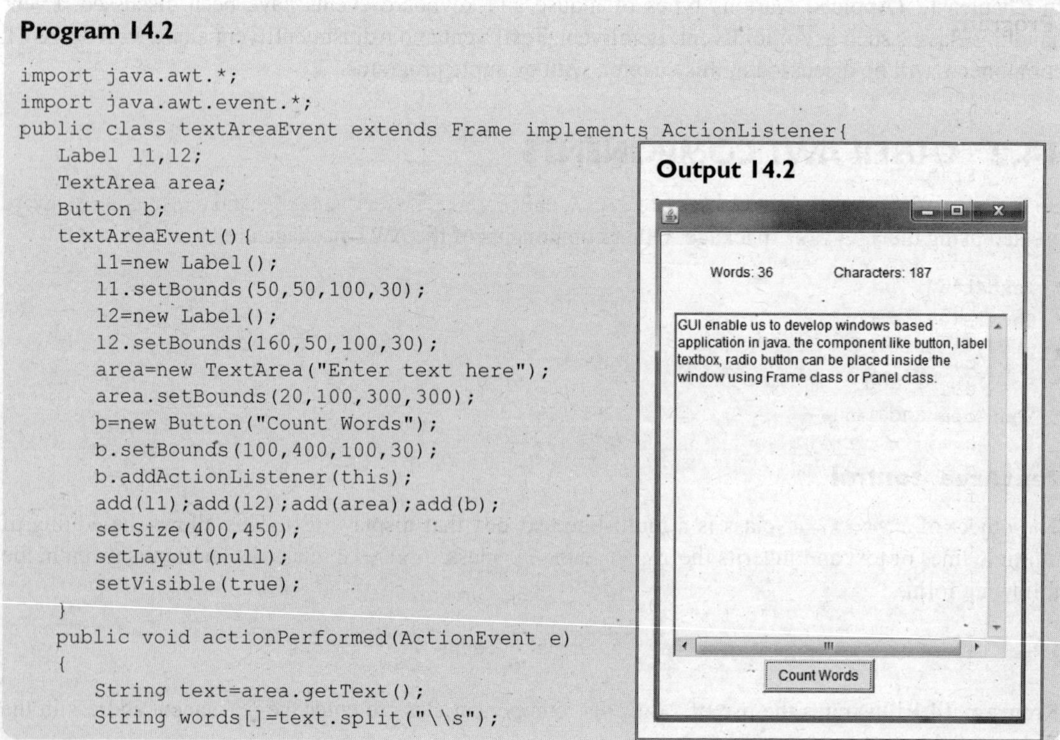

Program 14.2

```
import java.awt.*;
import java.awt.event.*;
public class textAreaEvent extends Frame implements ActionListener{
    Label l1,l2;
    TextArea area;
    Button b;
    textAreaEvent(){
        l1=new Label();
        l1.setBounds(50,50,100,30);
        l2=new Label();
        l2.setBounds(160,50,100,30);
        area=new TextArea("Enter text here");
        area.setBounds(20,100,300,300);
        b=new Button("Count Words");
        b.setBounds(100,400,100,30);
        b.addActionListener(this);
        add(l1);add(l2);add(area);add(b);
        setSize(400,450);
        setLayout(null);
        setVisible(true);
    }
    public void actionPerformed(ActionEvent e)
    {
        String text=area.getText();
        String words[]=text.split("\\s");
```

Output 14.2

```
        l1.setText("Words: "+words.length);
        l2.setText("Characters: "+text.length());
    }
    public static void main(String[] args) {
        new textAreaEvent();
    }
}
```

Program 14.2 demonstrates the use of the `TextArea` component with `ActionEvent`. A `Frame` is created and the `TextArea` component is initialised by creating an object for this class. Then a button with the name `Count Words` is created to perform an action. These controls are added into the `Frame` using the `add()` method. The `TextArea` control has the capacity to get multi-line editable text as shown in the output. By clicking the button, `ActionEvent` class method `actionPerformed()` is invoked and displays the counted words, characters, using `Label` controls.

`Choice` control

The `Choice` class is used to show a menu of choices. It provides a list of choices but only one choice is selected at a time by the user. Only the user's selection is shown on the top of the menu. For instance, if a menu contains five items in the list, then the top of the list item is visible to the user with a down arrow symbol. It inherits `Component` class. AWT `Choice` class declaration is as follows.

```
public class Choice extends Component implements ItemSelectable, Accessible
```

Program.14.3 illustrates the `Choice` control and its appearance.

Program 14.3

```
public class choiceExample {
    choiceExample() {
        import java.awt.*;
        import java.awt.event.*;
        Frame f = new Frame("Choose
        favorite choco using Choice");
        final Label label = new Label();
        label.setAlignment(Label.CENTER);
        label.setSize(400, 100);
        final Choice c = new Choice();
        c.setBounds(100, 100, 75, 75);
        c.add("1:Dairymilk");
        c.add("2:Munch");
        c.add("3:Milkybar");
        c.add("4:Perk");
        c.add("5:KitKat");
        f.add(c);
        f.add(label);
        f.setSize(400, 400);
        f.setLayout(null);
        f.setVisible(true);
        c.addItemListener(new
        ItemListener() {
            public void itemStateChanged(ItemEvent e) {
                String data = "You Selected: " + c.getItem(c.getSelectedIndex());
```

Output 14.3

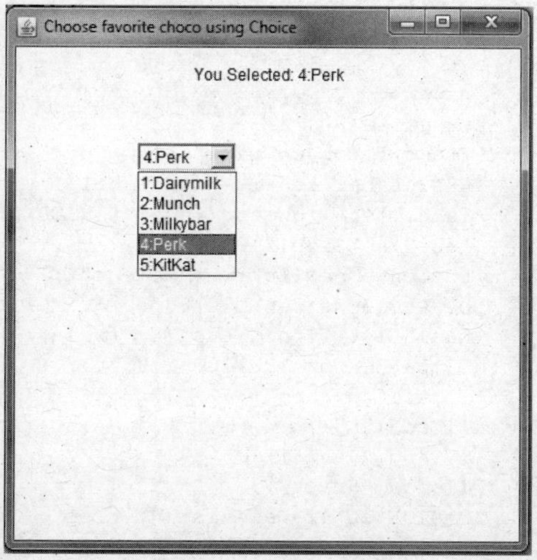

Choose favorite choco using Choice

You Selected: 4:Perk

4:Perk

1:Dairymilk
2:Munch
3:Milkybar
4:Perk
5:KitKat

```
            label.setText(data);
         }
      });
   }
   public static void main(String args[]) {
      new choiceExample();
   }
}
```

Program 14.3 illustrates the `Choice` control to display the list of chocolates in a popup menu. To do this, the `Frame` and `Choice` classes are created and then the choice item details are added (such as Munch, Milkybar and so on) using the `add()` method. Then the choice object is added into the `Frame` object by invoking `add()` method. The program output is as shown. When a specific chocolate is chosen by the user, the `ItemEvent` is triggered and its `Listener` method `itemStateChanged()` is invoked, then the result is stored in `Label`.

`List` control

The objects of `List` class represent a list of text items. With the help of the list, a user can choose either one item or multiple items. Unlike `Choice` control, all the `List` items are visible to the user at altogether. It inherits `Component` class. AWT `List` class declaration is given below.

```
public class List extends Component implements
ItemSelectable, Accessible
```

Program 14.4 demonstrates the `List` control of the AWT package to display a set of programming languages.

Program 14.4

```
import java.awt.*;
import java.awt.event.*;
public class listExample
{
   listExample(){
      Frame f1= new Frame("List your skills");
      final Label label = new Label();
      label.setAlignment(Label.CENTER);
      label.setSize(500,100);
      Button b=new Button("Select");
      b.setBounds(200,150,80,30);
      final List l1=new List(4, false);
      l1.setBounds(100,100, 70,70);
      l1.add("python");
      l1.add("R");
      l1.add("Java");
      l1.add("Scala");
      final List l2=new List(4, true);
      l2.setBounds(100,200, 70,70);
      l2.add("MVC");
      l2.add("Spring");
      l2.add("Hibernate");
      l2.add("JSF");
```

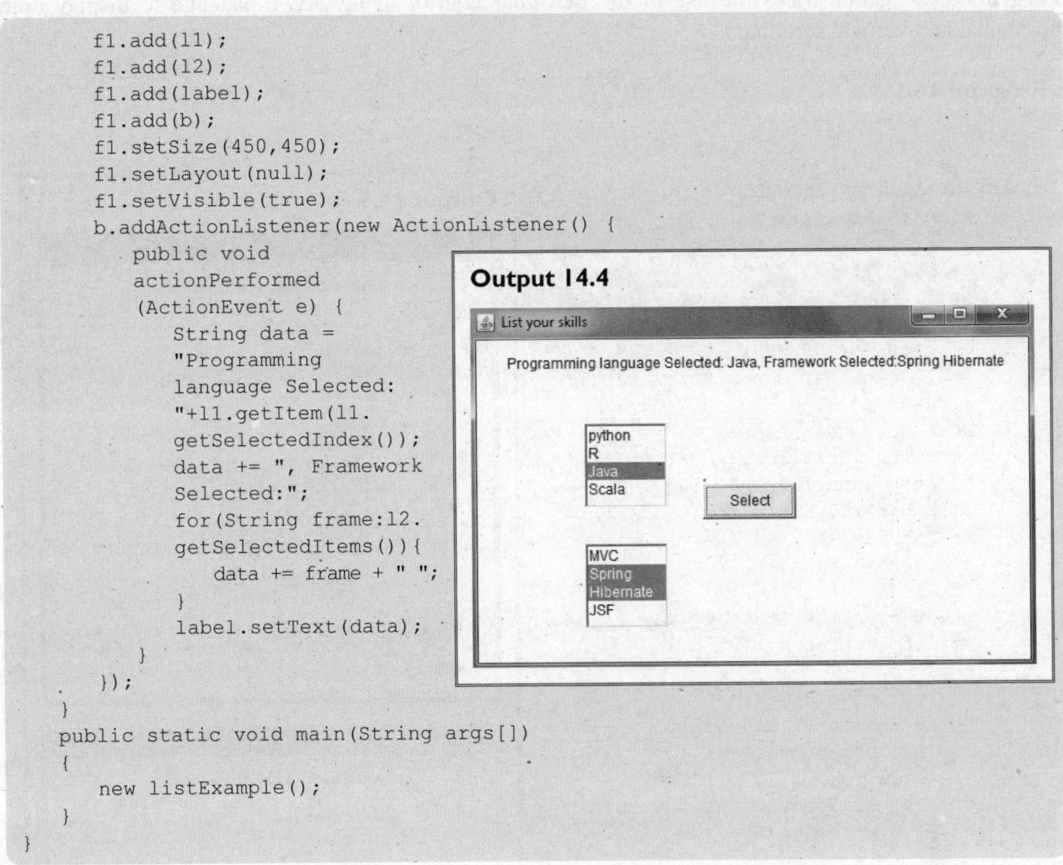

```
        f1.add(l1);
        f1.add(l2);
        f1.add(label);
        f1.add(b);
        f1.setSize(450,450);
        f1.setLayout(null);
        f1.setVisible(true);
        b.addActionListener(new ActionListener() {
            public void
            actionPerformed
            (ActionEvent e) {
                String data =
                "Programming
                language Selected:
                "+l1.getItem(l1.
                getSelectedIndex());
                data += ", Framework
                Selected:";
                for(String frame:l2.
                getSelectedItems()){
                    data += frame + " ";
                }
                label.setText(data);
            }
        });
    }
    public static void main(String args[])
    {
        new listExample();
    }
}
```

Output 14.4

Program 14.4 demonstrates the use of the `List` component class to display the programming languages in one list and the frameworks in Java in another list. To do this, first a `Frame` and then two `List` class objects `l1, l2` are created. The `List l1` has `False` as one parameter in the object initialisation which means the multiple selection of items in the list is not possible. For List `l2`, that parameter is `true`, hence multiple selections of items is possible. Using `l1` and `l2` objects, the `add()` method is used to insert the list of items. To perform an action, a button is created and the `actionPerformed()` method is invoked. `l1,l2` and a button `b` are added into the `Frame` object using the `add()` method. The program output is as shown.

`Scrollbar` control

The object of `Scrollbar` class is used to add horizontal and vertical scrollbars. `Scrollbar` is a GUI component that allows the user to see the rows and columns that are not visible because they lie outside the visible area of the window. For instance, if the Word file contains five pages of contents and the user is able to see only one page or half of the page, it depends on the design of the page. If the user wants to see the remaining page contents, they need to scroll down horizontally or vertically. This functionality can be provided by adding the `Scrollbar` control. AWT `Scrollbar` class declaration is given below.

```
public class Scrollbar extends Component implements Adjustable, Accessible
```

Program 14.5 demonstrates the use of the Scrollbar control of the AWT package to display both horizontal and vertical scrollbars.

Program 14.5

```
import java.awt.*;
import java.awt.event.*;
class scrollbarExample{
   scrollbarExample(){
      Frame f1= new Frame("Scrollbar
      Example");
      final Label l1 = new Label();
      l1.setAlignment(Label.CENTER);
      l1.setSize(400,100);
      final Scrollbar s=new Scrollbar();
      s.setBounds(100,100, 50,100);
      final Scrollbar s1=new
      Scrollbar(Scrollbar. HORIZONTAL);
      s1.setBounds(100,200, 150,100);
      f1.add(s);f1.add(s1);f1.add(l1);
      f1.setSize(400,400);
      f1.setLayout(null);
      f1.setVisible(true);
      s.addAdjustmentListener(new
      AdjustmentListener()
      {
         public void
         adjustmentValueChanged
         (AdjustmentEvent e) {
            l1.setText("Vertical
            Scrollbar Adjusted with:"+
            s.getValue());
         }
      });
      s1.addAdjustmentListener(new
      AdjustmentListener()
      {
         public void
         adjustmentValueChanged
         (AdjustmentEvent e) {
            l1.setText("Horizontal
            Scrollbar Adjusted with:"+
            s1.getValue());
         }
      });
   }
   public static void main(String args[]){
      new scrollbarExample();
   }
}
```

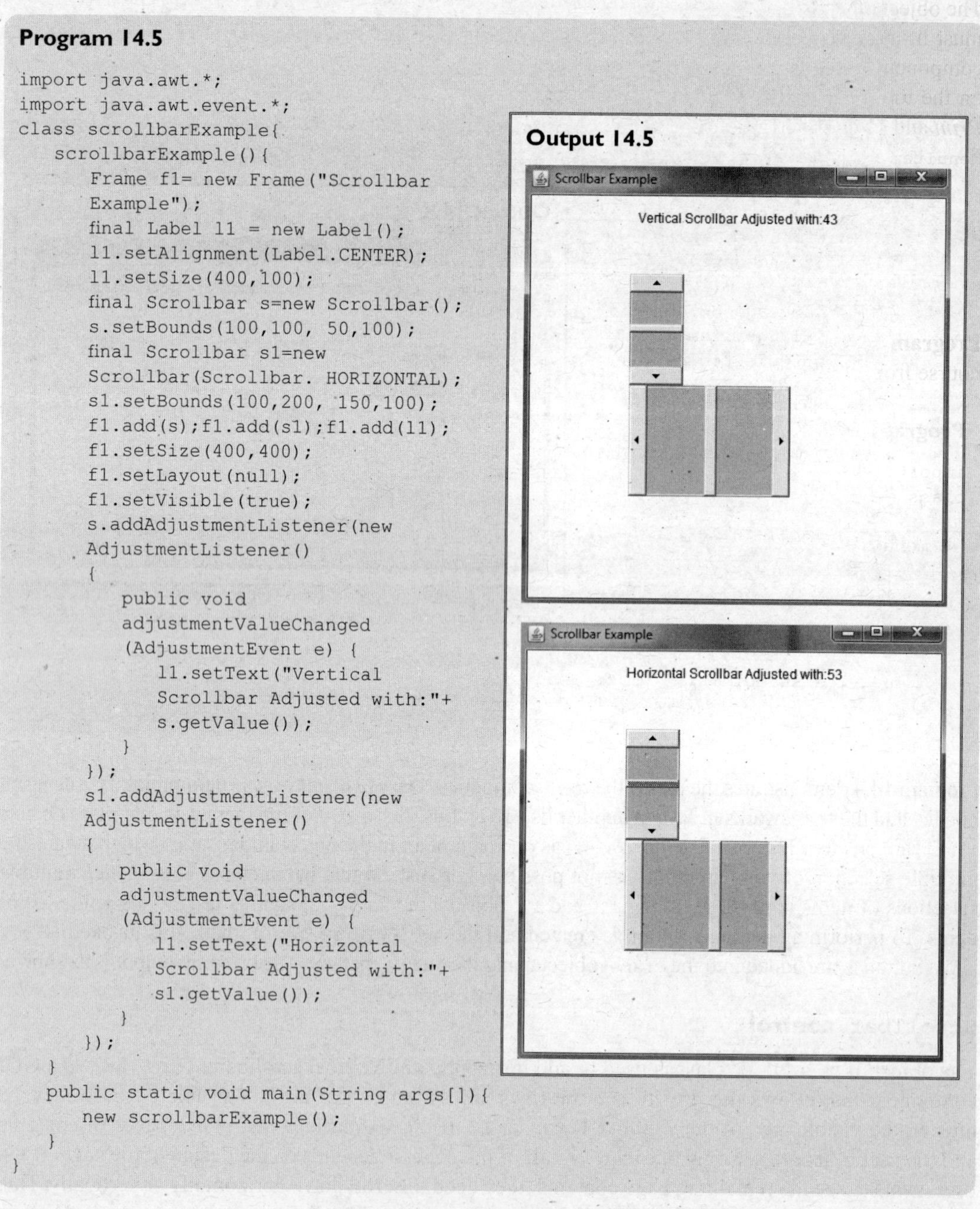

Program 14.5 uses both horizontal and vertical `Scrollbar` controls. They are created by passing the value to the `Scrollbar` class as `Scrollbar.HORIZONTAL` or `Scrollbar.VERTICAL`. `Scrollbar` has its own `Event` class called `AdjustmentEvent`. The method `adjustmentValueChanged()` is invoked by dragging the button shaped box inside the scrollbar control.

`Menu` and `MenuItem` control

The object of `MenuItem` class includes a labelled menu item on the menu bar. The items used in a menu must fit into the `MenuItem` or any of its subclasses. The object of the `Menu` class is a pulldown menu component and is displayed on the menu bar. For instance, the *Notepad* application contains *File* option on the top of the window below the title bar. This file also contains submenus such as *Open*, *Close*, *Print* and so on. To create such a menu in AWT, `Menu` and `MenuItem` classes are available. It inherits the `MenuItem` class. The class declarations are as follows.

```
public class MenuItem extends MenuComponent
implements Accessible
public class Menu extends MenuItem implements
MenuContainer, Accessible
```

Program 14.6 demonstrates the use of `MenuBar` and `MenuItem` control of the AWT package to select a course from a menu.

Program 14.6

```
import java.awt.*;
class menuExample
{
   menuExample(){
      Frame f= new Frame("Menu, MenuItem Example");
      MenuBar mb=new MenuBar();
      Menu menu=new Menu("Course");
      Menu submenu1=new Menu("UG");
      Menu submenu2=new Menu("PG");
      MenuItem iu1=new MenuItem("B.Sc,CS");
      MenuItem iu2=new MenuItem("B.C.A");
      MenuItem iu3=new MenuItem("B.Sc,IT");
      MenuItem ip1=new MenuItem("M.Sc,CS");
      MenuItem ip2=new MenuItem("M.Sc,IT");
      MenuItem ip3=new MenuItem("MCA");
      submenu1.add(iu1);
      submenu1.add(iu2);
      submenu1.add(iu3);
      submenu2.add(ip1);
      submenu2.add(ip2);
      submenu2.add(ip3);
      menu.add(submenu1);
      menu.add(submenu2);
      mb.add(menu);
      f.setMenuBar(mb);
      f.setSize(400,400);
      f.setLayout(null);
      f.setVisible(true);
   }
   public static void main(String args[])
   {
      new menuExample();
   }
}
```

Output 14.6

Program 14.6 illustrates the `Menu` and `MenuItem` controls of AWT. Course is created as the main menu using `Menu` class object. Then, submenus UG and PG are created using the same `Menu` class. `MenuItem` class is used to add items into `submenu1` and `submenu2`. These `MenuItems` are added into submenus using the `add()` method. Again, these submenus are added into `Menu` object using the `add()` method. The output is as shown above.

14.3 AWT GRAPHICS CLASSES

In the general form, a window is a container for information. Though output text to a window has been already demonstrated in the preceding examples, the advantage of a window's ability to represent high-quality text and graphics has not yet been utilised. Indeed, much of the power of the AWT comes from the support of Graphics. In the rest of this chapter we will discuss the colour, image and font-handling capabilities of Java. As mentioned earlier, AWT text is drawn using the `paint()` method of the Applet class.

14.3.1 AWT Colour

The `java.awt.Color` class is used to generate new colours and predefines a few colour constants. Colour is encapsulated by the `Color` class. Java allows the creation of up to 24 million diverse colours. Because the human eye has three kinds of neurons that react primarily to red, green and blue, it is possible for computer monitors to create all colours using the RGB system. The RGB system that Java uses, has combinations of red, green and blue in amounts represented by a number from 0 to 255. For example, red colour has the combination `255, 0, 0` that means 255 units of red with no green and blue. White is `255, 255, 255` and black is `0,0,0`.

Constant colour

Java initially defined a few colour constant names in lowercase, which violates the naming regulation of using uppercase for constants. These constant colours are best to use because they are available in all versions of Java. Some of the constants are `Color.black, Color.darkGray, Color.gray, Color.lightGray, Color.white, Color.magenta, Color.red, Color.blue, Color.green, Color.orange, Color.yellow, Color.pink, Color.cyan` and so on.

The new versions of Java added proper uppercase names for constants. Some of them are `Color.BLACK, Color.GRAY, Color.DARK_GRAY, Color.LIGHT_GRAY, Color.WHITE, Color.MAGENTA, Color.RED, Color.ORANGE, Color.PINK, Color.YELLOW, Color.GREEN, Color.CYAN, Color.BLUE` and so on.

Constructor

The most commonly used forms are shown here:

```
Color(int red, int green, int blue)
Color(int rgbValue)
Color(float red, float green, float blue)
```

The first form creates a new `Color` object that is a combination of red, green and blue. The second form contains values of each colour that must be in the range 0–255. The final constructor, `Color (float, float, float)`, takes three float values (between 0.0 and 1.0) that specify the relative mix of red, green and blue.

A `Color` object is created only to be passed as a parameter. Once the object is created for a `Color` class, it is used to set the foreground and/or background colour by using the `setForeground( )` and `setBackground( )` methods. For example,

```
Color c = new Color(255, 255, 240);
this.setBackground(c);
this.setForeground(c);
```

Additional constructors use single packed `int` or floating point values. In addition, there is support for the HSB (Hue, Saturation, Brightness) colour model and transparency.

The *hue-saturation-brightness (HSB)* colour model is an alternative to *red-green-blue (RGB)* for specifying a particular colour. Symbolically, *hue* is a wheel of colour. The *hue* is specified with a number between 0.0 and 1.0 (the colours are approximately red, orange, yellow, green, blue, indigo and violet. *Saturation* is another element ranging from 0.0 to 1.0, representing light pastels to intense hues. *Brightness* values also range from 0.0 to 1.0, where 1 is bright white and 0 is black. `Color` supplies two methods to convert between RGB and HSB. They are as follows:

`HSBtoRGB(float hue, float saturation, float brightness)`: This method returns a packed RGB value compatible with the `Color(int)` constructor.

`RGBtoHSB(int red, int green, int blue, float values[ ])`: This method returns a float array of HSB values corresponding to RGB integers.

In both the case, the array contains the hue at index 0, saturation at index 1, and brightness at index 2.

Obtaining RGB colour

The colour components of red, green and blue combinations independently may be obtained by using `getRed( )`, `getGreen( )` and `getBlue( )` methods as shown below.

```
int getRed( )
int getGreen( )
int getBlue( )
```

Each of these methods returns the RGB colour component found in the `Color` object in the lower 8 bits of an integer. To obtain a packed RGB representation of a colour, use `getRGB()`, shown here:

```
int getRGB()
```

To set the Current Graphics Colour (by default, graphics objects are drawn in the current foreground colour), one needs to call the method `setColor()` of the `Graphics` class:

```
void setColor(Color newColor)
```

Here, `newColor` specifies the new drawing colour. To obtain the current colour by calling `getColor()`, shown here:

```
Color getColor( )
```

Program 14.7 demonstrates the `Color` class and its methods.

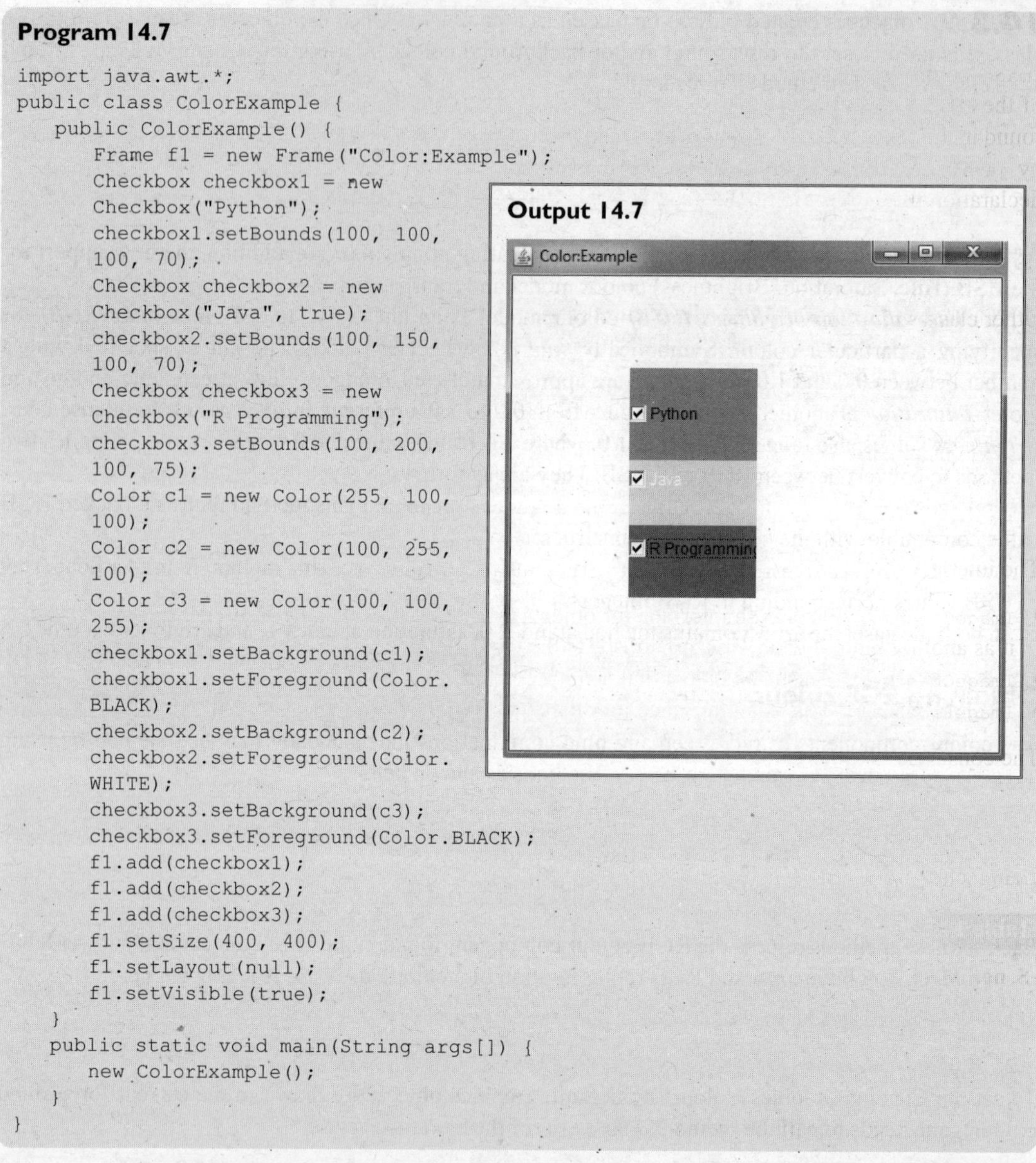

Program 14.7

```
import java.awt.*;
public class ColorExample {
    public ColorExample() {
        Frame f1 = new Frame("Color:Example");
        Checkbox checkbox1 = new
        Checkbox("Python");
        checkbox1.setBounds(100, 100,
        100, 70);
        Checkbox checkbox2 = new
        Checkbox("Java", true);
        checkbox2.setBounds(100, 150,
        100, 70);
        Checkbox checkbox3 = new
        Checkbox("R Programming");
        checkbox3.setBounds(100, 200,
        100, 75);
        Color c1 = new Color(255, 100,
        100);
        Color c2 = new Color(100, 255,
        100);
        Color c3 = new Color(100, 100,
        255);
        checkbox1.setBackground(c1);
        checkbox1.setForeground(Color.
        BLACK);
        checkbox2.setBackground(c2);
        checkbox2.setForeground(Color.
        WHITE);
        checkbox3.setBackground(c3);
        checkbox3.setForeground(Color.BLACK);
        f1.add(checkbox1);
        f1.add(checkbox2);
        f1.add(checkbox3);
        f1.setSize(400, 400);
        f1.setLayout(null);
        f1.setVisible(true);
    }
    public static void main(String args[]) {
        new ColorExample();
    }
}
```

Output 14.7

Program 14.7 demonstrates the use of the `Color` class representation for checkbox control. This also gives multiple ways of setting the colours of the components. First, within `Frame` object, three checkboxes have been created with the values of names of programming language such as Python, Java, R Programming. Initially, three `Color` objects are created as `c1`, `c2` and `c3` which have number value representation of colour. These colours have been set for the checkboxes as background colour by invoking `setBackground()` method. The text colour of checkboxes means that the foreground colour is applied using the direct property `Color.BLACK`. The program the output is as displayed.

14.3.2 AWT Image

`Image` control is the superclass for all image classes representing graphical images. Images are objects of the `Image` class and it is part of the `java.awt` package. Images are manipulated using the classes found in the `java.awt.image` package. There are a large number of image classes and interfaces defined by `java.awt.image`. Some of the image classes and interfaces will be discussed in this section. The declaration for `java.awt.Image` class is:

```
public abstract class Image extends Object
```

Other classes to work with images are listed below.

```
CropImageFilter
MemoryImageSource
FilteredImageSource
PixelGrabber
ImageFilter
RGBImageFilter
```

The interfaces to be used with `Image` class are listed below.

- `ImageConsumer`: This is an interface for objects that want to take pixel data from images and supply it as another kind of data. This, obviously, is the opposite of `ImageProducer`.
- `ImageObserver`: This is an object that can monitor an image while it loads.
- `ImageProducer`: This is an interface for objects that want to produce data for images.

The constructor for the image class is as follows:

```
Image()
```

`Image` class methods are listed in Table 14.2.

Table 14.2 Methods of `Image` class

S. no.	Method and description
1	`void flush()`: Flushes all reconstructable resources being used by this Image object.
2	`float getAccelerationPriority()`: Returns the current value of the acceleration priority hint.
3	`ImageCapabilities getCapabilities(GraphicsConfiguration gc)`: Returns an `ImageCapabilities` object that can be inquired upon as to the capabilities of this Image on the specified GraphicsConfiguration.
4	`abstract Graphics getGraphics()`: Creates a graphics context for drawing an off-screen image.
5	`abstract int getHeight(ImageObserver observer)`: Determines the height of the image.
6	`abstract Object getProperty(String name, ImageObserver observer)`: Gets a property of this image by name.
7	`Image getScaledInstance(int width, int height, int hints)`: Creates a scaled version of this image.
8	`abstract ImageProducer getSource()`: Gets the object that produces the pixels for the image.
9	`abstract int getWidth(ImageObserver observer)`: Determines the width of the image.
10	`void setAccelerationPriority(float priority)`: Sets a hint for this image about how important acceleration is.

File formats

Initially the web images were in the GIF file format. It is easy to make it possible for images to be viewed while online, so it was well suited to the internet. However, GIF images can have only up to 256 colours each. This limitation caused the major browser vendors to add support for JPEG images. The JPEG format was created by a group of photographic experts to store full-colour-spectrum, continuous-tone images. The images in the JPEG file format can be of much higher reliability and more highly compressed than a GIF encoding of the same source image. Another file format is PNG, which is another alternative to GIF. The Java image classes abstract the differences behind a clean interface.

Image operations

There are three common operations to be performed when you work with images: creating an image, loading an image, and displaying an image. In Java, the `Image` class is used to refer to images in memory and to images that must be loaded from external sources.

(i) *Creating an Image Object:* When creating a memory image using the following code, an error occurred:

```
Image test = new Image(100, 100);
// Error
```

Because images must be painted on a window to be seen, the `Image` class doesn't have enough information about its environment to create the proper data format for the screen. Therefore, the `Component` class in `java.awt` has a factory method called `createImage()` that is used to create `Image` objects. The `createImage( )` method has the following general form:

```
Image createImage(int width, int height)
```

This form returns a blank, that is, an empty image that has the specified width and height. For example,

```
Canvas s = new Canvas();
Image test = s.createImage(100, 100);
```

This creates an instance of Canvas and then calls the `createImage()` method to actually make an image object. At this point, the image is blank. Now let's see how to write or load an image.

(ii) *Loading an Image:* To obtain an image means loading the image. One way to do this is to use the `getImage()` method defined by the `Applet` class. It has the following forms.

```
Image getImage(URL url)
Image getImage(URL url, String imageName
```

The first form returns an `Image` object that encapsulates the image found at the location specified by `url`. The second form returns an `Image` object that encapsulates the image found at the location specified by `url` and having the name specified by `imageName`.

(iii) *Displaying an Image:* An image can be displayed by using `drawImage()`, which is a member of the `Graphics` class. It has several forms. The one we will be using is:

```
boolean drawImage(Image imgObj, int left, int top, ImageObserver imgOb)
```

This displays the image passed in `imgObj` with its upper-left corner specified by `left` and `top`. `imgOb` is a reference to a class that implements the `ImageObserver` interface. This interface is implemented by all AWT components. With `getImage()` and `drawImage()`, it is actually quite easy to load and display an image. **Program 14.8** illustrates the `Image` class and its methods to create, load and display an image.

Program 14.8

```
import java.awt.*;
import java.awt.event.*;
import java.awt.image.BufferedImage;
import java.io.File;
import java.io.IOException;
import javax.imageio.ImageIO;
public class ImageDemo {
   private Frame mainFrame;
   private Label headerLabel;
   private Label statusLabel;
   private Panel controlPanel;
   public ImageDemo(){
      prepareGUI();
   }
   public static void main(String[] args){
      ImageDemo awtControlDemo = new ImageDemo();
      awtControlDemo.showImageDemo();
   }
   private void prepareGUI(){
      mainFrame = new Frame("ImageExample");
      mainFrame.setSize(400,400);
      mainFrame.setLayout(new GridLayout(3, 1));
      mainFrame.addWindowListener(new WindowAdapter() {
         public void windowClosing(WindowEvent windowEvent){
            System.exit(0);
         }
      });
      headerLabel = new Label();
      headerLabel.setAlignment(Label.CENTER);
      statusLabel = new Label();
      statusLabel.setAlignment(Label.CENTER);
      statusLabel.setSize(100,100);
      controlPanel = new Panel();
      controlPanel.setLayout(new FlowLayout());
      mainFrame.add(headerLabel);
      mainFrame.add(controlPanel);
      mainFrame.add(statusLabel);
      mainFrame.setVisible(true);
   }
```

```
    private void showImageDemo(){
       headerLabel.setText("Image Demo");
       controlPanel.add(new ImageComponent("C:\\ Penguins.jpg"));
       mainFrame.setVisible(true);
    }
    class ImageComponent extends Component
    {
       BufferedImage img;
       public void paint(Graphics g) {
          g.drawImage(img, 0, 0, null);
       }
       public ImageComponent(String path)
       {
          try {
             img = ImageIO.read(new
             File(path));
          }
          catch (IOException e) {
             e.printStackTrace();
          }
       }
       public Dimension getPreferredSize()
       {
          if (img == null) {
             return new Dimension(100,100);
          }
          else {

             return new Dimension(img.getWidth(), img.getHeight());
          }
       }
    }
}
```

Output 14.8

ImageExample

Image Demo

Program 14.8 demonstrates the important graphics components of `Image` class. Since `Image` is considered a graphics component, it is not directly drawn to the window. There is a need to use the `Graphics` class to draw an image in the window. `Panel` is the best choice to work with `Graphics` classes. The first step is to load an image using the `ImageComponent` class. Within this class, the image name and its file format is loaded as `Penguins.jpg`. The second step is to draw an image into the `Panel` using the `Graphics` object method `drawImage()`. The third step is to display the image by adding `ImageComponent` object into `Panel` object. The program output is as shown.

14.3.3 AWT Font

The `java.awt.Font` class is used to create `Font` objects to set the font for drawing text, labels, text fields, buttons, and so on. Font is usually used to represent the text data in different styles such as bold, italic, underlined and font faces and varied sizes. There are three *logical/generic font names* that are given in Table 14.3. Java will select a font in the system that matches the general characteristics of the logical font.

Table 14.3 Generic font names

Serif	This text is in a serif font. Often used for blocks of text (example, Times New Roman).
sansserif	This text is in a SansSerif font. Often used for titles (example, Arial or Helvetica).
monospaced	This text is in a Monospaced font, often used for computer text (example, Courier).

The methods used to get a list of the *system fonts* on the host computer are listed below. The font information is obtained from the current graphics environment.

```
GraphicsEnvironment ge = GraphicsEnvironment.getLocalGraphicsEnvironment();
```

Get an array of font names (smaller than the number of fonts),

```
String[] fontNames = ge.getAvailableFontFamilyNames();
```

Get an array of fonts. It is preferable to use the names above.

```
Font[] allFonts = ge.getAllFonts();
```

The constructor for the `Font` class is given as,

```
Font f = new Font(name, style, size);
```

The parameters for the constructor take the following possible values (Table 14.4).

Table 14.4 Font values for name, style and size

String name	int style	int size
serif, sansserif, monospaced or a system font	Font.PLAIN Font.BOLD Font.ITALIC Font.BOLD+Font.ITALIC	Integer point size: typically in the range 10–48.

For example,

```
JButton b = new JButton("OK");
b.setFont(new Font("sansserif", Font.BOLD, 32));
```

Program 14.9 illustrates how to use the `Font` class.

Program 14.9

```
import java.awt.*;
public class FontDemo {
   public static void main(String[] args) {
      Frame f = new Frame("Font Example");
```

```
        String FontList[];
        String msg = "";
        TextArea area1 = null;
        GraphicsEnvironment ge
        = GraphicsEnvironment.
        getLocalGraphicsEnvironment();
        FontList =
        ge.getAvailableFontFamilyNames();
        for (int i = 0;i < FontList.
        length;
        i++) {
           msg += FontList[i] + " ";
           area1 = new TextArea(msg);
        }
        area1.setBounds(70, 100, 300,
        300);
        f.add(area1);
        f.setSize(400, 400);
        f.setLayout(null);
        f.setVisible(true);
    }
}
```

Output 14.9

Font Example

Aparajita
Arabic Typesetting
Arial
Arial Black
Arial Narrow
Arial Rounded
MT Bold
Arial Unicode
MS Baamini
Baskerville Old Face
Batang
BatangChe
Bauhaus 93
Bell MT Berlin Sans FB
Berlin Sans FB Demi
Bernard MT Condensed
Bitstream Vera Sans Mono
Blackadder ITC

Program 14.9 illustrates the `Graphics` class known as `Font`. This program lists all the available font faces in the system, such as Arial, Times New Roman, and so on. To do this, a String array object `Fontlist[]` and String `msg` are created to display the fonts. With the help of `GraphicsEnvironment` class, the `getAvailableFontFamilyNames()` method has been invoked and it is stored in `Fontlist` of String object. The `for` loop is used to print one by one, the name of all the fonts which are stored in `Fontlist` array. The data is displayed in the `TextArea` component as shown in the output window.

Getting font information

To obtain the information about a particular font, first get the current font by calling the `getFont()` method. This method is defined by the Graphics class,

```
Font getFont()
```

To retrieve the desired font information, various methods defined by `Font` class is used. **Program 14.10** displays the name, family, size and style of the currently selected font.

Program 14.10

```
// Display font info. import java.applet.*;
import java.awt.*;
/*
<applet code="FontInfo" width=350 height=60>
</applet>
*/
public class FontInfo extends Applet {
    public void paint(Graphics g) {
        Font f = g.getFont();
        String fontName = f.getName();
```

```
        String fontFamily = f.getFamily();
        int fontSize = f.getSize();
        int fontStyle = f.getStyle();
        String msg = "Family: " + fontName;
        msg += ", Font: " + fontFamily;
        msg += ", Size: " + fontSize + ",
        Style: ";
        if((fontStyle & Font.BOLD) == Font.
        BOLD)
        msg += "Bold ";
        if((fontStyle & Font.ITALIC) ==
        Font.ITALIC)
        msg += "Italic ";
        if((fontStyle & Font.PLAIN) ==
        Font.PLAIN)
        msg += "Plain ";
        g.drawString(msg, 4, 16);
    }
}
```

Output 14.10

Applet Viewer: awtt/FontInfo.class

Applet

Family: Dialog, Font: Dialog, Size: 12, Style: Plain

Applet started.

Program 14.10 demonstrates how to get the details of a font family using `Font` class. `Font` class object `f` is created with `Graphics` object `g` which invokes the `getFont()` method. This method retrieves the details of the current font and stores it in `f`. Then, by invoking the `getName()`, `getSize()`, `getStyle()` methods, the details of the font are printed as shown in the output.

14.4 OTHER SWING CONTROLS

Most of the components in the Swing package are similar to the AWT package components. Moreover, the Swing package provides special components that are not provided in the AWT. Some of them are listed below.

- `JPasswordField`
- `JTable`
- `JOptionPane`
- `JTabbedPane`
- `JTree`
- `JProgressBar`

For other components such as `JScrollPane`, `JComboBox`, `JMenu` and `MenuItem`, there are equivalent components in the AWT Package.

14.4.1 JPasswordField

The object of a `JPasswordField` class is a text component specialised for password entry. It allows the editing of a single line of text. It inherits the `JTextField` class. This component is not available in the AWT package. `JPasswordField` class declaration is as follows:

```
public class JPasswordField extends JTextField
```

Constructors in the `JPasswordField` class are listed below:

- `JPasswordField()`: Constructs a new `JPasswordField`, with a default document, null starting text string, and 0 column width.

- `JPasswordField(int columns)`: Constructs a new empty `JPasswordField` with the specified number of columns.
- `JPasswordField(String text)` : Constructs a new `JPasswordField` initialised with the specified text.
- `JPasswordField(String text, int columns)`: Constructs a new `JPasswordField` initialised with the specified text and columns.

Program 14.11 illustrates the login application using `JPasswordField` class.

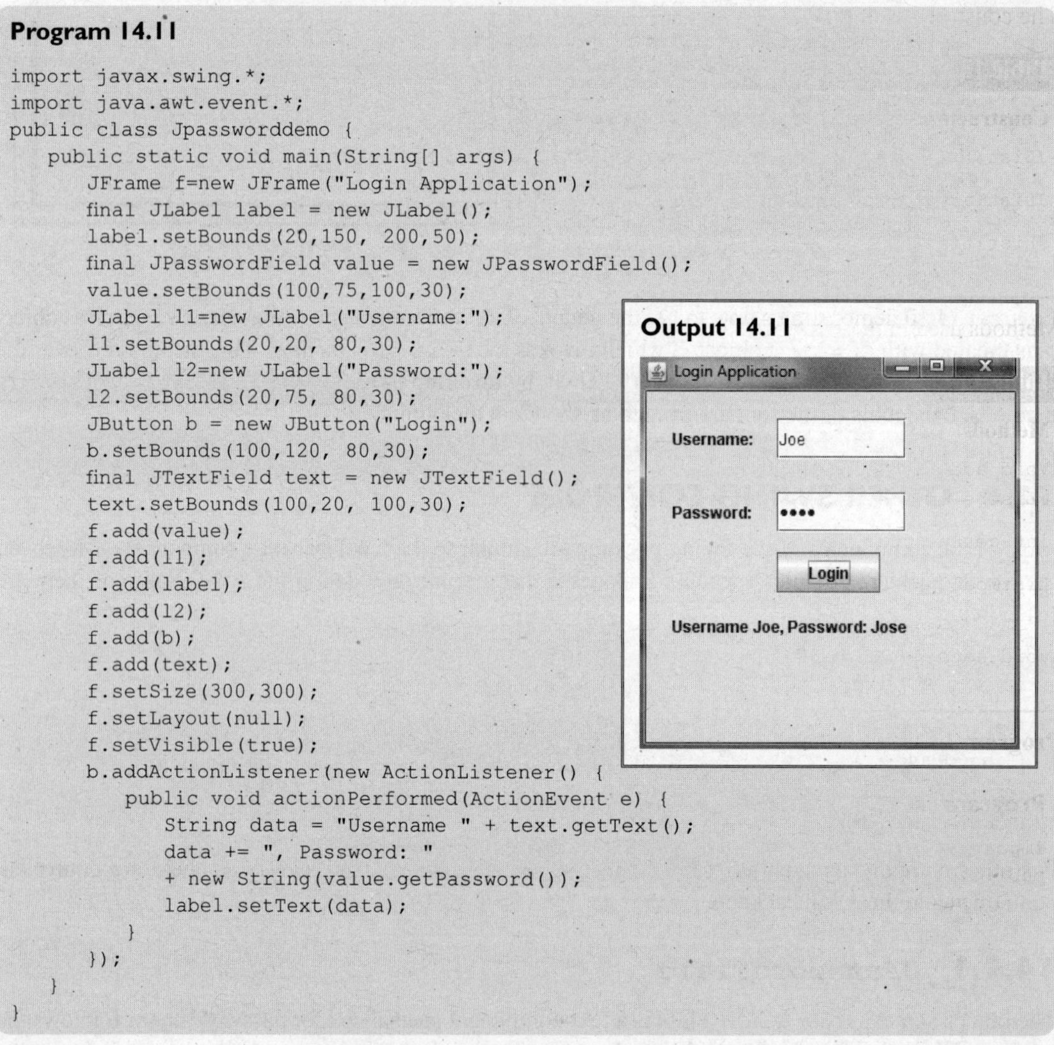

Program 14.11

```
import javax.swing.*;
import java.awt.event.*;
public class Jpassworddemo {
   public static void main(String[] args) {
      JFrame f=new JFrame("Login Application");
      final JLabel label = new JLabel();
      label.setBounds(20,150, 200,50);
      final JPasswordField value = new JPasswordField();
      value.setBounds(100,75,100,30);
      JLabel l1=new JLabel("Username:");
      l1.setBounds(20,20, 80,30);
      JLabel l2=new JLabel("Password:");
      l2.setBounds(20,75, 80,30);
      JButton b = new JButton("Login");
      b.setBounds(100,120, 80,30);
      final JTextField text = new JTextField();
      text.setBounds(100,20, 100,30);
      f.add(value);
      f.add(l1);
      f.add(label);
      f.add(l2);
      f.add(b);
      f.add(text);
      f.setSize(300,300);
      f.setLayout(null);
      f.setVisible(true);
      b.addActionListener(new ActionListener() {
         public void actionPerformed(ActionEvent e) {
            String data = "Username " + text.getText();
            data += ", Password: "
            + new String(value.getPassword());
            label.setText(data);
         }
      });
   }
}
```

Output 14.11

Program 14.11 demonstrates the use of `JPasswordField` to hide the details entered in the field. The Login application here has two textfields, `Username` with normal `JTextField` another hidden Textfield known as `JPasswordField`. A `JButton` is created to perform `ActionEvent` to display the entered values in `JLabel`. When a button is clicked, the method `actionPerformed()` of `ActionEvent` class is generated. The program output is as shown.

14.4.2 `JList` Class

The object of `JList` class represents a list of text items. The list of text items can be set up so that the user can choose either one item or multiple items. It inherits the `JComponent` class. Let's see the declaration for the `javax.swing.JList` class.

- `public class JList extends JComponent implements Scrollable, Accessible`
- `public class JList extends JComponent implements Scrollable, Accessible`

The constructors in the `JList` class are listed in Table 14.5.

Table 14.5 List of constructors in JList

Constructor	Description
`JList()`	Creates a `JList` with an empty, read-only, model.
`JList(ary[] listData)`	Creates a `JList` that displays the elements in the specified array.
`JList(ListModel<ary> dataModel)`	Creates a `JList` that displays elements from the specified non-null model.

Methods used in the `JList` class are listed in Table 14.6.

Table 14.6 List of methods used in JList class

Methods	Description
`Void addListSelectionListener (ListSelectionListener listener)`	It is used to add a listener to the list, to be notified each time a change to the selection occurs.
`int getSelectedIndex()`	It is used to return the smallest selected cell index.
`ListModel getModel()`	It is used to return the data model that holds a list of items displayed by the `JList` component.
`void setListData(Object[] listData)`	It is used to create a read-only `ListModel` from an array of objects.

Program 14.12 illustrates the use of this `JList` component of Swing.

Program 14.12

```
import javax.swing.*;
public class JListexample {
    JListexample() {
        JFrame f = new JFrame("JList demo");
        String items[] = {"python", "scala",
        "java", "Android"};
        final JList l1 = new JList(items);
        l1.setBounds(100, 100, 70, 70);
        f.add(l1);
        f.setSize(400, 400);
        f.setLayout(null);
        f.setVisible(true);
    }
    public static void main(String args[]) {
        new JListexample();
    }
}
```

Output 14.12

Program 14.12 demonstrates the `JList` component in Swing. Initially the programming language names are given as values to the String array. Then within the `JList` constructor, the array object is passed as argument. Finally, by adding the JList object into the Frame window and executed, the program will display the data as shown in the output window in a list view.

14.4.3 `JScrollPane` Class

A `JScrollPane` provides a scrollable view of a component. When screen real estate is limited, a scroll pane can be used to display a component that is large or one whose size can change dynamically. Other containers used to save screen space include split panes and tabbed panes.

The code to create a scroll pane can be minimal. The example is illustrated in the following `JTable` component. The other example using `JTextArea` Scrollbar is created using `JScrollPane` is given in **Program 14.13.**

Program 14.13

```
import java.awt.BorderLayout;
import java.awt.Dimension;
import javax.swing.JFrame;
import javax.swing.JScrollPane;
import javax.swing.JTextArea;
public class Jscrolldemotextarea
{
    public static void main(String[]
    args)
    {
        new Jscrolldemotextarea();
    }
    public Jscrolldemotextarea()
    {
        JTextArea textArea = new JTextArea();
        textArea.setText("Hi \n this \n is \n
        an\n example\n of \n Jscrollpane\n \n in
        JTextArea\n");
        JScrollPane scrollPane = new
        JScrollPane(textArea);
        JFrame frame = new JFrame("JScrollPane Test");
        frame.getContentPane().add(scrollPane, BorderLayout.CENTER);
        frame.setDefaultCloseOperation(JFrame.EXIT_ON_CLOSE);
        frame.setSize(new Dimension(240, 180));
        frame.setVisible(true);
    }
}
```

Output 14.13

JScrollPane Test

Hi
this
is
an
example
of
Jscrollpane

in JTextArea

Program 14.13 illustrates the `JScrollPane` class. This is similar to the scrollbar of AWT control. `JScrollPane` will dynamically resize the window based on the component placed in the Frame. Here `JTextArea` is created and values are given. Based on the content in the text area, the vertical scrollpane is resized by passing the `JTextArea` object to the `JScrollPane` constructor. Executing the program will display the output as shown.

14.4.4 `JTable`

The `JTable` class is used to display data in tabular form. It is composed of rows and columns. `JTable` is a component that displays rows and columns of data. The column boundaries can be dragged to resize columns, is depending on its configuration. It is possible to select a row, column, or cell within the table, and to change the data within a cell. `JTable` has many classes and interfaces associated with it. These are packaged in `javax.swing.table`. The `JTable` common constructor is as shown below.

```
JTable(Object data[ ][ ], Object colHeads[ ])
```

Program 14.14 demonstrates the use of a `JTable` with Employee details.

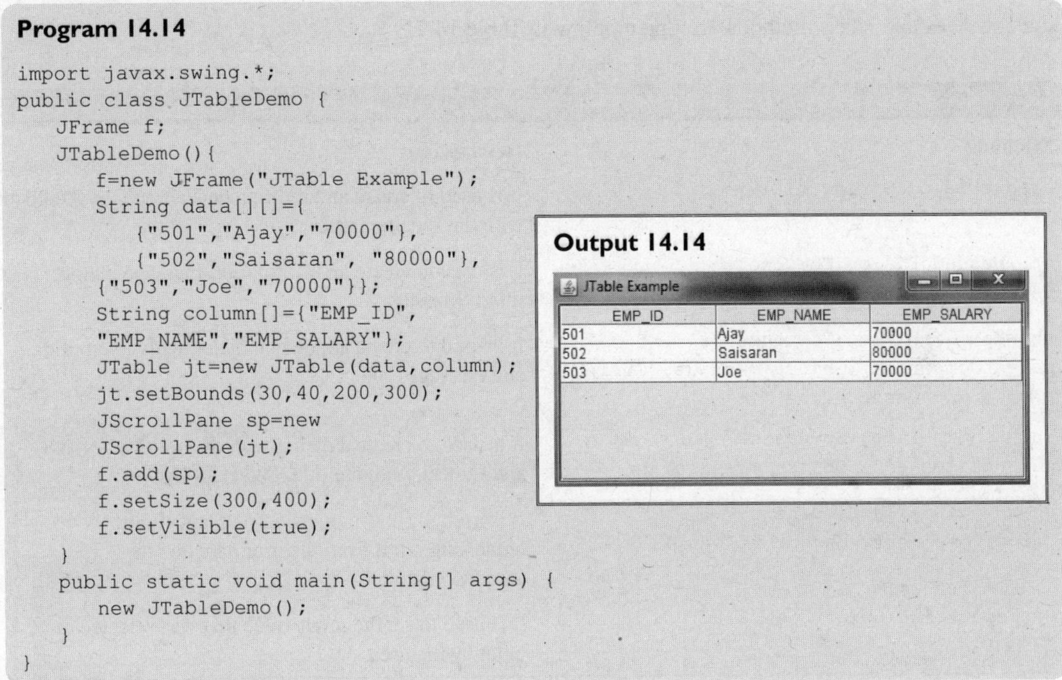

Program 14.14

```
import javax.swing.*;
public class JTableDemo {
    JFrame f;
    JTableDemo(){
        f=new JFrame("JTable Example");
        String data[][]={
            {"501","Ajay","70000"},
            {"502","Saisaran", "80000"},
        {"503","Joe","70000"}};
        String column[]={"EMP_ID",
        "EMP_NAME","EMP_SALARY"};
        JTable jt=new JTable(data,column);
        jt.setBounds(30,40,200,300);
        JScrollPane sp=new
        JScrollPane(jt);
        f.add(sp);
        f.setSize(300,400);
        f.setVisible(true);
    }
    public static void main(String[] args) {
        new JTableDemo();
    }
}
```

Output 14.14

Program 14.14 demonstrates the concept of a `JTable`. Usually the table contains rows and columns. In this program, the employee details are given in a table using the `JTable` component. To do this, `String array data[][]` is declared and the values initialised. This data array contains three rows and three columns of employee details. To define the header row for this array data, another one dimensional `String array column[]` is declared and initialised with with `EMP_ID`, `EMP_NAME` and `EMP_SALARY`. An object is created for `JTable jt` which has two parameters—row as `column[] array` and column as `data[] []`. These two arrays are passed into `JTable` class initialisation. Then the `JTable` object is included in the `JScrollPane` class. `JScrollpane` is similar to the `Scrollbar` of the AWT class, with the help of which dynamic resizing of the component can be done. The output is displayed.

14.4.5 JOptionPane

This `JOptionPane` class is used to supply standard dialog boxes in various forms such as message dialog box, confirm dialog box and input dialog box. These are used to show information or obtain input from the user, and so on. The `JOptionPane` class inherits the `JComponent` class. The `JOptionPane` class declaration is given below.

```
public class JOptionPane extends JComponent implements Accessible
```

Constructors in `JOptionPane` class

`JOptionPane()`: It is used to create a text message.

`JOptionPane(Object message)`: It is used to create an instance to display a message.

`JOptionPane(Object message, int messageType)`: It is used to create an instance to display a message with specified message type and default options.

The `JOptionPane` class methods are given below in Table 14.7.

Table 14.7 Methods in `JoptionPane` class

Methods	Description
`createDialog(String title)`	It is used to create and return a new parentless JDialog with the specified title.
`showMessageDialog(Component parentComponent, Object message)`	It is used to create an information-message dialog titled 'Message'.
`showMessageDialog(Component parentComponent, Object message, String title, int messageType)`	It is used to create a message dialog with given title and messageType.
`showConfirmDialog(Component parentComponent, Object message)`	It is used to create a dialog with the options Yes, No and Cancel; with the title, Select an Option.
`showInputDialog(Component parentComponent, Object message)`	It is used to show a question-message dialog requesting input from the user parented to parentComponent.
`setInputValue(Object newValue)`	It is used to set the input value that was selected or input by the user.

Program 14.15 illustrates how to display an alert message using `JOptionPane` class.

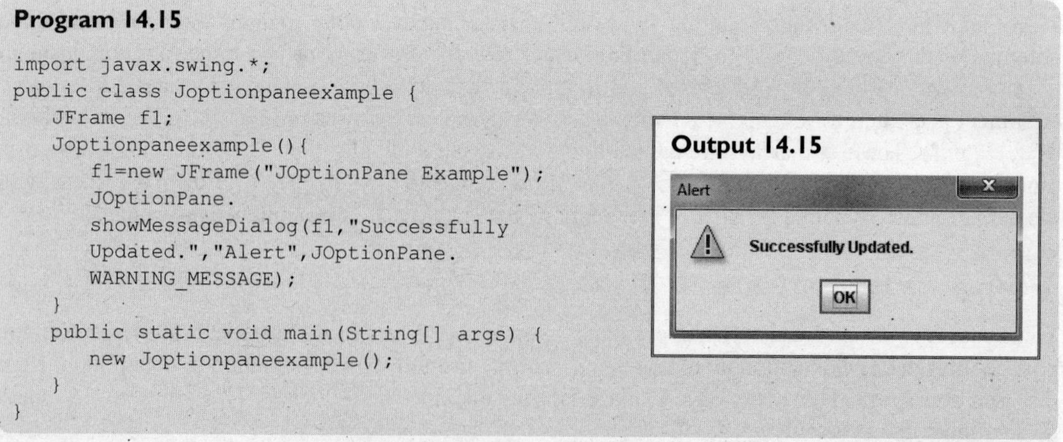

Program 14.15

```
import javax.swing.*;
public class Joptionpaneexample {
    JFrame f1;
    Joptionpaneexample(){
        f1=new JFrame("JOptionPane Example");
        JOptionPane.
        showMessageDialog(f1,"Successfully
        Updated.","Alert",JOptionPane.
        WARNING_MESSAGE);
    }
    public static void main(String[] args) {
        new Joptionpaneexample();
    }
}
```

Output 14.15

The `JOptionPane` component class control is used to display messages like alerts, confirmations and for getting input from the user. Unlike in other controls, it is not necessary to create an object for this class. The method `showMessageDialog` is invoked by passing four parameters to this method. The first parameter is `f1` which is the frame object, the second is the message to be displayed, the third parameter is the type of symbol or icon to be displayed along with the message; here an alert is specified. The fourth is the type of message such as `WARNING_MESSAGE`. The program output is shown.

14.4.6 JTree

The `JTree` class is used to display the tree structured data or hierarchical data. `JTree` is a multifaceted component. Similar to Tree in Data Structure, it has a 'root node' at the top which is a parent for all nodes in the tree. It inherits the `JComponent` class. The declaration for `javax.swing.JTree` class:

```
public class JTree extends JComponent implements Scrollable, Accessible
```

The constructors in the `JTree` class are listed below.

`JTree()`: Creates a `JTree` with a sample model.
`JTree(Object[] value)`: Creates a `JTree` with every element of the specified array as the child of a new root node.
`JTree(TreeNode root)`: Creates a `JTree` with the specified TreeNode as its root, which displays the root node.

Program 14.16 illustrates the `JTree` component class.

Program 14.16

```
import javax.swing.*;
import javax.swing.tree.DefaultMutableTreeNode;
public class JTreedemo {
   JFrame f;
   JTreedemo(){
      f=new JFrame("JTree Project");
      DefaultMutableTreeNode j=new
      DefaultMutableTreeNode("Java");
      DefaultMutableTreeNode awt=new
      DefaultMutableTreeNode("AWT Components");
      DefaultMutableTreeNode swin=new
      DefaultMutableTreeNode("SWING Components");
      j.add(awt);
      j.add(swin);
      DefaultMutableTreeNode b=new
      DefaultMutableTreeNode("Button");
      DefaultMutableTreeNode l=new
      DefaultMutableTreeNode("Label");
      DefaultMutableTreeNode c=new
      DefaultMutableTreeNode("Checkbox");
      DefaultMutableTreeNode ch=new
      DefaultMutableTreeNode("Chioce");
      DefaultMutableTreeNode jta=new DefaultMutableTreeNode("JTable");
      DefaultMutableTreeNode jo=new DefaultMutableTreeNode("JOptionPane");
      DefaultMutableTreeNode jpa=new DefaultMutableTreeNode("JPasswordField");
      DefaultMutableTreeNode jpr=new DefaultMutableTreeNode("JProgressBar");
```

Output 14.16

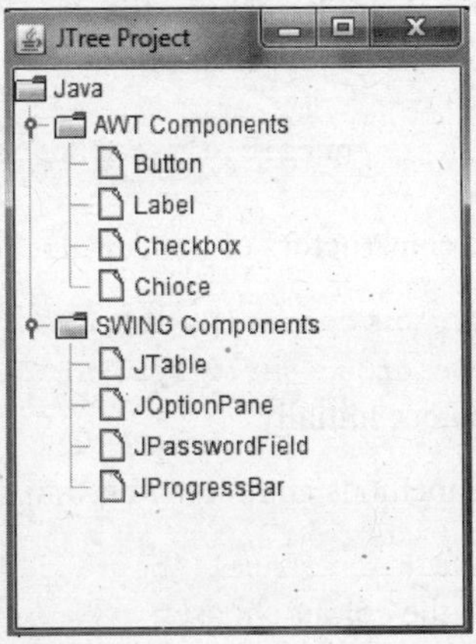

JTree Project
Java
AWT Components
Button
Label
Checkbox
Chioce
SWING Components
JTable
JOptionPane
JPasswordField
JProgressBar

```
        awt.add(b);
        awt.add(l);
        awt.add(c);
        awt.add(ch);
        swin.add(jta);
        swin.add(jo);
        swin.add(jpa);
        swin.add(jpr);
        JTree jt=new JTree(j);
        f.add(jt);
        f.setSize(200,200);
        f.setVisible(true);
    }
    public static void main(String[] args) {
        new JTreedemo();
    }
}
```

Program 14.16 illustrates how the `JTree` component of the `Swing` package acts as a directory or folder. A directory may contain subdirectories or subfolders. Swing's tree component subclass called `DefaultMutableTreeNode` class is used to create the directory structure. The first object `j` is created for this class and is considered as the main folder. The next two objects are created as `awt` and `swin`. These two objects are added under the first folder `Java`. Likewise, many subfolders can be added by using the same `DefaultMutableTreeNode` class. Then `JTree` object is created by including the main directory object `j`. The output displays the tree structure.

14.4.7 JColorChooser

The `JColorChooser` class is provided to create a colour chooser dialog box so that the user can select any colour. It inherits the `JComponent` class. `JColorChooser` class declaration for `javax.swing.JColorChooser` class is,

```
public class JColorChooser extends JComponent implements Accessible
```

The constructors of `JColorChooser` component class are:

- `JColorChooser()`: It is used to create a colour chooser panel with white colour initially.
- `JColorChooser(color initialcolor)`: It is used to create a colour chooser panel with the specified colour initially.

The methods commonly used in `JColorChooser` class are:

- `addChooserPanel(AbstractColorChooserPanel panel)`: It is used to add a colour chooser panel to the colour chooser.
- `showDialog(Component c, String title, Color initialColor)`: It is used to show the colour chooser dialog box.

Program 14.17 illustrates `JColorChooser` component class.

Program 14.17

```
import java.awt.event.*;
import java.awt.*;
import javax.swing.*;
public class colorchooserdemo
extends JFrame implements
ActionListener {
    JButton b;
    Container c;
    colorchooserdemo(){
        c=getContentPane();
        c.setLayout(new
        FlowLayout());
        b=new JButton("click to add
        colorchooser");
        b.addActionListener(this);
        c.add(b);
    }
    public void
    actionPerformed(ActionEvent e)
    {
        Color initialcolor=Color.
        RED;
        Color color=JColorChooser.
        showDialog(this,"Select a
        color",initialcolor);
        c.setBackground(color);

    }
    public static void
    main(String[] args) {
        colorchooserdemo ch=new
        colorchooserdemo();
        ch.setSize(400,400);
        ch.setVisible(true);
        ch.setDefaultCloseOperation
        (EXIT_ON_CLOSE);
    }
}
```

Output 14.17

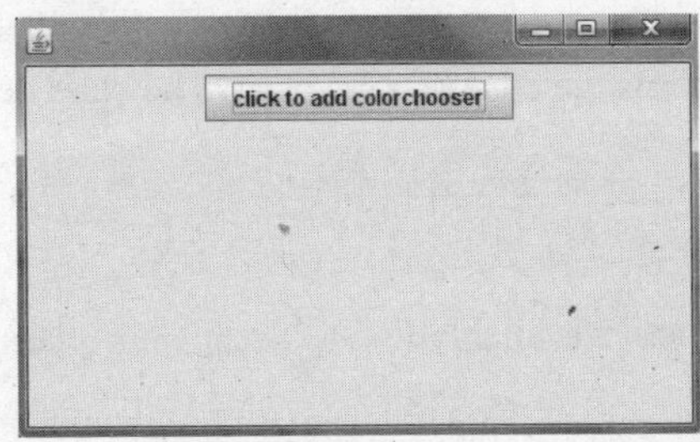


```
By clicking the button another dialog window
will be opened which is like
```

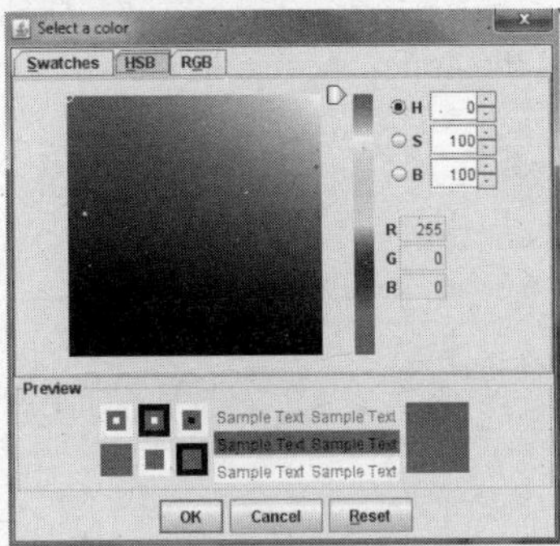


```
Selecting any color from the above window, and
clicking the OK button will set the background
color for the first window as shown below.
```

A Color class object is created and the method `showDialog` is invoked using `JColorChooser` class. The button is created to get the JColorChooser dialog box. This dialog box is already defined by the `JColorChooser` class and the colours are available for selection. On the click of a button, the `ColorChooser` window opens, as shown in the output. The initial colour red is already set and passed to the `showDialog` method. Selecting a colour from the dialog box and then clicking the `OK` button, sets the selected colour as the background colour of the first window.

14.4.8 JFileChooser

The object of the `JFileChooser` class is used to have a dialog window from which the user can select a file. It inherits the `JComponent` class. The class declaration for `javax.swing.JFileChooser` class is,

```
public class JFileChooser extends JComponent implements
Accessible
```

The Constructors available for `JFileChooser` class are:

- `JFileChooser()`: Constructs a `JFileChooser` pointing to the default directory.
- `JFileChooser(File currentDirectory)`: Constructs a `JFileChooser` using the given file as the path.
- `JFileChooser(String currentDirectoryPath)`: Constructs a `JFileChooser` using the given path.

Program 14.18 illustrates the use of the `JFileChooser` class to open a particular file.

Program 14.18

```
import javax.swing.*;
import java.awt.event.*;
import java.io.*;
public class Jfilechooserdemo extends
JFrame implements ActionListener{
  JMenuBar mb;
  JMenu file;
  JMenuItem open;
  JTextArea ta;
  Jfilechooserdemo(){
    open=new JMenuItem("Choose
    the file to open");
    open.addActionListener(this);
    file=new JMenu("File");
    file.add(open);
    mb=new JMenuBar();
    mb.setBounds(0,0,600,30);
    mb.add(file);
    ta=new JTextArea(600,600);
    ta.setBounds(0,30,600,600);
    add(mb);
    add(ta);
  }
  public void
  actionPerformed(ActionEvent e) {
    if(e.getSource()==open){
      JFileChooser fc=new
      JFileChooser();
      int i=fc.
      showOpenDialog(this);
      if(i==JFileChooser.
      APPROVE_OPTION){
        File f=fc.
        getSelectedFile();
        String filepath=f.
        getPath();
```

Output 14.18

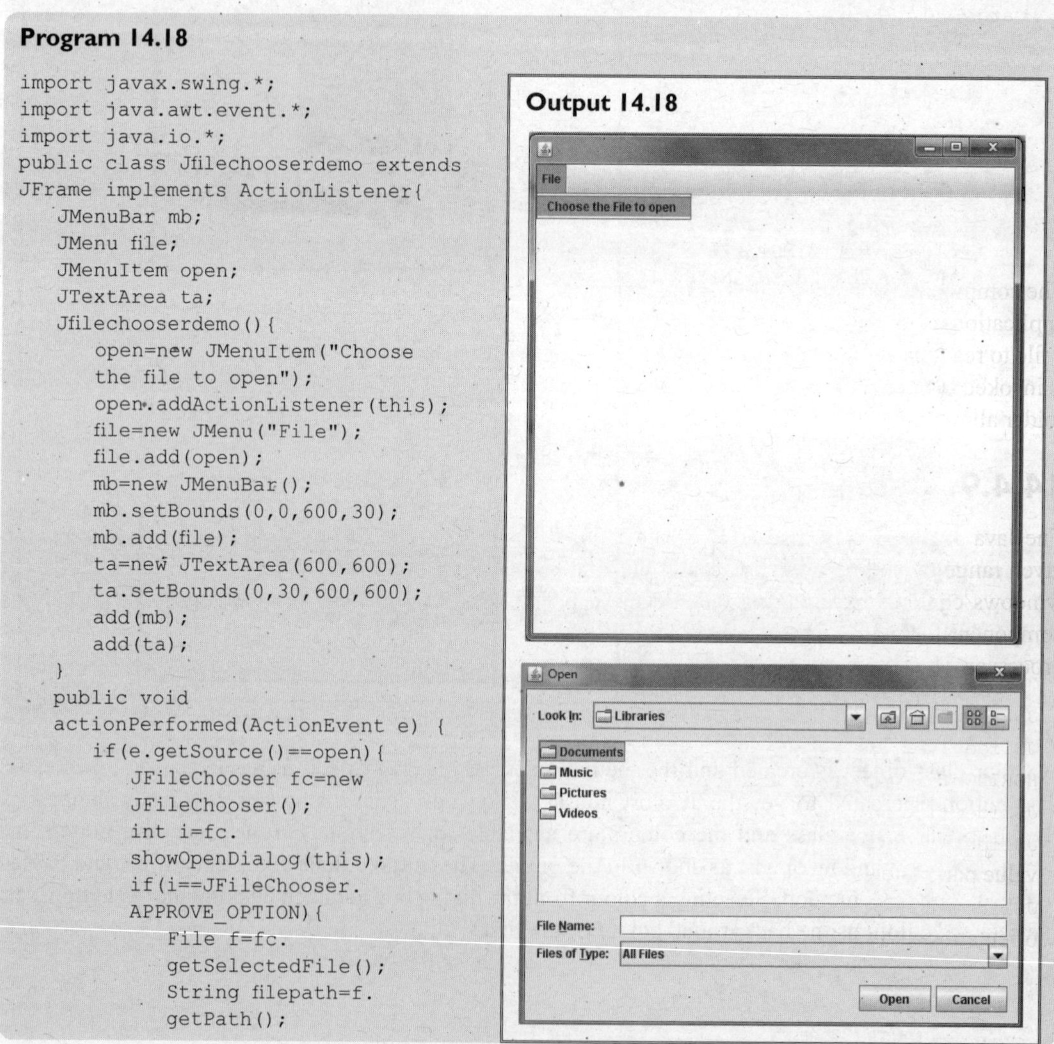

```
        try{
            BufferedReader br=new BufferedReader(new
            FileReader(filepath));
            String s1="",s2="";
            while((s1=br.
            readLine())!=null){
                s2+=s1+"\n";
            }
            ta.setText(s2);
            br.close();
            }catch (Exception ex)
             {ex.printStackTrace();
            }
        }
    }
}
public static void main(String[]
args) {
    Jfilechooserdemo om=new
    Jfilechooserdemo();
    om.setSize(500,500);
    om.setLayout(null);
    om.setVisible(true);
    om.setDefaultCloseOperation(EXIT_ON_CLOSE);
}
}
```

Output 14.18

```
File
package org.me.calculator;

import javax.jws.WebMethod;
import javax.jws.WebParam;
import javax.jws.WebService;

/**
 *
 * @author User
 */
@WebService()
public class CalculatorWS {

    /**
     * Web service operation
     */
    @WebMethod(operationName = "add")
    public int add(@WebParam(name = "i") int i, @WebParam(name = "j") int j) {
        return i + j;
    }

}
```

The common file operations are *Open*, *Save* and *Close*. These operations can be performed on the Swing application using the `JFileChooser` class. A menu is created for the file operation. This program opens a file to read the selected file. `JFilechooser` class object is created and the `showOpenDialog()` method is invoked to open a file. The output shows the open file dialog window. Selecting a file from any specific folder allows the contents to be viewed and edited inside the `JTextArea` component.

14.4.9 JSlider

The Java `JSlider` class is used to create a slider. Using the `JSlider`, a user can select a value from a given range by sliding a knob. Usually the application of the slider is to zoom-in and zoom-out of the windows contents by dragging the slider point. For instance, the word processor contains this slider component for margin adjustment and also to zoom-in and zoom-out of the content area of the word processor. The commonly used Constructors of the `JSlider` class are:

- `JSlider()`: It is used to create a slider with the initial value of 50 and a range of 0 to 100.
- `JSlider(int orientation)`: creating a slider with the given orientation by either `JSlider.HORIZONTAL` or `JSlider.VERTICAL` with the range 0 to 100 and an initial value 50.
- `JSlider(int min, int max)`: creating a horizontal slider using the given min and max values.
- `JSlider(int min, int max, int value)`: creating a horizontal slider using the given min, max and value parameters.
- `JSlider(int orientation, int min, int max, int value)`: creating a slider using the given orientation, min, max and value parameters.

The orientation of the `JSlider` is used in two ways to represent the component. The orientation has the pre-defined properties such as:

```
JSlider.HORIZONTAL JSlider.VERTICAL
```

Some of the `JSlider` class methods are listed below.

- `public void setMinorTickSpacing(int n)`: this is used to set the minor tick spacing to the slider.
- `public void setMajorTickSpacing(int n)`: this is used to set the major tick spacing to the slider.
- `public void setPaintTicks(boolean b)`: this is used to decide whether tick marks are painted.
- `public void setPaintLabels(boolean b)`: this is used to decide whether labels are painted.
- `public void setPaintTracks(boolean b)`: this is used to decide whether the track is painted.

Program 14.19 demonstrates the `JSlider` class.

Program 14.19

```
import javax.swing.*;
public class JSliderdemo extends JFrame{
    public JSliderdemo() {
        JSlider slider = new JSlider(JSlider.HORIZONTAL, 0, 50, 25);
        slider.setMinorTickSpacing(2);
        slider.setMajorTickSpacing(10);
        slider.setPaintTicks(true);
        slider.setPaintLabels(true);
        JPanel panel=new JPanel();
        panel.add(slider);
        add(panel);
    }
    public static void main(String s[]) {
        JSliderdemo frame=new JSliderdemo();
        frame.pack();
        frame.setVisible(true);
    }
}
```

Output 14.19

0 10 20 30 40 50

In Program 14.19, an object is first created for the `JSlider` class and the constructor intialised with orientation, minimum, maximum and its value. The orientation is given as horizontal and the slider points start from 0 to 50 that is given by the minimum and maximum value. Then the methods such as `setMinorTickSpacing()`, `setMajorTickSpacing()`, `setPaintTicks()` and `setPaintLabels()` are invoked by the `JSlider` object. Finally, the `JSlider` object is added to the Frame window and the program is executed to get the output.

14.4.10 `JProgressBar`

The `JProgressBar` class is used to display the progress of the task. It inherits the `JComponent` class. For instance, when one application is involved in some lengthy process, then the status of the process can be monitored by the progression of the process. An example of this kind of progress bar can be seen when Netbeans IDE is opened. To start with, IDE does not provide a working window directly; instead it displays a mini window while loading or preparing the GUI window. It takes some time to load the actual. The user sees a red line at the bottom, which grows as the task progresses. When the line reaches the other end, it signifies that the progression is complete and the IDE window has opened fully with working space and other components. A `JProgressBar` class declaration is as follows.

```
public class JProgressBar extends JComponent implements
SwingConstants, Accessible
```

Various Constructor forms of `JProgressBar` class are given below:

- `JProgressBar():` It is used to create a horizontal progress bar but no string text.
- `JProgressBar(int min, int max):` It is used to create a horizontal progress bar with the specified minimum and maximum values.
- `JProgressBar(int orient):` It is used to create a progress bar with the specified orientation, which can be either vertical or horizontal, by using `SwingConstants.VERTICAL` and `SwingConstants.HORIZONTAL` constants.
- `JProgressBar(int orient, int min, int max):` It is used to create a progress bar with the specified orientation, minimum and maximum values.

The methods in `JProgressBar` class are:

- `setStringPainted(boolean b):` It is used to determine whether the string should be displayed.
- `setString(String s):` It is used to set a value to the progress string.
- `setOrientation(int orientation):` It is used to set the orientation, which may be either vertical or horizontal, by using the constants `SwingConstants.VERTICAL` and `SwingConstants.HORIZONTAL`.
- `setValue(int value):` It is used to set the current value on the progress bar.

Program14.20 illustrates the use of `JProgressBar` class.

Program 14.20

```
import javax.swing.*;
public class Jprogressbardemo extends JFrame{
   JProgressBar jb;
   int i=0,num=0;
   Jprogressbardemo(){
      jb=new JProgressBar(0,2000);
      jb.setBounds(40,40,160,30);
      jb.setValue(0);
      jb.setStringPainted(true);
      add(jb);
      setSize(250,150);
      setLayout(null);
   }
   public void iterate(){
      while(i<=2000){
         jb.setValue(i);
         i=i+20;
         try{Thread.sleep(150);}catch(Exception e){}
      }
   }
   public static void main(String[] args) {
      Jprogressbardemo m1=new Jprogressbardemo();
      m1.setVisible(true);
      m1.iterate();
   }
}
```

Output 14.20

36%

In Program 14.20, an object is first created for the `JProgressBar` with minimum and maximum values in the object intialisation. Then the methods `setValue()` and `setStringPainted()` are invoked by the `JProgressBar` object. The `Thread` class method `sleep()` is invoked to provide time duration to complete the process progression. The program output is as shown.

14.4.11 JTabbedPane

The `JTabbedPane` class is used to switch between a group of components by clicking on a tab with a given title or icon. An example is a browser application having the option to open multiple new tabs in the same window. It inherits the `JComponent` class. The declaration for `javax.swing.JTabbedPane` class is,

```
public class JTabbedPane extends JComponent implements
Serializable, Accessible, SwingConstants
```

The constructors of the `JTabbedPane` are:

- `JTabbedPane()`: Creates an empty `JTabbedPane` with a default tab placement of `JTabbedPane` on top of the window.
- `JTabbedPane(int tabPlacement)`: Creates an empty `JTabbedPane` with a specified tab placement.
- `JTabbedPane(int tabPlacement, int tabLayoutPolicy)`: Creates an empty `JTabbedPane` with a specified tab placement and tab layout policy.

Program 14.21 demonstrates the use of `JTabbedPane` class for displaying three tabs related to course details.

Program 14.21

```
import javax.swing.*;
public class JTabdemo {
    JFrame f;
    JTabdemo(){
        f=new JFrame("JTabbedPane Demo");
        JTextArea ta=new JTextArea(200,200);
        JLabel l1=new JLabel("3 yrs UG Course");
        JLabel l2=new JLabel("2 yrs PG Course");
        JLabel l3=new JLabel("2 or 3 yrs PG
        Course");
        JPanel p1=new JPanel();
        p1.add(l1);
        p1.add(l2);
        p1.add(l3);
        JTabbedPane tp=new JTabbedPane();
        tp.setBounds(50,50,200,200);
        tp.add("B.Sc",l1);
        tp.add("M.Sc",l2);
        tp.add("MCA",l3);
        f.add(tp);
        f.setSize(400,400);
        f.setLayout(null);
        f.setVisible(true);
    }
    public static void main(String[] args) {
        new JTabdemo();
    }
}
```

Output 14.21

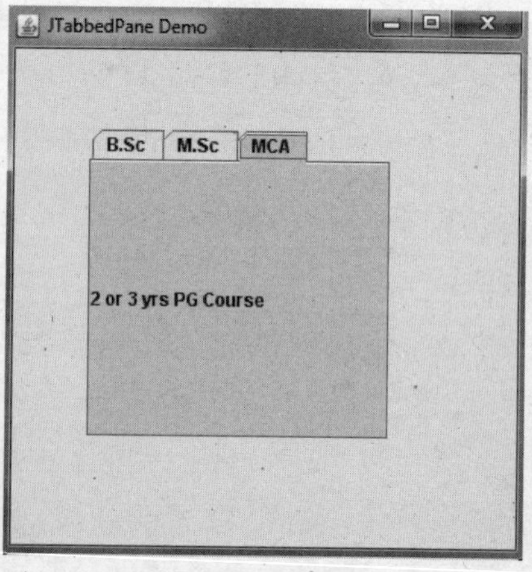

Program 14.21 demonstrates the use of the `JTabbedPane` class to display the list of courses in each tabbed window. To display the text according to the tab clicked by the user, `JTextArea` class is created and three label values are added into the `JPanel`. Then a `JTabbed` window is created which contains B.Sc, M.Sc and MCA as the three tabs. These tabs are added into the Frame window. The program output is as shown.

14.5 SIMPLE APPLICATIONS USING SWING AND AWT

In Chapter 13, various basic AWT controls and Swing components were explained with simple examples. Based on Swing and AWT controls, the user can create simple desktop applications using Swing and AWT controls. Let us first create the arithmetic calculator (similar to Program 13.18 in Chapter 13) using Swing components. To construct an arithmetic calculator, the user has to design the application using `JLabel`, `JTextField` and `JButton` controls of the Swing package and to perform the `ActionEvent` when the button is clicked. **Program 14.22** demonstrates the arithmetic calculator using Swing components.

Program 14.22

```
import java.awt.*;
import java.awt.event.*;
import javax.swing.*;
class Swingcalc implements ActionListener
{
    JFrame f;
    JButton b1,b2,b3,b4,b5;
    JTextField t1,t2,t3;
    JLabel l,l1;
    Swingcalc()
    {
        f=new JFrame("Listener");
        t1=new JTextField("");
        t2=new JTextField("");
        t3=new JTextField("");
        b1=new JButton("Add");
        b2=new JButton("Sub");
        b3=new JButton("Mul");
        b4=new JButton("Div");
        l=new JLabel();
        l1=new JLabel();
    }
    public void awt1()
    {
        f.setLayout(new GridLayout(3,2));
        f.setVisible(true);
        f.add(t1);
        f.add(t2);
        f.add(t3);
        f.add(b1);
        f.add(b2);
        f.add(b3);
```

```
        f.add(b4);
        f.add(l);
        f.add(l1);
        b1.addActionListener(this);
        b2.addActionListener(this);
        b3.addActionListener(this);
        b4.addActionListener(this);
        f.pack();
    }
    public void actionPerformed(ActionEvent e)
    {
        String s=new String(e.getActionCommand());
        l.setText(s);
        if((s).equals("Add"))
        {
            int a=Integer.parseInt(t1.getText());
            int b=Integer.parseInt(t2.getText());
            Integer c=a+b;
            t3.setText(c.toString());
        }
        else if((s).equals("Sub"))
        {
            int a=Integer.parseInt(t1.getText());
            int b=Integer.parseInt(t2.getText());
            Integer c=a-b;
            t3.setText(c.toString());
        }
        else if((s).equals("Mul"))
        {
            int a=Integer.parseInt(t1.getText());
            int b=Integer.parseInt(t2.getText());
            Integer c=a*b;
            t3.setText(c.toString());
        }
    }
    public static void main(String args[])
    {
        Swingcalc a=new Swingcalc();
        a.awt1();
    }
}
```

Output 14.22

Listener		
17	25	42
Add	Sub	Mul
Div	Add	

Program 14.22 illustrates performing an arithmetic calculation for any two given numbers. To design this application, one `JLabel`, three `JTextFields` and four `JButton` controls of Swing have been used. After creating the Swing components, all of them are added into the `JFrame` window using the `add()` method. Finally, the logic of the program such as addition, subtraction operations are performed using the `actionPerformed()` method as shown in the code.

The next application is to calculate the addition of two numbers using the `JOptionPane` class and its methods in Swing. **Program 14.23** illustrates this.

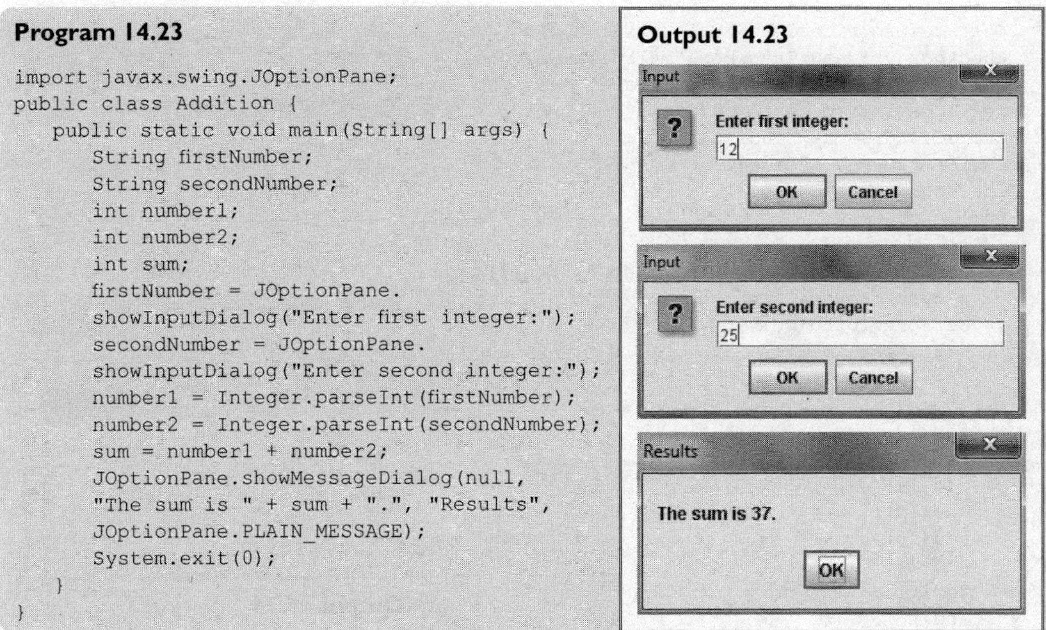

Program 14.23

```
import javax.swing.JOptionPane;
public class Addition {
    public static void main(String[] args) {
        String firstNumber;
        String secondNumber;
        int number1;
        int number2;
        int sum;
        firstNumber = JOptionPane.
        showInputDialog("Enter first integer:");
        secondNumber = JOptionPane.
        showInputDialog("Enter second integer:");
        number1 = Integer.parseInt(firstNumber);
        number2 = Integer.parseInt(secondNumber);
        sum = number1 + number2;
        JOptionPane.showMessageDialog(null,
        "The sum is " + sum + ".", "Results",
        JOptionPane.PLAIN_MESSAGE);
        System.exit(0);
    }
}
```

Output 14.23

Program 14.23 performs the addition of two given numbers using the `JOptionPane` class to display the prompt messages in any application. During the prompt, the user is able to give some input and perform some operation. The code contains the two `showInputDialog()` method of the `JOptionPane` class to receive the two numbers as input from the user during run time. Usually the inputs are in `String` type in Java and need to convert into `Integer` using the `Integer.parseInt()` method. Then addition is performed and the output is displayed using `showMessageDialog()` method of JOptionPane class.

Program 14.24 shows the design of a Student Registration form using various AWT Controls. Note that this application is performing an Event but the data is not stored anywhere in the database or any other storage medium. Only design of the application is demonstrated.

Program 14.24

```
import java.awt.*;
import java.applet.*;
import java.awt.event.*;
public class student1 extends Frame implements ActionListener
{
    String msg;
    Button b=new Button("submit");
    Label l11=new Label("Student Details",Label.CENTER);
    Label l1=new Label("Name",Label.LEFT);
    Label l2=new Label("age",Label.LEFT);
    Label l3=new Label("Gender(M/F)",Label.LEFT);
    Label l4=new Label("Address",Label.LEFT);
    Label l5=new Label("Course",Label.LEFT);
    Label l6=new Label("Semester",Label.LEFT);
    Label l7=new Label("",Label.RIGHT);
    TextField t1=new TextField();
    Choice c1=new Choice();
```

```
CheckboxGroup cbg1=new CheckboxGroup();
Checkbox ck1=new Checkbox("Male",false,cbg1);
Checkbox ck2=new Checkbox("Female",false,cbg1);
TextArea t2=new TextArea("",160,80,TextArea.SCROLLBARS_VERTICAL_ONLY);
Choice course=new Choice();
Choice sem=new Choice();
Choice age=new Choice();
public student1()
{
   addWindowListener(new myWindowAdapter());
   setBackground(Color.cyan);
   setForeground(Color.black);
   setLayout(null);
   add(l11);
   add(l1);
   add(l2);
   add(l3);
   add(l4);
   add(l5);
   add(l6);
   add(l7);
   add(t1);
   add(t2);
   add(ck1);
   add(ck2);
   add(course);
   add(sem);
   add(age);
   add(b);
   b.addActionListener(this);
   add(b);
   course.add("B.Sc c.s");
   course.add("B.Sc maths");
   course.add("B.Sc physics");
   course.add("B.A English");
   course.add("B.COM");
   sem.add("1-I");
   sem.add("2-II");
   sem.add("3-III");
   sem.add("4-IV");
   sem.add("5-V");
   sem.add("6-VI");
   age.add("17");
   age.add("19");
   age.add("18");
   age.add("21");
   age.add("20");
   l1.setBounds(25,65,80,20);
   l2.setBounds(25,90,80,20);
   l3.setBounds(25,120,80,20);
   l4.setBounds(25,185,80,20);
   l5.setBounds(25,260,80,20);
   l6.setBounds(25,290,80,20);
   l7.setBounds(25,260,80,20);
   l11.setBounds(10,40,270,20);
   t1.setBounds(120,65,160,20);
```

Output 14.24

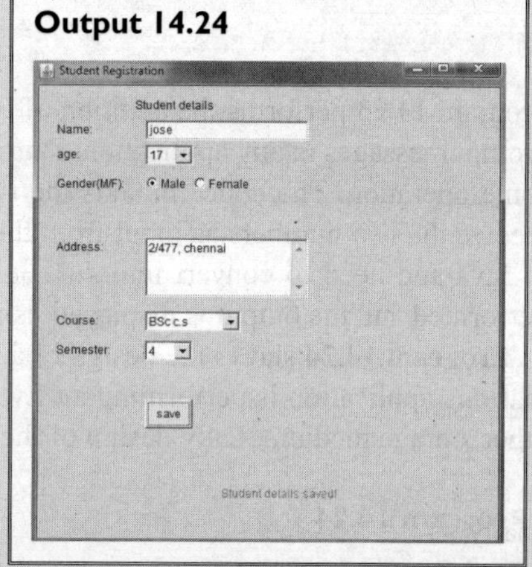

```
        t2.setBounds(120,185,160,60);
        ck1.setBounds(120,120,40,20);
        ck2.setBounds(170,120,50,20);
        course.setBounds(120,260,90,20);
        sem.setBounds(120,290,40,20);
        age.setBounds(120,90,40,20);
        b.setBounds(120,350,40,30);
    }
    public void paint(Graphics g)
    {g.drawString(msg,200,450);}
    public void actionPerformed(ActionEvent ae)
    {if(ae.getActionCommand().equals("save"))
        {
            msg="Student details saved!";
            setForeground(Color.red);
        }
    }
    public static void main(String g[])
    {student1 stu1=new student1();
        stu1.setSize(new Dimension(450,450));
        stu1.setTitle("Student Registration");
        stu1.setVisible(true);
    }
}
class myWindowAdapter extends WindowAdapter
{public void windowClosing(WindowEvent we)
    {
        System.exit(0);
    }
}
```

Program 14.24 uses different AWT controls to design the form for student registration application. The above code consists of `Label`, `TextField`, `Choice`, `Checkbox`, `TextArea` and `Button` controls of AWT. After creating objects for these controls, the position of each of the controls has been set using the `setBounds()` method. Then, the controls are added into the Frame window using the `add()` method. Finally, to perform an action when the button is clicked by the user, `actionPerformed()` method is created. The output is shown.

SUMMARY

1. This chapter discusses event handling of various components, such as, performing an `ActionEvent` for the `Button` component, `ItemEvent` for `Choice` and `List` components, and `AdjustmentEvent` on the `Scrollbar` component.
2. Other AWT components such as `Choice`, `List`, `TextArea`, `Scrollbar` and `Menu`, `MenuItem` controls are explained along with event handling classes and methods that are demonstrated with the necessary programs.
3. The `Graphics` class plays an important role in creating a window-based application. Some important graphics classes have been discussed, such as `Color`, `Image` and `Font` classes.
4. `Color` class provides various predefined methods such as `setBackgroundColor`, `setForeGround` and so on, to get and set the colours for all the components.
5. `Image` is a complex control that has three major steps to display the image on the

window. First the image is loaded from the system, then using the graphics `drawImage()` method, the image is drawn on the window and then displayed on the window using the `add()` method.

6. `Font` is an important class to display all the text details of components in different font faces, styles, sizes, and so on.
7. Various advanced Swing components have been discussed such as `JPasswordField`, `JOptionPane`, `JTable`, `JTree`, `JColorChooser`, `JFileChooser`, `JSlider` and `JTabbedPane`. These components are explained with relevant programs. With the help of these controls, complete window-based applications can be developed by the programmer.

SHORT QUESTIONS

1. What is event handling?
2. List out the event handling classes.
3. Describe `Choice` control.
4. Define `Scrollbar` control with an example.
5. How can one obtain RGB colours?
6. What are the two methods to convert between RGB and HSB?
7. Describe the `Color` class with its constructors.
8. What are the interfaces used in the `Image` class?
9. What are the file formats available in AWT?
10. List the generic font names.

COMPREHENSIVE QUESTIONS

1. Elaborate on the other AWT classes with examples.
2. Explain `Scrollbar` control briefly with an example.
3. Explain `Menu` and `MenuItem` controls in detail.
4. Explain AWT `Color` control class with an example.
5. Explain `Image` class operations with an example.
6. Explain AWT `Font` class with an example.
7. Elaborate on the `JTable` class with an example.
8. Explain the `JProgressBar` constructors and their methods in detail.
9. Explain `JColorChooser` class and `JFileChooser` class.
10. Illustrate `JTable` and `JTabbedPane` with examples.

SOLVED PROGRAMS

1. Display the color names in Tree view using `DefaultMutableTreeNode` class.

```
import javax.swing.*;
import javax.swing.tree.*;
public class TreeComponent{
  public static void main(String[] args) {
      JFrame frame = new JFrame("Creating a JTree Component!");
      DefaultMutableTreeNode parent = new DefaultMutableTreeNode("Color", true);
      DefaultMutableTreeNode black = new DefaultMutableTreeNode("Black");
      DefaultMutableTreeNode blue = new DefaultMutableTreeNode("Blue");
      DefaultMutableTreeNode nBlue = new DefaultMutableTreeNode("Navy Blue");
      DefaultMutableTreeNode dBlue = new DefaultMutableTreeNode("Dark Blue");
```

```
        DefaultMutableTreeNode green =
        new DefaultMutableTreeNode("Green");
        DefaultMutableTreeNode white = new
        DefaultMutableTreeNode("White");
        parent.add(black);
        parent.add(blue);
        blue.add(nBlue);
        blue.add(dBlue);
        parent.add(green );
        parent.add(white);
        JTree tree = new JTree(parent);
        frame.add(tree);
        frame.setSize(200,200);
        frame.setVisible(true);
    } }
```

Output

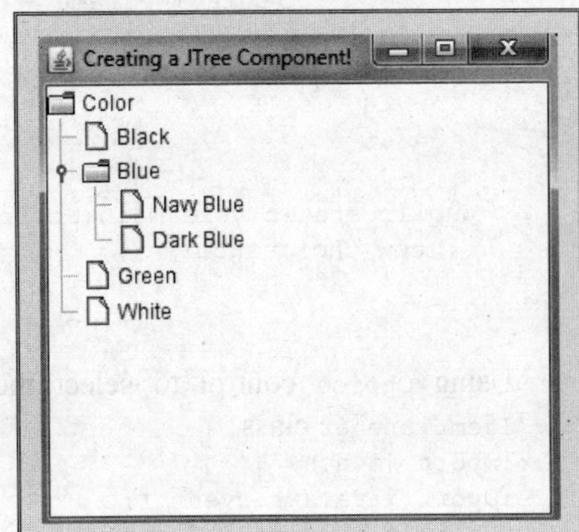

2. To display the gender and sports of interest as selected using the List component.

```
import java.awt.Button;
import java.awt.Choice;
import java.awt.Frame;
import java.awt.Label;
import java.awt.List;
import java.awt.event.ActionEvent;
import java.awt.event.ActionListener;
import java.awt.event.ItemEvent;
import java.awt.event.ItemListener;
public class ChoiceandList {
  ChoiceandList(){
       Frame f1= new Frame("List your
       skills");
       final Label label = new Label();
       label.setAlignment(Label.LEFT);
       label.setSize(500,100);
       Button b=new Button("Select");
       b.setBounds(200,150,80,30);
       final List l1=new List(4, false);
       l1.setBounds(100,100, 70,70);
       l1.add("Male");
       l1.add("Female");
       final List l2=new List(4, true);
       l2.setBounds(100,200, 70,70);
       l2.add("Cricket");
       l2.add("Shuttle");
       l2.add("Tennis");
       l2.add("Football");
       f1.add(l1); f1.add(l2); f1.add(label); f1.add(b);
       f1.setSize(450,450);
       f1.setLayout(null);
       f1.setVisible(true);
       b.addActionListener(new ActionListener() {
          public void actionPerformed(ActionEvent e) {
              String data = "\tGender: "+l1.getItem(l1.getSelectedIndex());
              data += ", Hobbies:";
```

Output

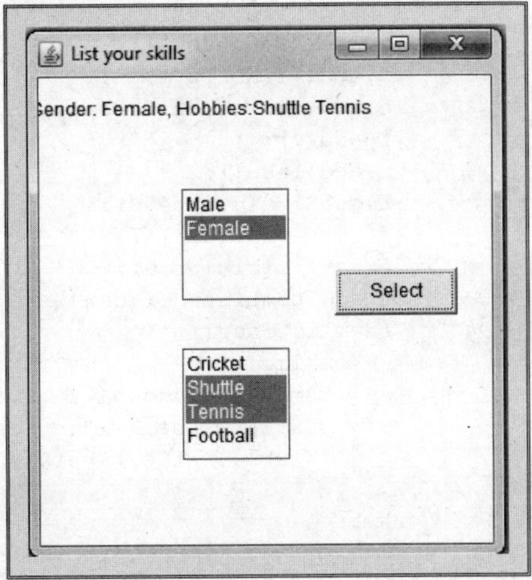

```
            for(String frame:l2.getSelectedItems()){
               data += frame + " ";
            }
            label.setText(data);
         }
      } );
   }
   public static void main(String[] args) {
      new ChoiceandList();
   }
}
```

3. Using `Choice` control to select the role model and display the selected role model using `ItemListener` class.

```
import java.awt.*;
import java.awt.event.*;
public class choiceExample {
   choiceExample() {
      Frame f = new Frame("Choose favorite Role Models");
      final Label label = new Label();
      label.setAlignment(Label.
      CENTER);
      label.setSize(400, 100);
      final Choice c = new Choice();
      c.setBounds(100, 100, 75, 75);
      c.add("1:A.P.J");
      c.add("2:Gandhi");
      c.add("3:Nehru");
      c.add(«4:Mother Tresa»);
      f.add(c);
      f.add(label);
      f.setSize(400, 400);
      f.setLayout(null);
      f.setVisible(true);
      c.addItemListener(new
      ItemListener() {
         public void
         itemStateChanged(ItemEvent e) {
            String data = "You Selected: " + c.getItem(c.getSelectedIndex());
            label.setText(data);
         }
      } );
   }
   public static void main(String args[]) {
      new choiceExample();
   }
}
```

Output

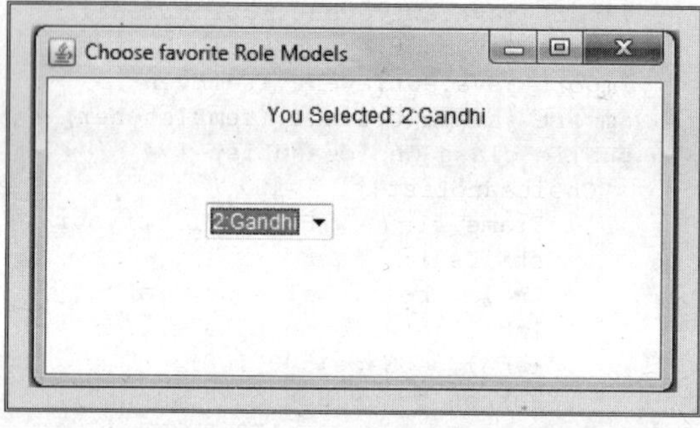

4. Using `JTabbedPane`, display the degree with its description.

```
import javax.swing.*;
public class JTabdemo {
   JFrame f;
   JTabdemo(){
      f=new JFrame("JTabbedPane Demo");
      JTextArea ta=new JTextArea(200,200);
```

```
        JLabel l1=new JLabel("You Choose UG");
        JLabel l2=new JLabel("You Choose
        PG");
        JLabel l3=new JLabel("You Choose
    M.Phil");
        JPanel p1=new JPanel();
        p1.add(l1);
        p1.add(l2);
        p1.add(l3);
        JTabbedPane tp=new
        JTabbedPane();
        tp.setBounds(50,50,200,200);
        tp.add("UG",l1);
        tp.add("PG",l2);
        tp.add("M.Phil",l3);
        f.add(tp);
        f.setSize(400,400);
        f.setLayout(null);
        f.setVisible(true);
    }
    public static void main(String[]
    args) {
        new JTabdemo();
    }
}
```

Output

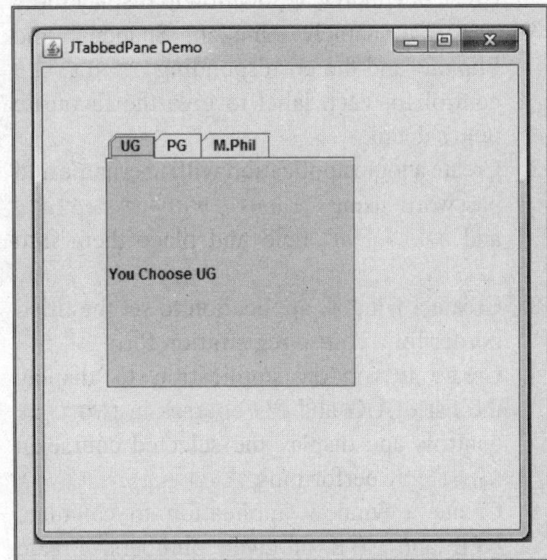

5. Displaying Student details using `JTable` class.

```
package newprogramsawt;
import javax.swing.*;
public class JTableDemo {
    JFrame f;
    JTableDemo(){
        f=new JFrame("JTable Example");
            String data[][]={ { "501","Ajay","01/05/1999","111-222-333"} ,
            { "502","Saisaran","01/01/1999","332-897-546"} ,
        { "503","Joe","02/08/1998","000-233-432"} } ;
        String column[]={ "STU_ID","STU_NAME","STU_DOB","STU_PHONE"} ;
        JTable jt=new JTable(data,column);
        jt.setBounds(30,40,200,300);
        JScrollPane sp=new JScrollPane(jt);
        f.add(sp);
        f.setSize(300,400);
        f.setVisible(true);
    }
    public static void main(String[] args) {
        new JTableDemo();
    }
}
```

Output

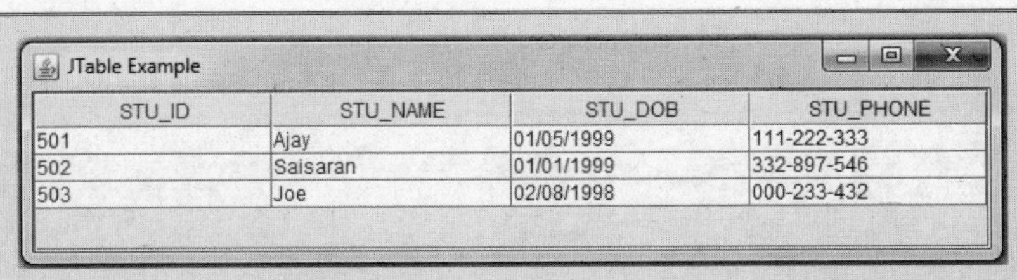

STU_ID	STU_NAME	STU_DOB	STU_PHONE
501	Ajay	01/05/1999	111-222-333
502	Saisaran	01/01/1999	332-897-546
503	Joe	02/08/1998	000-233-432

PROGRAMMING EXERCISES

1. Create a window application to display three `Jlabels` namely Amazon, Snapdeal and Flipkart and the corresponding `JTextField` control for each label to give the favourite item's detail.
2. Create a login application with username and password using `Jlabel` with `JTextField` and `JPassword` field and place them into `JPanel`.
3. Create a window application to set the titled border for a course registration form.
4. Create a window application to display the list of UG and PG courses in two `List` controls and display the selected course in `Labels` by performing `ItemEvent`.
5. Create a window application to calculate NPR and NCR of given numbers. Create two textfields to give `n` value and `r` value as inputs. To perform the calculations, create two buttons named Permutation and Combination. Create another textfield to display the results.
6. Create a window application to calculate employee salary using Swing class controls. Create three labels namely Name, Department and Salary. Create the corresponding textfields, then create a button to perform the calculation and then display the calculated salary in another textfield.
7. Create a tree view for the theory subjects as one folder and programming subjects as another folder and place the subject details under these folders using `JTree` component class.
8. Create a window application to display the student marks details using `JTable` class.

CHAPTER

15

Java Database Connectivity

Most of the Java-based applications today need access to databases. Java DataBase Connectivity (JDBC) provides interfaces and classes for creating database-independent connectivity between Java applications and a wide range of databases such as Oracle, MySQL, Sybase, PostgreSQL and DB2. It is database-independent since JDBC has not been developed for connecting with only a particular type of DB. JDBC, developed by JavaSoft, a subsidiary of Sun Microsystems, is an API specially designed for Java-based applications to connect and interact with different databases. JDBC provides a complete set of APIs that can be used by different types of Java-based application such as,

- desktop applications,
- web and enterprise applications,
- mobile applications, and
- micro applications.

All the above types of Java-based applications are able to use a JDBC driver to access a database, and take advantage of the stored data. The JDBC library is included in the `java.sql package`. Java applications developed with JDBC are platform- and vendor-independent. With JDBC, the Java-based application developer uses the JDBC API and never uses any proprietary API of a vendor-specific database. Almost all types of RDBMS support SQL; JDBC helps the Java developer to send SQL queries to all relational databases.

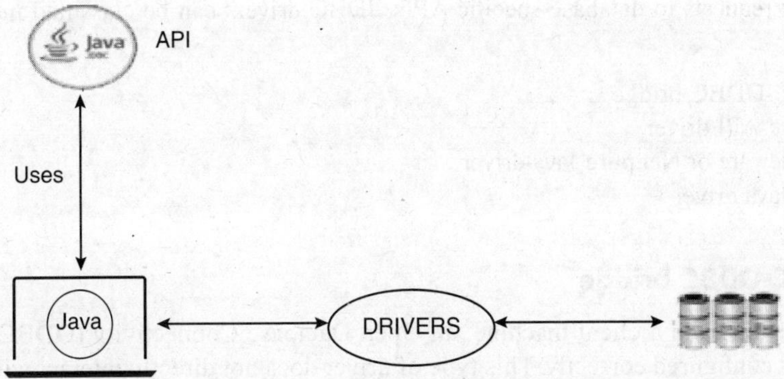

Fig. 15.1 Java app with DB connectivity through JDBC

Figure 15.1 depicts how the Java application uses the JDBC API for developing database enabled Java applications by implementing the `java.sql` package. Through the driver of a particular database, the Java application can connect and interact with databases such as MySQL and ORACLE. The driver manager holds the driver for each such type of database. If the Java application connects with ORACLE, the driver manager finds and connects an ORACLE driver with the application. A driver manager does the job of locating a particular driver for database connectivity on behalf of an application. Without a driver manager, the application will face the extra burden of locating the database. The driver manager and driver of a particular database fill the gaps between the database and the Java application. The JDBC driver manager ensures that the correct driver is used to access each data source.

Table 15.1 JDBC vs ODBC

JDBC API	ODBC API
Developed by Sun	Developed by Microsoft
JDBC API is developed in Java	ODBC API is developed in C
Language dependent	Language independent
Platform independent	Platform dependent—specifically for Windows

In the next section, various types of drivers that are responsible for database connectivity are explained.

15.1 TYPES OF DRIVERS

Almost all types of databases can be accessed by the Java-based applications. To access a particular type of database, the developer should know the classes and interfaces of the database. Different databases come with different sets of classes and interfaces, which are difficult for developers to remember. The JDBC API hides these issues in its architecture, so that the developer can concentrate on only developing the application which can access any database, with few modifications. The class/interface which provides a means to access a particular DB is called a JDBC driver. Each database has its own driver. These drivers are provided freely by the database vendors. The Driver Manager contains a driver for each type of database such as ORACLE and MySQL, and is used to obtain a connection with a particular database. The JVM uses the JDBC drivers provided by each database vendor to translate database access requests to database-specific APIs. JDBC drivers can be classified into four types as given below.

- *Type 1:* JDBC-ODBC bridge
- *Type 2:* Native-API driver
- *Type 3:*Middleware or Net pure Java driver
- *Type 4:*Pure Java driver

Type 1: JDBC-ODBC bridge

To use a Type 1 driver in a client machine, an Open Database Connectivity (ODBC) driver should be installed and configured correctly. This type of driver does not directly interact with the database.

To interact with the database, it needs a JDBC-ODBC bridge driver. It translates JDBC method calls into ODBC method calls. Even though this connects with all type of databases, its performance degrades because of two reasons—the client which uses a Type 1 driver should install an ODBC driver and all the JDBC method calls should be converted into ODBC method calls before they are processed.

Type 2: Native-API driver

Type 2 drivers are database vendor-specific native-APIs written partially in Java and partially in native code. The native-API of each database should be installed in the client system before accessing a particular database. So in this way, a native-API driver is a database-specific driver. These APIs are available from the database vendors. For instance, ORACLE will have the native-API for its database. If the client machine wants to access some other database, it should install a native-API of that database. This is slightly faster than the Type 1 driver, because it doesn't convert the JDBC method calls into ODBC method calls. Instead, it directly converts the JDBC method calls into database-specific calls. Type 2 drivers cannot be used for the web.

Type 3: Middleware or net pure Java driver

In a Type 3 driver, the JDBC driver on the client machine uses the socket to communicate with the middleware at the server. The middleware acts as a gateway for various other database servers. The client database access requests are sent through the network to the middleware or server and then the middleware converts the request to the database-specific API. The middleware or server may in turn make use of other types of drivers.

Type 4: Pure Java driver

The Type 4 driver is a purely Java-based driver. It directly communicates with the database-specific API through a socket. The API for that database is provided by the vendor. Type 4 is the best performing API compared with the other three APIs.

15.1.1 Choosing a Driver for the Application

Even though database access of an application seems to be the same, in reality it differs in many ways. For example, if an application accesses the database via a network, it cannot use any type of driver, because it has a specialised need to access a DB. Types of drivers discussed here are not applicable to all sorts of situations. The following points offer suggestions to the developer on choosing the right driver for database access.

- Prefer a Type 4 driver when the application is going to use only one type of database for the rest of its life such as MySQL, MS SQL, and so on.
- If the application needs to access multiple databases, Type 3 drivers are a better choice.
- When Type 3 and Type 4 drivers are not available, Type 2 drivers can be used.
- Type 1 driver is used for development and testing situations only and is not considered for deployment.

The next section elaborates on the architecture of the JDBC.

15.2 JDBC ARCHITECTURE

JDBC architecture is sometimes classified as two-tier and three-tier architecture for database access. In general, JDBC architecture consists of two layers:

- JDBC API: This provides the application-to-JDBC Manager connection.
- JDBC Driver API: This supports the JDBC Manager-to-Driver connection.

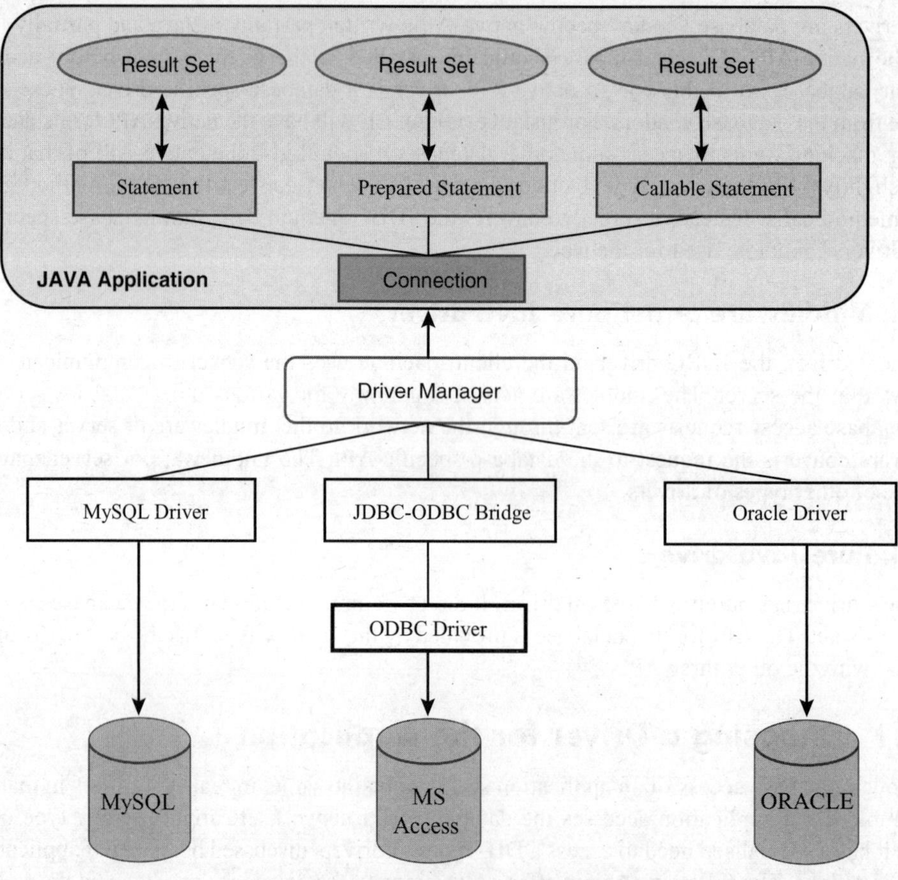

Fig. 15.2 General JDBC architecture

Figure15.2 shows a typical Java application that contains JDBC API to interact with all sorts of databases. JDBC API of an application provides the necessary classes and interfaces to connect the application with the driver manager. As mentioned earlier, the driver manager contains the driver for each type of database. Whenever a new vendor-specific database is introduced to the system, the driver manager configures the driver for that database in its list of available drivers. When the application tries to connect with the database, the driver manager checks the connection statement in the application and establishes a connection between the application and the database-specific driver. Before establishing the connection between application and driver, the driver manager makes sure that the driver is already available in the system. The driver for a particular database, such as MySQL, performs database related operations for the application.

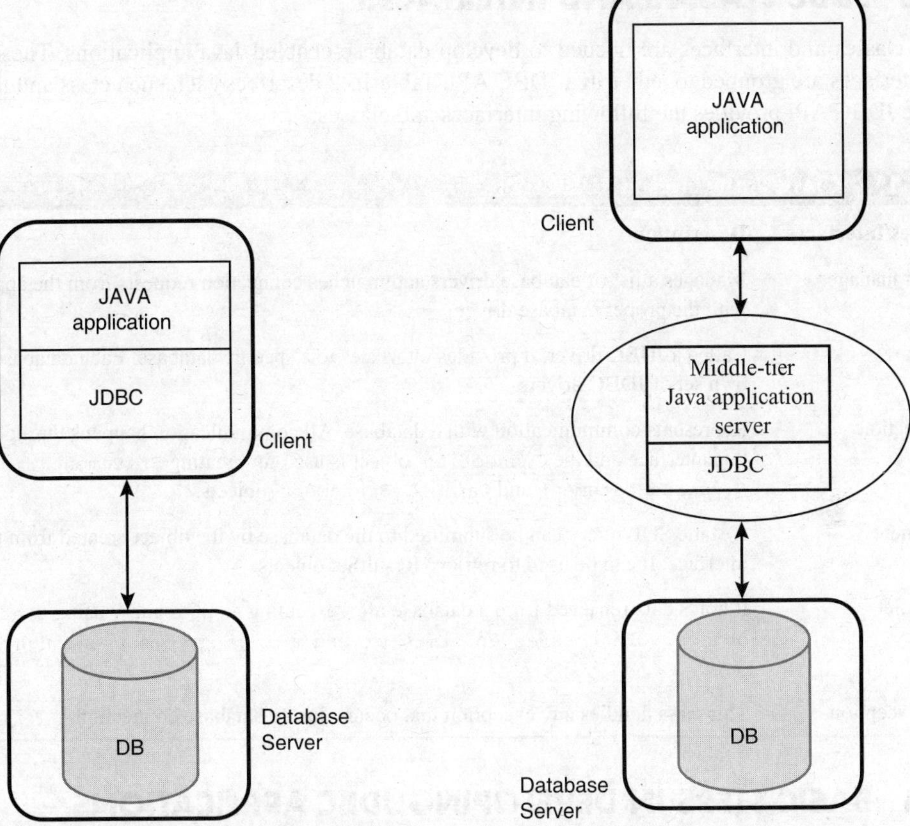

Fig. 15.3 Two-tier model

Fig. 15.4 Three-tier model

The two-tier model (Fig. 15.3) is the simplest JDBC model and enables the Java application to interact directly with the data source (database). In this model, the first tier consists of the client program with JDBC and the second tier is the database server. The JDBC driver provides the request/response communication between these two tiers. The application and database server may be on the same machine or on different machines. Type 2 and Type 4 drivers are based on this type of model. It can handle only a small scale of client database access requests; when the client rate increases, it struggles to manage all the requests at a time. So the two-tier model suffers from scalability issues. In the three-tier model (Fig. 15.4) the client application is called the first tier or the presentation tier which actually needs data from a database and the second tier is a logic tier which is an application server with JDBC which contains business logic and interacts with the DB on behalf of the application. Finally, there is the data tier which has a database server. In this model, the application communicates with the middle-tier services, from which the commands are again sent to the data source. The results are sent back to the middle tier, and from there to the application. The middle tier is usually written in C or C++, or JAVA. Type 1 and Type 3 drivers follow the three-tier model. Using the three-tier model, more than one database request can be fulfilled at a time, because the database access request is handled by the middle-tier. Web application is the best of the three-tier model implementation, where the client sends the database access request using JSP or Servlets and then the database request is received by the application server which has business logic and it queries the data from the database. Finally it forms the response with data and sends it to the client.

15.3 JDBC CLASSES AND INTERFACES

Many classes and interfaces are needed to develop database-enabled Java applications. These classes and interfaces are grouped together in a JDBC API. Table 15.2 describes each such class and interface.

The JDBC API provides the following interfaces and classes:

Table 15.2 Classes/interfaces in JDBC API

Classes/Interfaces	Description
Driver manager	Manages a list of database drivers and matches connection requests from the application with the proper database driver.
Driver	Called a JDBC driver, it provides interfaces to a specific database. Each database has its own set of JDBC drivers.
Connection	Represents communication with a database. All communication happens through this interface and the `Connection` object is used for creating `Statement`, `PreparedStatement` and `CallableStatement` objects.
Statement	A static SQL query can be submitted to the database by the object created from this interface. It can be used to retrieve ResultSet objects.
ResultSet	It holds data retrieved from a database after executing an SQL query using `Statement objects. It acts as an iterator and allows movement through its data.`
SQLException	This class handles any exception that occurs during database connection

15.4 BASIC STEPS IN DEVELOPING JDBC APPLICATIONS

Interacting with the database is a tedious job. This is because the developer should know information apart from the database driver such as data source name, authentication details, and so on. Merely knowing these details will not help the developer to establish a successful connection with the database. The developer should follow well-defined steps to develop a database-enabled application. The following steps are involved in creating a JDBC application.

(i) Importing the required packages.
(ii) Register the JDBC driver.
(iii) Formulate the Database URL and establish a connection.
(iv) Execute a query.
(v) Extract data from the result set.
(vi) Clean up the environment.

15.4.1 Importing the Required Packages

Before starting the application development, the required packages containing JDBC classes and interfaces must be included in the program. To use the standard JDBC package which allows performing the CRUD (Create, Read, Update and Delete) operations, the following package should be included in the source code:

```
import java.sql.* ;
```

The above statement includes the necessary classes and interfaces for developing database enabled Java programs. It should be imported before developing, otherwise the compiler can't recognise the connectivity and SQL statements in the program.

15.4.2 Register the JDBC Driver

The driver is a piece of software that knows how to interact with the data source. The driver of a particular database should be registered in the beginning itself. The registration of a driver is done once and not repeated anywhere in the program. The most common approach to register a driver is by using `Class.forName(String class name)` method, it returns the class. The driver `classname` of a database is specified as a parameter for a `forName()` method. By doing so, it automatically creates a driver instance and registers it with the driver manager. Each database has its own driver provided by the database vendor. For example, if MySQL database is going to be used in the program, the parameter for a `forName()` method should be specified as given below:

```
Class.forName("com.mysql.jdbc.Driver");
```

The above statement will dynamically load a driver class for the MySQL database. Table 15.3 shows the driver names and URL formats of frequently used databases. Note that a single Java program may have more than one driver loaded at the same time.

15.4.3 Formulate the Database URL and Establish Connection

After loading and registering the driver, a connection with the database can be established using the statement `DriverManager.getConnection()`; the `getConnection()` method is contained in the `DriverManager` class. `getConnection()` has three overloaded methods:

- `getConnection(String url)`
- `getConnection(String url, Properties p)`
- `getConnection(String url, String un, String pw)`

Each of the above overloaded methods needs a database URL, which is an address that points to the actual database. Forming a database URL is where most of the problems related to establishing a connection occur. The URL always starts with `jdbc:`. The format of the rest of the JDBC URL varies from database to database. `DriverManager` uses the database URL to find the JDBC driver, which in turn uses the URL to find the correct database. The connection statement can be declared in one of the following two ways:

First:

```
Connection cnn = DriverManager. getConnection("jdbc:mysql://
localhost:3306/ test","root","root");
URL: jdbc:mysql://localhost:3306/test
User Name: root
Password: root
```

Second:

```
String URL = " jdbc:mysql://localhost:3306/test";
String USER = "root";
String PASS = "root"
Connection cnn = DriverManager.getConnection(URL, USER, PASS);
```

The above code establishes a connection with the data base `test` of MySQL DB. The connection object `cnn` encapsulates a connection to a specific database and is also used for firing SQL queries. The driver manager searches the database with the registered drivers until a match is found. To manage a connection with a database, `Connection` object provides many useful methods. Table 15.3 describes the methods available to handle a database connection with a `Connection` object. A frequently used method with `Connection` object is `createStatement()`.

Table 15.3 Methods for database connection management

S. no.	Method	Description
1	`public Statement createStatement()`	Used to create a statement with `Connection` object to access database.
2	`public PreparedStatement parepareStatement(String s)`	Used to execute a repeated SQL query.
3	`public void setAutoCommit(Boolean)`	Used to set the auto commit on transaction.
4	`public void commit()`	When the transaction is successfully completed, this method is called to make changes in all the tables.
5	`public void rollback()`	If a transaction fails, this method will be triggered to roll back to the previous state.
6	`public void close()`	Used to close the database connection.

Table 15.4 JDBC driver names and URL formats

RDBMS	JDBC driver name	URL format
MySQL	`com.mysql.jdbc.Driver`	`jdbc:mysql://hostname/ databaseName`
ORACLE	`oracle.jdbc. driver. OracleDriver`	`jdbc:oracle:thin:@ hostname:portNumber:databaseName`
JavaDB/Derby	`org.apache. derby.jdbc. ClientDriver`	`jdbc:derby:net://[host]:[port]/ [database]`
Microsoft SQL server	`com.microsoft. sqlserver.jdbc. SQLServerDriver or com.microsoft. jdbc.sqlserver. SQLServerDriver`	`jdbc:jtds:sqlserver://<host>:<port> /<database_name>`
MS Access	`sun.jdbc.odbc.JdbcOdbcDriver`	`jdbc:odbc:<database_name>`

Table 15.4 lists the driver name for each type of RDMS. As mentioned earlier, it is unique to that database. For example, the driver `com.mysql.jdbc.Driver` is used only for the database MySQL and can't be used by any other database. The driver manager uses this unique drive name to recognise the vendor-specific database. Like the driver name, the URL which points to the data source is also in a unique format. So the developer should be careful when using different vendor-specific databases. When changing from one database to another, the driver name and URL format should be modified carefully. Even though the URL format varies from database to database, it has some common characteristics and can be divided into four parts.

- First: prefix *jdbc:*.
- Second: name of the database for instance MySQL, Oracle.
- Third: hostname and optional port number.
- Fourth: name of the data source.

15.4.4 Execute a Query

Once a connection with a database is established, the application can interact with the database. The following interfaces define the methods and properties used to query the data from the database. Table 15.5 describes the interfaces used for the `Statement` object creation.

Table 15.5 Interfaces used to create statements

Interfaces	Description
`Statement`	Used for general purpose database access. It doesn't accept parameters.
`PreparedStatement`	Used when SQL statements need to be used many times. This interface accepts input parameters at runtime.
`CallableStatement`	Used to access the database stored procedures. This interface also accepts runtime input parameters.

Using `Statement` interface

Before using a `Statement` object to execute a SQL statement, it must be created using the `Connection` object's `createStatement( )` method, as given below

```
Class.forName("com.mysql.jdbc.Driver");
Connection cnn = DriverManager.getConnection("jdbc:mysql://
localhost:3306/ test","root","root");
Statement st=cnn.createStatement();
```

In the above code snippet, the driver name `com.mysql.jdbc.Driver` for MySQL database is passed as a parameter to the `forName()` method. Once the method is triggered, the driver manager searches for `mysql` in its list. If it is available, the driver manager connects the application with the mysql. Now the stage has been set for the connectivity, the first line only establishes a connection with MySQL, not with the database. The URL is given below.

```
jdbc:mysql://localhost:3306/test","root","root"
 1st part      2nd part 3rd part  4th part
```

1st part: prefix `jdbc:` and vendor-specific database `mysql`
2nd part: host name `localhost` and optional port number `3306`
3rd part: data source or database name `test`
4th part: Username `root` and password `root`

This points to the exact data source in the MySQL database and this URL is passed as a parameter in the `getConnection()` method and triggered using the `DriverManager` object. If the data source `test` is available in the MySQL database, it returns the database to `Connection` object `cnn`. An object of

`Statement` interface is needed to execute the SQL queries. The `Statement` object `st` is created through statement `Statement st=cnn.createStatement()`. The `createStatement()` method is called using `Connection` object and in turn it is assigned the `Statement` object `st`.

Once the object of the `Statement` is obtained, it can be used to execute the SQL queries. To execute the SQL statements, one of the following methods will be used.

- `boolean execute (String SQL)`
- `int executeUpdate (String SQL)`
- `ResultSet executeQuery (String SQL)`

The `booleanexecute()` method will be used mostly to execute SQL DDL statements and it returns either true or false. The `executeQuery()` method is used to execute a `SELECT` statement and returns a `ResultSet` with the number of rows selected. The `executeUpdate()` is used to execute SQL statements such as `INSERT`, `UPDATE` or `DELETE` and it returns the number of rows affected. The above three methods need a SQL query to execute. The query will be passed as a parameter specified directly or as a string variable.

```
String sql = "SELECT * FROM emp";
ResultSet rs = st.executeQuery(sql);
```

In the above code, `Statement` object `st` is created with `createStatement()` of a `connection` object `cnn`. Through statement object `executeQuery()` method is triggered and query is passed by string variable `sql`. It returns the rows to the `ResultSet` object `rs`.

```
String sql = "UPDATE emp set age=30 WHERE id=103";
int r = st.executeUpdate(sql);
```

Here, `statement` object `st` is used to trigger `executeUpdate()` and it returns the number of rows affected. The values for the variable in the `UPDATE` statement are assigned during development. `Statement` interface doesn't allow the SQL statements to supply values for its variables during runtime. For this operation, `PreparedStatement` is used.

Using `PreparedStatement` interface

This interface is mostly used to execute repeated SQL statements. Just like the `Statement` interface, it accepts all the SQL statements. One additional feature of this interface is the ability to supply a parameter's value of the SQL statement at run time. To specify a parameter value of any SQL statement, the *parameter marker ?* is used. All the parameters values must be assigned before executing a SQL statement. Each parameter marker is referred by its ordinal position. The first marker represents position 1, the next position 2, and so forth. The `setXXX()` method is used to set the parameter value. The `XXX` represents the datatype of a value that is going to be set for the parameter. For example, refer to the code given below.

```
String sql = "UPDATE emp set age=? WHERE id=?";
preparedStatementst = cnn.prepareStatement(sql);
st.setInt(1, 29);
st.setInt(2, 501);
int r = st.executeUpdate();
```

In the above code segment, parameters `age` and `id` of `UPDATE` query are set with parameter marker ? and values for those parameters will be set by `setInt()` method because the `age` and `id` parameters are integer type. In the first `setInt(1, 29),` method, 1 represents the position in the query, here it points to the `age` and its value is 29. And the second `setInt(2, 501)` method, 2 represents the `id` and its value is 501.

Using `CallableStatement`

`CallableStatement` object is used to invoke the stored procedure of a database. Before employing a `CallableStatement` in a program, the purpose of stored procedures in database connectivity is known in advance. A stored procedure is a segment or subroutine just like a conventional programming language code which is stored in the database. A stored procedure contains a segment of SQL statements. It can be called by more than one application at a time. Creation of stored procedures differs from database to database. Stored procedures help in reducing traffic between the application and the database. Instead of sending the same SQL statement again and again to the database, the application needs to send only the name and parameters of the stored procedure which has a SQL statement to the database. A typical stored procedure created in MySQL server, is given below.

```
CREATE PROCEDURE demo.getrecords()
BEGIN
SELECT * FROM emp;
END
```

In the above code segment, `demo` is the name of the database and `getrecords()` is the name of a stored procedure. An application that needs to access all the records from the table `emp` can use the `getrecords()` stored procedure. It contains only one SQL statement which selects all the records from the table. The `CallableStatement` object uses three types of `IN`, `OUT` and `INOUT` parameters. The `IN` parameter works just like `setXXX()` method and `OUT` parameter functions as `getXXX()` method. `INOUT` parameter is a combination of both `IN` and `OUT` parameters. A statement `cn.prepareCall()` method is used to create an object for `CallableStatement`.

```
String SQL = "{call getrecords()}";
CallableStatementcst = cn.prepareCall (SQL);
```

In the above code, string variable `SQL` represents the stored procedure. The string variable `SQL` is passed as a parameter for the `prepareCall()` method and is triggered using the `Connection` object `cn`. Like the `Statement` interface object used for traversing the `ResultSet`, the `CallableStatement` interface object is used to interact with the stored procedures.

15.4.5 Extract Data from Result Set

`ResultSet`

Each row is a Record, and is returned by executing a SQL statement, will be stored in the object of a `ResultSet`. The `ResultSet` object is created by executing an SQL statement. The commonly used SQL statement for collecting all the records from the table is the `SELECT` statement. Once the `ResultSet` object is created, the cursor will be positioned just before the first row. The cursor is a pointer which points to one row at a time and is used to move across the table of data. If some specific data or row needs to be retrieved from the table, the cursor should be placed at the row using methods of `ResultSet` interface given in Table 15.7. Methods used to manipulate the `ResultSet` can be categorised into three types, such as navigating, viewing and updating.

Types of ResultSets

The desired type of `ResultSet` can be generated by supplying the `ResultSet` type and constant values in the following connection methods.

- `createStatement(int RSType, int RSConcurrency);`
- `prepareStatement(String SQL, int RSType, int RSConcurrency);`
- `prepareCall(String sql, int RSType, int RSConcurrency);`

The `RSType` argument indicates the type of a `ResultSet` object and the `RSConcurrency` argument is used to specify one of two `ResultSet` constants for specifying whether a result set is read-only or updatable. The `ResultSet` can be broadly categorised into scrollable and non-scrollable. Table 15.6 describes each type of `ResultSet`. The default `ResultSet` type is `TYPE_FORWARD_ONLY`.

Table 15.6 ResultSet types

S. no.	ResultSet type	Description
1	`ResultSet.TYPE_FORWARD_ ONLY`	It allows moving the cursor only forward from beginning to end.
2	`ResultSet.TYPE_SCROLL_ SENSITIVE`	It allows moving the cursor forward and backward through the records. It can detect any changes made on the records after creating the `ResultSet`.
3	`ResultSet.TYPE_SCROLL_ INSENSITIVE`	It allows moving the cursor forward and backward through the records. It never worries about any changes made on the records after creating `ResultSet`.

The second and third type of `ResultSet` uses two constants to specify whether a `ResultSet` is read only or updateable. The default constant is read only. The constants are given below:

- `ResultSet.CONCUR_READ_ONLY` - sets the `ResultSet` as read only.
- `ResultSet.CONCUR_UPDATABLE`- sets the `ResultSet` as updatable.

Scrollable vs non-scrollabe ResultSet

`ResultSet` can be set as scrollable or non-scrollable. If the `ResultSet` is specified as `TYPE_FORWARD_ONLY` then it becomes a non-scrollable result set. The cursor in the non-scrollable `ResultSet` moves only in the forward direction. It can't move its cursor in a random order or back and forth. Non-scrollable is a default type for `ResultSet` interface. If the cursor needs to be moved in a random order or back and forth, a scrollable `ResutltSet` should be opted for. A scrollable `ResultSet` can be created by specifying it to be either as `TYPE_SCROLL_SENSITIVE` or `TYPE_SCROLL_INSENSITIVE` (for more information, refer Table 15.6). The following examples show how to create a read only Scrollable ResultSet and an updatable one.

Example 1: Scrollable `ResultSet` that can update data.

```
Statement st = cnn.createStatement( RecordSet.TYPE_
SCROLL_SENSITIVE, ResultSet.CONCUR_UPDATABLE);
```

Example 2: Scrollable `ResultSet` that is read only.

```
Statement st = cnn.createStatement( RecordSet.TYPE_
SCROLL_INSENSITIVE, ResultSet.CONCUR_READ_ONLY);
```

In both of the above examples, a cursor can be moved back and forth. But, only the Scrollable `ResultSet` that has constant value `CONCUR_READ_ONLY` is able to update data while traversing. The following table provides the complete set of methods for navigating a cursor all over the record set.

Table 15.7 Navigation methods of `Resultset` interface

S. no.	Method	Description
1	`next()`	Takes the cursor to the next row. If there is no row available, it returns False.
2	`previous()`	Takes the cursor to the previous row. If there is no row available, it returns False.
3	`first()`	Shifts the cursor to the first row of a record set. Returns Boolean values True or False.
4	`last()`	Shifts the cursor to the last row of a record set. Returns Boolean values True or False.
5	`absolute(int row)`	Takes the cursor to the specified row in the record set.
6	`relative(int row)`	Moves the cursor a specified number of rows forward or backward from its current position.
7	`getRow()`	Returns the row number of where the cursor is currently positioned.
8	`isAfterLast()`	Retrieves information on whether the cursor is after the last row in this `ResultSet` object. This method is optional for `ResultSet`s with a result set type of `TYPE_FORWARD_ONLY`. Returns Boolean values True or False.
9	`isBeforeFirst()`	Retrieves information on whether the cursor is before the first row in this `ResultSet` object. This method is optional for `ResultSet`s with a result set type of `TYPE_FORWARD_ONLY`. Returns Boolean values True or False.
10	`isClosed()`	Retrieves information on whether this `ResultSet` object has been closed. A ResultSet is closed if the method close has been called on it, or if it is automatically closed. Returns True if this ResultSet object is closed; False if it is still open.
11	`isFirst()`	Returns True if the cursor is on the first row; False otherwise. This method is optional for ResultSets with a result set type of TYPE_FORWARD_ONLY.
12	`isLast()`	Returns True if the cursor is on the last row; False otherwise. This method is optional for ResultSets with a result set type of TYPE_FORWARD_ONLY.
13	`afterLast()`	Moves the cursor to just after the last row.
14	`beforeFirst()`	Moves the cursor to just before the first row.

`ResultSet` interface provides various methods to bring data from a table. There is a `get` method or `getXXX()` for each type of datatype; `XXX` represents the datatype of data to be extracted. If a data is of the integer type, then get method will be `getInt()`. Each `get` method either takes a column name or index to get data (Table 15.8).

Table 15.8 Methods for viewing data from a ResultSet

S. no.	Method	Description
1.	`getInt(String columnName)`	Gets the data from a specified column name.
2.	`getInt(int columnIndex)`	Gets the data from a specified column index. Note here that the column index starts at 1.

`ResultSet` interface also provides many useful methods for updating specific data from a table. It provides `update` methods with required datatypes such as `updateString()`, `updateInt()`. The `update` method modifies the data either by column name or column index. Table 15.9 gives the complete set of methods available for updating data.

Table 15.9 Methods for updating records

S. no.	Method	Description
1	`updateString(int columnIndex, String d)`	Updates a string type data in the specified column number with the data specified.
2	`updateInt(String columnName, Int s)`	Updates a specified column with integer type data.
3	`deleteRow()`	Deletes the current row.
4	`refreshRow()`	Refreshes the RecordSet to reflect changes make to it.
5	`insertRow()`	This method inserts a new row.

So far, various issues related to `RecordSet` have been discussed in detail. The remaining section explains how to extract data from a `RecordSet` object. The following code segment is frequently used for extracting data from a table.

```
while(rs.next())
{
    //Extract data by column name intregno = rs.getInt("reg");
    String name = rs.getString("name");
    String course=rs.getString("degree");
    int year = rs.getInt("year");
    String dept = rs.getString("department");
    //Output the values System.out.print("ENROLL NO: " + regno);
    System.out.print("NAME: " + name);
    System.out.print("YEAR: " + year);
    System.out.println("DEPARTMENT: " + dept);
}
```

The `while` loop is used to move through the record set one by one using the parameter `rs.next()` and `rs` is an object of `RecordSet` interface. The `next()` method is used to move the cursor to the next record of the table through looping. When the cursor reaches the last record in `ResultSet`, the loop is stopped.

The statements inside the `while` loop are divided into two segments. The first segment is for extracting data from the `ResultSet` through its object `rs` and storing the data in the local variables, while the second segment displays the data to the user. Local variables such as `regno,name,course,year, dept` are declared to store the data retrieved from the result set.

To get data from a specific column, `getXXX()` method is called using object `rs`, where `XXX` represents the datatype of the data to be retrieved from the column. In the statement `int regno = rs.getInt("reg")`, the local variable `regno` is declared to receive data and `rs.getInt("reg")` extracts the data from column name `reg` and assigns it to the variable `regno`. In this code segment, `get` method is an integer type and `reg` is the column name in a table. Datatype of `get` method and datatype of the column should match each other. Another important thing is to specify the exact column name as the parameter of a `get` method. Likewise, all other statements are used to extract data from each column of the table until the cursor reaches the row next to the last record.

Table 15.10 shows the various datatypes used for getting, setting and updating data through `RecordSet` object.

Table 15.10 Frequently used datatypes for getting, setting and updating data

Datatype	getXXX()	setXXX()	updateXXX()
INTEGER	getInt()	setInt()	updateInt()
TINYINT	getByte()	setByte()	updateByte()
SMALLINT	getShort()	setShort()	updateShort()
BIGINT	getLong()	setLong()	updateLong()
FLOAT	getFloat()	setFloat()	updateFloat()
REAL DOUBLE	getDouble()	setDouble()	updateDouble()
CHAR VARCHAR LONGVARCHAR	getString()	setString()	updateString()
BIT	getBoolean()	setBoolean()	updateBoolean()
DATE	getDate()	setDate()	updateDate()
TIME	getTime()	setTime()	updateTime()
CLOB	getClob()	setClob()	updateClob()
BLOB	getBlob()	setBlob()	updateBlob()

15.4.6 Cleaning up the Environment

The `close()` method of `Connection` object is used to explicitly close all connections with the current database session. Closing the database connection is a good coding practice, unless the `Resultset` may be damaged by some other things. Examples of close () are,

```
rs.close();
st.close();
cnn.close();
```

`rs.close()` closes the connection with the recordset, after which no other operation can be carried out in the future. Likewise the `st.close()` and `cnn.close()` statements close the connection with `Statement` and `Connection` objects.

Program 15.1 demonstrates how to connect and interact with the database. Information about the database and table are given below.

DB Name: `demo`
Table Name: `studinfo`
The table has already been filled with some data.

regno	name	course	year	dept
121501	KUMAR	BCA	1	CA
121502	ANUSHA	BCA	2	CA
121503	KEERTHIGA	BCA	3	CA
121504	RAKSHITA	BSc	1	MATHS

Program 15.1

```
import java.sql.*;
public class JAVADB1
{
    public static void main(String[] args) throws SQLException, ClassNotFoundException
    {
        try
        {
            Class.forName("com.mysql.jdbc.Driver");
            System.out.println("Establishing a connection
            with the database....");
            Connection cn = DriverManager.
            getConnection("jdbc:mysql://localhost:3306/
            demo","root","root");
            System.out.println("Creating statement
            object...");
            Statement st = cn.createStatement();
            String sql;
            sql = "SELECT * FROM studinfo";
            ResultSet rs = st.executeQuery(sql);
            while(rs.next())
            {
                //Extracting data from table using column
                name int r=rs.getInt("regno");
                String n=rs.getString("name");
                String c=rs.getString("course");
                int y=rs.getInt("year");
                String d=rs.getString("dept");
                //Displaying data System.out.
                println("ENROLLMENT NO: " + r);
                System.out.println("NAME: " + n);
                System.out.println("COURSE: "+ c);
                System.out.println("YEAR: " + y +" YEAR");
                System.out.println("DEPARTMENT: " + d);
            }
        }
        catch(Exception e)
        {
            System.out.println("An Exception has occurred :"+e);
        }
    }
}
```

Output 15.1

```
Establishing a
connection with the
database.... Creating
statement object...
ENROLLMENT NO: 121501
NAME: KUMAR
COURSE: BCA
YEAR: 1 YEAR
DEPARTMENT: CA
ENROLLMENT NO: 121502
NAME: ANUSHA
COURSE: BCA
YEAR: 2 YEAR
DEPARTMENT: CA
ENROLLMENT NO: 121503
NAME: KEERTHIGA
COURSE: BCA
YEAR: 3 YEAR
DEPARTMENT: CA
ENROLLMENT NO: 121504
NAME: RAKSHITA
COURSE: BSc
YEAR: 1 YEAR
DEPARTMENT: MATHS
```

The driver for MySQL database is loaded first using the statement `Class.forName()`, and the parameter of `forName()` method expresses what type of database is going to be used in the application. The driver of the MySQL database will be used to convert the queries triggered in the application into method calls understandable by the database. The next step is to locate the database and the respective table for querying data. The statement `DriverManager.getConnection()` helps to locate the database, whether in the local system or in the remote system. The database URL is passed as a parameter through the `getConnection()` method. The database URL has all the details needed to locate the database, such as database, hostname, optional port number and name of the database created by the developer. As has already been explained, all database URLs must start with the word `jdbc`. The `DriverManager` uses this URL passed by `getConnection()` method to locate and identify the vendor specific database from its list, as the driver manager keeps a record of all the available vendor specific databases in the system. After successfully establishing a connection with the database, in the very next statement `Statement st = cn.createStatement(); createStatement()` method is called using an object `cn` while declaring an object `st` for Statement. The object `st` is used for triggering an SQL query. Method `executeQuery()` is invoked using an object `st` with the SQL query as parameter (here SQL query was assigned to a String type variable `sql` and specified in the method). In the code `segmentResultSet rs = st.executeQuery(sql); executeQuery()` method executes the `SELECT` query and then assigns the result set(containing records) to an object `rs` of `ResultSet` interface. So the result of executing a query will be stored in the `ResultSet` object. The `ResultSet` object `rs` can be used for many database-related operations such traversing, extracting, updating and inserting. The remaining code segment extracts the data row by row from a `ResultSet` object `rs` using a `while` (`rs.next`) loop. The parameter of `rs.next()` (refer Table 15.7 for more on `next()` method) in the `while` loop traverses the cursor from the first row till the last row. Inside the `while` loop, the code segment `int r=rs.getInt("regno")` and similar code is used to extract specific data from the column of a table. In the code, `r` is an integer type variable to hold the data extracted from the table and `rs.getInt("regno")` extracts data from a column named `regno` and assigns it to the variable `r`. So the `while` loop extracts data row by row and displays it to the user.

Program 15.2 exhibits the insert, delete, update and search operations. The information about the database and table are given below.

DB Name: `demo`
Table Name: `emp`

The table has already been filled with some data.

Eid	Ename	Dept	exp	desig
561702	anbu	computer application	5	assistant professor
561703	kanchana	commerce	6	assistant professor
561704	sathish	management studies	8	assistant professor
561705	anitha	economics	9	assistant professor
561706	kumar	english	3	assistant professor
561707	karthik	software technology	5	assistant professor

Program 15.2

```
import java.io.*;
import java.sql.* ;
public class EmpDB
{
   static final String DRIVER = "com.mysql.jdbc.Driver";
   static final String URL = "jdbc:mysql://
   localhost:3306/demo";
   static final String USER = "root";
   static final String PASS = "root";
   public static void main(String[] args) throws
   ClassNotFoundException, SQLException, IOException
   {
      try
      {
         Class.forName(DRIVER);
         Connection conn = DriverManager.
         getConnection(URL,USER,PASS);
         Statement stmt = conn.createStatement();
         PreparedStatement stmt2;
         String sql = "SELECT * FROM emp";
         ResultSet rs = stmt.executeQuery(sql);
         InputStreamReader r=new
         InputStreamReader(System.in);
         BufferedReader in=new BufferedReader(r);
         System.out.println("Enter your
         choice(1:display, 2:insert, 3: delete,
         4:update, 5:Search) ");
         String data=in.readLine();
         int ch=Integer.parseInt(data);
         switch(ch)
         {
            case 1:
            while(rs.next())
            {
               //Retrieve by column name int id =
               rs.getInt("eid");
               String name = rs.getString("ename");
               String dept = rs.getString("dept");
               int exp=rs.getInt("exp");
               String desig = rs.getString("desig");
               //Display values System.out.
               println("Employee ID: " + id);
               System.out.println("Employee Name: " +
               name);
               System.out.println("Department: " +
               dept);
               System.out.println("Experience: " +
               exp);
               System.out.println("Designation:
               "+desig);
               System.out.println();
            }
            break;
            case 2:
            System.out.println("Enter Employee ID");
```

Output 15.2

```
Run-1
Enter your
choice(1:display,
2:insert,
3: delete, 4:update,
5:Search)
1
Employee ID: 561702
Employee Name: anbu
Department: computer
application Experience:
5
Designation: assistant
professor
Employee ID: 561703
Employee Name: kanchana
Department: commerce
Experience: 6
Designation: assistant
professor
Employee ID: 561704
Employee Name: sathish
Department: management
studies
Experience: 8
Designation: assistant
professor
Employee ID: 561705
Employee Name: anitha
Department: economics
Experience: 9
Designation: assistant
professor
Employee ID: 561706
Employee Name: kumar
Department: english
Experience: 3
Designation: assitant
professor
Employee ID: 561707
Employee Name: karthik
Department: software
technology
Experience: 5
Designation: assistant
professor
```

```
String i=in.readLine();
int id=Integer.parseInt(i);
System.out.println("Enter Employee Name: ");
String en=in.readLine();
System.out.println("Enter the Department: ");
String dept=in.readLine();
System.out.println("Enter the
Experience:");
String e=in.readLine();
int exp=Integer.parseInt(e);
System.out.println("Enter the
Designation:");
String desig=in.readLine();
stmt2=conn.prepareStatement("insert into
emp values(?,?,?,?,?)");
stmt2.setInt(1, id);
stmt2.setString(2, en);
stmt2.setString(3, dept);
stmt2.setInt(4, exp);
stmt2.setString(5, desig);
int g = stmt2.executeUpdate();
if(g> 0)
System.out.print("SAVED successfully");
break;
case 3:
System.out.println("Enter Employee ID");
String idd=in.readLine();
int did=Integer.parseInt(idd);
while(rs.next())
{
    if(did==rs.getInt("eid"))
    {
        String sn=rs.getString("ename");
        stmt2=conn.prepareStatement("DELETE
        FROM emp WHERE eid = ? ");
        stmt2.setInt(1, did);
        stmt2.executeUpdate();
        System.out.println("Employee named :
        "+sn+" is removed from DB");
        break;
    }
    else if(rs.isLast())
    {
        if(did!=rs.getInt("eid"))
        {
            System.out.println("No Such
            Data");
        }
    }
}
break;
case 4:
System.out.println("Enter Employee ID");
String ei=in.readLine();
int id2=Integer.parseInt(ei);
System.out.println("Enter Employee Name: ");
String en2=in.readLine();
```

Output 15.2

```
Run-2
Enter your
choice(1:display,
2:insert,
3: delete, 4:update,
5:Search)
5
Enter Employee ID
561705
Employee Name: anitha
Department: economics
Experience: 9
Designation: assistant
professor
Run-3
Enter your
choice(1:display,
2:insert,
3: delete, 4:update,
5:Search)
5
Enter Employee ID
561709
No Such Data
Run-4
Enter your
choice(1:display,
2:insert,
3: delete, 4:update,
5:Search)
3
Enter Employee ID
561709
No Such Data
Run-5
Enter your
choice(1:display,
2:insert,
3: delete, 4:update,
5:Search)
3
Enter Employee ID
561702
Employee named: anbu is
removed from DB
```

```
            System.out.println("Enter the Department: ");
            String dept2=in.readLine();
            System.out.println("Enter the Experience:");
            String e2=in.readLine();
            int exp2=Integer.parseInt(e2);
            System.out.println("Enter the Designation:");
            String desig2=in.readLine();
            stmt2=conn. prepareStatement("UPDATE emp SET ename=?, dept=?, exp=?,
            desig=? WHERE eid =?");
            stmt2.setString(1, en2);
            stmt2.setString(2, dept2);
            stmt2.setInt(3, exp2);
            stmt2.setString(4, desig2);
            stmt2.setInt(5, id2);
            stmt2.executeUpdate();
            break;
            case 5:
            System.out.println("Enter Employee ID");
            String e1=in.readLine();
            int eid=Integer.parseInt(e1);
            while(rs.next())
            {
               if(eid==rs.getInt("eid"))
               {
                  //Display values
                  System.out.println("Employee Name: " + rs.getString("ename"));
                  System.out.println("Department: " + rs.getString("dept"));
                  System.out.println("Experience: " + rs.getInt("exp"));
                  System.out.println("Designation: "+rs.getString("desig"));
                  System.out.println();
                  break;
               }
               else if(rs.isLast())
               {
                  if(eid!=rs.getInt("eid"))
                  {
                     System.out.println("No Such Data");
                  }
               }
            }
            break;
            default:
            System.out.println("SORRY NO SUCH OPERATION");
         }
         rs.close();
         stmt.close();
         conn.close();
      }
      catch(SQLException se)
      {
         se.printStackTrace();
      }
   }
}
```

The driver, database URL, user name and password have been assigned to the predefined variables `DRIVER`, `URL`, `USER` and `PASS`. Just like the previous program, the driver is identified by passing the variable `DRIVER` to the `Class.forName()` method as a parameter and then the program is connected with the respective database using a statement `Connection conn = DriverManager.getConnection (URL,US- ER,PASS)`. Here, two statement objects are created to execute the SQL queries. The first one, `stmt`, is created by invoking `createStatment()` method, so it can only fetch data from a table. The second `stmt2` is created by invoking the `prepareStatment()` and declared inside cases of `switch` structure for performing the DML operations with runtime parameters. After successfully setting up a connection with a database, the user choice for performing a particular DML operation is received using `input stream reader` and `buffered reader`. Based on the choice entered by the user, the case in the switch structure will be chosen and the required operation carried out. The switch structure is created with 5 cases. Case 1 fetches the data from a table as in the previous program.

Case 2 inserts the data using the `INSERT` query and the parameters for the respective columns are set using `setXXX()` method (if the column is integer type then `setXXX()` method is invoked with datatype of the column, that is, `setInt()`. For more information, refer to Table 15.10). Case 3 performs the delete operation based on employee id entered by the user through stream; first it checks whether the given employee id exists or not. If it exists, the respective record will be removed permanently from the table and immediately breaks out of the case. If it doesn't exist, it will show the message as 'No such data'. It checks the existence of employee id by navigating till the last record.

Case 4 performs the updation operation using the same `setXXX()` method. Case 5 searches for the record with the given employee id, it navigates the record set using a `while (rs.next())` loop. If the record is found, it displays that particular record and breaks out of the loop. If not, the message stating 'No such data' will be displayed. To check for the existence of a record, the two conditions `rs.isLast() and eid!=rs.getInt("eid")` are used. The first one checks whether the cursor has reached the end of the record set or not; if so, the control enters into the `if` block. Inside the second condition it is checked whether the given `eid` is equivalent or not, if not equal the `eid` doesn't exist in the table. If the user enters a choice apart from the 5, the default block is executed and then program execution is terminated.

Program 15.3 demonstrates how to use two tables from the same database in the same program. Details of the database and tables are given below.

DB Name: `stud`
First_Table: `sprofile`
Second_Table: `staff`

The two tables have been filled up with some records.

Program 15.3

```
import java.sql.*;
public class Twotable
{
    static final String JDBC_DRIVER = "com.mysql.jdbc.Driver";
    static final String DB_URL = "jdbc:mysql://localhost/stud";
    // Database credentials
    static final String USER = "root";
    static final String PASS = "root";
    public static void main(String[] args)
```

```
{
    try
    {
        Class.forName(JDBC_DRIVER);
        System.out.println("Connecting to database...");
        Connection cn1 = DriverManager. getConnection(DB_URL,USER,PASS);
        System.out.println("Creating statement...");
        Statement st= cn1.createStatement();
        String sql,sql1;
        sql = "SELECT * FROM sprofile";
        ResultSet rs = st.executeQuery(sql);
        System.out.println("FROM FIRST TABLE: sprofile");
        while(rs.next())
        {
            int r = rs.getInt("regno");
            String n=rs.getString("name");
            String c=rs.getString("course");
            String d=rs.getString("dept");
            String co=rs.getString("college");
            //Display values
            System.out.println("REGISTER NO: " + r);
            System.out.println("NAME: " +n);
            System.out.println("DEGREE: " + c);
            System.out.println("DEPARTMENT: " + d);
            System.out.println("COLLEGE: " + co);
            System.out.println();
        }
        sql1="SELECT * FROM staff";
        ResultSet rs1 = st.executeQuery(sql1);
        System.out.println("FROM SECOND TABLE:
        staff");
        while(rs1.next())
        {

            int i = rs1.getInt("ID");
            String n=rs1.getString("name");
            String d=rs1.getString("desig");
            String de=rs1.getString("dept");
            String ex=rs1.getString("expert");
            String doj=rs1.getString("doj");
            //Display values System.out.
            println("STAFF ID: " + i);
            System.out.println("NAME: " +n);
            System.out.println("DESIGNA
            +TION: " + d);
            System.out.println("DEPARTMENT: " + de);
            System.out.println("EXPERT IN: " + ex);
            System.out.println("DATE OF JOINING: " +doj);
            System.out.println();
        }
    }
    catch(Exception e){System.out.println("An Exception has occurred:"+e);}
  }
}
```

Output 15.3

```
Connecting to database...
Creating statement...
FROM FIRST TABLE: sprofile
REGISTER NO: 56121
NAME: kannan
DEGREE: BCA
DEPARTMENT: CA
COLLEGE: SHC
REGISTER NO: 56122
NAME: kumutha
DEGREE: MSc
DEPARTMENT: maths
COLLEGE: MKJC
FROM SECOND TABLE: staff
STAFF ID: 76701
NAME: babu
DESIGNATION: lecturer
DEPARTMENT: CS
EXPERT IN: JAVA
DATE OF JOINING: 2010-07-15
STAFF ID: 76702
NAME: thilagawathi
DESIGNATION: assistant
professor
DEPARTMENT: CA
EXPERT IN: .NET
DATE OF JOINING: 2014-06-23
```

The driver name and URL are assigned in static string type variables `JDBC_DRIVER`, `DB_URL` respectively and authentication details are assigned in string type variables `USER` and `PASS`. The database driver is loaded through the statement `Class.forName(JDBC_DRIVER)` and connection object `cn1` is created using the statement `Connection cn1 = DriverManager.getConnection (DB_URL,USER,PASS)`. If everything is set perfectly, the driver manager establishes a connection with the database. The `createS- tatement()` is invoked through `Connection` object `cn1` and assigned to the `Statement` object `st`. Two string type variables `sql`, `sql1` have been declared for the SQL query `SELECT` statement. The first variable `sql` is assigned a `SELECT` statement which extracts all the records from the table `sprofile` and the second variable `sql1` is assigned with another `SELECT` statement to extract all the records from the table `staff`. The `executeQuery()` method is invoked to execute the SQL query in the variable `sql` through `Statement` object `st`. All the extracted records are stored in the `ResultSet` object `rs`. So the `ResultSet` object `rs` contains all the records extracted from the table `sprofile`. The records are traversed using the `rs.next()` statement and placed in the brackets of the `while` loop. The `next()` method sets the cursor to the row just before the first row and then moves the cursor row by row in each iteration. During each iteration of the `while` loop, the records are extracted column by column. For instance, the statement `int r = rs.getInt("regno")` extracts the integer type data from the column `ID` and assigns it to the integer type variable `r`. Similarly, all other statements in the `while` loop extract the data from each of the columns and assign it to the respective variables. During each iteration, data from each row is extracted and assigned to the variables, and then these values are displayed row by row. So each iteration of the `while` loop extracts a row from the table until the cursor moves to the last row. To extract data from the second table `staff`, the same procedure is repeated. The `ResultSet` object is `rs1` and assigned with statement `st.executeQuery(sql1)`, the parameter `sql1` is a string type variable which has a `SELECT` statement for extracting data from the table `staff`. To traverse each row, `rs1.next()` is called in the `while` loop and it continues its execution until the last row is reached. While traversing each row, the data from each column is extracted and assigned to the respective variable and after extracting the data from last column, the entire row is displayed. The `while` loop extracts and displays the data row by row until the last row is reached.

Program 15.3 demonstrated how to use two different tables from the same database. **Program 15.4** exhibits the use of two different databases in the same program. One table from each database is used to extract records. Information about the databases and tables are given below.

Database 1: `stud`
Database 2: `test`
Table1: `sprofile` from first database
Table 2: `event` from second database

Program 15.4

```
import java.sql.*;
public class TwoDB
{
    static final String JDBC_DRIVER = "com.mysql.jdbc.Driver";
    static final String URL = "jdbc:mysql://localhost/stud";
    static final String URL1 = "jdbc:mysql://localhost/test";
    // Database credentials
    static final String USER = "root";
    static final String PASS = "root";
```

```
public static void main(String[] args)
{
    try
    {
        Class.forName(JDBC_DRIVER);
        System.out.println("Connecting to database...");
        Connection cn = DriverManager. getConnection(URL,USER,PASS);
        Connection cn1 = DriverManager. getConnection(URL1,USER,PASS);
        System.out.println("Creating statement...");
        Statement st= cn.createStatement();
        String sql,sql1;
        sql = "SELECT * FROM sprofile";
        ResultSet rs = st.executeQuery(sql);
        System.out.println("FROM FIRST DB: stud");
        while(rs.next())
        {
            int r = rs.getInt("regno");
            String n=rs.getString("name");
            String c=rs.getString("course");
            String d=rs.getString("dept");
            String co=rs.getString("college");
            //Display values System.out.
            println("REGISTER NO: " + r);
            System.out.println("NAME: " +n);
            System.out.println("DEGREE: " + c);
            System.out.println("DEPARTMENT: " + d);
            System.out.println("COLLEGE: " + co);
            System.out.println();
        }
        Statement st1= cn1.createStatement();
        sql1="SELECT * FROM event";
        ResultSet rs1 = st1.executeQuery(sql1);

        System.out.println("FROM SECOND DB: test");
        while(rs1.next())
        {
            int i = rs1.getInt("eid");
            String t=rs1.getString("title");
            Date d=rs1.getDate("date");
            String v=rs1.getString("venue");
            //Display values System.out.println("EVENT
            ID: " + i);
            System.out.println("EVENT NAME: " +t);
            System.out.println("DATE: " + d);
            System.out.println("VENUE: " + v);
            System.out.println();
        }
    }
    catch(Exception e){System.out.println("An Exception has occurred:"+e);}
}
}
```

Output 15.4

```
Connecting to
database...
Creating statement...
FROM FIRST DB: stud
REGISTER NO: 56121
NAME: kannan
DEGREE: BCA
DEPARTMENT: CA
COLLEGE: SHC
REGISTER NO: 56122
NAME: kumutha
DEGREE: MSc
DEPARTMENT: maths
COLLEGE: MKJC
FROM SECOND DB: test
EVENT ID: 818301
EVENT NAME:
inauguration
association
DATE: 2016-07-02
VENUE: DBIS
EVENT ID: 818302
EVENT NAME: Teachers
day celebration
DATE: 2016-09-05
VENUE: Corrino Hall
```

The database driver is just the same and it is assigned to the string type variable `JDBC_DRIVER`. This variable is assigned as parameter to the `forName()` method to load the MySQL driver. Here only one vendor-specific database is used, so there is no need for two drivers. However, two URLs are needed to locate two different databases. To load the two databases, the string variables `URL`, `URL1` are declared. The variable `URL` holds the URL for first database `stud` and the second `URL1` variable holds the URL for accessing the second database `test`. Two `Connection` objects `cn`, `cn1` are declared to connect with the databases. The object `cn` establishes a connection with database `stud` using the statement `Connection cn = DriverManager.getConnection(URL,USER,PASS)` and the `cn` object is further used to create `Statement` object `st` using the statement `st= cn.createStatement();` the `st` object will be used to execute the `SELECT` query to extract all the records from the table `sprofile`. In the statement `ResultSet rs = st.executeQuery(sql)`, the `executeQuery()` method is called with parameter `sql`, the string type variable that contains a `SELECT` query, and then extracted records are assigned to the `ResultSet` object `rs`. As already explained in the previous example, the `while` loop with parameter `rs.next()` extracts the data row by row until the cursor reaches the last record and displays the data to the user. Likewise, the same procedures are repeated to extract data from a table `event` of database `test`. The object `cn1` is assigned with the URL of the table `event` and then the `Statement` object `st1` is created while calling the `createStatement()` method using `cn1`.The result set is created using the statement `ResultSet rs1 = st1.executeQuery(sql1)`, where the `Statement` object `st1` triggers the `executeQuery(sql1)` method with the parameter `sql1`. All the records from the table `event` are then extracted and assigned to the `ResultSet` object `rs1`. The record set is traversed using the `while` loop with parameter `rs1.next()` and during each iteration, the entire row is extracted column by column and displayed to the user.

Programs 15.3 and 15.4 showed how to interact with the databases and tables in the same machine. **Program 15.5** implements the networking concepts. The client program sends a customer ID to the server program. The server program has the code for receiving the ID from a client, interacting with the DB, and it then sends back the result to the client.

Program 15.5

```
Server Program import java.net.*;
import java.io.*;
import java.sql.*;
public class NDBServer
{
   static final String driver = "com.mysql.
   jdbc.Driver";
   static final String url = "jdbc:mysql://
   localhost:3306/ abook";
   static final String UN = "root";
   static final String PW = "root";
   public static void main(String[] args)
   {
      try
      {
         Class.forName(driver);
         System.out.println("Connecting
         with DB....");
         Connection cn = DriverManager.
         getConnection(url,UN,PW);
         Statement st =
         cn.createStatement();
         ServerSocket ss=new
         ServerSocket(2020);
         System.out.println("Waiting for
         client request.....");
```

ServerOutput 15.5

```
Connecting with DB....
Waiting for client request.....
Connected with the client.
ClientProgram
import java.net.*;
import java.io.*;
public class NDBClient
{
public static void main(String[]
args)
{
try
{
int id;
Socket s=new
Socket("127.0.0.1",2020);
System.out.println("Connected with
SERVER...");
InputStream is=s.getInputStream();
DataInputStream dis =new
DataInputStream(is);
```

```
        Socket s=ss.accept();
        System.out.println("Connected
        with the client.");
        InputStream is=s.
        getInputStream();
        DataInputStream dis =new
        DataInputStream(is);
        OutputStream os=s.
        getOutputStream();
        DataOutputStream dos=new
        DataOutputStream(os);
        int id=dis.readInt();
        String SQL;
        SQL = "SELECT * FROM caddress";
        ResultSet rs =
        st.executeQuery(SQL);
        while(rs.next())
        {
            if(id==rs.getInt("ID"))
            {
                String msg="AVAILABLE";
                dos.writeUTF(msg);
                dos.writeInt(rs.
                getInt("ID"));
                dos.writeUTF(rs.
                getString("name"));
                dos.writeInt(rs.
                getInt("doorno"));
                dos.writeUTF(rs.
                getString("street"));
                dos.writeUTF(rs.
                getString("place"));
                dos.writeInt(rs.
                getInt("pincode"));
                dos.writeUTF(rs.
                getString("district"));
                dos.writeUTF(rs.
                getString("state"));
                dos.writeUTF(rs.
                getString("mobile"));
                dos.writeUTF(rs.
                getString("email"));
                break;
            }
            else if(rs.isLast())
            {
                if(id!=rs.getInt("ID"))
                {
                    String msg="Customer
                    with ID: "+id+" does
                    is not exist";
                    dos.writeUTF(msg);
                }
            }
        }
    }
```

```
OutputStream os=s.getOutputStream();
DataOutputStream dos=new
DataOutputStream(os);
InputStreamReader reader=new
InputStreamReader(System.in);
BufferedReader br=new
BufferedReader(reader);
System.out.println("Enter the customer
ID:");
id=Integer.parseInt(br.readLine());
dos.writeInt(id);
String m=dis.readUTF();
if(m.equals("AVAILABLE"))
{
System.out.println("CUSTOMER ID:
"+dis. readInt());
System.out.println("NAME: "+dis.
readUTF());
System.out.println("DOOR NO: "+dis.
readInt());
System.out.println("STREET: "+dis.
readUTF());
System.out.println("PLACE: "+dis.
readUTF());
System.out.println("PINCODE: "+dis.
readInt());
System.out.println("DISTRICT: "+dis.
readUTF());
System.out.println("STATE: "+dis.
readUTF());
System.out.println("MOBILE NO: "+dis.
readUTF());
System.out.println("E-MAIL: "+dis.
readUTF());
}
else
{
System.out.println(m);
}
}
catch(Exception e){System.out.
println("An
Exception has occurred: "+e);}
}
}
```

Client Output 15.5

```
Run - 1
Connected with SERVER...
Enter the customer ID:
125
CUSTOMER ID: 125
NAME: meganathan
DOOR NO: 84
STREET: cinnakulam street
```

```
        catch(Exception e)
        {System. out.println("An Exception
        has occurred"+e);}
    }
}
```

```
PLACE: tirupattur
PINCODE: 635601
DISTRICT: vellore STATE: tamil nadu
MOBILE NO: 999756482
E-MAIL: megatpt@gmail.com
Run - 2
Connected with SERVER... Enter the
customer ID:
129
Customer with ID No: 129 does not
exist
```

In the server program, the driver name, URL of the database and authentication details are assigned to variables `driver`, `url`, `UN` and `PW` respectively just before the `main()` method. The driver for the MySQL database is loaded using the `forName()` method. The `Connection` object and `Statement` object are created one after the other, to interact with the database. The ServerSocket object `ss` is created with the specified port number 2020 using the `ServerSocket` constructor. Using the `ss` object, the server program listens for incoming client requests on the port number 2020. So, the object `ss` is used only for connecting with the client. In the statement `Socket s=ss.accept()`, the `accept()` method is invoked using the `ss` object; this method is actually listening for incoming client requests. If the client request has arrived, the object of client socket will be connected with `Socket` object `s`. The remaining statements of the program will be executed based on whether the client request has arrived or not. Once the request has arrived on the port number, the remaining statements are executed, otherwise the execution waits here for any incoming request. The `InputStream` object `is` is assigned while invoking the `getInputStream()` method through `Socket` object `s`. This method extracts the id which was sent by the client program and assigns it to the object `is` as bits. To make the data readable, the object `is` should be assigned to the `DataInputStrame` object `dis` through its constructor. The statement `dis.readInt()` extracts the id from the object `dis` and assigns it to the local variable `id`. The `SELECT` query is created to get the record from the table and assigned to the string type variable `SQL`. Using the statement `ResultSet rs = st.executeQuery(SQL)` the `executeQuery()` method with parameter `SQL` is called using the object `st` and extracted records are stored in the `ResultSet` object `rs`. As usual, the `while` loop with parameter `rs.next()` is used to read the records one by one. But here, the record which matches the given `id` is needed. So the given `id` value is compared with the data in the table using the statement `if(id==rs.getInt("ID"))` and if a match is found, the server sends the message 'AVAILABLE' to the client and then the entire row which matches the `id` is extracted column by column. Each data unit is sent to the client program. If a match is not found, the server sends another message stating that the given `id` is not available. On the other hand, the client program creates a `Socket` object with the IP and port number of the server machine and server program. First the client program gets the `id` through `InputStreamReader` and `BufferedReader`. Using the `OutputStream` and `DataOutputStream` it sends the `id` to get the details. If a match is found, the server first sends the available message, after which all other data is sent one by one. The client then checks the first received data. If the message states that the id is available, the remaining data is received and displayed one by one, otherwise the server sends the message to the client that the `id` is not available. The client receives the messages and displays it to the user. The server waits for another client request.

15.5 CREATING A NEW DATABASE AND TABLE WITH JDBC

A new database or a table in the existing database can also be created in the program itself. Using a SQL query in DDL (Data Definition Language), a database or table is created with slight modifications in the physical connection with the database server. The existence of a database or a table can be checked using an interface `java.sql.DatabaseMetaData` (Section 15.7 discusses the database metadata). The same basic steps explained in Section 15.5 can be used here, but the database name should not be specified in the database URL. So the parameter of the `getConnection()` method is passed without a database name. In Program 15.6 the existence of a database has not been checked, so the existence of a database has to be manually checked or the database metadata used. **Program 15.6** creates a new database which does not exist in the MySQL database server.

Program 15.6

```
import java.io.*;
import java.sql.*;
public class NewDB
{
   static final String DRIVER = "com.mysql.jdbc.Driver";
   static final String URL = "jdbc:mysql://localhost:3306/";
   public static void main(String[] args)
   {
      try
      {
         Class.forName(DRIVER);
         String UN="root";
         String PW="root";
         Connection cn = DriverManager.
         getConnection(URL,UN ,PW );
         Statement st = cn.createStatement();
         st.executeUpdate("CREATE DATABASE firstdb");

         System.out.println("DATABASE HAS BEEN CREATED, Check the MySQL Server");
      }
      catch(Exception e){System.out.println("An Exception has occurred"+e);}
   }
}
```

Output 15.6

```
DATABASE HAS BEEN CREATED,
Check the MySQL Server
```

The two static variables `DRIVER` and `URL` have been declared in the beginning itself for assigning a MySQL DB driver name and database URL. In the database URL, the name of the database has not been specified because a new database is going to be created in that server; that's why it is left empty. The `DRIVER` variable is assigned as a parameter in the `Class.forName()` method for establishing a connection with the MySQL server. String variables `UN` and `PW` contain a username and password respectively. After the connection is established with MySQL Server, a `Connection` object `cn` is created by passing `URL`, UN and `PW` as parameters through the `DriverManager.getConnection()` method. If the driver manager identifies a particular database in the MySQL server, it will try to connect with the application using the username and password. If the connection is successfully established, the application can interact with the database server and if not, an exception will be triggered. A `createStatement()` is invoked and assigned to a `Statement` object `st`. By using `Statement` object `st`, `executeUpate()` method is called with a SQL query for creating a database as a parameter. The DriverManager creates a new database named `firstdb` in MySQL server. **Program 15.7** creates a new table in the database `firstdb`.

Program 15.7

```
import java.sql.*;
/*
* It creates a new table einfo in the database which was created in the program
15.6
*
*/
public class NewTable
{
   static final String DRIVER = "com.mysql.jdbc.Driver";
   static final String URL = "jdbc:mysql://localhost:3306/firstdb";
   public static void main(String[] args)
   {
      try
      {
         Class.forName(DRIVER);
         String UN="root";
         String PW="root";
         Connection cn = DriverManager.
         getConnection(URL,UN ,PW );
         Statement st = cn.createStatement();
         st.executeUpdate("CREATE TABLE einfo(eid INTEGER not Null,"
         + "title VARCHAR(100)not Null ,"
         + "date DATE not Null, time INTEGER not Null,"
         + " venue VARCHAR(100) not Null,"
         + "PRIMARY KEY(eid))");
         System.out.println("TABLE HAS BEEN CREATED, Check the MySQL Server");
      }
      catch(Exception e){System.out.println("An Exception has occurred"+e);}
   }
}
```

Output 15.7

```
TABLE HAS BEEN CREATED,
Check the database in MySQL
Server
```

This program is just like the previous one, but it creates a new table `einfo` in the database `firstdb` which was created in Program 15.6. The table `einfo` is created with five columns, all the five columns have been specified as not `null`. After successfully creating a table in the database `firstdb`, a message will be displayed. This program just demonstrates how to create a new table through a program instead of creating it in the database server. All the DML SQL queries can be used to manipulate the table. To perform insertion, deletion and updation operations with the table, refer to Program 15.2.

15.6 WORKING WITH DATABASE METADATA

Generally, metadata means data about data. Metadata describes the data or database. Much useful data can be gathered through the metadata. For example, if the metadata is gathered from a particular document, it gives the details such as date and time when created or last modified, type of document, privileges, author's name, title, category, size. The `DatabaseMetaData` interface in the `java.sql` package provides various methods to gather metadata. Table 15.11 describes various methods available in `DatabaseMetaData` interface. Before using the methods to extract the metadata, first an object of `DatabaseMetaData` should be created using the `getMetaData()` method of `Connection` interface.

Table 15.11 Methods in DatabaseMetaData interface

S. no.	Methods	Description
1	`getDriverName()`	Gets the name of the JDBC driver.
2	`getDriverVersion()`	Brings the version number of the JDBC driver.
3	`getUserName()`	Returns the user name of the databse.
4	`getDatabaseProductName()` `getDatabaseProductVersion()`	The first one returns the database product name and the second one returns the version.
5	`ResultSet getTables( String catalog,String schemaPattern, String tableNamePattern, String[] types)`	Returns the table description and other useful information. The types may be TABLE, VIEW, ALIAS, SYSTEM TABLE, and so on.

Program 15.8 retrieves the metadata for the given database and tables available in the database.

Program 15.8

```
import java.sql.*;
public class DBMetadata
{
   static final String DRIVER = "com.mysql.jdbc.Driver";
   static final String URL = "jdbc:mysql://localhost:3306/demo";
   static final String USER = "root";
   static final String PASS = "root";
   public static void main(String[] args)
   {
      try
      {
         Class.forName(DRIVER);
         Connection cn = DriverManager.getConnection(URL,USER,PASS);
         DatabaseMetaData md=cn.
         getMetaData();
         System.out.println("Name of the
         Driver: "+md.getDriverName());
         System.out.println("Version of the
         Driver: "+md.getDriverVersion());
         System.out.println("USER NAME:
         "+md.getUserName());
         System.out.println("DB
         Product Name: "+md.
         getDatabaseProductName());
         System.out.println("DB
         Product Verison: "+md.
         getDatabaseProductVersion());
         String t[]={"TABLE"};
         ResultSet rmd=md.getTables(null, null, null, t);
         System.out.println("TABLES IN A DB:");
         while(rmd.next())
         {
            System.out.println("Table name is : "+rmd.getString(3));
         }
         cn.close();
      }
      catch(Exception e){System. out.println("An Exception has occurred"+e);}
   }
}
```

Output 15.8

```
Name of the Driver: MySQL-AB JDBC
Driver
Version of the Driver: mysql-
connector-java-5.1.23 ( Revision:
${bzr.revision-id} )
USER NAME: root@localhost
DB Product Name: MySQL
DB Product Verison: 5.6.26-log
TABLES IN A DB: Table name is : emp
Table name is : studinfo
```

As already explained, two important pieces of information are needed for establishing a connection with the database. The first thing is the driver and the second one is the database URL which points to the actual database. These two pieces of information are assigned to the static type String variables `DRIVER` and `URL`. To retrieve metadata about the database, an object of `DatabaseMetaData` needs to be created. The `getMetaData()` method is invoked with the `Connection` object `cn` and assigned to `DatabaseMetaData` object `md`. With the help of the `md` object, metadata such as driver name, driver version, and product name can be retrieved. Using the output stream, all these metadata are displayed one by one. Program 15.8 retrieved the information about the database. **Program 15.9** uses the `DatabaseMetaData` to list the available tables in a specified database.

Program 15.9

```
import java.sql.*;
public class LISTTB
{
    static final String DRIVER = "com.mysql.jdbc.Driver";
    static final String URL = "jdbc:mysql://localhost/test";
    static final String UN = "root";
    static final String PW = "root";
    public static void main(String[] args)
    {
        try
        {
            Class.forName(DRIVER);
            System.out.println("Connecting database...");
            Connection cn = DriverManager.
            getConnection(URL, UN, PW);
            System.out.println("Connected successfully...");
            Statement st = cn.createStatement();
            DatabaseMetaData dbmd = cn.getMetaData();
            String[] types = {
            "TABLE" };
            ResultSet rs = dbmd.getTables(null, null, null, types);
            while (rs.next())
            {
                String tn = rs.getString(3);
                String tc = rs.getString(1);
                System.out.println("TABLE NAME: "+tn);
                System.out.println("TABLE CATALOG: "+tc);
            }
        }

        catch(Exception e){System.out.println("An Exception has occurred: "+e);}
}}
```

Output 15.9

```
Connecting database...
Connected successfully...
TABLE NAME: demo
TABLE CATALOG: test
TABLE NAME: event
TABLE CATALOG: test
```

The driver name, URL and database credentials are assigned to the predefined static type string variables `PW`, `URL`, `UN` and `DRIVER`. The `Try.... Catch` block is used to handle the `SQLExceptions`. As usual, the driver for the MySQL database is loaded with the `forName()` method. The connection with the database is established through the statement `Connection cn = DriverManager.getConnection(URL, UN, PW)` and passes the result to the `Connection` object `cn`. This `Connection` object is used to create a `Statement` object `st` through the `Statement st = cn.createStatement()`. The `getMetaData()` method is invoked using the `Connection` object `cn` and all the metadata will be stored in the object `dbmd`. String type array variable `types` with predefined value 'TABLE' is used, to be passed as a parameter in the `getTables()` method. The `getTables(null, null, null, types)` method has four parameters, each referred to by its sequence number, like parameter 1, 2, 3 and 4. Parameter 1 represents the database name, Parameter 3 represents the table and the last one specifies what type of information is retrieved, such as TABLE, VIEW, here values TABLE and it is stored in String type array `types`. The statement `ResultSet rs = dbmd.getTables(null, null, null, types)` of the `dbmd` object triggers the `getTables()` method. It stores all the metadata about the table in the `ResultSet` object `rs`. The `while` loop traverses the metadata by each iteration. In each iteration, the database name is retrieved using `String tn = rs.getString(3)` and the table name is retrieved using `String tc = rs.getString(1)`.

Program 15.10 checks for the existence of a table in the database.

Program 15.10

```
import java.sql.*;
import java.io.*;
public class TBEXIT
{
   static final String DRIVER = "com.mysql.jdbc.Driver";
   static final String URL = "jdbc:mysql://localhost/test";
   static final String UN = "root";
   static final String PW = "root";
   public static void main(String[] args)
   {
      try
      {
         Class.forName(DRIVER);
         System.out.println("Connecting database...");
         Connection cn = DriverManager.getConnection(URL, UN, PW);
         System.out.println("Connected successfully...");
         DatabaseMetaData dbmd = cn.getMetaData();
         String[] types = {
         "TABLE" };
         InputStreamReader reader=new
         InputStreamReader(System.in);
         BufferedReader br=new BufferedReader(reader);
         System.out.println("Enter the table name to
         know the existence: ");
         String dtable=br.readLine();
         ResultSet rs = dbmd.getTables(null, null,
         null, types);
         while (rs.next())
         {
            String tn = rs.getString(3);

            if(tn.equals(dtable))
            {
               System.out.println("TABLE EXISTS");
               break;
            }
            else if(rs.isLast())
            {
               if(tn !=dtable)
               {
                  System.out.println("TABLE doesn't EXIST");
               }
            }
         }
      }
      catch(Exception e){System.out.println("An Exception has occurred: "+e);}
   }
}
```

Output 15.10

```
Connecting database...
Connected
successfully...
Enter the table name
to know the existence:
stud
TABLE doesn't
EXIST Connecting
database... Connected
successfully... Enter
the table name to know
the existence:
event
TABLE EXISTS
```

This program checks for the existence of a given table from the catalog. After establishing a successful connection with the database, the `DatabaseMetaData` object `dbmd` is declared while calling the `getMetaData()` using the `Connection` object `cn`. The `DatabaseMetaData` object `dbmd` triggers the `getTables()` method with String type array `types`. As already mentioned, the 3rd parameter of the `getTables()` method represents the table, therefore, only the 3rd parameter is referred to here. The table name is received from the user through `InputStreamReader` and `BufferedReader` and stored in a string type variable `dtable`. The received table is then compared with the information presented in the `ResultSet` object `rs` using the `while` loop. In each iteration of the `while` loop, the `getString(3)` method is called with parameter 3 and the retrieved table name is stored in the variable `tn` and then compared with `dtable`. If found equal, the 'table exists' message will be displayed otherwise the 'table doesn't exist' message will be displayed. **Program 15.11** lists the available databases and checks for the existence of a given database.

Program 15.11

```
import java.sql.*;
import java.io.*;
public class DBEXIST
{
    static final String DRIVER = "com.mysql.jdbc.
    Driver";
    static final String URL = "jdbc:mysql://
    localhost:3306/";
    static final String UN = "root";
    static final String PW = "root";
    public static void main(String[] args)
    {
        try
        {
            Class.forName(DRIVER);
            System.out.println("Connecting
            database...");
            Connection cn = DriverManager.
            getConnection(URL, UN, PW);
            System.out.println("Connected
            successfully...");
            DatabaseMetaData dbmd = cn.getMetaData();
            ResultSet rs = dbmd.getCatalogs();
            System.out.println("LIST OF AVAILABE
            DATABASES");
            while (rs.next())
            {
                String cat = rs.getString(1);
                System.out.println("* "+cat);
            }
            InputStreamReader reader=new
            InputStreamReader(System.in);
            BufferedReader br=new
            BufferedReader(reader);
            System.out.println("Enter the Database name
            to know the existence: ");
            String db=br.readLine();
            ResultSet rs1 = dbmd.getCatalogs();
```

Output 15.11

```
Run - 1
Connecting database...
Connected successfully...
LIST OF AVAILABE DATABASES
* information_schema
* karthik
* mysql
* performance_schema
* stud
* sys
* test
Enter the Database name to
know the existence:
event
event DATABASE doesn't
EXIST
Run - 2
Connecting database...
Connected successfully...
LIST OF AVAILABE DATABASES
* information_schema
* karthik
* mysql
* performance_schema
* stud
* sys
* test
Enter the Database name to
know the existence:
stud
stud DATABASE EXISTS
```

```
        while (rs1.next())
        {
            String cat = rs1.getString(1);
            if(cat.equals(db))
            {
                System.out.println(db+ " DATABASE EXISTS");
                break;
            }
            else if(rs1.isLast())
            {
                if(cat !=db)
                {
                    System.out.println(db+" DATABASE doesn't EXIST");
                }
            }
        }
    }
    catch(Exception e){System.out.println("An
    Exception has occurred: "+e);}
  }
}
```

This program lists all the available databases from the MySQL server and checks for the existence of a given database. Like the previous programs it also creates the `DatabaseMetaData` object `dbmd`. This object is used to call the `getCatalog()` method and the statement `ResultSet rs = dbmd.getCatalogs()` retrieves all the available databases from the database server and assigns to the `ResultSet` object `st`. The `ResultSet` object `st` is traversed using the `while` loop; two `while` loops are used here. The first one extracts all the databases one by one and displays to the user in each iteration. The second one compares the given database name with the databases presented in the `ResultSet` object `rs`; if a match is found, it displays a message that the database exists otherwise it displays a message that the database doesn't exist.

`ResultSetMetaData` interface

An object created for `ResultSet` interface contains an entire set of records from the specified table. Using an object of `ResultSetMetaData` interface, a lot of useful information about the table can be retrieved. Table 15.12 shows the various methods provided by `ResultSetMetaData`. Just like `DatabaseMetaData`, an object needs to be obtained through invoking a `getMetaData()` method of `ResultSet` interface.

Table 15.12 Methods in `ResultSetMetaData` interface

S. no.	Methods	Description
1.	`getColumnCount()`	Gives the total number of columns in a table.
2.	`getColumnName(int index)`	Gets the column name of the specified column index.
3.	`getColumnTypeName(int index)`	Returns the datatype of a column of the specified index.
4.	`getTableName(int index)`	Returns the table name.

Program 15.12 demonstrates various metadata about the table through ResultSet.

Program 15.12

```
import java.sql.*;
public class TableMD
{
   /*
   *This program demonstrates about various metadata about table through *
   ResultSet
   */
   static final String DRIVER = "com.mysql.jdbc.Driver";
   static final String URL = "jdbc:mysql://
   localhost:3306/demo";
   static final String USER = "root";
   static final String PASS = "root";
   public static void main(String[] args)
   {
      try
      {
         Class.forName(DRIVER);
         Connection cn = DriverManager.
         getConnection(URL,USER,PASS);
         Statement s=cn.createStatement();
         ResultSet r=s.executeQuery("SELECT * FROM
         emp");
         ResultSetMetaData rd=r.getMetaData();
         System.out.println("Table Name: "+rd.
         getTableName(1));
         System.out.println("Total Number of Columns
         in the table: "+rd.getColumnCount());
         System.out.println("Name of Column
         1 and datatype and its size:
         "+rd.getColumnName(1)+" "+rd.
         getColumnTypeName(1)+" "+rd.
         getColumnDisplaySize(1));
         System.out.println("Name of Column
         2 and datatype and its size:
         "+rd. getColumnName(2)+" "+rd.
         getColumnTypeName(2)+" "+rd.getColumnDisplaySize(2));
         System.out.println("Name of Column 3 and datatype and its size:
         "+rd. getColumnName(3)+" "+rd.getColumnTypeName(3)+" "+rd.
         getColumnDisplaySize(3));
         System.out.println("Name of Column 4 and datatype and its size:
         "+rd. getColumnName(4)+" "+rd.getColumnTypeName(4)+" "+rd.
         getColumnDisplaySize(4));
         System.out.println("Name of Column 5 and datatype and its size:
         "+rd. getColumnName(5)+" "+rd.getColumnTypeName(5)+" "+rd.
         getColumnDisplaySize(5));
         cn.close();
      }
      catch(Exception e){System.out.println("An Exception has occurred"+e);}
   }
}
```

Output 15.12

```
Table Name: emp
Total Number of
Columns in the table:
5
Name of Column 1 and
datatype and its size:
eid INT UNSIGNED 10
Name of Column 2 and
datatype and its size:
ename VARCHAR 45
Name of Column 3 and
datatype and its size:
dept VARCHAR 45
Name of Column 4 and
datatype and its size:
exp INT UNSIGNED 10
Name of Column 5 and
datatype and its size:
desig VARCHAR 45
```

After successfully establishing a connection with the database, a `ResultSet` object `r` is created by invoking an `executeQuery ()` method through `Statement` object `s`. An SQL query which extracts all the records from the table `emp` is specified as a parameter in an `executeQuery()` method. The `ResultSet` object `r` contains all the records from the table `emp`. So far, the `ResultSet` objects were used for accessing and manipulating data from a table. But here the `ResultSet` object `r` will be used to retrieve the metadata about the table `emp`. The `getMetaData()` method of a `ResultSet` interface helps to retrieve the metadata. Through the statement `ResultSetMetaData rd=r.getMetaData(),` all the metadata about the table `emp` is passed down to the object `rd` of `ResutSetMetaData`. The `ResultSetMetaData` interface contains many useful methods to mine metadata from the given `ResultSet` object (for more information on this, see Table 15.13). For example, the statement `rd.getTableName()` extracts the table name. Likewise, all other methods mentioned in Table 15.13 extract other useful information about the table. Using the OutputStream method, this information is displayed one by one.

SUMMARY

1. JDBC is an API (Application Programming Interface) specially designed for Java-based applications to connect and interact with different databases.
2. The class/interface which provides a mean to access particular DB is called a JDBC driver. Each database has its own driver.
3. JDBC drivers can be classified into four types such as, *Type 1:* JDBC-ODBC bridge, *Type 2:* Native-API driver, *Type 3:* Middle-ware or Net pure java driver, *Type 4:* Pure Java driver.
4. JDBC architecture is sometimes classified as two-tier and three-tier.
5. The driver is a piece of software that knows how to interact with the data source.
6. The most common approach to register a driver is by using `Class.forName` (*String class name*) method.
7. A connection with the database can be established using the statement `DriverManager. getConnection()`.
8. Records (each row is a record) returned by executing a SQL statement will be stored in the object of a ResultSet.
9. ResultSet can be set as scrollable or non-scrollable. If the ResultSet is specified as TYPE_FORWARD_ONLY then it becomes a non-scrollable result set.
10. Metadata means data about data. It describes the data or database.

SHORT QUESTIONS

1. What is JDBC?
2. What is the role of drivers in JDBC?
3. What is `ResultSet`?
4. List the various types of drivers available in JDBC.
5. Compare JDBC-API and ODBC-API.
6. Differentiate between two-tier and three-tier architecture.
7. Compare a scrollable and a non-scrollable `ResultSet`.
8. List the basic steps to develop an application with JDBC.
9. Compare the following JDBC statements:
   (a) `Statement`
   (b) `PreparedStatement`
   (c) `CallableStatement`
10. How can a programmer create and establish a connection with a database?
11. What is metadata?
12. Tabulate the methods available to establish and manage a connection with the database.
13. What is a stored procedure?
14. How can a programmer extract metadata about the database?
15. Write a code segment to extract data from a `ResultSet` object.

COMPREHENSIVE QUESTIONS

1. Illustrate the two-tier and three-tier architecture of a JDBC with a neat diagram.
2. Give a brief note on the various types of drivers.
3. Draw a diagram showing the general architecture of a JDBC and explain the interaction among components.
4. Explain the following classes/interfaces available in JDBC-API.
   (a) `DriverManager`
   (b) `Driver`
   (c) `Connection`
   (d) `Statement`
   (e) `ResutlSet`
5. Explain the basic steps in developing a JDBC application.
6. Give a detailed note on `ResultSet`.
7. Explain the methods used to navigate a cursor in a `ResultSet`.
8. Briefly explain `DatabaseMetadata` with an example.
9. Give a note on `ResultSetMetaData` interface.
10. Explain the methods used for viewing and updating data in a `ResultSet`.

SOLVED PROGRAMS

1. The Program 1demonstrate the creation of new Database and subsequent programs create table and performs CRUD operations in this database. It creates the database *deptcs* in MySQL.

```
import java.sql.*;
public class SIRDB
{
  static final String JDBC_DRIVER = "com.mysql.jdbc.Driver";
  static final String DB_URL = "jdbc:mysql://localhost/";
  static final String USER = "root";
  static final String PASS = "root";
  public static void main(String[] args)
  {
     Connection cn = null;
     Statement st = null;
     try
     {
        Class.forName("com.mysql.jdbc.Driver");
        System.out.println("Connecting to database...");
        cn = DriverManager.getConnection(DB_URL, USER, PASS);
        System.out.println("Creating database...");
        st = cn.createStatement();
        String sql = "CREATE DATABASE DEPTCS";
        st.executeUpdate(sql);
        System.out.println("Database created successfully...");
     }
     catch(Exception e){ System.out.println("An Exception has been occurred"+e);}
  }
}
```

Output

```
Connecting to database...
Creating database...
Database created
successfully...
```

2. The Program 2 creates a new table *sir* in the database *deptcs* which was created in the previous program.

```
import java.sql.*;
public class SIRTABLE
{
```

```
static final String DRIVER = "com.mysql.jdbc.Driver";
static final String URL = "jdbc:mysql://localhost/deptcs";
static final String UN = "root";
static final String PW = "root";
public static void main(String[] args)
{
  Connection cn = null;
  Statement st = null;
  try
  {
    Class.forName("com.mysql.jdbc.Driver");
    System.out.println("Connecting to a database...");
    cn = DriverManager.getConnection(URL, UN, PW);
    System.out.println("Connected successfully...");
    System.out.println("Creating table...");
    st = cn.createStatement();
    String sql = "CREATE TABLE SIR " +
    "(regno INTEGER not NULL, " +
    " name VARCHAR(100) not NULL, " +
    " year INTEGER, " +
    " sex VARCHAR(25) not NULL, " +
    "religion VARCHAR(25) not NULL, "+
    " PRIMARY KEY ( regno ))";
    st.executeUpdate(sql);
    System.out.println("Table has been created....");
  }
  catch(Exception e){ System.out.println("An Exception has been occurred"+e);}
}
}
```

Output

```
Connecting to a database...
Connected successfully...
Creating table...
Table has been created....
```

3. The Program 3 inserts five records into the table sir which was created in the previous program.

```
import java.sql.*;
public class SIRINSERT
{
  static final String DRIVER = "com.mysql.jdbc.Driver";
  static final String URL = "jdbc:mysql://localhost/deptcs";
  static final String UN = "root";
  static final String PW = "root";
  public static void main(String[] args)
  {
    Connection cn = null;
    Statement st = null;
    try
    {
      Class.forName(DRIVER);
      System.out.println("Connecting
      database...");
      cn = DriverManager.getConnection(URL, UN, PW);
      System.out.println("Connected successfully...");
      System.out.println("Inserting records...");
      st = cn.createStatement();
      String sql = "INSERT INTO sir " +
      "VALUES (1215671, 'Anandhi', 2012, 'FEMALE', 'HINDU')";
      st.executeUpdate(sql);
      sql = "INSERT INTO sir " +
      "VALUES (1215672, 'Joseph', 2010, 'MALE', 'CHRISTIAN')";
      st.executeUpdate(sql);
```

Output

```
Connecting database...
Connected successfully...
Inserting records...
Inserted successfully...
```

```
        sql = "INSERT INTO sir " +
        "VALUES (1215673, 'Rani', 2013, 'FEMALE', 'CHRISTIAN')";
        st.executeUpdate(sql);
        sql = "INSERT INTO sir " +
        "VALUES (1215674, 'Arun', 2009, 'MALE', 'HINDU')";
        st.executeUpdate(sql);
        sql = "INSERT INTO sir " +
        "VALUES (1215675, 'Perumal', 2011, 'MALE', 'HINDU')";
        st.executeUpdate(sql);
        System.out.println("Inserted successfully...");
     }
     catch(Exception e){ System.out.println("An Exception has been occurred"+e);}
  }
 }
```

4. The Program 4 fetches all the records from the table *sir* and displays it to the user row by row.

```
import java.sql.*;
public class SIRDISPLAY
{
  static final String DRIVER = "com.mysql.jdbc.Driver";
  static final String URL = "jdbc:mysql://localhost/deptcs";
  static final String UN = "root";
  static final String PW = "root";
  public static void main(String[] args)
  {
     Connection cn = null;
     Statement st = null;
     try
     {
        Class.forName(DRIVER);
        System.out.println("Connecting database...");
        cn = DriverManager.getConnection(URL, UN, PW);
        System.out.println("Connected successfully...");
        st = cn.createStatement();
        String sql = "SELECT * FROM sir";
        ResultSet rs = st.executeQuery(sql);
        System.out.println("Fetching records...");
        while(rs.next())
        {
           //Retrieve by column name
           int r = rs.getInt("regno");
           String n = rs.getString("name");
           int y = rs.getInt("year");
           String s = rs.getString("sex");
           String re = rs.getString("religion");
           //Display values
           System.out.print("Register No: " + r);
           System.out.print(" Name: " + n);
           System.out.print(" Year: " + y);
           System.out.print(" Sex: " + s);
           System.out.print(" Religion: " + re);
           System.out.println();
        }
        rs.close();
     }
     catch(Exception e){ System.out.println("An Exception has been occurred:
"+e);}
```

```
    }
  }
```

Output

```
Connecting database...
Connected successfully...
Fetching records...
Register No: 1215671 Name: Anandhi Year: 2012 Sex: FEMALE Religion: HINDU
Register No: 1215672 Name: Joseph Year: 2010 Sex: MALE Religion: CHRISTIAN
Register No: 1215673 Name: Rani Year: 2013 Sex: FEMALE Religion: CHRISTIAN
Register No: 1215674 Name: Arun Year: 2009 Sex: MALE Religion: HINDU
Register No: 1215675 Name: Perumal Year: 2011 Sex: MALE Religion: HINDU
```

5. This program updates the name *rani* into *reeta* which was inserted in the program 3.

```
import java.sql.*;
public class SIRUPDATE
{
  static final String DRIVER = "com.mysql.jdbc.Driver";
  static final String URL = "jdbc:mysql://localhost/deptcs";
  static final String UN = "root";
  static final String PW = "root";
  public static void main(String[] args)
  {
    Connection cn = null;
    Statement st = null;
    try
    {
      Class.forName(DRIVER);
      System.out.println("Connecting database...");
      cn = DriverManager.getConnection(URL, UN, PW);
      System.out.println("Connected successfully...");
      st = cn.createStatement();
      String sql = "UPDATE sir SET name = 'Reeta' WHERE regno =1215673";
      st.executeUpdate(sql);
      sql = "SELECT * FROM sir";
      ResultSet rs = st.executeQuery(sql);
      System.out.println("Fetching records...");
      while(rs.next())
      {
        //Retrieve by column name
        int r = rs.getInt("regno");
        String n = rs.getString("name");
        int y = rs.getInt("year");
        String s = rs.getString("sex");
        String re = rs.getString("religion");
        //Display values
        System.out.print("Register No: " + r);
        System.out.print(" Name: " + n);
        System.out.print(" Year: " + y);
        System.out.print(" Sex: " + s);
        System.out.print(" Religion: " + re);
        System.out.println();
      }
      rs.close();
```

```
    }
    catch(Exception e){ System.out.println("An Exception has been occurred:
"+e);}
  }
 }
```

Output

```
Connecting database...
Connected successfully...
Fetching records...
Register No: 1215671 Name: Anandhi Year: 2012 Sex: FEMALE Religion: HINDU
Register No: 1215672 Name: Joseph Year: 2010 Sex: MALE Religion: CHRISTIAN
Register No: 1215673 Name: Reeta Year: 2013 Sex: FEMALE Religion:
CHRISTIAN
Register No: 1215674 Name: Arun Year: 2009 Sex: MALE Religion: HINDU
Register No: 1215675 Name: Perumal Year: 2011 Sex: MALE Religion: HINDU
```

6. The Program 6 deletes the record from the table based on the give *regno*.

```
import java.sql.*;
public class SIRDEL
{
  static final String DRIVER = "com.mysql.jdbc.Driver";
  static final String URL = "jdbc:mysql://localhost/deptcs";
  static final String UN = "root";
  static final String PW = "root";
  public static void main(String[] args)
  {
    Connection cn = null;
    Statement st = null;
    try
    {
      Class.forName(DRIVER);
      System.out.println("Connecting database...");
      cn = DriverManager.getConnection(URL, UN, PW);
      System.out.println("Connected successfully...");
      st = cn.createStatement();
      String sql = "DELETE FROM sir WHERE regno = 1215675";
      st.executeUpdate(sql);
      sql = "SELECT * FROM sir";
      ResultSet rs = st.executeQuery(sql);
      System.out.println("Fetching records...");
      while(rs.next())
      {
        //Retrieve by column name
        int r = rs.getInt("regno");
        String n = rs.getString("name");
        int y = rs.getInt("year");
        String s= rs.getString("sex");
        String re = rs.getString("religion");
        //Display values
        System.out.print("Register No: " + r);
        System.out.print(" Name: " + n);
        System.out.print(" Year: " + y);
        System.out.print(" Sex: " + s);
```

```
            System.out.print(" Religion: " + re);
            System.out.println();
         }
         rs.close();
      }
      catch(Exception e){ System.out.println("An Exception has been occurred:
"+e);}
   }
 }
```

Output

```
Connecting database...
Connected successfully...
Fetching records...
Register No: 1215671 Name: Anandhi Year: 2012 Sex: FEMALE Religion: HINDU
Register No: 1215672 Name: Joseph Year: 2010 Sex: MALE Religion:
CHRISTIAN
Register No: 1215673 Name: Reeta Year: 2013 Sex: FEMALE Religion:
CHRISTIAN
Register No: 1215674 Name: Arun Year: 2009 Sex: MALE Religion: HINDU
```

PROGRAMMING EXERCISES

1. Create a database `Result` and a table `studResult` in that database. Develop a program to retrieve the result of a particular student based on a register number and DOB.
2. Create two tables for storing student profiles and marks details in a database student. Extract the records from these two tables and display them.
3. Create a table for storing staff profiles in database `DB1` and create another table for storing subjects handled by staff in database `DB2`. Extract the records from both tables from `DB1` and `DB2`.
4. Perform the following operations in one program.
   (a) Create a database `Business`.
   (b) Create a table `clientaddress` in the database `Business`.
   (c) Insert the records into the table `clientaddress`.
   (d) Display the records.
   (e) Truncate a table.
   (f) Drop a table.
   (g) Drop a database.
5. Modify Exercise 1 using the networking concept. Instead of retrieving the result from the same program, develop a server program which can interact with the database and table, and develop a client program which gets the register number and DOB from the user and send this data to the server to get the result.
6. Write a program to check for the existence of a table in the database.
7. Write a program to list all the tables in the given database.
8. Write a program to list all the databases available in the database server.
9. Write a program to check for the existence of the database in the database server.
10. Write a program to check for the existence of the table. If the table does not exit, create a table and perform the insertion, updation, sorting and searching operations.

CHAPTER

16

Collections

Java provides an integrated architecture, known as a *collections framework,* for representing and manipulating groups of objects. A *collection* is basically a container that encapsulates multiple objects into a single unit. Examples include a list of employees, a set of numbers, a set of processes, a queue of requests, and so on. Every collections framework primarily contains three parts—*interfaces, implementation classes for interfaces* and *algorithms.* The majority of Java collections are located in the `java.util` package. This is one of Java's largest, most powerful concepts for handling groups of objects. The collections framework defines a set of interfaces and their implementations to manipulate collections, which serves as a container for a group of objects. The collections framework also allows storing, retrieving and updating a set of objects. It provides an API to work with the data structures such as lists, trees, maps and sets. In this chapter, sophisticated details on the set of interfaces, classes and its implementation will be discussed.

16.1 OVERVIEW OF COLLECTION FRAMEWORK

The collections framework is made up of a set of interfaces to work with groups of objects. Each interface describes different types of groups. While the user always needs to create specific implementations of the interfaces, access to the actual collection should be restricted to the use of the interface methods; this allows changing the underlying data structure, without altering the rest of the code. Figure 16.1 shows the hierarchy of the collections framework interface.

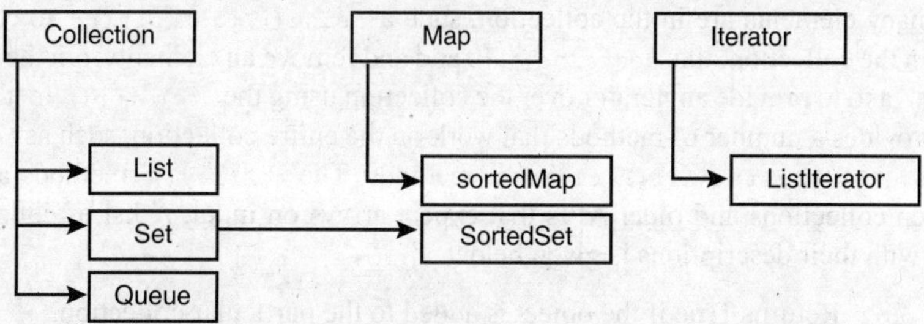

Fig. 16.1 Interfaces in the collections framework hierarchy

The `Collection` is the main interface. `List` and `Set` are sub-interfaces of the `Collection` interface. The other interfaces are `Map` and `Iterator`. `Set`, `Map` and `Iterator` interfaces have sub-interfaces in the sequence of `SortedSet`, `SortedMap` and `ListIterator`.

Java collections framework interface provides the abstract data type to represent collections. `java.util.Collection` is the root interface of collections framework. This is the top of the collections framework hierarchy and contains important methods such as `size()`, `iterator()`, `add()`, `remove()`, `clear()` that every `Collection` class must implement. Some important interfaces are `java.util.List`, `java.util.Set`, `java.util.Queue` and `java.util.Map`. `Map` is the only interface that does not inherit from the `Collection` interface but it is a part of the collections framework. All the collections framework interfaces are present in the `java.util` package. Table16.1 lists the description of interfaces shown in Fig. 16.1.

Table 16.1 Description of interfaces in the collections framework

Interface	Description
Collection	Collection of elements
• List	Sequence of elements
• Queue	Special type of list
• Set	Collection of unique elements
• SortedSet	Sorted collection of unique elements
Map	Collection of key-value pairs; unique
• SortedMap	Sorted collection of unique key-value pairs
Iterator	Objects to traverse via collection
• ListIterator	Sequence of objects to traverse via collection

These interfaces are used to represent the group of objects. Objects and their values are handled by various methods available in each interface. The operations performed using collection interfaces are given in the following section.

16.2 COLLECTION INTERFACE

This is the basis of the collection hierarchy. A collection presents a group of objects known as elements. Java does not provide any direct implementations of `Collection` interfaces. The interface has methods to notify how many elements are in the collection, such as, `size()`, `isEmpty();` to check whether a given object is in the collection, like `contains()`; to add and remove an element from the collection, like `add()`, `remove()` and to provide an iterator over the collection using the `iterator()` method. Collection interface also provides a number of methods that work on the entire collection, such as `containsAll()`, `addAll()`, `removeAll()`, `retainAll()`, `clear()` methods. The `toArray()` methods are provided as a bridge between collections and older APIs that expect arrays on input. A list of collection interface methods along with their descriptions is given below.

- `add(Object ob):` Returns True if the object is added to the particular collection.
- `addAll(Collection c):` Returns True if all objects in the collection is added to the particular collection.
- `clear():`Removes all elements in the specified collection.
- `contains(Object ob):` Returns True if the collection holds the element.
- `containsAll(Collection c):` Returns True if the collection holds all the elements in the specified collection.

- `equals(Object ob)`: Returns True if the particular object matches with an object in the collection.
- `hashCode()`:Returns the hashCode for the collection.
- `isEmpty()`:Returns True if the collection is empty.
- `iterator()`:Returns an iterator over the elements in the collection.
- `remove(Object ob)`: Returns True if the particular element is present in the collection and removes the object from the collection.
- `removeAll(Collection c)`: Returns True if all the elements in the collection c are removed from the collection.
- `retainAll(Collection c)`: Returns True if all the elements in the collection c are retained from the collection.
- `size()`:Returns the number of elements in the collection.
- `toArray()`:Returns an array of objects if the array holds all the elements in the collection.
- `toArray(Object[] a)`: Returns an array containing all of the elements in the collection; the runtime type of the returned array is that of the specified array. A new array is allocated with the runtime type of the specified array and the size of the collection.

`Set` interface

A `Set` is a collection that does not hold duplicate elements. This interface is designed on the mathematical set abstraction and is used to represent sets such as a bunch of cards in hand. The `Set` interface extends the `Collection` interface and holds the methods that are inherited from the `Collection` interface. Since the `Set` interface does not allow duplicate elements, the `add()` method returns False if adding a duplicate element to the collection. Java has three general-purpose `Set` implementation classes—`HashSet`, `TreeSet`, and `LinkedHashSet`. The `Set` interface does not allow random access to an element in the collection. An iterator or a `for-each` loop is used to traverse the elements of a set.

`SortedSet` interface

`SortedSet` is a sub interface of the `Set` interface that maintains its elements in ascending order. Several operations are provided to utilise the advantages of ordering. Sorted sets are used for obviously ordered sets. The supplementary methods defined by set are as follows.

- `comparator()`: Returns the `comparator` object. If the elements in the `SortedSet` are in ascending order then it returns null.
- `first()`: Returns the first element from the `SortedSet`.
- `headSet(Object to_element)`: Returns the number of elements less than that of the elements specified using the to_element object. The elements are returned from the sorted set.
- `last()`: Returns the last element from the `SortedSet`.
- `subSet(Object from_element, object to_element)` : Returns the elements between the range of particular objects.
- `tailSet(Object from_element)`: Returns the elements from a sorted set that are greater than or equal to the from_element value.

`List` interface

List is an ordered collection and can contain duplicate elements. Accessing an element in the list is done by using its index position. The List interface is similar to an array with dynamic length. List is one of the most used collection type. ArrayList and LinkedList are implementation classes of List interface. Collections class provides an useful algorithm for list, such as sort, shuffle, reverse, binarySearch , and so on.

`List` interface gives useful methods to add an element at a particular index, remove or replace an element based on the index and to get a sub-list using the index. These methods are described below.

- `add(int index, Object ob)`: Adds the element `ob` in the particular index of the list.
- `addAll(int index, Collection c)`: Adds all the elements of collection `c` in the particular index of the list.
- `get(int index )`: Returns the element in the particular index of the list.
- `indexOf(Object ob)`: Returns index of object `ob` in the list.
- `lastIndexOf(Object ob)`: Returns the last index of object `ob` in the list.
- `listIterator()`:Returns a list iterator of the element.
- `remove(int index)`: Removes an element at the particular index value.
- `set(int index, Object ob)`: Replaces the element at the specified index value with the particular element.
- `subList(int startindex, int endindex)`: Returns the elements from the particular start index to the end.

`Queue` interface

`Queue` is a collection used to hold multiple elements prior to processing. The elements are released in the order in which the elements are inserted. A queue provides insertion, extraction and inspection operations. Queues order the elements in a first-in, first-out (FIFO) manner. However, priority queues order the elements according to a supplied comparator or the elements in natural ordering. As in the case of Queue Data Structure, irrespective of the ordering used, the head of the queue is the element that would be removed by a call to remove or poll. In a FIFO queue, all new elements are inserted at the tail of the queue. The `Queue` interface method descriptions are given below.

- `element()`: Returns the element at the head of the queue. In this, the element still exists until removed. If the queue is empty then `element()` throws an exception `NoSuchElementException`.
- `offer(Object ob)`: Attempts to add an element to the queue. It is similar to `add()` method of list.
- `peek()`: Returns the element at the head of the queue. The element is not removed yet. If the queue is empty, `peek()` returns null.
- `poll()`: Returns the element at the head of the queue after removing the element. If the queue is empty, `poll()` returns null.
- `remove()`: Returns the element at the head of the queue after removing the element. If the queue is empty, `remove()` throws an Exception `NoSuchElementException`.

`Map` interface

`Map` corresponds to key-value pairs. The keys are unique and each key can map at the most one value. However, this does not ensure that the elements are ordered. To interoperate with other collection classes or interfaces, it provides three collection views, which allow a map's contents to be viewed as a set of keys, collection of values, or set of key-value mappings. A map is an object that maps keys to values. This is also known for key-value mapping. A map cannot have duplicate keys. Java Collections Framework provides three general-purpose `Map` implementations, which are `HashMap`, `TreeMap` and `LinkedHashMap`. The basic methods of `Map` are `put`, `get`, `containsKey`, `containsValue`, `size` and `isEmpty`. The other methods are described below.

- `clear()`: Removes all the mappings from a map.
- `entrySet()`: Returns the key-value pair enclosed in this map.

- `equals(Object ob)`: Returns True if the particular object maps with an object of a `Map` interface.
- `keySet()`: Returns the keys in a map. If removing a key from the map, the corresponding value is also removed.
- `putAll(Map m)`: Copies all the individual key-value pairs from a map to the map with which it is currently working.
- `remove(Object ob)`: Removes the particular key from the map.

`SortedMap` interface

As map maintains its key-value pair in ascending key order, the SortedMap extends the `Map` interface and is similar to SortedSet. Sorted maps are used for logically ordered collections of key-value pairs, such as dictionaries and telephone directories. The methods in `SortedMap` are given below.

- `comparator()`: Returns the comparator of the sorted map. If the sorted map uses natural ordering for the keys, then it returns null.
- `firstKey()`: Returns the first key of the sorted map.
- `headMap(Object ob)`: Returns the keys of the sorted map that are less than the specified end object.
- `lastKey( )`: Returns the last key of the sorted map.
- `subMap(Object start, Object end)`: Returns the keys of the sorted map that are between the specified start and end objects.
- `tailMap(Object start)`: Returns the keys of the sorted map that are greater than or equal to the start object.

`Iterator` interface

The `iterator()` method of the `Collection` interface returns an Iterator. With the `Iterator` interface methods, the user can traverse a collection from start to finish and safely remove elements from the underlying `Collection` interface. The `Iterator` interface methods are given below.

- `hasNext( )`: Returns True if the collection holds more than one element.
- `next( )`: Returns the next element from the collection.
- `remove( )`: Returns the current element from the collection.

The `remove()` method is optionally supported by the underlying collection. When called, and supported, the element returned by the last `next()` call is removed. To demonstrate, the following code shows the use of the `Iterator` interface for a general collection:

```
Collection collection = ...;
Iterator iterator = collection.iterator();
while (iterator.hasNext()) { Object element = iterator.next();
    if (removalCheck(element))
    {
        iterator.remove( );
    }
}
```

In the above code, `collection` contains a list of elements or values. To read the data one after other, the `Iterator` class is used. This class is similar to a `for` loop. The list of elements are accessed by `next()` method of the `Iterator` class.

`ListIterator` interface

In an `Iterator` interface, an element is inserted only at the end of the list. If there is a need to insert an element at the desired location of the list, then `ListIterator` interface is used. The `ListIterator` interface extends the `Iterator` interface. `ListIterator` contains a method named `add(int index, Object ob)`. This method allows the programmer to assign an element at the required position based on the index value.

`ListIterator` allows a programmer to traverse the list in either direction, modify the list during iteration and attain the iterator's current position in the list. A `ListIterator` has no current element; its cursor position always lies between the element that would be returned by a call to `previous()` and the element that would be returned by a call to `next()`.
Implementation classes: Collections provide the central part of implementation classes for `Collection` interfaces. These classes are used to create different types of collections in a Java program. The important collection classes are `ArrayList, LinkedList, HashMap, TreeMap, HashSet, TreeSet`. These classes resolve most of programming needs but if there is a need for some special collection class, then this can be extended by creating custom collections classes. All the collection classes are present in the `java.util` and `java.util.concurrent` packages. The implementation classes of `Collection` interfaces are explained in the following section.

16.3 COLLECTIONS IMPLEMENTATION CLASSES

Java does not provide any implementation for the root interface `Collection`. Instead it provides implementations of collection classes for more specific interfaces such as `Set`, `List`, `Queue` and so on. The classes exist in the collections framework to implement the `Collection` interface and the sub-interfaces. These classes also implement the `Map` and `Iterator` interfaces. The following list shows various `Collection` interfaces and their corresponding implementation classes.

- `Collection - AbstractCollection`
- `List - AbstractList`
- `Queue - AbstractQueue`
- `List - AbstractSequentialList`
- `List - LinkedList`
- `List, Cloneable and Serializable - ArrayList`
- `Set - AbstractSet`
- `Set - EnumSet`
- `Set - HashSet`
- `Queue - PriorityQueue`
- `Set - TreeSet`
- `List, Cloneable and Serializable - Vector`
- `List, Cloneable and Serializable - Stack`
- `Map, Cloneable and Serializable - HashTable`

`AbstractCollection` class

This class implements the root interface `Collection`. The `AbstractCollection` class provides the basis for the concrete collections framework classes. While it is free to implement all the methods of the `Collection` interface, this class also provides implementations for all the methods, except for the `iterator()`, `size()` methods that are implemented in the appropriate subclass. Optional methods like `add ()` will throw an exception if the subclass doesn't override the behaviour.

AbstractList and AbstractSequentialList classes

There are two abstract List implementations classes that are AbstractList and AbstractSequentialList. These classes override the equals() and hashCode() methods to make sure two equal collections return the same hash code. Two sets are equal if they are the same size and hold the same elements in the same order. The hashCode() implementation is specific in the List interface definition and implementation.

Besides the equals() and hashCode() implementations, AbstractList and AbstractSequentialList provide partial implementation of the remaining List methods. They make the construction of concrete List implementation easier for random-access and sequential-access data sources respectively. The set of methods that are needed to be defined depends on the behaviour of the List elements. Table 16.2 should help to remember which methods need to be implemented. There is no need to provide an implementation of the Iterator iterator() method.

Table 16.2 List of methods implementation

Mode of access	AbstractList	AbstractSequentialList
unmodifiable	Object get(int index) int size()	ListIterator listIterator(int index) - boolean hasNext() - Object next() - int nextIndex() - boolean hasPrevious() - Object previous() - int previousIndex()
modifiable	Object get(int index) int size() Object set(int index, Object element)	int size() ListIterator listIterator(int index) - boolean hasNext() - Object next() - int nextIndex() - boolean hasPrevious() - Object previous() - int previousIndex() - int size() ListIterator - set(Object element)
variable-size and modifiable	Object get(int index) int size() Object set(int index, Object element) add(int index, Object element) Object remove(int index)	ListIterator listIterator(int index) - boolean hasNext() - Object next() - int nextIndex() - boolean hasPrevious() - Object previous() - int previousIndex() int size() ListIterator - set(Object element) ListIterator - add(Object element) - remove()

Two important list implementation classes are ArrayList and LinkedList. ArrayList implementation is discussed in the following section.

16.3.1 ArrayList Class

There are two common List implementations in the collections framework. They are ArrayList and LinkedList and these types of lists are used according to specific needs. If there is a requirement to support random access with no insertion or removal of elements from any place other than the end, then ArrayList offers the optimal collection. ArrayLists are used like arrays, but there are some distinctions. First, the definition of the class ArrayList is not provided by the default package. Instead, this has been provided in the java.util package, and any program that makes use of the class ArrayList must contain the following statement at the start of the file:

```
import java.util.ArrayList;
```

An ArrayList is created and named in the same way as an object of any class, except for specifying the base type using a new notation. The basetype is any primitive type of data and it is optional. The syntax for ArrayList is given below,

```
ArrayList<basetype> obj = new ArrayList<basetype>();
```

Program 16.1 explains the implementation of List using an ArrayList class. The problem is to print the address. The class name is ArrayListExample and it consists of an address object, where address is of type ArrayList.

Program 16.1

```
import java.util.*;
public class ArrayListExample {
    public static void main(String args[]) {
        //ArrayList Example
        List address = new ArrayList();
        address.add("Name:Kadhi Craft");
        address.add("Gandhi Nagar");
        address.add("VLR");
        address.add("Contact No:1111111111");
        // Print all the address values
        System.out.println("Address:"+ address);
        //print only the 3rd position value using get()
        System.out.println("3 position:" +address. get(3));
        // print only the 0th position value using get()
        System.out.println("0 position:" +address.get(0));
    }
}
```

Output 16.1

```
Address: [Name:Kadhi Craft, Gandhi
Nagar, VLR, Contact No:1111111111]
3 position: Contact
No:1111111111
0 position: Name:Kadhi craft
```

This program demonstrates that the object address is created for ArrayList class using the List interface. And then using the add() method, values are inserted into the address object. Now all the values are stored in the address object. By printing the address object, the entire contents of ArrayList object are retrieved. If there is a need to print the particular value in an element, then get() method is used by specifying the index position of an array, in the same way as get(3) and get(0) values are retrieved in the above program.

The next type of List interface implementation is LinkedList class explained below.

16.3.2 LinkedList Classes

If there is a requirement to frequently add and remove elements from the middle of the list and access the list elements only in a sequential order, then `LinkedList` provides a better implementation. In addition, `LinkedList` includes many methods to work with the elements at the end of the list.

The methods are as follows,

- `addFirst(Object ob)`
- `addLast(Object ob)`
- `getFirst( )`
- `getLast( )`
- `removeFirst( )`
- `removeLast( )`

By using these new methods, the `LinkedList` can easily be handled as a stack, queue or other end-oriented data structure. Syntax for `LinkedList` with queue and stack is given below.

```
LinkedList queue = ...;
queue.addFirst(element);
Object object = queue.removeLast();
LinkedList stack = ...;
stack.addFirst(element);
Object object = stack.removeFirst();
```

The general structure of `LinkedList` class for Queue and Stack accessibility is given above. The `LinkedList` class implementation is demonstrated in **Program 16.2**. The problem is to display the person's details. The class name is `ListExample`. The object is to be created for the LinkedList class and the necessary methods are invoked.

Program 16.2

```
import java.util.*;
public class ListExample {
    public static void main(String args[]) {
        //LinkedList example: Person Details
        LinkedList queue = new LinkedList();
        queue.addFirst("Joe");
        queue.addFirst("Saga");
        queue.addLast("UI Designer");
        queue.addLast("Chennai");
        System.out.println(queue);
        //Print all the values in the queue
        System.out.println(queue.getFirst());
        // Print first value in the queue
        System.out.println(queue.getLast());
        // Print last value in the queue
        queue.removeLast();
        // Remove last value in the queue
        queue.removeFirst();
        // Remove first value in the queue
        System.out.println(queue);
    }
}
```

Output 16.2

```
[Saga, Joe, UI Designer,
Chennai]
Saga
Chennai
[Joe, UI Designer]
```

This program illustrates the concept of `LinkedList` class. First, an object is created for the `LinkedList` class. The object name is `queue`. Using `addFirst()` method, two values are inserted into `queue` and then using the `addLast()` method, two values are added into `queue`. By printing the `queue` object, the entire contents are retrieved and the values are printed. Then `removeFirst()` and `removeLast()` methods are invoked and the values removed. The final output is displayed which contains only `Joe` and `Uidesigner` values in the list.

16.3.3 ArrayList vs LinkedList

`ArrayList` and `LinkedList` implement the `List` interface and manage the insertion order. Both types of Lists are non-synchronised classes. But, there are several differences between `ArrayList` and `LinkedList` classes (Table 16.3).

Table 16.3 ArrayList vs LinkedList

ArrayList	LinkedList
1. Internally `ArrayList` uses dynamic arrays to store the elements.	Internally `LinkedList` uses doubly linked list to store the elements.
2. Handling `ArrayList` is slow as it internally uses arrays. If any element is removed from the array, all the bits are shifted in memory.	Handling `LinkedList` is faster than `ArrayList` as it uses doubly linked lists so no bit shifting is required in memory.
3. `ArrayList` class can only work as a list since it implements List only.	`LinkedList` class can work as both list and queue since it implements `List` and `Deque` interfaces.
4. `ArrayList` is best for storing and accessing data.	`LinkedList` is best for manipulating data.

Program 16.3 demonstrates the use of both `ArrayList` and `LinkedList`. The program aims to display the world's famous cities using these two classes.

Program 16.3

```
import java.util.*;
public class ListExample {
    public static void main(String args[]) { List list = new ArrayList();
        //Add values in array position like 0,1,2,3,etc
        list.add("Berlin");
        list.add("Paris");
        list.add("NewYork");
        list.add("London");
        list.add("Melbourne");
        System.out.println("Using ArrayList:"+list);
        System.out.println("2: " + list.get(2));
        System.out.println("0: " + list.get(0));
        //Add values in Queue:First in First Out[FIFO]
        LinkedList queue = new LinkedList();
        queue.addFirst("Berlin");
        queue.addFirst("Paris");
        queue.addFirst("NewYork");
        queue.addFirst("London");
        queue.addFirst("Melbourne");
        System.out.println("Using LinkedList:"+queue);
        queue.removeLast();
        queue.removeLast();
        System.out.println(queue);
    }
}
```

Output 16.3

```
Using ArrayList:[Berlin,
Paris, NewYork, London,
Melbourne]
2: Newyork
0: Berlin Using
LinkedList:[Melbourne,
London, NewYork, Paris,
Berlin]
[Melbourn, London, NewYork]
```

This program illustrates the values being added into the `ArrayList` sequentially with index position, whereas with `LinkedList` class, the values are added in a queue order. The output clearly shows how the values are stored in `ArrayList` and `LinkedList`.

In the next section, `Set` interface implementation classes are explained with examples.

16.3.4 HashSet, LinkedHashSet and TreeSet Classes

The collections framework provides two general-purpose implementations of the `Set` interface. These are `HashSet` and `TreeSet`. This `Set` interface will use a `HashSet` for storing a duplicate-free collection. For efficiency, objects added to a `HashSet` need to implement the `hashCode()` method in a manner that properly distributes the hash codes. At the same time most system classes override the default `hashCode()` method implementation in objects. When creating custom classes to add to a `HashSet` remember to override `hashCode()`.

`LinkedHashSet` class is used to store the values sequentially and this will perform all the operations supported by `LinkedList` but it avoids duplicate values. `LinkedHashSet` manages a linked list of the entries in the set, in the order in which the elements are inserted. This allows insertion-order iteration over the set. That is, when cycling through a `LinkedHashSet` using an iterator, the elements will be returned in the order in which the elements were inserted.

The `TreeSet` implementation is realistic when there is a requirement to extract elements from a collection in a sorted order. To organise the elements to work properly, elements are added to a `TreeSet` as it is sortable. Generally it is faster to add elements to a `HashSet`, then convert the collection to a `TreeSet` for sorted traversal. Both `HashSet` and `TreeSet` implement the `Cloneable` interface.

To illustrate the use of the concrete Set classes, **Program 16.4** creates a `HashSet` and adds a group of names, including one name twice and then prints the names in the set (list of state's capitals), demonstrating that a duplicate name is not present. Next, the same Program treats the set as a `TreeSet` and displays the list in a sorted manner.

Program 16.4

```
import java.util.*;
public class SetExample {
   public static void main(String args[]) { Set setobj = new HashSet();
       setobj.add("Chennai");
       setobj.add("Bangalore");
       setobj.add("Ahmedabad");
       setobj.add("Cochin");
       setobj.add("Hyderabad");
       setobj.add("Hyderabad");
       System.out.println("Using HashSet:"+setobj);
       Set ls=new LinkedHashSet();
       ls.add("Chennai");
       ls.add("Bangalore");
       ls.add("Ahmedabad");
       ls.add("Cochin");
       ls.add("Hyderabad");
       ls.add("Hyderabad");
       System.out.println("Using LinkedHashSet:"+ls);
       Set sortedset = new TreeSet(setobj);
       System.out.println("Using TreeSet:"+sortedset);
   }
}
```

Output 16.4

```
Using HashSet:[Cochin,
Bangalore, Chennai,
Hyderabad, Ahmedabad]
Using LinkedHashSet:[Chennai,
Bangalore, Ahmedabad, Cochin,
Hyderabad]
Using TreeSet:[Ahmedabad,
Bangalore, Chennai, Cochin,
Hyderabad]
```

Program 16.4 demonstrates three classes involved in `Set` interface implementation. The first class is `HashSet` class. The city names are added into `HashSet` class. Similarly, `LinkedHashSet` and `TreeSet` class are implemented. The purpose of using the `Set` interface is to remove the duplicate values. 'Hyderabad' is added twice in the `HashSet` class and in the `LinkedHashSet` class. Since the value is duplicated, it is automatically avoided by the Set implementation classes. This can be shown in the output of the program. The third implementation class of `Set` interface is the `TreeSet` class which is used to arrange the data elements in sorted order. The given city names are arranged in ascending order which is shown in the output.

16.3.5 PriorityQueue Class

The `Queue` interface orders the elements in First In First Out (FIFO) approach. Various methods involved in the `Queue` Interface are given below.

- `add(object);`
- `offer(object);`
- `remove();`
- `poll();`
- `element();`
- `peek();`

PriorityQueue class

The `PriorityQueue` class provides the capacity to implement `Queue` interface. But it does not order the elements in FIFO approach. The use of this class is demonstrated in **Program 16.5.**

Program 16.5

```
import java.util.Iterator;
import java.util.PriorityQueue;
public class PriorityQueueExample {
    public static void main(String args[])
    {
        PriorityQueue<String> queue=new PriorityQueue<String>();
        queue.add("Java");
        queue.add("Android");
        queue.add("Dot Net");
        queue.add("R programming");
        queue.add("python programming");
        System.out.println("head:"+queue.element());
        System.out.println("head:"+queue.peek());
        System.out.println("ITERATING THE
        ELEMENTS:");
        Iterator itr=queue.iterator();
        while(itr.hasNext()){ System.out.
        println(itr.next());
        }
        queue.remove();
        queue.poll();
        System.out.println("AFTER REMOVING TWO ELEMENTS:");
        Iterator<String> itr2=queue.iterator();
        while(itr2.hasNext()){ System.out.println(itr2.next());
        }
    }
}
```

Output 16.5

```
head:Android
head:Android
ITERATING THE ELEMENTS:
Android
Java
Dot Net
R programming
python programming
AFTER REMOVING TWO ELEMENTS:
Java
R programming
python programming
```

This program illustrates the use of `PriorityQueue` class. An object is created for the class `PriorityQueue`. Then the element values are added into the queue object. The method `element()` of `Queue` interface is invoked to set the head element in the queue which means the first priority is given to this head element. Here the head element is 'Android'. Using the `peek()` method, the head element value is returned. The elements in the queue are printed by iterating the elements in `Iterator` class. Then `remove()` and `poll()` methods are invoked to delete an element from the queue. After deleting the head element in the queue, the remaining elements are displayed using the `Iterator` class.

The next section demonstrates the `Map` interface implementation classes. The classes are `HashMap`, `LinkedHashMap` and `TreeMap` classes. Through the Map implementation classes, the user can work with key-value pairs of elements.

16.3.6 HashMap, LinkedHashMap and TreeMap Classes

The collections framework provides two general-purpose Map implementations—`HashMap` and `TreeMap`. Which implementation is to be used, depends on the specific needs. For inserting, deleting and locating elements in a Map, the `HashMap` offers the best alternative.

`LinkedHashMap` class extends `HashMap` and manages a linked list of the entries in the map in the order in which they were inserted. This allows insertion to be in-order arrangement over the map. That is, when iterating a `LinkedHashMap`, the elements will be returned in the order in which they were inserted.

If there is a need to traverse the keys in a sorted order, then `TreeMap` is the better alternative. Depending upon the size of the collection, it may be faster to add elements to a `HashMap`, then convert the map to a `TreeMap` for sorted key traversal. Using a `HashMap` requires that the class of key added has a well-defined `hashCode()` implementation. With the `TreeMap` implementation, elements added to the map must be sortable. Both `HashMap` and `TreeMap` implement the `Cloneable` interface. This is demonstrated in **Program 16.6** where temperature details of various cities in Tamil Nadu are represented. The city name and its temperature is given as a keyname–value pair. City acts as a keyname and temperature is given as its value.

Program 16.6

```
import java.util.HashMap;
import java.util.LinkedHashMap;
import java.util.TreeMap;
public class MapExample {
  public static void main(String args[])
  {
     HashMap m = new HashMap();
     // Put elements to the map
     m.put("Chennai", new Double(97.3));
     m.put("Vellore", new Double(105.2));
     m.put("Ooty", new Double(16.5));
     m.put("Kanyakumari", new
     Double(78.6));
     m.put("Kovai", new Double(100.8));
     System.out.println("HashMap(keyvalue
     pair):"+m);
     System.out.println("Key
     elements:"+m.keySet());
     System.out.println("Value
     elements:"+m.values());
     System.out.println();
     LinkedHashMap lm=new
     LinkedHashMap();
```

Output 17.6

```
HashMap(keyvalue pair):{Ooty=17.5,
Chennai=97.3, Kovai=100.8,
Vellore=105.2, Kanyakumari=78.6}
Key elements:[Ooty, Chennai, Kovai,
Vellore, Kanyakumari]
Value elements:[17.5, 97.3,
100.8, 105.2, 78.6]
LinkedHashMap(keyvalue
pair):{Chennai=97.3, Vellore=105.2,
Ooty=17.5, Kanyakumari=78.6,
Kovai=100.8}
Key elements:[Chennai, Vellore,
Ooty, Kanyakumari, Kovai]
Value elements:[97.3,
105.2, 17.5, 78.6, 100.8]
TreeMap(keyvalue pair):{Chennai=97.3,
Kanyakumari=78.6, Kovai=100.8,
Ooty=17.5, Vellore=105.2}
Key elements:[Chennai, Kanyakumari,
Kovai, Ooty, Vellore]
Value elements:[97.3, 78.6,
100.8, 17.5, 105.2]
```

```
        lm.put("Chennai", new Double(97.3));
        lm.put("Vellore", new Double(105.2));
        lm.put("Ooty", new Double(16.5));
        lm.put("Kanyakumari", new Double(78.6));
        lm.put("Kovai", new Double(100.8));
        System.out.println("LinkedHashMap(keyvalue pair):"+lm);
        System.out.println("Key elements:"+lm.keySet());
        System.out.println("Value elements:"+lm. values());
        System.out.println();
        TreeMap tm=new TreeMap(lm);
        System.out.println("TreeMap(keyvalue pair):"+tm);
        System.out.println("Key elements:"+tm.keySet());
        System.out.println("Value elements:"+tm. values());
    }
}
```

This program illustrates all three implementation classes of `Map` interface. First, an object is created for `HashMap` class. The element values are added using `put()`, passing two parameters, city name which act as keyname and temperature value which acts as value in the keyname-value pair. By printing object `m`, all the values in the `HashMap` objects are displayed. If there is need to display the key and value separately, `KeySet()` method is used to return the key name alone and `values()` method is used to return only the values of the elements. Likewise `LinkedHashMap` and `TreeMap` classes are implemented and their outputs are given.

16.4 Hashtable AND Hashmap VS Hashtable SORTING

`Hashtable` was part of the original `java.util` and is a concrete implementation of a dictionary. `Hashtable` implements the `Map` interface. Thus, `Hashtable` is now integrated into the collections framework. It is similar to `HashMap`, but is synchronised.

Like `HashMap`, `Hashtable` stores key/value pairs in a hash table. When using a `Hashtable`, specify an object that is used as a key, and the value to be linked to that key. The key is then hashed, and the resulting hash code is used as the index at which the value is stored within the table.

The `Hashtable` implementation is a generic dictionary that permits storing any object as its key or value (besides null). `Hashtable` is a synchronised Map; using `Hashtable` is slightly faster than using a synchronised `HashMap`. The Properties implementation is a specialised `Hashtable` for working with text strings. While having to cast values retrieved from a `Hashtable` to the desired class, the `Properties` class allows getting text values without casting. The class also supports loading and saving property settings from an input stream or to an output stream. The most commonly used set of properties is the system properties list, retrieved by `System.getProperties()`. `Hashtable` implementation is demonstrated in **Program 16.7.**

Program 16.7

```
import java.util.Enumeration;
import java.util.Hashtable;
public class HashtableExample {
    public static void main(String[] args) { Hashtable capital = new Hashtable();
        Enumeration names;
        String str;
        capital.put("Tamilnadu","Chennai");
```

```
        capital.put("Karnataka", "Bangalore");
        capital.put("Andhra","Amaravathi" );
        capital.put("Telangana","Hyderabad") ;
        capital.put("Kerala", "Trivandrum");
        names = capital.keys();
        while(names.hasMoreElements()) {
            str = (String) names.nextElement();
            System.out.println(str + ": " +capital.get(str));
        }
        System.out.println();
    }
}
```

Output 16.7

```
Tamilnadu: Chennai
Telangana: Hyderabad
Karnataka: Bangalore
Kerala: Trivandrum
Andhra: Amaravathi
```

The program shows object capital created for the `Hashtable` class. And then using the `put()` method, the key–value pair of the state and its capital are added into `Hashtable`. Then, using `Enumeration` class the elements are returned from `Hashtable` and it is printed as given in the output.

`HashMap` vs `Hashtable`

Even though both `HashMap` and `Hashtable` process the key–value pair of elements, there are significant differences between `HashMap` and `Hashtable` (Table 16.4).

Table 16.4 Comparison between `HashMap` and `Hashtable`

HashMap	Hashtable
1. `HashMap` is *not synchronised*. It is not-thread safe and can't be shared between many threads without proper synchronisation code.	`Hashtable` can be *synchronised*. It is threadsafe and can be shared with many threads.
2. `HashMap` allows one null key and multiple null values.	`Hashtable` does not allow any null key or value.
3. `HashMap` is a new class introduced in higher versions of JDK.	`Hashtable` is a legacy class.
4. `HashMap` is faster than Hashtable.	`Hashtable` is slower than `HashMap`.
5. `HashMap` is synchronised by calling this code Map m = Collections.synchronizedMap(hashMap);	`Hashtable` is internally synchronised and can't be unsynchronised.
6. `HashMap` is passed through by Iterator.	`Hashtable` is passed through by Enumerator and Iterator.
7. Iterator in `HashMap` is fail-fast.	Enumerator in `Hashtable` is not fail-fast.
8. `HashMap` inherits `AbstractMap` class.	`Hashtable` inherits `Dictionary` class.

16.5 SORTING IN COLLECTION

Collections class provides static methods for sorting the elements of a collection. If collection elements are of Set type, it can be sorted using `TreeSet` class. When `List` interface is used, the elements cannot be sorted. Collections class provides methods for sorting the elements of List type elements. Sorting the elements in Java can be applied to three types of objects.

- String objects.
- Wrapper class objects.
- User-defined class objects.

Sorting the elements common to all the interfaces in a collection can be done using CollectionsSort(). The method is given below.

- `public void sort(List list):` is used to sort the elements of List. List elements must be of comparable type.

`String` class and wrapper classes implement the `Comparable` interface. **Program 16.8** demonstrates sorting String objects of the List type elements. This program contains a list of programming languages and the aim is to sort the programming languages that are added into the `ArrayList` class.

Program 16.8

```
import java.util.*;
public class SortElementsofList {
   public static void main(String[] args) { ArrayList<String> li=new
   ArrayList<String>();
      li.add("Java progrmming");
      li.add("R programming");
      li.add("Python Programming");
      li.add("C# programming");
      System.out.println("List of Programming
      Languages in Sorted Order");
      Collections.sort(li);
      Iterator itr=li.iterator();
      while(itr.hasNext()){ System.out.println(itr.next());
      }
   }
}
```

Output 16.8

```
List of Programming Languages
in Sorted Order
C# programming
Java programming
Python Programming
R programming
```

This program demonstrates how to sort the String object. Instead of sorting the elements using `TreeSet` and `TreeMap` classes, the shortest way to sort the elements is done by invoking the `sort()` method of `Collections` interface directly. Then `Iterator` is used to return the values and they are printed. The elements are arranged in ascending order as shown in the output.

Program 16.9 demonstrates the sorting of wrapper class objects of List type elements. Here the wrapper class of the Integer object is to be sorted.

Program 16.9

```
import java.util.*;
public class NumberSorting {
   public static void main(String[] args) { ArrayList li=new ArrayList();
      li.add(Integer.valueOf(450));
      li.add(Integer.valueOf(250));
      li.add(650);
      //internal conversion into objects as Integer.valueOf(230)
      Collections.sort(li);
      Iterator itr=li.iterator();
      while(itr.hasNext()){ System.out.println(itr.next());
      }
   }
}
```

Output 16.9

```
250
450
650
```

This program illustrates the sorting of wrapper class objects. Integer is one of the wrapper classes. The integer values are added using `ArrayList` object. The given values are converted either by invoking the valueOf() method or by internal conversion done on the integer values. These two types of conversion are demonstrated in the program code. Then by invoking the sort() method of Collections interface the objects are arranged in ascending order. The output shows that the integer values are sorted.

User-defined class objects are sorted by Comparable interface in collections. This is discussed in the following section.

16.6 COMPARABLE VS COMPARATOR INTERFACES

Comparable interface

The Comparable interface in the java.lang package comes into use when a class has a natural ordering. Given a collection of objects of the same type, the interface allows you to order the collection into that natural ordering.

The compareTo() method compares the current instance with an element passed in as an argument. If the current instance comes before the argument in the ordering, a negative value is returned. If the current instance comes after, then a positive value is returned. Otherwise, zero is returned. A zero return value does not indicate the equality of elements. A zero return value just signifies that two objects are ordered at the same position.

Program 16.10 illustrates the implementation of Comparable interface.

Program 16.10

```
import java.util.*;
class Student implements Comparable<Student>{
   int rollno;
   String name;
   int age;
   Student(int rollno,String name,int age){
      this.rollno=rollno;
      this.name=name;
      this.age=age;
   }
   public int compareTo(Student st){
      if(rollno==st.rollno)
      return 0;
      else if(rollno>st.rollno)
      return 1;
      else
      return -1;
   }
}
public class ComparableExample {
   public static void main(String[] args) { ArrayList<Student> al=new
   ArrayList<Student>();
      al.add(new Student(101,"Saga",23));
      al.add(new Student(106,"Joe",24));
      al.add(new Student(105,"Jose",25));
      System.out.println("Sort by Rollno");
      Collections.sort(al);
      for(Student st:al){
         System.out.println(st.rollno+" "+st.name+" "+st.age);
      }
   }
}
```

Output 16.10

```
Sort by Rollno
101  Saga 23
105  Jose 25
106  Joe 24
```

This program demonstrates the concept of user-defined object sorting using the `Comparable` interface. `Student` class is created with a set of data members which implement the `Comparable` interface. The interface method `compareTo()` is defined within `Student` class. Then the Java `main` class is created.

With the help of `ArrayList` class, values are assigned to the `Student` class object. Three sets of data are added into the `ArrayList` object. The `compareTo()` method is used to compare the currently added rollno value with the previous one. With this comparison, the data elements are sorted based on rollno. Then the `sort()` method is invoked and the sorted values are printed.

`Comparator` interface

Java `Comparator` interface is used to order the objects of a user-defined class. This interface is found in `java.util` package and contains two methods—`compare (Object obj1,Object obj2)` and `equals(-Object element)`. It provides multiple sorting sequences, that is, the elements can be sorted on the basis of any data member, for example rollno, name, age or anything else.

The collections framework provides a special `Set` interface for maintaining elements in a sorted order by `SortedSet`. The methods in the `SortedSet` interface are as follows.

- `comparator()`
- `first()`
- `last()`
- `headSet(Object toElement)`
- `subSet(Object fromElement,Object toElement)`
- `tailSet(Object fromElement)`

The interface provides access methods to the ends of the set as well as to subsets of the set. When working with subsets of the list, changes to the subset are reflected in the source set. In addition, changes to the source set are reflected in the subset. This works because subsets are identified by elements at the end points, not indices. In addition, if the `fromElement` is part of the source set, it is part of the subset. However, if the `toElement` is part of the source set, it is not part of the subset.

The elements added to a `SortedSet` must either implement `Comparable` or you must provide a `Comparator` to the constructor of its implementation class `TreeSet`. To demonstrate this, **Program 16.11** uses the reverse order `Comparator` available from the `Collections` class.

Program 16.11

```
import java.util.*;
class Student {
   int rollno;
   String name;
   int age;
   Student(int rollno,String name,int age){
      this.rollno=rollno;
      this.name=name;
      this.age=age;
   }}
class AgeComparator implements Comparator{
   public int compare(Object o1,Object o2)
   { Student s1=(Student)o1;
      Student s2=(Student)o2;
      if(s1.age==s2.age) return 0;
      else if(s1.age>s2.age)
      return 1;
      else
      return -1;
   }}
```

```
class NameComparator implements Comparator{
   public int compare(Object o1,Object o2){
      Student s1=(Student)o1;
      Student s2=(Student)o2;
      return s1.name.compareTo(s2.name);
   }}
public class ComparatorExample {
   public static void main(String[] args) {
      ArrayList al=new ArrayList();
      al.add(new Student(101,"saga",23));
      al.add(new Student(106,"joe",24));
      al.add(new Student(105,"jose",25));
      System.out.println("Sorting by Name...");
      Collections.sort(al,new NameComparator());
      //compare()method of NameComparator invoked
      Iterator itr=al.iterator();
      while(itr.hasNext()){
         Student st=(Student)itr.next();
         System.out.println(st.rollno+" "+st.name+" "+st.age);
      }
      System.out.println("sorting by age");
      Collections.sort(al,new AgeComparator());
      //compare()method of AgeComparator invoked
      Iterator itr2=al.iterator();
      while(itr2.hasNext()){
         Student st=(Student)itr2.next();
         System.out.println(st.rollno+" "+st.name+" "+st.age);
      }}}
```

Output 16.11

```
Sorting by Name...
106 joe 24
105 jose 25
101 saga 23
sorting by age...
101 saga 23
106 joe 24
105 jose 25
```

This program illustrates another way of sorting user-defined objects using `Comparator` interface. Program 16.10 is modified by splitting Student class into two classes, namely `AgeComparator` and `NameComparator`. Instead of implementing `comparable` interface, `Comparator` interface is implemented in both the classes. For method definition, the `compare()` method is used instead of `compareTo()` to compare the objects. The first class compares the values based on Age and the second class compares the values based on Name, then invokes the `sort()` method to arrange the objects in ascending order. Finally, using `Iterator` interface, the values are retrieved and printed.

Difference between `Comparable` and `Comparator`

`Comparable` and `Comparator` are both interfaces and can be used to sort collection elements. But there are many differences between `Comparable` and `Comparator` interfaces (Table.16.5).

Table 16.5 `Comparable` vs `Comparator` **interface**

Comparable	Comparator
`Comparable` provides a **single sorting sequence.** The collection can be sorted on the basis of a single element such as id, name, price, and so on.	`Comparator` provides **multiple sorting sequence.** The collection can be sorted on the basis of multiple elements such as id, name and price.
`Comparable` **affects the original class**, that is, actual class is modified.	`Comparator` **doesn't affect the original class**, that is, the actual class is not modified.
`Comparable` provides `compareTo()` **method** to sort elements.	`Comparator` provides `compare()` **method** to sort elements.
`Comparable` is found in `java.lang` package.	`Comparator` is found in `java.util` package.
We can sort the list elements of Comparable type by `Collections.sort(List)` method.	We can sort the list elements of Comparator type by `Collections.sort(List,Comparator)` method.

SUMMARY

1. The collections Framework provides a well-designed set of interfaces and implementations for representing and manipulating groups of elements.
2. Understanding the capabilities of this framework reduces the effort required to design and implement a comparable set of APIs.
3. By developing the concept of collections, groups of data elements can be managed in various aspects like arranging the data, inserting, deleting and finding the data elements in an easy manner.
4. The interfaces which are available in collections frameworks are `List`, `Set`, `Map` and so on. These are demonstrated with programs. `Collection` interfaces provide the set of methods to process the groups of data.
5. The interfaces are provided with Abstract level methods to implement and manipulate the groups of data.
6. The collection implementation classes are used to manage the data. The classes which are implemented using collections framework are `HashSet`, `LinkedHashSet`, `TreeSet`, `HashMap`, `TreeMap`, `PriorityQueue` and their use is demonstrated with programs. The difference between the interfaces and implementation classes is illustrated clearly.

SHORT QUESTIONS

1. What is the `Vector` class?
2. What is the `Set` interface?
3. What is the `Dictionary` class?
4. What is the `HashTable` class?
5. What is the difference between `HashSet` and `TreeSet`?
6. What are the three major parts of the collections framework?
7. Write down the methods of the `List` interface.
8. Define implementation class.
9. Differentiate between `HashMap` and `HashSet`.
10. Define `Comparable` and `Comparator` interfaces.

COMPREHENSIVE QUESTIONS

1. Explain `set` iinterface and `sorted` interface.
2. Differentiate between `array` list and `linked` list.
3. Explain priority `Queue` classes.
4. Differentiate between `HashTable` and `HashMap`.
5. Explain sorting in collections.
6. Differentiate between `Comparable` interface and `Comparator` interface.
7. Elaborate on the `SortedMap` interface methods.
8. Explain `Map` interface methods.
9. Explain the methods available in `Queue` interface.
10. Elucidate the `list` interface methods.
11. Explain the `Collection` interface.
12. Explain in detail the collection implementation classes.
13. Explain `HashSet`, `LinkedHashSet` and `TreeSet` classes with examples.
14. Illustrate `HashMap`, `LinkedHashMap` and `TreeMap` classes.
15. Explain `HashTable` classes and differentiate between `HashTable` and `HashMap`.
16. Explain in detail `Comparable` interface and `Comparator` interface.

SOLVED PROGRAMS

1. Display mobile handset details using Comparable interface.

```
package Collections;
import java.util.*;
class Product implements java.lang.Comparable<Product>{
  int p_id;
  String p_name;
  int p_price;
  Product(int pid,String pname,int price){
     this.p_id=pid;
     this.p_name=pname;
     this.p_price=price;
  }
  public int compareTo(Product pt){
     if(p_price==pt.p_price)
     return 0;
     else if(p_price>pt.p_price)
     return 1;
     else
     return -1;
  }
}
public class Comparable {
  public static void main(String[] args) {
     ArrayList<Product> al=new ArrayList<Product>();
     al.add(new Product(101,"Samsung",50000));
     al.add(new Product(110,"Oppo",25000));
     al.add(new Product(105,"Vivo",20000));
     System.out.println("Sort by Product Price");
     Collections.sort(al);
     for(Product pt:al){
        System.out.println(pt.p_id+" "+pt.p_name+" "+pt.p_price);
     }
  }
}
```

Output

```
Sort by Product Price
105  Vivo 20000
110  Oppo 25000
101  Samsung 50000
```

2. Display the hobbies of a person using HashMap class.

```
import java.util.HashMap;
public class HashMapExample {
  private int id;
  private String firstName;
  private String lastName;
  private HashMap hobbies;
  public HashMapExample()
  {
  }
  public HashMapExample(int id,String fname, String lname)
  {
     this.id=id;
     this.firstName = fname;
     this.lastName = lname;
     this.hobbies=hobbies;
  }
  public static void main(String[] args) {
     HashMap set1 = new HashMap();
```

```
        set1.put("Listening","Musics");
        set1.put("Reading", "Books-Newspaper");
        set1.put("Writing", "Story-Poems");
        HashMapExample emp1=new
        HashMapExample(1,"Joe","Smith");
        System.out.println("Id="+emp1.id);
        System.out.println("Firstname="+emp1.
        firstName);
        System.out.println("LastName="+emp1.
        lastName);
        System.out.println("Type="+set1.keySet()+"
        Values ="+set1.values());
    }
  }
```

Output

```
Id=1
Firstname=Joe
LastName=Smith
Type=[Reading, Listening,
Writing]
Values =[Books-Newspaper,
Musics, Story-Poems]
```

3. Create a collection using HashTable class for Electronic items.

```
import java.util.Enumeration;
import java.util.Hashtable;
public class HashTable {
   public static void main(String[] args) {
      Hashtable electronic = new Hashtable();
      Enumeration names;
      String str;
      double bal;
      electronic.put("Phones","Vivo-Oppo-Samsung");
      electronic.put("Laptops", "Lenovo-Wipro-HP");
      electronic.put("Tab","Samsung-Lenovo-Intex" );
      names = electronic.keys();
      while(names.hasMoreElements()) {
         str = (String) names.nextElement();
         System.out.println(str + ": " +
         electronic.get(str));
      }
      System.out.println();
   }
  }
```

Output

```
Tab: Samsung-Lenovo-Intex
Phones: Vivo-Oppo-Samsung
Laptops: Lenovo-Wipro-HP
```

4. Grouping countries and their weather details using HashMap, LinkedHashMap and TreeMap classes.

```
import java.util.HashMap;
import java.util.LinkedHashMap;
import java.util.TreeMap;
public class MapExample {
   public static void main(String args[])
   {
      HashMap m = new HashMap();
      // Put elements to the map
      m.put("India", new Double(97.3));
      m.put("America", new Double(105.2));
      m.put("Pakistan", new Double(17.5));
      m.put("China", new Double(78.6));
      m.put("Japan", new Double(100.8));
      System.out.println("HashMap(keyvalue pair):"+m);
      System.out.println("Key elements:"+m.keySet());
      System.out.println("Value elements:"+m.values());
      System.out.println();
```

```
        LinkedHashMap lm=new LinkedHashMap();
        lm.put("India", new Double(97.3));
        lm.put("America", new Double(105.2));
        lm.put("Pakistan", new Double(17.5));
        lm.put("Canada", new Double(78.6));
        lm.put("Greece", new Double(100.8));
        System.out.println("LinkedHashMap(keyvalue pair):"+lm);
        System.out.println("Key elements:"+lm.keySet());
        System.out.println("Value elements:"+lm.values());
        System.out.println();
        TreeMap tm=new TreeMap(lm);
        System.out.println("TreeMap(keyvalue pair):"+tm);
        System.out.println("Key elements:"+tm.keySet());
        System.out.println("Value elements:"+tm.values());
    }
}
```

Output

```
HashMap(keyvalue pair):{Pakistan=17.5, China=78.6, Japan=100.8, America=105.2,
India=97.3}
Key elements:[Pakistan, China, Japan, America, India]
Value elements:[17.5, 78.6, 100.8, 105.2, 97.3]
LinkedHashMap(keyvalue pair):{India=97.3, America=105.2, Pakistan=17.5,
Canada=78.6, Greece=100.8}
Key elements:[India, America, Pakistan, Canada, Greece]
Value elements:[97.3, 105.2, 17.5, 78.6, 100.8]
TreeMap(keyvalue pair):{America=105.2, Canada=78.6, Greece=100.8, India=97.3,
Pakistan=17.5}
Key elements:[America, Canada, Greece, India, Pakistan]
Value elements:[105.2, 78.6, 100.8, 97.3, 17.5]
```

5. Display five country names and perform the remove operation using PriorityQueue class.

```
import java.util.Iterator;
import java.util.PriorityQueue;
public class PriorityQueueExample {
  public static void main(String args[])
  {
    PriorityQueue<String> queue=new
    PriorityQueue<String>();
    queue.add("America");
    queue.add("India");
    queue.add("Canada");
    queue.add("China");
    queue.add("Japan");
    System.out.println("head:"+queue.
    element());
    System.out.println("head:"+queue.peek());
    System.out.println("ITERATING THE
    ELEMENTS:");
    Iterator itr=queue.iterator();
    while(itr.hasNext()){
       System.out.println(itr.next());
    }
    queue.remove();
    queue.poll();
```

Output

```
head:America
head:America
ITERATING THE ELEMENTS:
America
China
Canada
India
Japan
AFTER REMOVING TWO ELEMENTS:
China
India
Japan
```

```
        System.out.println("AFTER REMOVING TWO ELEMENTS:");
        Iterator<String> itr2=queue.iterator();
        while(itr2.hasNext()){
            System.out.println(itr2.next());
        }
    }
}
```

PROGRAMMING EXERCISES

1. Write a program to implement the `List` interface for Product Details.
2. Write a program to display three students' details using the `ArrayList` class.
3. Write a program to implement student details using the `Set` interface.
4. Write a program to display college details using the `Iterator` class.
5. Write a program to implement book details using the `Map` interface.
6. Write a program to implement comparable interface for `BankAccount` details.
7. Write a program to display all the states of India and their weather information using `HashMap` and `LinkedHashMap` classes.
8. Write a program to display the staff member name as value and department as key using `HashTable` class.
9. Write a program to sort the employee details based on name and experience by implementing `Comparator` interface.
10. Write a program to sort UG departments based on name by implementing `Comparable` interface.

CHAPTER

17

Design Patterns

In the year 1994, a book was published with the title *Design Patterns—Elements of Reusable Object-Oriented Software* written by Erich Gamma, Richard Helm, Ralph Johnson and John Vlissides. Before the publication of this book, no one knew about the use of design patterns in solving object-oriented software development problems. This book introduced a whole new concept, *design patterns*, in the OOP world. The people who wrote the book are called the *Gang of Four* (GOF). In software engineering terms, a design pattern is a solution to frequently occurring problems in software design. It is not an end product that can be directly used or applied in the program code. However, the design pattern provides a template that can be used in different situations to provide solutions to repeatedly occurring problems. A definition given by the *Christopher Alexander* provides a direct view of design patterns, 'Each pattern describes a problem which occurs over and over again in our environment, and then describes the core of the solution to that problem'. As the definition suggests, one thing that should be remembered is that a design pattern is an idea to solve frequently occurring software design problems and not an implementation. Design patterns are language independent, which means that they can be utilised by all types of object-oriented programming languages. Remember that a design pattern may be language-independent but it can be applied only in an object-oriented environment, which means that object-oriented programming languages alone can use these patterns. By implementing the design patterns while developing a program, a developer can make the code more flexible and reusable. If one wants to become an effective object-oriented software developer, one should know or use design patterns in the programming practice. Once again, a design pattern does not provide direct code to merge with an existing program to solve a problem, but it provides an idea to develop a program that can solve the software design issues. For example, consider a situation where the developer/programmer wants to declare a class that can be instantiated only once and used by all other classes. So the requirement is that it stops further creation after the instantiation of the class. There is a solution to solve this problem through design pattern; a commonly used design pattern for this type of problem is a *singleton pattern*, which provides a programming idea to solve the above stated problem.

17.1 INTRODUCTION

Benefits of using design patterns

As mentioned earlier, design patterns do not provide direct implementation; rather, they suggest programming ideas that are reusable in many software development scenarios. Design patterns have evolved through years of programming experiences by trial and error. So the solutions provided by these patterns are drawn from real-time experiences. They are proven and tested solutions. Design patterns provide common solutions to the object-oriented software developer and it is based on the best practices evolved over a long period of time, by experienced and specialised programmers across the industry.

Parts of a design pattern

A design pattern is not an entity; rather it is collection of various design patterns. Each such pattern has the following elements:

- Name,
- Problem,
- Solution, and
- Consequences.

Each design pattern is named based on what type of problem it can solve. It gives a picture of when and how to use a particular design pattern. The solution gives a common template to solve the particular problem. Even though a design pattern provides a solution, it may sometimes have unexpected consequences, which are documented as part of the description.

The next section discusses various types of design pattern.

17.2 CATALOGUE FOR DESIGN PATTERN

A design pattern is not a single entity, rather, it is a class of many different patterns. Each of such patterns describes a solution to a particular problem in object-oriented software development. There are roughly twenty-four design patterns available to solve specific design issues, and based on the nature of these patterns, they are grouped together under three categories—*creational, structural* and *behavioural patterns*.

Creational design patterns

There are five different patterns that come under creational design patterns. These patterns suggest five different ways to instantiate or declare an object for a class instead of creating an object in the usual way. This provides a programmer more flexibility in the creation of an object. Hence the object can be created based on the need or situation. In general, patterns that come under creational patterns are concerned with the ways of creating an object. These patterns are used when a decision is made at the time of instantiation. Patterns that fall under creational design pattern are:

- factory method pattern,
- prototype pattern,
- singleton pattern,
- builder pattern, and
- abstract factory pattern.

Factory method pattern defines an interface or abstract class for creating an object but lets the subclasses decide which class to instantiate. *Prototype pattern* suggests cloning an existing object and customising it as per the needs, instead of creating a whole new one. *Singleton pattern* talks of declaring a class that has only one object and making a global access point. *Builder pattern* constructs a complex object from a simple one using a step-by-step approach. *Abstract factory pattern* defines an interface or abstract class to instantiate a family of similar objects.

Structural design patterns

Factory method patterns are concerned with the way of creating objects, whereas the structural design patterns are concerned with how classes and objects are composed to form larger structures. For example, multiple inheritance combines the various classes into one single class. The advantage of inheriting multiple classes is that a single class can access all the properties and methods of those classes. The primary focus of these structural patterns is on how the classes inherit and are composed from other classes. It simplifies the structure of inheritance by recognising the relationships among the various classes in a structure. There are seven different patterns that exist in the structural category:

- adapter pattern,
- bridge pattern,
- composite pattern,
- decorator pattern,
- façade pattern,
- flyweight pattern, and
- proxy pattern.

An *adapter pattern* suggests just converting the interface of a class into another interface that a client wants. *Bridge pattern* decouples an abstraction from its implementation so that the two can vary independently. A *composite pattern* talks of just allowing clients to operate in a generic manner on objects that may or may not represent a hierarchy of objects.

Decorator pattern dynamically attaches flexible and or additional responsibilities to an object. A *facade pattern* talks of providing an unified and simplified interface to a set of interfaces in a subsystem; therefore it hides the complexities of the subsystem from the client. The *flyweight pattern* reuses similar kinds of existing objects by storing and creating new ones when no similar objects are found. *Proxy pattern* creates an object which represents other objects, so the original object is hidden from the outside.

Behavioural design patterns

These kinds of patterns describe the communication between classes and objects. Behavioural class patterns use inheritance to distribute behaviour between classes, behavioural object patterns use object composition rather than inheritance. The primary concern among patterns in the behavioural category is to avoid tightly coupled patterns and to provide an easy communication among objects and classes with loosely coupled ones. By implementing loosely-coupled communication, a client can avoid hard coding and dependency. There are twelve design patterns that come under this category—(i) chain of responsibility pattern, (ii) command pattern, (iii) interpreter pattern, (iv) iterator pattern, (v) mediator pattern, (vi) memento pattern, (vii) observer pattern, (viii) state pattern, (ix) strategy pattern, (x) template pattern, (xi) visitor pattern, and (xii) null object pattern.

In *command pattern,* the call for an operation is enfolded under an object as a command and passed to the invoker object. The invoker object searches for the appropriate object that can handle this command and passes to it for execution. The *interpreter pattern* provides a way to evaluate language grammar or expression. The *iterator pattern* provides a way to access the elements of a collection object in a sequential manner without any need to know its underlying representation. The *mediator pattern* reduces the communication complexities among objects. The *memento pattern* helps to restore the state of an object to the previous state. If one-to-many relationships exist among objects, changes made to one object will reflect changes in its dependent objects. The *observer pattern* helps to implement this type of relationship among objects. The *state pattern* allows an object to change its behaviour when changes are made to its internals. In *strategy pattern*, the behaviour of the class is changed during execution. In *template pattern*, abstract class provides a way or template to run its methods and its subclasses can override the methods as per requirement, but the invocation should be the same as defined in the abstract class. In the *chain of responsibility pattern*, the sender sends a request to a chain of objects and that request will be handled by any object in the chain. The *visitor pattern* changes its execution algorithms when the visitor of the class changes. The *null object pattern* replaces the check for NULL object instance.

The genesis and types of design patterns in general have been discussed. An elaborate discussion of all the twenty-four patterns in this chapter alone is not possible, but the subsequent sections introduce some of the design patterns that are necessary and frequently used. Before looking at each pattern in depth, there are certain concepts that a developer needs to understand such as class and object, inheritance and interface, that are prerequisites to understanding design patterns.

17.3 FACTORY METHOD PATTERN DEFINITION

A factory pattern or factory method pattern affirms that it is advisable to just '*define an interface or abstract class for creating an object but let the subclasses decide which class to instantiate*', as given by GOF.

In an object-oriented environment, not all objects that are created are utilised during the development or compile time; only one or two are used at run time. This kind of unhealthy programming practice causes a wastage of memory due to creating too many objects and not using all of them. Some of the objects are never used in the program's lifetime. Factory method pattern is a programming technique developed to resolve such object creation problems. Here, the creation of objects is delegated to the subclasses. Instead of creating all necessary objects while developing a program, it creates only an object that is required during run time. So, objects that are not needed at run time are avoided. Figure 17.1 illustrates the factory method pattern.

Where to use the factory method pattern

- When a base class doesn't know which subclasses will be needed to create an object.
- When a class needs its subclasses to decide which object is to be created.
- When the parent classes leave the creation of objects to their subclasses.

UML diagram

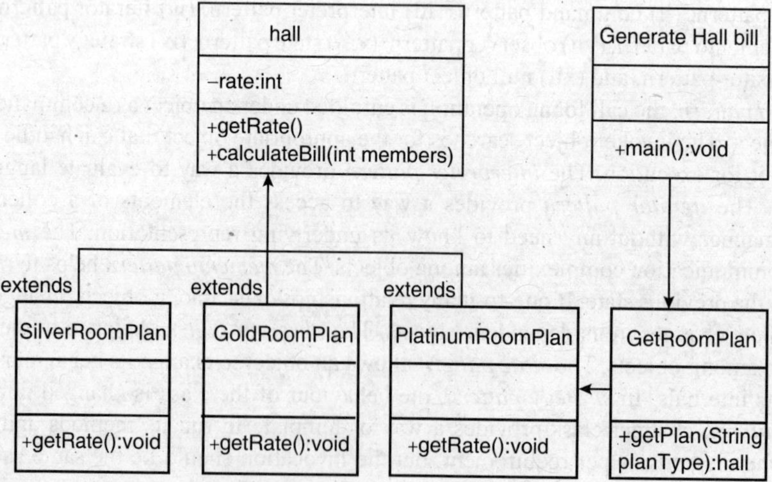

Fig. 17.1 Factory method pattern

Steps involved

STEP 1: Create an interface or abstract class.

```
abstract class hall
{
    protected int rate;
    abstract void getRate();
    public void calculateBill(int members)
    { System.out.println(members*rate);
    }
}
```

STEP 2: Develop a concrete class to inherit an abstract class.

```
class SilverRoomPlan extends hall
{ void getRate()
    {
        rate=800;
    }
}
class GoldRoomPlan extends hall
{
    void getRate()
    {
        rate=1400;
    }
}
class PlatinumRoomPlan extends hall
{
    void getRate()
    {
        rate=2000;
    }
}
```

STEP 3: Develop a factory class to an generate object for concrete class based on the given choice.

```
class GetRoomPlan
{
    public hall getPlan(String planType)
    {
        if(planType == null)
        {
            STEP 4
            return null;
        }
        if(planType.equalsIgnoreCase("APRC"))
        {
            return new SilverRoomPlan();
        }
```

```
        else if(planType.equalsIgnoreCase("INDOOR"))
        {
           return new GoldRoomPlan();
        }
        else if(planType.equalsIgnoreCase("BOSCO"))
        {
           return new PlatinumRoomPlan();
        }
        return null;
}}
```

Use the factory to get an object of concrete class by passing the type.

```
public class Generate Hall bill
{
   public static void main(String[] args) throws IOException
   {
      GetRoomPlan planFactory = new GetRoomPlan();
      System.out.print("WELCOME TO HALL BOOKING");
      System.out.print("Enter the Type of HALL: ");
      BufferedReader br=new BufferedReader(new InputStreamReader(System.in));
      String planName=br.readLine();
      System.out.print("Enter the number of DAYS: ");
      int members=Integer.parseInt(br.readLine());
      hall p = planFactory.getPlan(planName);
      System.out.print("Bill amount for "+planName+" of "+members+" members
      is: ");
      p.getRate();
      p.calculateBill(members);
   }
}
```

```
Output
WELCOME TO HALL BOOKING
Enter the Type of HALL: Bosco
Enter the number of DAYS: 4
Bill amount for Bosco of 4
members is: 8000
```

An abstract class `hall` is declared with three concrete classes namely `SilverRoomPlan`, `GoldRoomPlan` and `PlatinumRoomPlan`. A factory creator class `GetRoomPlan` is declared to create a factory of objects. The abstract class `hall` lets the subclasses decide which class is to be instantiated. A factory creator takes care of object creation based on the given option. The client class `Generate Hall bill` receives the option for booking a hall for a given number of days, from the user through a buffered reader. It creates an object `planFactory` for the factory class. Through the statement hall `p = planFactory.getPlan(planName)`, the type of room to be booked is sent to the factory creator and then the object is created for the concrete class based on the option received and returned. The object returned will be assigned to object `p` of the abstract class `hall`. For example, if the user enters the `bosco` hall to be booked, the received hall name will be sent to the factory creator. The factory creator class creates an object `bosco` for the `Platinum- RoomPlan` and returns it. Through the object `p`, `getRate()` method is invoked, it should be noted here that the object `p` is already assigned with an object created by the factory creator, so only the method which belongs to the respective concrete class is invoked and the corresponding rate is sent to the abstract class. The `calculate()` method of the abstract class is invoked to perform the calculation. The received bill amount is then displayed to the user. By using the factory method, memory is saved by avoiding the creation of too many objects. If the usual manner is followed, the developer will have to create three objects per type of room. Not all three objects will be used, because the user will book only one hall at a time.

17.4 PROTOTYPE PATTERN

In the prototype pattern, a new object is created by cloning an existing object. The newly created object can be customised as per the needs of the developer. If not, the newly created object is just a replica of the existing object. This type of pattern is suitable where creating an object is an expensive task. It allows the user to insert or delete objects during execution. The prototype pattern avoids the creation of subclasses. Figure 17.2 illustrates the prototype pattern.

Where to use the prototype pattern

- When object creation is done during execution.
- When creating an object is expensive or complicated.
- To keep a minimum number of classes in the application.
- To hide object creation and its representation from the user.

UML

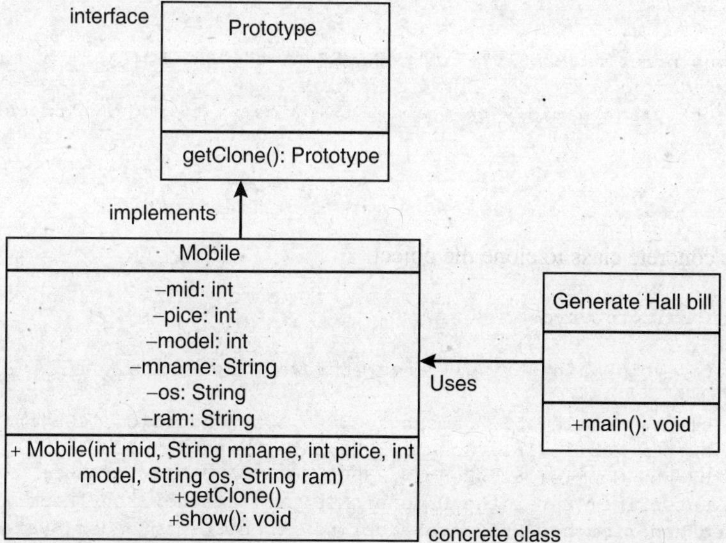

Fig. 17.2 Prototype pattern

Steps involved

STEP 1: Create an abstract class or interface with a method that is used to clone an object.

```
import java.io.BufferedReader;
import java.io.IOException;
import java.io.InputStreamReader;
interface Prototype
{
    public Prototype getClone();
}
```

STEP 2: Create a concrete class that inherits an abstract class or interface.

```
class Mobile implements Prototype
{
   int mid, price, model;
   String mname,os,ram;
   public Mobile(int mid, String mname, int price, int model,String os,String ram)
   {
      this.mid = mid;
      this.mname = mname;
      this.price = price;
      this.model = model;
      this.os = os;
      this.ram = ram;
   }
   public Prototype getClone()
   {
      return new Mobile(mid,mname,price,model,os,ram);
   }
   public void show()
   { System.out.println("Mob_ID"+"\t"+"MNAME"+"\ t"+"PRICE"+"\t"+"MODEL"+"\t"+"OS"
   +"\t"+"RAM"+"\t");
      System.out.println(mid+»\t»+mname+»\t»+price+»\ t»+model+»\t»+os+»\t»+ram
      +»\t»);
   }
}
```

STEP 3: Use the concrete class to clone the object.

```
public class Mobileprototype
{
   public static void main(String[] args) throws IOException
   {
      Mobile b1=new Mobile(151,"Samsung",23000,2014,"Android","4GB");
      Mobile b2=new Mobile(161,"Sony",23000,2014,"Windows","2GB");
      Mobile b3=new Mobile(181,»Redmi»,23000,2015,»Android»,»4GB»);
      System.out.print("Enter the Name of MOBILE:(Samsung, Sony,Redmi): ");
      BufferedReader br=new BufferedReader(new InputStreamReader(System.in));
      String btype=br.readLine();
      if(btype.equalsIgnoreCase("Samsung"))
      {
         Mobile e4=(Mobile) b1.getClone();
         e4.show();
      }
```

```
        else if(btype.equalsIgnoreCase("Sony"))
        {
            Mobile e4=(Mobile) b2.getClone();
            e4.show();
        }
        else if(btype.
        equalsIgnoreCase("Redmi"))
        {
            Mobile e4=(Mobile)
            b3.getClone();
            e4.show();
        }
    }
}
```

```
Output
Enter the Name of MOBILE: (Samsung, Sony,
Redmi): Redmi
 Mob_ID  MNAME  PRICE  MODEL    OS     RAM
  181    Redmi  23000  2015  Android  4GB
```

An interface `Prototype` is created with the `getClone()` method of type `Prototype`. This method is used to clone the object whenever required. A concrete class `Mobile` which inherits an interface `Prototype` is declared with integer type data members `mid`, `price` and `model` and string type data members `mname`, `os` and `ram`. The concrete class also has member functions such as `Mobile` constructor, `getClone()` method and `show()` methods. The `Mobile` constructor receives data from the client when an object is created for this class and assigns it to the local data members. The `getClone()` method clones the object resulting in the required object. The `show()` method displays all the data to the user. In the public class `Mobile-prototype`, three objects `b1`, `b2` and `b3` are created for the concrete class `Mobile`. These three objects have been assigned data about different mobiles, while being created through constructors. The `b1` object holds the information about the mobile Samsung, `b2` about Sony, and `b3` about Redmi respectively. These three objects will be cloned whenever the user wants to know the price of the particular mobile. The String type variable `btype` receives the mobile type from the user through a buffered reader. After receiving the mobile type, it is checked with an `if…else` ladder. If the type equals 'Samsung', then the first `if` block is executed, otherwise the subsequent `else…if` blocks will be executed. If the user enters the mobile type as 'Samsung' the `if` block is chosen and the statement inside the block `Mobile e4=(- Mobile) b1.getClone()` clones `b1` object and then assigns it to the newly created object `e4` of Mobile concrete class and the `show()` method is invoked with the newly created object `e4`. The `e4` object will have the same data as the cloned object `b1`. So the `e4` object is just a replica of `b1` object and it displays the same data from `b1` object to the user.

17.5 SINGLETON PATTERN

In this type of pattern, a class is allowed to be instantiated only once and further instantiation is not allowed. A single object of that class can be used by all other classes. This class provides a public access point to use its single object. It saves memory because the object is not created at each request and a single object is reused.

Two things should be monitored here—the first is to make a single object easily accessible by all other classes and the second is to monitor the further instantiation of the class. A better solution is to make the class itself responsible for keeping track of its sole instance. The class can ensure that no other instance can be created (by intercepting requests to create new objects), and it can provide a way to access the instance. Figure 17.3 illustrates the functioning of a Singleton pattern. There are two forms of the Singleton design pattern.

- **Early instantiation:** creation of instance at load time.
- **Lazy instantiation:** creation of instance when required.

UML

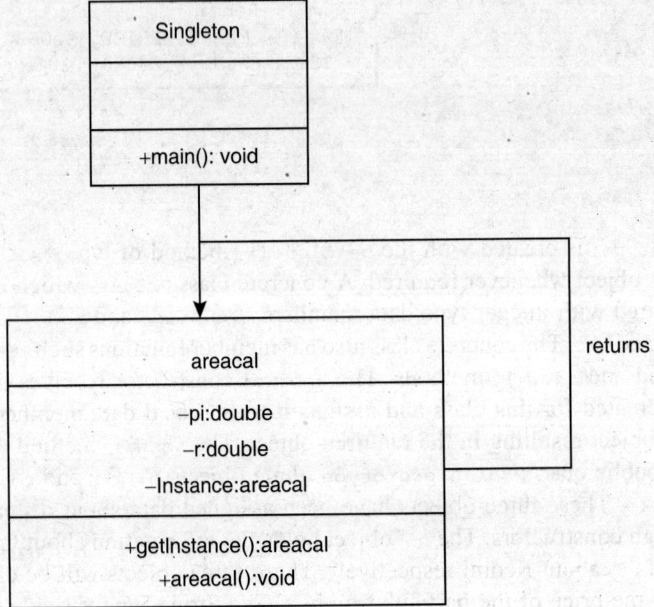

Fig. 17.3 Singleton pattern

Steps involved

STEP 1: Create a singleton class.

```
import java.io.*;
class areacal
{
    double pi=3.14,r;
    private static areacal instance = new areacal();
    private areacal(){}
    public static areacal getInstance()
    {
        return instance;
    }
}
```

STEP 2: Get the single object from the Singleton class.

```
public class Singleton
{
    public static void main(String[] args) throws
    IOException
    {
        //areacal obj =new areacal();
        areacal obj = areacal.getInstance();
        BufferedReader br=new BufferedReader(new
        InputStreamReader(System.in));
        System.out.print("Enter the radius value:");
        String r=br.readLine();
        obj.r=Double.parseDouble(r);
        double pi=obj.pi;
        double aoc=pi*(obj.r*obj.r);
        System.out.println("The Area of circle for the given radius value = "+obj.
        r+" is "+aoc);
    }
}
```

```
Output
Enter the radius value: 7.5
The Area of circle for the
given radius value = 7.5 is
176.625
```

A class `areacal` is created with the data members `pi`=3.14, `r` of type double and this class will be made singleton by making the constructor of this class private. By making the constructor private through the statement `private areacal(){}` , object creation for this class is blocked. So the constructor is declared with a private access modifier. But without the object of the class, its members can't be accessed from outside. A single object `instance` is declared to access the data members of this class and a `getInstance()` method of type `areacal` is declared to return the single object `instance`. Whenever the `getInstance()` method is invoked, it returns the single object `instance`. If another class needs to access the data members `pi` and `r` of the class `areacal`, it should use the single object `instance` by invoking the `getInstance()` method. A public class `Singleton` is declared to use the single object `instance` to access its data members. In the first statement `areacal obj =new areacal()`, a new object `obj` is created as usual to access the data members. When the program is executed, it will invoke an exception. In the very next statement, `areacal obj = areacal.getInstance()` an object `obj` is created by invoking the `getInstance()` method; this method returns the single object `instance` to the object `obj`. Through the object `obj`, all the operations will be carried out. The `BufferedReader` and `InputStreamReader` are used to get the radius value from the user. The received radius value will be assigned to the double type variable `r`. The `r` variable is a data member of singleton class `areacal`, so it is called through the object `obj`. After receiving the radius value, the area of the circle is calculated for which the pi value is needed; the pi value is stored in the double type variable `pi` of singleton class `areacal`. A local `pi` variable of type double is declared to retrieve the `pi` value through the statement `obj.pi`. So far the radius value and pi value have been received and stored in the respective variables. Through the statement `double aoc=pi*(obj.r*obj.r)` the area of the circle is calculated and stored in the double type variable `aoc`. The result is then displayed to the user.

17.6 PROXY PATTERN

In proxy pattern, an object is created to represent another object and this hides the original object. An object that represents another object is called a proxy object. According to GOF, a proxy pattern 'provides the control for accessing the original object'. Using this pattern, many useful operations can be performed, such as, *hiding the information of the original object*, on demand loading, and so on. This pattern is also known as *Surrogate* or *Placeholder.* Figure 17.4 illustrates the proxy pattern.

Where to use the proxy pattern

- **Virtual proxy**—Proxy pattern can be used when more than one database access request arrives to extract a large size image. This type of situation will create multiple proxies and consume vast memory. The original object is created only once when the first request arrives, after which the proxy object is used to serve another request.
- **Protective proxy**—Here a proxy pattern can be used as an authorisation layer to verify whether the actual user has access to appropriate content. For example, a proxy server restricts some internet access. Only the websites and content that are valid will be allowed and the remaining ones will be blocked.
- **Remote proxy**—A remote proxy can be thought of as the stub in the RPC call. The remote proxy provides a local representation of the object that is present in a different address location. Another example can be, providing an interface for remote resources such as web service or REST resources.
- **Smart proxy**—A smart proxy provides an additional layer of security by interposing specific actions when the object is accessed. For example, to check whether the real object is locked or not before accessing it, so that no other objects can change it.

UML

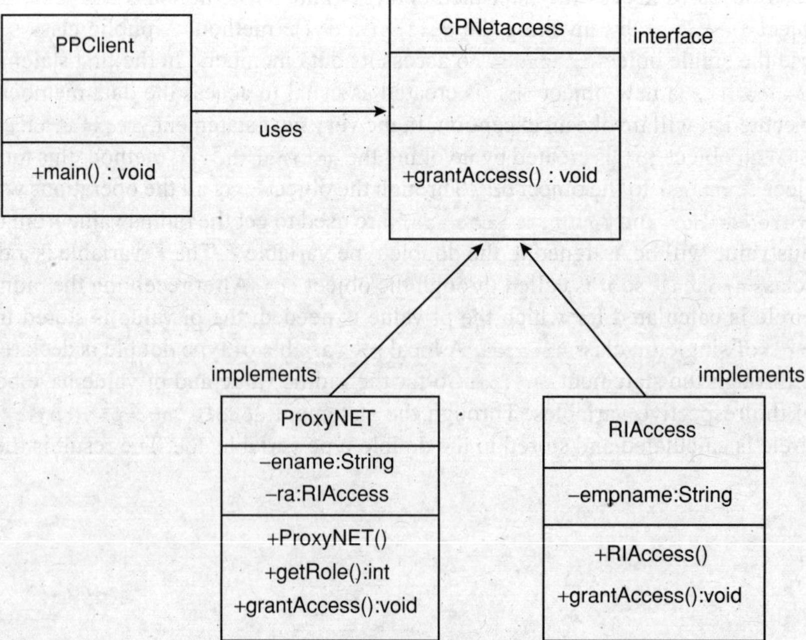

Fig. 17.4 Proxy pattern

Steps involved

STEP 1: Create an interface.

```
interface CPNetaccess
{
   public void grantAccess();
}
```

STEP 2: Create a class which actually provides a service that implements an interface.

```
class RIAccess implements CPNetaccess
{
   private final String empname;
   public RIAccess(String s)
   {
      empname = s;
   }
   public void grantAccess()
   {
      System.out.println("NET Access granted for : "+
      empname);
   }
}
```

STEP 3: Create a proxy class which represents the original class that implements an interface.

```
class ProxyNET implements CPNetaccess
{
   public ProxyNET(String ename) {
      this.ename = ename;
   }
   private String ename;
   private RIAccess ra;
   public int getRole(String emplName)
   {
      return 9;
   }
   public void grantAccess()
   {
      if (getRole(ename) > 4)
      {
         ra = new RIAccess(ename);
         ra.grantAccess();
      }
      else
      {
         System.out.println("can't grant access for employee
         below 5");
      }
   }
}
```

STEP 4: Declare a client which requests NET access.

```
public class PPClient
{
    public static void main(String[] args)
    {
        CPNetaccess ac = new ProxyNET
        ("POOVIZHI");
        ac.grantAccess();
    }
}
```

```
Output
NET Access granted for: POOVIZHI
```

An interface `CPNetaccess` is created with one member function `grantAccess()` method and that method is used by the two concrete classes `RIAccess` and `ProxyNET` respectively. The ProxyNET is actually a proxy class that represents the original class and *RIAccess* is the original class. Both concrete classes inherit the properties of `CPNetaccess` interface. The `RIAccess` has one data member `empname` of string type and two member functions such as `RIAccess` constructor and `grantAccess()` method. The `ProxyNET` concrete class has two data members `ename` of String type and `ra` of `RIAccess`. It has three member functions such as `ProxyNET()` constructor, `getrole()` and `grantAccess()`. A public class named `PPClient` is declared to use the proxy class to grant access. The statement,

```
CPNetaccess ac = new ProxyNET("POOVIZHI")
```

creates an object `ac for` the concrete class `ProxyNET` with the parameter value `POOVIZHI`, and as soon as it is created the `ProxNET` constructor receives the string and stores it in the local variable `ename` of string type. After receiving the employee name, the `getrole()` method returns the value 9. Through the object `ac`, the `grantAccess()` method is invoked and inside it the role of the employee is checked through `if ... else`. In the `if` block, the condition is checked by invoking `getrole()` with parameter value `ename` and if the returned value is greater than 4, the `if` block is executed otherwise the `else` block will be executed. Inside the `if` block, an object `ra` for the concrete class `RIAccess()` is created and with that `grantAccess()` method is invoked. The `grantAccess()` method in the `RIAccess` sends the message stating that NET access is granted for the employee. When the `grantAccess()` method of `ProxyNET()` is called, it forwards that request to the same method in the `RIAccess` concrete class which is actually granting permission to the user. In this way, the proxy object `ac` represents the original object `ra` and returns the message from the original object to the user.

17.7 ITERATOR PATTERN

It is one of the behavioral patterns that provides a way to access the elements from the collection without exposing its internal structure. A collection of items is useful when it gives way to access its elements without worrying about internal representation. This pattern provides a uniform interface for traversing different collections without exposing their internal structure (Fig. 17.5).

Participants of iterator design pattern

- **Iterator**: It is an interface which provides a way to traverse the collection and concrete iterator class must implement the methods declared in this interface.
- **Concrete iterator:** Implementing all the methods declared in the iterator interface and keeping track of the current position in traversal.
- **Aggregate:** It is also an interface that can create an iterator object.
- **Concrete aggregate:** Implements the aggregate interface and its method.

UML diagram

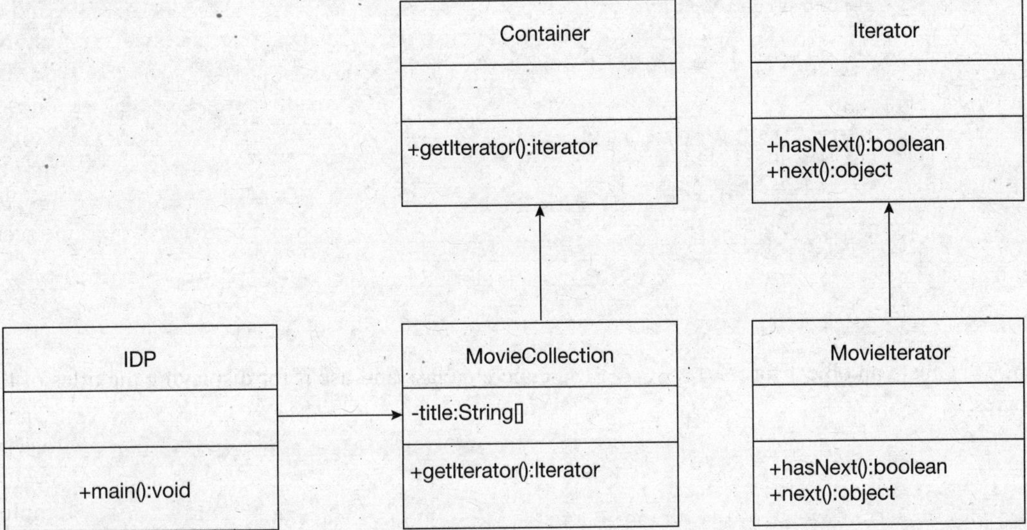

Fig. 17.5 Iterator pattern

Steps involved

STEP 1: Create iterator and container interfaces in two separate Java files.

```
public interface Iterator
{
   public boolean hasNext();
   public Object next();
}
public interface Container
{
   public Iterator getIterator();
}
```

STEP 2: Create `MovieCollection` concrete class implementing the `container` interface and it has inner class `MovieIterator` implementing the `Iterator` interface.

```
public class MovieCollection implements Container
{
   public String title[] = {"Jeens" , "Iruvar" ,"Titanic" , "Avatar", "Devadass"};
   @Override
   public Iterator getIterator()
   {
      return new MovieIterator();
   }
    private class MovieIterator implements Iterator
   {
      int index;
      @Override
      public boolean hasNext() {
         if(index < title.length){
            return true;
         }
         return false;
      }
      @Override
      public Object next() {
         if(this.hasNext()){
            return title[index++];
         }
         return null;
      }
   }
}
```

STEP 3: Create an object for `MovieCollection` concrete class and use it for displaying the titles of the movies.

```
public class IDP
{
   public static void main(String[] args)
   {
      MovieCollection mc = new MovieCollection();
      for(Iterator iter = mc.getIterator(); iter.hasNext();)
      {
         String title = (String)iter.next();
         System.out.println("Movie Title : " + title);
      }
   }
}
```

```
Output
Movie Title : Jeens
Movie Title : Iruvar
Movie Title : Titanic
Movie Title : Avatar
Movie Title : Devadass
```

The `MovieCollection` is a concrete class that implements the iterator and container interfaces to traverse the collection of movies. An object has been declared in the Main class to traverse the collection and to print the movie titles.

SUMMARY

1. Each pattern describes a problem that occurs over and over again in our environment, and then describes the core of the solution to that problem.
2. Design patterns are language independent, which means all types of object-oriented programming languages can use the design patterns.
3. Design patterns have evolved from years of programming experiences by trial and error.
4. Design patterns provide common solutions to the object-oriented software developer

and they are the best practices evolved over a long period of time from the experienced and specialised programmers from the industry.

5. Design patterns are grouped together under three categories, namely creational, structural and behavioural patterns.
6. Factory method pattern defines an interface or abstract class for creating an object but lets the subclasses decide which class to instantiate.
7. Prototype pattern states that an existing object be cloned and customised as per needs instead of creating a whole new one.
8. Singleton pattern says that a class be declared with only one object and a global access point made.

SHORT QUESTIONS

1. Give the definition of design pattern proposed by Christopher Alexander.
2. A design pattern is a well-proven solution for solving specific problems/tasks. Do you agree? Justify your answer.
3. Write the advantages of design patterns.
4. When should we use design patterns?
5. State the sole purpose of the creational, structural and behavioural patterns.
6. Where can we apply the factory method pattern? Give an example.
7. Give a brief note on prototype pattern.
8. Compare the creational pattern and structural pattern.
9. List the patterns available under creational pattern.
10. Write short note on behavioural patterns.

COMPREHENSIVE QUESTIONS

1. Give a detailed note on design patterns.
2. Explain the patterns in creational pattern.
3. Where can we use the prototype pattern?
4. How is object creation restricted in singleton pattern? Explain with the help of a program.
5. Demonstrate cloning of an existing object with a program.
6. Expalin the patterns in structural pattern.
7. List the patterns available in behavioural pattern and give a brief note on each.
8. Draw a UML class diagram for the adapter pattern and write a program to implement it.
9. Draw a UML class diagram for the proxy pattern and write a program to implement it.
10. Explain the factory pattern with the help of a program.

SOLVED PROBLEMS

1. The Program 1 prepares the EB Bill using the Factory Method Pattern.

Directory Structure

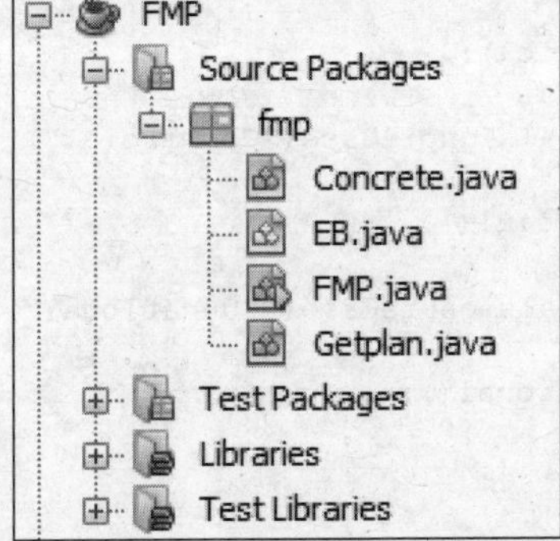

Abstract Class: ***EB.java***

```
package fmp;
abstract class EB
{
  protected double rate;
  abstract void getRate();
  public void calculateBill(Double reading)
  {
     System.out.println(reading*rate);
  }
}
```

Concrete Class to inherit Abstract Class: ***Concrete.java***

```
package fmp;
class Domestic extends EB
{
  void getRate()
  {
     rate=2.5;
  }
}
class Commercial extends EB
{
  void getRate()
  {
     rate=5.6;
  }
}
class Educational extends EB
{
  void getRate()
  {
     rate=1.5;
  }
}
```

Factory Class to generate objects: ***Getplan.java***

```
package fmp;
public class Getplan
{
  public EB getPlan(String planType)
  {
     if(planType == null)
     {
        return null;
     }
     if(planType.equalsIgnoreCase("Domestic"))
     {
        return new Domestic();
     }
     else if(planType.equalsIgnoreCase("Commercial"))
     {
        return new Commercial();
     }
     else if(planType.equalsIgnoreCase("Educational"))
     {
        return new Educational();
     }
```

Output

```
Enter the Type of Connection: Domestic
Enter the reading: 415
Bill amount for Domestic is 1037.5
```

```
        return null;
    }
  }
Main Class: FMP.java
package fmp;
import java.io.*;
public class FMP
{
  public static void main(String[] args) throws IOException
  {
      Getplan plan= new Getplan();
      System.out.print("Enter the Type of Connection: ");
      BufferedReader br=new BufferedReader(new InputStreamReader(System.in));
      String planName=br.readLine();
      System.out.print("Enter the reading: ");
      Double reading=Double.parseDouble(br.readLine());
      EB p = plan.getPlan(planName);
      System.out.print("Bill amount for "+planName+" is ");
      p.getRate();
      p.calculateBill(reading);
  }
}
```

PROGRAMMING EXERCISES

1. Calculating the **Fixed Deposit** interest based on the number of years of deposit. ***Interest rates are given below***

Years	Interest Rate
Upto 1 year	6.5 %
Above 1 year and less than 2 years	6.75%
Above 2 years and less than 3 years	7.00%
3 years and above	7.5%

2. A hall can be booked for a particular function on the basis of the number of people arriving. At a time only one hall can be booked. ***Hall capacity is given below:***

Capacity	Name of the Hall
<=60	Micro Hall
60> && <=150	Zambi bar Hall
150>&&<=500	Lakzvi Hall
Above 500	Navaland Hall

3. Choose an appropriate pattern to develop program for preparing the bill for supermarket purchases.
4. Choose an appropriate pattern to develop a program for purchasing a bike based on the company model and engine capacity.
5. Use Factory method pattern to book a cab for travel based on the km, distance, location and car type.
6. Develop a program to calculate the area of a circle using Proxy Pattern.
7. Write a program to display the product details as per the Factory method pattern.
8. When purchasing a car through a dealer, the dealer fixes the price based on the manufacturer of the car. Choose the correct pattern to resolve this problem and develop a program as per the pattern.
9. Choose the correct pattern to develop a program to calculate EB bill based on the type of connection.
10. Develop a program to calculate maturity amount and interest earned in a fixed deposit using Adapter pattern.

CHAPTER

18

Servlets

Servlets are protocol- and platform-independent server-side software components. Like applets, servlets are also Java classes; applets are used to implement the client-side of a client-server application whereas servlets are used at the server-side which is run inside a Java enabled server or application server such as the WebSphere application server. Before Servlet, CGI (Common Gateway Interface) scripting language was popular as a server-side programming language. Servlets are loaded and executed within the Java Virtual Machine (JVM) of the Web server or application server, in much the same way as applets are loaded and executed within the JVM of the Web client. Since servlets run inside the servers they do not need a graphical user interface (GUI).

18.1 BASICS OF SERVLET

Servlet can be described in many ways, depending on the context. Servlet is a technology used to create web applications. Servlet is an API that provides many interfaces and classes including documentation. It is an interface that must be implemented for creating any servlet. It is a class that extends the capabilities of the servers and responds to the incoming requests. It can respond to any type of request. Servlet is a web component that is deployed on the server to create dynamic web pages. A servlet implements a common request/response paradigm for handling the messaging between the client and the server. The Java Servlet API defines a standard interface for the handling of these request and response messages between the client and server. Figure 18.1 shows a high-level client-to-servlet process flow.

- The client sends a request to the web server.
- The web server interprets it and forwards it to the corresponding servlet.
- The servlet processes the request, then builds a response, generates the output and sends it back to the web server.
- The web server sends the response back to the client. The browser then displays it on the screen.

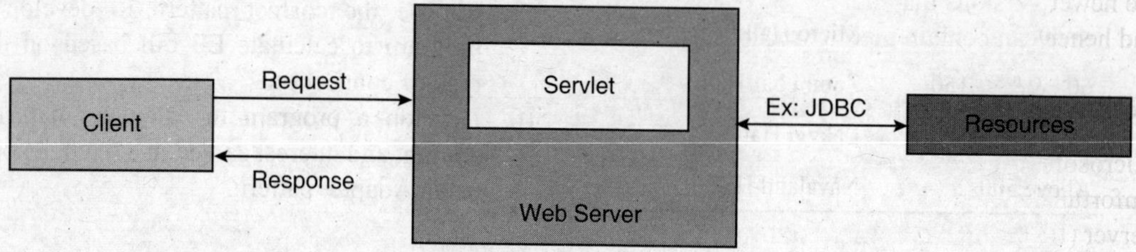

Fig. 18.1 Execution of a Java servlet

It runs entirely within the Java Virtual Machine (JVM). Since it runs on the server and may be designed to generate simple outputs which even older versions of browsers can interpret, there is no browser incompatibility.

Applets, upon download from the server, run in the client's browser. They will function properly provided a proper Java Runtime Environment (JRE) is installed in the client's browser. If the client uses an old browser and the applets use advanced features, the browsers may fail to execute them. Servlets, on the other hand, run on the server machine and usually generate simple HTML code. So, even an older version of the browser can display these HTML pages correctly. Applets cannot access local resources such as files and databases. Servlets, if configured properly, have full access to system resources. Therefore, servlets are more powerful than applets. However, since applets and servlets are used at opposite ends of a client–server application, making a direct comparison between them should be avoided.

18.2 SERVLET ALTERNATIVES

Numerous parallel technologies to servlets exist. However, each has its own set of problems. Some of the other server-side technologies are discussed in this section.

Common Gateway Interface (CGI)

CGI is one of the most common server-side solutions. Although widely used, CGI scripting technology has a number of shortcomings, including platform dependence and lack of scalability. A CGI application is an independent program that receives requests from the web server and sends them back to the web server. Some of the common problems of this technology are as follows.

- A new process is created every time the web server receives a CGI request. Since a new process is created and initialised, it may result in a considerable increase in response time. Servers may also run out of memory if not configured properly.
- Although a CGI application can be written in almost every language, most of them are not platform-independent. The most common platform-independent language is Perl. Although Perl is a very powerful text processing language, it requires a new interpreter to be started for every request. This increases the overall response time.
- Since a CGI application is a completely separate process, if it terminates abnormally before responding, the web server has no way to identify what happened there. Consequently, it fails to service the request made by the client.

Proprietary APIs

Many proprietary web servers have built-in support for server-side programming. Examples include Netscape's NSAPI, Microsoft's ISAPI, and O'Reilly's WSAPI. However, none of these APIs are free and the newer versions may not be backward compatible. Most of these are developed in C/C++ languages and hence can contain memory leaks and core dumps that can crash the web server.

Active Server Pages (ASP)

Microsoft's Active Server Pages (ASP) is another technology that supports server-side programming. Unfortunately, the only web server that supports this technology is Microsoft's Internet Information Server (IIS), which is not free. Although some third-party products support ASP, they are not free either.

Server-side JavaScript

Server-side JavaScript is another alternative to servlets. However, the only known servers that support it are Netscape's Enterprise and FastTrack servers. This ties one to a particular vendor and hence, if possible, should be avoided.

18.3 SERVLET STRENGTHS

Java servlet technology has some distinct advantages over other competent technologies. Truly speaking, except JSP (which is in fact an extension to servlet), no technology can compete with servlet technology. The following are some advantages of Java servlet technology.

Efficient

When a servlet gets loaded on the server, it remains in the server's memory as a single object instance. Each new request is then served by a lightweight Java thread spawned from the servlet. This is a much more efficient technique than creating a new process for every request, as done in CGI. Servlets also have more alternatives for optimisations, such as caching the previous computation and keeping the database/socket connections open, and so on.

Persistent and performance

Servlets can maintain the session by using session tracking/cookies, a mechanism that helps them track information from request to request. Critical information can also be saved to a persistent storage and can be retrieved from it when the servlet is loaded the next time.

Portable and platform independent

Servlets are written in Java and so they are portable across operating systems and server implementations. This allows servlets to be moved across new operating systems seamlessly. A programmer can develop a servlet on a Windows machine running the Tomcat or any other server and later it is possible to deploy that servlet effortlessly on any other operating system such as a Unix machine running an iPlanet/Netscape application server. So, servlets are truly *Write Once Run Anywhere* (WORA) programs.

Robust

Since servlets can use the entire rich Java library, they can provide extremely robust solutions. Java has a very powerful exception handling mechanism and provides a garbage collector to handle memory leaks. It also has a very large and rich class library with network and file support, database access, distributed object components, DOM support, security, utility packages, and so on.

Extensible

Servlets are written Java technology, which is popular for its features such as platform independence, garbage collection, exception handling, and extremely powerful utility packages. Servlets can also make use of Java's object orientation features, especially inheritance. A subclass inherits all the features of its super class. Additional features and methods can be added and hence it is easily extendable.

Secure

Servlets run in a Java-enabled web server. So it can use security mechanisms from both the web server and the Java Security Manager.

Cost-effective

There are a number of free web servers available for personal and commercial use. Java Development Kit (JDK) is also free and can be downloaded from http://java.com. So, applications can be developed practically without any cost.

Table 18.1 **Standalone web servers**

Product	Source	Product	Source
Apache Web Server	Apache	Web server	ZEUS
WebSphere Application Server	IBM	iPlanet	Netscape
Weblogic Application Server	BEA	J Application server	GenStone

Table 18.2 **Add-on servlet engine**

Product	Source	Product	Source
Tomcat	Jakarta project	JRun web server	Allaire
JServ	Java-Apache project	ServletExec	New Atlanta

18.4 SERVLET ARCHITECTURE

Servlet architecture consists of two packages, namely, `javax.servlet` and `javax.servlet.http`. The first package contains top-level interfaces and classes that are used and extended by all other servlets either directly or indirectly. The `javax.servlet` package also contains classes to support generic protocol-independent servlets. This means that servlets can be used for many protocols, for example, HTTP and FTP. The second package is provided for servlets that can handle HTTP requests. The `javax.servlet.http` package extends the functionality of the base package to include specific support for the HTTP protocol. Figure 18.2 shows the Servlet architecture.

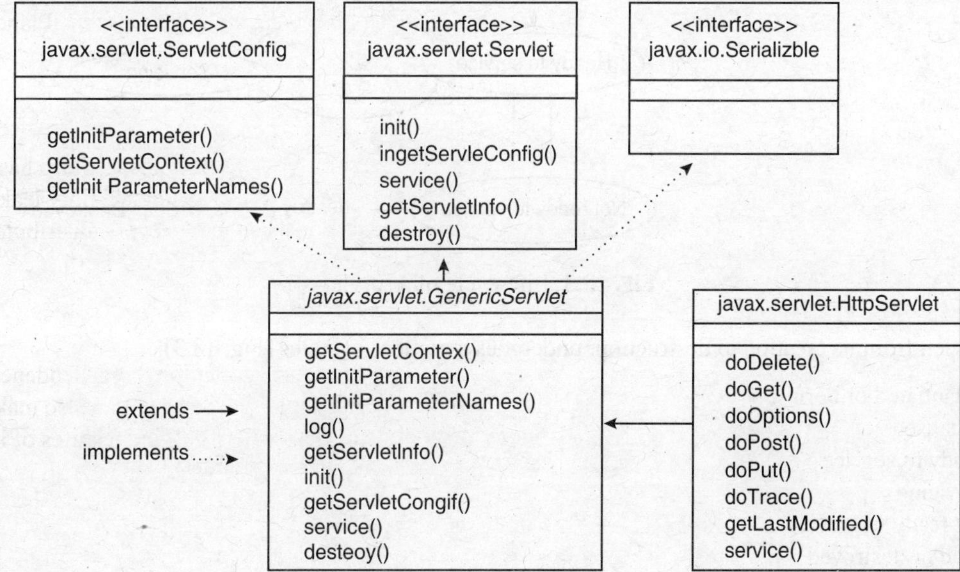

Fig. 18.2 Servlet architecture

The top-level interface of the servlet architecture is `javax.servlet.Servlet`. It provides the basic functionalities of all the servlets that are created by implementing this interface directly or indirectly. For example, the `init()` method initialises the servlet, the `service()` method serves the client request, and the `destroy()` method shuts the servlet down. The `GenericServlet` class implements this interface and defines a generic protocol-independent servlet. To write an HTTP servlet for use on the Web, the programmer can even use a more specialised class of `GenericServlet` called `HttpServlet`. `HttpServlet` provides additional methods for the processing of HTTP requests such as GET (doGet method) and POST (doPost method).

18.5 SERVLET LIFE CYCLE

The container in which the servlet has been deployed supervises and controls the life cycle of the servlet. Typically, this container is referred to as a web server. When the container receives a request from a client and determines that the request should be handled by a servlet, it performs the following steps.

- If an instance of the target servlet does not exist, the container does the following:
- Finds and loads the servlet class.
- Creates an instance of the servlet class.
- Calls the `init()` method on this servlet instance to initialise it.
- The container then invokes the `service()` method on the servlet which is newly created or on an existing servlet, passing a `ServletRequest` type object and a `ServletResponse` type object.
- If the container decides that the servlet is no longer needed, it removes and finalises the servlet by calling the servlet's `destroy()` method.

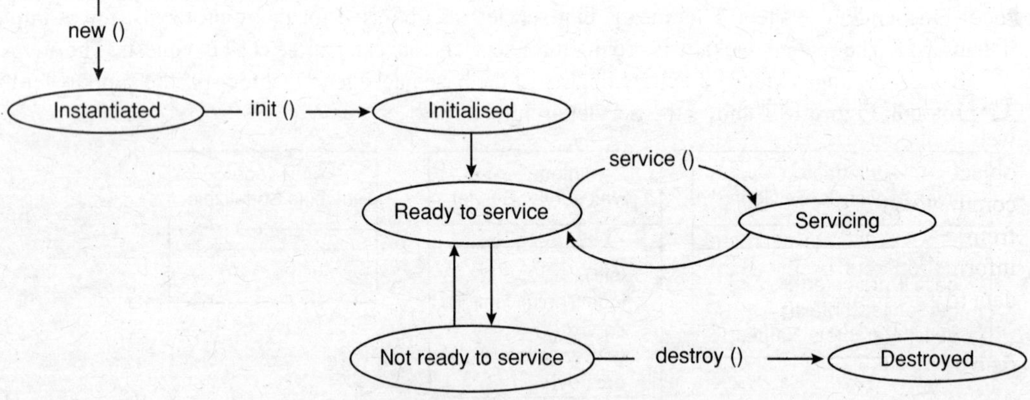

Fig. 18.3 Life cycle of a servlet

A servlet, from its creation to destruction, undergoes a number of states (Fig. 18.3).

- Instantiated or born
- Initialised
- Ready to service
- Servicing
- Not ready to service
- Dead or destroyed

The entire period when a servlet remains alive is called the life cycle of the servlet. The class `Servlet` provides a framework where the servlets can run. It has a set of methods to control and supervise the smooth execution of sevlets, as described in Fig. 18.3. These methods are called in a specific order during a servlet's entire life cycle. A servlet must override these methods to do a designated task. Even though life cycle methods are called automatically by the container, programmers should have a sound knowledge about when they are called and what can be done with these methods. The following is a brief description of these life cycle methods.

init()

A servlet's life begins here. This method is called only once by the web container, just after it instantiates and loads the servlet. So, it is a good idea to read the persistent configuration data, initialise resources that will be used during the rest of the time and perform any other one-time activity by overriding the `init()` method. Once the servlet is initialised, it becomes ready to handle the client's request. The syntax of the `init()` method is as follows:

```
void init(ServletConfig)
```

The web container passes a `ServletConfig` object, which contains the startup configuration for this servlet, such as initialisation parameters. To serve requests, this `init()` method must be completed and return successfully.

service()

This is the most important method and the syntax is as follows:

```
void service(ServletRequest request, ServletResponse response)
```

This method gets called each time the web container receives a request intended for this servlet. The web container calls the `service()` method on a servlet with two objects: a `ServletRequest` type object `request` and a `ServletResponse` type object `response`. The `request` object encapsulates the communication from the client to the server, while the `response` object encapsulates the communication from the servlet back to the client. The `ServletRequest` interface provides methods to retrieve information sent by the clients. Similarly, the `ServletResponse` interface provides methods to send data to the clients.

destroy()

The general format of this method is as follows:

```
void destroy();
```

This method gets called when the web container uninstalls the servlet. This method is overridden to clean up the resources that were allocated to this servlet. It also makes sure that any persistent state is synchronised with the servlet's current in-memory state.

Other methods

The `javax.servlet.Servlet` interface also provides the following methods to inspect the properties of a servlet at runtime.

```
ServletConfig getServletConfig();
```

This returns a `ServletConfig` object, which contains the initialisation parameters and startup configuration used for this servlet. The returned object is the object that was passed to the `init()` method during the servlet's instantiation.

```
String getServletInfo();
```

This returns a String object containing information about the servlet, such as its version, author, copyright, and so on.

18.6 GENERIC SERVLET

The class `javax.servlet.GenericServlet` implements the `javax.servlet.Servlet` interface and for convenience, the `javax.servlet.ServletConfig` interface. A `servlet` class is usually created by extending either the `GenericServlet` class or its descendant `javax.servlet.http.HttpServlet` class unless the servlet needs another class as a parent. If a servlet does need to be a subclass of another class, it must implement the `Servlet` interface directly. This would be necessary when, for example, RMI or CORBA objects act as servlets. In such a case, the `servlet` class must implement all the methods of the `Servlet` interface. The `GenericServlet` class defines a generic protocol-independent servlet, in the sense that it can be extended to provide implementation of any protocol, such as HTTP, FTP and SMTP. The `GenericServlet` class was created to make writing servlets easier. It provides implementations of the life cycle methods `init()` and `destroy()`, as well as methods in the `ServletConfig` interface. The servlet writer has to implement only the `service()` method. This is required because it is the method that is called every time a client requests for the servlet. The general format of this method is shown as follows.

```
public void service(javax.servlet.ServletRequest request
javax.servlet.ServletResponse response) throws javax.
servlet.ServletException, java. io.IOException;
```

This method expects two arguments. The `ServletRequest` type object request encapsulates the client request and is used to extract information from the client's request. On the other hand, `ServletResponse` type object response contains information to be sent back to the client.

18.7 HTTPSERVLET

The `HttpServlet` class extends `GenericServlet` and provides a framework for handling HTTP requests. Servlets to handle only HTTP requests are usually created by extending this class. It provides an implementation for the `service()` method. So, there is no need to implement the `service()` method if the programmer extends the `HttpServlet` class. The `service()` method in the `HttpServlet` class reads the method type stored in the HTTP request message and invokes a specific method based on this value. Specifically, if the method type is GET, it calls `doGet()`; if the method type is POST, it calls `doPost()`; and so on. These are the methods that need to be overridden. Default implementations of these methods are also provided. The list of all such methods is given in Fig. 18.4.

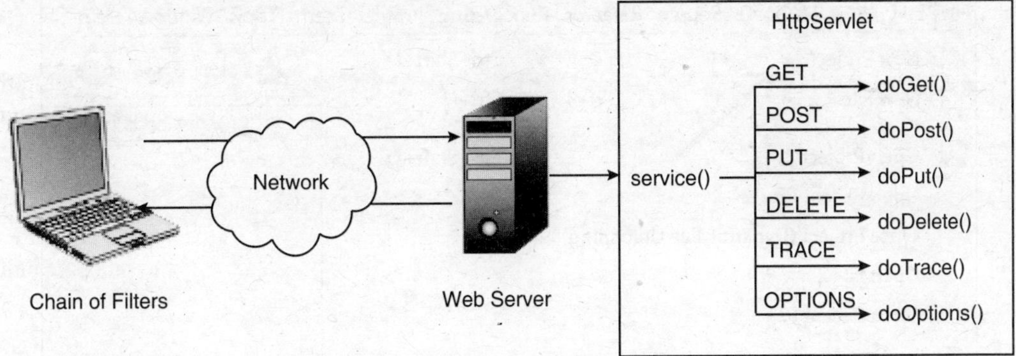

Fig. 18.4 HTTP servlet in action

Each of these methods takes two arguments: an `HttpServletRequest` type object and an `HttpServletResponse` type object. The following is the syntax of the `doGet()` method:

```
void doGet(HttpServletRequest request, HttpServletResponse response)
```

The `HttpServletRequest` interface extends the `ServletRequest` interface and provides all the functionality of the `ServletRequest` interface. Additionally, it provides methods to retrieve HTTP-specific information such as headers, method, URL, cookies sent, and so on. The `HttpServletResponse` interface extends the `ServletResponse` interface and provides all the functionality of the `ServletResponse` interface. Additionally, it provides methods to send HTTP-specific information back to the client. Servlets created by extending the `HttpServlet` class can handle multiple simultaneous requests. For each request, a thread is created, which runs its `service()` method. If there is a need to create a single-threaded servlet then the servlet must implement the `SingleThreadModel` interface as follows:

```
public class SimpleServlet extends HttpServlet implements SingleThreadModel{ }
```

The interface `SingleThreadModel` does not define any method. It is used to merely declare that the servlet should use a single thread.

18.8 FIRST SERVLET

Creating the first servlet application using Netbeans IDE

An IDE is an Integrated Development Environment and it makes creating applications a lot easier. It is the simplest way to create servlet applications. An IDE is a software application that provides facilities to computer programmers for software development. Eclipse, MyEclipse, Netbeans are examples of some popular Java IDEs. This section deals with creating servlet applications on Netbeans IDE.

The following are the steps to create a servlet application in Netbeans IDE.

1. Open Netbeans IDE, Select `File` → `New Project`.

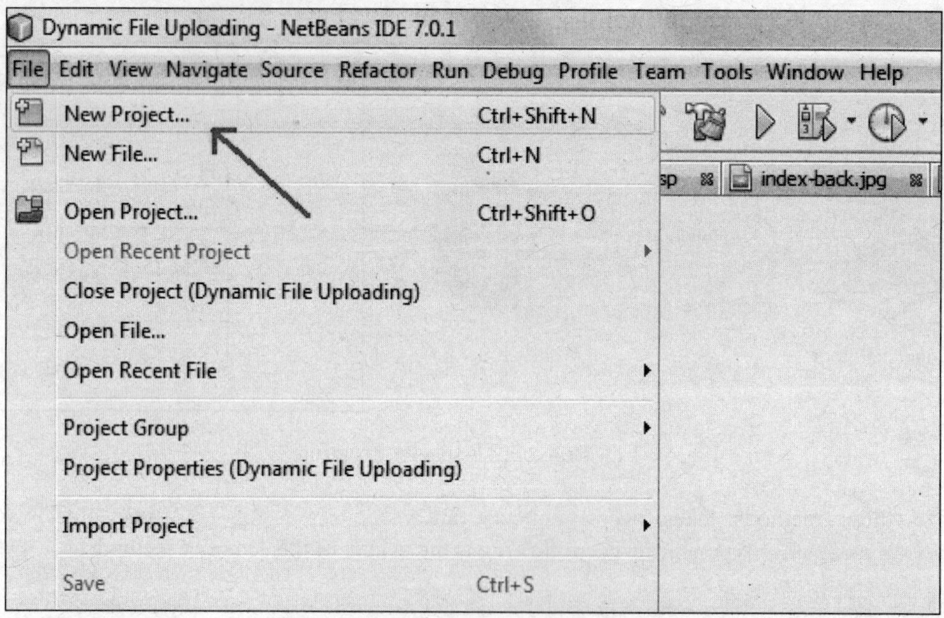

2. Select `Java Web` → `Web Application` and then click on `Next`.

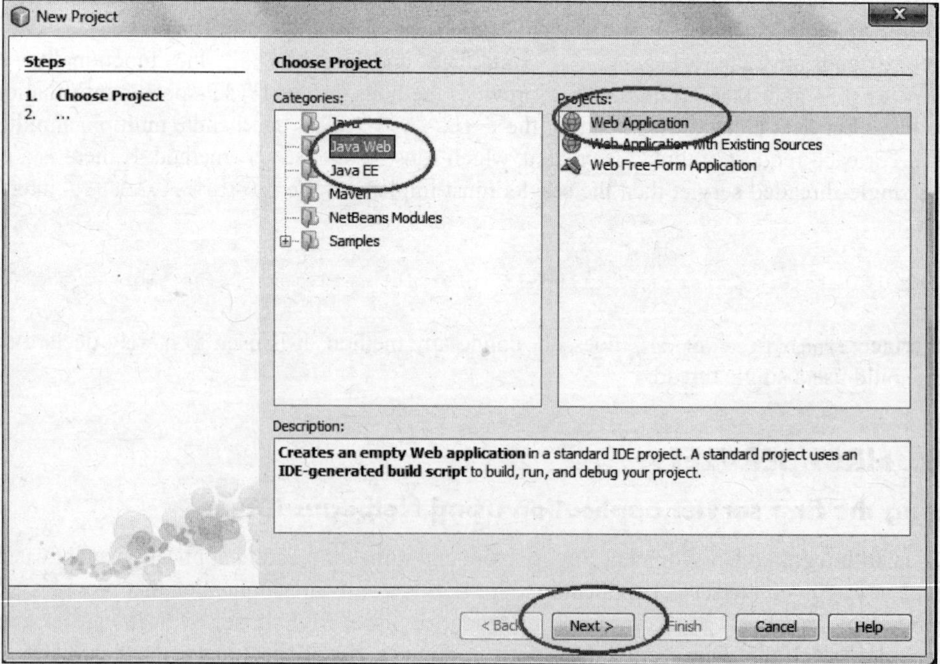

3. Give a name to the project and click on `Next`.

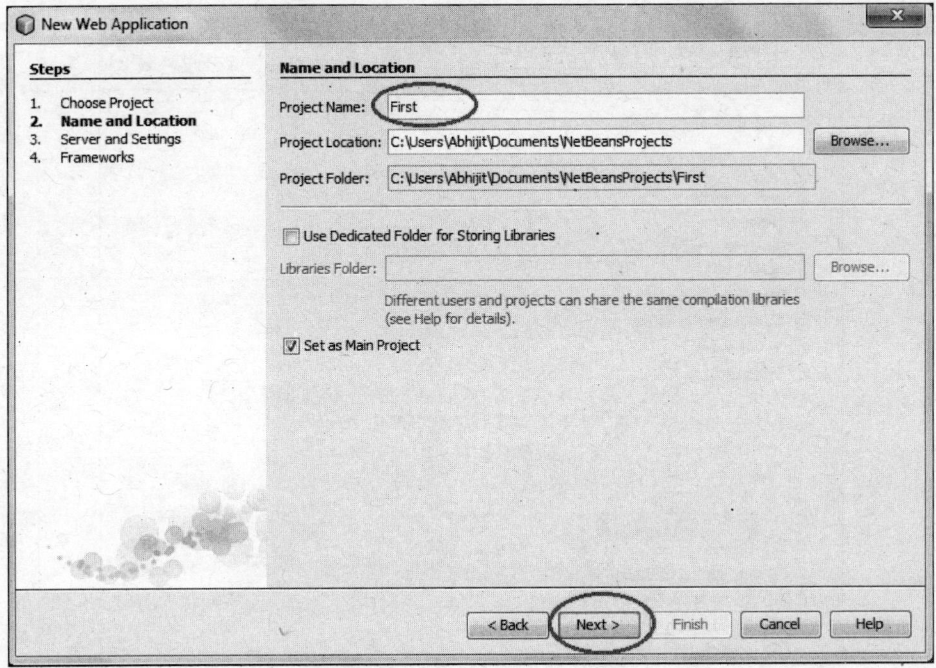

4. Select the Server such as GlassFish or Tomcat and Click `Finish`.

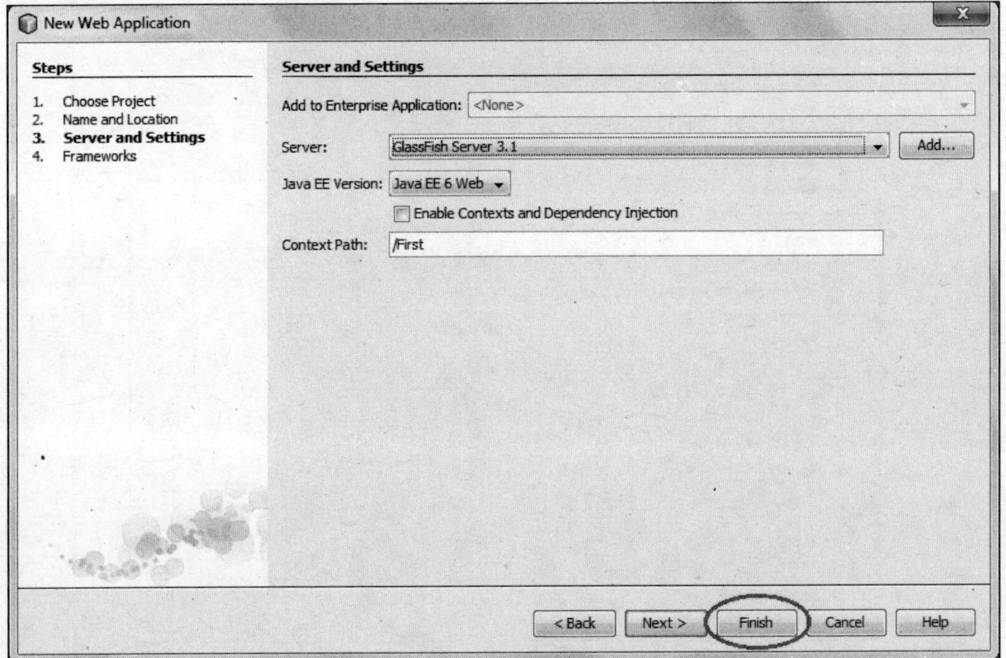

5. The complete directory structure required for the Servlet Application will be created automatically by the IDE.

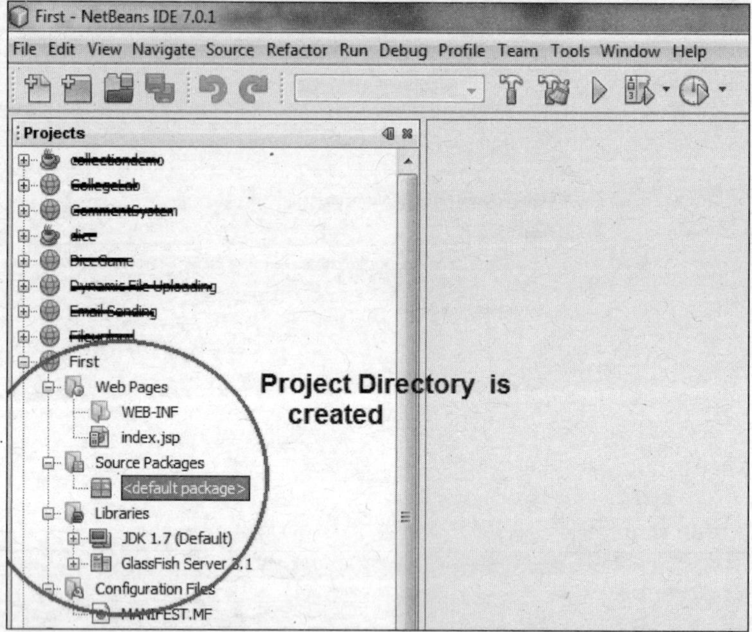

6. To create a Servlet, open `Source Package`, right click on default packages → `New` → `Servlet`.

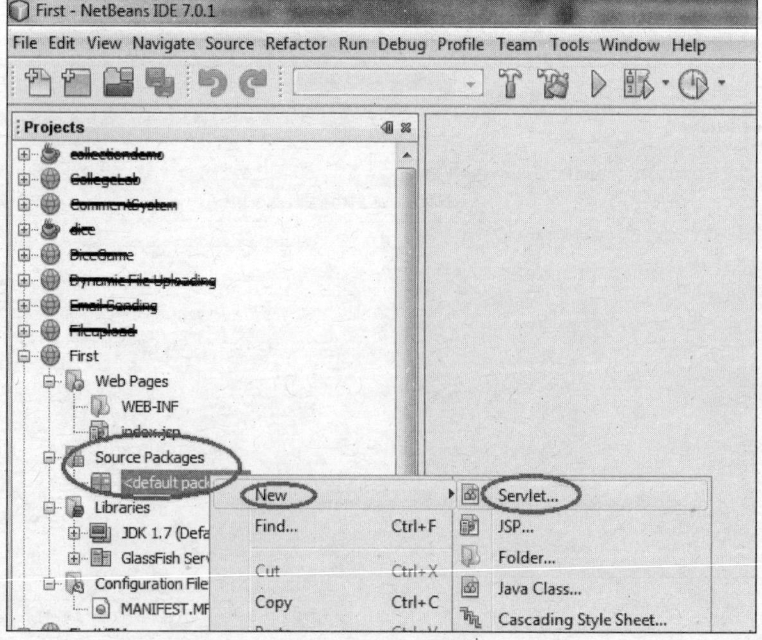

7. Provide a name to the Servlet class file and click next.

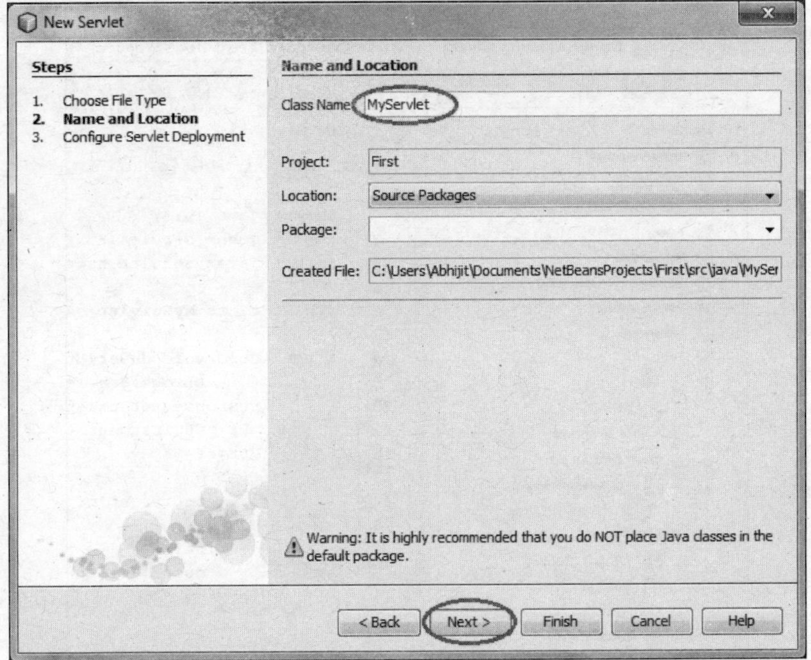

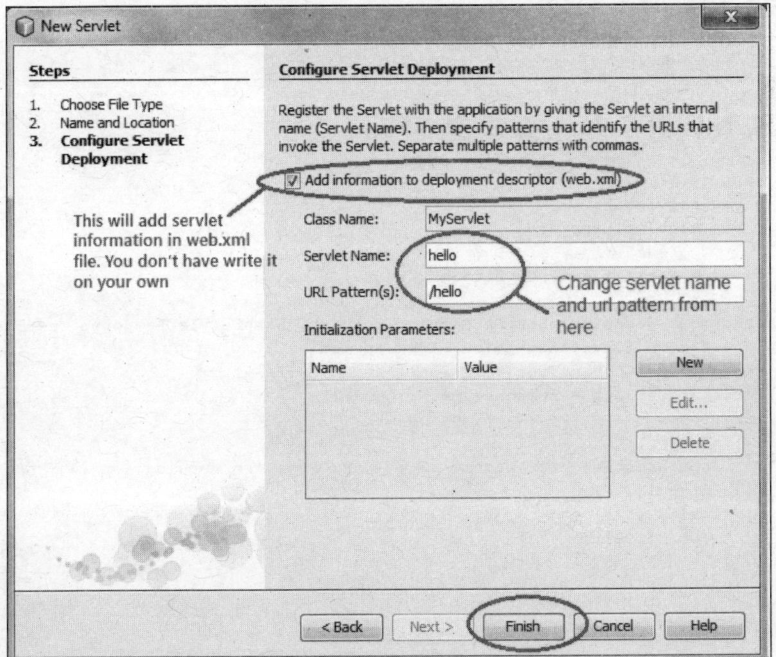

Provide Servlet name and URL pattern as shown and click next.

8. Servlet class is ready and you just need to change the method definitions.

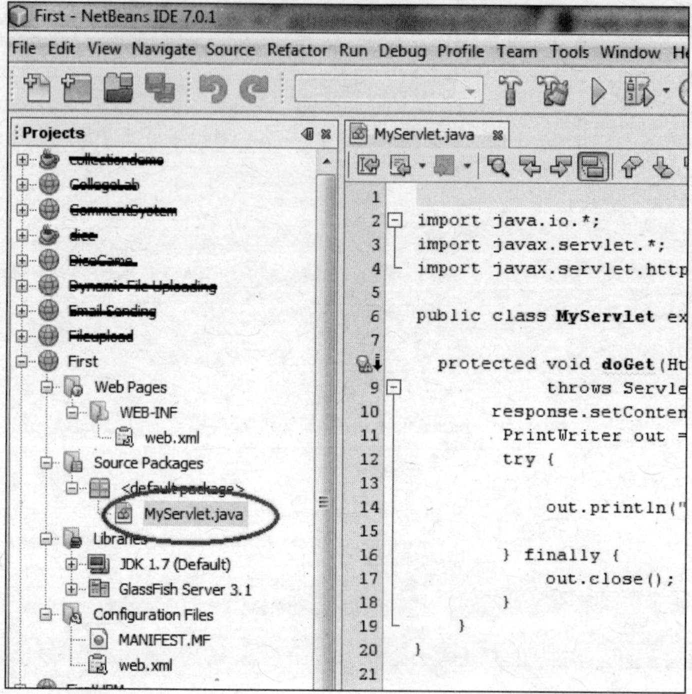

9. Write some code inside the Servlet class.

```
import java.io.*;
import javax.servlet.*;
import javax.servlet.http.*;

public class MyServlet extends HttpServlet {

  protected void doGet(HttpServletRequest request, HttpServletResponse response)
          throws ServletException, IOException {
      response.setContentType("text/html;charset=UTF-8");
       PrintWriter out = response.getWriter();
       try {

           out.println("<h2>Welcome to my first servlet application in NetBeans</h2>");

       } finally {
           out.close();
       }
    }
}
```

10. Create an HTML file, right click on `Web Pages` → `New` → `HTML`.

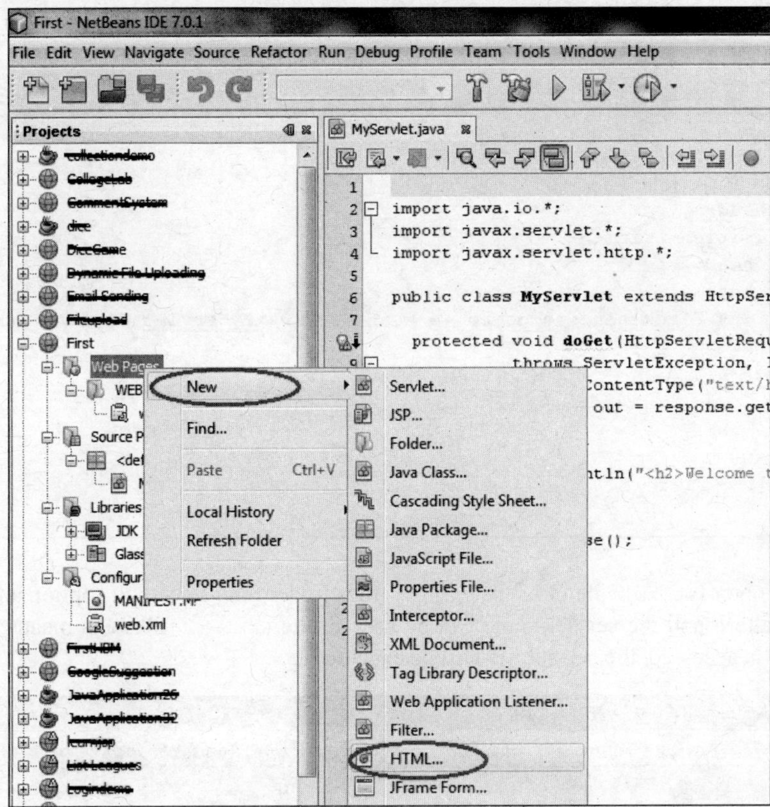

11. Provide a name for the HTML file. It is preferred to use `index` as the name, because the browser will always pick up the `index.html` file automatically from a directory.

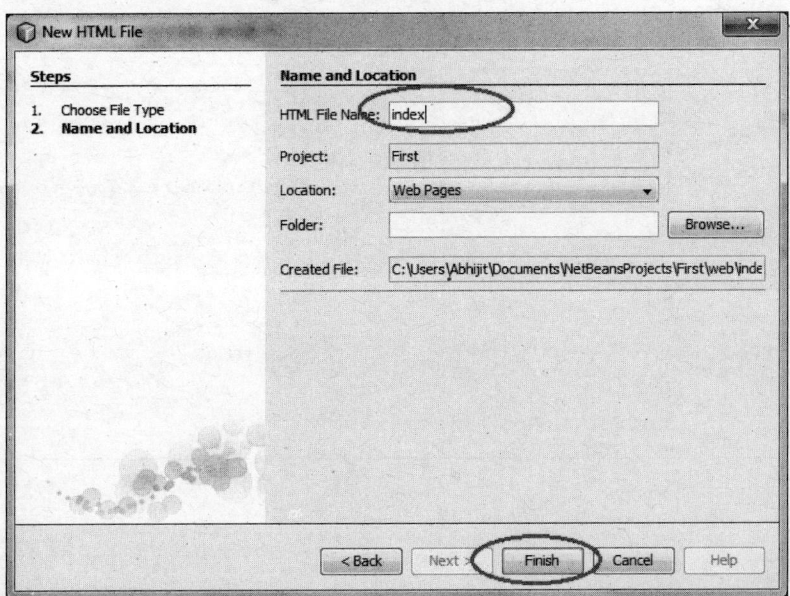

12. Write some code inside the HTML file. In this example, a hyperlink is created to the servlet, in the HTML file.

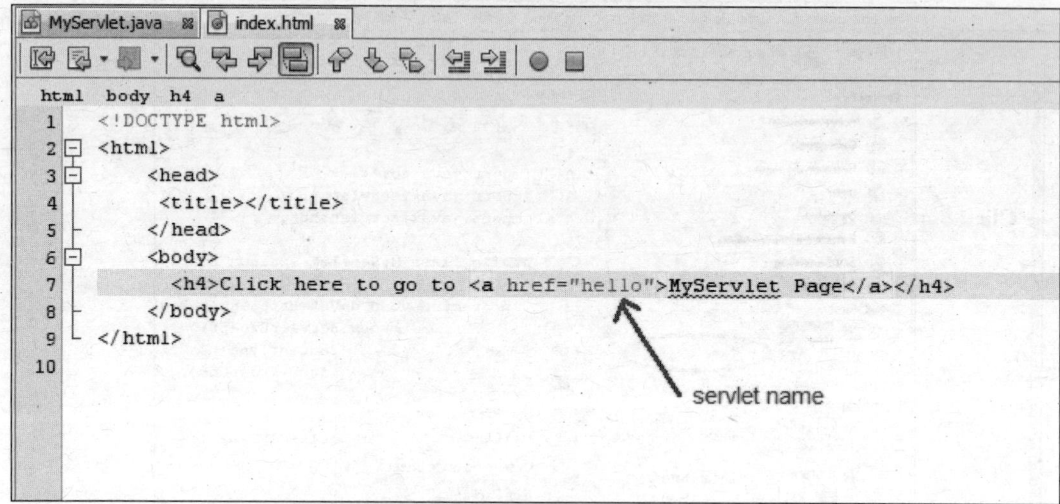

13. Click and open `web.xml` file in `Configuration` files folder then select `XML` option and edit the file. The url pattern and the servlet-name can be seen in the `web.xml` file; this means that when the `hello` url is accessed, the servlet file will be executed.

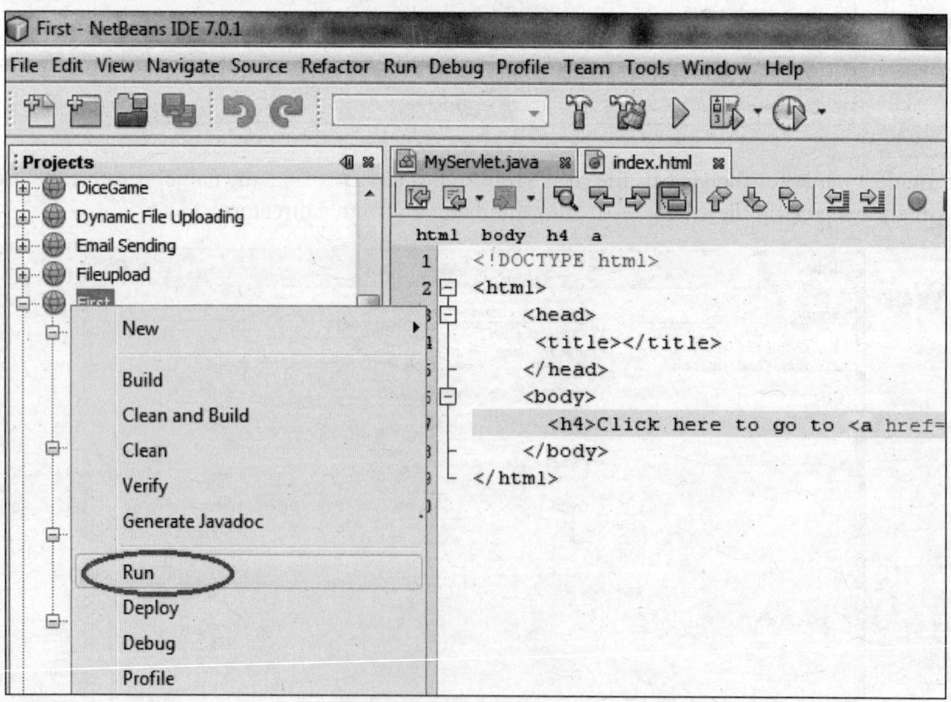

14. To run the application right click on `Project` and select `Run`.
15. Click on the link created, to open the servlet.

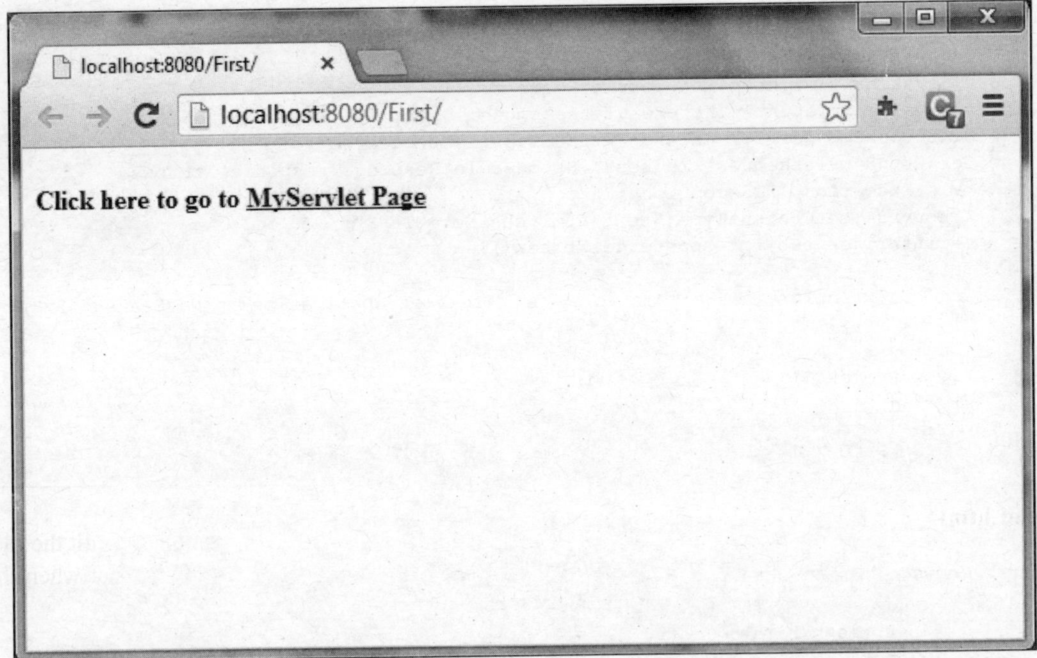

16. The servlet class is running in the browser.

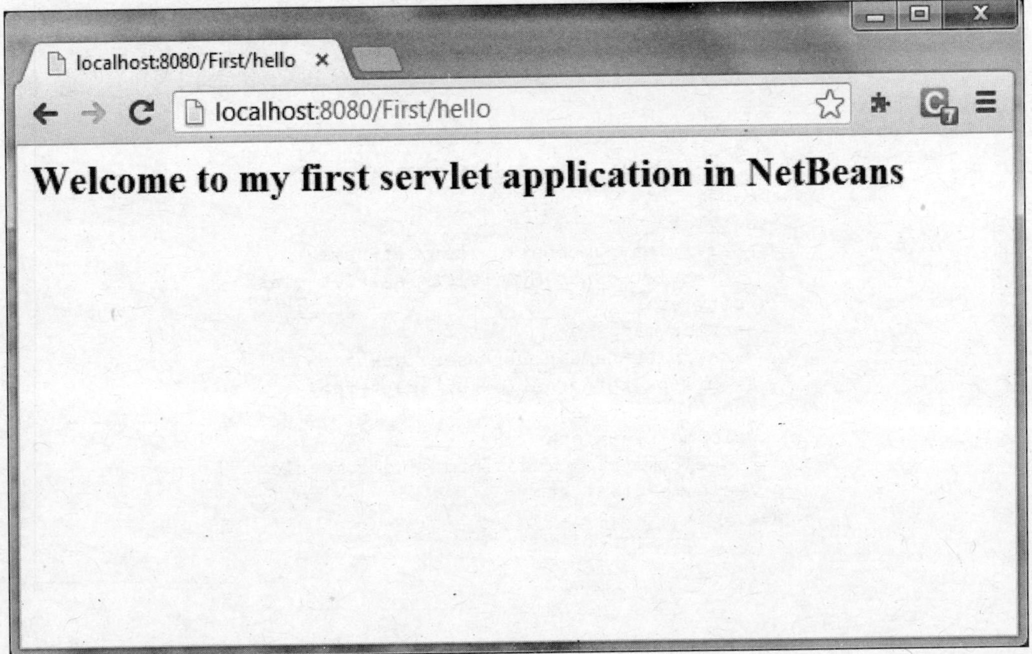

MyServlet.java

```
import java.io.IOException;
import java.io.PrintWriter;
import javax.servlet.ServletException;
import javax.servlet.http.HttpServlet;
import javax.servlet.http.HttpServletRequest;
import javax.servlet.http.HttpServletResponse;
   public class MyServlet extends HttpServlet { protected void
   doGet(HttpServletRequest request, HttpServletResponse response) throws
   ServletException, IOException {
      response.setContentType("text/html;charset=UTF-8");
      PrintWriter out = response.getWriter();
      try {
         out.println("<h2>Welcome to my first servlet application in NetBeans</h2>");
      }
      finally {
         out.close();
      }
   }
}
```

index.html

```
<html>
   <head>
      <title></title>
      <meta http-equiv="Content-Type" content="text/html; charset=UTF-8">
   </head>
   <body>
      <h4> Click to go <a href="hello">MyServlet Page</a></h4>
   </body>
</html>
```

web.xml

```
<?xml version="1.0" encoding="UTF-8"?>
<web-app>
   <servlet>
      <servlet-name>hello</servlet-name>
      <servlet-class>MyServlet</servlet-class>
   </servlet>
   <servlet-mapping>
      <servlet-name>hello</servlet-name>
      <url-pattern>/hello</url-pattern>
   </servlet-mapping>
   <welcome-file-list>
      <welcome-file> index.html</welcome-file>
   </welcome-file-list>
</web-app>
```

18.9 PASSING PARAMETERS TO SERVLETS

Like command line arguments, parameters can be passed to servlets. Servlets can access those parameters and customise their tasks. This helps servlets to function differently in different situations without the need to recompile the source code. There are two ways in which parameters can be passed to a servlet: using URLs and using the HTML form. The disadvantage of passing parameters using URLs is that users can view the parameter names with their values passed. So, it is not safe to send sensitive information using this method. Moreover, the number of parameters that can be passed is also limited. HTML forms can be used to pass parameters in a convenient way. The following HTML code can be used to pass parameters.

```
<html>
   <head>
   <title></title>
      <meta http-equiv="Content-Type" content="text/html; charset=UTF-8">
   </head>
   <body>
      <form action="hello" method="get">
         Name: <input type="text" name="username"/><br/><br/>
         Password: <input type="password" name="userpass"/><br/><br/>
         <input type="submit" value="Login"/>
      </form>
   </body>
</html>
```

18.10 RETRIEVING PARAMETERS

The three methods of the `ServletRequest` interface may be used to retrieve parameters. The syntax is as follows:

```
public abstract java.lang.String getParameter(java. lang.String);
public abstract java.lang.String[ ] getParameterValues(java.lang.String);
public abstract java.util.Enumeration getParameterNames();
```

The `getParameter()` method returns the value of the specified parameter. Make sure that the parameter has exactly one value. If there are multiple parameters with the same name, use the `getParameterValues()` method, which returns an array of string values of the specified parameter. The `getParameterNames()` method returns all the parameters as an enumeration. The values of the individual parameters can be obtained by iterating through the enumeration and using the `getParameter()` method for each of these parameters. The following example shows how to retrieve the values of two parameters, username and password, then return to the client.

```
// MyServlet.java
import java.io.IOException;
import java.io.PrintWriter;
import javax.servlet.ServletException;
import javax.servlet.http.HttpServlet;
import javax.servlet.http.HttpServletRequest;
import javax.servlet.http.HttpServletResponse;
```

```
public class MyServlet extends HttpServlet {
protected void doGet(HttpServletRequest request,
HttpServletResponse response) throws ServletException,
IOException {
   response.setContentType("text/html;charset=UTF-8");
   PrintWriter out = response.getWriter();
   try {
      String name=request.getParameter("username");
      String pass=request.getParameter("userpass");
      out.println("The username is:"+name);
      out.println("The password is:"+pass);
   }
   finally {
      out.close();
   }
 }
}
```

```
//index.html
<html>
   <head>
   <title></title>
      <meta http-equiv="Content-Type" content="text/html; charset=UTF-8">
   </head>
   <body>
      <form action="hello" method="get">
         Name: <input type="text" name="username"/><br/><br/>
         Password: <input type="password" name="userpass"/><br/><br/>
         <input type="submit" value="Login"/>
      </form>
   </body>
</html>
```

```
//web.xml
<?xml version="1.0" encoding="UTF-8"?>
<web-app>
   <servlet>
      <servlet-name>hello</servlet-name>
      <servlet-class>MyServlet</servlet-class>
   </servlet>
   <servlet-mapping>
      <servlet-name>hello</servlet-name>
      <url-pattern>/hello</url-pattern>
   </servlet-mapping>
   <welcome-file-list>
      <welcome-file> index.html</welcome-file>
   </welcome-file-list>
</web-app>
```

While executing the application, the following form of output is obtained.

`Passing parameter`

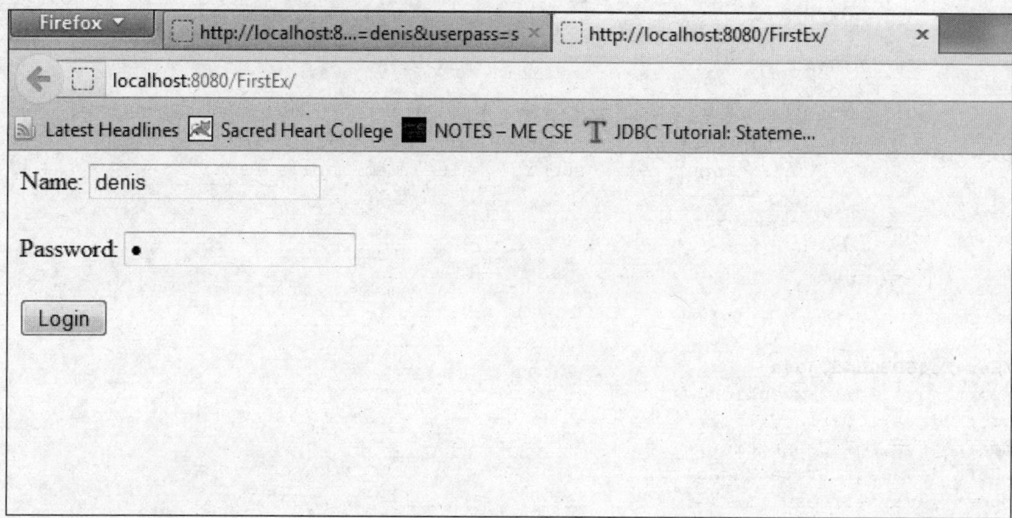

Enter name and password then click `Login`.

`Retrieving parameter`

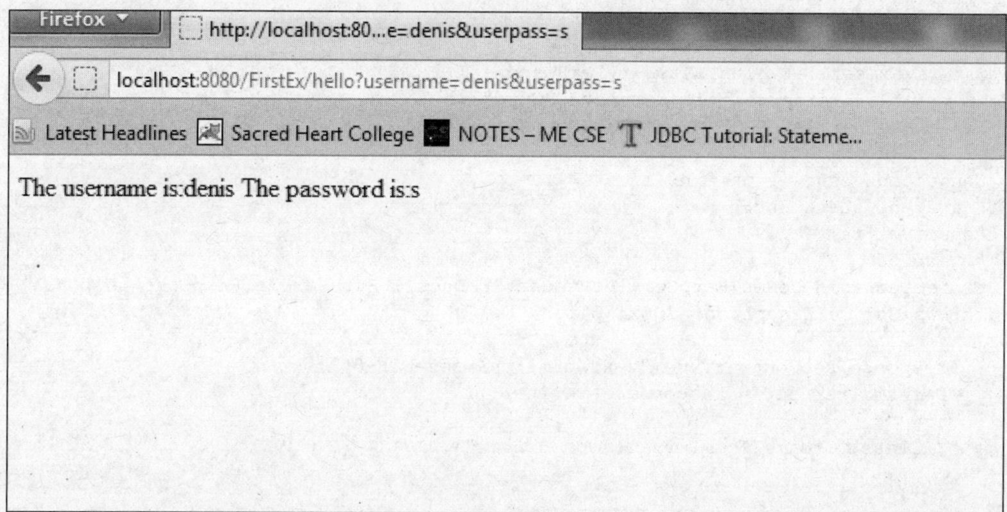

Working with JDBC from a servlet

There are some prerequisites to developing an application with JDBC from a servlet. In general, the database and web server are the core components required. In the following example, the database is MySQL and Server is Apache; both are available under open source software, XAMPP. Therefore, any version of the XAMPP installer can be downloaded and installed.

The database `testDB` is created, which consists of the `product` table with 4 fields and the values are inserted. The next task is to retrieve the values using JDBC from the servlet. Follow the same steps that have been used for creating the *First Servlet in Netbeans*, (as discussed in Section 18.9).

```
//index.html
<html>
   <head>
      <title> JDBC Servlet</title>
   </head>
   <body>
      <center>
         <form action="ServletJDBCfind" method="get">
            <input type="submit" value="Get Mobile Datails">
         </form>
      </center>
   </body>
</html>
```

```
//ServletJDBCfind.java
import java.io.IOException;
import java.io.PrintWriter;
import java.sql.Connection;
import java.sql.DriverManager;
import java.sql.ResultSet;
import java.sql.SQLException;
import java.sql.Statement;
import javax.servlet.ServletException;
import javax.servlet.annotation.WebServlet;
import javax.servlet.http.HttpServlet;
import javax.servlet.http.HttpServletRequest;
import javax.servlet.http.HttpServletResponse;
@WebServlet(urlPatterns = {"/ServletJDBCfind"})
public class ServletJDBCfind extends HttpServlet
{
   Connection connection = null;
   Statement statement;
   ResultSet rs;
   @Override
   protected void doGet(HttpServletRequest request, HttpServletResponse response)
   throws ServletException, IOException
   {
      response.setContentType("text/html;charset=UTF-8");
      PrintWriter out = response.getWriter();
      try
      { Class.forName("com.mysql.jdbc.Driver");
         try
         {
   Connection=DriverManager.getConnection("jdbc:mysql://localhost/testDB ","root","");
            // default username is root and password is empty
         }
         catch(SQLException ex)
         {
            ex.getMessage();
         }
         statement = connection.createStatement();
         rs = statement.executeQuery("Select * from product");
         out.println("<html><head><title>Mobile Details</title></head>");
         out.println("<body>");
         out.println("<ul>");
```

```
        while(rs.next())
        {
            out.println("<li>" + rs.getString("Model")+ " "
            + rs.getString("Brand")+ " "
            + rs.getString("Config")+ " "
            +rs.getString("Price"));
        }
        out.println("</ul>");
        out.println("</body></html>");
    }
    catch(ClassNotFoundException e)
    {
        out.println("driver error");
    }
    catch(SQLException e)
    {
        out.println("SQLEXception:"+e.getMessage());
    }
  }
}
```

```
//web.xml
<web-app>
<servlet>
<servlet-name>ServletJDBCfind</servlet-name>
<servlet-class>ServletJDBCfind</servlet-class>
</servlet>
<servlet-mapping>
<servlet-name>ServletJDBCfind</servlet-name>
<url-pattern>/ServletJDBCfind</url-pattern>
</servlet-mapping>
</web-app>
```

After coding as above, the MySQL driver has to be loaded to the project. Select and right click the `Libraries` folder then select `Add Library`.

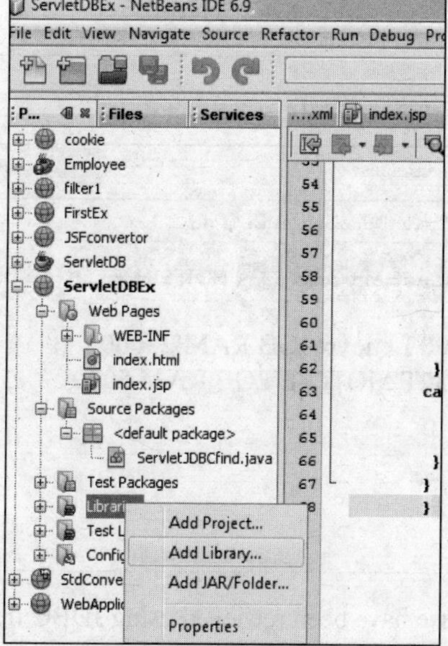

Select `MySQL JDBC Driver` and click `Add Library`.

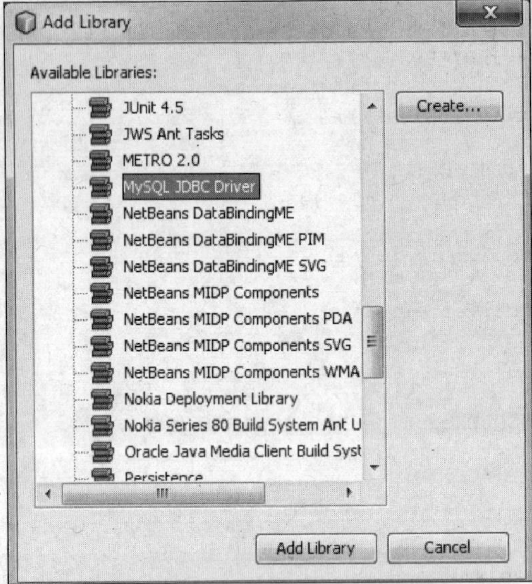

After the completion of these steps, right click the project and select the Run option, and the following output will be displayed.

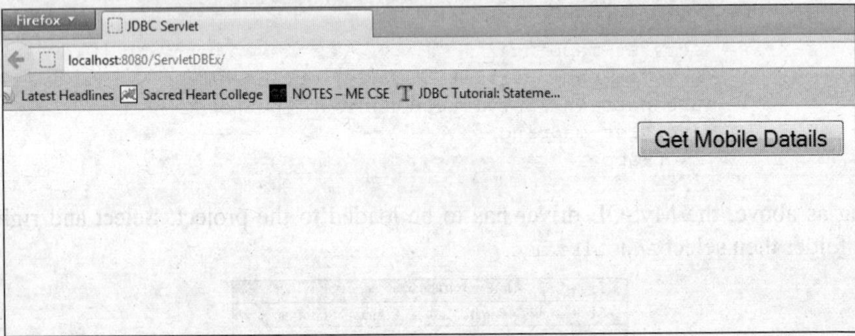

Click the button `Get Mobile Details`.

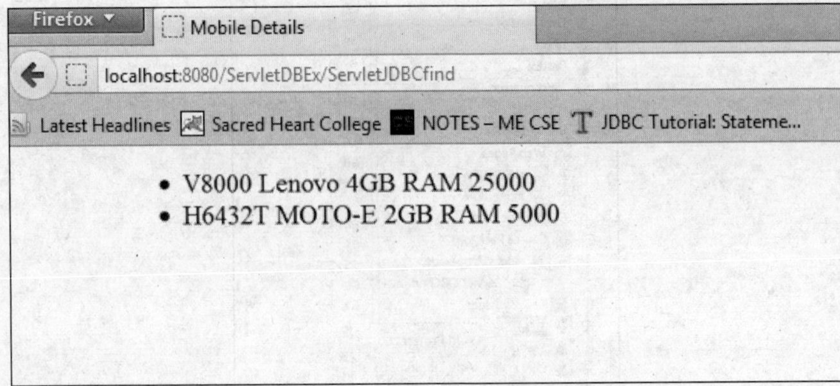

The inserted values in the database have been retrieved using JDBC from the servlet.

18.11 COOKIES

HTTP is stateless. This means that every HTTP request is different from others. Sometimes it is necessary to keep track of a sequence of related requests sent by a client to perform some designated task. This is called session tracking. Cookies are one of the solutions to session tracking. A cookie is a [key, value] pair created by the server and is installed in the client's browser when the client makes a request for the first time. A browser also maintains a list of cookies installed in it and sends it to the server as a part of subsequent HTTP requests. The server can then easily identify that this request is a part of a sequence of related requests. This way, cookies provide an elegant solution to session tracking. The servlet API supports cookies. A cookie is represented using the `javax.servlet.http.Cookie` class and is created using the following constructor:

```
Cookie(String key, String value)
```

A cookie is added by the `addCookie()` method of the `HttpServletResponse` class. Similarly, the server can get all cookies sent by the web browser using the `getCookies()` method of the `HttpServletRequestclass`. There are two types of cookies in servlets, namely non-persistent cookies and persistent cookies. A non-persistent cookie is valid for a single session and it is removed each time the user closes the browser. A persistent cookie however is valid for multiple sessions and it is not removed when the user closes the browser. A cookie can be defined as a small piece of information that persists across multiple client requests. The following example illustrates the handling of servlet cookies.

```
//index.html
<form action="servlet1" method="post">
   Name:<input type="text" name="userName"/><br/>
   <input type="submit" value="go"/>
</form>
```

```
//FirstServlet.java
import java.io.*;
import javax.servlet.*;
import javax.servlet.http.*;
public class FirstServlet extends HttpServlet { public void
doPost(HttpServletRequest request, HttpServletResponse response)
   {
      try
      { response.setContentType("text/html");
         PrintWriter out = response.getWriter();
         String n=request.getParameter("userName");
         out.print("Welcome "+n);
         Cookie ck=new Cookie("uname",n);//creating cookie object
         response.addCookie(ck);//adding cookie in the response
         //creating submit button
         out.print("<form action='servlet2' method='post'>");
         out.print("<input type='submit' value='go'>");
         out.print("</form>");
         out.close();
      }
      catch(Exception e){System.out.println(e);}
   }
}
```

```
//SecondServlet.java
import java.io.*;
import javax.servlet.*;
import javax.servlet.http.*;
public class SecondServlet extends HttpServlet {
   public void doPost(HttpServletRequest request, HttpServletResponse response){
      try{ response.setContentType("text/html");
         PrintWriter out = response.getWriter();
         Cookie ck[]=request.getCookies();
         out.print("Hello "+ck[0].getValue());
         out.close();
      }catch(Exception e){System.out.println(e);}
   }
}
```

```
//web.xml
<web-app>
   <servlet>
      <description>This is the description of my J2EE component</description>
      <display-name>This is the display name of my J2EE component</display-name>
      <servlet-name>Servlet1</servlet-name>
      <servlet-class>FirstServlet</servlet-class>
   </servlet>
   <servlet>
      <description>This is the description of my J2EE component</description>
      <display-name>This is the display name of my J2EE component</display-name>
      <servlet-name>SecondServlet</servlet-name>
      <servlet-class>SecondServlet</servlet-class>
   </servlet>
   <servlet-mapping>
      <servlet-name>Servlet1</servlet-name>
      <url-pattern>/servlet1</url-pattern>
   </servlet-mapping>
   <servlet-mapping>
      <servlet-name>SecondServlet</servlet-name>
      <url-pattern>/servlet2</url-pattern>
   </servlet-mapping>
   <welcome-file-list>
      <welcome-file>index.html</welcome-file>
   </welcome-file-list>
</web-app>
```

The output will be as follows:

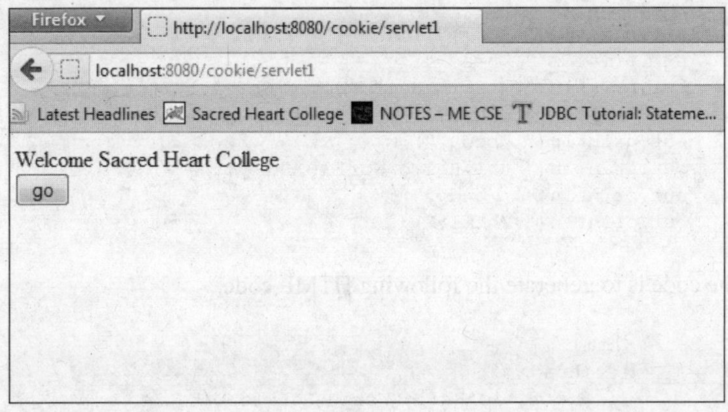

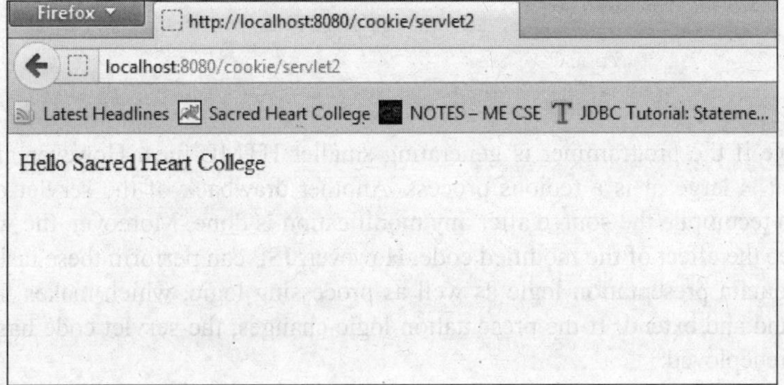

Limitations of cookies

Cookies work correctly provided the web browsers have enabled cookie support. In addition to security concerns, there are some technical limitations:

- Cookies can carry small pieces of information and are not a standard means of communication.
- Some web browsers limit the number of cookies in general to 20 per web server. To avoid this problem, more than one block of information may be sent per cookie.
- The value of a cookie should never exceed 4 KB. If the value of a cookie is larger than 4 KB, it should be trimmed to fit.
- Cookies cannot identify a particular user. A user can be identified by a combination of user account, browser and computer. So, users who have multiple accounts and use multiple computers/browsers have multiple sets of cookies. Consequently, cookies cannot differentiate between multiple browsers running on a single computer.
- Intruders can snoop, steal cookies and attack sessions. This is called session hijacking.

18.12 PROBLEMS WITH SERVLETS

Servlets are not useful for generating presentation content such as HTML. Consider the following piece of code.

```
out.println("<html>");
out.println(" <head>");
out.println(" <title>Hello World Servlet</title>");
out.println(" </head>");
out.println(" <body>");
out.println(" <h1>Hello World!</h1>");
out.println(" </body>");
out.println("</html>");
```

The purpose of the code is to generate the following HTML code.

```
<html>
   <head>
      <title>Hello World Servlet</title>
   </head>
   <body>
      <h1>Hello World!</h1>
   </body>
</html>
```

This is acceptable if the programmer is generating smaller HTML files. However, if the size of the HTML document is large, it is a tedious process. Another drawback of the servlet over Java Server Pages (JSP) is to recompile the source after any modification is done. Moreover, the web server has to be restarted to see the effect of the modified code. However, JSP can perform these tasks automatically. Servlets often contain presentation logic as well as processing logic, which makes the code difficult to read, understand and extend. If the presentation logic changes, the servlet code has to be modified, recompiled and redeployed.

SUMMARY

1. Servlet is a Java technology for server-side programming. A servlet is a Java module that runs inside a Java-enabled web server and service requests obtained from a web server.
2. Java servlet technology has some distinct advantages over other competent technologies in terms of efficiency, persistence, portability, robustness, extensibility, and so on.
3. Servlets run in the server machine and usually generate simple HTML code. Therefore, even a very old browser can display the generated HTML pages correctly.
4. The basic servlet architecture consists of two packages: `javax.servlet` and `javax.servlet.http`. The first package contains top-level interfaces and classes that are used and extended by all other servlets. The second package is provided for use with servlets that can handle HTTP requests.
5. The container in which the servlet is deployed, supervises and controls the life cycle of a servlet. During its lifetime, methods such as `init()`, `service()`, and `destroy()` are called in some specific order.
6. The `GenericServlet` class defines a generic protocol-independent servlet, in the sense that it can be extended to provide the implementation of any protocol such as HTTP, FTP and SMTP. On the other hand, `HttpServlet` class extends `GenericServlet` and provides a framework for handling HTTP requests.
7. There are two ways to pass parameters to a servlet: using a URL and using an HTML form. One of the disadvantages of passing parameters using URLs is that users can

view the parameter names along with their values passed. So, it is not safe to send sensitive information using this method. Moreover, the number of parameters that can be passed is also limited. HTML forms can be used to pass parameters in a convenient way. The methods of the `ServletRequest` interface are used to retrieve parameters.

8. Server-Side Include (SSI) allows embedding servlets within HTML pages, using SSI directives. This allows the inclusion of dynamically generated content in an existing HTML file, without having to serve the entire page via a CGI program or other dynamic technologies.
9. Sometimes, it is necessary to keep track of a sequence of related requests sent by a client to perform some designated task. This is called session tracking. Cookies are one of the solutions to session tracking.
10. Filters are objects that are installed between clients and servers to inspect requests and responses. They can transform requests or modify responses.

SHORT QUESTIONS

1. What is a servlet? How does it differ from a Java Application?
2. What are the advantages of servlets over CGI?
3. What is the significance of the `GenericServlet` class?
4. What kind of exceptions does `ServletException` handle?
5. What are initialisation parameters? When are they used?
6. What is a cookie? What are the real-life uses of cookies?
7. What is the task of the `javax.servlet.Servlet` interface?
8. What are the two objects that a servlet receives when it accepts a call from a client?
9. What types of constraints can `ServletResponse` interface set on the client?
10. Mention some uses of servlets.

COMPREHENSIVE QUESTIONS

1. Briefly explain the life cycle of a servlet.
2. Describe how an HTTP servlet handles its client requests.
3. What are the differences between servlets and applets?
4. How can you invoke other web resources such as servlets/JSPs?
5. How can you include other resources in the response?
6. What information does the `ServletResponse` interface give to servlet methods for replying to the client?
7. What do you understand by servlet mapping?
8. What is session hijacking?
9. Explain the concept of cookies.
10. Give an account of servlet architecture.

SOLVED PROBLEMS

1. Write a Java program with Servlets to create a dynamic HTML form to accept and display the user name and password with the help of get() and post() methods.

Serv.java

```
import java.io.*;
import javax.servlet.http.*;
import javax.servlet.*;
public class serv extends HttpServlet {
```

```
  protected void doPost(HttpServletRequest req, HttpServletResponse
  resp) throws
  ServletException, IOException
  {
    String un= req.getParameter("username");
    String pwd= req.getParameter("pwd");
    resp.setContentType("text/html");
    PrintWriter pw=resp.getWriter();
    pw.println("<h2>Welcome,"+un+"</h2>");
    pw.println("<h2>Your Password is,"+pwd+"</h2>");
    pw.close();
  }
}
```

Postreq.html

```
<html>
  <body>
    <form action= 'serv' method='post'>
      Enter User Name:
      <input type='text' name='username'> <br/><br/>
      Enter Password:
      <input type='text' name='pwd'> <br/><br/>
      <input type='submit' value='Click here to submit this form'>
      <br/><br/>
    </form>
  </body>
</html>
```

Web.xml

```
<servlet>
  <servlet-name>s<servlet-class>s
</servlet>
<servlet-mapping>
  <servlet-name>s<servlet-class>s
</servlet-mapping>
```

2. Write a Java Servlet program for 'auto refreshing' the webpage after given period of time.

```
import java.io.*;
import javax.servlet.*;
import javax.servlet.http.*;
import java.util.*;
// Extend HttpServlet class
public class refr extends HttpServlet {
  // Method to handle GET method request.
  public void doGet(HttpServletRequest request, HttpServletResponse response)
  throws
  ServletException, IOException
  {
    // Set refresh, autoload time as 5 seconds
    response.setIntHeader("Refresh", 5);
    // Set response content type
    response.setContentType("text/html");
    // Get current time
    Calendar calendar = new GregorianCalendar();
    String am_pm;
    int hour = calendar.get(Calendar.HOUR);
    int minute = calendar.get(Calendar.MINUTE);
    int second = calendar.get(Calendar.SECOND);
    if(calendar.get(Calendar.AM_PM) == 0)
```

```
am_pm = "AM";
else
am_pm = "PM";
String CT = hour+":"+ minute +":"+ second +" "+ am_pm;
PrintWriter out = response.getWriter();
String title = "Auto Page Refresh using Servlet";
String docType =
"<!doctype html public \"-//w3c//dtd html 4.0 " +
"transitional//en\">\n";
out.println(docType +
"<html>\n" +
"<head><title>" + title + "</title></head>\n"+
"<body bgcolor=\"#f0f0f0\">\n" +
"<h1 align=\"center\">" + title + "</h1>\n" +
"<p>Current Time is: " + CT + "</p>\n");
}
// Method to handle POST method request.
public void doPost(HttpServletRequest request,
HttpServletResponse response)
throws ServletException, IOException {
doGet(request, response);
}
}
```

3. Write a Java Servlet program to demonstrate the use of cookies.

Cookie.html

```
<html>
  <head>
    <title>Cookies Example in Servlets</title>
  </head>
  <body bgcolor=wheat>
    <center>
      <h1>Cookies Example in Java</h1>
      <form action="createcookie" method="post">
        First name: <input type="text" name="fname">
        Last name: <input type="text" name="lname">
        <input type="submit"value="SUBMIT">
      </form>
    </center>
  </body>
</html>
```

createcookie.java

```
import javax.servlet.*;
import javax.servlet.http.*;
import java.io.*;
public class createcookie extends HttpServlet
{
  public void doPost(HttpServletRequest req,HttpServletResponse res) throws
  ServletException,IOException
  {
    String fname=req.getParameter("fname");
    String lname=req.getParameter("lname");
    Cookie f=new Cookie("first_name",fname);
    Cookie l=new Cookie("last_name",lname);
    res.addCookie(f);
    res.addCookie(l);
  }
```

```
}
reetrivecookie.java
import javax.servlet.*;
import javax.servlet.http.*;
import java.io.*;
public class retrievecookie extends HttpServlet
{
  public void doGet(HttpServletRequest req,HttpServletResponse res) throws
  ServletException,IOException
  {
     PrintWriter pw=res.getWriter();
     pw.println("<h1>");
     Cookie[] c=req.getCookies();
     for(k=0;k<2;k++)
     {
        pw.println(c[k].getValue());
     }
     pw.println("</h1>");
  }
}
```

4. To write HTML code and a servlet to demonstrate invoking a servlet from html.

PostParam.java

```
import java.io.*;
import java.util.*;
import javax.servlet.*;
public class PostParam extends GenericServlet
{
  public void service(ServletRequest request,ServletResponse response) throws
  ServletException,IOException
  {
     PrintWriter pw = response.getWriter();
     Enumeration e = request.getParameterNames();
     while(e.hasMoreElements())
     {
        String pname = (String)e.nextElement();
        pw.print(pname + " = ");
        String pvalue = request.getParameter(pname);
     pw.println(pvalue); }
pw.close(); } }
```

index.html

```
<HTML>
  <head>
     <TITLE>INVOKING SERVLET FROM HTML</TITLE>
  </head>
  <BODY>
     <CENTER>
        <FORM name = "PostParam" method = "Post" action=" PostParam">
           <TABLE>
              <tr>
                 <td><B>Employee</B>
                 </td>
                 <td><input type = "textbox" name="ename" size="25" value="">
                 </td>
              </tr>
              <tr>
                 <td><B>Phone</B>
```

```
                </td>
                <td><input type = "textbox" name="phoneno" size="25"
                value=""></td>
            </tr>
        </TABLE>
        <INPUT type = "submit" value="Submit">
    </FORM>
    </CENTER>
  </body>
</html>
```

5. To create the login form using a servlet.
   Create a table userreg with name and pass fields. Moreover, it must contain some data. The table should be created as: create table userreg(name varchar2(40),pass varchar2(40));

   index.html

```
<form action="servlet1" method="post">
  Name:<input type="text" name="username"/><br/><br/>
  Password:<input type="password" name="userpass"/><br/><br/>
  <input type="submit" value="login"/>
</form>
```

   FirstServlet.java

```
import java.io.IOException;
import java.io.PrintWriter;
import javax.servlet.RequestDispatcher;
import javax.servlet.ServletException;
import javax.servlet.http.HttpServlet;
import javax.servlet.http.HttpServletRequest;
import javax.servlet.http.HttpServletResponse;
public class FirstServlet extends HttpServlet {
  public void doPost(HttpServletRequest request, HttpServletResponse response)
  throws ServletException, IOException {
      response.setContentType("text/html");
      PrintWriter out = response.getWriter();
      String n=request.getParameter("username");
      String p=request.getParameter("userpass");
      if(LoginDao.validate(n, p)){
          RequestDispatcher rd=request.getRequestDispatcher("servlet2");
          rd.forward(request,response);
      }
      else{
          out.print("Sorry username or password error");
          RequestDispatcher rd=request.getRequestDispatcher("index.html");
          rd.include(request,response);
      }
      out.close();
  }
}
```

   LoginDao.java

```
import java.sql.*;
public class LoginDao {
  public static boolean validate(String name,String pass){
      boolean status=false;
      try{
          Class.forName("com.mysql.jdbc.Driver");
          Connection=DriverManager.getConnection("jdbc:mysql://localhost/
          testDB","root","");
```

```
            PreparedStatement ps=con.prepareStatement("select * from userreg where
            name=? and pass=?");
            ps.setString(1,name);
            ps.setString(2,pass);
            ResultSet rs=ps.executeQuery();
            status=rs.next();
        } catch(Exception e){ System.out.println(e);}
        return status;
    }
}
```

WelcomeServlet.java

```
import java.io.IOException;
import java.io.PrintWriter;
import javax.servlet.ServletException;
import javax.servlet.http.HttpServlet;
import javax.servlet.http.HttpServletRequest;
import javax.servlet.http.HttpServletResponse;
public class WelcomeServlet extends HttpServlet {
  public void doPost(HttpServletRequest request, HttpServletResponse response)
  throws ServletException, IOException {
      response.setContentType("text/html");
      PrintWriter out = response.getWriter();
      String n=request.getParameter("username");
      out.print("Welcome "+n);
      out.close();
  }
}
```

PROGRAMMING EXERCISES

1. Develop a servlet to create a web page that brings the user's address to the client from the server.
2. Write an HTML form to submit the name of an employee to a servlet. The servlet should open a database and retrieve that employee's new record corresponding to this employee in the appropriate database. It should then inform the client that the details of the new employee have been added to the database.
3. Write a HTML form to submit the name of a new employee and the branch office in which he is appointed. The servlet should insert a Subject ="Java" to the client. Also write another servlet to read back the cookies from the client. Report the retrieved values to the client through a web page.
4. Write a servlet to add the cookies (Name = "Denis", Phone No="1234567890") and phone number. Then it should construct and send back a web page containing the employee's name and phone number.
5. Write a program to perform the CRUD operations using JDBC from a servlet.

CHAPTER

19

Java Server Pages

Java Server Pages (JSP) is a server-side technology that enables web programmers to generate web pages dynamically in response to client requests. Among many server-side technologies used to build dynamic web applications, JSP is the one that has grabbed the attention of web developers due to several reasons. JSP is basically a high-level extension to the Java servlet technology. It enables inserting pure Java code in a HTML document directly. These pages are executed under the supervision of an environment called the *web container*. The web container first compiles the page on the server and generates a servlet that is loaded in the Java Runtime Environment (JRE) automatically. The interesting part is that the web container only generates the servlet from the page if its last modification time is newer than the time when the servlet was generated last. The servlet serves the client requests in the usual way. This makes the development of web applications convenient, simple and fast. Maintenance also becomes very easy. JSP technology provides excellent server-side programming for web applications that need database access. JSP not only provides cross-web-server and cross-platform support, but also integrates the WYSIWYG (What You See Is What You Get) features of static HTML pages with the extreme power of Java technology. JSP also allow the separation the dynamic content of web pages from the static HTML content. The programmer can write regular HTML files in the usual way and then insert Java code for the dynamic parts using special tags, which usually start with <% and end with %>. Usually, JSP files have the extension `.jsp`.

19.1 OVERVIEW

JSP technology was developed by Sun Microsystems to separate the development of dynamic Web page content from static HTML page design. The result of this separation means that the page design can change without the need to alter the underlying dynamic content of the page. This is useful in the development life-cycle because the web page designers do not have to know how to create the dynamic content, but simply have to know where to place the dynamic content within the page. To facilitate embedding of dynamic content, JSPs use a number of tags that enable the page designer to insert the properties of a JavaBeans object and script elements into a JSP file. The advantages of using JSP technology over other methods of dynamic content creation are as follows.

Separation of dynamic and static content

This allows for the separation of application logic and Web page design, reducing the complexity of website development and maintenance of the site.

Platform independence

Because JSP technology is Java-based, it is platform independent. JSPs can run on nearly any web application server. JSPs can be developed on any platform and viewed by any browser because the output of a compiled JSP page is in HTML.

Component reuse

Using JavaBeans and Enterprise JavaBeans, JSPs leverage the inherent reusability offered by these technologies. This enables developers to share components with other developers or their client community, which can speed up website development.

Scripting and tags

JSPs support both embedded JavaScript and tags. JavaScript is typically used to add page-level functionality to the JSP. Tags provide an easy way to embed and modify JavaBeans properties and to specify other directives and actions.

19.2 JSP HTTP AND ENGINES

Java Server Pages specification extends the idea of Java servlet API, to provide a robust framework to developers of web applications for creating dynamic web content. Currently, JSP or servlet technology supports only HTTP. However, a developer may extend the idea of servlet or JSP to implement other protocols such as FTP or SMTP. Since JSP uses HTML, XML and Java code, the applications are secure, fast and independent of server platforms. It allows the programmer to embed pure Java code in a HTML document. It is important that the JSP specifications are defined on top of the Java servlet API. Consequently, it follows all servlet semantics and has all powers that a servlet has.

The life cycle and many of the capabilities, especially the dynamic aspects of JSP pages, are exactly the same as those of Java servlet technology.

To process JSP pages, a web container that can understand JSP (sometimes referred to as a JSP engine) code is needed. The JSP engine is a specialised servlet that runs under the supervision of the servlet engine. This JSP engine is typically connected with a web server or can be integrated inside a web server or an application server. Many such servers are freely available and can be downloaded for evaluation and/or development of web applications. Some of them are Tomcat, Java Web Server, WebLogic and WebSphere. Once a JSP-capable web server or application server is downloaded and installed on a machine, it is better to know where to place the JSP files, what their URLs will be and how to access them from the web browser or another application using those URLs. A web server like GlassFish is an open source available in Netbeans itself, and can be used to run all the JSP pages.

Tomcat

Tomcat implements servlet 2.2 and JSP 1.1 specifications. It is very easy to install and can be used as a small stand-alone server for developing and testing servlets and JSP pages. For large applications, it is usually integrated into the more powerful Apache web server.

Java web server

The Java System web server by Sun is a leading web server that delivers secure infrastructure for medium and large business technologies and applications. Sun claims that it delivers 8x better performance than

Apache 2.0 with Tomcat. It is available on all major operating systems and supports a wide range of technologies such as JSP and Java Servlet technologies, PHP and CGI.

WebLogic

WebLogic by BEA Systems of San Jose, California, is a J2EE application server and also a HTTP server for Microsoft Windows, Unix/Linux and other platforms. WebLogic supports DB2, Oracle, Microsoft SQL Server and other JDBC-compliant databases. The WebLogic server also includes the .NET framework for interoperability and allows integration of the following native components:

- CORBA connectivity,
- COM+ connectivity,
- J2EE connector architecture,
- IBM's WebSphere MQ connectivity, and
- native JMS messaging for enterprise.

Data Mapping functionality and Business Process Management are also included in WebLogic Server Process Edition.

WebSphere

IBM attempted to develop software to set up, operate and integrate electronic business applications that can work across multiple computing platforms, using Java-based web technologies. The result is the WebSphere Application Server (WAS). It includes both run-time components and tools that can be used to develop robust and versatile applications that will run on WAS.

19.3 WORKING OF JSP

Java Server Pages are made operable by contents (HTML tags, JSP tags and scripts) translated into a servlet by the application server. This process is responsible for translating both the dynamic and static elements declared within the JSP file into Java servlet code that delivers the translated contents through the web server output stream to the browser. Because JSPs are server-side technology, the processing of both, the static and dynamic elements of the page, occurs in the server. The architecture of a JSP/servlet enabled web site is often referred to as *thin-client* because most of the business logic is executed on the server. The following process outlines the tasks performed on a JSP file on the first invocation of the file or when the underlying JSP file is changed by the developer (Fig. 19.1).

- The web browser makes a request to the JSP page.
- The JSP engine parses the contents of the JSP file.
- The JSP engine creates a temporary servlet source code based on the contents of the JSP. The generated servlet is responsible for rendering the static elements of the JSP specified at design time in addition to creating the dynamic elements of the page.
- The servlet source code is compiled by the Java compiler into a servlet class file.
- The servlet is instantiated. The init and service methods of the servlet are called and the servlet logic is executed.
- The combination of static HTML and graphics combined with the dynamic elements specified in the original JSP page definition are sent to the web browser through the output stream of the servlet's response object.

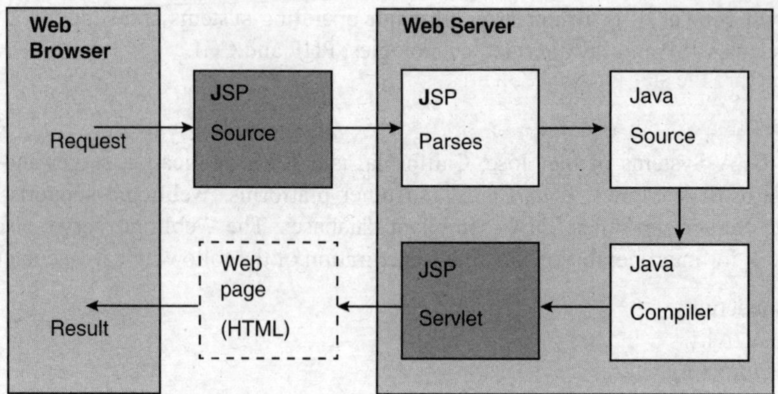

Fig. 19.1 The JSP processing life-cycle on first-time invocation

Subsequent invocations of the JSP file will simply invoke the service method of the servlet created by the above process to serve the content to the web browser. The servlet produced as a result of the above process remains in service until the application server is stopped, the servlet is manually unloaded, or a change is made to the underlying file, causing recompilation.

19.4 ANATOMY OF A JSP PAGE

A JSP page basically consists of two parts: HTML/XML markups and JSP constructs. A large per cent of the JSP page, in many cases, just consists of static HTML/XML components, known as template text. Consequently, it is possible to create and maintain JSP pages using traditional HTML/XML tools. There are three primary types of JSP constructs in a typical JSP page—*scripting elements, directives*, and *actions*.

Java code that will become an integral part of the resultant servlet is inserted using scripting elements. Directives are used to control the overall structure and behaviour of the generated servlet. Actions allow using existing components and otherwise controlling the behaviour of the JSP engine. There are three kinds of scripting elements—*scriptlets, declarations* and *expressions*. Scriptlets allow the programmer to insert any Java-server relevant API in the HTML or XML page, provided the syntax is correct. Declarations allow declaring variables and methods. Expressions are used to print the value of Java expressions.

19.5 JSP SYNTAX

The syntax of JSP is similar to that of XML. All JSP tags must conform to the following general rules:

- tags must have their matching end tags,
- attributes must appear in the start tag, and
- attribute values in the tag must be quoted.

White spaces within the body text of a JSP page are preserved during the translation phase. To use special characters such as '%', add a '\' character before it. To use the '\' character, add another '\' character before it.

19.6 CREATING A SIMPLE JSP PAGE

The following are the steps involved in creating a JSP file in Netbeans IDE.

1. Open `Netbeans IDE`, Select `File` → `New Project`.

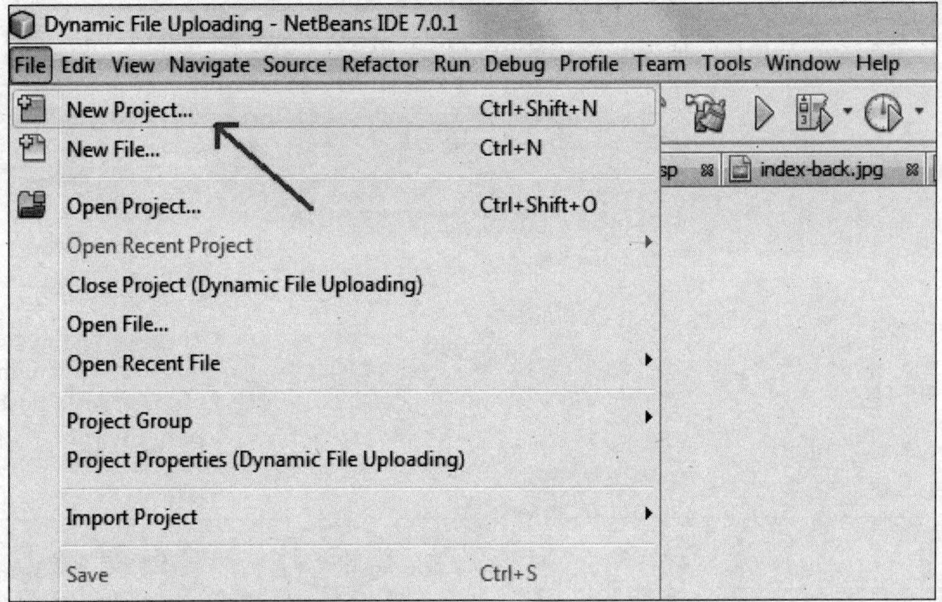

2. Select `Java Web` → `Web Application` and then click on `Next`.

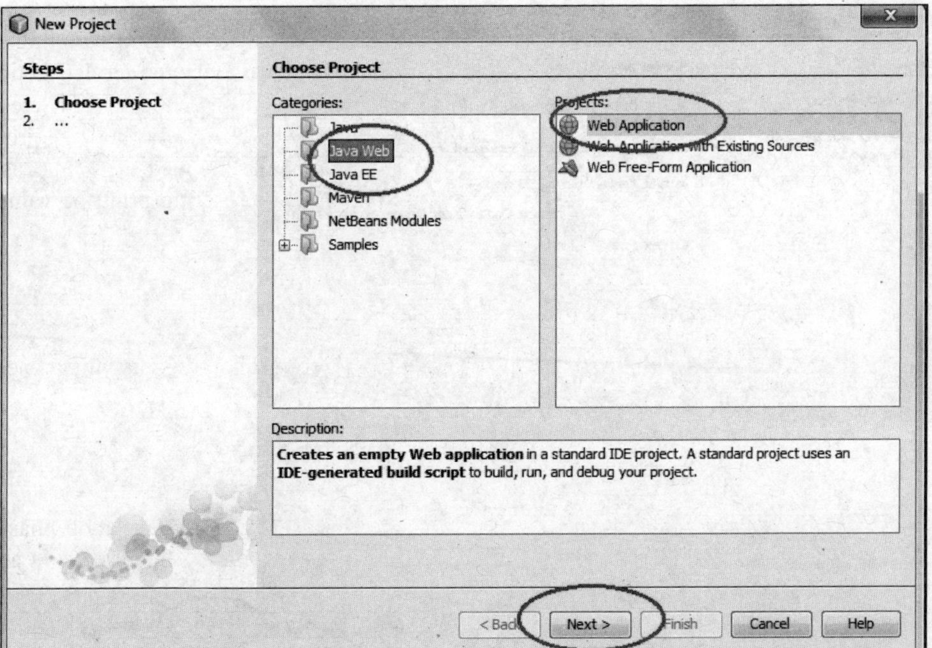

3. Give a name to the project and click on `Next`.

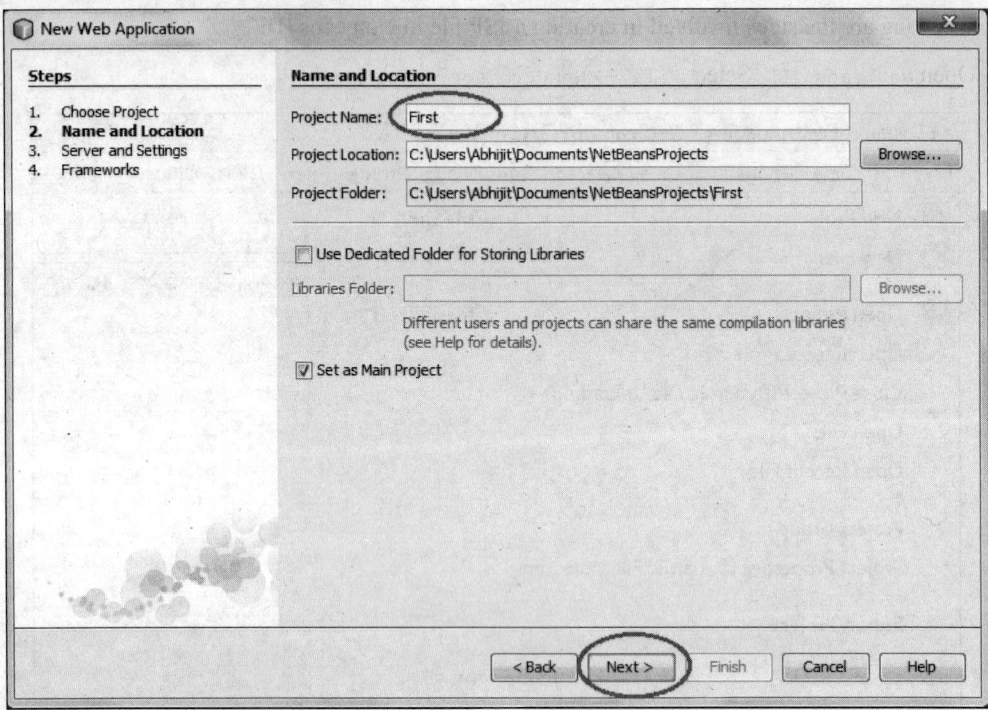

4. Select the `Server GlassFish` and click `Finish`.

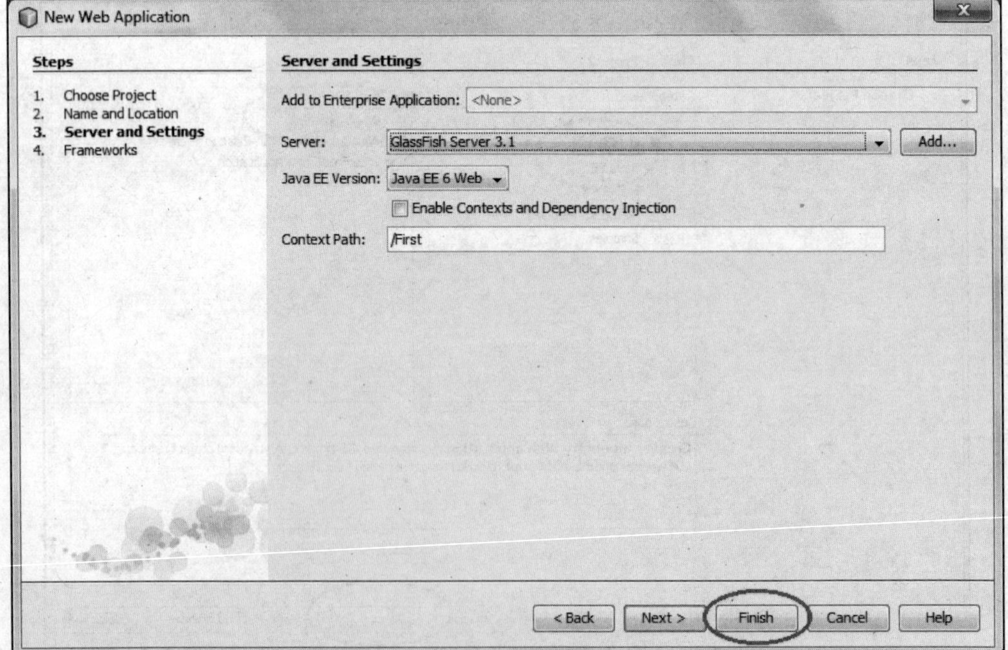

5. The complete directory structure required for JSP application will be created automatically by the IDE. A default `index.jsp` file is created under the folder `Web Pages`.

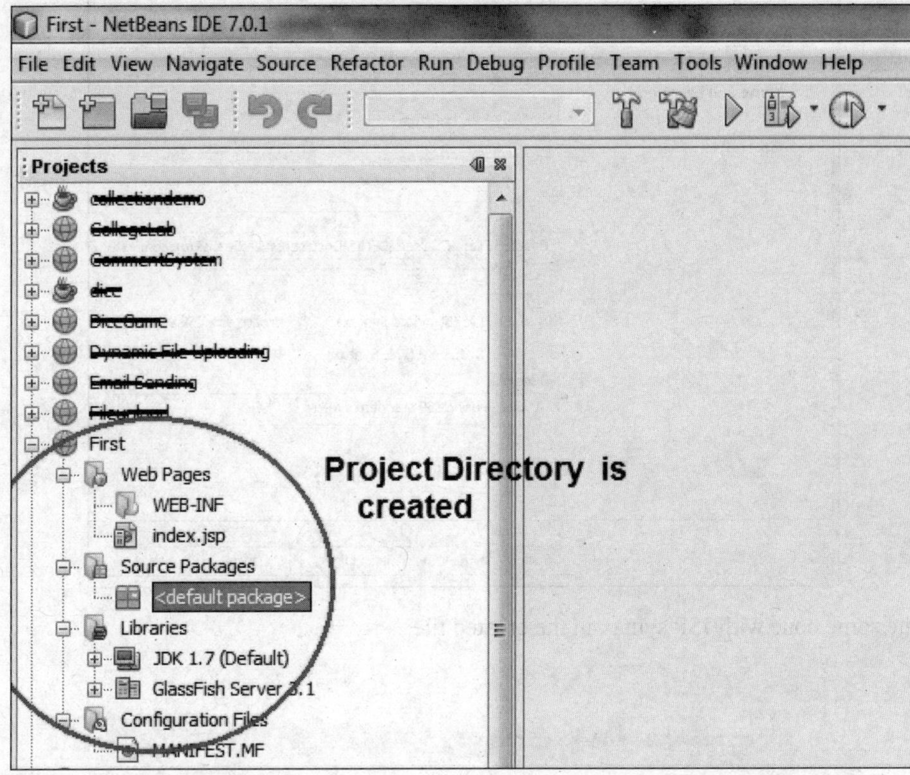

6. To create a JSP file, right-click on `Web Pages` folder, → select `New` → `JSP` option.

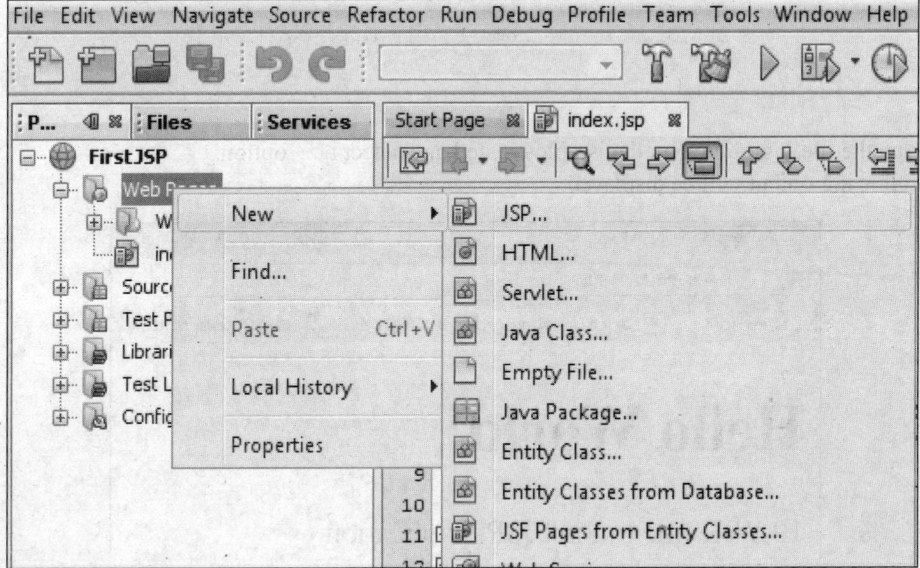

7. Give a file name as shown below and click `Finish`.

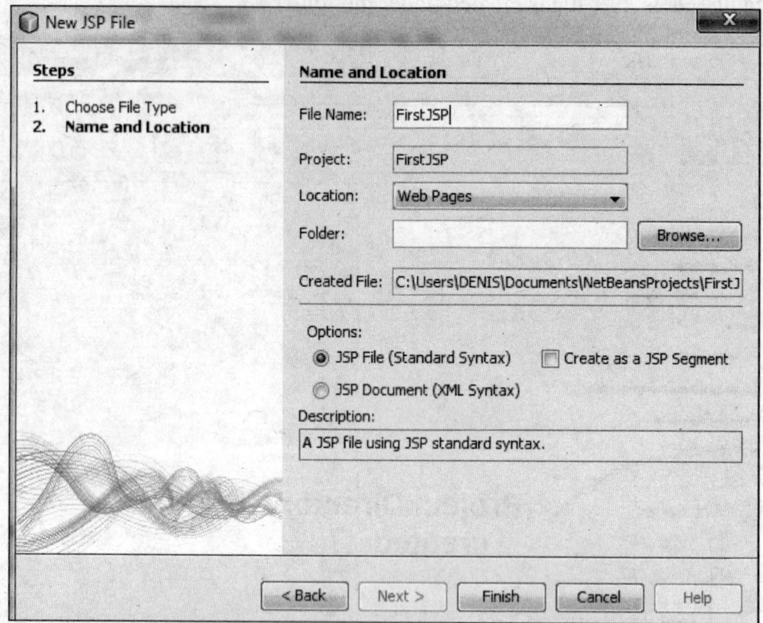

8. Write some code with JSP syntax in the created file.

```
<html>
   <head>
      <title>JSP Page</title>
   </head>
   <body>
      <h1>Hello World!</h1>
      <% out.print(2*5); %>
      <% out.println();%>
      <% out.println("Welcome to First JSP Application");%>
   </body>
</html>
```

9. To run the file, right-click on the jsp file created and select `Run` option.
The following output will be displayed.

19.7 COMPONENTS OF JSP

Java Server Pages are composed of standard HTML tags and JSP tags. A JSP page consists of the following components:

- directives,
- scripting elements,
  - declarations,
  - expressions,
  - scriptlets,
- actions.

This section describes each of these categories in more detail. Table 19.1 lists some JSP tags and their meanings.

Table 19.1 JSP tags and their meanings

JSP tag	Meaning
<%@...-%>	Used for JSP directives such as page and include.
<%!...%>	Used for variables, methods and inner class declarations.
<%=...%>	Used for JSP expressions.
<%...%>	Used for JSP scriptlets that can contain arbitrary Java statements.

19.7.1 Directives

A JSP directive is a global definition sent to the JSP engine that remains valid regardless of any specific requests made to the JSP page. A directive always appears at the top of the JSP file, before any other JSP tags. This is because of the way the JSP parsing engine produces servlet code from the JSP file. Directives do not generate any output directly, but tell the JSP engine how to handle the JSP page. They are enclosed within the <%@ and %> tags. The commonly used directives are `page`, `include`, and `taglib`.

The syntax of a directive is:

```
<%@ directive directive_attr_name = value %>
```

page directive

The `page` directive defines page dependent attributes to the JSP engine. The `page` directive has many attributes, which can be specified in any order. The following is the syntax of the `page` directive:

```
<%@ page language="java" buffer="none"
isThreadSafe="yes" errorPage="/error.jsp" %>
```

import

The value of this attribute is a list of fully qualified names of classes separated by commas (,), to be imported by the JSP file. To import all the classes of a package, use '.*' at the end of the package name. The following directive imports all the classes in the `java.io` and `java.reflect` packages and the class `Vector` that belongs to the `java.util` package.

```
<%@ page import="java.io.*, java.reflect.*, java.util.Vector" %>
```

The classes can then be referred from declarations, expressions and scriptlets within the JSP document, without using the package prefix. The programmer must import a class before using it. It is possible to use `import` as many times as required, in a JSP file. For example, the line of code just discussed can be written as three directives, as follows:

```
<%@ page import=»java.io.*» %>
<%@ page import=»java.reflect.*» %>
<%@ page import=»java.util.Vector» %>
```

Those directives are converted to the corresponding import statement in the generated servlet file. There is no need to import the classes of the packages `java.lang, javax.servlet, javax.servlet. http` and `javax.servlet.jsp` as they are imported implicitly.

session

This attribute indicates whether the JSP file requires a HTTP session. The following syntax is used:

```
session="true | false"
```

If true is specified (this is the default value), the JSP file has a session object that refers to the current or new session. If the value is false, no `session` object is created. If the JSP file does not require a session, the value should be set to false for performance considerations.

buffer

Syntax:

```
buffer="none | sizekb"
```

The `buffer` attribute indicates the size in kilobytes (default is 8 KB) of the output buffer to be used by the JSP file. The value 'none' indicates a buffer with zero size. In such a case, the output is written directly to the output stream of the response object of the servlet.

autoFlush

Syntax:

```
autoFlush="true | false"
```

The `autoFlush` attribute specifies whether the buffer should be flushed automatically when it is full. If set to false, a buffer overflow exception is thrown when the buffer becomes full. The default value is true. The value of `autoFlush` can never be set to false when the buffer is set to none.

isThreadSafe

Syntax:

```
isThreadSafe="true | false"
```

This attribute indicates whether the JSP page can handle multiple threads simultaneously. If set to true, the JSP container is allowed to send multiple concurrent client requests to this JSP page. This is to ensure that the access to shared resources by multiple concurrent threads is effectively synchronised. If set to false, the JSP container sends clients' requests one by one using a single thread. This attribute basically provides information to the underlying servlet on whether it should implement the `SingleThreadModel` interface or not.

info

Syntax:

```
info="text"
```

It allows the programmer to specify descriptive information about the JSP page. This information can be retrieved using the `Servlet.getServletInfo()` method.

contentType

Syntax:

```
contentType="MIMEType [ ;charset=characterSet ]"
```

It specifies the MIME type and encoding used in the generated response to be sent to the client. MIME types and encoding supported by the JSP container can only be specified. The default MIME type and character encoding are text/html and ISO-8859-1, respectively.

errorPage and isErrorPage

Syntax:

```
errorPage="relativeURL"
isErrorPage="true | false"
```

When an uncaught exception occurs in a JSP page, the JSP container sends information explaining the exception, which is undesirable for some cases such as commercial sites. The `errorPage` attribute specifies the relative path name of another JSP page to be displayed, in case an error occurs in the current page. In the error page, the `isErrorPage` attribute must be set to true. The error page can access the implicit exception variable that represents the exception that has occurred, as well as other implicit variables. It can then, by consulting those objects, send some message that can be understood by the clients.

include directive

This directive inserts the contents of a file in a JSP page, during the translation phase when the JSP page is compiled.
Syntax:

```
<%@ include file="relativeURL" %>
```

If the file to be included is a HTML or text file, its contents are directly included in the place of the `include` directive. The following example includes a HTML file `header.html` in a JSP page.

```
<%@ include file="header.html" %>
```

If the included file is a JSP file, it is first translated and then included in the JSP page.

```
<%@ include file="login.jsp" %>
```

Make sure that the tags in the included file do not conflict with the tags used in including the JSP page. For example, if the including JSP page contains tags such as `<html>` and `<body>`, the included file must not contain those tags. The include process is said to be static as the file is included at compilation time.

```
//index.jsp
<h2>this is index page</h2>
<jsp:include page="printdate.jsp" />
<h2>end section of index page</h2>
```

```
//printdate.jsp
<% out.print("Today is:"+java.util.Calendar.getInstance( ).getTime( )); %>
```

Comments

Comments are used to document the JSP pages and can be inserted anywhere in the JSP page. The general syntax is as follows:

```
<%-- JSP comment --%>
```

Anything between `<%--` and `--%>` is ignored by the JSP engine and is not even added to the servlet's source code. For example:

```
<%-- Prints current date and time --%>
<%= new java.util.Date(); %>
```

The Java-like comments may also be used in scriptlets and declarations. They are added to the servlet but not interpreted, and hence are not sent to the client.

```
<%
//get all cookies
Cookie[ ] cookies = request.getCookies();
/*
The following code checks whether the request contains a cookie having
the name "user"
*/
String user = null;
for(int i = 0; i < cookies.length; i++) if(cookies[i].getName().
equals("user")) user = (String)cookies[i].getValue(); if(user != null) {
   //proceed
}
%>
```

The HTML comments are enclosed in <!-- and --> and added to the servlet source code as well as to the response, but browsers do not display it on the screen. Consider the following code:

```
<!-- This page was generated at server on
<%= (new java.util.Date()) %>
-->
```

This generates the following HTML comment. This is sent to the client, but not displayed on the screen.

```
<!-- This page was generated at server on
Fri Mar 24 04:14:07 PDT 1917
-->
```

taglib

The `taglib` directive allows custom extensions to be made to the tags known to the JSP engine. The JSP `taglib` directive is used to define a tag library that defines many tags. Programmers use the TLD (Tag Library Descriptor) file to define the tags.
Syntax:

```
<%@ taglib uri="uritaglibrary" prefix="prefixtaglibrary" %>
```

In the following example, the tag used is named currentDate. To use this tag, the `taglib` directive must be specified so the container gets information about the tag.

```
<html>
    <body>
        <%@ taglib uri="http://www.javatutorial.com/tags" prefix="mytag" %>
        <mytag:currentDate/>
    </body>
</html>
```

19.7.2 Scripting Elements

The scripting elements provide the ability to insert java code in the JSP. There are three types of scripting elements:

- scriptlet tag,
- expression tag, and
- declaration tag.

Scriptlets

JSP supports embedding of Java code fragments within a JSP by using a scriptlet block. Scriptlets are used to embed small code blocks within the JSP page, rather than to declare entire methods as in a declarations block. The syntax for a scriptlet is:

```
<% scriptlet %>
```

The following example uses a scriptlet to output an HTML message based on the time of day. The HTML elements appear outside the script declarations.

```
<% if (Calendar.getInstance().get(Calendar.AM_PM) == Calendar.AM)
{%>
   How are you this morning ?
<% } else
{ %>
   How are you this afternoon ?
<% } %>
```

In the following example, two files have been created, `index.html` and `welcome.jsp`. The `index.html` file gets the username from the user and the `welcome.jsp` file prints the username with the welcome message.

```
//index.html
<html>
   <body>
      <form action="welcome.jsp">
         <input type="text" name="uname">
         <input type="submit" value="go"><br/>
      </form>
   </body>
</html>
//welcome.jsp
<html>
   <body>
      <%
         String name=request.getParameter("uname");
         out.print("welcome "+name);
      %>
      </form>
   </body>
</html>
```

Several scriptlets and templates can be merged to do some designated task. The following example illustrates this:

```
<%
int no = (int) (Math.random( )*10);
if(no % 2 == 0) {
   %> Even
   <% } else { %> Odd
<% } %>
```

This code gets converted into something like,

```
int no = (int) (Math.random()*10);
if(no % 2 == 0) { out.write("\r\n"); out.write("Even\r\n");
   } else { out.write("\r\n"); out.write("Odd\r\n");
}
```

Expressions

Expressions are scriptlet fragments whose results can be converted to String objects and subsequently fed to the output stream for display in a browser. They are generally used to insert a small piece of data in a JSP page, without using the `out.print()` or `out.write()` statements. It is a faster, easier and clearer way to display the values of variables/parameters/expressions in a JSP page. The general syntax of JSP expressions is as follows:

```
<%= expressions %>
```

The expression is embedded within the tag pair <%= and %>. There is no semicolon at the end of the expression. The expression is evaluated, converted to a String and inserted in place of the expression using an `out.print()` statement. For example, to add 3 and 4 and display the result, the programmer must write the JSP expression as follows:

```
3 + 4 = <%= 3+4 %>
```

The expression is translated into the following Java statements in servlet source code.

```
out.write("3 + 4 = ");
out.print( 3+4 );
```

The following output is displayed:

```
3 + 4 = 7
```

The expression can be anything, as long as it can be converted to a string. For example, the following expression uses a `java.util.Date` object.

```
Date and time is : <%= new java.util.Date() %>
```

JSP expressions can be used as attribute values as well as tag names of JSP elements. Consider the following JSP code.

```
<%
    java.util.Date dt = new java.util.Date(); String dateStr = dt.toString();
    String time = "currentTime";
%>
<<%= time %> value="<%= dateStr %>" />
```

This generates the following tag:

```
<currentTime value="Sun Mar 26 09:12:50 PDT 1917" />
```

JSP also has an equivalent tag for expressions:

```
<jsp:expression>
    expressions
</jsp:expression>
```

In the following example, the index.html file gets the username and sends the request to the `welcome.jsp` file, which displays the username.

```
//index.jsp
<html>
    <body>
        <form action="welcome.jsp">
            <input type="text" name="uname"><br/>
            <input type="submit" value="go">
        </form>
    </body>
</html>
```

```
//welcome.jsp
<html>
    <body>
        <%= "Welcome "+request.getParameter("uname") %>
    </body>
</html>
```

Declarations

A declaration block contains Java variables and methods that are called from an expression block within the JSP file. The code within a declaration block is usually written in Java, and is often used for additional processing on the dynamic data generated by a JavaBeans property. The syntax of a declaration is:

```
<%! declarations %>
```

For example:

```
<%! int sum = 0; %>
<%! int x, y , z; %>
<%! java.util.Hashtable table = new java.util.Hashtable();%>
```

These variable declarations are inserted into the body of the `Servlet` class, that is outside the `_jspService()` method that processes the client requests. So, variables declared in this way become instance variables of the underlying servlet.

```
<%! int sum = 0; %>
```

The following is an example of JSP declaration tag, where a method is defined which returns the cube of given number; this method is called from the JSP expression tag.

```
// index.jsp
<html>
    <body>
    <%!
        int cube(int n){
            return n*n*n*;
        }
    %>
    <%= "Cube of 3 is:"+cube(3) %>
    </body>
</html>
```

19.7.3 Standard Actions

There are many JSP action tags or elements. Each JSP action tag is used to perform some specific tasks. The action tags are used to control the flow between pages and to use JavaBeans. Table 19.2 gives a list of JSP action tags.

Table 19.2 JSP action tags

JSP action tags	Description
`jsp:forward`	Forwards the request and response to another resource.
`jsp:include`	Includes another resource.
`jsp:useBean`	Creates or locates a bean object.
`jsp:setProperty`	Sets the value of property in the bean object.
`jsp:getProperty`	Prints the value of property of the bean.
`jsp:plugin`	Embeds another component such as an applet.
`jsp:param`	Sets the parameter value. It is used mostly in forward and include.
`jsp:fallback`	Can be used to print the message if plugin is working. It is used in jsp:plugin.

The JSP engine provides programmers with many built-in sophisticated functions for easy development of web applications. These functions include instantiating objects in a JSP page, communicating with other JSP pages and servlets, and so on. JSP actions are XML tags that can be used in a JSP page to use these functions. The same thing can be achieved by writing Java code within scriptlets. However, JSP action tags are convenient ways to use those functions. It also promotes component framework as well as application maintainability. The following section describes the commonly used JSP action tags.

include

This action tag provides an alternative way to include a file in a JSP page. The general syntax of the include action tag is:

```
<jsp:include page="relativeURL | <%=expression%>" flush="true" />
```

For example, the following code includes the file `header.jsp` in the current page:

```
<jsp:include page="header.jsp" />
```

It is similar to the `include` directive but instead of inserting the text of the included file in the original file at compilation time, it actually includes the target at run-time. It acts like a subroutine where the control is passed temporarily to the target. The control is then returned to the original JSP page. The result of the included file is inserted in the place of `<jsp:include>` action in the original JSP page. The included file should be a JSP file, servlet or any other dynamic program that can process the parameters. The optional attribute `flush` can only take the value True. The following example illustrates the concept. Suppose the contents of `date.jsp` are as given here.

```
Date and time: <%= new java.util.Date() %>
```

Consider the file `include.jsp`, which has included the `date.jsp` file using the `<jsp:include>` action tag as follows:

```
Before<br>
<jsp:include page="date.jsp" />
<br>After
```

This generates the following result:

```
Before
Date and time: Sun Mar 26 19:56:54 IST 1917
After
```

The value of the `page` attribute may be a dynamically generated file name, as the following example illustrates:

```
<%
    String fileName = "sortByName.jsp";
    String criteria = request. getParameter("sortCriteria");
    if(criteria != null) fileName = criteria + ".jsp";
%>
<jsp:include page="<%=fileName%>" />
```

So, if the `include.jsp` page is invoked using the URL `http://127.0.0.1:8080/net/include.jsp?sortCriteria=sortByRoll`, the include action effectively becomes:

```
<jsp:include page="sortByRoll.jsp" />
```

The file `sortByRoll.jsp` must exist. Otherwise, an exception will be thrown. If the `include.jsp` page is invoked using the URL `http://127.0.0.1:8080/net/include.jsp`, the include action effectively becomes,

```
<jsp:include page="sortByName.jsp" />
```

param

The JSP `<jsp:param>` action allows the programmer to append additional parameters to the current request. The general syntax is as follows:

```
<jsp:param name="parameterName"
value="parameterValue | <%=expression%>" />
```

The `name` and `value` attributes of the `<jsp:param>` tag specify the case sensitive name and value of the parameter, respectively. It is typically used with the `<jsp:include>` and `<jsp:forward>` action tags. For example, the following code passes the control to the JSP page `process.jsp` temporarily, with two additional parameters, `user` and `sessionId`.

```
<jsp:include page="process.jsp">
    <jsp:param name="user" value="monali" />
    <jsp:param name="sessionId" value="12D43F3Q436N43" />
</jsp:include>
```

The value of the `value` attribute may be a dynamic value, but the value of the `name` attribute must be static. The following example illustrates this:

```
<% String user = request.getParameter("user"); %>
<jsp:include page="process.jsp">
    <jsp:param name="user" value="<%=user%>" />
    <jsp:param name="sessionId" value="<%=System.currentTimeMillis()%>" />
</jsp:include>
```

forward

This action tag hands over the current request to the specified page internally at the server side. If the current page has already generated some output, it is suppressed. The output will only be caused by the page that has handled the request last in the forward chain. The control is never returned to the original page. The general syntax of the JSP forward action tag is,

```
<jsp:forward page="relativeURL | <%=expression%>" />
```

Consider the `forward.jsp` file, which forwards the current request to the `date.jsp` file using the `<jsp:forward>` action as follows:

```
Before<br>
<jsp:forward page="date.jsp" />
<br>After
```

This transfers the control to the `date.jsp` page. The result that the file `forward.jsp` has generated so far (`Before<br>`) is cleared. The output is due to the page `date.jsp` only, as follows.

```
Date and time: Sun Mar 26 09:31:15 PDT 1917
```

Like the `<jsp:include>` action tag, the value of the `page` attribute of `<jsp:forward>` may be a dynamic file name. The following example illustrates this:

```
<% String mailbox = request.getParameter("mailbox") + ".jsp";%>
<jsp:forward page="<%=fileName%>" />
```

Additional parameters may be specified using the `<jsp:param>` action as follows:

```
<%
String mailbox = request.getParameter("mailbox") + ".jsp";
String user = request.getParameter("user");%>
<jsp:forward page="<%=fileName%>" >
<jsp:param name="user" value="<%=user%>" />
<jsp:forward>
```

plugin

The <jsp:plugin> action is used to generate a HTML file that can download the Java plug-in on demand and execute applets or JavaBeans. It is an alternative way to deploy applets through the Java plug-in. Since JSP pages are dynamic in nature, the developers of web applications can make use of the Java plug-in to generate browser-specific tags to insert applets on the fly in a much easier and flexible way. The <jsp:plugin> action generates the `embed` or `object` tag for the applet to be executed, depending upon the browser used. When the JSP is translated, the <jsp:plugin> action element is substituted by either an <embed> or an <object> HTML tag. The following code specifies an applet.

```
<jsp:plugin type="applet" code="Message" >
<jsp:params>
<jsp:param name="message" value="Hello World!"/>
</jsp:params>
<jsp:fallback>
<p> Unable to start Plug-in. </p>
</jsp:fallback>
</jsp:plugin>
```

The `type` attribute of the <jsp:plugin> tag specifies the type (bean or applet) of plug-in to be used and the `code` attribute specifies the name of the file (without extension) containing the byte code for this plug-in. In the above example, the <jsp:plugin> action inserts an applet whose code can be found in the class file `Message.class`.

The <jsp:plugin> action tag has a similar set of attributes as the <applet> tag. The <jsp:params> and <jsp:param> actions are used to pass parameters to the plug-in. The <jsp:fallback> tag specifies the message to be displayed if the Java plug-in fails to start due to some unavoidable reason. The source code for the `Message` applet (`Message.java`) is:

```
public class Message extends java.applet.Applet { String msg;
    public void init() {
        msg = getParameter("message");
    }
    public void paint(java.awt.Graphics g) {
        g.drawString(msg, 19, 19);
    }
}
```

This applet takes a single parameter message and displays its value at location (19, 19) on the browser's screen, relative to the applet window. The web server generates either an <embed> or an <object> tag, depending upon the browser that requested the JSP page.

jsp:useBean

The `jsp:useBean` tag is used to declare a JavaBean object to use within the JSP. This declaration must be done before using the `jsp:getProperty` and `jsp:setProperty` tags. When the `jsp:useBean` tag is processed, the application server performs a lookup of the specified given Java object using the values specified in the id and scope attributes. If the object is not found, it will attempt to create it using the values specified in the scope and class attributes. The syntax for inserting a JavaBean is:

```
<jsp:useBean id="beanInstanceName" scope="page|request|session|application" typespec>
   optional scriptlets and tags
</jsp:useBean>
```

Here, `typespec` can be declared using any of the following variations:

```
class="package.class"
type="package.class"
type="package.class" beanName="package.class"
```

There can also be embedded scriptlets and tags such as `jsp:getProperty` within the `jsp:useBean` declaration that will be executed upon creation of the bean. This is often used to modify the properties of a bean immediately after it has been created.

An example of a simple form of bean instantiation is:

```
<jsp:useBean id ="DateDisplayBean" class="itso.servjsp.jspsamples.DateDisplayBean"/>
```

This example tries to locate an instance of the `DateDisplayBean` class. If no instance exists, a new instance is created. The instance can then be accessed within the JSP using the specified id of `DateDisplayBean`.

jsp:getProperty

Once the bean has been declared with `jsp:useBean`, the programmer can access its exposed properties through the `jsp:getProperty` tag, which inserts the String value of the primitive type or object into the output stream. For primitive types, the conversion to String is performed automatically. For object types, the `toString` method of the object is called. The syntax for the `jsp:getProperty` tag is:

```
<jsp:getProperty name="beanName" property="propertyName"/>
```

jsp:SetProperty

The properties of beans can be set by using the `jsp:setProperty tag`. The syntax for this tag is:

```
<jsp:setProperty name="beanName" prop_expr/>
```

19.8 IMPLICIT OBJECTS

Web container allows a programmer to directly access many useful objects defined in the `_jspService()` method of the JSP page's underlying servlet. These objects are called implicit objects as they are instantiated automatically. The implicit objects contain information about request, response, session, configuration, and so on. Some implicit objects are described in Table 19.3. The following code snippet is an example of accessing the `out` implicit object to display a line of text in the browser:

```
out.println("Here is the <b>Date Display JSP</b>");
```

Table 19.3 JSP implicit objects

Variable	Class	Description
out	javax.servlet.jsp.JspWriter	Output stream of the JSP page's servlet.
request	Subtype of javax.servlet. ServletRequest	Current client request being handled by the JSP page.
response	Subtype of javax.servlet. ServletResponse	Response generated by the JSP page to be returned to the client.
config	javax.servlet.ServletConfig	Initialisation information of the JSP page's servlet.
session	javax.servlet.http.HttpSession	Session object for the client.
application	javax.servlet.ServletContext	Context of the JSP page's servlet and other web components contained in the same application.
exception	java.lang.Throwable	Represents error. Accessible only from an error page.
page	java.lang.Object	Refers to JSP page's servlet processing the current request.
pageContext	javax.servlet.jsp.PageContext	The context of the JSP page that provides APIs to manage the various scoped attributes. It is extensively used by the tag handlers.

request

This object refers to the `javax.servlet.http.HttpServletRequest` type object that is passed to the `_jspService()` method of the generated servlet. It represents the HTTP request made by a client to this JSP page. It is used to retrieve information sent by the client such as parameters (using the `getParameter()` method), HTTP request type (GET, POST, HEAD) and HTTP request headers (cookies, referrer, and so on). This implicit object has `request` scope.

```
<%
String name = request.getParameter("name");
out.println("Hello " + name);
%>
```

A JSP page can retrieve parameters sent through an HTML form. Consider the following form:

```
<form method='post' action='jsp/add.jsp'>
<input type='text' name='a' size='4'>+
<input type='text' name='b' size='4'>
<input type='submit' value='Add'>
</form>
```

The code for the `add.jsp` file is,

```
<%
int a = Integer.parseInt(request. getParameter("a")); int b = Integer.
parseInt(request.getParameter("b")); out.println(a + " + " + b + " = " + (a + b));
%>
```

response

This object refers to the `javax.servlet.http.HttpServletResponse` type object that is passed to the `_jspService()` method of the generated servlet. It represents the HTTP response to the client. This object is used to send information such as HTTP response header and cookies. This implicit object has page scope.

pageContext

This `javax.servlet.jsp.PageContext` type object refers to the current JSP page context. It is used to access information related to this page such as request, response, session, application and underlying servlet configuration. This implicit object has page scope.

session

This `javax.servlet.http.HttpSession` type object refers to the session used by the JSP page. There is no `session` object created if the `session` attribute of the page directive is turned off and any attempt to refer to this object causes an error. It is used to access session-related information such as creation time and ID associated with this session. This implicit object has session scope.

Application

This `javax.servlet.ServletContext` object refers to the underlying application and is used to share data among all pages under this application. This implicit object has application scope.

out

It denotes the character output stream that is used to send data back to the client. It is a buffered version of `java.io.PrintWriter` called `javax.servlet.jsp.JspWriter` type object. The object `out` is used only in scriptlets. This implicit object has page scope.

```
<% out.println("Hello World!"); %>
```

JSP expressions are placed in the output stream automatically and hence do not use this `out` object there explicitly.

config

This `javax.servlet.ServletConfig` type object refers to the configuration of the underlying servlet. It is used to retrieve initial parameters, servlet name, and so on. This implicit object has page scope.

Page

This object refers to the JSP page itself. It can be used to call any instance of the JSP page's servlet. This implicit object has page scope.

Exception

This represents an uncaught exception, which causes an error page to be called. This object is available in the JSP page for which the `isErrorPage` attribute of the page directive is set to true. This implicit object has page scope.

SUMMARY

1. JSP allows direct embedding of Java code in HTML pages. To process JSP pages, a JSP engine is needed. The JSP engine is a specialised servlet that runs under the supervision of the servlet engine. The commonly used JSP engines include Apache's Tomcat, Java Web Server, IBM's WebSphere, and so on.
2. JSP technology has been built on top of servlet technology. The JSP pages are finally converted to servlets automatically. A JSP page basically consists of static HTML/XML components called template text as well as JSP constructs. JSP constructs consist of directives, declarations, expressions, scriptlets and actions.
3. A JSP page may contain instructions to be used by the JSP container to indicate how the page is interpreted and executed. Those instructions are called directives. Expressions are used to insert small pieces (usually) of data in a JSP page without using `out. print()` or `out.write()` statements. It is possible to insert an arbitrary piece of Java code using JSP scriptlet constructs in a JSP page.
4. JSP declarations are used to declare one or more variables, methods or inner classes that can be used later in the JSP page.
5. JSP actions are XML tags that can be used in a JSP page to use functions provided by the JSP engine.
6. The scope of a JSP object is defined as the availability of that object for use from a particular place in the web application. There are four object scopes—page, request, session and application.
7. A web container allows a programmer to directly access many useful objects defined in the `_jspService()` method of the JSP page's underlying servlet. These objects are called implicit objects as they are instantiated automatically.
8. The implicit objects contain information about request, response, session, configuration, and so on.
9. JavaBeans are reusable Java components called beans which allow us to separate business logic from presentation logic. There are three action elements that are used to work with beans. A JSP action element `<jsp:useBean>` instantiates a JavaBean object into the JSP page. The `<jsp:setProperty>` action tag assigns a new value to the specified property of the specified bean object. The `<jsp:getProperty>` action element retrieves the value of the specified property of the specified bean object.
10. There are many ways to track sessions in JSP. Hidden fields may be used to send information back and forth between server and client to track sessions, without affecting the display. This is another simple but elegant method to track sessions and is widely used. Cookies are also used to track sessions. JSP technology (and its underlying servlet technology) provides a higher level approach for session tracking.

SHORT QUESTIONS

1. List some advantages of JSP over servlets.
2. What is the key difference between `HttpServletResponse.sendRedirect()` and `<jsp:forward>`?
3. What is the function of a JSP engine?
4. What is the purpose of `include` directive in a JSP page?
5. What is the difference between a declaration and a scriplet?
6. What do you mean by the scope of JSP objects?
7. What is the usage of session and application implicit objects?
8. Explain the method of passing data between two JSP pages.
9. Write a short note on the anatomy of a JSP page.
10. Write the syntax of a JSP page.

COMPREHENSIVE QUESTIONS

1. Explain how JSP works.
2. Discuss the life cycle of JSP.
3. Give an account on JSP components.
4. Explain the directives in JSP.
5. What are the scripting elements in JSP? Explain its types.
6. Illustrate the JSP action tags.
7. Describe the implict JSP objects.
8. Briefly describe the structure of a JSP page.
9. What are the different session tracking technologies available in JSP?
10. Write the steps to create a simple JSP application in Netbeans IDE.

SOLVED PROGRAMS

1. Program to handle static contents in JSP.

index.jsp
```
<html>
  <head>
    <title>JSP Page</title>
  </head>
  <body>
    <h1>Hello World!</h1>
    <%@include file="static.html" %>
  </body>
</html>
```
static.html
```
<html>
  <head>
    <title></title>
  </head>
  <body>
    <p> this is paragraph</p>
  </body>
</html>
```

2. Find current date and time using JSP.
```
<html>
  <head>
    <title>JSP Page</title>
    <%@ page import="java.util.*" %>
  </head>
  <body>
    <h2>The date is::</h2>
    <% Date date=new Date();
    out.println(date); %>
  </body>
</html>
```

3. Program to handle sesssions in JSP.

GetName.html
```
<HTML>
  <BODY>
    <FORM METHOD=POST ACTION="SaveName.jsp">
      What's your name? <INPUT TYPE=TEXT NAME=username SIZE=20>
      <P><INPUT TYPE=SUBMIT>
```

```
      </FORM>
   </BODY>
</HTML>
```

SaveName.jsp

```
<%
String name = request.getParameter( "username" );
session.setAttribute( "theName", name );
%>
<HTML>
   <BODY>
      <A HREF="NextPage.jsp">Continue</A>
   </BODY>
</HTML>
```

NextPage.jsp

```
<HTML>
   <BODY>
      Hello, <%= session.getAttribute( "theName" ) %>
   </BODY>
</HTML>
```

4. Comparison operators in JSP.

conditions.jsp

```
<html>
   <head>
      <title>EL Conditions</title>
      <style>
         body, td { font-family:verdana;font-size:10pt;}
      </style>
   </head>
   <body>
      <h2>EL Conditions</h2>
      <table border="1">
         <tr>
            <td><b>Concept</b></td>
            <td><b>EL Condition</b></td>
            <td><b>Result</b></td>
         </tr>
         <tr>
            <td>Numeric less than</td>
            <td>${ '${ '} 1 &lt; 2} </td>
            <td>${ 1 < 2} </td>
         </tr>
         <tr>
            <td>Numeric greater than</td>
            <td>${ '${ '} 1 &gt; 2} </td>
            <td>${ 1 > 2} </td>
         </tr>
         <tr>
            <td>Numeric less than</td>
            <td>${ '${ '} 1 lt 2} </td>
            <td>${ 1 lt 2} </td>
         </tr>
         <tr>
            <td>Numeric greater than</td>
            <td>${ '${ '} 1 gt 2} </td>
            <td>${ 1 gt 2} </td>
         </tr>
```

```
<tr>
   <td>Numeric Greater than or equal</td>
   <td>${ '${ '} 1 &gt;= 1} </td>
   <td>${ 1 >= 1} </td>
</tr>
<tr>
   <td>Numeric Less than or equal</td>
   <td>${ '${ '} 1 &lt;= 1} </td>
   <td>${ 1 <= 1} </td>
</tr>
<tr>
   <td>Numeric less than or equal</td>
   <td>${ '${ '} 1 le 1} </td>
   <td>${ 1 le 1} </td>
</tr>
<tr>
   <td>Numeric greater than or equal</td>
   <td>${ '${ '} 1 ge 1} </td>
   <td>${ 1 ge 1} </td>
</tr>
<tr>
   <td>Numeric equal to</td>
   <td>${ '${ '} 1 == 1} </td>
   <td>${ 1 == 1} </td>
</tr>
<tr>
   <td>Numeric equal to</td>
   <td>${ '${ '} 1 eq 1} </td>
   <td>${ 1 eq 1} </td>
</tr>
<tr>
   <td>Numeric not equal to</td>
   <td>${ '${ '} 1 != 2} </td>
   <td>${ 1 != 2} </td>
</tr>
<tr>
   <td>Numeric not equal to</td>
   <td>${ '${ '} 1 ne 2} </td>
   <td>${ 1 ne 2} </td>
</tr>
<tr>
   <td>Alphabetic less than</td>
   <td>${ '${ '} 'abe' &lt; 'ade'} </td>
   <td>${ 'abe' < 'ade'} </td>
</tr>
<tr>
   <td>Alphabetic greater than</td>
   <td>${ '${ '} 'abe' &gt; 'ade'} </td>
   <td>${ 'abe' > 'ade'} </td>
</tr>
<tr>
   <td>Alphabetic equal to</td>
   <td>${ '${ '} 'abe' eq 'abe'} </td>
   <td>${ 'abe' eq 'abe'} </td>
</tr>
<tr>
```

```
            <td>Alphabetic not equal to</td>
            <td>${ '${ '} 'abe' ne 'ade'} </td>
            <td>${ 'abe' ne 'ade'} </td>
         </tr>
      </table>
   </body>
</html>
```

5. Example of a JSP CheckBox.

jspCheckBox.jsp

```
<html>
  <h2>Select Languages:</h2>
  <form ACTION="jspCheckBox.jsp">
     <input type="checkbox" name="id" value="Java"> Java<BR>
     <input type="checkbox" name="id" value=".NET"> .NET<BR>
     <input type="checkbox" name="id" value="PHP"> PHP<BR>
     <input type="checkbox" name="id" value="C/C++"> C/C++<BR>
     <input type="checkbox" name="id" value="PERL"> PERL <BR>
     <input type="submit" value="Submit">
  </form>
  <%
  String select[] = request.getParameterValues("id"); if (select != null &&
  select.length != 0) {  out.println("You have selected: ");
     for (int i = 0; i < select.length; i++) {
        out.println(select[i]);
     }
  }
  %>
</html>
```

6. Passing values from JSP pages.

index.jsp

```
<html>
  <head>
     <title>JSP Page</title>
  </head>
  <body>
     <center>
        <h2>Entry Form!</h2>
        <form action="result.jsp" method="post">
           <table>
              <tr>
                 <td>
                    User Name:
                 </td>
                 <td>
                    <input type="text" name="username"/>
                 </td>
              </tr>
              <tr>
                 <td>
                    Pass Word:
                 </td>
                 <td>
                    <input type="password" name="password"/>
                 </td>
              </tr>
```

```
                <tr>
                    <td>
                        Email Id:
                    </td>
                    <td>
                        <input type="text" name="emailid"/>
                    </td>
                </tr>
                <tr>
                    <td colspan="2">
                        <input type="submit" name="Enter..."/>
                    </td>
                </tr>
            </table>
        </form>
    </center>
  </body>
</html>
```

result.jsp

```
<html>
    <title>JSP Page</title>
  </head>
  <body>
    <center>
        <h2>Welcome to this page!</h2>
        <form action="" method="post">
            <table>
                <tr>
                    <td>
                        User Name:
                    </td>
                    <td>
                        ${ param.username}
                    </td>
                </tr>
                <tr>
                    <td>
                        Pass Word:
                    </td>
                    <td>
                        ${ param.password}
                    </td>
                </tr>
                <tr>
                    <td>
                        Email Id:
                    </td>
                    <td>
                        ${ param.emailid}
                    </td>
                </tr>
                <tr>
                    <td colspan="2">
                        Go to the <a href="index.jsp">main</a> page!
                    </td>
                </tr>
```

```
            </table>
        </form>
    </center>
  </body>
</html>
```

7. Program to include a `jsp` file in another `jsp` file

index.jsp

```
<html>
  <head>
      <title>JSP Page</title>
  </head>
  <body>
      <TABLE BORDER=5 ALIGN="CENTER">
          <TR><TH CLASS="TITLE"> Include Tag!</TABLE>
      <P>
          Information about our products and services.
      <%@ include file="/include.jsp" %>
  </body>
</html>
```

include.jsp

```
<%@ page import=»java.util.Date» %>
<%-- The following become fields in each servlet that results from a JSP page that
includes this file. --%>
<%!
private int accessCount = 0;
private Date accessDate = new Date();
private String accessHost = "<I>No previous access</I>";
%>
<P>
<HR>
This page &copy; 2017
<A HREF="http//www.my-company.com/">my-company.com</A>. This page has been
accessed <%= ++accessCount %>
times since server reboot. It was most recently accessed from
<%= accessHost %> at <%= accessDate %>.
<% accessHost = request.getRemoteHost(); %>
<% accessDate = new Date(); %>
```

PROGRAMMING EXERCISES

1. Create a webpage to search for students by roll number using JSP.
2. Write a HTML code to create a form for customer registration for an online shopping portal.
3. Design a simple JSP page to display current date and time from the system.
4. Create a calculator application using JSP tags.
5. Create an application for an organisation with Employee as table name and have Eno, Ename, Salary, PF, Experience, as fields. Insert five rows of values in the table. Then retrieve the values from the database using a JSP form.
6. Write a JSP program to display the grade of a student by accepting the marks of five subjects.
7. Create a JSP page to calculate and display simple interest based on inputs.
8. Write a program to illustrate the components of JSP.
9. Design a `registration.jsp` page with input for user registration details.
10. Write a JSP program to convert currency.

CHAPTER

20

Introduction to MVC

MVC (Model View Controller) is a design pattern, not a full-fledged application. It separates an application into following:

- A **Model** that has Data and Business Logic for the application.
- A **View** part of the MVC pattern carries out the following tasks.
  - Interacting with the user.
  - Uses the **Model** for presenting the data and output to the user.
- A **Controller** that acts as an interface between the Model and View.
  - The main job is choosing the right model to persist and manipulate the data given by the user.
  - Choosing one of the Views to present the output to the user.

The MVC pattern can be implemented with Java and .Net platforms. In Java, the following technologies are used for each part.

- **JavaBean** is used to represent the Model.
- **JSP** acts as a View.
- **Servlet** plays the role of the Controller.

Some of the popular MVC-based web frameworks are given below:

- Struts
- Spring MVC
- Ruby on Rails
- Django
- Laravel
- CakePHP
- CherryPy

Need of MVC framework for web application development

In Java-based web application development, the JSP and Servlet are used to handle data manipulation and presentation of results. Neither JSP nor Servlet are efficient for server-side manipulation. Servlet is efficient in controlling the HTTP requests but is very inefficient in preparing the HTTP response back to the user. However, JSP is excellent in making HTTP response, but is lacking in controlling HTTP requests. The MVC design pattern combines the controlling abilities of Servlet and the presentation capabilities of JSP along with JavaBean for the Java based web application development.

20.1 STRUCTURE OF MVC FRAMEWORK

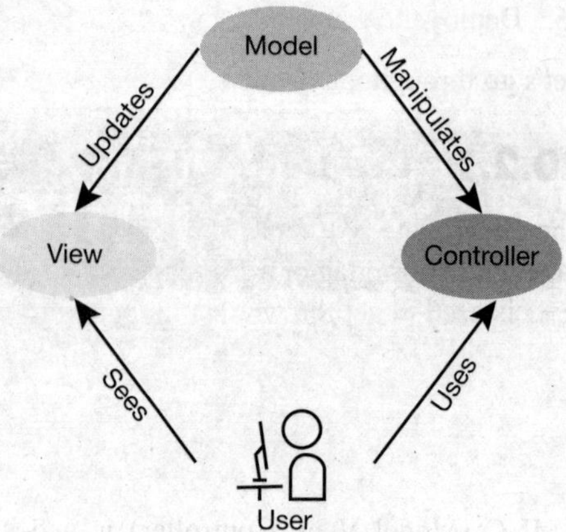

Fig. 20.1 Structure of MVC

(i) The webclient makes a http request by submitting form data, this http request will be sent to the controller of the MVC based web application. Here, the view is an ordinary HTML page.
(ii) After the http request is received, the controller extracts the data sent in the http header, especially form data, and stores them in the local variables. Soon after all the form data are saved in the local variables, the controller will create an object for the Java class in the model layer. Now the controller has to choose which view will prepare a response and send it to the webclient. Before forwarding the request to that view, the controller creates a http request attribute which carries the object of the class. At last the controller forwards the request to the view with the request attribute which has an object of the class.
(iii) The Java class of the model layer receives the data sent by the controller and stores them in the local variables. The Java class will carry out the following two tasks on the data received from the controller. Both are optional, based on the design and development of the web application.
  (a) The first task is applying business logic and producing the desired result.
  (b) The second task is to store the data in the table of the database server such as MySQL.
(iv) The model interacts with the RDBMS to perform the CRUD operations with the data received from the controller.
(v) After sending the data of the webclient to the Java class in the model, the controller also sends an object of that Java class while forwarding the request of the webclient to the view.
(vi) When the request is received at the view from the controller, the view creates a new object for the same Java class from the object received though the forwarded request. With that object, the view accesses the properties of the Java class and prepares a response to be sent back to the webclient.
(vii) Finally the view sends a response to the webclient which carries the data and results from the Java class of the model layer.

This how the heart of MVC functions for every http request triggered by the webclient. It is not compulsory to use only one *Model*, *View* and *Controller* while developing a web application. At a time, any number of models, views and controllers can be used to develop MVC based web application. But without proper linking, the web application will not work.

20.2 DEVELOPING WEB APPLICATIONSWITH MVC DESIGN PATTERN

Since MVC integrates three different Java Technologies to develop a web application, it is better to follow the well-defined steps which help the developer to begin and end the application development in a correct way.

1. Create a client page (HTML or JSP).
2. Create a Java package under source packages.
3. Create a Java Bean in the package and declare the properties and optional methods.

4. Create a Servlet class under the Java package which is created in step 2.
5. Create a JSP page under Web pages section.
6. Deploy the web application.

Let's go through the above steps one-by-one.

20.2.1 Create a Client Page (HTML or JSP)

The client page will make the http request to the controller. This webpage maybe an ordinary HTML page with a form tag or a JSP page with only HTML tags. Here, an ordinary HTML page named `index.html` is used to get the whole number from the client to check the eligibility of the voter.

```
<html>
   <head>
      <title>Web Application with MVC</title>
   </head>
   <body>
      <form action="VServlet" method="POST"><br>
         Enter Your Name:<input type="text" name="n"><br>
         Enter Your Age(in years):<input type="text" name="y"><br>
         <input type="submit" value="FIND">
      </form>
   </body>
</html>
```

The `action` attribute of the form tag has the name of the servlet, that is *controller*,which was given during the Servlet creation. Be careful and note down the exact name of the Servlet. Just specify name of the servlet file without the *.java* extension. Here, the name for the controller servlet is given as *VServlet*.

20.2.2 Create a Java Package Under Source Packages

Open the project folders and click the + sign against the *Source Packages*. The right-hand side of the IDE. va class of the Model layer, you can find the *default package*. Now right-click on the *default package* and click *New*, then select the *Java Package*. If you don't find the package, then click *Other* and then choose Java in the *Categories* section and choose *Java Package* at the bottom of the *File Types* section. Now enter the name for the Java Package, given here as *MC*. After entering the name for the Java package, click the Finish button at the bottom of the wizard. Now we can find the created package under Source Packages in the screen-shot given below.

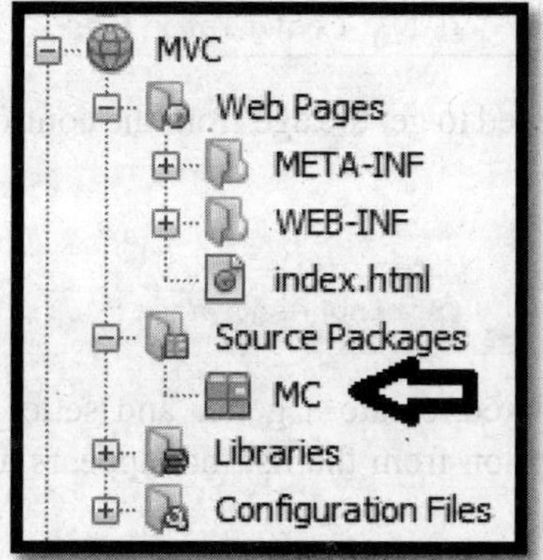

20.2.3 Create a Java Bean in the MC Package and Declare the Properties and Optional Methods

To create a Java Bean, right-click on the newly created package (*MC*), created under the *Source Packages*. Now click *New* from the list that appears and choose the *Java Class*. If it is not there, then click *Other* and then choose Java in the *Categories* section and select *Java Class* from the *File Types* section. In the wizard that appears, give the name for the new Java class; here, *VOTER* is given as the Java Bean name.

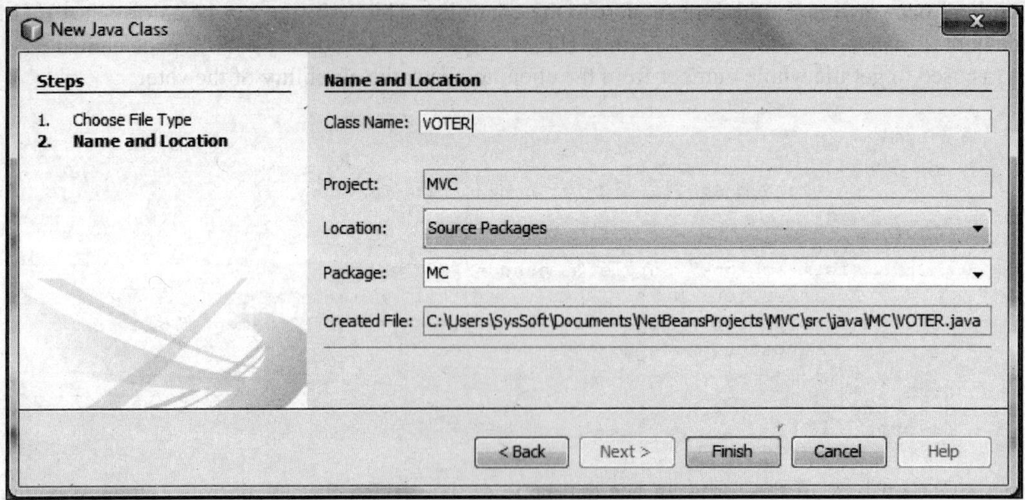

Click the Finish button at the bottom of the wizard to create a Java class.

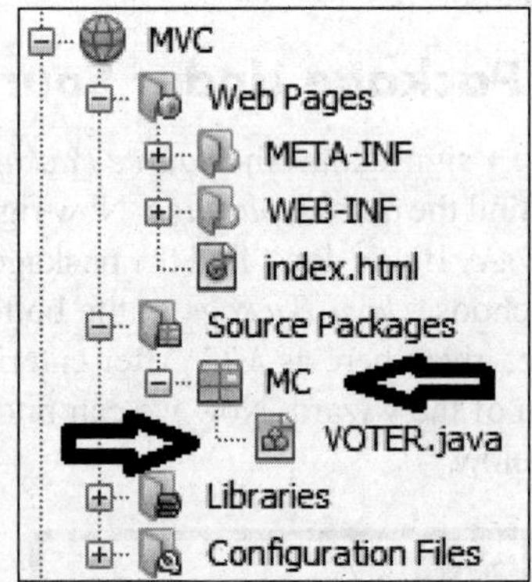

Now declare a property which is needed to get the age from the controller. Here, the following properties have been created.

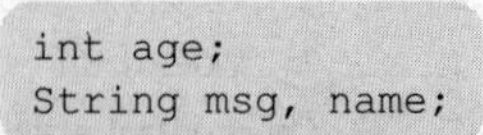

```
int age;
String msg, name;
```

As soon as the properties are declared, create a getter and setter methods by right-clicking on the properties. Click the *Insert Code* option from the list that appears and choose *getter and setter* option as shown below.

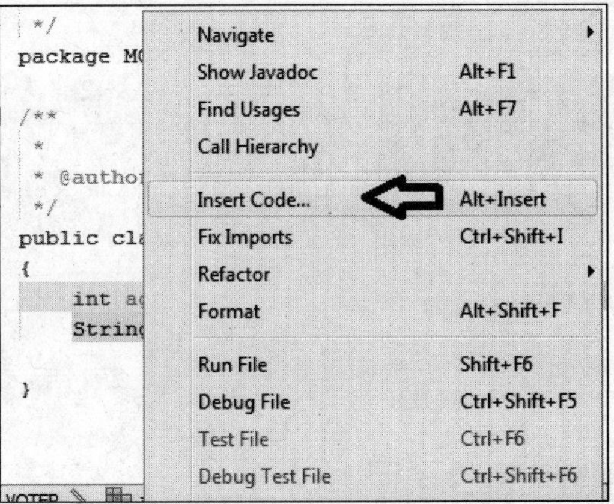

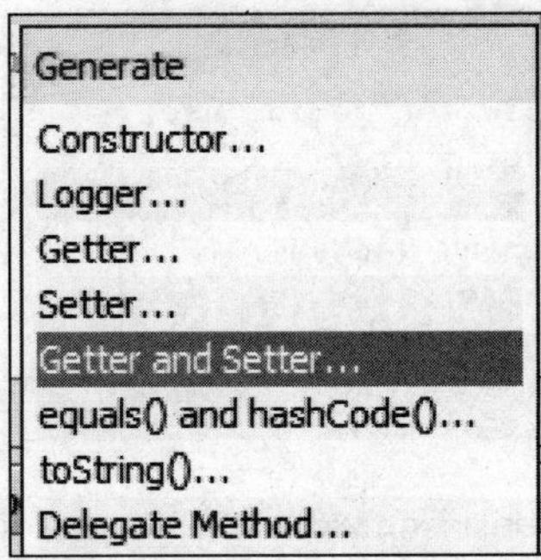

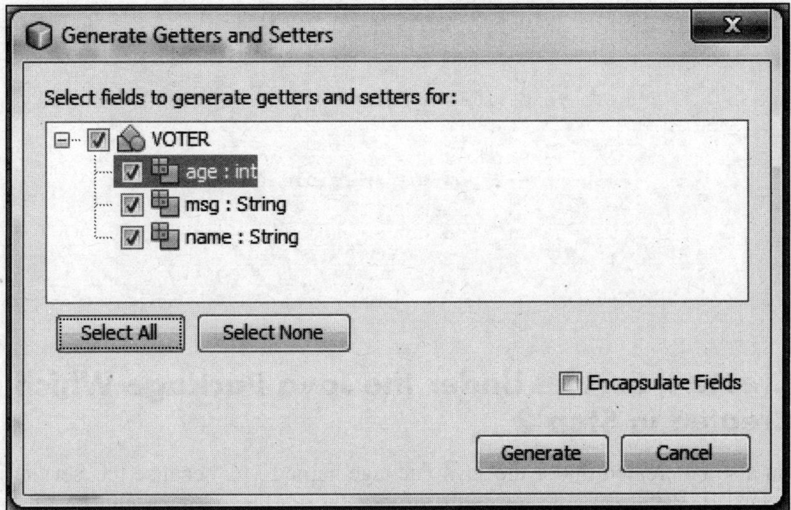

Now, a method is needed to declare the business logic to find whether the person is eligible to vote or not and send the result to the viewer. Here, an optional method named *validate* is declared with the following business logic.

```
public void validate()
{
    if ( age >= 18 )
    msg=name+" you are eligible to vote";
    else
    msg=name+" you not are eligible to vote";
}
```

Now, the Java Bean will look like:

```
package MC;
public class VOTER
{
    int age;
    String msg, name;
    publicintgetAge() {
        return age;
    }
    public void setAge(int age) {
        this.age = age;
    }
    public String getMsg() {
        returnmsg;
    }
    public void setMsg(String msg) {
        this.msg = msg;
    }
    public String getName() {
        return name;
    }
    public void setName(String name) {
        this.name = name;
    }
    public void validate()
    {
        if ( age >= 18 )
        msg=name+" you are eligible to vote";
        else
        msg=name+" you not are eligible to vote";
    }
}
```

20.2.4 Create a Servlet Under the Java Package Which is Created in Step 2

The Servlet can also be created under the Java Package named *MC* because the Servlet is also a Java Class just like Java Bean, possessing an ability to handle the http request and response. To create a Servlet, right-click on the *MC* package and click *New* and in the list that appears, choose *Servlet*. If the Servlet option doesn't show up, then choose the *Other* option at the bottom of the list. In the wizard that appears, choose *Web* from the *Categories* section on the left-hand side and choose *Servlet* on the *File Types* on the right-hand side and click the *Next* button. The following wizard will appear, give a name for the Servlet. Here, *VServlet* is given as the Servlet name.

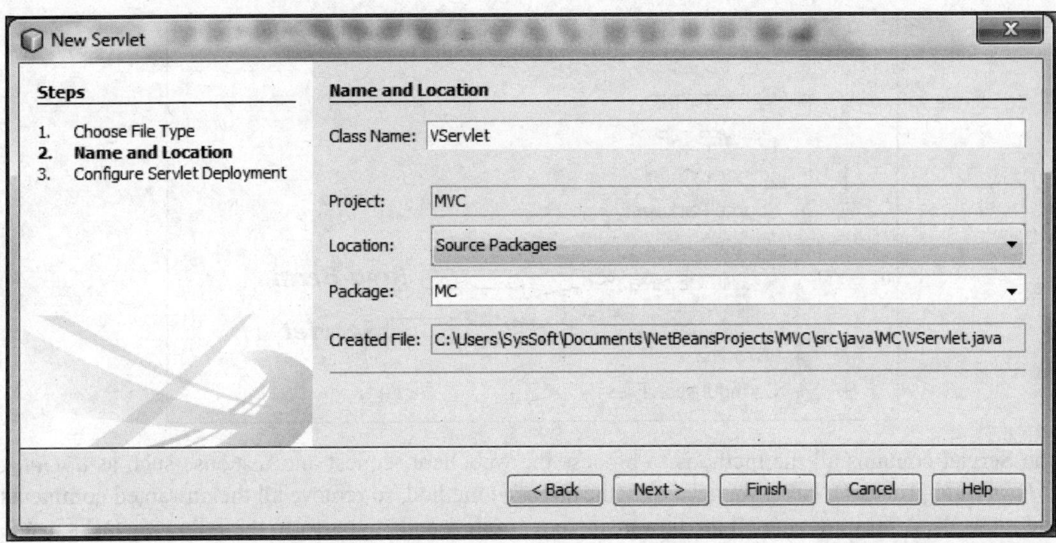

Click the *Next* button and in the second wizard check the *web.xml* check box and give the Servlet name and URL pattern. If you don't want to give a new name, then leave the default name. Note that the Servlet name given in this wizard will be specified in the action attribute of the form tag of *index.html*.

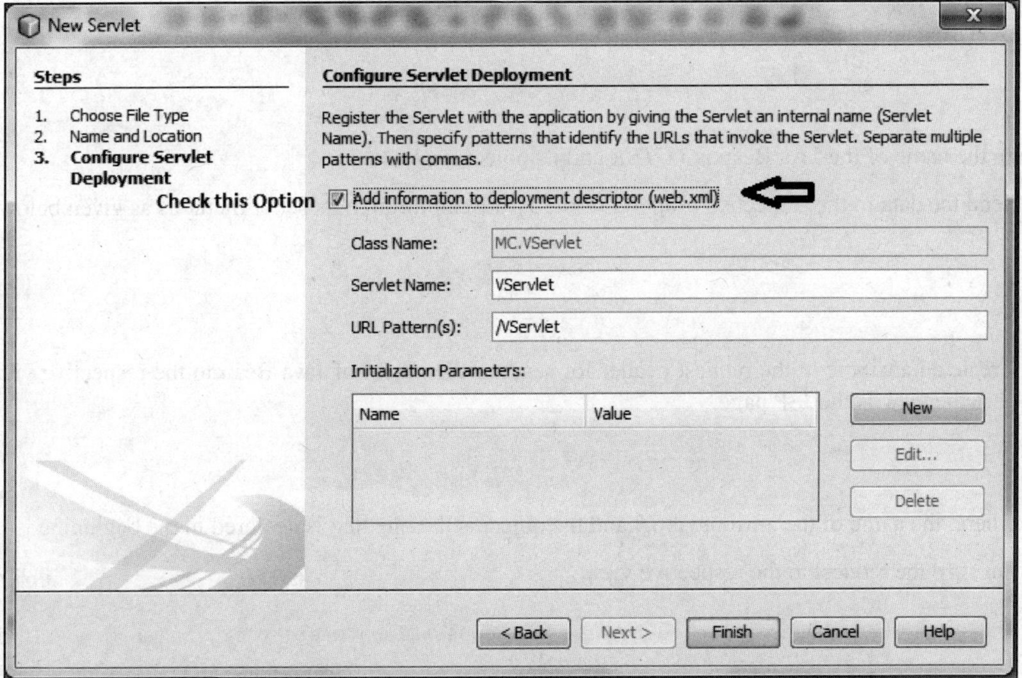

Now click the *Finish* button to close the wizard and check the *Directory Folder*.

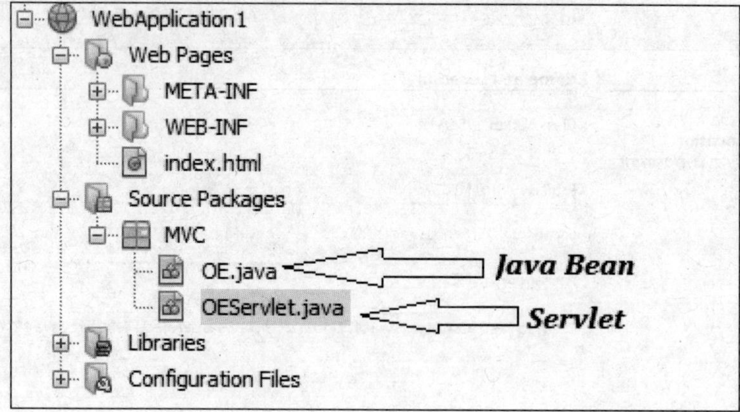

The Servlet contains all the methods to process the webclient request and response such as *doGet*(), *doPost*() and process(). Here, we need only the *doPost*() method, so remove all the unwanted comments and methods. After removing all the unwanted code, write a code to perform the following tasks inside the *doPost*() method.

- Request processing and storing data

```
int a=Integer.parseInt(request.getParameter("y"));
String n=request.getParameter("n");
```

- Declaring an object for the Java Bean

```
VOTER obj=new VOTER();
```

Here the name of the Java Bean is *VOTER* and its object is *obj*.

- Send the data to the respective property of the Java Bean through its setter methods as given below.

```
obj.setName(n);
obj.setAge(a);
```

- Create an attribute in the request header for sending the object of Java Bean to the respective view, here the view is the JSP page.

```
request.setAttribute("JB", obj);
```

where, the name of the attribute is *JB* and the object is the one that is declared in the beginning.

- Forward the request to the respective view.

```
RequestDispatcherrd=request.getRequestDispatcher("view.jsp");
rd.forward(request, response);
```

The complete code of the Servlet which covers all the above tasks is given below.

```
package MC;
importjava.io.IOException;
importjavax.servlet.RequestDispatcher;
importjavax.servlet.ServletException;
importjavax.servlet.http.HttpServlet;
import javax.servlet.http.*;
public class VServlet extends HttpServlet
{
    @Override
    protected void doPost(HttpServletRequest request, HttpServletResponse response)
    throwsServletException, IOException
    {
        String n=request.getParameter("n");
        int a=Integer.parseInt(request.getParameter("y"));
        VOTER obj=new VOTER();
        obj.setName(n);
        obj.setAge(a);
        request.setAttribute("JB", obj);
        RequestDispatcherrd=request.getRequestDispatcher("view.jsp");
        rd.forward(request, response);
    }
}
```

20.2.5 Create a JSP Page Under the Web Pages Section

To create a JSP page, right-click on the Web Pages folder and click *New*, choose the JSP page. In the wizard that appears, give the name for the JSP page; here, it is given as *view.jsp*.

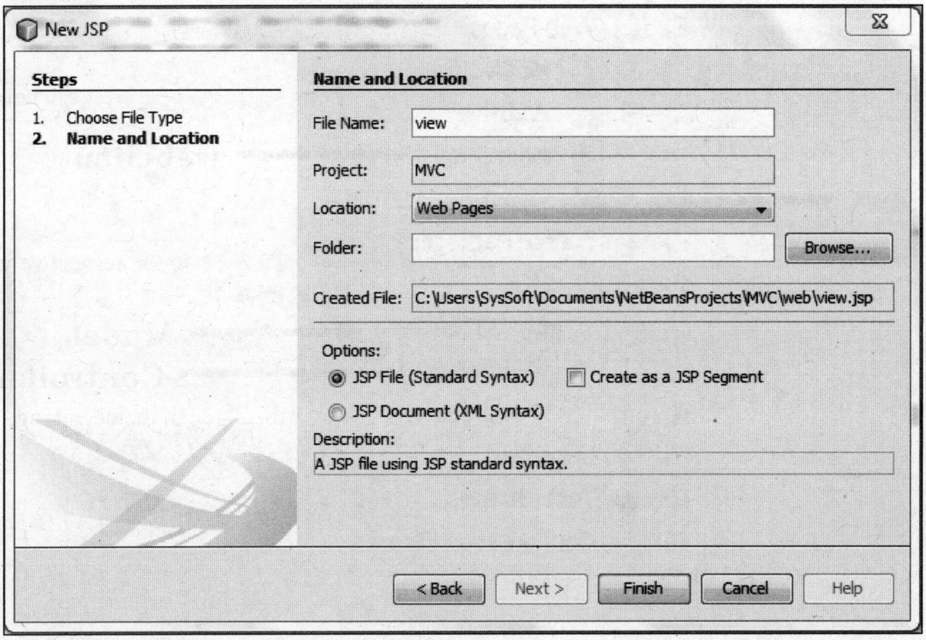

Click the *Finish* button. The *view.jsp* plays the view role and it does the following tasks on its behalf.

- Creating an object with the object received from the controller *VServlet.java*

```
VOTER obj=(VOTER)request.getAttribute("JB");
```

Here the newly created object is *bean* with the object sent by the controller *JB*.

- Invoking the validate method of Java Bean class

```
obj.validate();
```

- Sending the response back to the webclient

```
out.println(obj.getMsg());
```

Finally the JSP page will look as shown below.

```
<%@page import="MC.VOTER"%>
<%@page contentType="text/html" pageEncoding="UTF-8"%>
<%
VOTER obj=(VOTER)request.getAttribute("JB");
obj.validate();
out.println(obj.getMsg());
%>
```

The final directory structure of the web application is given below.

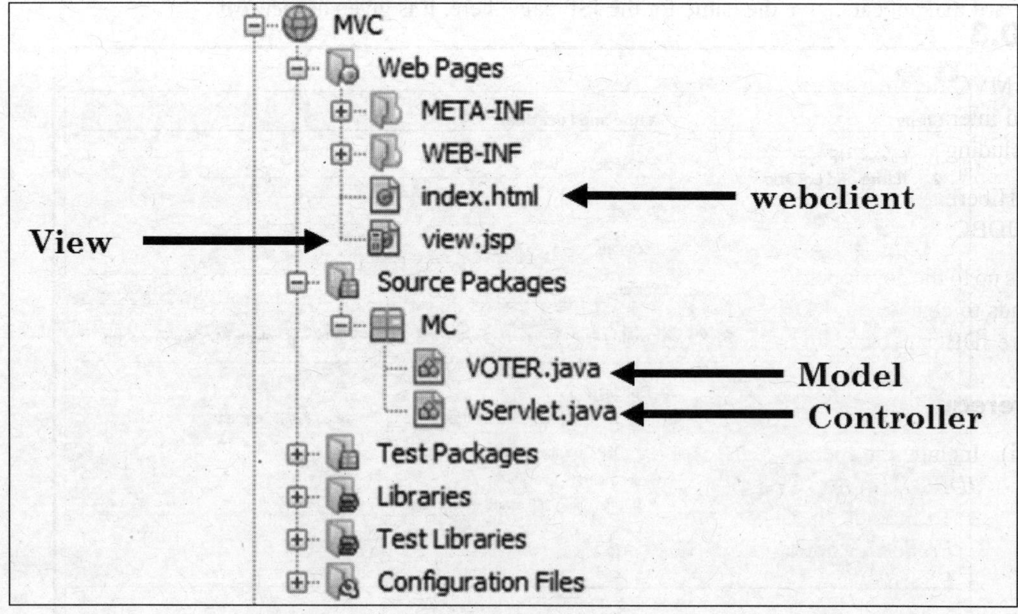

20.2.6 Deploy the Web Application

To run the application, right-click on the root-folder of the project and click *Run*.

OUTPUT

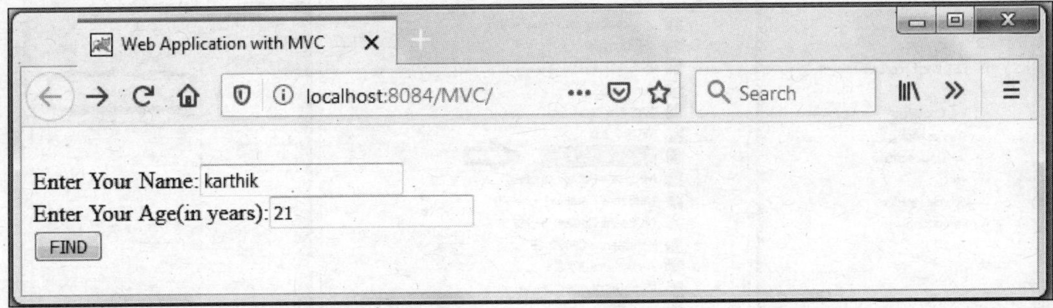

20.3 MVC WITH DB ACCESS

In MVC design pattern, we can interact with database from the Java Bean that is Model. To connect and interact with the RDBMS, the following two are the universal ways in all Java based applications including web applications.

- Hibernate
- JDBC

It is up to the developer to choose either of the above DB connectivity mechanisms. If the web application tends to change the RDBMS often, it is better go for the Hibernate, otherwise JDBC is perfect. Here, core JDBC mechanism is used to connect and interact with the RDBMS.

Prerequisites for DB access from JavaBean

(i) Include the specific JDBC driver into the Project Directory as shown below (*In our case MySQL JDBC Driver*).
  - To include the JDBC Driver for MySQL, right-click on the Project Directory and click the *Properties* option.
  - Choose *Libraries* under the category section on the left-hand side.

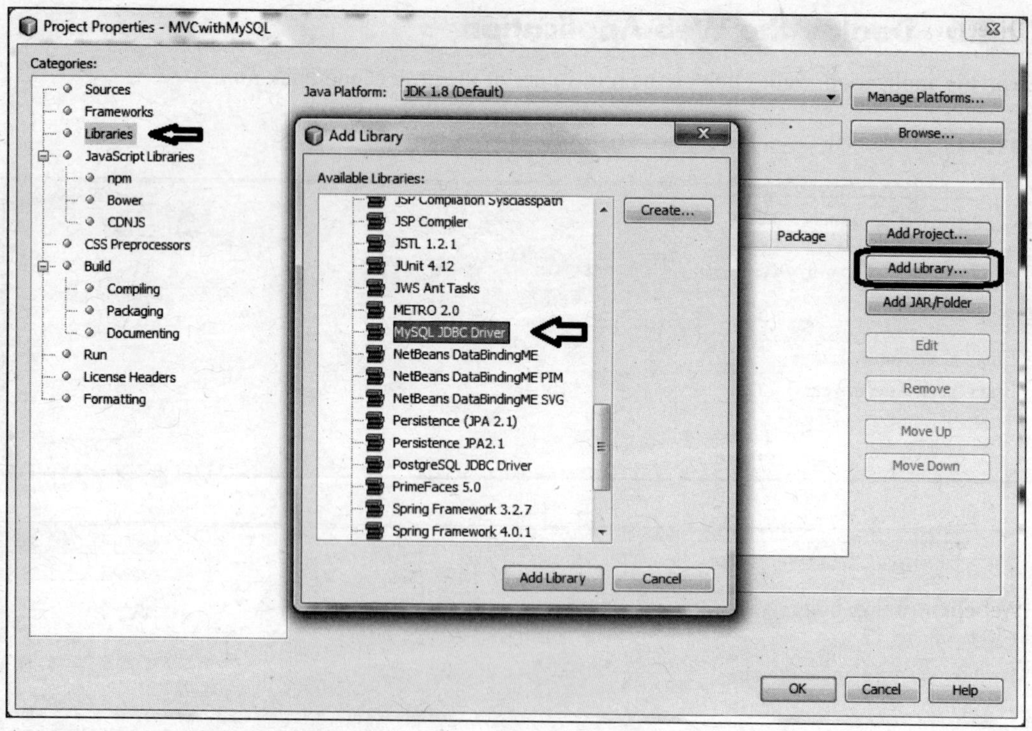

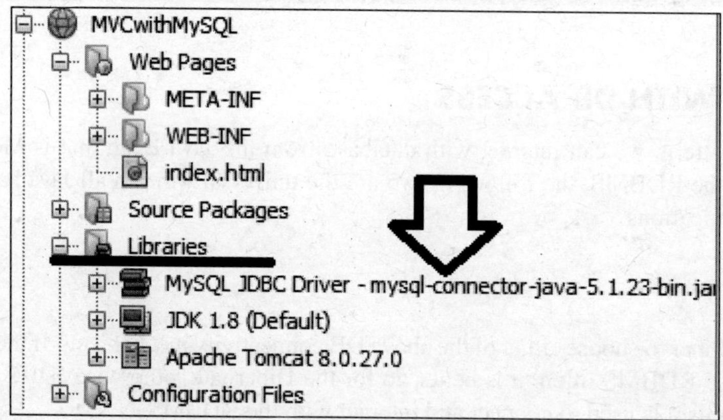

Program 20.1 demonstrates how to fetch a specific record from the database using JDBC from JavaBean of MVC design pattern.

Program 20.1

MySQL table: contact

#	cid	name	mobile	email
1	101	Anu	6655120000	anurosy@gmail.com
2	102	poovizhi	7788665500	poo2020@yahoo.com

Directory structure:

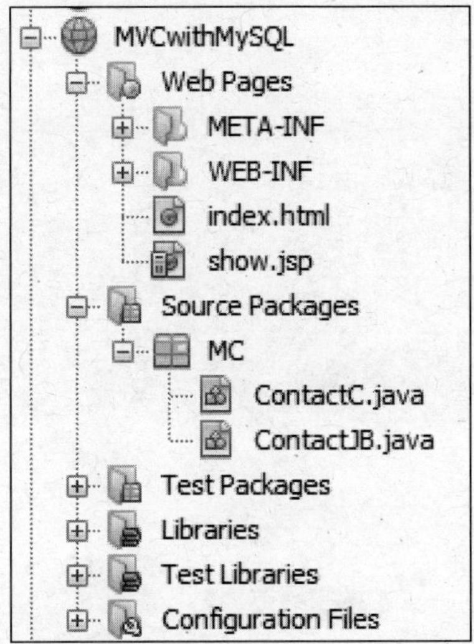

Webclient page: index.html

```
<html>
    <head><title>INPUT PAGE</title></head>
    <body>
        <form action="ContactC" method="POST">
            Enter Contact ID:<input type="text" name="cid"/>
            <input type="submit" value="FETCH"/>
        </form>
    </body>
</html>
```

Model: ContactJB.java

```
package MC;
importjava.sql.*;
public class ContactJB
{
    String DRIVER = "com.mysql.jdbc.Driver";
    String URL = "jdbc:mysql://localhost:3306/karthik";
    String UN = "root";
    String PW = "";
    Connection cn;
    PreparedStatementpst;
    intcid;
    String name, mobile, email, msg;
    publicintgetCid() {
        returncid;
    }
    public void setCid(intcid) {
        this.cid = cid;
    }
    public String getName() {
        return name;
    }
```

```
    public void setName(String name) {
        this.name = name;
    }
    public String getMobile() {
        return mobile;
    }
    public void setMobile(String mobile) {
        this.mobile = mobile;
    }
    public String getEmail() {
        return email;
    }
    public void setEmail(String email) {
        this.email = email;
    }
    public String getMsg() {
        returnmsg;
    }
    public void setMsg(String msg) {
        this.msg = msg;
    }
    public void fetch() throws ClassNotFoundException, SQLException
    {
        Class.forName(DRIVER);
        cn = DriverManager.getConnection(URL, UN, PW);
        pst=cn.prepareStatement("select * from contact where cid=?");
        pst.setInt(1, cid);
        ResultSetrs=pst.executeQuery();
        if(!rs.isBeforeFirst())
        {
            msg="There is no contact in this ID";
        }
        else
        {
            while(rs.next())
            {
                cid = rs.getInt(1);
                name = rs.getString(2);
                mobile=rs.getString(3);
                email=rs.getString(4);
            }
        }
    }
}
```

View: show.jsp

```
<%@page import="MC.ContactJB"%>
<%@page contentType="text/html" pageEncoding="UTF-8"%>
<%
ContactJBobj=(ContactJB)request.getAttribute("JB");
obj.fetch();
String msg=obj.getMsg();
if(msg == null)
{
    out.println("Contact ID: "+obj.getCid()+"<br>");
```

```
        out.println("Name: "+obj.getName()+"<br>");
        out.println("Mobile: "+obj.getMobile()+"<br>");
        out.println("E-mail: "+obj.getEmail()+"<br>");
    }
    else
    {
        out.println(obj.getMsg());
    }
    %>
```

Controller: ContactC.jsp

```
package MC;
importjava.io.IOException;
importjavax.servlet.RequestDispatcher;
importjavax.servlet.ServletException;
import javax.servlet.http.*;
public class ContactC extends HttpServlet
{
    @Override
    protected void doPost(HttpServletRequest request, HttpServletResponse response)
    throwsServletException, IOException
    {
        int id=Integer.parseInt(request.getParameter("cid"));
        ContactJBobj=new ContactJB();
        obj.setCid(id);
        request.setAttribute("JB", obj);
        RequestDispatcherrd=request.getRequestDispatcher("show.jsp");
        rd.forward(request, response);
    }
}
```

Output 20.1

Run-1

INPUT PAGE

localhost:8084/MVCwit

Enter Contact ID: 101 FETCH

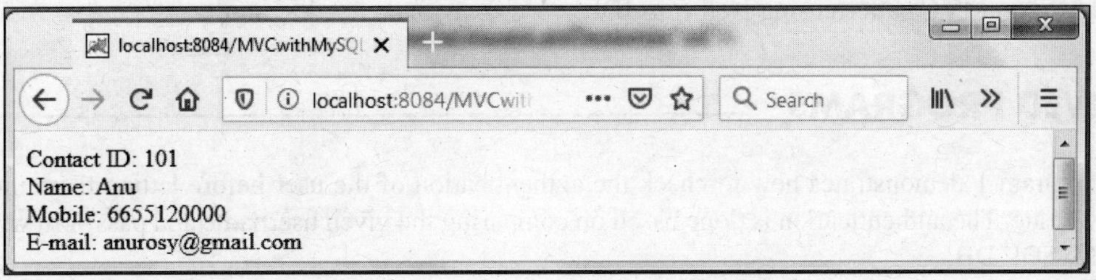

localhost:8084/MVCwithMySQL

localhost:8084/MVCwit

Contact ID: 101
Name: Anu
Mobile: 6655120000
E-mail: anurosy@gmail.com

Run-2

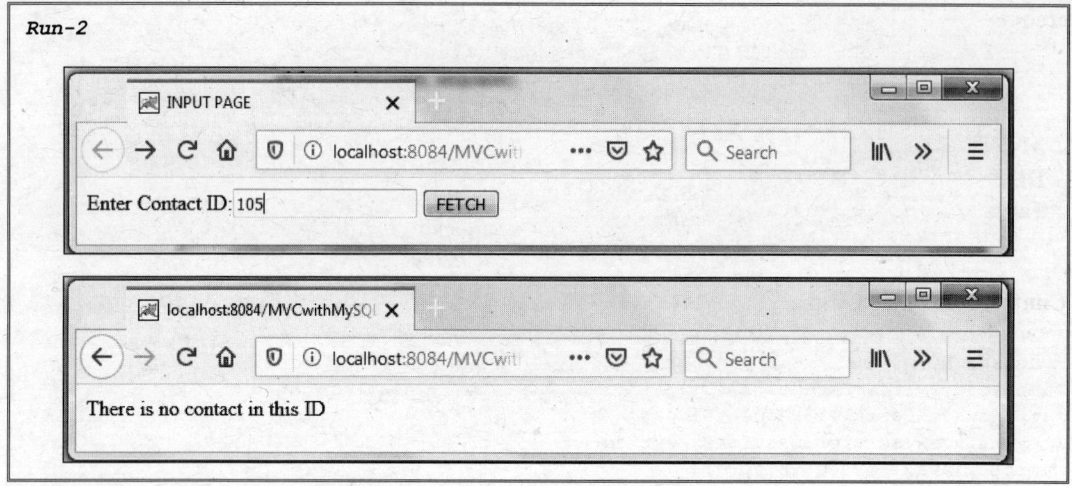

SUMMARY

1. The MVC design pattern combines the controlling abilities of Servlet and the presentation capabilities of JSP along with Java Bean for the Java-based web application development.
2. A Model has data and business logic for the application.
3. A View interacts with the user as well as presents the data and output to the user.
4. A Controller acts like an interface between the Model and View.
5. It is not compulsory to use only one Model, View and Controller while developing a web application. At a time any number of models, views and controllers can be used to develop an MVC based web application.

SHORT QUESTIONS

1. Write the components of an MVC Pattern.
2. Compare the merits and demerits of Servlet and JSP.
3. List out various MVC based design patterns.

COMPREHENSIVE QUESTIONS

1. Write the steps to develop a web application based on MVC pattern using Netbeans IDE.
2. Illustrate the structure of the MVC pattern with a neat diagram.

SOLVED PROGRAMS

1. Program 1 demonstrates how to check the authentication of the user before letting them into the website. The authentication is done based on comparing the given username and password with the MySQL DB.

Prerequisites

- Create Database and Table
- Include the MySQL JDBC driver into the project directory structure

MySQL DB
DB Name: karthik
Table Name: login

#	uname	pword
1	admin	niki
2	C251	rakshita
3	DP102	JKP
4	QC187	RJS

Directory Structure

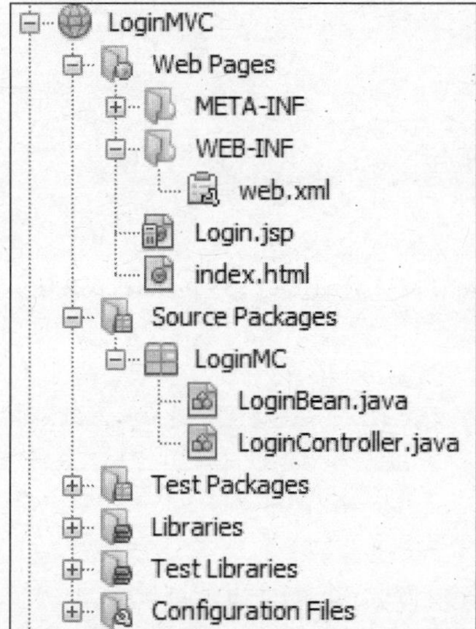

Deployment Descriptor: web.xml

```
<?xml version="1.0" encoding="UTF-8"?>
<web-app>
    <servlet>
        <servlet-name>LoginController</servlet-name>
        <servlet-class>LoginMC.LoginController</servlet-class>
    </servlet>
    <servlet-mapping>
        <servlet-name>LoginController</servlet-name>
        <url-pattern>/LoginController</url-pattern>
    </servlet-mapping>
    <session-config>
        <session-timeout>
            30
        </session-timeout>
```

```
</session-config>
   <welcome-file-list>
      <welcome-file>
         index.html
      </welcome-file>
   </welcome-file-list>
</web-app>
```

Client Page: index.html

```
<html>
   <head>
      <title>Login Page</title>
   </head>
   <body>
      <form action="LoginController" method="post">
         User Name:<input type="text" name="u"/></br>
         Password:<input type="password" name="p"/></br>
         <input type="submit" value="Login"/>
         <input type="reset" value="Cancel"/>
      </form>
   </body>
</html>
```

Model: LoginBean.java

```
package LoginMC;
import java.sql.*;
public class LoginBean
{
   String un,pw,res;
   String DRIVER = "com.mysql.jdbc.Driver";
   String URL = "jdbc:mysql://localhost:3306/karthik";
   String UN = "root";
   String PW = "";
   Connection cn;
   PreparedStatement pst;
   public String getUn() {
      return un;
   }
   public void setUn(String un) {
      this.un = un;
   }
   public String getPw() {
      return pw;
   }
   public void setPw(String pw) {
      this.pw = pw;
   }
   public String getRes() {
      return res;
   }
   public void setRes(String res) {
      this.res = res;
   }
   public void validate() throws ClassNotFoundException, SQLException
   {
      Class.forName(DRIVER);
      cn = DriverManager.getConnection(URL, UN, PW);
```

```
        pst=cn.prepareStatement("select * from login");
        ResultSet rs=pst.executeQuery();
        while(rs.next())
        {
           if(un.equals(rs.getString(1))&&pw.equals(rs.getString(2)))
           {
              res="true";
              break;
           }
           else
           {
              res="false";
           }
        }
     }
  }
```

View: Login.jsp

```
<%@page contentType="text/html" pageEncoding="UTF-8"%>
<%@page import="LoginMC.LoginBean"%>
<html>
   <head>
      <title>Login Page</title>
   </head>
   <body>
      <%
         LoginBean obj=(LoginBean)request.getAttribute("JB");
         obj.validate();
         String msg=obj.getRes();
         if(msg == "true")
         {
            out.println("Welcome to our site");
         }
         else
         {
            out.println("SORRY No such User Name or Password");
         }
      %>
      <a href="index.html"><input type="button" value="Go Back"/></a>
   </body>
</html>
```

Controller: LoginController.java

```
package LoginMC;
import java.io.IOException;
import javax.servlet.*;
import javax.servlet.http.HttpServlet;
import javax.servlet.http.HttpServletRequest;
import javax.servlet.http.HttpServletResponse;
public class LoginController extends HttpServlet
{
   @Override
   protected void doPost(HttpServletRequest request, HttpServletResponse response)
   throws ServletException, IOException
   {
      String un,pw;
      un=request.getParameter("u");
```

```
        pw=request.getParameter("p");
        LoginBean obj=new LoginBean();
        obj.setUn(un);
        obj.setPw(pw);
        request.setAttribute("JB", obj);
        RequestDispatcher rd=request.getRequestDispatcher("Login.jsp");
        rd.forward(request, response);
    }
}
```

Output

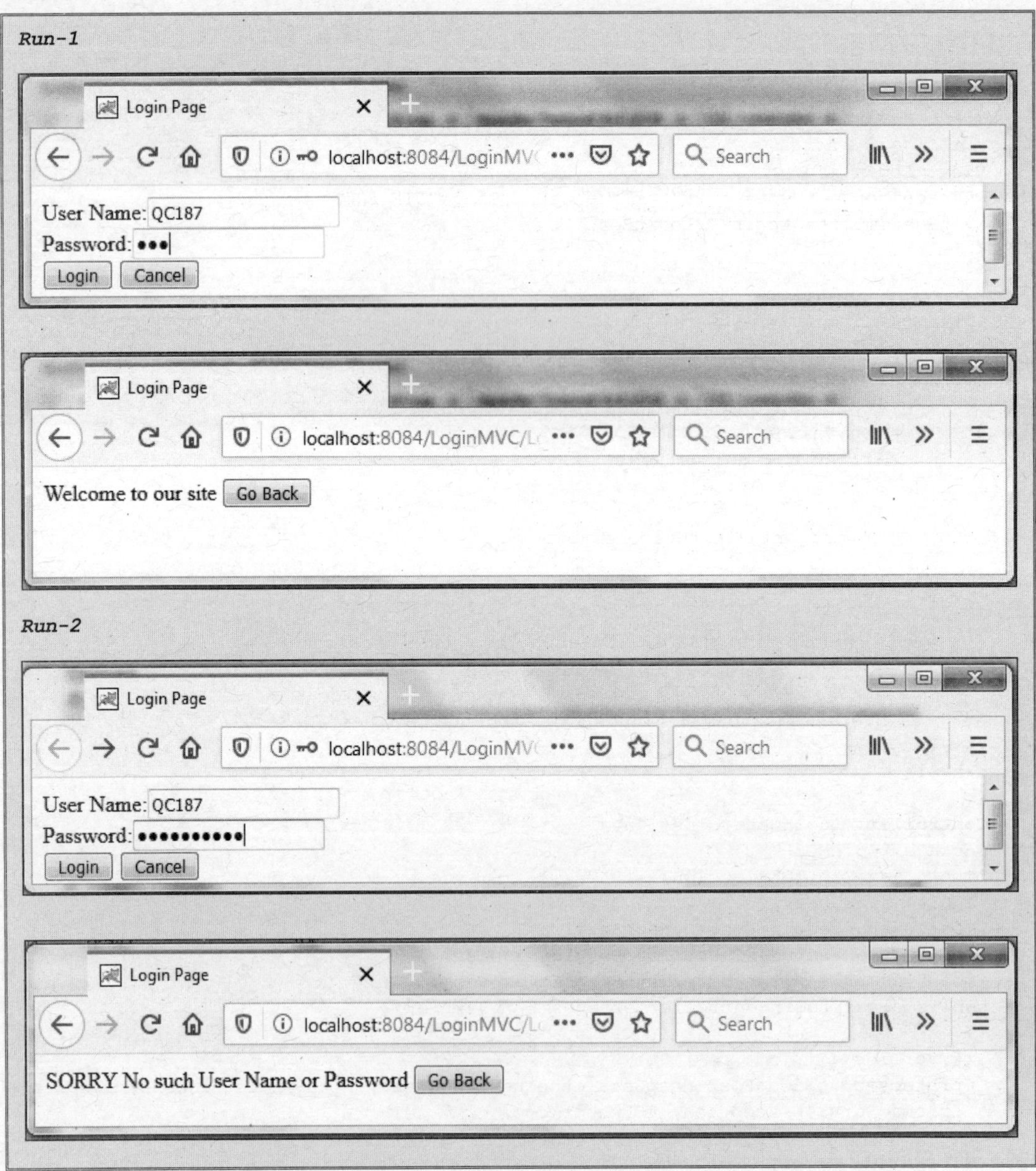

2. Program 2 demonstrates how to fetch the result of the student, based on the given register number and DOB from the MySQL DB.

Prerequisites

- Create Database and Table
- Include the MySQL JDBC driver into the project directory structure

MySQL DB
DB Name: karthik
Table Name: result

#	regno	Lang1	English	Mathematics	Science	SocialScience	dob
1	121453	56	65	47	70	80	05/01/2006
2	121501	70	85	54	60	67	14/07/2007
3	187543	80	91	98	95	97	11/08/2005
4	191402	70	71	78	76	74	15/05/2007
5	201541	84	83	89	88	81	20/09/2007

Directory Structure

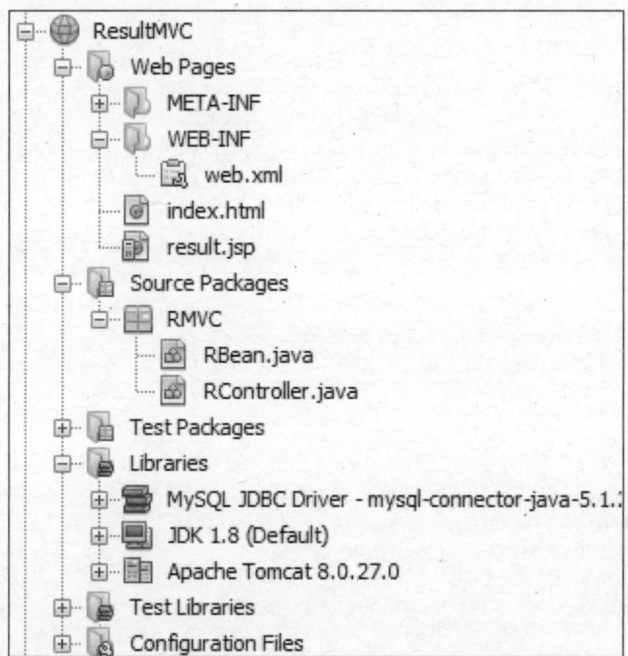

Deployment Descriptor: web.xml

```
<?xml version="1.0" encoding="UTF-8"?>
<web-app>
   <servlet>
      <servlet-name>RController</servlet-name>
      <servlet-class>RMVC.RController</servlet-class>
   </servlet>
   <servlet-mapping>
      <servlet-name>RController</servlet-name>
      <url-pattern>/RController</url-pattern>
```

```
    </servlet-mapping>
    <session-config>
        <session-timeout>
            30
        </session-timeout>
    </session-config>
    <welcome-file-list>
        <welcome-file>
            index.html
        </welcome-file>
    </welcome-file-list>
</web-app>
```

Client Page: index.html

```
<html>
    <head> <title>INPUT PAGE</title> </head>
    <body>
        <form action="RController" method="POST">
            Reg No:<input type="text" name="r"/></br>
            DOB:<input type="text" name="d"/></br>
            <input type="submit" value="Fetch"/>
            <input type="reset" value="Clear"/>
        </form>
    </body>
</html>
```

Model: RBean.java

```
package RMVC;
import java.sql.Connection;
import java.sql.DriverManager;
import java.sql.PreparedStatement;
import java.sql.ResultSet;
import java.sql.SQLException;
public class RBean
{
    String DRIVER = "com.mysql.jdbc.Driver";
    String URL = "jdbc:mysql://localhost:3306/karthik";
    String UN = "root";
    String PW = "";
    Connection cn;
    PreparedStatement pst;
    int reg, lang1,eng,math,sci,ssci;
    String msg,dob;
    public String getDob() {
        return dob;
    }
    public void setDob(String dob) {
        this.dob = dob;
    }
    public String getMsg() {
        return msg;
    }
    public void setMsg(String msg) {
        this.msg = msg;
    }
    public int getLang1() {
        return lang1;
    }
    public void setLang1(int lang1) {
```

```
        this.lang1 = lang1;
    }
    public int getEng() {
        return eng;
    }
    public void setEng(int eng) {
        this.eng = eng;
    }
    public int getMath() {
        return math;
    }
    public void setMath(int math) {
        this.math = math;
    }
    public int getSci() {
        return sci;
    }
    public void setSci(int sci) {
        this.sci = sci;
    }
    public int getSsci() {
        return ssci;
    }
    public void setSsci(int ssci) {
        this.ssci = ssci;
    }
    public int getReg() {
        return reg;
    }
    public void setReg(int reg) {
        this.reg = reg;
    }
    public void fetch() throws ClassNotFoundException, SQLException
    {
        Class.forName(DRIVER);
        cn = DriverManager.getConnection(URL, UN, PW);
        pst=cn.prepareStatement("select * from result ");
        ResultSet rs=pst.executeQuery();
        while(rs.next())
        {
            if(reg==rs.getInt(1)&&dob.equals(rs.getString(7)))
            {
                msg="true";
                reg = rs.getInt(1);
                lang1 = rs.getInt(2);
                eng=rs.getInt(3);
                math=rs.getInt(4);
                sci=rs.getInt(5);
                ssci=rs.getInt(6);
                break;
            }
            else
            {
                msg="false";
            }
        }
    }
}
```

View: result.jsp

```
<%@page contentType="text/html" pageEncoding="UTF-8"%>
<%@page import="RMVC.RBean"%>
<html>
  <head>
     <title>Result Page</title>
  </head>
  <body>
     <%
        RBean obj=(RBean)request.getAttribute("JB");
        obj.fetch();
        String msg=obj.getMsg();
        if(msg == "false")
        {
           out.println("There is NO such Register Number and DOB");
        }
        else
        {
           %>
           <h2>
           <% out.println("Register Number: "+obj.getReg());%> <br>
           <% out.println("Language 1: "+obj.getLang1());%> <br>
           <% out.println("English: "+obj.getEng());%> <br>
           <% out.println("Mathematics: "+obj.getMath());%> <br>
           <% out.println("Science: "+obj.getSci());%> <br>
           <% out.println("Social Science: "+obj.getSsci());%> <br>
           <%
        }
     %>
</h2>
</br>
<a href="index.html"><input type="button" value="Go Back"/></a>
</body>
</html>
```

Controller: RController.java

```
package RMVC;
import java.io.IOException;
import javax.servlet.RequestDispatcher;
import javax.servlet.ServletException;
import javax.servlet.http.HttpServlet;
import javax.servlet.http.HttpServletRequest;
import javax.servlet.http.HttpServletResponse;
public class RController extends HttpServlet
{
  @Override
  protected void doPost(HttpServletRequest request, HttpServletResponse response)
  throws ServletException, IOException {
     int reg=Integer.parseInt(request.getParameter("r"));
     String dob=request.getParameter("d");
     RBean obj=new RBean();
     obj.setReg(reg);
     obj.setDob(dob);
     request.setAttribute("JB", obj);
     RequestDispatcher rd=request.getRequestDispatcher("result.jsp");
     rd.forward(request, response);
  }
 }
```

Output

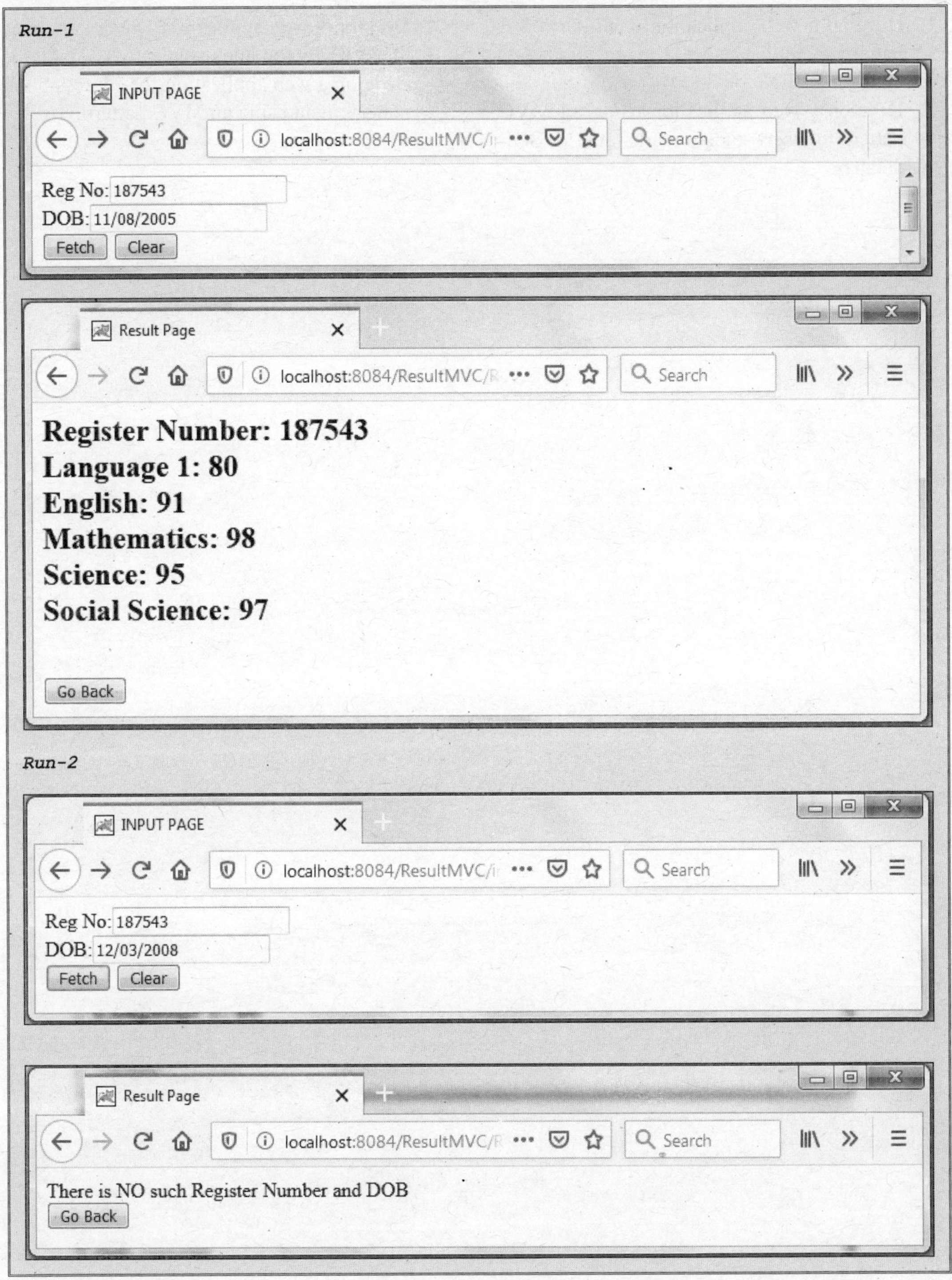
Run-1
INPUT PAGE
localhost:8084/ResultMVC/i
Search
Reg No: 187543
DOB: 11/08/2005
Fetch
Clear
Result Page
localhost:8084/ResultMVC/R
Search
Register Number: 187543
Language 1: 80
English: 91
Mathematics: 98
Science: 95
Social Science: 97
Go Back
Run-2
INPUT PAGE
localhost:8084/ResultMVC/i
Search
Reg No: 187543
DOB: 12/03/2008
Fetch
Clear
Result Page
localhost:8084/ResultMVC/R
Search
There is NO such Register Number and DOB
Go Back

PROGRAMMING EXERCISES

1. Develop a web application using an MVC pattern to find whether a given number is ODD or EVEN.
2. Develop a web application using an MVC pattern to insert student marks into MySQL database.
3. Develop a web application which simulates the LOG-IN module using an MVC pattern.
4. Develop a web application for address book management using an MVC pattern.

Index

I

J

K

L

M

N

O

P

Q

R

S

T

U

V

W

Z